Montenegro

WITHDRAWN

the Bradt Travel Guide

Annalisa Rellie
Updated by Rudolf Abraham

www.bradtguides.com

edition
5

Bradt Travel Guides Ltd, UK
The Globe Pequot Press Inc, USA

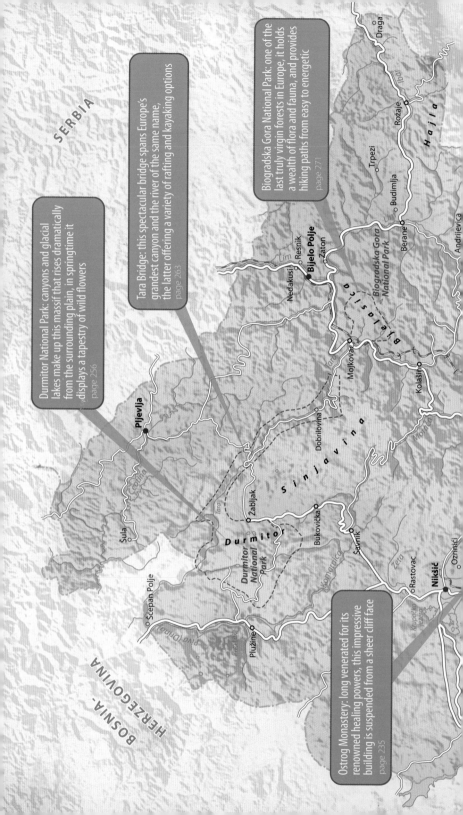

Durmitor National Park: canyons and glacial lakes make up this massif that rises dramatically from the surrounding plain, in springtime it displays a tapestry of wild flowers
page 256

Tara Bridge: this spectacular bridge spans Europe's grandest canyon and the river of the same name, the latter offering a variety of rafting and kayaking options
page 263

Biogradska Gora National Park: one of the last truly virgin forests in Europe, it holds a wealth of flora and fauna, and provides hiking paths from easy to energetic
page 271

Ostrog Monastery: long venerated for its renowned healing powers, this impressive building is suspended from a sheer cliff face
page 235

SERBIA

BOSNIA-HERZEGOVINA

Draga

Ibar

Rožaje

Hajla

Trpezi

Budimlja

Andrijevica

Berane

Biogradska Gora National Park

Resnik

Bijelo Polje

Zaton

Lim

Nedakusi

Bjelasica

Mojkovac

Kolašin

Dobrilovina

Tara

Morača

Sinjavina

Žabljak

Durmitor

Durmitor National Park

Bukovička

Šavnik

Komarnica

Rastovac

Zeta

Nikšić

Oznići

Pljevlja

Ćehotina

Šula

Ščepan Polje

Pivsko Jezero

Plužine

Piva (Drina)

Župadko Jezero

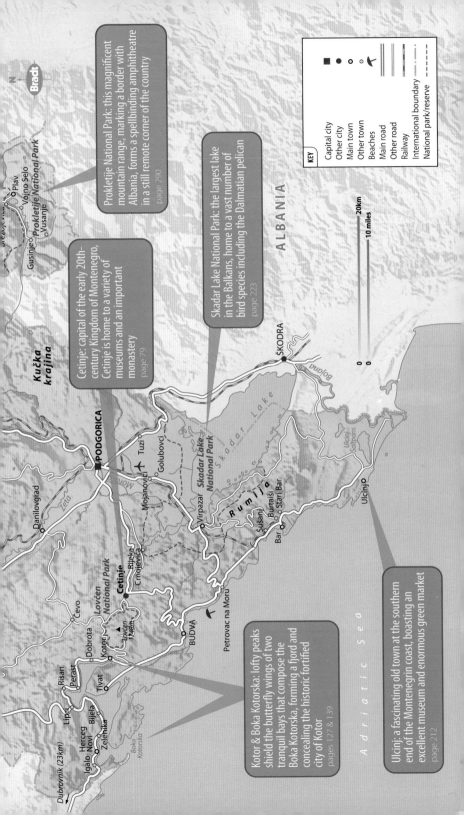

Prokletije National Park: this magnificent mountain range, marking a border with Albania, forms a spellbinding amphitheatre in a still remote corner of the country
page 290

Cetinje: capital of the early 20th-century Kingdom of Montenegro, Cetinje is home to a variety of museums and an important monastery
page 79

Skadar Lake National Park: the largest lake in the Balkans, home to a vast number of bird species including the Dalmatian pelican
page 223

Kotor & Boka Kotorska: lofty peaks shield the butterfly wings of two tranquil bays that compose the Boka Kotorska, forming a fjord and concealing the historic fortified city of Kotor
pages 127 & 139

Ulcinj: a fascinating old town at the southern end of the Montenegrin coast, boasting an excellent museum and enormous green market
page 212

KEY

Capital city
Other city
Main town
Other town
Beaches
Main road
Other road
Railway
International boundary
National park/reserve

ALBANIA

ŠKODRA

PODGORICA

Danilovgrad

Tuzi

Golubovci

Mojanovići

Virpazar

Rumija

Šušanj
Burtaiši
Bar · Stari Bar

Ulcinj

Skadar Lake

Skadar Lake National Park

Bojana

Ulcinj
Saltpans

Kučka krajina

Gusinje
Vusanje
Vojno Selo
Plav
Prokletije National Park

Zeta
Morača

Cetinje

Rijeka Crnojevića

Lovćen National Park

Cevo

Dobrota

Risan
Perast

Lipci
Herceg Novi
Igalo
Zelenika
Bijela
Tivat
Kotor
Lovćen

Budva

Petrovac na Moru

Boka Kotorska

Adriatic Sea

Dubrovnik (23km)

0   10 miles
0   20km

Bradt

Montenegro
Don't
miss...

Stunning old towns
Wander through the narrow
streets of towns like Budva
(NTOM) pages 165–77

Exploring Montenegro's
national parks
Discover Durmitor National
Park, one of Montenegro's five
breathtaking national parks
(RA) pages 256–63

Spectacular vistas

With some of Europe's finest mountain ranges, canyons and rivers, it's hard not to stumble across one of the innumerable jaw dropping views. Pictured here is the Crnojevica River in Skadar Lake National Park
(LM/S) pages 223–31

Local festivals and traditions

Come and watch the locals celebrating Fašinada, a ritual procession of boats filled with stones and trees around the island of Gospa od Škrpjela, near Perast
(NTOM) page 59

Kotor

The architecture of UNESCO-listed Kotor reflects its Western European and Byzantine history
(O/S) pages 139–48

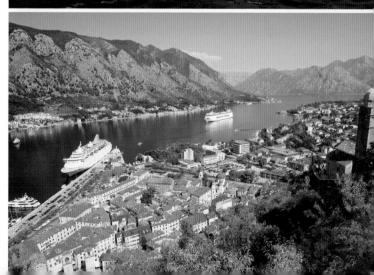

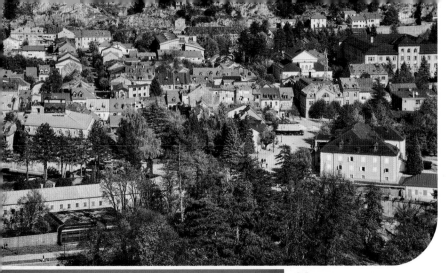

Montenegro
in colour

above   The former administrative capital for 500 years, Cetinje is Montenegro's cultural and historical capital (MV/S) pages 79–90

left   Kotor's clocktower was built at the start of the 17th century, and the clock itself was added in 1810 (NTOM) page 146

below   Podgorica's Millennium Bridge, which opened in 2005 in honour of Montenegro's National Day, has become a symbol of the city (NTOM) page 98

above Until 50 years ago, Sveti Stefan was a pretty little fishing village. Now it's a unique and luxurious hotel (BZG/S) pages 186–9

right The town of Herceg Novi changed hands many times over the centuries (RA) pages 115–23

below The harbour at Perast is a delightful place for a stroll (AC/AWL) pages 134–7

We're 40...
how did that happen?

How did it all happen? George (my then husband) and I wrote the first Bradt guide – about hiking in Peru and Bolivia – on an Amazon river barge, and typed it up on a borrowed typewriter. We had no money for the next two books so George went to work for a printer and was paid in books rather than money.

Forty years on, Bradt publishes over 200 titles that sell all over the world. I still suffer from Imposter Syndrome – how did it all happen? I hadn't even worked in an office before! Well, I've been extraordinarily lucky with the people around me. George provided the belief to get us started (and the mother to run our US office). Then, in 1977, I recruited a helper, Janet Mears, who is still working for us. She and the many dedicated staff who followed have been the foundations on which the company is built. But the bricks and mortar have been our authors and readers. Without them there would be no Bradt Travel Guides. Thank you all for making it happen.

Hilary Bradt

AUTHOR AND UPDATER

AUTHOR Following her childhood education in a seaside convent, **Annalisa Rellie** studied theatre at the Guildhall School of Music and Drama in London, after which the casting couch of early marriage spared her an actor's breadline and led to a quarter of a century happily exploring the world with her diplomat husband. When they settled back in London she turned her hand to journalism, writing in a freelance capacity for magazines about travel and food.

Her passion for Montenegro, which began with a press trip in spring 2000, continued to grow exponentially as she worked tirelessly on four editions of this, the first English-language guide dedicated exclusively to the country. Annalisa died in early 2014.

UPDATER Rudolf Abraham (*www.rudolfabraham.co.uk*) is an award-winning travel writer and photographer specialising in Croatia and eastern Europe. He is the author of several books, including the first English-language hiking guides to Croatia and Montenegro; co-author of *Istria; The Bradt Travel Guide*; and has updated the Bradt guides to Croatia and Transylvania. His work is published widely, including BBC News, BBC *Countryfile*, *Canvas*, CNN *Traveller*, *Discover Britain*, *France*, *Hidden Europe*, *National Geographic Traveller*, *OE*, *Wanderlust* and *Vanity Fair*. He has been a frequent visitor to southeast Europe since the late 1990s, when he lived and worked in neighbouring Croatia for two years.

AUTHOR'S STORY

I went to Montenegro the first time in the year of the millennium as part of a press group. The object was to write a thousand words for a magazine article. I came away and wrote 70,000 (yet even this new edition's 160,000 or so still doesn't say it all). Hilary Bradt's response to my suggestion for a guide was at once positive: 'Montenegro – it sounds a Bradt Travel Guide sort of place'.

Others at that time were not so aware of the little country and when the first edition appeared, every bookshop and library I visited found me shifting copies, sometimes from the Caribbean section, other times out of Africa. Happily this is no longer the case and all the world now knows about the land of the Black Mountain, its wild beauty, so neatly encapsulated by the PR guys. Gathering together the guide was a labour of love: equal emphasis on both the 'l' words. They say no-one can write a biography without falling a little in love with the subject. The same must surely apply to a single-country travel book. The only difference with Montenegro was that for me, it was love at first sight.

People often ask just what it is about Bradt. The answer is simple: they allow their authors to tell the story as well as to write the guide.

Regrets, I've had a few … It would be nice to be handy with a camera. It would also be lovely to know more about flowers and trees, instead of having pockets ever filled with leaves too crumbled for identification. And why can no-one tell me the name of the shrub that shades the Šetalište Pet Danica at Herceg Novi, its creamy blossom in May filling the town with the sweetest scent?

PUBLISHER'S FOREWORD   *Adrian Phillips, Managing Director*

Independence seems to suit Montenegro. Rocketing visitor numbers have propelled this ever-evolving state to the forefront of eastern European countries and Bradt is proud to have been the first publisher to produce a dedicated guide.

It was with great sadness that we learnt of the recent death of Annalisa Rellie, who worked tirelessly on four editions of her guide, and whose passion for Montenegro and its people came through in every page. In this fifth edition, her dedicated work has been continued by regional specialist Rudolf Abraham.

Fifth edition published January 2015
First published 2003

Bradt Travel Guides Ltd, IDC House, The Vale, Chalfont St Peter, Bucks SL9 9RZ, England
www.bradtguides.com
Print edition published in the USA by The Globe Pequot Press Inc, PO Box 480, Guilford, Connecticut 06437-0480

Text copyright © 2015 Annalisa Rellie
Maps copyright © 2015 Bradt Travel Guides Ltd
Photographs copyright © 2015 Individual photographers (see below)
Project managers: Tricia Hayne and Claire Strange
Cover research: Pepi Bluck, Perfect Picture

ISBN: 978 1 84162 857 8 (print)
ISBN: 978 1 78477 111 9 (ePub)
ISBN: 978 1 78477 211 6 (mobi)

British Library Cataloguing in Publication Data
A catalogue record for this book is available from the British Library

Photographers Rudolf Abraham (RA); Alamy (A): World Pictures/Alamy (WP/A); AWL: Alan Copson (AC/AWL), Neil Farrin (NF/AWL), Walter Bibikow (WB/AWL); FLPA (FLPA): / Imagebroker/FLPA (/I/FLPA), Do van Dijk, Nis/Minden Pictures/FLPA (DVDN/MP/FLPA), F1online/F1online/FLPA (F1O/F1O/FLPA); National Tourist Organisation of Montenegro (NTOM); Shutterstock: Bildagentur Zoonar GmbH (BZG/S), BTRSELLER (B/S), ddsign (D/S), Lenar Musin (LM/S), Madrugada Verde (MV/S), Misa Maric (MM/S), ollirg (O/S), Pelevina Ksinia (PK/S), saiko3p (S3P/S), vojkan-photography (VP/S), Vlada Z (VZ/S); SuperStock (SS)
Front cover Stari Grad (Old Town), Budva (AC/AWL)
Back cover Bukumirsko Lake is one of Montenegro's smallest lakes (NTOM)
Title page A stone carving in Budva (NF/AWL); in Kotor's old town (AC/AWL); Stoliv lies on the Bay of Kotor (NTOM)

Maps David McCutcheon FBCart S; colour map relief base by Nick Rowland FRGS; includes map data © OpenStreetMap contributors

Typeset from the author's disk by Wakewing, High Wycombe
Production managed by Jellyfish Print Solutions; printed in India
Digital conversion by the Firsty Group

DEDICATION

To the memory of Annalisa Rellie
whose spirit of adventure, commitment to this guide, and above all love of
Montenegro continue to shine through

Annalisa Rellie was a woman of many parts. In a full and eventful life, she was an author, wife, and mother, and a warm and faithful friend and colleague, but will always be remembered for her contribution to Slavonic Studies as the founder-author of the Bradt Guide to Montenegro. The first volume of her book appeared in 2003, and it immediately became the most authoritative guide in any language to the newly emerging state. With its excellent photographs and clear and sensitively written text, it was much more than a travel guide in the technical sense and helped define the identity of emerging Montenegro in the English-speaking world.

Her book described for the first time in English – at least since 19th-century travellers like Revd W Denton – many places scarcely ever visited by foreigners, and she made a strong stand for the protection of the wonders of the Montenegrin natural environment against the depredations brought on some part of the coast by modern mass tourism. She will be deeply missed by all who were fortunate enough to know her.

Professor James Pettifer

ACKNOWLEDGEMENTS

ANNALISA RELLIE (4th edition) It's rather hard to know where to start – I'm enormously indebted to so very many who have helped and supported me in the production of both this guide and those that preceded it. Had it not been for the encouragement of three people – Julian Peel Yates, former Head of the OSCE/ODIHR mission in Podgorica, who in spring 2000 invited me to participate in a press visit he was organising; Bojan Šarkić, who was at that time Head of Mission for the Republic of Montenegro here in the United Kingdom; and Alun Evans, ex-Foreign and Commonwealth Office, then with British Airways – the project would never have got off the ground.

I would like to thank again all those who so assiduously answered dozens of my questions and assisted me with this and previous editions. To the Bradt team I can only repeat what I said last time: it simply would not have been possible without their wisdom, kindness and flexibility.

RUDOLF ABRAHAM (5th edition) Thanks to Emma and Ben Heywood in Virpazar, Hayley Wright in Herceg Novi, the ever-helpful Kirsi Hyvaerinen, and to my wonderful wife and daughter. And to Annalisa, who I only had the opportunity to meet once, briefly, in late 2013, before her untimely death a few months later – and so never got to tell her how much I enjoyed reading and updating her book, or how those creamy blossoms along the waterfront in Herceg Novi she wrote of were still flowering in profusion early the following spring.

Contents

LIST OF MAPS

FEEDBACK REQUEST AND UPDATES WEBSITE

At Bradt Travel Guides we're aware that guidebooks start to go out of date on the day they're published – and that you, our readers, are out there in the field doing research of your own. You'll find out before us when a fine new family-run hotel opens or a favourite restaurant changes hands and goes downhill. So why not write and tell us about your experiences? Contact us on ℡ 01753 893444 or e info@bradtguides.com. We will forward emails to the author who may post updates on the Bradt website at www.bradtupdates.com/montenegro. Alternatively you can add a review of the book to www.bradtguides.com or Amazon.

ATTENTION WILDLIFE ENTHUSIASTS

For more on wildlife in Montenegro why not check out Bradt's *Central and Eastern European Wildlife*. Go to www.bradguides.com and key in MONTWILD40 at the checkout for your 40% discount while stocks last.

FOLLOW BRADT

For the latest news, special offers and competitions, subscribe to the Bradt newsletter via the website www.bradtguides.com and follow Bradt on:

- www.facebook.com/BradtTravelGuides
- @BradtGuides
- @bradtguides
- pinterest.com/bradtguides

HOW TO USE THIS GUIDE

AUTHOR'S FAVOURITES Finding genuinely characterful accommodation or that unmissable off-the-beaten-track café can be difficult, so the author and updater have chosen a few of their favourite places throughout the country to point you in the right direction. These 'author's favourites' are marked with a ✳.

CONTACT INFORMATION Unless it's somewhere very fancy, no-one would think of booking at most restaurants or cafés in Montenegro, and calling without speaking Serbian/Montenegrin wouldn't get you very far anyway. Thus phone numbers – and email addresses – have been included only where they might be useful. It's worth noting that some commercial organisations – such as car-hire companies, and even some hotels and restaurants – give mobile numbers either as an alternative to land lines or even as a preferred method of contact.

ADDRESSES Where the letters 'bb' appear in a street address, it means that the building has no number.

SPELLINGS Historically, the language spoken throughout Montenegro displayed slight variations between the east and the west of the country, with attendant differences in spellings, particularly of proper nouns; for example Peter and Petar, Bura and Bora. In this guide we have attempted to maintain a consistency for ease of approach, although for proper names in minority areas with non-Slav roots (eg: Albanian or Turkish), Serbian spellings have generally been adopted.

MAPS The road network in Montenegro is constantly being upgraded, old gravel tracks repaved, etc, so travellers are strongly advised to use the maps in this guidebook only in conjunction with the most recent maps available (see page 68).

KEYS AND SYMBOLS Maps include alphabetical keys covering the locations of those places to stay, eat or drink that are featured in the book. Note that regional maps may not show all hotels and restaurants in the area: other establishments may be located in towns shown on the map.

GRIDS AND GRID REFERENCES Several maps use grid lines to allow easy location of sites. Map grid references are listed in square brackets after the name of the place or sight of interest in the text, with page number followed by grid number, eg: [103 C3].

Introduction

The Balkans ... is, or was, a gay peninsula filled with sprightly people who ate peppered foods, drank strong liquors, wore flamboyant clothes, loved and murdered easily and had a splendid talent for starting wars. Less imaginative westerners looked down on them with secret envy, sniffing at their royalty, scoffing at their pretensions, and fearing their savage terrorists. Karl Marx called them 'ethnic trash.' I, as a footloose youngster in my twenties, adored them.

C L Sulzberger *The New York Times*, 1950
Copyright © The New York Times Co. Reprinted with permission.

The year 2006 was to be a memorable one for Montenegro, or Crna Gora as she is properly called in her *Maternji Jesik* ('mother tongue'), for that May the state slipped the yoke that coupled her with Serbia. The federation had constituted the rump of former Yugoslavia but now the smaller partner emerged a fully independent country, and is well placed to join the eager throng pacing the waiting room of the European Union. It had been nearly a century since, in the wake of World War I, the then Kingdom of Montenegro lost her sovereignty and became united with Serbia, Bosnia, Croatia and Slovenia to form the Kingdom of Serbs, Croats and Slovenes (renamed in 1929 Yugoslavia).

Under the leadership of Josip Broz Tito in the 30-odd years after World War II, the greater Yugoslavia fared reasonably well economically, particularly in the field of tourism, and if there was little individual wealth it did not follow that people felt especially poor. A Montenegrin will maintain that in common with all Mediterranean lands his country possesses an incalculable asset, the 'trinity' of vine, olive and grain – add to that an unfailing supply of fish – and because of this he need never go hungry.

But a pre-millennium decade of conflict in the Balkans inflicted a toll. Resources were stretched to the limit and much of the infrastructure fell into disrepair, leading to a significant drop in tourist numbers, in particular an absence of visitors from western Europe and North America.

For Montenegrins, a large proportion of whom have at least some Serbian blood, the question of separation had never been an easy one. It was impossible not to review the past as they looked to the future: the ancient heraldic emblem depicting a bicephalous eagle spoke for a population almost equally divided as to whether to pursue a political path in partnership with the republic with whom historically they shared so much of their birthright, or to go for full independence. In the event the referendum that led to the latter conclusion was – as expected – close run, but credit to all parties involved, including Serbia, once the results were announced and the decision made, differences were put aside and the mood was both jubilant and forward looking. As someone who was there reported on the evening following the plebiscite: 'It was fantastic, emotional and unrealistic. All the young people and elderly Montenegrins were voting in national costumes, Podgorica and Cetinje were covered in red and gold flags – a hundred thousand people on the streets of Podgorica. Two hours waiting in the car to get out of Cetinje after the celebration ... Mission accomplished.

The new independence was received by the international community as confirmation of stability and within months external investment in Montenegro had increased exponentially. Privatisations were widespread: everything but grandmothers was up for sale and prices for real estate in the coastal plain were soaring. Overnight it seemed everyone had become an entrepreneur. The wise ones sat on their land and waited; others chose to sell quickly. Some, fearing a country overrun by speculators, didn't want to sell at all and, whatever the cost or lack of it, preferred to maintain the status quo.

Almost a decade on and the dust has settled – and dust is an appropriate word: for far too much of the coast has become a construction site. The government has had to address planning restrictions before it is too late, to avoid the verdant coastline sacrificing its unique character and beauty to overdevelopment.

Similar reservations with regard to the speed and sheer scale of reconstruction cannot be said to apply inland, either in the mountains or in the eastern corners of the country, where progress is altogether a more gradual process. However, with the assistance and support of such international bodies as the European Union, the United Nations Development Programme, USAID, the Organisation for Security and Cooperation in Europe and the European Bank for Reconstruction and Development, and more importantly through their own enthusiasm and energies, these municipalities will catch up one fine day.

Meanwhile, some great hotels offering state-of-the-art facilities have opened, others have been refurbished and have extended their services. The number of small family-run establishments is on the increase and everywhere there is an upbeat sense of revival, underpinning the Montenegrin tradition of hospitality to all comers.

Inland, the splendid Hussein Pasha Mosque in Pljevlja, its soaring minaret a landmark, has also risen from its renovations. Small eco-villages are providing peaceful rest for travellers in the beautiful wilderness of the mountains, and the sublime Prokletije has been recognised at last as a national park.

Within this guide there is frequent reference to the indomitable spirit of the Montenegrins, their strength in repelling invaders in total contrast to the openhearted welcome with which they greet all friendly visitors. Tall in stature, they mirror their mountains, and what a land those towering mountains hide, a wilderness of canyons plunging to torrential rivers, primeval forests and glacial lakes but also Arcadian pasture where established traditions in animal and crop husbandry are upheld.

Crna Gora means 'Black Mountain' and it is often said to be a reflection on the forbidding appearance of the great and symbolic Mt Lovćen, clad in pines, as it appears rising from the sea. A more likely explanation is that the name derives from Ivan Crnojević, the last ruler of the medieval state of Zeta, who in 1482 led his people to refuge from the Ottoman forces in the mountain fastness of Cetinje, at the foot of Mt Lovćen. Over centuries of heroic self-defence and bloodshed Montenegrins have become inured to the ultimate – to death – and to some extent this has numbed its sting. You have only to encounter them on their highways to recognise that for them life is balanced on the fulcrum; something of a gamble, where to win nevertheless means all. To a Montenegrin the values that count are honour, courage and loyalty, but these lofty ideals are sweetly laced with humanity.

It is important to understand that until very recently this was essentially a tribal society regulated by archaic customs and traditional rules, where the blood feud was incontrovertible and justice was meted out according to its dictate. In Hubert Butler's perceptive essay 'The Last Izmerenje' it is clear how recently this stuff has been going on (*izmerenje*, or more usually *izmirenje*, means 'reconciliation'). Some would argue that vestiges of these mores linger even today.

> The Montenegrin love of liberty and fair play and the Montenegrin sense of honour have made me feel more at home in this far corner of Europe than in any other foreign land.

So said Edith Durham in her 1904 book, *Through the Lands of the Serb*. The British have a natural understanding and respect for Montenegro; we too value our independence and have traditionally been prepared to fight tooth and nail to retain it. Like us, figuratively at least, they are a small island, though much of their sea is of limestone and granite. Montenegro's national and revered hero is Petar II Petrović Njegoš, a statesman and writer respected for his direction and justification of difficult choices on the noble path of survival. We too have our national heroes who on occasion have taken responsibility for sometimes controversial decisions. One of these was Winston Spencer Churchill, also a writer, a poet and certainly a statesman.

Lord Byron is frequently quoted, more often misquoted. That he found the country beautiful is beyond dispute. Maybe, like this author, he found the place so spellbinding he was simply at a loss for words.

* * *

They rose to where their sovereign eagle sails,
They kept their faith, their freedom, on the height,
Chaste, frugal, savage, arm'd by day and night
Against the Turk; whose inroad nowhere scales
Their headlong passes, but his footstep fails,
And red with blood the Crescent reels from fight
Before their dauntless hundreds, in prone flight
By thousands down the crags and thro' the vales.
O smallest among peoples! rough rock-throne
Of Freedom! warriors beating back the swarm
Of Turkish Islam for five hundred years,
Great Tsernogora! never since thine own
Black ridges drew the cloud and brake the storm
Has breathed a race of mightier mountaineers.

Montenegro, Alfred Lord Tennyson, 1877
(Internet Modern History Sourcebook,
www.fordham.edu/halsall/mod/tennyson-montenegro.html)

Part One

GENERAL INFORMATION

MONTENEGRO AT A GLANCE

Location On the Adriatic coast, with Serbia to the north, Albania to the southeast and Croatia and Bosnia and Herzegovina to the northwest

Status Republic

Size 13,812km²

National parks Durmitor (39,000ha); Lovćen (6,200ha); Biogradska Gora (5,650ha); Skadar Lake (40,000ha); Prokletije (16,630ha)

Climate Mediterranean on coast; more extreme on central plain; subalpine in mountains

Population 625,266 (2011 census)

Capital Podgorica (population 185,937)

Historical and cultural capital Cetinje

Other major cities Herceg Novi, Ulcinj, Budva, Nikšić, Kotor, Bar and Pljevlja

Total length of roads 5,174km

Length of railway 249km

Major earners Bauxite and aluminium; beer and wine; ship repair; hydro-electric power; agriculture including timber; tourism

Language Montenegrin

Religion Most Montenegrins are, at least nominally, Christian, but there is also a significant Muslim minority. Main Christian denomination is Eastern Orthodox, subdivided into Montenegrin Orthodox and Serbian Orthodox; sizeable Roman Catholic presence; also small minorities of Protestants and Jews.

Currency Euro €1 = £0.79 = US$1.28 (autumn 2014)

Time GMT+1; daylight saving +1 hour from last Sunday in March to last Sunday in October

International telephone code +382 (Serbia retains the old shared number, +381)

Email national designation .me (formerly cg.yu)

Electricity 220 volts AC. Sockets are round two-pin.

Flag The golden eagle of King Nikola on a red field with a golden frame, on the chest of the eagle a lion backed with green and blue (adopted 12 July 2004)

Anthem Based on the traditional folk song 'Oh Bright Dawn in May' (*Oj Svijetla Majska Zoro*)

National holidays 1–2 January, 7 January, 8 March, Easter Sunday & Monday, 1–2 May, 9 May, 21–2 May, 13 July, 29–30 November, 25 December

1

Background Information

GEOGRAPHY

Montenegro is a former constituent republic of Yugoslavia. It lies on the Adriatic coast, between Croatia and Albania; it also borders on Bosnia and Herzegovina, Serbia and Kosovo. Roughly equal in circumference to Cyprus or Connecticut, Montenegro, with such a concertina of mountains, is in terms of surface area far bigger than either. At 13,812km², it is nevertheless a small country. The length of the coastline is 293km, of which 73km are beach. The length of the borders is 614km. The highest mountain, Bobotov kuk (Mt Durmitor), is 2,523m, although some claim that peaks in the Prokletije, on the border with Albania, are higher. The largest lake, Skadar, is 391km². The deepest canyon, Tara, is 1,300m.

The complete geographical picture of the country is marvellously diverse: in effect, a narrow coastal plain, a lofty Dinaric hinterland and an interior karst plain mottled with stubbly, *maquis*-covered hills. Karst is the limestone constituent present in the Alps themselves, which are in turn part of the range that extends parallel with the Adriatic coast, forming a spondylitic backbone to the Balkan peninsula. As a result of the ground's characteristic porosity, rain water rapidly disappears, leaving a landform stony and barren. Some lakes dry up completely in summer and underground is a honeycomb of channels and caves.

The 277km narrow coastal plain is defined by beaches and inlets and what is invariably referred to as the Mediterranean's only 'fjord', the awesome Boka Kotorska, characterised by high mountains – 'hyacinth-pale', as writer Simon Winchester so aptly described them – rising almost perpendicularly from the gulf and, on its seaward, westerly coast, the untamed Luštica Peninsula with its secluded coves and iridescent blue grotto. The seashores, most of which provide excellent facilities for bathing, diving, sailing and almost all water sports, are a mix of white pebble and, in the far south beyond the pirates' domain of Ulcinj, over 13km of broad, unbroken, sandy beach. The mild Mediterranean climate the entire coast enjoys makes for long hot summers and the promise of a five- to six-month swimming season.

Skadar Lake, only 40km from the sea, is the largest lake in the Balkans and rich in flora and fauna. It's both a fisherman's and an ornithologist's paradise, its adjacent marshland being one of the most extensive in the Mediterranean.

The northern region is theatrically mountainous and alpine, intersected by fast-flowing rivers in deep, narrow valleys, ravines and narrow plateaux, glacial lakes and virgin forests. With a canyon grand enough to be compared to Colorado's and an assembly of peaks over 2,000m, it is no surprise that historically it has proved ideal guerrilla country, as centuries of invaders, most recently the Nazis, have found to their cost. While the north remains economically the least developed area of Montenegro, it holds, in the Durmitor National Park alone, 200km of marked hiking trails, challenging mountain climbing and some skiing, the latter at particularly advantageous prices. In the nearby Bjelasica–Komovi highlands, another small ski centre operates within easy reach of the centrally located town of Kolašin, and a network of 'green paths' for long-distance walking has been mapped, with Biogradska Gora, close by, one of the few surviving primeval forests in Europe. A third small ski station is situated not far from Nikšić in the central region. Further east the mighty Prokletije Massif, bordering on Albania, constitutes an extraordinary wilderness terrain (see also pages 290–1 and 302).

CLIMATE

The narrow coastal belt enjoys a Mediterranean climate, with long dry summers and short mild winters. Average July maximum temperatures are around 28°C; the January average is 9°C. Annual sunshine amounts to over 2,500 hours with a summer average of 300-plus hours per month – or ten hours a day. November is generally the wettest month.

The central plain is colder in winter and warmer in summer than the coast. Podgorica averages a January temperature of 5°C and a July temperature of 26.5°C. The maximum can reach 40°C and the minimum –10°C.

AVERAGE AIR/SEA TEMPERATURES & SUNSHINE

	Coastal strip				Inland		Mountains		
	Air temperature °C (average max)	Air temperature °C (average min)	Hours of sunshine per day	Sea temperature °C	Air temperature °C (average max)	Air temperature °C (average min)	Air temperature °C (average max)	Air temperature °C (average min)	Hours of sunshine per day
Winter									
December	13.2	6.1	3.4	14.8	8.9	0	3.2	-5.2	-
January	11.9	4.5	3.7	13.0	7.1	-1.5	2.0	-7.3	2.6
February	12.4	5.1	4.3	12.5	8.3	-1.0	4.1	-5.8	3.4
Spring									
March	14.8	7.1	5.3	13.9	11.8	3.7	8.1	-2.5	4.4
April	18.7	9.7	6.5	16.1	16.0	5.7	12.4	1.0	5.3
May	22.3	13.6	8.2	20.4	21.2	9.9	17.8	5.1	6.2
Summer									
June	26.1	16.8	9.6	23.7	24.9	11.8	20.8	8.1	6.8
July	28.6	19.3	10.9	24.4	28.5	15.4	23.3	9.3	8.5
August	28.8	19.2	10.0	25.1	28.5	15.1	23.5	9.1	7.9
Autumn									
September	25.8	16.6	8.2	23.8	24.4	11.9	20.0	6.2	6.5
October	21.6	13.1	6.2	21.3	18.9	7.4	14.9	2.4	-
November	13.7	9.3	4.0	18.2	12.9	3.5	8.8	-1.1	-

The high karst mountain area consists of plains at around 1,700m rising to peaks at around 2,000m. The climate is subalpine with cold snowy winters (up to 5m in the mountains) and moderate summers averaging 270 hours of sunshine per month. Winter maximum temperatures are around 3°C and minima around –6°C. In the summer months, temperatures range from 23°C to 9°C.

NATURAL HISTORY AND CONSERVATION

FAUNA According to a report written in 2001 by the Wildlife Conservation Society of Yugoslavia, it is still possible to find bears, wolves, lynx and jackals in the wilder parts of Montenegro.

Bears The number of Balkan brown bears at large is said to be around a hundred, largely spread across the mountainous areas of the north. Montenegrin bears generally live between 900m and 2,600m, concentrated in the 1,000–1,500m band. They prefer broad-leaf forests to conifers and like human presence to be minimal, but they do not mind a few sheep and cattle in the summer and they fancy some orchards and fields in the vicinity. Plums are a particular favourite.

Bears are only aggressive, says the society, when they are protecting their cubs or their food supply, or if they are scared or surprised. And they don't like dogs much.

Human attacks are very rare, but in 2001 some children were attacked while collecting mushrooms near Rožaje. Montenegrin hunting laws protect only females with cubs under two years old in the winter months, but males as well as females in the summer.

Wolves There are believed to be 200–300 wolves in the northern hilly/mountain areas. They like deciduous forests with a few glades and meadows and are not averse to some livestock in the vicinity. There is said to be no recent record of a wolf attacking a human, except occasionally when they are rabid – though it is not necessarily easy to tell at a distance whether they are in this state.

Wolves are unprotected in Montenegro, because of the threat they pose to sheep, and indeed in some places they attract a €15 bounty. When a wolf is killed in Rožaje, it is customary to put it on the roof rack and drive around town on a lap of victory. An estimated 300 wolves were shot in 1980, although numbers killed are rather lower today. (This situation may not tally with the fact that Montenegro has declared its intention to better its record in ecological terms, but it at least has aspirations.)

Lynx and jackals A small number of lynx are believed to inhabit the area around Plužine. They prefer to live between 550m and 2,500m in scarcely populated, rocky areas of oak or beech forest. They are not known to attack humans but will occasionally go for a dog. Like jackals, lynx avoid the home bases of the bigger and stronger wolf. A few jackals exist in southern Mediterranean and sub-Mediterranean areas but they do not bother anyone much.

Snakes Snakes are not much more likely than wolves to cause problems for the visitor. The two poisonous land snakes, both members of the viper family, are the *poskok* (nose-horned viper) and the *šarka* (common viper or adder).

The *poskok* – by far the more venomous of the two – is thin and green with a nasty little horn on its nose. The *šarka* is bigger, the colour and circumference of a good cigar. Both will get out of your way if they possibly can, but they quite like lying in the sun on warm rocks or tracks.

Birds The variety of terrain and climate in Montenegro means that, despite its small size, it is home to an astonishingly large variety of birds. It is reliably reported that over 300 bird species (of a total of 526 European species) can be found regularly in the country. Of these, some 200 actually nest in Montenegro, including raptors, forest and wetland species.

The coast attracts waders, cormorants and pelicans, as well as – on the Ulcinj Saltpans – flamingoes. Freshwater lakes, such as Šasko Lake, host many different species of swamp bird, as well as a heron colony, while at Skadar Lake National Park, eagles, ibis, bitterns, herons, warblers, ducks, pelicans, owls and buntings are among the 290 recorded species, with wintering flocks numbering some 200,000 birds.

The virgin deciduous–coniferous forest of Biogradska Gora National Park is home to a profusion of forest birds, including eagles, owls, woodpeckers, thrushes, larks, nightingales, tits, buntings and partridges, while the mountainous Durmitor National Park, with its thick coniferous forest, claims 167 different species of bird.

PROJECT CANTERBURY

In 1861 the Rev J M Neale MA, Warden of Sackville College, published an account of his visit to Cetinje in Notes, Ecclesiological and Picturesque, on Dalmatia, Croatia, Istria, Styria, with a Visit to Montenegro:

'We were very anxious to pay, however hurriedly, a visit to Montenegro; which, though shorn of its interest since the alteration of its hierarchical government, has yet sufficient difference from every other European state, to render a visit, though it may be brief, an entrance, as it were, into a perfectly novel scene.

Having hired three horses for ourselves (permission having been obtained for Dundich) and one as a sumpter animal, we rode out of Cattaro about 7 in the morning. The pavement of the city is so extremely slippery, that, to prevent accidents, our baggage was not packed till we were fairly outside the walls, in the place where the Montenegrins usually hold their market. Almost the very moment that Cattaro is left, the ascent of the mountain begins, admirably engineered by a series of zigzags, and presenting at each turn a nobler and nobler prospect – at first, of the Canal, afterwards of the eastern coast, and, finally, of mountain-range behind mountain-range, stretching onward to the interior. This road was a work of the Austrian Government; and, though followed by the Montenegrins in ascending it, it is utterly neglected by them in the descent, when, however heavily loaded, they jump down from parapet to parapet, endeavouring merely to strike out the shortest, without any regard to the easiest, line. For the first three-quarters of an hour, the citadel of Cattaro towers high above you on the right hand; and, before you attain its elevation, you pass the small Morlaceo hamlet of Spigliari. Here a road strikes off to the right, which eventually leads to Budua, and the southernmost extremity of the Austrian dominions in Turkey; but a few miles off. This hamlet contains nine houses; and there is a tradition that, should that number ever be exceeded, the place will at once be destroyed. The Austrian frontier extends some way beyond this; and the moment we pass that, the mountain-road end [sic]. We are forced to dismount, and our horses clamber as well as they can through watercourses and over rocks; so utterly bad [a] road that I think Portugal could not match it.

For more information on the birds of Montenegro as a whole there are three excellent websites: www.birdwatchingmn.org (**The Centre for Protection and Research of Birds**, Montenegrin only); www.fatbirder.com/links_geo/europe/montenegro.html and www.birdtours.co.uk/tripreports/serbia/mont1/montenegro97.html. For details of birdwatching, see pages 63–4.

FLORA Montenegro, especially in spring and summer, is filled with a wide variety of wild flowers, some unique to this corner of the Balkans, and at all times is host to an extensive range of plants. Serious botanists would do well to arm themselves with a book such as Oleg Polunin's *Flowers of Greece and the Balkans*; the rest of us should probably take a Latin dictionary as well. What follows concentrates only on a few of the more recognisable species.

Dalmatian coast The Dalmatian coast climate of generally hot dry summers, mild damp winters and early springs means the vegetation is attractive and quite

It is almost impossible to imagine, without having seen, the marvellous effect of those mountain-ranges, tossed in the wildest confusion one behind the other, as you look to the Herzegovina and to Bosnia. It is no uncommon thing to make out fifteen or sixteen lines of mountain at once. About four hours from Cettigne, we came on a kind of desolate plateau, where was a miserable cottage, dignified by our servant with the name of 'The Hotel'. It consists of one room, into which fowls, horses, and men have promiscuous entrance. The poor people that keep it belong to the Eastern Church, and there was the little icon of S. Mary, hanging in the corner of their room – the place of honour here as in Russia. A wretched daub it was; but it received as much veneration from the Montenegrin muleteers, who were dining while we fed our beasts, as the most precious relique in the most gorgeous church could ever enjoy. Since it is necessary to walk for some four or five miles, the road being all but impassable for horses. There is one most glorious prospect towards Scutari and Antivari; the track there makes a tremendous dip into a narrow ravine, and, on the left hand, at the commencement of the succeeding mountain, is the little village of S. George. Here I made acquaintance with the priest, and was introduced to his wife. Miserably poor they were; his income amounting – so far as the Church is concerned – to about thirty florins a-year: but, as he said, he would not change situations with any 'pastor' – to use his own term – in Christendom. He told me that neither he nor any of the Montenegrin priests ever preached, except some of the more learned ones at Christmas and Easter. I counted his library: it consisted of eight volumes. His church was built in the seventeenth century: there is nothing whatever noticeable in it, though the iconostasis has somewhat better paintings than might be expected in such an out-of-the-way spot.

Thus we proceeded all day, with no further variation than the different degrees of savageness of each succeeding ravine. But the water-shed of the mountains once passed, the scenery improved, and several of the glens were covered with bushes and low underwood, and then, as we penetrated more and more into the country, with really fine trees. The latter – now at the very end of May – were almost in full leaf; but here and there the snow lay in patches under them. At length, about 6 o'clock, we stood on the summit of the last mountain-range, and saw the long, narrow plain of Cettigne stretching at our feet.'

The flora of Montenegro is one of the most diverse of any comparable-sized temperate or subtropical region in the world. The country is mostly mountainous, with only 10% of its land area below 200m elevation. Montenegro is generally classified as having a Mediterranean climate along the coast and continental climate inland, though microclimates can be found along the coast, valleys, mountains, and plateaus, creating a diversity of habitats with subtropical to alpine floras. The geological features form three distinct floristic zones: the inland mountains, the central lowland plain and the Adriatic coast. The diverse climate and relief features create a high degree of biological diversity in a very small territory.

The coastal hinterlands dip into a rugged, yet friendly coastline, with mountains holding a flora typical of Mediterranean climates. Familiar herbs in the mint family (Lamiaceae or Labiatae), such as winter savory (*Satureja montana* L.), sage (*S. officinalis* L.), thyme (*Thymus* spp.), and oregano (*Origanum vulgare* L.), abound in the dry rocky soils, under the shadow of the spires of Italian cypress (*Cupressus sempervirens* L., Cupressaceae), basking beneath the hot Mediterranean sun. Here thickets of wild figs (*Ficus carica* L., Moraceae), chaste tree (*Vitex agnus-castus* L., Verbenaceae), wild pomegranate (*Punica granatum* L., Punicaceae), and Scotch broom (*Cytisus scoparius* L., Fabaceae) surround ancient olive groves on mountain slopes that dip into the turquoise waters of the Adriatic below.

Montenegro's tradition of harvesting wild medicinal herbs dates back centuries, if not millennia. Dalmatia is the origin for much of the world's common **garden sage** – 'Dalmatian sage', the familiar culinary herb and phytomedicine. More than 50% of the world's supply is still wild – harvested along the Adriatic coast from Albania in the south to the Croatian coastal mountains north of Montenegro. As an understorey subshrub, sage is a dominant floristic element in the coastal mountains, with its azure blue flowers covering the dry rocky landscape.

Montenegro has 3,136 vascular plants, of which 659 species are medicinal. In the coastal region approximately 174 species have recognised medicinal value. In the central highlands, as many as 540 medicinal plant species are found, and in the Balkans to the north, at least 479 species can be documented as medicinal plants. Three of the top 15 best-selling herbs on world markets are wild-harvested in Montenegro, including St John's wort (*Hypericum perforatum* L., Clusiaceae), valerian (*Valeriana officinalis* L., Valerianaceae) and bilberry (*Vaccinium myrtillus* L., Ericaceae). In addition, the Adriatic coast from Albania to Montenegro is the world's largest production region of wild-harvested Dalmatian sage (*Salvia officinalis* L., Lamiaceae).

The distinct silver-grey leaves of **olive** (*Olea europea* L., Oleaceae), now valued for their antioxidant and antihypertensive activity, are a familiar sight along the coastal region. Among the nearly 500,000 olive trees in ancient groves along the Montenegrin coast is a special treat for those who make their way to the village of Mirovica just north of Bar, where a local park protects a 2,000-year-old olive tree – one of the oldest in the world. Legend holds that before marrying, men must plant ten olive trees, which has resulted in nearly 500,000 olive trees growing today in ancient groves along the Montenegrin coast.

Throughout Montenegro, **St John's wort** commonly blooms from late May to August, depending upon the region and the elevation. Along the Montenegrin coast in July and August, one may come across an occasional vendor selling bottles of *Kanatrionovo Ulje* – St John's wort oil. The red-coloured oil is used to treat first-degree burns, along with bruises and other skin conditions. Once known to pharmacists as 'red oil' or 'Hypericum liniment', it is still available in European pharmacies. In Montenegro, it is sold as a kind of 'tanning oil' to create a dark tan, though in light-skinned individuals this practice could cause an unpleasant dermatitis.

In late June, heading inland towards Skadar, a dominant flowering plant is *Helichrysum italicum* (Roth) G. Don, Asteraceae. The flowering tops are collected by villagers along the coastal mountains and the Skadar Lake region and sold to buyers for distillation of the essential oil. Known regionally as *immortelle*, or in the American nursery trade as '**curry plant**', the essential oil has been shown to have significant antibacterial activity as well as anti-inflammatory and antioxidant activity. Aromatherapists use the essential oil to facilitate the healing of wounds and scars. One of the reasons it has not gained more popularity is its great expense compared with other essential oils.

Driving north towards the Sinjavina Massif, one transitions from a Mediterranean to a continental flora and high alpine slopes, some over 2,500m tall, with familiar medicinal plants typical of central Europe such as **linden** (known in some areas by the common name 'lime tree', *Tilia* spp., Tiliaceae), **bilberry** and **gentian** (*Gentiana lutea* L., Gentianaceae). Climbing the steep truck-choked main highway up Mt Sinjavina, one reaches a continental divide where water flows west towards the Adriatic on the western slopes and towards the Black Sea from the eastern slopes. This eastern slope holds the headwaters of the Tara River valley. The azure blue waters, considered the cleanest in Europe, cut through the Biogradska Gora National Park towards the Durmitor Massif, with 49 peaks over 2,000m atop a vast plateau. Here in the calcareous soils of the high mountain glades and plateaux is the home of **yellow gentian** (*G. lutea* spp. *symphandra* [Murb.] Hayek), the root of which has long been valued as a bitter tonic. Yellow gentian is one important medicinal plant which has become threatened in Montenegro and throughout its range, due to factors ranging from relative scarcity in a limited high-mountain habitat to overharvest. The export of the root is now banned. Today former traders in gentian root are keenly interested in its conservation. One such, Mr Veselin Vicinić, is the owner of Flores, a herb tea, bulk herb and essential oil producer in Mojkovac. For some years, he has been encouraging villagers and seasonal shepherds in remote mountain hamlets – where there are no tractors, mowing machines or hay balers – to let the plants go to seed. This informal conservation effort serves to help increase awareness of the plant and its sustainable development.

Further north and east in the city of Plav, the annual Bilberry Festival celebrates the harvest season of this native wild fruit, known locally as 'blueberry'. Bilberry jam and juice products are widely available in markets in Montenegro. Since imposition of UN sanctions in the early 1990s, the bilberry harvest has fallen to less than half of its former tonnage, and the regional government for Plav and business concerns began the Bilberry Festival in an effort to redevelop this wild-harvested crop.

Author, photographer and consultant, Steven Foster, is co-author (with Rebecca Johnson) of Desk Reference to Nature's Medicine *(2006, National Geographic Society, Washington, DC), produced with support from USAID and the Booz Allen Montenegro Competitiveness Project (MCP). Abridged from* Herbal Grain, *the Journal of the American Botanical Council. © American Botanical Council; used with kind permission.*

varied. There are a lot of evergreen trees, small, greyish aromatic shrubs and brightly coloured flowers, especially in the spring and at the beginning of autumn, and a high degree of cultivation. Sometimes the land suffers from deforestation or overgrazing. The trees are often varieties of pine or less familiar members of the oak family, as well as junipers and, of course, olives. There are also large areas of *maquis*, a sort of high dense scrub growing to 2–3m, composed largely of hard-leaved evergreen shrubs.

Maquis often results from deforestation and may just be a stage on the way to *garrigue*, which is a stunted version of *maquis*. In spring the *garrigue* can be quite colourful, but by high summer it is distinctly monochrome.

There are two main varieties of *maquis*, one in which myrtles predominate and the other characterised by holm oaks, which despite their family name are catkin-bearing evergreens. Myrtle leaves are a commonly used cooking herb, especially with lamb or goat, as well as being deployed homoeopathically as an antiseptic or astringent. But the most attractive of the *maquis* trees are the Scots and Aleppo pines, some of which manage to rise up through the underbrush.

The *maquis* and *garrigue* are full of climbing plants such as sarsaparilla, many of them prickly enough to make pedestrian progress hazardous. Among the other evergreens are heathers, briars, strawberry trees (nothing to do with strawberries except for a slight similarity in the appearance of the fruit) and bay (*Laurus nobilis*), the leaves of which are also used for robust meat flavouring, and the berries in eau-de-vie. Many of the flowering plants are typically European Mediterranean: sweet-scented wisteria, oleanders, mimosa and bougainvillea, with thyme and eucalyptus to confound the perfume.

The marshy areas are full of rushes and sedge but also have irises, kingcups and orchids.

Inland Further inland and at higher levels the characteristic vegetation of oaks, hornbeams, planes, willows, some elms and poplars with oleanders, birch and tamarisk is called by the botanists 'Mediterranean mixed deciduous'. There are also some big beech forests. Above about 600m one finds wide areas of fir and pine rising to nearly 2,000m, which is the treeline. The upland meadows, especially in May and June, are a Technicolor carpet including the protected gentian.

NATIONAL PARKS AND CONSERVATION There is no question that the country has made a unique pledge to adopt an ecologically protective policy, but it is taking time to implement. In the main this is because most of the infrastructure, water and drainage are still antiquated, though these issues are being addressed by the Montenegrins with such international aid as they at present receive. With the increase of tourists on the coast in the summer months, freshwater supplies have in the past been overstretched, but the situation is improving along the littoral.

There are five national parks, together incorporating a full 10% of the country, and all well worth visiting: Biogradska Gora (pages 271–4), Lovćen (pages 90–4), Skadar Lake (pages 223–31), Prokletije (pages 290–1) and Durmitor (pages 256–63). For further details, contact the **National Parks of Montenegro Public Enterprise** (*Podgorica;* \ *020 601015;* e *npcg@nparkovi.me; www.nparkovi.me*).

HISTORY

For a small country, Montenegro has an immensely complex history. However, bearing in mind that it sits in the middle of the Balkans, has been on or near the

DECLARATION ON THE ECOLOGICAL STATE OF MONTENEGRO

'We, members of the Parliament of the Republic of Montenegro, are aware that, in view of the threat to nature, protection of the identity of the land in which we live and work has become our most immediate and pressing task.

Bearing in mind our debt to nature, a source of health and our inspiration for freedom and culture, we are devoting ourselves to its protection for the sake of our survival and the future of our posterity.

We recognize that all our differences are less important than the changes in the environment we live in. Regardless of our national, religious, political and other sentiments and convictions we are fully aware that dignity and blessedness of a human being are intrinsically connected with blessedness and purity of nature.

Man and creation in him and around him are one in their depths, their meaning and denotation.

Thus the abuse of man has always entailed the abuse of nature. And being committed to the struggle for the dignity of man, we are also called upon to struggle for the dignity of nature.

By adopting this Declaration, Montenegro defines its attitude towards nature as a state policy and calls upon all the people to show wisdom and prevent an impending ecological catastrophe.'

This declaration was made at Žabljak on 20 September 1991.

front lines of a series of more or less despotic empires including the Roman, the Ottoman, the Austro-Hungarian, the Napoleonic, the Nazi and the Soviet, and that its people are said to take seriously only God and war, this may not be much of a surprise.

ILLYRIANS, ROMANS AND SLAVS Signs of Balkan civilisation date back to the 7th millennium BC. Agriculture, pottery and copper smelting supported the establishment of small towns and by the end of the 4th millennium BC there was active trade with eastern Europe. By 600BC the Illyrians were settled in what is now Montenegro, utilising iron technology for both swords and ploughshares and dealing extensively with the Greek city states. By 400BC Celts were moving in from the north, closely followed by the Romans. In AD9 the Illyrians were subdued though the territory remained Illyrium. The Romans built roads, aqueducts, forts and all the usual trappings of empire.

When the Emperor Theodosius died in AD395, the Roman Empire split into two, roughly from the site of the present Budva and up the Sava and Danube rivers. Rome lost control of the eastern half, which became the Byzantine Empire. The western half remained Roman. The Goths and the Huns displaced the Romans over the next 200 years, but the overall military masters of the region were the Avars and Bulgars under the nominal rule of Constantinople.

During the 6th century AD Slavs from Poland and the Baltic, attracted partly by the Mediterranean climate, moved into the province of Praevalitana. They found Roman settlements already established at what are now Kotor, Budva, Ulcinj, Bar and Duklija, and were gradually converted to Christianity by the existing populace. One can still trace many hundreds of Baltic and Polish place names, rivers and mountains which correspond to those in the Balkans.

1

In AD625 the Emperor Heraclius formed an alliance with two of the stronger Slavic tribes already in the region, the Croats and the Serbs, who took control of the Dalmatian coast. Because Dalmatia was rugged and lacking in minerals, the interior became something of a haven for refugee tribes, living mostly as extended family groups (*zadruge*) governed by a fairly democratically selected patriarch (*župan*). Sometimes several of these *zadruge* would unite under a senior *župan*, who might even adopt the title of king. The first Serb mini-state duly emerged in about 850 under a senior *župan* called Vlastimir, who resisted Bulgar expansion and acknowledged Byzantine suzerainty. The 9th century also saw a gradual adoption of Christianity, and the introduction of the Cyrillic alphabet, which spread from the territories of the First Bulgarian Empire, where it had been developed by disciples of the Byzantine missionaries Sts Cyril and Methodius.

THE KINGDOM OF DUKLIJA Following Vlastimir's death there was a period of general disorganisation, but in 1017 his nephew, King Vojislav, set up the vassal state of Duklija (or Doclea) named after the Illyrian tribe who once lived there. In 1042 he beat the Byzantines at the battle of Bar and won independence. By 1077 his son Mihailo governed a kingdom which included most of Montenegro, Albania and Herzegovina and he was acknowledged by Pope Gregory VII as *Sclavorum Regi* – King of the Slavs.

The kingdom of Duklija gradually weakened until in 1169 a senior *župan* called Stefan Nemanja established a vassal state in the region of Raška. His son, Stefan Provencani ('first crowned'), became the first real Serb king in 1217. The dynasty steadily expanded until the ninth king, Stefan Dušan (1331–55), ruled over an area including Montenegro, Albania, Macedonia, much of Bosnia and Serbia, as well as Epirus and Thessaly. A key to this expansion was the family's success in promoting religious and cultural cohesion under the Orthodox Church and in codifying the law. See also page 112.

THE ARRIVAL OF THE OTTOMANS The Ottoman Empire established a foothold on mainland Europe in 1354 and began to expand northwards. Slav leaders were disunited and competitive, constantly making and breaking alliances with the Turks and with each other. The Turks regarded all Muslims as belonging to a single community of the faithful and so anyone could join the ruling group by converting to Islam.

The Ottomans took Serbia at the battle of Kosovo in 1389, occupied Bosnia in 1463 and Herzegovina in 1483. The Crnojević dynasty, who by now ruled most of present-day Montenegro, moved the capital from Žabljak Crnojevići (see also page 230) on Skadar Lake to the hill town of Cetinje in 1482 to resist the invaders more easily. The territory began for the first time to be known as Crna Gora and, though its boundaries had contracted, it established traditions of independent sovereignty and culture, with Cetinje becoming the home of the first printing press in southern Europe in 1494. For tactical reasons King Stefan concluded an alliance with Venice in 1455.

THE PRINCE-BISHOPS In 1516 there was a major constitutional shift in Montenegro. The last of the Crnojević dynasty married a Venetian and retired to Venice, conferring the succession upon the prince-bishop (*vladika*) of Cetinje. This formal link between Church and State ensured national stability, lending the *vladika* authority in the eyes of the peasants and minimising the risk of competitive alliances between local leaders and the Turks. War with the Ottoman Empire

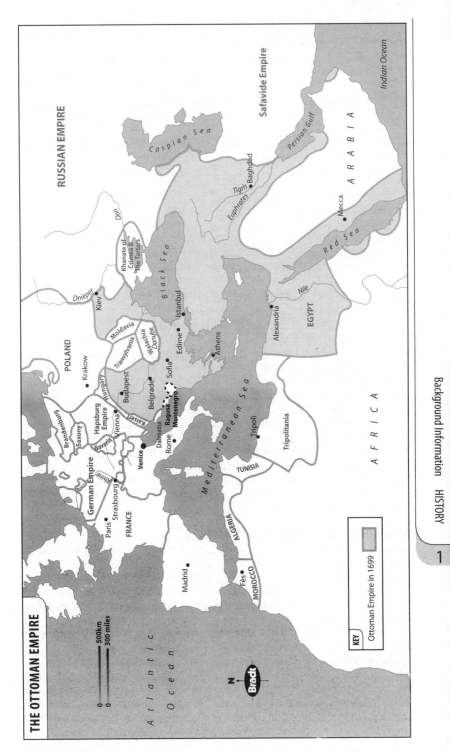

THE OTTOMAN EMPIRE

KEY

Ottoman Empire in 1699

… just friends and brave enemies.

Thomas Jefferson, 1806

In accordance with the 1878 Congress of Berlin, Prince Nikola set about implementing the provisions it had directed and ensuring political and religious rights were granted to the Muslim inhabitants of Montenegro. He appointed a *mufti* (Islamic scholar) to oversee those of the Islamic faith and a period of peace ensued between the Principality of Montenegro and the Ottoman Empire, shattered only with the outbreak of the Balkan wars of 1912–13.

In the course of several amicable visits between Constantinople and Cetinje, presents were exchanged. Prince Nikola received a yacht, a white Arabian steed and a palace on the Bosphorus. Diplomacy not being without its little ironies, that mansion was later sold in order that the (by this time) king could keep himself during his years of exile (1916–21).

continued, but although Cetinje was sacked in 1623, 1687 and again in 1712, the Turks were never able to subjugate the Montenegrins.

As Orthodox bishops the *vladikas* were required to be celibate, and initially the succession was elective, but when Danilo acceded in 1696 he won the right to nominate his own heir. Subsequently the hereditary theocracy remained vested in the Petrović clan, invariably passing from uncle to nephew.

In July 1712 Danilo won a notable victory over a 35,000-man Turkish army at Carev Laz. Five thousand Turks died and the battle became a landmark in Montenegro's Wars of Independence.

As well as being a successful general, Danilo was a successful diplomat. As Venetian power declined, he paid a visit in 1715 to Peter the Great. The resulting Russian alliance brought financial aid and modest territorial gains, but Danilo was still outshone by Petar I Petrović Njegoš, who acceded in 1782. He defeated the Turks in a series of battles, using guerrilla tactics to compensate for his much smaller forces. By 1799 the Ottoman Porte had had enough and formally recognised Montenegrin independence.

MONTENEGRO AND RUSSIA VERSUS NAPOLEON
In 1806 Montenegro and Russia combined to beat Napoleon at Kotor, then Montenegro won unilateral battles against him at Cavtat and Herceg Novi. The Montenegrins also beat the French at Kotor Bay, utilising ammunition supplied by Britain and Russia, but the subsequent Congress of Vienna in 1814 nevertheless gave Kotor Bay to Austria. Despite the part it had played in the downfall of Napoleon, Montenegro still lacked the access to the sea it so badly wanted.

When Petar I died in 1830, he was proclaimed a saint of the Montenegrin Orthodox Church, St Petar of Cetinje (Sv Petar Cetinskji).

The early 19th century saw considerable social change in Montenegro, especially after the succession of Petar II Petrović Njegoš. By general consensus Petar II was the most outstanding of all Montenegrin rulers and he laid the foundations of the subsequent kingdom and indeed of modern Montenegro. He organised a central government comprising a senate, a 32-man *guardia* who acted as travelling magistrates, and a *perjanici*, who were a police force. He organised taxes, despite predictable opposition from individualistic Montenegrins, and he was an epic poet whose *magnum opus*, *The Mountain Wreath*, distilled in the vernacular the essence of Montenegrin wisdom and philosophy.

Petar II died in 1851, but his nephew Danilo II was already betrothed and therefore could not succeed him as *vladika*. Instead he became *gospodar* (prince) and by ensuring that this remained a hereditary position he effectively separated Church and State. In 1860 he was assassinated at Kotor, quite possibly at Austrian instigation, and was succeeded by the 19-year-old Nikola Petrović, who had spent the previous two years being educated in Venice.

PRINCE NIKOLA PETROVIĆ The francophile court that had sent Nikola to Venice favoured French language and French etiquette. Nikola shared this admiration, although his wife was a good Montenegrin. Together they had three sons and nine daughters. Six of the latter married royal or aristocratic Europeans, including Grand Duke Petar of Russia and King Victor Emmanuel of Italy, and became invaluable political assets (see box, page 94). This was insufficient, however, to keep the Turks quiet, and after an intermittent series of wars and treaties Montenegro and Serbia jointly declared war on Turkey in 1876, with Russia joining in a year later.

Between 1876 and 1878 Prince Nikola led the Montenegrin army to a series of victories. The Congress of Berlin in 1878 confirmed most of the resulting territorial gains, including the towns of Podgorica, Bar, Ulcinj and Nikšić. Montenegro virtually doubled in size and its new borders were internationally recognised. It had access to the sea at last.

Nikola was also a social reformer. He introduced free elementary education and a girls' institute for elementary teachers, an agricultural college, post and telegraph offices, a network of roads and railways and freedom of the press. Foreign capital, especially Italian, flooded in; business boomed and a number of embassies opened in Cetinje.

Great Britain was among the countries ready to establish good relations with the principality and in 1887 the Duke of Edinburgh, son of Queen Victoria, visited Cetinje on a five-day state visit, together with his duchess (Maria Alexandrovna, sister of the Tsar Alexander) and his nephew George (later to become King George V).

In 1910 parliament proclaimed Nikola king. But 1912 saw the start of the Balkan wars against Turkey. Montenegro was again victorious and the Treaty of London brought more territorial gains on the Albanian and Kosovan borders, but the Montenegrins paid a high price in casualties.

WORLD WAR I When World War I broke out in 1914, Montenegro immediately invaded the recently established state of Albania and then, in support of Serbia, declared war on Austria. This was a mistake as by late 1915 both countries were occupied by Austro-German troops. Most of the Serbian army escaped to Corfu and lived to fight another day, but the Montenegrin army did not stage a tactical retreat, unlike King Nikola who took some of his ministers to Rome and put himself under the protection of his son-in-law, the king of Italy.

In 1918 King Petar of Serbia, another son-in-law of Nikola, exploited the post-war chaos to enter Montenegro with his troops. At first the Serbs were welcomed as liberators and allies in the expectation that the Montenegrin government would be restored as part of the new Confederation of Slavic States. But when Serbia's role as an army of occupation became clear and Serbia announced the annexation of Montenegro, Montenegrins staged a national uprising on the Orthodox Christmas, 7 January 1919. Nikola died in Antibes in 1921 (though in 1989 his remains, along with those of his queen, were reinterred in Cetinje in the Chapel of Cipur), but this Montenegrin war continued until 1926 and ended only because the leaders believed the promises of the Allies to restore liberty and independence. Lloyd George, Poincaré and Wilson all publicly pledged Montenegrin independence, but actions did not match words and Montenegro became the only Allied country to lose its freedom as a result of World War I. Emigration, especially to the USA, accelerated.

THE BIRTH OF YUGOSLAVIA Between the two world wars, Montenegro disappeared from the map and suffered from malign neglect at the hands of Serbia, which turned itself into Yugoslavia in 1929. The assassination of Yugoslavia's King Alexander by a Croat in 1934 and his replacement by the Regent Prince Paul, uncle of King Petar II, made little difference to the centrist Belgrade regime. An effective programme of land reform turned Yugoslavia into a reasonably prosperous country of small farmers. As Germany under Hitler led the interwar European economic revival, Hitler deliberately built links with Yugoslavia and by 1938, 53% of Yugoslav exports went there. Following that year's *Anschluss*, Yugoslavia worked hard to maintain its political independence in the face of German pressure to join the Axis. The invasions of Czechoslovakia and, by the Italians, Albania added to the pressure, as did the 1939 Nazi–Soviet non-aggression pact. In March 1941 Prince Paul finally caved in and signed the Tripartite Pact with Germany and Italy.

WORLD WAR II AND THE PARTISANS The popular response was one of outrage, leading to a bloodless coup fronted by the air force. The regent was exiled and King Petar II's immediate accession was proclaimed by the Government of National Unity. Within a month Germany invaded and Petar fled to London with his government-in-exile. Yugoslavia was split up and shared between Germany, Italy, Hungary and Bulgaria. Most of Montenegro was handed to the Italians, the rest to Italian-ruled Albania. An ill-starred Italian attempt to restore a puppet monarchy in Montenegro was short-lived. An enlarged and autonomous Croatia under the fascist Ante Pavelić and his Ustaša movement adopted a policy of extreme racial purification, exterminating what may have amounted to hundreds of thousands of Jews, gypsies and Serbs. The rump of the Royal Yugoslav Army went into hiding and formed the Chetniks under Dragoljub Mihailović. The third and much the most significant resistance force were the Communist Partisans led by Josip Broz, using the *nom de guerre* of Tito.

These three military groups were coming from totally different directions. Ustaša troops acted as little more than an adjunct of the Axis armies. The objective of the Chetniks was to maintain the prospect of a reunified Yugoslavia which could be handed back to King Petar when the war finally ended. The Partisans, on the other hand, waged all-out guerrilla war almost regardless of casualties or reprisals, aimed both at taking some pressure off the beleaguered Soviet Union and at establishing a communist state in post-war Yugoslavia. Their success in harassing the Axis can be judged by the savagely high reprisal tariff of 50 executed Yugoslavs for every wounded Axis soldier and 150 executed Yugoslavs for every killed Axis soldier.

Inevitably all three groups clashed with each other, especially the Ustaše and the Partisans. Britain did what it could to support resistance but initially the shortage of supplies and transport meant that support was largely moral. At first Churchill and the Special Operations Executive (SOE) inclined instinctively towards the royalist Chetniks and their London-based leader, but as intercepted signals traffic made it increasingly obvious that only the Partisans were inflicting significant casualties on the Axis troops, so British and (in due course) American assistance swung behind Tito. By early 1944 all the Allied backing was going to him and the presence since 1941 of a British military mission on the ground (albeit a small one), led first by Bill (later Sir William) Deakin and then by Fitzroy (later Sir Fitzroy) Maclean, gave Britain something of a unique relationship.

Montenegro's relatively isolated position and mountainous interior, together with the strength of the local Communist Party and the country's warlike traditions, made it an ideal operating zone for the Partisans. When Italy surrendered in 1943 the Partisans in Montenegro became even better placed as they took over huge quantities of Italian weapons and ammunition.

By the summer of 1944 the end of the war was in sight. Tito met Churchill in Naples in August and then flew without notice to Moscow. There, plans were laid for the liberation of Yugoslavia. With Russian assistance the Partisans liberated Belgrade in October and quickly took possession of the rest of the country.

TITO BECOMES PRESIDENT The Partisans were now in an enviable position of power. They had 800,000 men in uniform, an effective civil administration and no occupying troops. King Petar unwillingly agreed not to return until there had been a plebiscite on the monarchy, though three members of the London government-in-exile joined the Belgrade government under Prime Minister Tito. In November 1945, in a high poll, 90% of voters backed a new constitution setting up the Federal People's Republic of Yugoslavia. Full communist control was imposed and the authoritarian State Security Service (UDBA) ensured that there was no meaningful opposition.

Partly as a reward for its heroic role in wartime resistance, Montenegro became one of the six republics in the new Yugoslavia and acquired additional territory

SIR WILLIAM DEAKIN

In the years before the war, which led to his parachuting by night on to Mt Durmitor in the midst of a major military operation, Bill Deakin was a fellow and tutor in history at Wadham College, Oxford, and also literary assistant to Sir Winston Churchill when the latter was writing his life of Marlborough.

Deakin was seconded to the Special Operations Executive (SOE) from the Queen's Own Oxfordshire Hussars, serving in Egypt before he went to Yugoslavia (see above). When the war ended, after a year at the embassy in Belgrade, he went back to Oxford and in 1950 became the first Warden of St Antony's, staying there until he retired to the south of France in 1968.

Among his decorations are a DSO awarded in 1943; a Partisan Star 1st class; a Russian Order of Valour; a Légion d'Honneur; and, in 1958, a German Grosse Verdienstkreuz. He was knighted in 1975.

He died, aged 91, on 22 January 2005.

Sir Fitzroy Maclean, Bart, is another British SOE operative whose name is associated with Partisan support in World War II. He was romantically described at the time by the Nazi press:

> So this is Tito's Grey Eminence ... His career developed according to the schemes of British plutocratic tradition: Eton and Cambridge, embassy attaché in Paris and Moscow, Eastern European department of the Foreign Office, Lieutenant of the Highlanders. Bribed elections in his native town of Lancaster gave him the possibility of imposing a by-election in which he was elected. When the war broke out this smart young man thought himself a hero.
>
> Apparently he cannot keep quiet, he is dreaming of adventures in foreign countries and of military glory, he remembers that he is an officer who renounced the exemption from military service to which he is entitled as a member of the House of Commons, and joins the Highlanders fighting in North Africa against Rommel.
>
> In short he is: an adventurer, who in the middle of the war remembers he is an officer. But he does not stay a long time with the Highlanders. He joins the parachute troops and is awarded the rank of colonel, for a landing behind the lines of the Italians, who were already demoralised at that time. He named his parachute company 'Mystery column'. This energetic youth was chosen by England, when the need was felt by His Britannic Majesty to send a mission to Tito's bands. An adventurer who dreams of glory and heroical deeds, in remote countries and who intends teaching Tito's bandits with a Kodak and a bush-knife the meaning of English culture ...
>
> *Donauzeitung*, 4 February 1944

Sir Fitzroy was a diplomat before World War II, serving for some time in the Soviet Union during the era of Stalinist show trials. An MP for over 30 years, he was Under Secretary for War in both the Churchill and the Eden governments, then went back to write books and farm in Argyllshire. He died on 15 June 1996.

along the Dalmatian coast. The other republics were Serbia, Croatia, Bosnia and Herzegovina, Macedonia and Slovenia. With six languages (Serbian, Croatian, Macedonian, Slovenian, Albanian and Hungarian) and three religions (Roman Catholic, Orthodox and Muslim) the new country faced a complex birth. But it was not only the strongest Balkan nation, it was also second only to the USSR in terms of power in eastern Europe.

Yugoslavia expected post-war Soviet support over boundary disputes, especially with Austria and Italy, and in the economic sphere. They also expected recognition for their heroic resistance to Hitler. But Stalin regarded Tito as a potential rival on the international stage. In 1948 he summoned representatives of Yugoslavia and Bulgaria to Moscow to reprimand them for the independence of their policies. Bulgaria submitted but Tito replied with his famous letter about different roads to socialism. By 1949 eastern and western Europe were divided by the Iron Curtain and Yugoslavia had been expelled from the Communist Bloc.

POST-TITO: THE FRAGMENTATION OF YUGOSLAVIA Tito devoted much of his energy to establishing himself as a leader of the Non-Aligned Movement and

Yugoslavia prospered well enough economically, particularly in the field of tourism. His achievement in bonding the country was immense and many former Yugoslavs look back with nostalgia on Yugoslavia's golden years and think fondly of Tito's role as a leader (with Castro, Nasser and Nehru) of the so-called Non-Aligned. The six republics enjoyed a fair degree of autonomy but development was uneven and in many respects Montenegro lagged behind.

When Tito died in May 1980 Yugoslavia began to fragment. Foreign debt and ethnic tensions both grew. By 1991 inter-republic relations were tense and Slovenia and Croatia, followed by Macedonia, all withdrew from the Federation. Heavy fighting broke out after the JNA (Yugoslav People's Army) entered Croatia, occupying around a quarter of the country and, along with Serbian irregulars, laying siege to Dubrovnik and Vukovar. In May 1992 a UN protective force was introduced but by 1995 over 200,000 Serbs had been forced to leave the territory and some half a million Croats had been displaced.

In Bosnia and Herzegovina the Muslim and Croat populations wished to secede from the Federation but the Serbs wanted to stay. This was a black period in Yugoslav history, involving civil war, atrocities, war crimes and widespread bloodshed. In 1992 Bosnia's independence was recognised. And then there were two; Montenegro and Serbia jointly proclaimed the new Federal Republic of Yugoslavia on 27 April 1992. Each of them had its own president, its own legislature and sovereignty over all matters not specifically assigned to the federal government.

THE MILOSEVIĆ YEARS Slobodan Milošević, who had been president of Serbia for ten years, took over as president of the Federation in 1997. He continued the policy of restricting the rights of ethnic Albanians in the region of Kosovo, whose autonomy had been abolished some seven years earlier, which provoked increasingly effective insurrection by the Kosovo Liberation Army. In March 1998, the Yugoslav army launched a counter-offensive and by the autumn the Kosovan force had been largely eliminated. NATO tried, ineffectively, to mediate and in March 1999 began a series of air strikes against targets in Montenegro, Serbia, Kosovo and the autonomous region of Vojvodina. Milošević made no concessions and forced some 800,000 Kosovans out of their territory and into Bosnia, Albania and Macedonia. NATO then deployed the Kosovo Force (KFOR) and Kosovo became a United Nations protectorate. Montenegro increasingly distanced itself from Milošević's Kosovo policies and offered a haven to tens of thousands of displaced persons.

In October 2000 Milošević was overthrown and replaced as federal president by Vojislav Kostunica, who called parliamentary elections, persuaded the United Nations to readmit Yugoslavia and established an interim coalition government. On 11 March 2006 Milošević was found dead in his cell in The Hague while on trial before the International Court of Justice, accused of war crimes.

MONTENEGRO TODAY On 14 March 2002 the federal and the two remaining republican governments of former Yugoslavia signed the Belgrade Agreement to form a new loose confederation, to be known henceforward as the State Union of Serbia and Montenegro. The constitutional charter of this alliance was signed on 4 February 2003, indicating a firm intention towards eventual integration into the European Union (EU). In the meantime each of the republics was broadly autonomous, with its own prime minister but joint federal ministries of defence, foreign affairs, human rights and internal trade. The economies, customs services and currencies remained separate, and indeed Montenegro adopted the euro when it was first introduced on 1 January 2002, while Serbia retained the dinar. The unicameral parliament had 91 Serbian seats and 35 Montenegrin.

Under the constitutional charter, either side had the right to hold a referendum after three years to consider national independence. In 2006, to no-one's surprise, Montenegro opted to exercise this right and, on 21 May 2006, under EU supervision and monitored by a multitude of international bureaucrats, the population duly voted 55.5% in favour of an independent Republic of Montenegro on an 86.5% turnout. This narrowly satisfied the agreed minimum majority of 55%. The EU and the US had jointly opposed the split on the grounds that 'Balkanisation' would encourage a further proliferation of small states such as Kosovo and would tend to push the area towards instability, but they accepted the transition with good grace and both the Montenegrins and the Serbs have been sensible enough to make the process painless and to maintain excellent bilateral relations throughout the separation process. Serbia inherited the old Yugoslav membership of the UN and other major multilateral bodies, but Montenegro has in most places been quickly elected alongside them.

Milo Đukanović had dominated Montenegrin politics since the Union was formed in 2002 and he was the victor of the referendum. Having won clear parliamentary endorsement he became the first state president, but stepped down in October of that year so he could be elected prime minister the following January. His Coalition for a European Montenegro consisted mainly of his own Democratic Party of Socialists (DPS) and the Social Democratic Party (SDP), but deliberately included representatives of all the main ethnic groups. In the first independent elections, held on 10 September 2006, the coalition won a narrow majority, securing 41 of the 81 parliamentary seats contested. The opposition, led by Pedrag Bulatović's pro-Yugoslavia Coalition for Changes, did poorly, dropping from 26 to 11 seats and finishing equal third to Andrija Mandić's Serb List who won 12. Nebojsa Medojević's new party, Movement for Changes, previously an NGO, also held 11 seats.

On 3 October 2006 Đukanović resigned and Željko Sturanović was named premier in his place, though Đukanović was reappointed prime minister in February 2008.

Filip Vujanović was elected president of Montenegro in May 2003 after Đukanović stepped down. He was reconfirmed president in April 2008 with 52% of the vote. Both domestic and international observers confirmed the legitimacy of these elections and, on 10 June 2009, Đukanović was re-elected by parliament to a sixth term and his coalition held a comfortable majority of 48 of the 81 seats. He nevertheless resigned in December 2010 and Igor Lukšić took over as prime minister. Still in his mid-30s Mr Lukšić, who has a doctorate in economics and had previously been minister of finance, became the youngest premier in the world. A linguist and a natural communicator, he brought the face of Montenegrin government into the 21st century. He was succeeded in December 2012 by Milo Đukanović, who was elected for a fourth term as prime minister, having become minister of finance in the Lukšić government. The current president is again Filip Vujanović.

In April 2009, the European Union approved Montenegro's application to become a candidate for membership, but such a step is still a year or two off; Croatia, at the head of the Balkan queue, became a member of the EU in 2013, and both Montenegro and Serbia may not be far behind, with the EU having opened accession talks with Montenegro in June 2012.

The future now bodes well for Montenegro to continue sailing smoothly out of her doldrum decade of isolation and frustration. Further democratic progress, prospects of continued privatisation, increases in tourism and fresh international investment initiatives look assured. Though there remain some local issues regarding uneven regional economic development, there is little serious friction between the various ethnic groups.

ECONOMY

Under Tito, Yugoslavia was by communist standards a moderately successful economy. There was a reasonably developed industry exporting to the Third World and eastern and western Europe, agriculture was doing quite well and tourism was booming along the Adriatic coast. After a rocky post-Tito period, things were starting to look up again until the flare-up of Milosević versus NATO, and bombs over former Yugoslavia. Embargoes became the order of the day and, despite distancing itself from the perceived political excesses of Serbia, Montenegro suffered quite a lot more than it deserved.

Economically it still misses its old socialist hinterland but its political ambitions within Europe are clear and sensible and Montenegro is on the way back. Towards the end of the Milosević era Montenegro removed its budget and economy from federal control, adopted the euro instead of the dinar as the official currency, established an independent central bank and set up its own customs regime. Unemployment is decreasing relatively quickly but remains uncomfortably high.

The Agency for Economic Restructuring and Foreign Investment in Podgorica is ambitiously slanted towards reconstruction fuelled by foreign investment, and the latter is starting to flow in. Tourism rightly comes high on the priority list. Purchase prices of existing establishments are often low, but prospective purchasers are expected to pour in significant further investment. Montenegro's eyes are on an increasingly upmarket clientele and will be encouraged that the World Travel and Tourism Council ranks Montenegro as the fastest-growing tourist destination anywhere, with a steady increase of 8% per annum forecast over the next decade. Those who are prepared to invest more than €500,000 in the country are rewarded with citizenship and tax breaks.

The single greatest contributor to GDP and export is the Podgorica Aluminium Plant, now privatised and belonging to the Russian-owned En+ Group. Agriculture remains important, as do docks and shipping. Other businesses have been sold to Western interests – Nikšić Brewery, for example, has been bought by Interbrew of Belgium, petrol retailer Jugopetrol Kotor by Hellenic Petroleum, Montenegro Bank by the Slovenian Nova Ljubljanska Bank, and Montenegro Telekom has gone to Matov of Hungary.

PEOPLE

The population at the 2011 census was 625,266, which marks a continuing decline. Unfortunately the last decade has seen a steady exodus of better-educated young Montenegrins looking for a higher standard of living abroad, though their remittances are a useful source of income. Around 58% of the population now lives in urban areas. The refugee problem is exacerbated by the age spread: a large number are either under 14 years of age or over 60 with only a comparatively small percentage falling within the more productive years in between.

The real ethnic and cultural differences between Serbian and Montenegrin are interminably debatable and interminably debated. There have been constant population shifts and intermarriage among the two and also with Croatians,

Albanians and Bosnians. The latest (2011) census puts ethnic Montenegrins at about 45%, Serbs at about 28%, with Albanians at 5%, Croats at about 1% and Bosnians at over 8%. A sizeable number of Montenegrins live in Serbia.

In a notable social shift, the farming percentage of Montenegro dropped from 61.5% of the population in 1953 to 7.4% in 1991. The vast majority of the working population is engaged in services, another sizeable percentage in industry and only a very small percentage in agriculture.

LANGUAGE

The name of the language spoken in Montenegro was for some years a subject of debate. Serbo-Croat was the language of Montenegro, Serbia, Bosnia and Herzegovina and Croatia, but Montenegro has now come into line with its fellow former Yugoslav republics and called the language Montenegrin after the state, a clear improvement on the previous infelicitous *Maternji Jezik* ('Mother Tongue') or the confusing suggestion by some academics to name it *South Slav*.

One difference between the languages spoken in Belgrade and Podgorica is that the latter has two extra letters. It is also characterised by its wide use of proverbs, metaphors and figurative speech.

The language – or languages – once known as Serbo-Croat actually comes in a western variant, spoken in Croatia and most of Bosnia and Herzegovina, and an eastern variant, spoken in Serbia. Montenegro has a bit of each, and it was generally referred to just as Serbian (*Srpsko*). Most writing is in the Latin alphabet but Cyrillic is increasingly widely used, especially away from the coast and, unlike in Serbia, both alphabets have equal status under the constitution. Foreign tourists, especially those travelling around by car or bike, will find it helpful to have a basic familiarity with the Cyrillic alphabet, or at least a phrasebook with a crib (see *Appendix 1*, page 315).

Along the coast there are a number of minor dialects that are not too different from the mother tongue, as well as at least two varieties which are non-comprehensible to monolingual Serbians. One is Paštrovski (strangely similar, it is claimed, to the dialect of Puglia in Italy; so much so that each can understand the other), spoken by the fiercely independent tribe who still predominate in the area around Petrovac; the other is Budva, spoken around that town. Neither is still widely used and intermarriage with outsiders poses a threat to their continuing viability.

Native Albanian speakers are concentrated in the eastern border areas of the country.

One thing Montenegro shares with every other country in the world is an appreciation of tourists who make an effort to speak at least a little of what – to us – looks and sounds a very unfamiliar sort of language, with a paucity of vowels. For information on pronunciation and a brief vocabulary, see *Appendix 1*, page 315.

English replaced Russian as the second language in schools some years ago and there are generally people around in the resort areas with a good, or at least reasonable command of the language. Elsewhere, if you need an interpreter it is a better bet to seek out a 30-something or younger. After Russian and English the most widely spoken foreign languages are Italian (for reasons of geography) and German (because of the relatively large number of tourists).

RELIGION

The population of Montenegro is approximately 70% Orthodox, 21% Islamic, 4% Roman Catholic, 2% Protestant, 3% other. Montenegro's various religions co-exist with no apparent signs of strife, although there is minor disagreement between those who espouse Serbian Orthodoxy and the small number who prefer to call themselves Montenegrin Orthodox. The fact that there is no discernible doctrinal difference does not preclude theological argument.

Any dispute arises from the premise that the Montenegrin Orthodox Church was independent from 1766 until 1920, when it was assimilated into the Serbian Church. An independent Montenegrin Orthodox Church was once again set up in 2000 but it is regarded as renegade by the global Orthodox faith, and the official Montenegrin Church remains part of the Serbian one.

Religious extremists of any persuasion are very rare. The Council for the Safeguarding of the Rights of National Minorities, chaired by the President of Montenegro, takes a particular interest in religious equality.

Most of the ethnic Slav **Muslims** come from the Sandžak area, which was partitioned between Montenegro and Serbia in 1913, while the ethnic Albanian Muslims live near the Albanian and Kosovan borders. Some Montenegrins were converted to Islam through force and some through bribery. Others were convinced. Most Montenegrin Muslims are Sunni, though a Dervish sect introduced in 1974 also has its adherents. The civic rights of Muslims are carefully protected and there are several Muslim members of Parliament.

The **Roman Catholic** Archdiocese of Bar is one of two covering the territories of Montenegro, Serbia and Macedonia. The current archbishop is Petar Perkolić. Bar was raised to the status of archbishopric by Pope Clement III in 1089. It supervises ten bishoprics. For historical reasons the Catholics tend to be concentrated along the coast, while the mountains have a higher proportion of Orthodox.

The predominant Montenegrin religion remains **Eastern Orthodox**, part of the family of Christian Churches in eastern Europe under the general primacy

---

BURIAL NOTICES

Within towns you may see white squares of paper pinned to roadside trees. These are bereavement notices: black-edged being for Orthodox, blue-edged for children and green-edged for Muslim. As the saying goes: 'I haven't seen Branko lately, not even on the olive tree …'

of the Patriarchate of Constantinople. It developed from the Greek Church of the Byzantine Empire and finally broke with Rome in 1054 over the issues of papal primacy and the language of the creed. The veneration of icons is central to Orthodox belief.

EDUCATION

In 1871 the little country had 40 schools. Montenegrins are proud to relate that by 1910 that number had increased to 136, as a result of reforms in social administration brought about by Prince, later to be King, Nikola.

Elementary education is free and compulsory for all children between the ages of six and 15. Various types of secondary education are available but the most popular include technical and vocational schools, with four-year courses designed to take pupils to university entrance. At secondary level there are art, apprentice and teacher-training schools, followed by post-secondary schools and the University of Montenegro at Podgorica. Graduate unemployment is high, as it is for most other socio-economic groups.

The normal language of instruction is Montenegrin, but Albanian is also used in some schools.

Adult literacy of Montenegrin nationals is over 90%. Despite the policy outlined above, current school enrolment is approximately 70% at the primary level, 65% at the secondary level and 25% at the tertiary level. The influx of refugees has made already serious overcrowding in schools even worse, but urgent steps are being taken to improve this situation.

CULTURE

NATIONAL COSTUME National costume is not much in evidence these days, even in the remoter areas. Around 75 years ago a highlander would typically be wearing a red embroidered waistcoat, a white coat, dark breeches and white leggings. Around his shoulders, pashmina-style, would be draped a wide all-purpose wrap. Arms were carried at all times, often extravagantly, including not just several pistols but knives and a sword as well. A man would not wish to be seen without his belt. On the head every male would, in keeping with his sovereign, wear a traditional black rimless hat (*képi*), its crown embroidered with red and gold. These colours were said to declare red for blood, gold for glory and black for remembrance. Until 1910, this was also his battle-dress.

ART AND ARCHITECTURE There is a strong Byzantine influence in Montenegrin medieval architecture and painting, visible in the thousands of square metres of frescoes in the monasteries and in the hundreds of icons. Other notable buildings include the Renaissance palaces at Kotor and Perast, and many examples of Venetian influence in the region of the Boka Kotorska. More recent administrative buildings tend to be Socialist Realist and not worth the detour.

Village houses in the Muslim areas usually have an Eastern appearance while in the Orthodox areas they are typically Mediterranean.

PAINTING AND SCULPTURE Montenegrin painting largely followed the religious tradition until the 19th century. The 20th century saw local artists increasingly drawn into the European modern mainstream, partly through visits to the country by significant foreign artists and partly through outward travels to Italy and France.

Today both the quality and quantity of art on display is impressive and pictures are among the best purchases to take home at the end of a visit.

There has, by contrast, never been much of a tradition of sculpture but you can find some collectable wood carvings, especially in the mountains.

MUSIC Much of Montenegrin music is an acquired taste to Western ears, though some of the choral works are easy to appreciate.

The vocal tradition features funeral laments, generally sung by women, centring on stories about the dead person, though the lilting songs of the Boka seamen are altogether more cheerful, and – around Kotor – easy to find on CD. The two national instruments are the flute, played by the mountain people who watch over the animals, and the single-string violin called the *gusle*, invariably played with a vocal accompaniment.

Montenegro offers such a theatrical backdrop, it is surprising that so far it has featured so little in opera (but see also the following section on literature).

In 2006 the government founded the Music Centre of Montenegro, and in December 2007 the new Montenegro Symphony Orchestra gave its premier performance in Cetinje under the baton of the Russian conductor Aleksey Shatsky. Since then the orchestra has performed regularly, often with leading international guests.

Another high point in current Montenegrin music is the guitar playing of Miloš Karadaglić, who has been described by the London *Daily Telegraph* as 'shining a brilliant light on the entire heritage of his instrument'. His first album, *Mediterráneo*, was issued in 2011; his latest, *Aranjuez*, in 2014.

LITERATURE AND PRINTING Montenegro has a strong literary tradition dating back nearly a thousand years. The oldest literary work, *Kingdom of Slavs*, was written in Bar in the 12th century by an anonymous Benedictine priest. Monasteries and other libraries contain a number of manuscripts from the 13th century, many

THE DIMITRIJEVIĆ–RAFAILOVIĆ ICON PAINTING SCHOOL

At the end of the 13th century and the beginning of the 14th, a decorated partition between the nave and the altar increasingly became an interior feature in church design. The painting of the incorporated wooden panels adhered to strict stylistic dictates, strongly Byzantine in influence but also frequently reflecting Greek, Romanesque, Gothic and Renaissance inspiration. The arrival of the Ottomans in Montenegro did not affect the idiom though in general artists were producing fewer works. In fact the 17th century is considered the golden era in iconography in Crna Gora, typified by Hilander (Mt Athos) master Georije Mitrovanović from Morača Monastery and also by the work of Radul. The pattern was continued by an extended group of artists from the Bay of Kotor, the Dimitrijević–Rafailović family of Risan, who, in the course of the 17th century through to the 19th, produced an exceptional body of work. Over five generations, the family produced 11 painters who created literally thousands of icons and almost a hundred iconostases, woodcarvings and fresco compositions, mainly in village churches. Though relatively unsophisticated on the grander scale, the paintings display great purity in conception and an infectious spiritual inspiration. What more could be desirable in a religious work of art?

illustrated with magnificent miniatures, but book production really stems from the introduction to Cetinje in 1494 of the first printing press in southern Europe, and one of the first anywhere on the continent. The first Montenegrin book, *Oktoih* (*The Book of Psalms*), was published in Cyrillic the same year, with intricate engravings. The Cetinje press, which was actually located at Obud just outside the nearby village of Rijeka Crnojevića, played a major role in diffusing literacy and culture in the area. As a consequence of Turkish attack this early press was closed in 1496. A subsequent one was installed in 1834 by Petar II Petrović Njegoš but during a Turkish siege in 1852 the type was melted down by the Montenegrins for deployment as bullets, as indeed was the roof of Njegoš's palace, Biljarda.

Poetry and history both ranked highly in Montenegrin book production, though the histories were sometimes quite blatantly spun. The earliest history of Montenegro, written by Prince-Bishop Vasilije and published in Moscow in 1754, was really an appeal for Russian military and financial support. Montenegrin rulers also used their literary efforts for political ends, leading the way in writing and encouraging books which served to unite the disparate clans in national solidarity against the Ottomans and in the pursuit of freedom. The work most highly regarded by Montenegrins even today is the 19th-century verse play *The Mountain Wreath*, written by *vladika* Petar II Petrović Njegoš. This philosophical piece gains little in translation.

Montenegro has often inspired authors from the rest of Europe and the United States, and books by Montenegrins were published abroad, especially in Venice and London. *Rime Vulgari* (*Vernacular Rhymes*), written by Ludovico Pasquali of Cattaro, was for some reason published in London in 1593. G Wheeler started the series of descriptive works on the area with his *A Journey to Dalmatia*, written in 1682, while the various wars of the 19th century inspired a number of works on both politics (including Gladstone's *Montenegro* in 1879 and a mediocre semi-political sonnet of the same name by Tennyson in 1877) and travel.

By the beginning of the 20th century a number of intrepid ladies were venturing into the Balkans. One of the books written in 1904 by Edith Durham, probably Rebecca West's only rival as *doyenne*, is prefaced by a publisher's note apologising that:

> Owing to the absence of Miss Durham in Macedonia, the following pages have not had the advantage of her revision in going through the press.

Various books and operas in the second half of the 19th century took up the theme of Montenegro the exotic. Franz Lehar's *The Merry Widow* is based on Prince Danilo and the romantic goings-on of the court at Cetinje. Alphonse Daudet borrowed the persona of a real-life Montenegrin con artist and lady-killer for *Tartarin de Tarascon*. Paris saw the operetta *The Montenegrins* in 1894. Pierre Loti drew upon his military experiences in the Boka, and a number of Italian authors profited from the traditional ties to feature things Montenegrin in miscellaneous works; indeed a Montenegrin bibliography published in 1993 lists no fewer than 1,043 Italian books on the country published in Italy between 1532 and 1941.

2

Practical Information

WHEN TO VISIT

The nicest seasons to visit Montenegro are spring and autumn: either between late March, by which time even in the high mountain regions the 'ice days' should have passed, and the end of June; or in September and October after the summer vacationers have dispersed, when the deciduous trees will be turning coppery but the sea will still be warm enough for bathing. July and August are the best months only for those who like family fun and crowds. As a local hotelier put it, speaking of the 'Montenegrin Riviera', while the under-30s will love the nightlife and buzz of the town beaches in July and August, those seeking a quieter ambience may prefer to visit the coast during the bridge months – April/May/June or September/October. In the mountains, July and August are guaranteed to be temperate.

HIGHLIGHTS

Montenegro, for its size, is a country of quite amazing diversity, where vast mountains and canyons fall steeply to an extraordinary 293km coastline and a series of brilliant blue inlets, the grandest of which is the ravishing Venetian Boka Kotorska.

Set back from the coastal plain, less-travelled peaks hide fascinating frescoed monasteries and intriguing archaeological sites. You will also find countless possibilities to hike, or ride your bike, or indeed the local bus, through untroubled wilderness, accessible for nine months of the year. For the other three, a scenic winter wonderland tempts visitors with challenging winter sports, and all at yesterday's prices.

In contrast but always within reach, the Adriatic provides dependable sunshine, restaurants and bars galore: glamour and nightlife to rival Ibiza. Ten years ago few had even heard of Montenegro, but the stars are out for the coming decade.

Because each is unique, the **five national parks** have to be high on a must-see itinerary; despite the twists and turns, sheer drops and terrifying abysses that may sometimes be involved in reaching them, try to take them all in, even if you are only here for a limited time. Skadar (pages 223–31), almost enclosed within Montenegrin and Albanian mountains, is the largest lake in the Balkans. Wonderfully tranquil, the shades of mist float just above the surface, dissolving into the far beyond. Equally a paradise for fishermen and ornithologists, it's also lovely for boat trips among the little islands. **Biogradska Gora** (pages 271–4) is mountains, lake and forest, 30% of the large area primeval and protected since 1878; no pruning, no planting, no clearing, but 2,000 different plant species make it scientifically important as well as beautiful.

Lovćen (pages 90–4) features the imposing mausoleum of Petar II Petrović Njegoš (1813–51), Montenegro's greatest ruler, philosopher and poet, high on the summit of Mt Jezerski and commanding a 360° view over his lands. This, the legendary Black Mountain, is sometimes referred to as Montenegro's Mt Olympus.

Durmitor (pages 256–63), a UNESCO Heritage Site since 1980, is at the mountainous heart of Crna Gora and was a centre of Partisan activity in World War II. It includes 27 peaks of over 2,200m and is bordered by two deep canyons, the Tara and the Piva. Rich in both fauna and flora, it is also the acme of the country's winter skiing.

The **Prokletije** (pages 290–1) is Montenegro's newest and arguably most breathtaking national park, its crenulated massif towering above deep glacial valleys and boasting Maja Kolata, at 2,528m just 5m higher than the mighty Bobotov kuk of Dumitor, rendering it the highest peak in the country. Largely undeveloped, this is a park for those who like spectacular scenery without many people, and are prepared to exercise their legs and lungs.

A second UNESCO Heritage Site is the city of **Kotor** (pages 139–48), deep in the Boka Bay. Often called a mini-Dubrovnik, its walls are even longer than those of its Croatian counterpart. A charming stone-clad maze of twisting alleys bathed in dawn shadows, it can feel like its only inhabitants are the cats. Venetian palaces and treasure-filled churches compete for your attention.

The country offers a wealth of possibilities for **walking**, and far beyond the borders of the national parks there is a wide variety of barely trodden trails where it is possible to find complete solitude and inspiring views. There are now established routes for **biking** through the mountains and canyons of the interior (maps should be available from local tourist offices as well as from the excellently equipped office of the regional tourist organisation at Kolašin for Bjelasica and Komovi).

Throughout the country there are partially explored **archaeological sites**, reflecting Montenegro's many successive influences – Illyrian, Greek, Roman, Byzantine, Slavic, Venetian and Turkish – while the coastal area from Herceg Novi in the northwest to Ulcinj in the far southeast has a romantic history of seafaring and pirates.

Montenegro offers excellent and competitively priced **spa facilities** in many of the hotels and a very wide range of treatments at the Mediterranean Health Centre in Igalo (page 124), adjacent to Herceg Novi, near the mouth of the Boka Kotorska. Here you will find ideal and discreet conditions for rest, recreation and medical care under expert supervision, with thalassotherapy a speciality. The location is particularly handy for those wishing to arrive and depart through Dubrovnik's Ćilipi Airport, and prices, so far, remain a steal.

SUGGESTED ITINERARIES

The majority of travellers arrive either by air into the capital Podgorica or by road from Croatia (having flown into Dubrovnik).

In principle, if you have a **free day** available in Podgorica you could take a local bus, or certainly a taxi, to visit the historic capital of Cetinje and its four main museums.

ONE DAY If you plan to spend only one day in the country, and if you are travelling from Croatia and join an **organised coach or taxi tour**, it is possible to travel through much of the Bay of Kotorska, climb the dizzying Ladder of Cattaro, lunch on the mile-high plateau of Njeguši and continue to the ancient capital of Cetinje before retracing your steps. You could also make the same itinerary by rental car or, if you are feeling energetic, by bike.

An alternative would be to travel down the coast via the stunning though short **Kamenari–Lepetane ferry**, on to Tivat with an opportunity to stroll through the impressive new Porto Montenegro development, and then to visit the restored city of Budva. Travelling by a relatively slow and infrequent local bus from Dubrovnik to Herceg Novi, the first big town over the border in Montenegro, would leave you very little time indeed to explore in a day.

A WEEKEND If you wish to plan a weekend in Montenegro and you are travelling **from Croatia** it is possible to travel more or less the length of the coast and back, with perhaps one overnight stay in each direction in either Kotor, Petrovac or Budva, all of which offer a wide choice of accommodation.

From Podgorica a tour of most of the coast, passing *en route* over Skadar Lake, could also be achieved in a weekend, but it would not allow much time for relaxation!

A WEEK OR LONGER With a **week** at your disposal it would perhaps be best to choose between exploring the coast quite fully, stopping at monasteries (accommodation within all price ranges should be available in coastal towns whatever the season), or instead concentrating mainly on the spectacular countryside inland. For example, a round trip allowing time for proper sightseeing could still include the Bay of Kotorska, but also the dramatic new road linking it, through Grahovo and Nikšić and the once remote Šavnik, to the high Durmitor range and the mighty Tara Canyon. There would be time to head to the far north to Pljevlja, with its beautiful mosque, before, if you are travelling by car or bike, taking the much-improved route down the eastern border to Bijelo Polje and the new Prokletije National Park. After this, travel through the Komovi mountains to Kolašin and later Podgorica and Skadar Lake.

If you have a **fortnight** you would comfortably be able to cover most of the country. Do keep in mind, though, that during the winter extensive touring using mountain roads is not recommended. At any time of the year the choice of accommodation will be limited in more remote areas.

TOURIST INFORMATION

The **National Tourism Organisation of Montenegro** (*Bulevar Sv Petra Cetinskog 130, 81000 Podgorica;* 📞 *077 100001;* e *info@montenegro.travel; www.montenegro.travel*) is the overall body providing general information and literature for travel throughout the country.

Tourist information centres in the municipalities are fair to excellent sources of information, generally but not invariably in English, on hotels, room rentals, restaurants, car and boat hire, adventure and sporting activities and local points of interest. At a time when tourist facilities are rapidly developing (which can mean both opening and closing) they are the best source of up-to-date listings and prices. They are typically open in summer 09.00–18.00 and in winter 09.00–14.00 (but expect a degree of flexibility in these hours).

There is a 24-hour tourist information **helpline** in English (📞 *1300*).

REGIONAL TOURIST OFFICES Please note that websites of a number of local tourist offices have recently switched from a .travel to a .me domain.

Bar Obala 13 jul bb; 📞 030 311633; e info@bar.travel; www.bar.travel

Berane Mojsije Zečevića 8; 📞 051 236664; e info@berane.travel; www.berane.travel

2

Budva Mediteranska 4; ☎033 402814; e info@budva.travel; www.budva.travel

Cetinje ☎041 230251; e info@cetinje.travel; www.cetinje.travel

Danilovgrad Sava Burića 2; ☎020 816016; e info@danilovgrad.travel; www.danilovgrad.travel

Herceg Novi Jova Dabovića 12; ☎031 350820; e info@hercegnovi.travel; www.hercegnovi.travel

Kolašin Mirka Vešovića 1; ☎020 864254; e info@kolasin.travel; www.kolasin.travel

Kotor Stari Grad 328; ☎032 325950; e info@kotor.travel; www.tokotor.me

Mojkovac ☎050 472428; e info@mojkovac.travel; www.mojkovac.travel

Nikšić Atrijum poslovic centar; ☎040 213262; e info@niksic.travel; www.niksic.montenegro.travel

Petrovac Stupovi bb, near bus station; ⏰ Jun–Sep, 08.00–20.00 Mon–Sat

Plav ☎051 252888; e info@plav.travel; www.plav.me

Pljevlja ☎052 300148; e info@pljevlja.travel; www.pljevlja.travel

Plužine ☎040 270069; e info@pluzine.travel; www.pluzine.travel

Podgorica Slobode 47; ☎020 667536; e info@podgorica.travel; www.podgorica.travel

Rožaje Maršala Tita bb; ☎051 270158; e info@rozaje.travel; www.rozaje.me (Montenegrin only)

Šavnik ☎040 266066; e info@savnik.travel; www.savnik.montenegro.travel/en/savnik

Tivat Palih boraca 8; ☎032 671324; e info@tivat.travel; www.tivat.travel

Ulcinj Marsala Tita bb; ☎030 412206; e info@ulcinj.travel; www.ulcinj.travel (Montenegrin only)

Žabljak Narodnih heroja 3; ☎052 361802; e info@zabljak.travel; www.zabljak.montenegro.travel/en/zabljak

Regional Tourism organisation for Bjelasica and Komovi Trg Boraca 2, Kolašin; ☎020 865110; e office@rtobik.co.me; www.bjelasica-komovi.me

TOUR OPERATORS

IN THE UK
Quite a few UK tour operators are now featuring package holidays to Montenegro in their brochures. The choice of packages & operators is steadily expanding & there is a reasonable choice. Currently the following are among the leaders in the field:

Balkan Holidays Ltd Sofia Hse, 19 Conduit St, London W1S 2BH; ☎020 7543 5555, 0845 130 1115 (brochure line), 0845 130 1114 (reservations); www.balkanholidays.co.uk. Flights from up to 10 UK airports. Holidays in Budva, Petrovac & elsewhere.

Cosmos Holidays ☎0843 227 1464; www.cosmos.co.uk

Discovery Travel Pope's Head Court Offices, Peter Lane, York YO1 8SU; ☎01904 632226; e info@discoverytravel.co.uk; www.discoverytravel.co.uk

Exodus Travels Ltd Grange Mills, Weir Rd, London SW12 0NE; ☎0845 287 3647; e sales@exodus.co.uk; www.exodus.co.uk. Walking in the Montenegrin mountains & on the coast, plus Bosnia & Herzegovina.

First Choice Diamond Hse, Peel Cross Rd, Salford, Manchester M5 4DT; ☎020 3451 2720; www.firstchoice.co.uk

Peregrine Adventures ☎0808 274 5438; e travel@peregrineadventures.com; www.peregrineadventures.co.uk

Ramblers Worldwide Holidays ☎01707 331133; e info@ramblersholidays.co.uk; www.ramblersholidays.co.uk

Regent Holidays 15 John St, Bristol BS1 2HR; ☎020 7666 1244; e regent@regentholidays.co.uk; www.regentholidays.co.uk

Thomson Holidays Greater London Hse, Hampstead Rd, London NW1 7SD; ☎0871 230 8181, 020 3451 2688; www.thomson.co.uk

Travelsphere Ltd Compass Hse, Rockingham Rd, Market Harborough LE16 7QD; ☎0844 273 7157; www.travelsphere.co.uk

IN MONTENEGRO
The following companies all have English-speaking staff:

Podgorica
✻ **Montenegro Adventures** Jovana Tomaševića 35, 81000 Podgorica; ☎020 208000; m 069 315601; e info@montenegro-adventures.com; www.montenegro-adventures.com. Arranges accommodation & travel for individual & group travel, whether for business or recreation, inc

conferences & team-building. A very professional & reliable outfit with knowledgeable, helpful staff that promotes sustainable tourism.

Montenegro Charter Company d.o.o. (yacht charter) bul Sv Petra Cetinjskog 92, 8100 Podgorica; ☎ 020 220195; m 069 070198; e info@montenegrocharter.com; www. montenegrocharter.com. All new boats based at the marina at Kotor.

Bijelo Polje
RAMS ☎ 050 432374; e rams@t-com.me, info@ ramstravel.co.me; www.ramstravel.co.me. See advert on page 76.

Budva
Adria Popa Jola Zeca bb, PO Box 49, Budva 85310; ☎ 033 402600; e adriaex@t-com.me; www. adriaex.com.Comprehensive range of services including airport transfers, accommodation, car hire, hiking, biking, jeeps, rafting, ecotours, birdwatching, boat trips, etc. Tailor-made programmes for groups & individuals, & business specialist.

Herceg Novi
* **Black Mountain Adventure Travel** e info@montenegroholiday.com; www. montenegroholiday.com. Internet-based company with can-do British owners; Russian & Montenegrin spoken. Dozens of eco-friendly outdoor activities throughout Montenegro & neighbouring areas.

Sveti Stefan
Levantin Travel Vukice Mitrović br 3; m 069 028436; e levantin@t-com.me; http://levantin.me/ travel-agency-st-stefan. Own adjacent boutique apartments; organise travel, car hire & excursions.

Kolašin
Eco Tours Donje Đokić 5; ☎ 020 860700; e eco-tours@t-com.me; www.eco-tours.co.me
Explorer Mojkovačka bb; ☎ 020 864200; e explorer@t-com.me; www.montenegroexplorer. co.me

Nikšić
Anitra Travel Agency Njegoševa 12; ☎ 040 200598; e info@anitra.me; http://tara-grab.com

Virpazar (Skadar Lake)
* **Undiscovered Montenegro** m 069 402364 (Montenegro), ☎ 020 3287 0015 (UK); e enquiries@undiscoveredmontenegro.com; www.undiscoveredmontenegro.com. UK-registered company run by British couple who have lived in the area for several years. Hiking, kayaking & other outdoor activities; wine & other tours; accommodation – all with an emphasis on sustainable local tourism.

Žabljak
Sv Đorđije (St George Travel) Jovana Cvijića 47; ☎ 052 361367; m 069 074367; e tasaint@t-com. me. Full knowledge of the region.

WORLDWIDE
Austria
Gruber Reisen Idlhofgasse 5–7, 8020 Graz; ☎ 316 70890; www.gruberreisen.at
Kompas Touristik Reiseveransitung GmbH Siebenterngasse 21, A-1070 Wien; ☎ 1 40 22042; e info@kompas.at; www.kompas.at

Belgium
Jetair Tui www.jetair.be

Canada
Bestway Tours 8678 Greenall Ave, Burnaby BC, V5J 3M6; ☎ 1 800 663 0844; www.bestway.com

Czech Republic
Cedok 11 135 Praha 1, Na Prikope 18; ☎ 800 112112; www.cedok.cz
Vitkovice Tours 1200 Praha, Myslikova 10; ☎ 800 567567; www.ckvt.cz

France
Clio Voyages Culturels 27 rue du Hameau, 75015 Paris; ☎ 01 53 68 82 82; www.clio.fr
Rivages du Monde 29 rue des Pyramides, 75001 Paris; ☎ 01 58 36 08 36; www.rivagesdumonde.fr
Top of Travel 4 Place Félix Eboué, 75583 Paris Cedex 12; www.topoftravel.fr

Germany
Mediterrana Tours Förstereistr 34, 01099 Dresden; ☎ 351 810 8758; e info@ mediterranatours.de; www.mediterranatours.de
ITS LTU Tourism GmbH, Humboldtstr 140–144, D-51149 Koln; www.its.de

2

TUI AG Karl Wiechert Allee 4, D-30625 Hannover; ☎0511 56780105; www.tui.com

Hungary
Quaestor Travel Bathori u 6, 1054 Budapest; ☎1 302 5010; www.quaestor.hu/travel

Ireland
Concorde 69 Upper O'Connell St, Dublin; ☎01 775 9300; e info@concordetravel.ie; www.concordetravel.ie

Israel
Flying Carpet 10 Nechama St, Tel Aviv; ☎3 515 1664; e Vickid1@flying.co.il; www.flying.co.il

Italy
Agestea 70126 Bari, via Liside 4; ☎080 558 4943
Eurotravel 11020 Quart (Aosta), Torrent de Maillod 15; ☎0165 773285
Kompas 00185 Roma, Piazza dell Esquilino 8/G; ☎06 4782 4267; www.kompas.it
Viaggi Prospettive 20158 Milano, via degli Imbriani 54; ☎02 393362

Russia
Bering 119034 Moscow, Precistenskii per, 22/4, office 11; ☎095 244 0506; e bering@mail.cnt.ru
Mosintur 109172 Moscow, Boljsie Kamensiki 19; ☎095 276 2675; e mosintur@arstel.ru

Slovakia
Globtour Rovniakova 34, Bratislava 85102; ☎2 6820 5810, 0850 166911; www.globtour.sk
Seneca Tours Blumentálska 11, Bratislava; ☎2 5249 4946; e seneca@seneca.sk; http://seneca.sk

Slovenia
Kompas Pražakova 4, 1514 Ljubljana; ☎01 2006 111; e info@kompas.si; www.kompas.si

USA
Affordable Tours 11150 Cash Rd, Stafford, TX 77477; ☎1 800 935 2620; www.affordabletours.com
Alexander & Roberts 53 Summer St, Keene, NH 03431; ☎1 800 221 2216; www.alexanderroberts.com
Witte Travel 3250 28th St SE, Grand Rapids, MI 49512; ☎1 800 469 4883; www.wittetravel.com

RED TAPE

VISAS Citizens of EU countries, Switzerland, Australia, Canada, New Zealand, USA, Israel, Japan and most countries of eastern Europe do not need visas for single-entry 90-day visits (for citizens of Russia, Albania and Ukraine the limit is 30 days). Make sure you get an entry stamp on arrival, however, or risk allegations of being an illegal immigrant when you leave. As with most countries, passports must be undamaged and valid for the length of the stay.

Would-be tourists from other countries, two particular examples being Malaysia and Taiwan, may experience unexpected and unexplained delays or even refusals. People from these countries should consider getting their visas before booking a non-refundable ticket. Nationals of countries not listed in the previous paragraph should contact their local Montenegrin consulate, if there is one, or their Serbian consulate as a fallback.

It is now routine and hassle-free to make side trips without visas to Serbia, Bosnia and Herzegovina, Croatia, Albania and Kosovo. For cross-border excursions, see *Chapter 9*.

EMBASSIES

OVERSEAS DIPLOMATIC OFFICES OF MONTENEGRO
Before the 2006 separation, Montenegrin diplomatic interests were formally in the hands of the joint embassies of Serbia & Montenegro, & Serbian embassies are to be found in most countries. Montenegro now has its own embassies in most major cities; elsewhere, the Serbian embassies have accepted some continuing responsibility & are a good place to start if you have any consular or other queries. Current Montenegrin offices include:

Ⓔ Albania Rr Jul Varibova 11, Tirana; ☎ +35 54 225 7406; e montenegroembassy@albmail.com
Ⓔ Austria Nibelungengasse 13/11, 1010 Vienna; ☎ +43 1 715 3102; e diplomat-mn@me-austria.eu
Ⓔ Belgium Rue de la Fusée 64, 1130 Brussels; ☎ +32 2705 2851
Ⓔ Bosnia & Herzegovina Talirovica 4, Sarajevo; ☎ +387 33 239925
Ⓔ China 3-1-12 San Li Tun Diplomatic Compound, Beijing 100600; ☎ +86 10 6532 7610; e embmontenegro@yahoo.com
Ⓔ Croatia Trg Nikole Šubica Zrinjskog 1, Zagreb; ☎ +385 1 4573 362
Ⓔ European Union Mission of the Republic of Montenegro to the EU, 34 rue Marie Thérèse, 1210 Brussels; ☎ +32 02 223 5561; e montenegrinmission@skynet.be
Ⓔ France Bd St Germain, Paris; ☎ +33 1 53 63 80 30
Ⓔ Germany Dessauerstr 28/29, D-10963 Berlin; ☎ +49 302 529 1996; e berlin@embassy-montenegro.de; Consulate-General of Montenegro, Zeil 5, 6013 Frankfurt/Main ☎ +49 698 484 4801
Ⓔ Hungary Jokai Ter 10.III.I, Budapest; ☎ +36 1311 0444; e amb.mne@hdsnet.hu
Ⓔ Italy Via Antonio Gramsci 9, Roma; ☎ +39 06 4544 3800, 4547 1660; e montenegro-roma@libero.it
Ⓔ Macedonia ul Vasil Stefanovski 7, Skopje; ☎ +389 23 227277
Ⓔ Russia Embassy of Montenegro, Mytnaya 3, ofis 23–25, 119049 Moskva; ☎ +74 99 230 1865; e ambassadac@ya.ru
Ⓔ Serbia Uzicka 1, Belgrade; ☎ +381 11 266 2300/8975; e ambasadacg@gmail.com
Ⓔ Slovenia Reseljeva cesta 40, Ljubljana; ☎ +386 1 439 5365; e embamon-lj@t-2.net
Ⓔ Switzerland 147 rue de Lausanne, 1202 Geneva; ☎ +41 22 732660, +41 22 732 6680; e missionofmontenegro@bluewin.ch
Ⓔ UK 18 Callcott St, London W8 7SU; ☎ +44 20 7727 6007; ⏰ embassy 09.00–17.00; consulate 11.00–13.00.
Ⓔ United Nations Mission of the Republic of Montenegro to the UN, 801 Second Av, 7th floor, New York, NY 10017; ☎ +1 212 661 3700
Ⓔ USA 1610 New Hampshire Av NW, Washington, DC 20009; ☎ +1 202 234 6108; e misijacg@msn.com; Consulate General of Montenegro, 801 Second Av, 7th floor, New York NY 10017 ☎ +1 212 661 3700/5400

FOREIGN EMBASSIES IN MONTENEGRO

Ⓔ Albanian Stanka Dragojevića 14, 81000 Podgorica; ☎ 020 667380; e embassy.podgorica@mfa.gov.alb; ⏰ 08.00–16.00 Mon–Fri
Ⓔ Austria Svetlane Kane Radević br 3, 81000 Podgorica; ☎ 020 201135; e podgorica-ob@bmaa.gv.at, podgorica-ob@bmeia.gv.at; ⏰ 08.00–16.00 Mon–Fri
Ⓔ Bosnia & Herzegovina Atinska 58, 81000 Podgorica; ☎ 020 618015; e amb.podgorica@mvp.gov.ba; ⏰ 09.00–17.00 Mon–Fri
Ⓔ Bulgaria Vukice Mitrović 10, 81000 Podgorica; ☎ 020 655009; e bg.embassy.me@abv.bg, embassy.podgorica@mfa.bg; ⏰ 09.00–15.30 Mon–Fri
Ⓔ China (PRC) Radosava Burića 4a, 81000 Podgorica; ☎ 020 609275; e chinaemb-me@mfa.gov.cn; ⏰ 08.30–15.00
Ⓔ Croatia Vladimira Četkovića 2, 81000 Podgorica; ☎ 020 269760; e croemb.podgorica@mvpel.hr; ⏰ 09.00–17.00 Mon–Fri. Consulate General, Šušanj 248, 82000 Kotor; ☎ 032 323127
Ⓔ France Atinska 35, 81000 Podgorica; ☎ 020 655348; e ambafrance@ambafrance.co.me; www.ambafrance-me.org; ⏰ 09.00–17.00 Mon–Fri
Ⓔ Germany Hercegovačka 10, 81000 Podgorica; ☎ 020 667285, 020 441018; e deutsche.botschaft@t-com.me, info@podgorica.diplo.de; www.podgorica.diplo.de; ⏰ 08.00–16.00 Mon–Thu, 08.00–14.00 Fri
Ⓔ Greece Atinska 4, 81000 Podgorica; ☎ 020 655544; e gremb.pod.mfa.gr; ⏰ 08.30–15.30 Mon–Fri
Ⓔ Hungary Kralja Nikole 104, 81000 Podgorica; ☎ 020 602910; e mission.pdg@kum.hu; ⏰ 08.00–16.30 Mon–Fri
Ⓔ Italy Džordža Vašingtona 83, 81000 Podgorica; ☎ 020 234661; e segreteria.podgorica@esteri.it; www.ambpodgorica.esteri.it; ⏰ 09.00–17.00 Mon–Thu, 09.00–14.00 Fri
Ⓔ Macedonia Hercegovačka 49/III, 81000 Podgorica; ☎ 020 667415 e podgorica@mfa.gov.mk; ⏰ 09.00–17.00 Mon–Fri
Ⓔ Poland Kozaračka 79, 81000 Podgorica; ☎ 020 608320; e podgorica.amb.sekretariat@msz.gov.pl; www.podgorica.msz.gov.pl; ⏰ 09.00–16.00 Mon–Fri
Ⓔ Romania Vukovice Mitrović 40, 81000 Podgorica; ☎ 020 618040; e ambs.romania.mne@t-com.me; ⏰ 09.00–13.00 Mon–Fri, 14.30–16.00 Wed

Russia Veliše Mugoše 1, 81000 Podgorica; ☏ 020 272460; e podgorica@dkf.ru, info@ambrus. me; ⏰ 08.00–13.30 Mon–Fri

Serbia Hercegovačka 18, 81000 Podgorica; ☏ 020 667305; e embassy.podgorica@mfa.rs; ⏰ 09.30–13.30 Mon–Fri

Slovenia Atinska 41, 81000 Podgorica; ☏ 020 618150; e kpg@gov.sl; ⏰ 08.00–16.00 Mon–Fri

Turkey Radosava Burića bb; ☏ 020 445700; e podgorica.be@mfa.gov.tr; ⏰ 10.00–16.00

Ukraine Serdara Jola Piletića 15; ☏ 020 227521; e emb-me@mfa.gov.ua; ⏰ 08.00–17.00

United Arab Emirates bul Svetog Petra Cetinskog 147; ☏ 020 411401; e uae@ podgoricaembassy.me ⏰ 09.00–15.00

United Kingdom Ulcinjska 8, Gorica C, 81000 Podgorica; ☏ 020 618010; e podgorica@ britishembassy.co.me, podgorica@fco.gov.uk; www. gov.uk/government/world/montenegro; ⏰ 08.30–16.00 Mon–Thu, 08.30–12.00 Fri. British Information Centre, Njegoševa 5, Podgorica; ☏ 020 243672

USA Dzona Dzeksona 2, 81000 Podgorica; ☏ 020 410500; e podgoricaACS@state-gov; http:// podgorica.usembassy.gov; ⏰ by appointment only

GETTING THERE AND AWAY

BY AIR

From the UK Montenegro Airlines (*27 Old Gloucester St, London WC1N 3AX; m 07701 012010; www.montenegroairlines.com*) operates flights (May–Sep) between London Gatwick and Podgorica, and London Gatwick and Tivat. Flights take three hours.

In 2014, **Ryanair** (*www.ryanair.com*) began four-weekly flights between Podgorica and Brussels Charleroi in June 2013, and in 2014 began direct flights between London Stansted and Podgorica. This is currently the easiest and (in common with all budget airlines, providing you book well in advance) the cheapest and most convenient way to get to Montenegro from the UK.

There are also flights from London to Podgorica with **Adria Airways** (*www. adria.si*).

Via Dubrovnik For many years, the favoured route to Montenegro for a good many travellers was to fly to Dubrovnik and cross the frontier overland. Flights from the UK are operated to Dubrovnik's Čilipi Airport by British Airways (*www. britishairways.com*), easyJet (*www.easyjet.com*), Aer Lingus (*www.aerlingus.com*) and Croatia Airlines (*www.croatiaairlines.com*).

Via Trieste or Split There are various more complicated and scenic ways to get to Montenegro. One is to fly to Trieste from London Stansted on Ryanair (*fares variable but can be economic*) and take a bus from Trieste to Rijeka (*2hrs; about €12*), from where you can catch a ferry to Dubrovnik with Jadrolinija ferries (*www. jadrolinija.hr; 22hrs; cabins from €60*). Another is to take a flight with easyJet or another carrier to Split (*fares vary according to season*) and continue by bus to Dubrovnik and on to Montenegro.

From mainland Europe In June 2013, Ryanair introduced four flights a week between Podgorica and Brussels. It is also possible to pick up a Podgorica-bound Montenegro Airlines flight in Belgrade, Copenhagen, Frankfurt, Ljubljana, Moscow, Niš, Paris, Rome, Vienna or Zurich, or to fly JAT or British Airways with a change in Belgrade. Montenegro Airlines also offers direct flights to Tivat: three a day from Belgrade, three a week from Moscow and two a week from Paris.

The only other scheduled airlines currently flying to Montenegro are **Adria Airways** (*www.adria.si*) from Ljubljana, Zurich, Paris, Copenhagen and Vienna;

Austrian Airlines (*www.austrian.com*) from Vienna; **Turkish Airlines** (*www. turkishairlines.com*) from Istanbul and **Air Berlin** (*www.airberlin.com*) from Nürnberg to Tivat).

Arriving in Montenegro
Most flights to Montenegro arrive at **Golubovci** (Podgorica) **Airport** (✆ *020 653003; www.montenegroairports.com; see pages 99–102*), which is 12km from Podgorica. Some flights, mostly charters, land at **Tivat Airport** (✆ *032 670930; www.montenegroairports.com; see pages 153–5*), which is 4km from Tivat itself, on the coast between Kotor and Budva. Tivat also has facilities for private aircraft. Until Ryanair started flying to Podgorica, the country's *de facto* third airport was – and out of season still is – **Dubrovnik** (Čilipi), (✆ *+385 (0)20 773100; www. airport-dubrovnik.hr*), 29km across the Croatian border from Herceg Novi.

There are **car-hire** desks at Podgorica Airport (see page 104) but they are not always manned unless someone with a prior reservation is expected; Tivat Airport also has car-hire desks (page 155). A number of other companies, including Europcar in Budva, will arrange an airport drop-off. Sometimes, especially off-season or for a two-week rental, they will not charge for this. The sensible option, unless you are feeling adventurous, is to book the car before you fly.

Standard **international departure tax** is €16 from both Podgorica and Tivat airports. This must be paid in cash at check-in and a receipt will be stapled to your boarding pass.

Getting from Čilipi Airport to Montenegro
The easiest way to get from Dubrovnik's Čilipi Airport to Montenegro is to arrange to be met by your hotel's transport. Most will charge in the region of €30–50 for this, depending on distance, but some provide a complimentary service, especially off-season or for stays of over a fortnight. Otherwise you can arrange car hire with either a Croatian or a Montenegrin company. Rates are similar, but the great advantage of using a Croatian company is that you avoid the pick-up and drop-off charges. Make sure your company does not charge for cross-border travel and that the car comes equipped with a Montenegrin ecological tax disc card. The better car-hire companies will treat all this as a matter of course and we have found no obvious disadvantages in having Croatian plates in Montenegro, but it is wise to take the full insurance option (about €35 per week).

In season there can be delays at the border (Debeli Brjeg) and the paperwork needs to be right, though Montenegrin ecological tax discs can be purchased without fuss from border posts (€10 for one year) if your hire company has not provided one.

There is a wide variety of **car-hire** desks at Čilipi (cross the car park in front of the terminal if they are not waiting for you on arrival) and all the big firms are represented. One that has proved exceptionally helpful and reasonably priced is

✱ **Best Buy Rent** ✆ +385 (0)20 422043; e davor.buric@du.t-com.hr. Run by Davor Burić, who speaks good English & will go to immense trouble if you have any kind of problem. He has a full range of cars, mostly Opels, & will charge about €190 per week in mid-season for a smallish car with full insurance if you pay cash.

It's also possible to take a **taxi** (✆ +385 (0)98 725769; e info@taxiservicedubrovnik. com) across the border. Typical fares from Čilipi Airport – for advance bookings only, they say – are Herceg Novi €50; Kotor or Tivat €80; Budva €100; Bar €130; and Podgorica or Ulcinj €150.

GETTING FROM ČILIPI AIRPORT TO DUBROVNIK If you want to do things the leisurely way and/or take a look at Dubrovnik, consider spending a night there. It is, however, 20km in the opposite direction to Montenegro, whereas Herceg Novi is only 29km. The airport kombi-bus to Dubrovnik (*30kn or €5; euros accepted*) stops just outside the arrivals terminal and is well signed. However, it is scheduled to connect with arrivals and departures of Croatia Airlines, so if your timings don't fit you may need to take a taxi, costing in the region of 260kn (€40). Drivers will accept euros but it's a good idea to have, as near as possible, the appropriate notes, and to round up the fare. Make sure the meter is running. The kombi-bus stops near the Pile Gate to the old town before going on to the bus station at Gruž, but will also let you off along the way if requested.

IN DUBROVNIK The **bus station** (*put Republike 19; information* \ *+385 020 357088; http://libertasdubrovnik.hr*) has a left-luggage office (*garderoba*) that is open 05.00–22.30 daily.

🏠 **Where to stay** There are numerous places to stay in and around the old city itself (*see www.tzdubrovnik.hr*). In addition, consider:

Petka Hotel www.hotelpetka.hr. 800m/10min walk from the bus station, a modern hotel with a seaport view. €€€€

Lero Hotel www.hotel-lero.hr. Nearer the old city but on the airport kombi route. €€€€

ℹ️ **Tourist information** A tourist information centre (*summer 08.00–20.00 daily; winter 08.00–20.00 Mon–Sat*) is located opposite the port, between the Petka and the bus station. Take local bus 1A or 1B from these hotels to the old town; otherwise a taxi costs approximately €8.

GETTING FROM DUBROVNIK TO MONTENEGRO
By bus There is a good service from the bus terminal to Ulcinj. Ask the driver nicely and he will drop you off at your hotel if it is *en route*. Buses to Ulcinj leave Dubrovnik daily at 10.30 and 20.30 (€21) and make stops in all the Montenegrin towns along the coast including Herceg Novi. This bus passes the airport on its way to Herceg Novi but there is no provision for getting on there. Try and flag it down on the main road if you want to, but don't be too optimistic.

There are also additional buses to Herceg Novi at 09.30 and 15.20 (€11), and to Budva (€15). That said, note that all bus timetables are subject to change, so it is always wise to check a short time before travel (\ *+385 (0)80 305070; for timetables see www.libertasdubrovnik.com*).

Buy your ticket at the office, not on the bus. Larger suitcases put in the luggage hold are €1 each. The buses themselves are big, new, comfortable and air conditioned. Staff at the ticket and information offices are efficient and speak good English.

By taxi (\ *+385 (0)98 725769;* e *info@taxiservicedubrovnik.com*) A town **taxi** hailed on the street will charge about €70 to Herceg Novi.

BY SEA There are regular car-ferry services between **Bar** and Bari (to which Ryanair flies from London Stansted), and from the beginning of July until mid-September between Bar and Ancona. Ferries are operated by **Montenegro Lines** in Bar (*030 312366*). There is at least one Bar–Bari sailing per day in high season and three per week in low season, generally leaving port (at both ends) between 21.00 and 23.00, arriving the next morning after an early breakfast (around 07.00–08.00). Ships leave Bar for Ancona on Wednesdays and Fridays at 16.00, arriving at 08.00, and returning the following day at the same times. One-way passenger fares to and from Bari range from about €60 for a reclining seat to €120 for the best cabin. Return (round-trip) fares give a significant saving. Cars are around €75 each way. Meals and modest embarkation taxes are extra. Ancona fares are about 20% higher. In midsummer, cabins (especially inside ones) can become very hot and stuffy, so consider camping on deck, or take along a small battery fan.

See also *Bar*, pages 203–4.

There are international customs and immigration entry facilities at **Bar**, **Budva**, **Kotor**, **Zelenika** and **Porto Montenegro in Tivat**. However, private vessels entering Montenegro from international waters are advised to check formalities with Zelenika Port Authority (*031 321698*).

Port offices

Bar *030 300600; www.lukabar.me.* Montenegro's main port, landing both cargo & passengers. Full customs & immigration.

Budva Stari Grad; *033 451227.* Registers boats, speedboats & jet skis. Extension of permits for international vessels. Customs & immigration (summer only).

Budva Marina MC-Marina, Mediteranska 4; *033 452281;* e info@marinabudva.com; www.marinabudva.com. Berth capacity for 300 speedboats & yachts not exceeding 25m in length.

Kotor *032 325572; www.portofkotor.*co.me. By the walls of old Kotor; busy with ferries & cruise ships in summer.

Kotor Marina Prčanj Near Hotel Splendid; www.marinaprcanj.me. 10 moorings, winter & summer.

Tivat Porto Montenegro *032 674660;* www.portomontenegro.com. Provides a comprehensive range of facilities for yachts of all sizes. Full customs & immigration service.

Zelenika *031 678642.* Full customs & immigration service.

BY TRAIN The only international railway link into Montenegro is through Belgrade (one of the world's most spectacular rail trips; see page 203). There is currently only one stopping day train and one express night train between the two, but schedules keep changing, so check with the railways before you make too many plans. Only the first will let you see the fantastic views. The journey is scheduled to take seven hours to Kolašin, eight to Podgorica and ten to Bar. Take a picnic (preferable) or buy light refreshments on the train. For online Railways of Montenegro timetables, visit www.zcg-prevoz.me but note that these times should always be confirmed in advance of travel, and that long-distance trains often arrive at least an hour late.

Fares are quite reasonable and unless you are on a tight budget it is worth buying a first-class ticket (around €25 to Podgorica, as opposed to €17 for second class; €27 or €19 to Bar). You can pay on the train, perhaps after inspecting the alternatives, but payment is in dinars only and no credit cards; you do, however, save the €3 seat reservation charge.

The business trains are the ones to choose if you have the option. On the non-business trains, accommodation is less salubrious and there is no refreshment car. In addition, although some carriages on the non-business trains are clearly marked as first-class (indicated with a '1'), it is pointless to buy a first-class ticket, as there is no perceptible difference between the two breeds and all passengers sit anywhere: seats are usually first come, first served. Some rolling stock is newer than others and in summer you should try to ensure that you are in a compartment where the window will open.

Podgorica Railway Station (☎ *020 441211*) boasts only a ticket office and a café, but the bus station (☎ *020 620430*) just across the road is much better endowed, with ATMs, a food shop, a post office, a reasonable restaurant and a left-luggage office (€2 per item). A taxi to the town centre from either should be about €2.

At present the following stations are open for passenger traffic:

Bar ☎030 301622	**Mojkovac** ☎050 472130
Bijelo Polje ☎050 478560	**Podgorica** ☎020 441211
Kolašin ☎020 441492	**Sutomore** ☎030 301691

Long-held rumours of a resumption of passenger traffic on the freight line from Nikšić via Danilovgrad to Podgorica are no longer considered likely to materialise.

If you really like trains, **European Rail** in London (☎ *020 7387 0444; www. europeanrail.com*) will book you a journey to Montenegro via Vienna, Budapest and Belgrade. It is said to be an efficient service and a memorable trip. And in case none of these alternatives appeals to you, drive to Düsseldorf and get the car train to Rijeka, Croatia, then motor along the Dalmatian coast (*see* **Autozug**, *www.dbautozug.de*).

BY ROAD

By bus There are international buses that link Montenegrin towns to Dubrovnik, Belgrade, Novi Sad, Subotica and Sarajevo. The following are examples of one-way bus fares to Podgorica:

Belgrade, Serbia €25–40
Sarajevo, Bosnia & Herzegovina €16.30–17.40
Novi Sad, Serbia €25.50

See also *Getting from Dubrovnik to Montenegro*, page 35.

By car Border posts have proliferated in the last three years on roads to neighbouring countries. For tourists they are normally a mere formality, but in high season there can be time-consuming queues on some routes.

Apart from the crossing from Dubrovnik (Croatia) at **Debeli Brjeg** (page 35), it is possible to enter from Serbia via **Čemerno** (near Jabuka) or **Dobrakovo** (north of Bijelo Polje); from Bosnia and Herzegovina via **Sitnica** (near Herceg Novi), **Vilusi**, **Vraćenovići**, **Šćepan Polje** or **Metaljika**; from Kosovo via the **Kulina Pass** between **Rožaje** and **Peć** or **Špiljani Draga**; or from Albania via **Bozaj** (Hani i Hotit), **Sukobin** or **Grnčar** near Plav (page 305).

CASINO ROYALE

The James Bond film claims to be partly set in Montenegro. The 'Montenegrin countryside' was shot in Italy, looks beautiful and could easily be where it purports to be. The 'Montenegrin towns' are in the Czech Republic and do not pass close examination. The 'Montenegrin train' bears as much resemblance to the real thing as a Rolls Royce does to a dodgem.

For more on driving, see pages 47–51 and for more about these border crossings see *Chapter 9*.

Confusingly, two different roads traversing Montenegro are referred to informally as the 'Adriatic Highway'. Most frequently the term is used for the coastal road linking Herceg Novi and Ulcinj; alternatively the phrase may sometimes be used for the road linking Belgrade (Serbia) with the coast.

HEALTH   *with Dr Felicity Nicholson*

IMMUNISATIONS AND DANGERS It is recommended that travellers from the UK be up to date on primary courses of vaccinations for diphtheria, tetanus and polio; these now come as an all-in-one vaccine (Revaxis), which lasts for ten years. Other vaccines to be considered are pneumococcal and flu vaccine in the elderly, as well as hepatitis A. Hepatitis B should also be considered for longer trips and definitely for those working in medical settings or with children. Vaccination against rabies is also recommended (see below).

Hepatitis A is more common in hotter countries and is spread by infected food and water. One dose of vaccine gives protection against the virus for a year. It can be boosted at least six months later, or at any time after that, to give 25 years' cover. It may be obtainable free of charge on the NHS so do ask well in advance of your trip.

Hepatitis B is spread through blood and other body fluids, so as well as being recommended for those working with children or in medical settings, it is classed as a disease of risky behaviour. Unsafe sex, tattooing, acupuncture, body piercing, etc are best avoided. For those aged 16 or over, three doses of vaccine can be given over a minimum of 21 days (Engerix B only). For younger travellers, at least two months must be allowed to get in all three doses. Whenever possible, if time allows, longer courses (ie: three doses over at least six months) give more sustainable protection.

Technically all visitors to Montenegro need a certificate confirming that they are HIV negative, but we know of no case where this rule has been enforced.

Tick-borne encephalitis
This is contracted from the bite of a tick and, less commonly, by consuming unpasteurised milk and milk products. Ticks are prevalent only between June and September, on the edge of forests and in long grass. If you're going to be walking in forests during the summer months, apply tick repellent and make sure you wear appropriate clothing: long trousers tucked into socks and boots, a hat and a long-sleeved top.

Ensure that you check yourself at the end of the day for ticks or – better – get a travelling companion to do it for you. Children are particularly susceptible to ticks in their hair or behind their ears, so make sure that these areas are checked too. (For advice on tick removal, see box, page 40.) An area of spreading redness around the bite site, or a rash or fever coming on a few days or more after the bite, would require a trip to the doctor.

Tick-borne encephalitis vaccine is now readily available in the UK. There is both an adult and junior form, which initially requires two doses given a minimum of two weeks apart. For those at continued risk, a third dose should be given at least five months later.

Rabies
Montenegro is classified as a high-risk country for rabies. That said, the chance of exposure is small if you avoid direct contact with warm-blooded mammals, in particular dogs that roam wild in the mountains (but note that any mammal can carry the disease). If you are unfortunate enough to be bitten,

Ticks should ideally be removed as soon as possible, as leaving them on the body increases the chance of infection. They should be removed with special tick tweezers that can be bought in good travel shops. Failing that you can use your fingernails by grasping the tick as close to your body as possible and pulling steadily and firmly away at right angles to your skin. The tick will come away completely as long as you do not jerk or twist it. If possible, douse the wound with alcohol (any spirit will do) or iodine. Irritants (such as Olbas oil) or lit cigarettes are to be discouraged as they can cause the ticks to regurgitate and therefore increase the risk of disease.

scratched or licked over an open wound by any mammal, even if they look well, seek medical help as soon as possible. In the interim, scrub the wound with soap and bottled/boiled water for a good 15 minutes, then pour on an antiseptic solution; even alcohol will do. This helps to stop the rabies virus entering the body and will guard against wound infections, including tetanus.

Although treatment should be given as soon as possible, it is never too late to seek help, as the incubation period for rabies can be very long. Tell the doctor if you have had pre-exposure vaccine, as this will change the treatment you receive. If you have not had the vaccine then you need a blood product called rabies immunoglobulin (RIG), which is both expensive and – more importantly – very hard to come by. You will also need five doses of vaccine after exposure. The vaccine itself is usually available, but you need both products to ensure successful post-exposure treatment.

If you are intending to work with animals, or plan to be more than 24 hours from medical help, then you would be wise to get the pre-exposure vaccine. This consists of three doses given over a minimum of 21 days, though ideally it should be over at least 28 days. Then if you do have a potential exposure you no longer need the RIG and only need two doses of vaccine given three days apart.

Food and water Care should be taken over food and water hygiene. Tap water is generally perfectly safe to drink but should be avoided in coastal resorts in high season (July–August) when the system can become overloaded. Even if it is safe it is better to drink bottled water as the mineral content may well be different and can lead to upset stomachs. The mountain water is delicious, though note that there have been some problems with potable water in Mojkovac, where there are said to be lead deposits in the town reservoir, and lately there have been reports of water shortages in Žabljak because of the rapidly growing population. (For those taking a side trip into Kosovo, Mitrovica is also said to have an unreliable potable water supply.) Bottled water, still or fizzy, is inexpensive and freely available. Restaurant food, including raw fruit and vegetables, very rarely causes health problems and hotel standards of hygiene are normally high. In the countryside the local people know which springs are safe for filling your water bottles.

Heat and heatstroke In high summer, the sun in Montenegro is intense. Use sunscreen and drink lots of liquids.

Snakebite Although snakebite is common, and it is very unpleasant to get bitten, the most important thing to remember is *don't panic*. It is likely that no venom has been dispensed and, even in the worst cases, the victim has hours or days to get to help, not a matter of minutes. He/she should be kept calm, with no exertions to pump venom around the blood system, while being taken rapidly to the nearest medical help. The area of the bite should be washed to remove any venom from the skin, and the bitten limb should be immobilised. Paracetamol may be used as a painkiller, but never use aspirin because it may cause internal bleeding.

TRAVEL CLINICS AND HEALTH INFORMATION A full list of current travel clinic websites worldwide is available on www.istm.org. For other journey preparation information, consult www.nathnac.org/ds/map_world.aspx (UK) or http://wwwnc. cdc.gov/travel/ (US). Information about various medications may be found on www.netdoctor.co.uk/travel. All advice found online should be used in conjunction with expert advice received prior to or during travel.

HEALTHCARE IN MONTENEGRO Foreigners do not generally have access to the domestic national-health system and in any case would probably prefer to use one of the growing number of private clinics, especially if they have health insurance (which is strongly recommended), but there is a reciprocal healthcare agreement for UK nationals that entitles them to free treatment in a genuine emergency. To get this treatment, UK nationals will need to show a UK passport. If you are a UK resident but not a UK national you will need a Certificate of Insurance from HM Revenue and Customs' Centre for Non-Residents (which has offices in all major UK towns).

For non-urgent treatment, there are general or specialist medical practices that are privately run and recommended for tourists. You can expect payment, often in cash, to be required.

Many doctors, especially those in the private clinics, will be overseas educated and thus will often speak English, but of course general practitioners frequently do not. The standard of care in the clinics is actually quite high. Availability of drugs is uncertain, however, so travellers should take with them a good supply of any medication on which they are dependent. Should you need to buy over-the-counter drugs from a pharmacy in an outlying place, be sure to check the use-by date.

Medical assistance Consuls and honorary consuls (pages 33–4) should be able to give good advice on the best place to seek medical assistance in an emergency.

If you are unlucky enough to need an ambulance you can dial ☎124 anywhere in Montenegro. Following are contact details for the major general hospitals:

✚ **Bar** ☎030 313428	✚ **Kotor** ☎032 352602
✚ **Berane** ☎051 230614	✚ **Nikšić** ☎040 244216
✚ **Bijelo Polje** ☎050 432411	✚ **Pljevlja** ☎052 281883
✚ **Budva** ☎033 451026	✚ **Podgorica** ☎020 225123 (children); 020
✚ **Cetinje** ☎041 231336	412412 (adults)
✚ **Herceg Novi** ☎031 640406	

SAFETY

The level of crime in Montenegro is low and it is generally safe to walk in towns after dark, at least in the central areas. There is some petty theft, for instance from pockets, beach bags or unattended cars, but very little personal violence. The approach to women is little short of chivalrous and the usual attitude of locals to foreign tourists is friendly and generous to a fault.

The laws regarding the use or possession of drugs, and the penalties for breaking them, are broadly similar to those in the UK. Possession as well as trafficking in drugs can mean a jail sentence.

The police and military do not like their personnel, buildings or vehicles to be photographed. If you don't want a row, have the charm ready.

There are no known landmines or unexploded ordnance within the national borders. However, see the warning on page 301.

The latest UK Foreign and Commonwealth Office travel advice (℡ *020 7008 0232/3; www.fco.gov.uk*) says somewhat cautiously (as it has done for some years) that 'most visits to Montenegro are trouble-free'. Indeed they are, but although both the UK and Montenegro have recognised Kosovo, Serbia so far has not, and in 2011

EARTHQUAKES

Although catastrophic earthquakes occur infrequently, Montenegro, in common with much of the eastern Adriatic seaboard, lies on a seismic fault line and tremors are not unusual.

On Sunday 15 April 1979 at 07.20 local time a strong earthquake registering 7.1 on the Richter scale occurred just off the Montenegrin coast. It was a sunny spring morning and many people were already up and about and out of doors. This factor, combined with the discernible vibration from a brief foreshock which provoked many residents to run out of their buildings, undoubtedly resulted in a lower death toll than might have been expected. As it was, 94 people were killed and over a thousand injured. More than 80,000 were left temporarily homeless. Most of Kotor and Budva collapsed, leaving a jigsaw of fallen historic buildings. It is a tribute to local perseverance and craftsmanship that the slow, painstaking challenge of piecing together treasured landmarks, bit by bit, has been accomplished. The restoration took several decades.

As well as the massive coastal disaster, internal communications were seriously disrupted. The railway between Nikšić and Podgorica and the main line from Bar to Belgrade were both cut. An eyewitness who was in the hills behind Budva recalls: 'It was like the end of the world. There was a long drawn-out roar of thousands of tonnes of stone falling to the ground. The sea turned red and seemed to boil. Then silence.'

The entire nation was speechless. Tito, who was always said to have a special affection for Montenegro because of the people's heroic Partisan activities under his leadership in World War II, was himself near Herceg Novi staying at his Villa Galeb. Five hours after the initial shock he found a way to address the population, broadcasting from Zagreb as Titograd (now Podgorica) Radio was off the air. He exhorted all Yugoslav republics to help the Montenegrins, to whom his message was: 'You are not alone.' The older generation who heard that speech remember it as one of his finest, reducing them to tears at his simple words of comfort.

On the principle that something good can be found in the worst situation, beneath the ruined cities much significant archaeological evidence was uncovered. In Budva the Hellenistic and Roman necropolises first stumbled upon in 1937 revealed no fewer than 4,000 additional relics; and in Kotor the existence of an early round church underneath St Tryphon's Cathedral was confirmed.

there were some minor problems at borders between those two countrie
travellers should be aware of this and exercise tact (but in reality are
encounter problems).

The road between Rožaje and Peć, over the Kulina Pass, is officially the only legal
crossing point between Montenegro and Kosovo, but in practice it is permissible
through Dračenovac near Špiljani Draga (page 308) for all EU nationals. If in any
doubt check with the authorities before you travel.

Travellers to Montenegro are required to register with the police within 24 hours
of arrival, though if you are staying in a hotel or official tourist accommodation this
will automatically be done for you.

WOMEN TRAVELLERS

Foreigners are in general treated as honoured guests in Montenegro. This applies
equally to males and females, and women will feel quite safe walking alone after
dark in busy tourist areas. Indeed, in cities such as Podgorica and Nikšić, joining
the evening *passeggiata* feels positively obligatory, even for the unaccompanied
traveller. That said, just as in Britain or the USA, it is common sense to exercise
reasonable caution with regard to lonely spots, either urban or rural. It is also
wise to think twice before diving into a rowdy male-dominated bar or club. In
Montenegro alcohol consumption by young women is rarely great, most preferring
juice, and any 'laddish' behaviour runs the risk of sending out the wrong message.

TRAVELLERS WITH LIMITED MOBILITY

Except for the higher-category new international hotels that are beginning to open,
there are as yet few facilities adapted for, or dedicated to, wheelchair users, and
toilet arrangements could prove a serious challenge. But for the undeterred, while
getting around would not by any means be straightforward, neither should it be too
hard to find willing volunteers to lend a hand. In Podgorica, pavement ramps have
recently been constructed at pedestrian traffic-light crossings, and some of Herceg
Novi's many flights of steps have ramps. However, the claim by many local hotels to
be 'disabled friendly' is often based on a very loose definition of the words.

GAY AND LESBIAN TRAVELLERS

Homosexuality in both sexes is accepted without much enthusiasm, so long as it
is not flaunted. There are few, if any gay clubs or bars, but the Residence Hotel in
Sveti Stefan (page 184) stands out for its unusually relaxed attitude to questions of
sexuality.

TRAVELLING WITH CHILDREN

Montenegrins, even restaurant and hotel proprietors, love children and will
generally make a fuss of them. That does not mean, however, that they often stock
cots, high chairs or car seats. If you are going to need any of these, it is as well
to check availability in advance. The bus station at Budva has a large soft-play
room, which makes it a worthy candidate for a stop for those travelling with young
children.

Baby food, disposable nappies and general chemist requirements are widely
available except in the most isolated places.

WHAT TO TAKE

These days it is possible to obtain almost everything in Montenegro, but finding what you want and your own brand is not always easy. You may also be some distance from shops. It is therefore wise to consider the following before travel:

- **Medication:** take an adequate supply of anything you depend on or use regularly. Local supplies may or may not be available.
- **Mosquito repellent** in summer
- **Towel,** especially if you want a large beach towel, as hotel linen is clean but often inadequate and on occasion bath towels might be confused with face flannels.
- **Plenty of underwear:** laundry may be tricky except in the grander establishments and sometimes by special arrangement in private houses.
- **Basin or bath plug:** this is often provided, but in self-catering accommodation there may be only a tub, without plug, plus maybe a plastic bowl and an immersion heater. (Useful tip: if you forget your plug and have a handful of coins, placing these in a face flannel or handkerchief will make an adequate stop-gap.)
- **Decanted bath cleaner**
- **J-cloths**
- **Sweeteners:** you may not need them for yourself but many ladies will be grateful for the gift as they are almost unobtainable locally.
- **Instant developing ('Polaroid') camera:** in rural areas people love pictures made to order
- **Torch and extra batteries**
- **Compass**
- **Candles**
- **Short-wave radio**
- **Bottles** for spring water and emergency petrol
- **Paper, notebook, drawing paper, watercolours**
- **Snorkel and mask**
- **Beach shoes** if you don't like walking on pebbles
- **Skates** in winter only
- **Warm nightwear** in winter: bedding may be inadequate

If you are planning to stay in private accommodation, tiny gifts typical of your own country often come in handy (see below).

CLOTHING/DRESS Dress is mainly very casual, but bear in mind that if you are a guest in a Montenegrin home your hosts will appreciate it if you dress to please. Montenegrins love labels just as much as New Yorkers – even if they are only M&S or Macy's (bear this in mind for presents too; see below). Bring warm clothes for the highlands – even at night in summer. Also consider a tracksuit with comfortable trousers. Better hotels and restaurants prefer long trousers for dinner.

Trainers are a sensible choice for light hiking, but for serious hill-walking, or anything more rigorous, boots are recommended. Shorts and bikinis are fine for beach areas, but not in towns or when visiting monasteries. In Muslim regions, modest attire is required. When entering a Muslim building it is customary to remove one's shoes (slippers at the door often serve as a useful reminder). Some monasteries now provide coveralls for the skimpily dressed.

GIFTS Montenegrins love gifts. If you find yourself empty-handed, pick wild hyacinth or blossom, but rather better for women are scented shelf liners, hand cream or homemade English marmalade. Monks like homemade treats too.

MONEY

The official **currency** in Montenegro is the euro, which replaced the Deutschmark in 2002. An unlimited amount of foreign currency may be brought into the country but not more than €2,000 may be re-exported unless it was declared on entry.

Euros in Montenegro, like euros everywhere, come in notes of five, ten, 20, 50, 100, 200 and 500 euros. The coins come in one, two, five, ten, 20 and 50 cents and one and two euros.

As with so many other things in Montenegro, the currency-exchange scene has been in a state of rapid change for the better. **Credit cards** are widely accepted by the bigger hotels, shops, restaurants, garages and travel agents. Beware, though: you can still get caught out. Visa and MasterCard are the most common, though not necessarily both in the same establishment. American Express is now quite widely accepted, having been unknown just a few years ago, and Diners Club limps in in fourth place.

There are now plenty of **cash machines** (called Bankomat) in Montenegro, including in the smaller towns. A few hotels and supermarkets and virtually all bank branches will have a Visa and/or MasterCard ATM. Most banks will also exchange pounds (*funte*) and dollars (*dolare*), though not many other currencies, and quite a few will exchange travellers' cheques, but they will often require you to show them your passport first. Scottish and Irish banknotes will attract a funny look but no euros.

For banking hours, see *Opening times*, page 63.

Bank policies are as follows (but be aware these are subject to change):

$ **Atlasmont Banka** 5% commission on both currency & travellers' cheques, except US & Swiss currency 3%. Visa/MasterCard ATMs.

$ **CKB** Will exchange currency up to £500, more by negotiation. Commission 3%. Will exchange travellers' cheques on the spot, also commission 3%. Visa & MasterCard ATMs.

$ **Hypobank** Commission-free currency exchange. Travellers' cheques 2%, euros or other. Visa & MasterCard ATMs.

$ **Komercijalna Banka** Currency exchanged for 3% commission. Travellers' cheques up to €100 per day, €5 fee, cashed immediately. Visa ATMs.

$ **Montenegro Banka** Commission-free currency exchange. Travellers' cheques 1.5% commission. All branches have Visa ATMs, up to €400.

$ **Nickšicka Banka** No foreign currency exchange.

$ **Opportunity Bank** The only currency exchanged is the dollar. Travellers' cheques 2% commission, min value €20, take 3 days to clear. Visa/MasterCard ATMs.

$ **Podgorička Banka** Will exchange only dollar bills, no other currency; commission 2%. No travellers' cheques. Visa ATMs.

BUDGETING An increasing number of British and other European travel companies are offering package holidays, chiefly in resorts along the Montenegrin coast such as Herceg Novi, Budva, Bečići and Petrovac. Although the star rating of accommodation is not yet always in accord with that of western Europe, hotels offered will in practice usually be the equivalent of three- or four-star category. High-season prices for a week, including air fare, transfers, and B&B in a shared double room will be in the region of £500–650. Allowing for excursions, beach equipment rental, snack lunch, evening meal and drinks you would probably need to budget a minimum of a further £30 per day per person.

Travelling under your own steam, not including air fare or car hire, and staying in private accommodation, one person, sharing a bedroom as part of a couple, or in a group, could comfortably hope to get by on €50 a day. For a single traveller, perhaps allow €55–60. Backpackers staying in hostels, biking or sticking to local transport, should be able to manage on less.

Needless to say if you choose a hotel such as the Aman-Sveti Stefan, Villa Miločer or the Splendid in Bečići, the sky could be your limit.

For the average prices of selected food and drink, see page 56. For information on tipping etiquette, see *Tipping*, page 56.

GETTING AROUND

BY BUS Within Montenegro there is a comprehensive service between most of the larger towns, but one cannot assume that it will be possible to travel directly from A to B; for example there is no official bus route between Kotor and Cetinje by the old road through Njeguši; instead one must travel via Budva. The bus network covers all of the coast and much of the mountainous region and it is safe to assume that there will be a link, though not necessarily more than once or twice a day nor on time, between neighbouring towns of any size.

Contact details for the main bus stations are as follows (stations indicated by * work 24 hours a day in the summer season):

🚌 **Bar** ✆030 346141
🚌 **Berane** ✆051 234828
🚌 **Bijelo Polje** ✆050 432219
🚌 **Budva*** ✆033 456000
🚌 **Cetinje** ✆041 21052
🚌 **Danilovgrad** ✆020 811711
🚌 **Herceg Novi*** ✆031 321225
🚌 **Kolašin** ✆020 864033
🚌 **Kotor*** ✆032 325809
🚌 **Mojkovac** ✆050 470133

🚌 **Nikšić** ✆040 213018
🚌 **Petrovac** ✆033 461510
🚌 **Pljevlja*** ✆052 323114
🚌 **Podgorica*** ✆020 620430; www.montenet. org/travel/timetable.htm#bus (unreliable)
🚌 **Sutomore** ✆030 373128
🚌 **Tivat** ✆032 672620
🚌 **Ulcinj** ✆030 413225
🚌 **Žabljak** ✆052 361318

In addition to the above, buses go to Banja Luca, Berkovici, Bileća, Bjeljina, Djakovića, Gacko, Gusinje, Kragujevac, Kraljevo, Nevesinje, Niš, Peć, Plav, Plužine, Prizen, Rožaje, Šavnik, Sribinje, Subotica, Trebinje and Užice.

Montenegrin buses are by most standards cheap, frequent, safe and fairly comfortable, though the inland buses can be a bit more rickety and a bit less punctual than those on the coast. Any risk is likely to come more from the driving rather than from the behaviour of your fellow passengers, to whom British and American tourists are still a welcome rarity and a subject of friendly interest. Bear in mind that it is much easier to catch a bus from a town, where you know the bus will stop, than from an intermediate location. Although the driver will happily drop you off at any point along the route, in rural areas picking up other than at a designated stop can depend on the whim of the driver or another passenger's wish to get off – or indeed whether the bus is full.

Bus companies, timetables and fares There are a number of different bus companies operating single-decker, coach-style vehicles. These are usually air conditioned and fairly comfortable, but such services are frequently supplemented by less comfortable minibuses.

Olimpia Express ℡020 451718. Run an efficient service in the Budva–Sveti Stefan–Petrovac coastal region, with hourly buses from early until late in high season; less frequent service in winter months.
Autoboka Kotor bus station; ℡032 322111. Operates within Montenegro as well as to Serbia &

Croatia. There is also a small travel company, **Boka Bay Travel**, at the same address.
Blue Line Igalo; ℡031 335100; www.blueline-mne.com. Serves Herceg Novi, Podgorica & Andrijevica.

Timetables are often posted in bus stations and sometimes at bus stops, but at the time of writing most are not available on the internet (but see above for Herceg Novi, Podgorica and Nikšić), and published copies, except sometimes in the newspapers, do not exist. A new timetable is produced every year but is not immune from change at short notice; in any case buses run more frequently in the summer, especially near the sea. At any time, schedules are notoriously subject to change; some are posted in the local press but it is best always to check, prior to travel, either with the local tourist office or the bus station. For a useful – though not always accurate or exhaustive – guide to schedules, see www.autobusni-kolodvor.com/en/terminal.aspx?d=499. For further information see also www.visit-montenegro.com.

For most destinations within Montenegro the one-way fare will be under €10. Generally you pay an extra euro on top of the fare if you buy your ticket at the bus station rather than on the bus, but the former will assure you of a seat. If you want a return ticket you'll need to buy it at the bus station. Please note that different bus companies charge different rates, and that there can be seasonal variations in price. Examples of one-way prices from Podgorica are:

Cetinje €4	**Herceg Novi** €8–9	**Žabljak** €7.50–9.50	**Nikšic** €3
Budva €6	**Kolašin** €4.50–6	**Bijelo Polje** €7–8	

Despite being on a bus route, some visitors have found that the only two ways of getting to their final destination are by taxi or by hitching a lift. (Note: though hitchhiking would never be recommended, in Montenegro it is generally accepted and on the increase.) In more isolated areas a private vehicle or a truck will often be prepared to carry a small group for negotiated payment. It is suggested you offer a little more than you believe you would have paid by bus and a little less than you would pay a taxi. Informal minibuses frequently complement the official service at a competitive price, but are of course unregulated.

BY CAR Montenegrins drive on the right, fearlessly and with verve. It is best not to call their bluff. (A wry comment from a reader: 'there seem to be only two kinds of drivers, the slow ones right in front of you and the fast ones right on your tail'.) Give priority to traffic from the right, as in France, unless there is a clear indication otherwise. Pedestrian crossings are often rather faintly marked, but drivers are still expected to stop when people want to cross. Exercise caution.

Roads are not always well signed and the signs themselves are sometimes obscured by political or advertising posters. Up-to-date **maps** are now quite widely available, for instance in filling stations. In the UK, the Map Shop (*15 High St, Upton-upon-Severn WR8 0HJ;* ℡ *01684 593146; www.themapshop.co.uk*) and Stanfords (*12–14 Long Acre, London WC2;* ℡ *020 7836 1321*) stock a good one published by Gizi at £7.95. Reasonable alternatives are those published by Merkur of Belgrade or by Kod and Kam, but no two maps seem to be precisely the same, and the smaller roads are still sometimes inaccurately represented. Very few establishments list a street address. The appearance of 'bb' in place of a street number is very common and means there are no street numbers. There is usually no alternative to finding the town and then asking directions.

Road surfaces can change disconcertingly and without warning from reasonable asphalt to rocky dirt. (It doesn't help that Montenegrins call rocky dirt roads '*macadam*'.) Many side roads are single-track and the terrain means there is no shortage of blind corners. Like roads everywhere, rain after a dry spell means slippery surfaces – and Montenegro has lots of dry spells. In the north in winter, secondary roads can be completely closed by snow, while prolonged rain may lead to rockfalls or small landslides. Rocks and pot-holes can be left for months and are hard to see at night, as well as causing local drivers to take unexpected evasive action on either side of the road.

The **speed limit** is 80km/h on motorways and 50km/h in built-up areas, or lower speeds as posted. Excessive speeding, defined as anything above 30km/h over the limit, may result in temporary confiscation of your licence and a fine of between €20 and €300. The Montenegrin police have a habit of parking in lay-bys to catch speeders. Montenegrin drivers have a corresponding habit of flashing their headlights at oncoming drivers to warn them of speed traps. It is still best not to rely on a friendly warning. Spot fines are the penalty for getting caught. **Roadside checks** to confirm legal ownership of a car are common and if you are in a rented car you will save time by remembering where you have put the registration papers.

Seat belts must be worn in the front seats and it is obligatory to have your headlights on at all times. Drivers may not use mobile phones while on the move (though not all bus drivers abide by this rule). For any of these offences there will sometimes be spot fines. The maximum blood alcohol limit is 0.05, which sounds low – and it is.

In high season coastal roads get congested and **parking** can be tricky. Do not assume that it is OK to park diagonally or on a pavement just because others have. Towing is still fairly rare but will cost you €50.

Most towns of any size have **fuel stations**, many of which take Visa and MasterCard, but there are few off the major roads. It is best to keep fairly well topped up. Premium 98 octane and unleaded 95 are both around €1.40 per litre; diesel €1.30.

The AMSCG (Automobile Association of Montenegro) **offers emergency roadside assistance** (✆ *19807*) and **travel advice** (✆ *020 234999*; e *ic.amscg@t-com. me; www.amscg.org*).

If you are driving a **rental car** you are in theory required to have an international driving licence. In practice, and over a good many years driving in Montenegro

DISTANCE TABLE

Distances in km (approx) between towns

	Podgorica	Andrijevica	Bar	Berane	Bijelo Polje	Budva	Danilovgrad	Žabljak	Kolašin	Kotor	Mojkovac	Nikšić	Plav	Plužine	Pljevlja	Rožaje	Tivat	Ulcinj	Herceg Novi	Cetinje	Šavnik
Podgorica	-	158	52	142	121	66	23	125	72	89	93	55	183	114	179	173	89	78	133	36	100
Andrijevica	158	-	210	16	48	224	181	137	86	247	65	213	25	234	151	47	247	236	291	194	162
Bar	52	210	-	194	173	40	75	177	124	63	145	107	235	166	231	225	63	26	107	70	152
Berane	142	16	194	-	32	208	165	121	70	231	49	197	41	218	135	31	231	220	275	178	146
Bijelo Polje	121	48	173	32	-	187	144	100	49	210	28	170	73	197	114	63	210	199	254	157	125
Budva	66	224	40	208	187	-	89	191	138	23	159	121	249	180	245	239	23	66	67	30	166
Danilovgrad	23	181	75	165	144	89	-	102	95	112	116	32	206	91	166	196	112	101	125	59	77
Žabljak	125	137	177	121	100	191	102	-	93	167	72	70	162	97	64	152	176	203	163	161	25
Kolašin	72	86	124	70	49	138	95	93	-	161	21	127	111	186	107	101	161	150	205	108	118
Kotor	89	247	63	231	210	23	112	167	161	-	182	97	272	156	231	262	9	89	44	53	142
Mojkovac	93	65	145	49	28	159	116	72	21	182	-	142	90	169	86	80	182	171	226	129	97
Nikšić	55	213	107	197	170	121	32	70	127	97	142	-	232	59	134	222	106	133	93	91	45
Plav	183	25	235	41	73	249	206	162	111	272	90	232	-	259	176	72	272	261	316	219	187
Plužine	114	234	166	218	197	180	91	97	186	156	169	59	259	-	161	249	165	192	152	150	72
Pljevlja	179	151	231	135	114	245	166	64	107	231	86	134	176	161	-	166	240	257	227	215	89
Rožaje	173	47	225	31	63	239	196	152	101	262	80	222	72	249	166	-	262	251	306	209	177
Tivat	89	247	63	231	210	23	112	176	161	9	182	106	272	165	240	262	-	89	53	53	151
Ulcinj	78	236	26	220	199	66	101	203	150	89	171	133	261	192	257	251	89	-	133	96	178
Herceg Novi	133	291	107	275	254	67	125	163	205	44	226	93	316	152	227	306	53	133	-	97	138
Cetinje	36	194	70	178	157	30	59	161	108	53	129	91	219	150	215	209	53	96	97	-	136
Šavnik	100	162	152	146	125	166	77	25	118	142	97	45	187	72	89	177	151	178	138	136	-

and a good many routine police checks, we have never had presentation of a UK licence queried. If you are driving your own car, ensure that you have Green Card insurance valid for Europe. Because Montenegro is not yet a member of the International Association of National Motor Insurers' Bureau, they have an agreement with Serbia that SRB (Serbia) will cover MNE (Montenegro). Border police should know this, but if you are unlucky enough to meet the exception you should purchase local insurance as instructed and with your receipt you can claim a refund at the National Bureau of Insurance of Montenegro (*PC Europoint, Bulevar Svetog Petra Cetinjskog 1A/11, Podgorica;* \ *020 243440; www.nbocg.me/cg*). Since June 2008 all cars in Montenegro have needed to display an ecological tax disc costing €10 per year (for a vehicle with up to eight seats) and designed to fund environmental projects. Hire cars normally have them; otherwise they can be bought at the border.

Car hire Government tourist information centres and travel agencies can often recommend good car-rental firms, but in high season reliable vehicles may be in short supply and it is always prudent to book in advance.

For a one-week rental, expect to pay in the region of €35 per day for a Yugo Cabrio, rising to €55 (Renault Clio) or €60 (Renault Thalia). Automatics are usually available on request but often cost more. 4x4s can be obtained but by no means yet in all locations and rates tend to approach double the daily rate for a regular small car. The insurance on offer is not standard so you should clarify precisely what the coverage is before you sign. Most rentals include unlimited mileage though some limit you to a maximum 200km free per day. Age limits, usually over 22, and experience requirements, usually two years' driving, are common. Child seats are generally but not always available at an extra cost.

There are several car-hire desks at **Podgorica Airport** but you will need to book in advance. **Tivat Airport** also has car-hire desks. For details of both, see pages 104 and 155, and www.montenegroairports.com.

The rental companies are generally ready to pick you or the car up from airports or hotels, some at no extra charge. For longer rentals this facility can extend into

BACK ROADS AND BYWAYS

The first thing to tell you about byways is that Montenegrins will tell you not to take them. They do not want to lose their valuable tourists gratuitously in the mountains. Byways meander, forget themselves and double back, twist into hopeless contortion or sometimes simply peter out. Asphalt without warning can give way to loose stone pitted with pot-holes and in winter weather some minor roads become simply impassable, even for 4x4s. Potential hazards notwithstanding, the rewards can be great: silence, Edenic unimagined surroundings and a deeper understanding of the rugged country these stalwart people have defended with such zeal.

Punctures are to be expected and before setting forth it would be incautious not to confirm that you have a serviceable spare tyre. Bikers need to be fully equipped (see box, page 65). For this kind of adventure you'll need the best maps available, and a compass is obviously a good idea.

There are myriad ways to go. Four of the least demanding in the mountain regions are briefly described on pages 243, 249, 258 and 299. For cyclists, see also pages 281 and 286–7.

neighbouring countries, including Dubrovnik's Čilipi Airport. If you are planning adventures off the beaten track it is wise to consider making an arrangement for a driver/guide. Ensure in advance that that person is familiar with the area you intend to explore.

To rent a **motorbike** (scooter) expect to pay from around €25 per day.

BY TAXI Taxis are quite cheap and are generally metered in the larger towns. Otherwise it is sensible to agree the fare in advance (as an example, Bijelo Polje–Plav was €25 for four people one way and €35 for two on the way back). As in many other countries not all meters necessarily register at the same speed.

BY TRAIN The internal rail network is only 249km long in total but prices are reasonable and views are often spectacular (see box page 203).

The Railways of Montenegro (↑ *020 441210; www.zcg-prevoz.me*) website is in English. It is quite a good guide, although it is not always up to date and some pages remain 'under reconstruction'. Railway information is available in Montenegrin on the following numbers:

Bar ↘030 301622	**Nikšić** ↘040 214480
Bijelo Polje ↘050 478560	**Podgorica** ↘020 441211
Kolašin ↘020 441492	**Sutomore** ↘030 301691
Mojkovac ↘050 472130	**Virpazar** ↘020 441435

Timetables are mostly in Cyrillic. They set targets for trains but bull's-eyes are rare, and in any case the targets are subject to frequent change, often at short notice. Trains run less often out of high season, between October and May.

Although tickets may be purchased on the train, they are cheaper at the station (the opposite of buses). Examples of one-way second-class prices from Podgorica are:

Bar €3.40
Bijelo Polje €4.30
Kolašin €2.20

As on the international route, so-called business trains cost a bit more but are quite a lot better than the ordinary versions. On standard trains, first class is a question of first come, first served, and not worth paying for, though some booking clerks are happy to sell you the notional ticket.

Carriages are reasonably clean and comfortable, but choose one where the windows are transparent and can be opened (especially in warm weather). Refreshments are frequently unavailable on regular trains so it is wise to carry water and snacks for your journey, though sometimes young entrepreneurs will have boxes of ice creams and snacks for sale on the platforms of country stations when trains stop.

BY SEA The Adriatic coast has increasingly good facilities for boat hire, but note that there is no organised maritime rescue service. Boats may be rented from:

Bar Miso Ostojić at Sveti Nikola; ↘030 313911; e omc@t-com.me; www.omcmarina.com

Bijela Branko Zgradić at Navar (no tel)

Kotor Marsenić Boat Hire; m 069 649749; Milo Bozović speaks English

BY ORGANISED TOUR There are numerous organised tours available – see the list of tour operators (pages 30–2), and at the beginning of each relevant section. Otherwise, consult your nearest tourist information office (pages 29–30). To whet your appetite, consider some excursions on offer at the time of writing:

Half-day trips

The Albanian border By bus. Views over the Bojana River, Skadar Lake and a visit to Ostros village.

Bus trip to Ulcinj and Ada Bojana Along the coast and past the 12km-long Velika Beach.

Excursion by bus to rural Montenegro With demonstrations of traditional folk customs and a visit to a typical country village.

Day trips

Tara Bridge (page 263) The highest in Europe at 150m. Train and bus through the Morača Canyon.

Ostrog Monastery (page 235) A dizzying drive to Montenegro's most atmospheric monastery, built into the side of a soaring cliff.

Cetinje (pages 79–90) Montenegro's old historic capital, cradled in the mountains.

Skadar Lake (pages 223–31) By bus to the lake and then by boat around it to view the fishing villages and wildlife.

By bus around Skadar Lake (pages 223–31) The Zeta River, Podgorica, Cetinje, Kotor and the Boka Kotorska. Includes visits to small fishing villages and lakeside fortresses, with opportunities for birdwatching and swimming. An outdoor lunch is provided.

By bus to Biogradska jezero (Biogradska Lake) (pages 271–4) Taking in Skadar Lake, Virpazar, the Morača Monastery and Kolašin, the route goes through the mountains with a number of bridges and tunnels. It includes stops in the small town of Virpazar and at the Morača Monastery as well as several at viewing points.

Adriatic coast by boat (pages 191–7) Cruising along the coast to the beach at Drobni Pijesak, near Petrovac. Drinks, games, music and a fish picnic are included.

Boka Kotorska by boat and bus (pages 127–48) After cruising along the coastline of the Bay of Kotor to a musical accompaniment, there is a stop at Gospa od Škrpjela (Our Lady of the Rock) to visit the small church. The boat will also anchor for a while to give passengers a chance to swim. Lunch and drinks are included.

Dubrovnik By bus and boat. The main features include the City Fortress, the Ducal Palace, the Church of St Blaise and Sponza Palace.

In addition to trips into Croatia, some cross-border excursions to Albania and Serbia can be found and offer much of interest. Local travel agencies and hotels will be only too pleased to advise on what is available.

ACCOMMODATION

It would be wrong to imply to travellers that standards of accommodation in Montenegro will invariably match the levels of western Europe. Montenegrin grades are not yet exactly the equivalent of international ratings, but new hotels of four- or five-star international standard are opening on the coast, in Podgorica and elsewhere. In no way do the few remaining state hotels, most of which need investment, measure up to western European standards, but they are rapidly being bought up and transformed. It is nevertheless important to bear in mind that – however antiquated the establishment, however dreary and overdue for a face-lift the interior, however noisy the plumbing – you can always expect fresh and clean linen. While at worst the bath towel may be of face-cloth proportions and the blankets only slightly larger, they will invariably be clean. You are unlikely to encounter bedbugs and you will never find a really filthy public lavatory (except maybe in a non-business train on the Bar to Belgrade railway!). As Rebecca West wrote in 1941, in *Black Lamb and Grey Falcon*: 'squalor is not a Montenegrin characteristic'.

Thus it is important to remember that Montenegro prides itself upon its hospitality and equally importantly that they do their level best for the comfort of their guests. To a Montenegrin, outward presentation, pride in appearance and the way the world views one is paramount. While he may inhabit a small, run-down – even condemned – establishment, the clothes he wears, his car and so on will be as near as he can make it to immaculate.

A few years ago small private hotels overtook the great multi-roomed state ones for comfort and detail, often appearing as Balkan versions of a decent British B&B. Now better-standard large hotels, both foreign and Montenegrin, are on the increase.

In Montenegrin hotel descriptions you will find the word 'apartment' is frequently used in place of 'suite', but it doesn't follow that the accommodation so listed will in every case include more than a bedroom, a bathroom and a sitting area. If cooking facilities are a requirement it is always wise to check.

While traditionally a *hotel garni* is assumed to be one that does not provide a full restaurant facility, or one that may cater for breakfast only, in Montenegro the term is used more loosely and more often than not applies to establishments *with* restaurants.

If any advertised hotel amenities are of particular importance to you, check before booking; not all rooms will necessarily have the stated facilities, whatever the brochure (or even this guide) may claim; circumstances can and do change. (This particularly applies to wheelchair access.)

While **breakfast** will usually be included in the overnight price with good bread, local jam and often ham and eggs in the deal, in some hotels tea or coffee will be an extra and not always a worthwhile one. Both will tend to come out of a large urn. In the less travelled regions, if you don't much like Turkish coffee for breakfast, you will do better to order cappuccino, which is invariably excellent. And try the *priganice* (fried dough balls) with honey if you can find them. Other meals in state-run hotels in the smaller centres can usually be described as 'institutional'. But these standards will all change and already food in private hotels is often very good indeed.

In high season coastal areas suffer from domestic daytime **water-supply shortages** and **electricity cuts**; again this situation is being addressed and is markedly improving. Some of the fancier new hotels have private supplies of both.

The in-room television, except in the newer establishments or the larger towns, will usually be in Serbian/Montenegrin and perhaps Italian only, but cable and satellite are on the increase, with CNN and sometimes BBC World becoming more frequently available.

By far the best times of year to visit are spring and autumn, but not every hotel will be open at these times. In July and August the seaside resorts become very crowded as this is the usual holiday time for Montenegrins and their Balkan neighbours, but head inland and into the mountains at this time of year and you'll leave the crowds far behind.

Away from the main seaside and skiing resorts, hotels (full or empty) are often quite scarce. Even off-season it is best not to leave it too late to find a room. By dusk the only option may be a private house (see below).

HOTEL PRICES Hotel prices vary widely by area, season and (sometimes) length of stay. A number of relatively expensive hotels have opened recently, especially in Podgorica and on the coast, but otherwise prices have remained fairly stable.

PRIVATE ACCOMMODATION Many rooms are available in private houses. Prices depend on the city, location and quality of the room as well as the season, and range from €10 to €30 per day. To find these either look out for signs on individual houses saying *sobe* ('rooms') or enquire at the nearest tourist office. Travel agents, especially in the resorts, will often offer a selection of private rooms, flats and villas.

There are said to be official regulations governing *sobe*, but their observation is informal. Private rooms are almost invariably clean and comfortable, if simple. Often they will include private bathrooms; indeed sometimes the family will move out to allow the traveller en-suite accommodation. The standard of hospitality is very high and landladies are invariably grateful for your custom, but phrasebooks generally come in handy.

EATING AND DRINKING

FOOD Montenegrin cuisine can be divided into northern, continental and Mediterranean. Nearly all produce is locally grown and much is organic, and tastes are distinctive. A traditional form of cooking is *ispod* – 'under the coals' – in a pot known as a *sač*.

The northern area features forest berries, blueberries, raspberries and strawberries, also herbal teas and wild mushrooms. They cook with sour cream (*kajmak*), yoghurt and both cow's and sheep's cheese. The finest *kajmak*, it is claimed, comes from Trsa, a high pasture in Durmitor. Naturally flavoured with wild herbs, it costs €20 per kilo and makes a delicious dip. Traditional dishes include *kačamak*, a rich cheese and potato dish reminiscent of fondue and popular in mountain areas; lamb cooked in milk; peppers in *kajmak*; and Durmitor steak. Montenegrins are noted carnivores, but lamb and veal are more common than beef. 'Steak' can often mean veal, frequently stuffed with ham and cheese.

The continental area uses a lot of fish from Skadar Lake and the rivers that feed it, especially carp, trout and eel; the fish is served smoked, fried and in salad. They prepare smoked ham, cheese in olive oil, sausages and dried mutton. Around Podgorica they stuff cabbage leaves with minced meat and rice, and carp with risotto and dried plums.

Olive oil is the basis of every meal with fish, salad and vegetables; and of sauces, with garlic and parsley. They harvest a large variety of sea fish as well as crustacea, and use a lot of vegetables: chicory, asparagus, leek, fennel and nettles. Popular seasonings are rosemary, wild sage and myrtle. A salad staple is *šopska*, consisting of chopped cucumber, lettuce, tomato and onion with grated cheese. Without cheese it is called *šrpska* salad. Soups are generally excellent, especially veal broth (*teleca čorba*).

The corner cafés unfortunately serve far too much pizza. It's not bad pizza, but when you get sick of it, turn to the local staples of delicious Njeguši ham, air-dried and smoked (warning: sometimes on menus *pršut* can also mean dried mutton which is properly defined as *kastradina*, more greasy and with a taste not to everyone's palate), fresh cheese and olives – and see what you have been missing. Omelettes are safe and good.

A useful tip for a quick snack on the move: purchase some sausage, ham or cheese and a loaf of bread from one of the many and excellent mini-markets. The salesperson will often be happy to cut it up and convert it into a sandwich, there and then. These stores are open for longer hours than just about anywhere else.

DRINK Montenegro produces both red (called *crna* – black, like the mountains) and white (*belo*) **wines**, but the former have more character. The terraced slopes of Crmnica are the source of the pick of the crop.

Vranac is the best known red and eminently drinkable, with a fine ruby colour and a Mediterranean character. 'Vranac pro cordem' is a Vranac with a high level of prothoanthocyanidol and is marketed as being good for your heart. The third popular variety is merlot. In the one or two restaurants run by the Plantaze vineyards you may be able to get a vintage Vranac at upwards of €50 per bottle. A wine tour around small local vineyards near Virpazar (page 227) is a great way to taste some good Vranac.

The nicest local dry white wine is Krstač, which competes with the local chardonnay and a very decent sauvignon.

The real **national drink** is *rakija* or *loza*. Rakija is a generic name, the liquor made from plums, mulberries or whatever fruit is plentiful, while *loza* is a white brandy always made from grapes. The slightly upmarket version is *kruna*, distilled in copper stills fired with vine twigs and wood, and the Podgorica variety is called *Crnogorski Prvijenac*. These are the universal mark of Montenegrin hospitality and a great source of goodwill.

A glass of *rakija* is the standard gesture of welcome when you visit a Montenegrin house. As a foreigner it is not obligatory to accept, but they will be pleased if you do. For extra marks, maintain eye contact during the toast. In the mountains people will treat an open wound with *rakija* to aid the healing process.

In summer most restaurants serve delicious homemade lemonade (*limonata*), fresh from the tree with water and sugar to taste.

In general Montenegrins are not heavy drinkers. Taxes on alcohol are low and prices for food, local beer and imported spirits notably lower than in the UK or USA.

RESTAURANTS There are as yet few really top-class international restaurants in Montenegro. Čatovića Mlini at Morinj on the Boka Kotorska is a notable exception, in which the ambience and the food could hold its own with the best anywhere. Vinjo Santo in Krtoli on the Luštica Peninsula is another. One at Porto Montenegro and the new assortment of restaurants at Aman Sveti Stefan/Miločer are also in a class of their own. But, aside from these, both in the capital Podgorica and on the coast it is perfectly possible to eat very well, with locally caught fish such as dentex, squid, sea bass, grey mullet, gilthead bream and St Pierre among a host of others all being usually of excellent quality. In seaside restaurants such as Bastion at Kotor you will find fish rather quaintly graded as first, second and third class; this does *not* apply to their freshness but simply to their rarity and value. The fish is almost invariably priced by grade and weight, so it is useful to know that one decent-sized fish for two should weigh about 500g and even in quite modest restaurants

can often cost €40–50. Meat, typically beef or lamb, is generally of good quality and nearly always cheaper than fish.

In the east of the country, where in recent times few tourists have ventured, good restaurants can be few and far between, though here too there are exceptions, for example Konoba Badanj in Virpazar (page 229), and the restaurant at Ali Pasha Springs near Plav and Gusinje, when and if it reopens.

Without fail, wherever you go, locally smoked prosciutto-style ham and cheese – often preserved in oil – will be delicious, with the finest cheese and ham arguably coming from the village of Njeguši below Mt Lovćen.

A note on *konoba* – a word that doesn't really translate. Originally it referred to the domestic wine cellar where the man of the house would entertain his friends while the women got on with their chores. Gradually it grew to describe a place where groups of both sexes could meet to eat, drink and relax.

Most restaurants in tourist areas are open every day in the main season, but opening hours may be less predictable out of season.

Prices Prices will generally be higher in coastal resorts and big towns, but for an order of magnitude think in terms of:

Cup of coffee €1.50–2.50
Bottle of beer €1–2.50
Bottle of local wine €8–15
Gin or whisky €2+
Grilled beefsteak €10–15
Grilled saltwater fish, 250g €15–25

Pasta (with meat) €8+
Pizza €7+
Salads (often quite substantial with ham, cheese, egg, etc) €7+
Typical tourist restaurant meal for two with wine €35–45

Tipping Montenegrins do not generally tip much, simply rounding up the total. Visitors will normally feel more comfortable leaving 10–15%. It will be appreciated.

BARS AND NIGHTLIFE Nightlife is not a feature of most Montenegrin towns, but in areas where foreign and domestic tourists congregate – specifically Podgorica, Ulcinj, Budva, Petrovac, Herceg Novi and Kotor, and now Tivat too, in part thanks to Porto Montenegro – there are quite a few seasonal bars and nightclubs to be found. In Budva, particularly, clubs tend to stay open as long as there are people in them – often until 05.00–06.00 – while in Podgorica the scene is more upmarket, with a jazz club that welcomes national and international musicians, and dozens of wine bars.

Alcohol consumption There is neither a minimum nor a maximum legal drinking age in Montenegrin bars, but one does not often see a drunken Montenegrin – even males – and never females.

PUBLIC HOLIDAYS AND FESTIVALS

PUBLIC HOLIDAYS

1–2 January	New Year
7 January	Orthodox Christmas Day
8 March	International Women's Day
Easter	5 April 2015, 27 March 2016, 16 April 2017
1–2 May	Labour Day
9 May	Victory in Europe Day
21–22 May	New Declaration of Independence in 2006
13 July	National Day, commemorating the anniversaries of the Recognition of Montenegrin Independence by the Congress of Berlin in 1878 and the Day of Anti-Fascist Rebellion in Montenegro in 1941
29–30 November	Republic Day
25 December	Christmas Day

Most Montenegrin Muslims observe Ramadan, and take part in the four-day festival of Bayram which marks the end of Ramadan.

While Sv Sava is the most important saint in the Serbian Orthodox Church, each Montenegrin family has its own patron saint. On his or her saint's special day, an individual is entitled to a day's leave from work and can be excused from housework and from labour in the fields.

FESTIVALS For many of the festivals listed below the specific date will alter from year to year so dates given may be approximate. Local tourist offices will often be able to give details.

January
Christmas Celebration (*6–8 Jan*) In almost every town in Montenegro. '*Mir božji, Hristos se rodi!*' ('God's peace, Christ is born!').

Orthodox New Year and Celebration of Sv Vasile the Great (*13 Jan*) Almost everywhere, with religious and entertainment programmes in town squares, in front of monasteries and churches.

Gitarijada (*www.bar.travel*) Bar Guitar Festival gathering the most successful guitar players and professors from the country and abroad.

February
Mimosa Festival (*Herceg Novi, Baošići, Djenovići & Kumbor; www.hercegnovi. travel; end Jan to beginning Mar*) In honour of the mimosa flower. Festivities include fishermen's fiestas, a sailing regatta, masked balls, carnivals, literary evenings, painting exhibitions, floral exhibitions, plays and even a mimosa-arranging session.

Kotor Carnival Carnival and masked ball in Kotor.

Nights of Boka Bay Carnival (Bokeljska Noć) (*Tivat; www.tivat.travel; 2nd half Feb*) Traditional winter carnival event organised by the Boka Navy from Tivat, including masked ball.

St Tryphon's Day (Dan Svetog Tripuna) (*Kotor; www.kotor.travel*) Religious festivities and a parade including Boka Marina Brass Band, folk bands and church choirs, dedicated to the patron saint of Kotor.

Prčanj Carnival (*www.kotor.travel*) Traditional winter carnival celebrations in Prčanj, near Kotor.

March

Camellia Days (*Kotor & Stoliv; www.kotor.travel; late Mar–early Apr*) Held in honour of the camellia flower. Floral exhibitions, painting exhibitions, plays, a camellia ball and a Lady of the Camellias contest.

International Para-Ski Cup (*Žabljak; www.zabljak.travel*) Organised by the Žabljak municipality for the Durmitor Cup.

April

Vrbica (*5 Apr 2015, 24 Apr 2016, 9 Apr 2017*) Orthodox Palm Sunday, the Sunday before Easter; processions with willow garlands.

Orthodox Easter (*12 Apr 2015, 1 May 2016, 16 Apr 2017*) Celebrated in most of Montenegro.

May

Žučenica Fest (*Tivat; www.tivat.travel*) Gastronomic festival of Boka cuisine, featuring *žučenica* (chicory).

Kićenje Mada (*Perast; 1 May at 08.00*) Decorating the oak tree in front of Sv Nikola's Church, to welcome the month of May.

Shooting the Kokot (rooster) (*Perast; www.kotor.travel; 15 May*) Celebrates the liberation of Perast from the Turks in 1654. The rooster represents the Turks and the first to shoot are sailors from the Boka Navy.

Vladimir's Cross (*Bar; www.bar.travel; 30 May*) The cross is kept in the Andrović family as a most precious relic. Each year on the Day of Holy Trinity, the cross is taken to the peak of Mt Rumija to the place where, according to legend, there used to be a church.

Days of Marko Miljanov (*Medun; www.podgorica.travel*) Literary events organised by the museum in Medun, near Podgorica.

Sutomore Motorcycle Race (*1st half May & mid Sept*) International motorcycle gathering.

Lim River Rafting Regatta (*Plav; www.toberane.me; last weekend May*) Rafting race from the source of the River Lim at Plav Lake to the confluence of the Lim and Milesevka rivers.

June

Montenegro Dance Festival (*www.montenegrodancefestival.com*) Held in Kotor, Tivat and Herceg Novi in late April/early May and late June/early July.

Ruke – Days of Creativity Festival of arts and crafts in Herceg Novi.

Boka Navy Day (*Kotor; www.bokeljskamornarica.org*) Celebration of 12 centuries of the Boka Navy since a ship brought St Valentine's relics to the town. Sailors dance the St Valentine's Wheel Dance.

Montenegro Amateur Drama Festival (*Bijelo Polje*) Long-running festival of amateur drama, established in 1970.

Southern Soul Festival (*Velika Plaza, Ulcinj; www.southernsoulfestival.com*) Big music festival, with soul, R&B, jazz and hip-hop spread over four nights, featuring top international names including the likes of Alex Barck, Rick Wilhite and Gilles Peterson.

Purgatorije – Tivat Cultural Summer (*end Jun to end Aug*) Theatre, music, literary and artistic programmes.

July

Budva's Summer Festival of Theatre (Festival Grad Teatar) (*www.gradteatar.me; around 2 months, mid-Jun to mid-Aug*) See box page 60.

Podgorica Cultural Summer (*Podgorica; www.podgorica.travel; from Jul to Sep*) Theatre, concerts and art exhibitions.

Bijelo Polje (White Field Jazz Festival) (*www.tobijelopolje.me; 2 days in mid-Jul*) Well-established jazz festival which has been running since 2006.

Sunčane Skale (Sunny Steps) (*Herceg Novi; www.suncaneskale.org; 3 nights early Jul*) International music festival on the stage of the Kanli kula.

Children's Theatre (*Kotor; early Jul*) Montenegrin and international festival of children's theatre, now running for over 20 years and including children's puppet shows, dancing, art and plays.

The Square of Books (*Herceg Novi*). Book fair in Belavista Square.

Fašinada (*Perast; www.kotor.travel; 22 Jul*) A ritual procession of boats around the island of Gospa od Škrpjela (Our Lady of the Rock) near Perast. See box page 137.

The Days of Mountain Flowers (*Žabljak; www.zabljak.travel*) Wedding on Crna jezera, flower show, art exhibition, scientific lectures, traditional and mountain sports.

The Durmitor Ring (*Žabljak; www.drumiputokazi.com*) Marathon mountain-bike championship.

Durmitor Ski/Snowboard Cup Held on Durmitor's Savin kuk.

2

It is said that as early as the Hellenistic period Budva had a thriving theatre, proof of which is believed to be small terracotta token-like objects found during the digging of foundations for the Avala Hotel, close to the old walled city. It is thought these would have been used to gain admittance to performances.

More recently, when painstaking repairs after the devastation of the 1979 earthquake were finally completed, the community of Budva had the idea of reinstating the tradition. The walls of the citadel were recognised to be an ideal backdrop for the staging of operas and plays and, starting from 1 July 1987, this came about with a series of productions including Shakespeare's *Richard III* and *Titus Andronicus*. In the same summer, Mozart's *Don Giovanni* and Verdi's *Otello* were both ambitiously and successfully performed on the nearby sandy Jaz Beach.

Since that time the annual festival (*Festival Grad Teatar; www.gradteatar. me*) has been steadily growing and works have additionally been staged in a variety of neighbouring locations, including monasteries and hotel gardens such as Villa Miločer, sister hotel to Sveti Stefan. The festival runs for around two months, from mid-June to mid-August.

Summer with Stars (*Budva; Jul/Aug*) Concerts by Montenegrin and ex-Yu singers.

Days of Mushrooms and Medicinal Herbs (Dani gljiva i ljekovitog bilja) (*Rožaje, 1 week in Jul*) See page 284.

Kotor Summer Carnival (*Kotor; http://kotor.me; end Jul/beginning Aug*) International summer carnival held in front of Kotor's old town, with carnival groups from Kotor, Montenegro and abroad.

Blueberry Festival (*Plav; www.toplav.me; end Jul*)

August

The Nights of Boka (*http://kotor.me*) Traditional parade of decorated boats in the waters of the Boka Kotorska, followed by fireworks in front of Kotor's old town. Dates back around three centuries.

Cetinje Jazz Festival (*www.cetinje.travel*) Jazz festival running since 2010 in Cetinje and (as of 2014) in Rijeka Crnojevića.

Montenegro Film Festival (*Herceg Novi; www.hercegfest.co.me; 1st week Aug*) Montenegro's top film festival, founded in 1987. Screenings in the Kanli kula.

Swimming Marathon (*Sutomore to Bar; www.bar.travel*) A 5km swimming marathon from the Hotel Sozina in Sutomore to the Hotel Topolica in Bar.

Ratković's Days of Poetry (*Bijelo Polje; www.bijelopolje.travel*) Gathering of writers.

Tivatsko Kulturno Ljeto (Tivat Cultural Summer) (*Tivat Riviera*) Plays, concerts, exhibitions, poetry readings, choirs and dance groups appear along the riviera, celebrating local culture.

Cetinje Festival (*Cetinje; www.cetinje.travel; mid Aug*) International festival of folk music and folk dancing.

Lastva Fiestas (*Gornja Lastva; www.tivat.travel*) Religious and traditional events, including carrying St Roko's statue through Donja Lastva.

Perast Klapa Festival (*Perast; www.festivalklapaperast.com; 3 days in Jun*) Festival of traditional klapa (a capella singing).

Port Cup (*Bar; www.bar.travel*) International women's volleyball contest.

International Festival of Tamburitza Orchestras (*Bijelo Polje; www.tobijelopolje.me*)

Koštanjada (*Stoliv; www.kotor.travel; end Aug/early Sep*) Gastronomic Chestnut Day.

September
Bayram For the Muslim community. Date changes every year.

Jazz Festival (*Petrovac; 1st week Sep*)

Herceg Novi Jazz Fest (*early Sep*) New jazz festival.

Montenegro Mediterranean Film Festival (MOFF) (*Kotor*) Film festival focusing on films from the Mediterranean region.

Meetings of Farmers, Grape Growers, Orchardists and Bee-keepers (*Virpazar; www.bar.travel*) Events promoting the agricultural produce of the Skadar Lake region.

Festival of Children's Poetry (*Danilovgrad*) Festival of children's literature and poetry.

Festival of International Alternative Theatre (FIAT) (*Podgorica, 1st half Sep*)

October
Days of Širun (*Budva; early Oct*) Annual fisherman's festival that has been running for almost 50 years.

Days of Pljevlja Cheese (*Pljevlja*) Festival of local highland cheese and dairy produce.

Podgorica International Marathon and Half Marathon (*www.maraton.co.me; www.podgorica.travel; late Oct/early Nov*)

November
Meeting Under an Olive Tree (*Mirovica, near Bar; www.bar.travel*) Traditional event dedicated to children's creativity. Children present their literary and painting interpretations of the theme 'Olive trees, peace and friendship'. Takes place at Mirovica, famous for its 2,000 year old olive tree.

The Olive Day (*Stari Bar; www.bar.travel*) Festival dedicated to the olive tree, with olive oil and other local products. Also exhibitions of traditional costumes, entertainment and culture.

December

DEUS – December Art Scene (*Podgorica; www.podgorica.travel*) Theatre, music, fine arts, literature and film. Formerly known as December Days of Culture.

Hrast Oak is associated with Christmas and it is customary throughout Montenegro to burn a celebratory oak log either in the garden or simply in the fireplace.

Christmas (*25 Dec*) For the Catholic community.

Festival of Wine and Bleak (*Virpazar*) Annual festival celebrating the local freshwater fish (bleak), wine and other produce from around Skadar Lake.

SHOPPING

The most interesting purchases in Montenegro are things to eat or drink, and handicrafts. Among the things to look out for are fruit and vegetables and fruit juices, which are all excellent, usually organic and inexpensive. Olive oil from the Bar area, light and delicious, is available in good produce stores in Podgorica and along the coast, or from the market in Bar, freshly bottled by the local producer. Honey is lovely, especially from the Bjelopavlići valley, between the Ostrog Monastery and Danilovgrad; expect to pay €4–5 a litre.

Mini-markets in Montenegro are wonderful places, with the widest selection of goods imaginable, all neatly displayed and individually priced and the shopkeeper taking proprietorial pride in the orderliness of his empire.

Many places have **food markets** where local farmers sell their produce (usually both fresh and cheap). There are often also **town markets** where bottom-range clothing and household goods, generally from Turkey or eastern Europe, are on sale at bottom-range prices.

Of the **handicrafts**, there are handmade wooden artefacts and utensils (particularly in Rožaje and to some extent in Žabljak and other mountainous regions); copies of icons and prints (found in monastery shops; in general museum shops have little as yet in the way of reproductions); local weaving and national costume (particularly in the northern towns); lacework (Dobrota, Boka Kotorska, Cetinje and Njeguši); musical instruments: *gusle*, the one-stringed fiddle, and the shepherd's double flute, found in northern areas near the border with Serbia; and original painting and sculpture, often at rock-bottom prices (Rožaje, Žabljak, Herceg Novi and Cetinje) – though note that antiquities may not be exported without a special licence.

The larger regional **tourist offices and the national park centres** will frequently stock a limited selection of local handicrafts. The retail outlet within each national park and some museums, such as that housed in the Royal Palace at Cetinje, have a selection of books, pictures and local guides.

OPENING TIMES

Museums are usually closed on a Monday, but they underfunded and by no means always adhere to fixed opening hours. **Churches** are frequently found to be locked and enquiries nearby may be to no avail. In such cases one can only assume that the key has either been lost or buried in the pocket of a past priest. As archaeologist Jovan Martinović in Kotor reflected, 'It is always the key: the key is always the question.' But it is of course dispiriting to keep a museum open and have no visitors. At present it is always wisest to check locally with the listed Montenegro **tourist offices** that can be found in all the main centres.

Shops are generally open 09.00–21.00 Monday–Saturday, although food shops often open as early as 06.00 and may open on Sundays as well. **Larger supermarkets** close on Sunday afternoons. In tourist centres, some shops stay open until midnight in season. **Banking hours** vary from town to town, bank to bank and sometimes season to season. A very rough guide would be 08.00–19.00 on weekdays, 08.00–13.00 on Saturdays, closed on Sundays. **Post offices** are usually open from Monday to Saturday, although sometimes Monday to Friday in eastern areas of the country.

ACTIVITIES

BALLOONING Podgorica boasts the **Ballooning Sports Club** Budućnost (m *067 234832;* e *balonarstvo@t-com.me*).

BEACH VOLLEYBALL Montenegro's sandy beaches are ideal for beach volleyball. The main clubs are in Budva (page 173) and Bar (page 206).

BIRDWATCHING Both the Montenegrin littoral and Skadar Lake provide outstanding opportunities for ornithologists. The country is situated on an important migratory route known as the Adriatic Flyway, one favoured by birds migrating between Europe and sub-Saharan Africa. Alongside these migratory birds there is also a huge number of resident species, all adding to Montenegro's avian diversity (see pages 6–7). One word of warning, however: in spite of efforts to control such activities, particularly in Ulcinj Solana (Ulcinj Saltpans, a popular site for migrating waders), illegal **hunting** remains rife.

There are five main areas for birdwatching:

The coast The coast itself attracts waders, cormorants and pelicans, especially Buljarica Beach and south of Ulcinj. Just inland, the newly declared nature reserve of the **Ulcinj Saltpans** is also a breeding site for the greater flamingo, though as there is a commercial salt extraction operation here you will need permission to go in. This should be a formality.

Other coastal highlights for waterbirds are the small **saltpan at Tivat** (Tivatska Solila, page 161), which in 2013 was declared a RAMSAR Site (Wetland of International Importance), and the area of marsh on the **Čanj wetland** near Petrovac (page 200).

Šasko Lake The small freshwater Šasko Lake, inland from Ulcinj and near the Albanian border, is also good for waterbirds, although access is a bit tricky and you will need to rent a boat from a local fisherman. Do so, and you'll be rewarded with sightings of many different species of swamp bird, as well as a heron colony (pages 221–2).

Skadar Lake National Park (pages 223–31) An ornithologist's dream, especially in the breeding season – but leave the border area with Albania to the smugglers. The best starting point by boat is Virpazar, from where there are several possible birding tours. Eagles, ibis, bitterns, herons, warblers, ducks, pelicans, owls and buntings are among the 290 recorded species in the lake area. The commonly quoted figure for wintering flocks is 200,000 birds.

With adequate notice, staff at the visitor centres in Virpazar and Vranjina on Skadar Lake can arrange birdwatching expeditions using small boats, as well as dedicated towers and hides (✆ 020 879103). Alternatively contact Undiscovered Montenegro (page 228).

Biogradska Gora National Park (pages 271–4) This virgin deciduous–coniferous forest, such as hardly exists anywhere else in Europe, is home to a profusion of forest birds. On a good one-day walk through the forest and around the lake you may be lucky enough to spot some from a list that includes eagles, owls, woodpeckers, thrushes, larks, nightingales, tits, buntings and partridges.

Durmitor National Park (pages 256–63) With mountains rising to 2,522m and a lot of thick coniferous forest, Durmitor claims 175 different species of birds. It isn't quite as remote or as undeveloped as Biogradska but is considerably more mountainous. On the heights, specials include the snowfinch, black redstart and alpine chough, while the forests are home to the nutcracker, firecrest and three-toed woodpecker, among others. Birds of prey include short-toed and golden eagles, honey buzzards and peregrine.

BOCANJE This Montenegrin version of Mediterranean bowls is mostly practised in the Boka Kotorska. There are several clubs in Tivat, where an annual 'Bocce Olympics' is held. Contact the tourist office for details (*http://tivat.travel/en/bocce/*).

CANYONING Though in its infancy as a guided extreme sport in Montenegro, canyoning in the narrow gorge of the Komarnica River (page 244) is spectacular. The team of instructors is highly experienced, but canyoning is not for the faint-hearted, and a decent level of fitness is mandatory.

CYCLING If you like pedalling up and down beautiful hills in the fresh air, this is your place. But mind the cars, the boulders, the unlit tunnels and the unfenced cliff edges.

The Tourism Ministry, in co-operation with the German Cycling Association, has produced a variety of maps and guidebooks as well as newly signed bicycle trails. Mountain biking, too, is attracting growing interest in Montenegro, with the implementation of many innovations including new signposting on recommended routes. At the same time a number of hotels have signed up to the 'Bed & Bike' scheme, usually advertised prominently on their walls, under which they guarantee to provide safe storage, washing and drying facilities, travel and luggage information, advice on local repair facilities and the loan of some tools. (Details are available on the website of the National Tourism Organisation, www.montenegro.travel.)

Wilderness Biking Montenegro, covering 17 trails over 1,700km, is available online from www.mapsolutions.de/MTB-book (German only) and from the tourist board website (*www.montenegro.travel*).

The *Guide to the Orjen Massif* by Željko Starčević and Dr Goran Komar (Mountaineering Club Subra, 2006) has an excellent section entitled 'Mountain biking guide', with details of routes. The book is available from the Salt Book Store in Herceg Novi old town. The authors make the point that although mountain bikes are one of the most ecologically non-damaging methods of travel, they nevertheless can have some harmful effects upon 'exposed earth terrain', and it is better where possible to limit their use to established tracks.

ON THE SUBJECT OF BICYCLES

It used to be comparatively simple to take a bicycle by air if hold space was available; more surprisingly it was said to be unusual to be charged extra for its transport. Not unexpectedly the situation has changed: charges are now levied and vary from one carrier to another. Check with your airline well in advance.

Environmentally concerned travellers are increasingly choosing bikes as a means of getting around. If someone wishes to avoid air travel to Montenegro it is possible to reach Kolašin, Podgorica or Bar from the rest of Europe by train. Howard Boyd, a Transport Policy Advisor to CTC (Cyclists' Touring Club) writes:

> At least one service a day from Belgrade to Podgorica takes bicycles at a small extra charge, currently a daytime service ... Bicycles do not need to be dismantled (although bags must be taken off) but they must be checked in at least an hour in advance and retrieved from the *magazine* at the destination.

However, he goes on to add there can be problems with Eurostar, including delays in unloading which can interfere with onward travel, in which case it may be necessary to dismantle the bike and bag it. On TGV lines there isn't always much available space, he adds. As the situation appears to be fluid, certainly so at the time of writing, anyone planning to travel to Montenegro with a bike is advised to check their travel arrangements very carefully in advance.

Boyd also suggests bringing a folding bike, such as the popular Brompton which, although in no way a substitute for a heavy-duty model and which even on coastal roads will necessitate a certain amount of walking and pushing, will nevertheless allow a considerable amount of flexibility, not least the option of folding it up and jumping on a bus. Needless to add that for a trip such as the one described on pages 286–7, a high-quality mountain bike is essential – with, Boyd stresses, tyres of a minimum 37mm.

Bicycles for purchase are sometimes available in the Big Market (*Velika Pijaca*) in Podgorica, for roughly the same price as a night in an expensive hotel, and heavy-duty bike rental companies are on the increase within the country.

The author would strongly advise those planning to use a bicycle of any type to avoid whenever possible the main 'express' highways, where the combination of unlit tunnels and juggernauts is potentially lethal, and instead to search out the quieter back roads.

As well as informative leaflets and route maps for wilderness biking throughout Montenegro (available from many of the regional tourist offices and downloadable from the National Tourist Office website, www.montenegro.travel), there are two excellent maps, entitled *Cycling Around Škodra/Skadar Lake*, prepared by Mark Rupa (e *rupa_mark@yahoo.co.uk*) and financed by HRK The German Rectors' Conference, GTZ Albania and GTZ Montenegro. The first map covers routes around the area described above and the second one includes the Komovi area. They contain other useful titbits and helpful tips for cyclists in the Balkans.

(For further information on the subject of mountain biking in Montenegro, see opposite.)

Practical Information   ACTIVITIES

2

The Annual Adventure Race, organised by Black Mountain but currently on hold, is a combination kayak, cycle and run, which raises money for local charities.

For further information contact the **Cycling Association of Montenegro** (*ul M Kucevica, PF 130, 84000 Bijelo Polje;* ☎ *050 431107*). For an individual account of cycling in Montenegro, see box, pages 286–7.

Biking tours

A number of travel companies already have road & off-road biking programmes in place. Most of those who arrange hiking will similarly offer biking tours. Already well established in this field are:

ACE Cycling & Mountaineering Centre
B Kramanović 51/8, 1800 Nis, Serbia; Krasici I/2, 85320 Tivat; e info@ace-adventurecentre.com; www.ace-adventurecentre.com. Organise guided bicycle tours in Montenegro, for which they supply bikes, but they do not rent otherwise.

Bicycle Club Rudar
Pljevlja; ☎ +052 321157. Rental.

Black Mountain Montenegro Ltd
Herceg Novi; e info@montenegroholiday.com; www.montenegroholiday.com. Specialises in eco-friendly & adventure tourism & is an associate of the 'Leave No Trace Organisation'.

Eco Tours
Kolašin; ☎ 020 860700; e eco-tours@t-com.me; www.eco-tours.co.me. Rental €10 per day or €6 per half day.

Montenegro Adventures
Jovana Tomaševića 35, 81000 Podgorica (just across the street from the Millennium Bridge); ☎ 020 208000; e info@montenegro-adventures.com; www.montenegro-adventures.com

Rams
Bijelo Polje; ☎ 050 432374; e rams@t-com.me; www.ramstravel.co.me

Summit
Žabljak; m 069 016502; www.summit.co.me. Rental.

✳ Tempo
Bratska i Jedinstva 57, Podgorica; ☎ 020 623632; e tempobike@t-com.me; www.tempo.co.me (Montenegrin only). Comprehensive repair service.

Undiscovered Montenegro
Virpazar; e info@undiscoveredmontenegro.com; www.undiscoveredmontenegro.com. Free use of bikes with accommodation at Villa Miela in Virpazar (page 228).

Bicycle transport

Bus: Blue Line Trebinjska 48, Igalo; ☎ 031 336006; www.blueline-mne.com (Dubrovnik–Podgorica €30)

Italy–Montenegro Ferry, Barska Plovidba Obala 13 jula bb, Bar; ☎ 030 311465; e online@barplov.com; www.montenegrolines.com (bicycle transport free)

Montenegro Airlines bul Ivana Crnojevića 55, 81000 Podgorica; ☎ 020 664411; www.montenegroairlines.com

Railways www.zcg-prevoz.me (Montenegrin only) (within Montenegro €5 per bike)

CAVING The mountains of Montenegro, being formed largely of limestone/karst, are an ideal location for the extreme sport of caving, and interest in this activity has been growing. There is much to be explored and significant caves lie close to Podgorica, notably **Lipska** at 3,410m and **Cetinjska Pećina** at 2,650m, both in the neighbourhood of Cetinje. In view of the potential hazards involved – flash-flooding being only one of them – it is highly advisable to seek access advice from local experts. Try the **Speleological Society of Montenegro** (☎ *040 242133;* e *speleologija@t-com.me*).

FISHING Fishing is popular on Skadar Lake, Black Lake (Crno jezero) and Biogradska Lake; on many rivers including the Morača, Tara, Bojana and Zeta; and of course on the Adriatic Sea. Freshwater fish include trout, grayling, chub, carp and bleak. Saltwater fish are abundant: mullet, St Pierre, sea perch and porgie, etc. Fishing licences, priced at €5–20 per day, must be obtained in advance from the fishing association; this law is enforced.

Sport-fishing associations include the following:

FLY-FISHING IN MONTENEGRO

As experienced by Kevin Lyne, British Ambassador at Podgorica 2007–09

As you might expect from the geography of Montenegro, there is spectacular fly-fishing for trout and grayling in the many rivers and mountain lakes. This has been relatively neglected by organised adventure holiday companies and the keen fisherman will need to spend some time planning and preparing.

The following locations are well worth checking out: the Morača and Cijevna rivers near Podgorica (and the tributary Mrtvica north of Podgorica); the River Zeta near Nikšić; the River Lim near Bijelo Polje; the River Tara in and near Kolašin; the Komarnica canyon and Trnovačko Lake near Plužine; and Plav Lake and the rivers that flow in and out of it. The season is from 1 April to 1 November, with some local variations. Licence fees will also vary from place to place and are reasonably priced, but foreigners pay more than Montenegrins. You will find free and friendly advice in specialist fishing-tackle shops, for example those in Podgorica near Marka Miljanova and Vukova streets. Hotels and tour operators should also be able to connect you with shops and guides. Tackle-wise, a four-weight rod with floating line should be adequate for most situations. Excellent locally tied flies can be obtained in the shops.

That's the good news. Less encouraging is the degree to which this outstanding fishing habitat is under threat from under-regulated development (eg: gravel extraction), pollution and overfishing. There are some courageous and pioneering fishing enthusiasts in Montenegro who are doing their best to resist this, including through the enforcement of catch-and-release policies. The fishing clubs in Plav and Kolašin deserve special mention in this regard. But it is tough going. Growing interest from foreign visitors should support their campaigns, so help them where you can.

Berane SFA Lim; m 067 544966; e obatovicz@t-com.me
Danilovgrad SFA Trabuco; m 069 027009; e ribolovici@t-com.me
Kolašin SFA Kolašin; ☎ 020 865314; e sportsko_ribolovni_klub_kolasin@yahoo.com
Mojkovac SFA Mojkovac; ☎ 050 472611

Nikšić SFA Nikšić; ☎ 040 241417
Pljevlja SFA Lipljen; m 069 990762
Plužine SFA Bajo Pivljanin; m 069 990762
Podgorica ☎ 020 623227; e spasop@t-com. me
Rožaje SFA Ibar; ☎ 051 272130
Šavnik SFA Komarnica; m 069 217601

GEOCACHING A number of 'treasure boxes' hidden around the country near spectacular viewpoints contain a notebook and pencil, as well as a few small gifts to exchange. Some can be reached by car or bike; others require access on foot, such as below Ledina Pećina, the extraordinary ice cave in the Durmitor Massif. Note that GPS is necessary to participate. The geocaching motto is 'cache in, trash out' – carry a bag to collect rubbish along the way: an ideal concept given Montenegro's ecological principles. For details, see www.geocaching.com.

HIKING, TREKKING, MOUNTAINEERING AND FREE-CLIMBING Much of the countryside provides magnificent opportunities for walking and trekking, with trails varying from easy to challenging. In particular, the Durmitor Massif has numerous peaks over 2,200m, several of them accessible without the use of special equipment, and the general area has 60km of marked paths, 20km of which are cleared.

2

A portion of the mountaineering transversal, **CT-1**, runs through the Biogradska Gora National Park. A total of 120km in length, it begins in Veruša and continues through Komovi, Trešnjevik and Lisa, skirting the slopes of Ključ past Raskrsnica, Vranjak to Biogradska Lake and on to Mojkovac and Sinjajevina, then Njegovuđa and finally Žabljak.

A new, second traversal – the 182km **CT-2** or Coastal Traversal – was established in 2009: a well-marked route from Herceg Novi, across Orjen, Lovćen and Rumija, to Bar.

Most recent is the **Peaks of the Balkans** trail, a well and truly epic, spectacular 192km route through the mountains of Montenegro, Albania and Kosovo. A detailed map, with a brief description of each stage, is available (*www.peaksofthebalkans. com*), and a new guide by Rudolf Abraham is due to be published in 2015.

Marked **free-climbing** trails are rated from 6+ to 8-, and competitions are now regularly organised.

Hiking maps and guidebooks
Walking possibilities throughout Montenegro and around its borders are boundless and a variety of suggestions can be found within this guide. There are also several dedicated publications.

The most detailed English-language guidebook available to hiking in Montenegro is Rudolf Abraham's *The Mountains of Montenegro* (see *Appendix 3*, page 326), which covers Durmitor, Biogradska Gora, Lovćen and Prokletije national parks, as well as several other areas including Orjen, Komovi and Kučka Krajina.

Another excellent little book, describing most of the mountainous areas within the country, was published in both English and Serbian in 2004: *The Mountains of Montenegro* by Daniel Vincek, Ratko Popović and Mijo Kovačević (see page 326). However, some of the information in this is now considerably out of date.

For suggested routes in the Bjelasica–Komovi region, look for the invaluable *Green Paths* trekking map, published on the initiative of the Montenegro Office of the Organization for Security and Co-operation in Europe, in collaboration with Naturefriends International, the Norwegian government and the Siemens group of companies.

Finding Your Way Through the Mountains of Bjelasica and Komovi, published by the Austrian–Montenegrin Partnership for Bjelasica and Komovi, is available free of charge from the Local Project Office in Kolašin (**e** *office@rtobik.co.me*, *www. bjelasica-komovi.com*).

Two other useful trekking guides, one for the Orjen Massif and one describing the high coastal transversal route linking Orjen–Lovćen–Rumija (see page 326), are available in good local bookshops such as the Salt Bookstore in Herceg Novi.

A carefully detailed, professionally compiled guide, *Durmitor and the Tara Canyon*, written by mountaineer Branislav Cerović and published by the Durmitor National Park, is particularly recommended, though some of the information is now out of date (including new huts which have opened and others which have closed; newly waymarked trails, etc); it is usually available from the park's shop at Crno jezero (Black Lake). Climbs to each of Durmitor's main peaks are featured, with special detail given to Bobotov kuk, Savin kuk, Crevena Greda, Meded and Planinica. For trekking guidebooks and maps featuring Prokletije, see page 326.

Organised trips
A number of travel agencies, including Black Mountain (page 118), organise wilderness trekking. For the latest information see www.montenegro. travel. Alternatively, contact one of the following organisations:

↟ Mountaineering Association of Montenegro ☎020 622220; e info@pscg.me; www.pscg.me

↟ Mountaineering club 'Pestingrad' Kotor; e pkpestingrad@yahoo.com; www.pestingrad.com

↟ PSK Komovi www.komovi.org.me

Subra Mountaineering Club e subra@t-com.me; www.pksubra.me

HUNTING AND SHOOTING The best-known shooting grounds are at Skadar Lake, Mt Durmitor, the Bjelopavlička Valley, Crmnica and Ulcinj (at Šas). Hunting is allowed, with a permit, seasonally for bears and wild boar, and without one, for wolves (some areas only), foxes and rabbits. For information on permits consult either the local tourist office or the **Montenegrin Hunting Association** (*Bulevar revolucije 48, Podgorica;* ☎*020 242213*). Note that hunting laws are constantly under review, but at the time of writing the shooting calendar reads:

capercaillie 15 Apr–15 May	**rabbit** 1 Oct–31 Dec	**wild boar** 1 Oct–20 Feb
duck 15 Aug–28 Feb	**rock partridge** 1 Oct–30 Nov	**wolf** 1 Oct–1 Mar
pheasant 1 Oct–31 Jan	**roe deer** 1 May–30 Sep	**woodcock** 1 Oct–28 Feb
quail 15 Aug–31 Dec	**turtle dove** 15 Aug–30 Sep	

KAYAKING There are plenty of opportunities for kayaking, suitable for all levels of experience, both on the coast (try Kayak Herceg Novi; *www.kayak-hercegnovi.com*) or on the enormous Skadar Lake (contact Undiscovered Montenegro; *www.undiscoveredmontenegro.com*).

MOTORBIKING Bikers (the motorised variety) have arrived in Montenegro. A system of planned routes taking from half a day to three days offers a wide variety of thrilling Montenegrin experiences. For details of recommended routes contact:

VG Racing Team Bar, contact Goran Grgić; m 068 607600

BU2 Budva, contact Senad Adrović; m 069 250221

Harley Davidson Budva, contact Kristo Niklanović; m 069 030180

Poseidon Budva, contact Vlado Bulatović; m 067 251400

Cruiser Herceg Novi, contact Nesko Krivokapić; m 067 812969

Oridjinali Kotor, contact Borka Zukić; m 069 049238

No Limit Bikers Podgorica, contact Ivan Bozović; m 067 232100

Pirates Ulcinj, contact Alen Alović; m 068 705514

There is also a dedicated bikers' 'Beer & Bike' club (*Slovenska Obala 10 – next to restoran Jadran, Budva*), which serves ten types of beer, eight types of sausage and pretzels. The owner and manager are themselves bikers. (It should be remembered that the maximum permitted driver blood-alcohol concentration limit in Montenegro is 0.05; in both the UK and USA it remains 0.08.)

OFF-ROADING For off-road exploring, contact specialist operator **Montenegro Trophy** in **Nikšic** (page 238), who organise an off-road rally on the Krnovo Plateau for the eponymous Montenegro Trophy.

PARAGLIDING To be found mostly on the coast (see box, page 173), but also in Durmitor.

🪂 MAC fly e montenegrofly@hotmail.co.uk; www.montenegrofly.com

🪂 Paragliding Montenegro e info@ paraglidingmontenegro.com; www. paraglidingmontenegro.com

RIDING Specialised activity organisations such as **Jelka Tours** (*Palih Partizanski bb, Kolašin;* ☎ *020 860150; www.vilajelka.co.me*) feature riding either from their own ranch or in combination with other sports such as camping and rafting, but organised stables are still rare even in places like Žabljak.

SAILING The main sailing centres are Budva, Bar, Herceg Novi, Kotor and Tivat. The National Tourist Organisation publishes a handy booklet, *International Yachting Guide*, which is an introduction and aid to navigating Montenegrin waters. It can be downloaded as a PDF from www.montenegro.travel.com. Organisations to contact are:

Budva
⚠ **MC Marina** ☎033 452281; e info@ marinabudva.com; www.marinabudva.com
⚠ **MennYacht** ☎033 452540; e montenegro@ mennyacht.com; www.mennyacht.com
⚠ **MIFIS** m 067 846844; e mfisworld@t-com. me; www.mifisworld.com

Herceg Novi
⚠ **Brodarsko drustvo Jugola Grakalić** ☎031 322205; e jugolagrakalic@t-com.me
⚠ **Herceg Novi Spinnaker** ☎031 323981; e ychmn@hotmail.com

Tivat
⚠ **Avel Yachting** Donja Lastva bb;☎032 684899; e info@avel.yachting.com; www.avel-yachting.com
⚠ **Kaliman Marina** ☎032 671039. Space for 240 boats.
⚠ **Porto Montenegro** ☎032 674660; e berths@portomontenegro.com; www. portomontenegro.com. Recommended (see also pages 159–60).

Bar
⚠ **OMC Marina Sv Nikola** ☎030 313911; e OMC@t-com.me; www.omcmarina.com

Kotor
⚠ **Monte Marine Yachting** ☎032 302736; e yachtmn@t-com.me
⚠ **Montenegro Charter Company** bul Sv Petra Cetinjskog 92, 81000 Podgorica, also at Kotor Marina;☎020 229585; e info@ montenegrocharter.com; www. montenegrocharter.com. All new boats, sailing & motorised. Recommended.
⚠ **SouthSail Charter** Kotor Marina, Prčanj I Morinj;☎032 684838; e southsail@t-com.me
⚠ **The Sailing Association of Montenegro** Stari Grad 494;☎032 330523. Founded in 1948, it includes clubs in Kotor (Lahor), Bečiči (Jovo Dabović), Meljine (Jedro), Herceg Novi (Jugole Grakalić) & Bar (Jadran). It organises races in Optimist, Laser Standard & Radijal Europe classes.

SCUBA DIVING Diving arrangements can be made at several locations along the Montenegrin coast. There are many small caves in the limestone cliffs and the average depth of the sea is about 35m. Summer water temperatures average 21–25°C and in winter it rarely drops below 13°C. Visibility is usually between 15m and 35m. Fish are plentiful.

The Boka Kotorska holds underwater potential for divers, with caves, springs and wrecks to be explored. There are almost no real beaches on its inner bays: it's sea wall all the way.

Montenegro has two underwater archaeological sites that are protected by law since 2011: the Bay of Bigovica near Bar, and the deep sea area off the coast of Risan between the Stripački and Murove headlands. There are a few archaeological finds which are not yet fully explored, as well as various wrecks, including *Sent Istvan* at the mouth of the Boka Kotorska; a military patrol vessel in Zanjik Valley; an unidentified two-master near Platamuni Cape; the World War II destroyer *Zenta* off Petrovac; King Nikola's yacht and a World War I Austrian naval ship, *Dag*, in Bar; and another Austrian naval vessel off the Great Beach at Ulcinj. All are accessible to divers except the *Zenta*, which lies at 70m.

For advice on scuba diving, underwater photography, spear fishing and even underwater hockey, contact the **Diving Association of Montenegro (Ronilački savez Crne Gore)** (*ul Jovana Tomaševića 23, 85000 Bar;* m *067 508009, 069 030448;* e *ronilacki.savezcg@t-com.me; www.mdiving.me – Montenegrin only*).

Among the many diving clubs on the coast are:

DC Hobotnica Bar; m 069 495604; e info@ divemontenegro.com; www.divemontenegro.com

DC Montenegro Čanj; www.ronjenje.net

SKIING Facilities are still in a fairly early stage of development but there are usually at least four months of decent snow and prices compare very favourably to most other countries in Europe or North America.

Skiing is centred on the Durmitor and Bjelasica mountains (pages 256–63 and 271) and the resorts of Žabljak and Kolašin. There's also a motel and three lifts at Vučje, near Nikšić (page 239), and near Berane, Lovke Ski Centre (page 280) has now reopened. Another small ski area – at Turjak, just outside Rožaje – has not been operating for a few years, but ski lifts, hotels and investors exist and the slopes will undoubtedly come back into action at some stage.

Ski Centar 1450, Kolašin Trg Borca br 1; 020 863100; e office@kolasin1450.com; www. kolasin1450.com

Ski Centar Durmitor 052 361144; www. durmitor.com

Skiing Association of Montenegro ul Nika Miljanica br 8, Nikšić; 040 244649; e montenegroski@t-com.me; www. montenegroexplorer.co.me

Snowboard Club Savinkuk m 069 477677

TENNIS The sport is widely played, especially along the coast, and a number of hotels have clay or cement courts. The main clubs are in Budva, Igalo, Tivat and Podgorica.

WHITE-WATER RAFTING Rafting by rubber Gemini-style or wooden raft is well organised in the Tara Canyon along 100km of the Tara River (pages 262–3), where tourist offices and better hotels can provide up-to-date details on the variety of rafting companies. There is also embryonic rafting activity on some other rivers, including the Morača (page 300).

WINDSURFING AND KITESURFING Windsurfing can be enjoyed at virtually all the coastal resorts as well as on Skadar Lake. Ask at your hotel or at the local tourist office or contact the **Windsurfing Club Pelikan** at Vranjina on Skadar Lake (069 020549, http://pelikansurf.me), who rent equipment and organise training and competitions. There is also kitesurfing at Ulcinj (see page 217).

MEDIA AND COMMUNICATIONS

NEWSPAPERS, RADIO AND TELEVISION The vernacular press includes three main newspapers, *Pobjeda* (*Victory*, pro-government), *Vijesti* (independent), and *Dan* (pro-Belgrade), as well as an influential weekly called *Monitor*. English-language newspapers in news-stand format are extremely rare in Montenegro, even in the big hotels, though **The Tobacco Shop**, just behind the Vardar Hotel in Kotor Old Town, has the *Financial Times* and the *International New York Times*. The electronic/internet versions that can be found in many other countries are also scarce, but may be ordered (minimum one week) through the bookshop **Gradska Knjižara** (e *nknjiga@gmail.com; www.novaknjiga.com*) at Porto Montenegro, or at their branch in Podgorica. An eclectic selection of English and American magazines is available in Podgorica and at one or two of the big foreign-owned hotels. The kiosk outside Kotor main gate sells *Le Monde*. Otherwise go online to **Newspaper Direct** (✆ *085 316704;* e *newspaperdirect.scg@gmail.com; www. newspaperdirect.com*).

There are two main Montenegrin radio stations (state-run Montenegro Radio and the independent Radio Elmag), two TV stations (Montenegro TV and the independent Montena) and a news agency, Montenafax. Satellite television is available in a growing number of hotels, some of which include English-language programmes; otherwise it can provide a useful opportunity to brush up your Italian.

TELEPHONE Prior to the separation of Montenegro and Serbia, the two countries shared the same international dialling code. Now Montenegro is +382, while Serbia has retained the old prefix of +381.

International dialling codes To get an overseas number, dial 00 (not 99) before the country code, eg:

UK ✆00 44	**Australia** ✆00 61
USA ✆00 1	**Canada** ✆00 1

Local dialling codes In 2009, all area codes were changed (and telephone numbers gained an extra digit).

Podgorica, Kolašin, Danilovgrad ✆020	**Nikšić, Plužine, Šavnik** ✆040
Bar, Ulcinj ✆030	**Cetinje** ✆041
Herceg Novi ✆031	**Bijelo Polje, Mojkovac** ✆050
Tivat, Kotor ✆032	**Berane, Rožaje, Plav, Andrijevica** ✆051
Budva ✆033	**Pljevlja, Žabljak** ✆052

MonteCards, for use in telephone booths, can be bought in post offices and newspaper kiosks and can make life much simpler as well as cheaper.

Mobile phones The three mobile companies – Telenor (*www.telenor.me*), T-Mobile (*www.t-mobile.me*) and M:tel (*www.mtel-cg.com*) – also sell vouchers for their charges. These too are available in kiosks as well as the appropriate telephone shops.

If you expect to use your own mobile much it's worth investing in a Montenegrin SIM card, costing from €5, preferably for use in a spare handset; an existing telephone can be unlocked, but generally takes at least half a day. Otherwise remember that text messages to a country like Montenegro (non-EU and a long way from many other places) are considerably cheaper than even brief telephone calls. Incoming calls, even if you do not answer and they go straight to your voicemail, cost about €1.80, so tell frequent callers that you will be away. If you have a smartphone, turn off data roaming before you get on the plane and use only a free Wi-Fi hotspot, otherwise at around €1.20 per MB you can spend several hundred per month. If you have to use your usual number for overseas calls, see whether your network operator has a discounted bundle, ie: a bulk rate for the country.

Useful telephone numbers
Emergency numbers These numbers can be used throughout Montenegro and **the** operator will connect you to the nearest appropriate facility:

Ambulance ✆124	**Fire** ✆123
Police ✆122	**Roadside assistance** ✆19807

Other useful numbers

Information (local) ✆1181	**Speaking clock** ✆125
Information (international) ✆1202	**Tourist information (English)** ✆1300
International calls ✆00	**Weather** ✆1325

INTERNET Internet facilities are fast growing in Montenegro. Most hotels have a Wi-Fi facility in the lobby if not in the bedrooms. Cyber-cafés can generally be found in the larger towns and resorts. The cafés open and close with regularity, however, so it is best to enquire about them locally. For example, in Budva during the summer there are temporary internet facilities on Slovenska Plaža. You can expect to pay more in hotels, although costs are generally moderate.

BUYING PROPERTY

Property prices have risen substantially as western Europeans notice Croatia's cheaper neighbour, but they are still ludicrously cheap by British standards and there are no legal restrictions on purchases by foreigners. But buyer beware, especially near the coast. Land titles are not well documented and are often unclear. The ownership of properties has often become fragmented and there has been steady emigration for enough generations to make the situation extremely uncertain in many cases. The market remains largely unregulated and somewhat speculative.

If you are interested in buying a house, a good way of finding out what might be on the market is to ask the locals. But at an early stage, consult a good lawyer. And before you sign anything, make very sure that you are covered against the possibility of a gentleman turning up in a year or two and demanding to know what you are doing in his house. At the end of the day the best source of advice on potential pitfalls is going to be another foreign national who has already been through the process.

There are now a number of estate agents in Montenegro who cater for foreign buyers. There are also an increasing number of foreign buyers, not least Russian and British, eager for a bargain and in some areas local resentment is understandably building up at the loss of their heritage.

CULTURAL ETIQUETTE

Traditionally, it was unwise to twitch a Montenegrin moustache; punishment could be as swift as it might be severe; today with facial hair generally in the decline, this seems a less likely temptation.

Montenegrins warm to efforts by visitors to master at least one or two words of the Montenegrin language. You will discover they quite frequently know more English than they admit to, especially the younger generation. In the south many speak a little English, some Italian and maybe some German. In general, though, Montenegrins don't like to say something in another language unless they feel sure they have the pronunciation just right. It is a matter of pride to pronounce foreign words faultlessly. They do not like getting things wrong (this of course ties in with the wish to create a good impression and the importance of appearance). A great deal of English is picked up from movies and television and since the breakdown of communism it has become the second language taught in schools.

Smoking, particularly among males, is widespread. There has been much talk about anti-smoking laws, but little action. Smoking remains popular, including among restaurant customers. Smaller cafés can get a real fug, but in season there is generally a terrace.

Montenegrins are hospitable by nature. If you visit their house, you will almost certainly be offered a glass of *rakija*. It is not essential to accept it, but they will be pleased if you do; and when they propose the inevitable toast, maintain eye contact with the toaster.

When driving past, wave to children only, or possibly policemen as well. Adults find it demeaning and the author was requested to desist.

Everyone in Montenegro will want to discuss politics and it is fine to do so. But remember that Tito is still widely held in high regard and communism, especially for the middle aged, is not a dirty word. Montenegrins sensibly dislike both losing an argument and interlocutors who bang relentlessly on.

You should not photograph military or police establishments, personnel or vehicles unless you want to see the inside of a police station. Otherwise you can photograph whatever you like and indeed many Montenegrins will be quite flattered that you want to take their picture home, but it is obviously polite to ask permission if you single individuals out. If you have an instant camera, presenting someone's photograph to them will generally be appreciated.

For information on tipping etiquette, see page 56.

- Try to accept with enthusiasm everything on offer. Within reason, of course!
- Montenegrins love a party or a celebration. A century ago when no-one was properly dressed unless he bore arms, the ebullience would traditionally be accentuated with volleys of gunfire directed skywards, the reciting of triumphant ballads and strumming of the *gusle*. Nowadays fireworks have to suffice, accompanied more often than not by Croatian or Serbian pop tunes. Serbia was victorious in the 2007 Eurovision Song Contest.
- Montenegrins are very physical and will grab your hand, arm, knee or whatever is nearest – but merely to make a point, not to expand a relationship. In this they are similar to Italians. A few years back, a stranger in an isolated region would be welcomed with a bear hug. Nowadays, a new reticence is detectable and a pat on the shoulder seems to suffice. Montenegrins frequently and spontaneously embrace, whether man to woman, man to man or woman to woman.
- Beware of national criticism: no-one wants to hear what the country lacks.
- When visiting homes it is customary to take a gift, however tiny. Imported things are especially welcome. Women love to receive hand cream, perfume or anything from your own country, but not chocolate or sweets.
- It is common sense that when visiting monasteries women should be reasonably dressed and men should abstain from beach singlets and shorts.

- When visiting a shrine, such as Sv Vasilij's remains at Ostrog, it is customary to walk out of the chapel backwards. In the Orthodox Church the normal practice is to bend and kiss the venerated relics. While you may well decline to participate, this should nevertheless be done gracefully. A small monetary token left in the box or dish usually provided is a nice gesture.
- Outdoor shoes are always removed in Muslim buildings and often in Christian ones, for practical reasons.
- Topless sunbathing is on the increase but be discreet and follow the locals' lead. Restrict nudism to secluded or designated areas.

TRAVELLING POSITIVELY

REFUGEES Like the British, the Montenegrins are proud, so anything offered should be done with discretion.

In addition to OSCE, the border town of **Rožaje** has a history of generosity towards refugees and is involved with supporting young people through a dance troupe, cultural work and an annual literary award (see also page 283).

OSCE (Organisation for Security and Co-operation in Europe) (*Bulevar Svetog Petra Cetinjskog 1a, 81000 Podgorica;* \ *020 406401;* e *omim@osce.org; www.osce. org/montenegro*) This inter-governmental agency is doing a magnificent job. It has identified a wide range of projects in all 21 municipalities covering health, industry, education, local government, media freedom, agriculture, culture, tourism, the environment and so forth. Solutions here are more likely to lie with charities or government than with individuals. But for individuals, donations to help with the problems still facing displaced people could well be directed through this organisation.

ENVIRONMENT
Balkans Peace Park Project (*67 Harcourt Rd, Redland, Bristol BS6 7RD;* e *enquiries@balkanspeacepark.org; www.balkanspeacepark.org*) A UK-registered charity endorsed by UNEP, IUCN and the Research Unit in South East European Studies, Peace Studies Dept, University of Bradford, Yorks. See also box page 292.

ARCHAEOLOGY The British professor who is principal archaeologist of the Butrint Foundation in Albania has recommended further international aid for the wealth

STUFF YOUR RUCKSACK – AND MAKE A DIFFERENCE

www.stuffyourrucksack.com is a website set up by TV's Kate Humble which enables travellers to give direct help to small charities, schools or other organisations in the country they are visiting. Maybe a local school needs books, a map or pencils, or an orphanage needs children's clothes or toys – all things that can easily be 'stuffed in a rucksack' before departure. The charities get exactly what they need and travellers have the chance to meet local people and see how and where their gifts will be used.

The website describes organisations that need your help and lists the items they most need. Check what's needed in Montenegro, contact the organisation to say you're coming and bring not only the much-needed goods but an extra dimension to your travels and the knowledge that in a small way you have made a difference.

of Crna Gora sites, marine as well as on land. It has even been suggested that the Montenegrin coast might yet yield the first Illyrian shipwreck (see box, page 139). At the time of writing these projects and their associated museums remain underfunded. Anyone wishing to help with money or muscle could choose from:

🏺 **Pljevlja** Director in Chief, Regional Museum, Radoman-Risto Manojlović, Tpr 13 Jyna bb, 84210 Pljevlja; 📞052 222002

🏺 **Stari Bar** Contact resident archaeologist, Mladen Zagarčanin; 📞030 315355 (museum)

Part Two

THE GUIDE

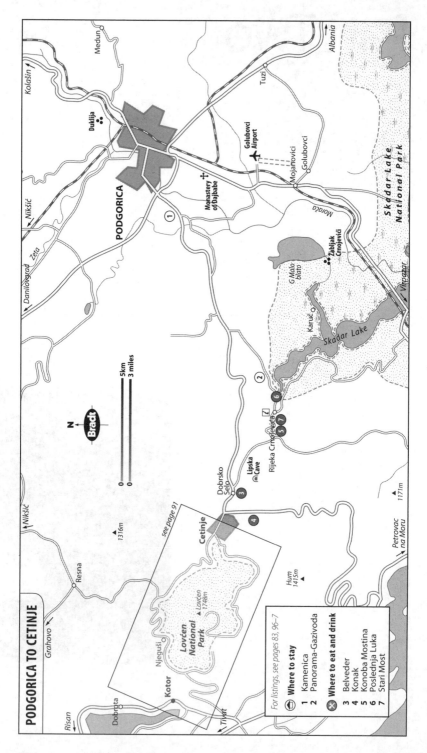

PODGORICA TO CETINJE

For listings, see pages 83, 96–7

Where to stay
1 Kamenica
2 Panorama-Gazivoda

Where to eat and drink
3 Belveder
4 Konak
5 Konoba Mostina
6 Poslednja Luka
7 Stari Most

Bradt

N

0 5km
0 3 miles

3

A Tale of Two Cities

CETINJE

Set deep in the Zetan Plain, Podgorica is certainly today's administrative capital but speak to any Montenegrin and you will quickly discover a visceral attachment to the mountain fastness of Cetinje that for 500 stormy years held that position. From the coast and from the plain, two roads climb dizzily to converge then briefly drop into the lap of mighty Lovćen, the black mountain whose summit bears the mausoleum of the *vladika* – Prince-Bishop Petar II Petrović Njegoš, the greatest Montenegrin of them all.

The climate in Cetinje is moderate – continental with cool dry summers and considerable winter snowfall. The city sits 670m above sea level.

HISTORY 'The storm-proof roof of Europe' was how Scottish traveller Mrs Will Gordon (*A Woman In The Balkans*) described her first sight of Cetinje only a few months after a certain Austrian Archduke, Franz Ferdinand, had his aspirations shot to pieces and all Europe was catapulted into war:

> as far as the eye can reach rise, tier upon tier, these mighty monsters of grey stone; as
> if a typhoon in the midst of its wild frenzy and at the climax of its fury had suddenly
> been frozen into these waves and peaks of stony grandeur.

She was not exaggerating. Beneath this thunderous panorama a doll's house city has with courage and ferocity dispatched all aggressors over the centuries; to say the Crnagorski (Montenegrins) are warriors is an understatement. Yet Cetinje was much more than a fortress; three times the Ottomans tried to invade but they never succeeded in conquering the town. The first time was in 1692, when the original monastery built by Ivan Crnojević was destroyed by the Montenegrins themselves who, as the Turks broke down the door, rather than capitulate, ignited a cache of gunpowder and blew up the building, the Turks and themselves. The second time, in 1714, the enemy succeeded in burning down the entire town before being forced into retreat by resistant Montenegrin tribes. Again they tried in 1785 and again they failed to overpower the indomitable Montenegrins.

The ethos of this, the very heart of Crna Gora, is infectious. A Croatian now living here points at an illustration of the new-old Montenegrin flag: 'See,' she exclaims, 'the wings of the Montenegrin eagle are raised – in acclamation that "we" never capitulated to the Turk, whereas the Serbian eagle's wings point downward.'

Now, in a city whose population is well below 20,000, there is a will to relocate some element of the national administration back here, including one or two government ministries, to restore something of the city's gallant political past.

The heir to the ruling house of Montenegro, Prince Nikola Petrović Njegoš, works as an architect in Paris but he regularly visits Cetinje where his base is in part of **Prince Danilo's Blue Palace**. Built during the 1890s this mansion served as a model for other royal palaces around the country, for example **Topolina** at Bar on the coast. Though it is clear Nikola Petrović feels a great allegiance to the country of his forefathers, he chooses to maintain a low profile and to use his particular skills supportively. One initiative, a **cultural biennial** with a theme based on optimism and reconstruction, ran from 1995 to 2004, but has since been stalled. However, since the country's declaration of independence in 2006, there has been suggestion of a greater role for the prince as 'its representative in dealings with other royal [families] and international organisations'. It has been made clear such a move would in no way affect Montenegro's status as a republic.

GETTING THERE Aside from hiring a car or taking on a tough bike ride, the only means of access to Cetinje is by bus, most easily from Podgorica, Budva, Tivat, Kotor or Herceg Novi. The **bus station** is at the northeastern extremity of town and a short walk from the marketplace, on ul Ivana Crnojevića. There are several buses a day to and from these towns, in theory every 10–25 minutes between 06.00 and 20.00, but there is no information desk or timetable. A ticket from Podgorica costs around €3, from Tivat €3.50 and from Kotor €4. Minibuses supplement these services but their timings are subject to variation. **Note:** at the time of writing there is no public transport from Kotor via the Ladder of Cattaro and Njeguši.

GETTING AROUND The linden-shaded boulevards are best explored **on foot**: everything is close to hand. There's a **car park** (*€2 per day*) at the tourist information office. For taxis try:

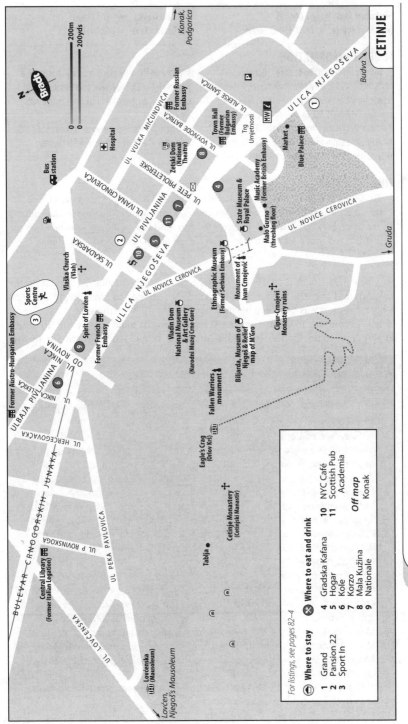

CETINJE

Konak, Podgorica

200m
200yds

N

Budva

ULICA NJEGOŠEVA

Former Russian Embassy

UL ALEKSE ŠANTIĆA

UL VULKA MIĆUNOVICA

Hospital

Bus station

Town Hall (Former Bulgarian Embassy)

Trg Umjetnosti

MW **i**

P

Zetski Dom (National Theatre)

UL VOJVODE BATRIĆA

UL PETE PROLETERSKE

8

Market

Blue Palace

4

State Museum & Royal Palace

Music Academy (Former British Embassy)

Malo Guvno (threshing floor)

UL NOVICE CEROVIĆA

Gruda

7

11

2

UL PIVLJANINA

5

UL SKADARSKA

10

Vlaška Church (Vlah)

ULICA NJEGOŠEVA

UL NOVICE CEROVICA

Ethnographic Museum (Former Serbian Embassy)

Monument of Ivan Crnojević

Cipur Crnojevi Monastery ruins

Sports Centre

3

Spirit of Lovćen

Former French Embassy

9

OD ROVINA

UL NIKCA

Former Austro-Hungarian Embassy

ULBAJA PIVLJANINA

UL NIKCA PIVLJENKA

6

UL HERCEGOVAČKA

Vladin Dom National Museum & Art Gallery (Narodni Muzej Crne Gore)

Biljarda, Museum of Njegoš & Relief map of M'Gro

Fallen Warriors monument

Eagle's Crag (Orlov Krš)

BULEVAR CRNOGORSKIH JUNAKA

UL P ROVINSKOGA

Central Library (former Italian Legation)

UL PEKA PAVLOVIĆA

Tablja

Cetinje Monastery (Cetinjski Manastir)

UL LOVĆENSKA

Lovćen, Njegoš's Mausoleum

Lovćenska Mausoleum

For listings, see pages 82–4

⊙ Where to stay
1 Grand
2 Pansion 22
3 Sport In

⊗ Where to eat and drink
4 Gradska Kafana
5 Hogar
6 Kole
7 Korzo
8 Mala Kužina
9 Nationale
10 NYC Café
11 Scottish Pub
    Academia

Off map
    Konak

81

🚕 **Robur Taxi** m 067 664455
🚕 **Taxi-Cetinje** m 068 045045/505050

🚕 **Taxi Desko** m 067 517400
🚕 **Terrae Taxi** m 068 045045

TOURIST INFORMATION

🗎 **Tourist information centre** Njegoševa 39; 📞041 230250; e info@cetinje.travel; www. cetinje.travel; ⏲ winter: 09.00–14.00 Mon–Fri; summer: 08.00–19.00. In the big car park below the monastery, near the Grand Hotel. They speak good Russian but minimal English, have limited information even on the town museums, & are situated on the only place in Cetinje to charge a parking fee (€2). They have a small selection of gifts, maps, postcards & illustrated local books for sale.

There are well-maintained, locked public toilets alongside the tourist office; ask for the key.

🏠 WHERE TO STAY   *Map, page 81.*

> The Grand is the only hotel in Yugoslavia … in which I have found hot water in both taps. It is the only hotel anywhere in which I have met a waiter who was familiar with *The Canterbury Tales*. And it is probably the only hotel in a capital city anywhere in which you would see a man draw a gun and shoot a mad dog dead in the dining room.

So wrote J A Cuddon in 1968. This legendary hotel, previously known as the Lokanda and once the residency of the American Mission to Montenegro, sadly no longer stands. It was damaged beyond repair in the 1979 earthquake.

Few people stay in Cetinje and most tend to visit as a day trip. If you do decide to stay, you could try the establishments listed below. An alternative is to find

---

NERO WOLFE

Rex Stout (1886–1975) was one of the most successful American crime writers in the 1930s–60s. He wrote over 40 novels, many of them filmed, featuring his Montenegrin detective Nero Wolfe.

In earlier editions I wrote that as Stout was born in Indiana and never visited Montenegro, it seemed puzzling that he invented a Montenegrin detective who reminisced about being taught maths by a teacher with a 30cm moustache and only ate out in a restaurant that served Balkan sausages. I suggested that it might just be that Montenegro has always seemed exotic, but perhaps the clue lies in Stout's two years in Paris after World War I, when it was home to many Montenegrin exiles, including the highly visible princes Petrović, sons of the exiled King Nikola. F Scott Fitzgerald mixed in the same Parisian circles as Stout and he too introduced Montenegro into his writing (see box, page 84).

The mystery, however, has now been solved by Mr Branko Terzić, Privy Councillor of HRH Crown Prince Alexander of Serbia. Mr Terzić was kind enough to send me an extract from John McAleer's *Rex Stout, a Biography* (Little, Brown, Boston, 1977), in which Stout is quoted as saying 'I got the idea of making Wolfe a Montenegrin from Louis Adamic. Louis told me that Montenegrin men are famous for being lazy.' He adds that everything he knew about Montenegro he got from his friend Adamic in person or from the latter's book, *The Native's Return*.

Indebted as I am to Mr Terzić, I can't help feeling Mr Stout would have preferred the Petrović version.

accommodation in a private house through the tourist information centre (opposite); some are listed on their website (*www.cetinje.travel*). A reader has recommended a room in a private house (*Nevenka Dankovic, Donji Kraj 34*; m *068 050018*), which they say is very reasonably priced, clean but 'very basic'. Another option would be to stay at Ivanova Korita in Lovćen National Park (page 93), 14km from Cetinje.

🏠 **Grand Hotel** (202 rooms, 8 apts) ul Njegoševa 1; ✆041 231651; m 067 312295; e office@hotelgrand.me; www.hotelgrand.me. A few totalitarian pretensions remain, like the name, but this old lady badly needs some botox. Tennis court, billiards, bowling alley, restaurant, snack bar & large terrace, & a conference hall with 420 seats. Room price inc quite a good bacon & egg approximation of an English b/fast. Visa & MasterCard accepted. €€€€

✳ 🏠 **Pansion 22** (8 rooms) Ivana Crnojevića 22; m 069 055473; e pansion22@t-com.me; www.pansion22.com. Comfortable, centrally

located small hotel in renovated townhouse, 200m from monastery; 5min walk to bus station. Recommended top-floor room with balcony & mountain view. Open all year. €€€

🏠 **Sport In** (10 rooms) Sportski Centar; ✆041 231177; e sportinct@t-com.me; www.hotel-sportin-cetinje.host22.com. Located in the Sportski Centar, beside the soccer stadium & basketball court, a few mins' walk from the centre of town & bus station. TV, minibar, Wi-Fi, use of internet at reception, free parking. Daytime staff speak English. Restaurant ⏰ 07.00–20.00; b/fast buffet. €€

✗ WHERE TO EAT AND DRINK

In addition to the places listed below, there is a selection of coffee shops and bars in the centre of town, near the palace. They mostly have big terraces and are pleasant in good weather but a bit gloomy in the rain.

In town
Map, page 81.

✗ **Gradska Kafana** ul Njegoševa bb; ⏰ 07.00–23.00. In the old Bulgarian Embassy, adjacent to the Royal Palace. Slightly run-down inside, but a big terrace. Local dishes inc *popeci* (veal stuffed with ham & cheese), smoked carp, trout & gilthead bream. €€€

✗ **Nationale** Nikac od Rovina bb; ✆041 234851; e information@callcentar.me; ⏰ 09.00–23.00. Opposite the president's residence. Many say this is the best restaurant in town. Fish specialities but great meat dishes too, & fair prices. Visa & MasterCard. €€€

✗ **Hogar** ul Njegoševa bb; ⏰ 10.00–24.00. Simple pizzas, pastas & a few grills; clean, staid & moderately priced. €€

✗ **Kole** ul Crnogorskih Junaka 12; m 069 035716; www.restaurantkole.me; ⏰ 07.00–24.00. Meat, grills, ham & other local specialities, plus homemade bread & a decent range of Montenegrin wines. Popular with locals. €€

✗ **Korzo** ul Njogoševa 24; ⏰ 07.00–23.00. A limited menu featuring good traditional local dishes & pizzas at reasonable prices, plus a friendly welcome. €€

✗ **Mala Kužina** ul Baja Pivljanina; ⏰ 09.00–23.00. Simple, good-value salads, steaks, sausages & hamburgers. €€

🍽 **NYC Café** Balčića pazar bb; www.caffenyc.me; ⏰ 08.00–24.00. Drinks, coffee, food inc b/fast, salads, pizzas, risotto, sandwiches & other snacks, amid unexpected New York & cowhide-themed décor. €€

🍷 **Scottish Pub Academia** ul Njogoševa bb. It has 3 apparent connections with Scotland; the non-English speaking staff wear saltires on their chests, there are pictures of lochs & glens on the walls, & the absentee Montenegrin owner is said to love the Highlands. He also serves Glenlivet. No food, no CCs, but a large & cheerful terrace on the main street, & free Wi-Fi. Very popular with the locals. Worth a visit.

Outside Cetinje
Maps, pages 78, 81.

✳ ✗ **Belveder** m 069 708866; e belveder@gmail.com; http://belveder.me; ⏰ 09.00–24.00. 2km on the road to Podgorica at Kruševo Ždrijelo, just off to the right & clearly signed, this nicely appointed restaurant has spectacular views from the big terrace high over Skadar Lake. Efficient service & decent food; atmospheric in the evening;

'those lights way out there are Albania', owner's son assures. Menu in English. €€€€

✱ ✖ Konak ◊041 241241; m 067 398000; e restorankonak@t-com.me; www.konak.me; ◷ 07.00–23.00. 4km outside town on the road to Budva. Popular & spotlessly clean with a big country-style terrace set back from the road. Good spoken English & a wide choice of food inc steak tartare & veal escalope. Try the mixed plate – fresh & matured local Njeguši cheese with carp, smoked *pršut* (local ham). Start – or end – with lovely *pranice* (tiny doughnuts) & honey from blackberry pollen. Immaculate lavatories. Diners Club & MasterCard accepted. €€€

OTHER PRACTICALITIES
Banks
$ **CKB** ul V Proleterske bb
$ **Hipotekarna Banka** Bajova 74
$ **Montenegrobanka** ul Njegoševa bb
$ **Podgorička Banka** ul Njegoševa br 138

Medical facilities
✚ **Cetinje Hospital** ◊041 231369

Pharmacies
✚ **Galateja** ul Njegoševa br 43; ◊041 234400
✚ **Montefarm** ul Njegoševa br 45; ◊041 231159

Other
▣ **Internet café** Gradjanska Kuca, Njegoševa 52; m 067 820087; e nikola_acm@hotmail.com
✉ **Post office** Titov trg, diagonally opposite the State Museum; ◊041 231026; ◷ 07.00–20.00, Mon–Sat
Public toilets At **tourist information** office (page 82); ◷ same hours

WHAT TO SEE

> Stern old King of the stark, black hills,
> Where the lean, fierce eagles breed,
> Your speech sings true as your good sword rings –
> And you are a king indeed!

Don Marquis, Nicholas of Montenegro, *1912*

The dusty paths, scumbled mansions and forgotten gardens are filled with ghosts. In Cetinje's *belle époque* a prince became a king, with a quiver-full of daughters attracting suitors from the grandest courts in Europe. Here people danced and spun their webs.

A useful aid to sightseeing in Cetinje has recently been installed by a mobile telephone company: **T-Mobile Tourist Guide** covers most significant landmarks. Look for a sign in front of each monument, museum or former embassy, then

---

MAJOR JAY GATSBY

In F Scott Fitzgerald's *The Great Gatsby*, the eponymous Major Gatsby boasts of his Danilo's Cross – named after an ancestor of Petar II Petrović Njegoš – while pursuing the delectable Daisy Buchanan around Long Island.

A surviving letter from Fitzgerald to his literary agent in New York in 1924 seeks assurances as to the appearance of the 'Danilo's Medal' and the possibility of its being awarded to a non-Montenegrin. Fitzgerald and Zelda were in the habit of visiting both Paris and Antibes, where the exiled Montenegrin royal family were then living. He was also friendly with the English author Joyce Cary, who himself visited Montenegro in 1913 at the time of the Second Balkan War and won a Danilo's Cross in the fighting around Skadar Lake.

simply dial 1555 on your phone and enter the number shown on the appropriate sign to find out about that location. The price of service for (Montenegrin) T-Mobile subscribers is €0.40 per call regardless of duration. Foreign users should check prices with their operators. Obtaining a local SIM card is straightforward and will obviously save you money (see pages 72–3).

Old diplomatic quarter In 1912, 11 foreign diplomatic missions had been accredited, half of them with purpose-built residences. All of these buildings but one (the US premises were lost in the earthquake of 1979) can be seen today. And in their individual detail each is still curiously identifiable.

In pole position across from the Royal Palace (home to the State Museum), what was once the **British Embassy** is now a music academy. It would not look out of place in Guildford, and sadly it served its diplomatic purpose for only four years. The building was designed by an English architect called Harty and completed in 1912, replacing temporary accommodation leased from the Germans. In 1916 the ambassador and his staff beat a fairly hasty retreat, shortly before the capitulation of Montenegro and its occupation by Austro-Hungary. After the Serbian annexation of Montenegro in 1918, the old embassy became first the governor's mansion, then the residence of the prime minister. Later it was a club for cultural workers, then the town library; now it is the Academy of Music.

Nearby, on Voyjvode Batrića, is the former **Russian Embassy.** Although architecturally reminiscent of St Petersburg, its late Baroque styling was in fact the work of Italian architect Corradini and it was built in 1903; while the **Italian Legation** itself, unmistakably Adriatic with its classical delineation, now contains the Central Library (Djuradj Crnojević). It is fun to pick them out. The Russian Embassy today serves as Montenegro University's Faculty of Fine Arts and the **Turkish** is the state school of drama. In the square of the Royal Palace, the **Bulgarian** has become a restaurant. For some years leading up to 1949, the **French**, a particularly fine building verging on the grandiose, housed the headquarters of the UDB, the State Security Service. The former British, French, Turkish and Austro-Hungarian embassies are all protected as historical landmarks.

Cetinje Monastery and around At the western end of town, sheltering beneath the rock, is **Cetinje Monastery (Cetinjski Manastir)** (⌚ 08.00–18.00). It dates from the 15th-century foundation of the city by Ivan Crnojević, the ruler of Zeta who moved to this high plateau with his followers in retreat from Ottoman invaders. The Turks pursued and three times the sombre stone edifice was destroyed and again rebuilt. In March, the low meadow before the monastery is a carpet of crocuses, purple for humility: nature's choice belies the riches that lie locked in its tiny chapel, including the alleged right hand of St John the Baptist and a shard from the crucifixion cross. And in the **Treasury Museum (Riznica Cetinjskog Manastira)** (⌚ 08.00–18.00; €2), as is customary in the Eastern Orthodox Church, the monastery holds a valuable historical record in the form of artefacts and literature that, in spite of its turbulent history, have somehow been preserved from the earliest days. Here, for example, you will find the staff and seal of Ivan Crnojević, metropolitan crowns and mitres bright with jewels and a remarkable collection of illuminated manuscripts (some even carried in the exodus from the churches of the old Zetan state on the plain below). Also to be found are printed books from the first Slavic printing house established at Obud, beside Rijeka Crnojevića (pages 96–7) in 1494, including the first south Slav Cyrillic *incunabula*, the *Oktoih of the First Voice*; an intricate ornamental cloth embroidered by Catherine the Great; and many icons, including one in particular, the

Montenegrin theocratic doctrine stated that, for a monk:

> the monastery is the centre of the universe. It is the manger wherein he is born, the shady tree under which he sits and from where the apple falls in his lap. From this tree he makes the cross on which he is crucified.

Under the *vladikas* – the prince-bishops – the bishop's role was extended to

> the riding of horses and leading the army. If it was necessary to cut off a head, then one must remember in so-doing to pray for the victim's salvation.

The philosophy is that while killing might be unavoidable, unforgiving hatred is unacceptable.

work of an unnamed master, depicting the Madonna and child gazing on each other with an expression of *umiljavanje* – literally, explains the monk, 'such sweetness' – but he adds that there is really no English equivalent for the expression, which he interprets as 'tears of joy'. Modest dress is expected.

Most monasteries produce their own *rakija* – fruit brandy – and this one is no exception. There are beehives too, which here interestingly yield honey from the flower of *pelen* – wormwood, as in absinthe.

On a small rise above the monastery is the site of the *tablja*, the tower on which the Turkish heads – trophies of battle – were once displayed. There are a number of caves in the karst cliffs to the north of the church.

Next door to the monastery, and now housing the Museum of Njegoš (page 89), stands the fortified residence built in 1838 for Petar II Petrović Njegoš. It is now known simply and quirkily as **Biljarda** [map, page 81] on account of its billiard table, a souvenir that the prince brought back from his travels in Italy. It can have been no mean feat hauling it from Kotor, far below, up the precipitous mule track that at that time was the only route into the capital from the coast.

Connected to Biljarda and housed in a glass pavilion is another curiosity, a **relief map** of Montenegro said to be comprehensive in its detail of the entire country: a veritable minigolf course created by the Austrian occupiers for strategic use during World War I.

Originally Biljarda had a strong lead roof but 20 years on, when Cetinje came under attack from Omar Pasha and his Ottoman forces, it was removed and melted down for bullets, along with the type from the recently installed printing press.

Between the monastery, Biljarda and the Royal Palace is **Malo Guvno** – the threshing floor. For mountain people the grain meant survival, therefore such a place was of great significance. Traditionally it filled many other purposes too. It was a general gathering ground where important assemblies were held, blood feuds settled, culprits punished, hostages exchanged and inter-tribal conflicts over cattle pastures resolved. In effect it was where the parliament had its origins. But it was also a stage for festivals, singing and the traditional circular dance, the *kolo*. Njegoš's greatest verse epic, *The Mountain Wreath*, was set in this place.

Between Biljarda and the Ecclesiastical Court is a monument designed by Vanja Radaus in memory of the patriots of Cetinje executed by firing squads in World War II.

Eagle's Crag (Orlov Krš) To the west of Malo Guvno, beyond the crocus meadow and the place known as *cipur* (vegetable garden), it is a short climb to **Orlov Krš** – Eagle's Crag – the outcrop surmounted by a monument to Bishop Danilo, the first of the Petrović Njegoš dynasty. From this peaceful point you will be able to appreciate the whole picture: the little town in its rocky nest. When the moon is high it is a magical sight; these times are described by the inhabitants of Cetinje as silver nights. Looking east, the baroque shape of the old **Government House (Vladin Dom)**, the largest building in Montenegro, is easily picked out. It now houses the **National Historical Museum** and the **Art Gallery of Montenegro** (page 89).

Cetinje centre From Malo Guvno, a very short walk east brings you to the centre of town, which essentially comprises two parallel streets shaded by lime trees adjoining a marketplace. Strolling north on the most easterly of the streets, ul Pivljanina, you will come to the **Vlaška Church,** built in 1450 before Cetinje had been settled. It gets its name from the shepherds who built it and who would bring their flocks to summer pasture here. In front of the church there are two tombstones, one of which, according to legend, marks the resting place of an infamous Montenegrin outlaw who nevertheless died defending Cetinje from the Turks. Facing the church is a proud monument, the **Spirit of Lovćen**, which shows a female figure holding in her right hand a sword raised skyward, and in her left a laurel wreath. It commemorates the Montenegrin emigrés who volunteered to return from the United States of America to help defend their homeland at the beginning of World War I. Sadly, their ship was sunk outside the northern Albanian port of San Giovanni di Medua, now called Shëngjin, and they were drowned. With grim prescience the monument was erected in 1939.

Further south on Baja Pivljanina you'll find the freshly white-painted portico of **Zetski Dom**, home to the National Theatre (\ *041 230525; www.zetskidom.me*). Designed in 1884 by architect Josip Slade (under whose supervision the dramatic road linking Kotor with Krstac pass to Lovćen had recently been constructed), it took a further eight years to complete. However the first show, *The Balkan Empress* – written by Prince Nikola himself – was staged in 1888, long before the building was finished. The state drama school is conveniently located across the street in the old building of the **Embassy of Turkey**, and the theatre provides a showcase for student productions.

Museums (🕐 *09.00–17.00 daily, but see below; combined ticket adult/child aged 7–18 & student €10/5; under 7s free*) These days Cetinje is predominantly a town of museums and students, making for a good mix. Despite official opening times, museums – a number of them painted a distinguishing grey and white – sometimes close early if they have no visitors (check with the tourist office, page 82). A combined ticket for the four museums is available from any of the museum ticket offices. See page 85 for information on the **Treasury Museum (Riznica Cetinjskog Manastira)**.

State Museum (*Royal Palace, trg Kralja Nikole;* \ *041 230555; adult/child €5/2.50*) Located next to the threshing floor, the State Museum is housed in the modest burnt-sienna palace, which was home to the last monarch of Montenegro, King Nikola I. The gilded period of his reign has been beguilingly recreated in salons arranged as they would have been (the original contents having been looted during World War II). In addition there are now romantic displays of arms, sparkling decorations, and banners including a company standard emotively riddled with

THE MALTESE FALCON

Since May 2002, a splendid icon with a fascinating history has been on display in the Blue Chapel of the National Museum of Montenegro at Cetinje (Vladin Dom).

The provenance of this icon is linked with the alleged right hand of St John the Baptist and also with what is claimed to be a fragment of Christ's cross. The latter two can now be found in the small church within Cetinje Monastery.

The painter of the beautiful icon, called the Madonna of Philermos, is unknown but there has been some speculation that it was St Luke the Evangelist. Certainly it appears to have been Hellenic and it was almost certainly acquired by the Order of St John Knights Hospitallers, which was established in Jerusalem by the Crusaders at the beginning of the 12th century. There the order came by a number of Christian relics and in 1187, after the fall of Jerusalem when the knights transferred their headquarters to the island of Rhodes, they carried these treasures with them. After Rhodes was conquered by the Turks in 1522 the Knights moved on via various Mediterranean havens, including Crete and Malta, and subsequently became known as the Knights of Malta. All the while they retained the holy relics. (In common with Montenegro, the tiny island of Malta, also in the sultan's sights and similarly greatly outnumbered, always succeeded in resisting Turkish subjugation.) Until 1798 the Madonna of Philermos was displayed in a specially dedicated chapel in the conventual church of the order; the hand of St John the Baptist was placed in the oratory of the same church. But when in that year Napoleon Bonaparte conquered Malta, the Grand Master of the order, Ferdinand Hampesh, was given permission to carry these relics to Rome where the Knights were to establish a further residence. (All the other valuables were seized by the French and taken away on board the warship *L'Orient* which was subsequently blown up by Nelson's fleet at Aboukir Bay in August that year.)

Shortly afterwards Tsar Pavle I contrived to become the new Grand Master of the knights and Hampesh passed on the relics, which were then placed in a convent at Vorontsov Palace in Russia. Thereafter the synod of the Russian Orthodox Church celebrated the receiving of these sacred objects in St Petersburg every October – surely a measure of their value.

After the 1917 revolution they were taken for protection by the mother of the murdered tsar, who carried them via Crimea, London and Denmark. They were then given to the head of the Russian Orthodox Church in exile who deposited them for safe keeping in the Karađorđević royal chapel in Belgrade. In 1941, after German troops occupied Serbia, they were taken to Ostrog Monastery where King Petar II Karađorđević of Yugoslavia had taken shelter. In 1952 Montenegrin police, searching for the gold that King Petar II was rumoured to have taken to Ostrog, found the relics and passed them to the National Museum at Cetinje (see opposite page). The hand and the particle of the cross were passed on to the monastery but not displayed until 1994, and now at long last the icon of the Madonna of Philermos can once again be viewed, in the National Museum.

Some of the earlier vicissitudes through which these relics travelled are believed to have provided a basis for the film *The Maltese Falcon*.

bullets from the major 19th-century encounter with the Turks at Vučji Do. It is interesting to note that before 1910 the Montenegrins did not have military uniform; they simply went into battle in their national dress. A man's weapons were his proudest possessions. Various intriguing sepia photographs portray the royal family splendidly arrayed and holding their own among such figures as the Russian tsar. The royal daughters married into some of the grandest families in Europe. Proof of the royal marksmanship is displayed in the king's bedchamber, festooned with pelts. He was, it is said, 'a wonderful pistol shot who could remove a cigarette from a man's mouth at twelve paces'.

A noteworthy recent acquisition hangs in the library. Painted in 1908 by Victorian military artist Richard Caton Woodville – who at that time was chiefly employed by *The Illustrated London News* – it shows Prince Nikola, as he then was, seated in judgement under his customary plane tree, surrounded by individuals mostly in Montenegrin dress but a small number in Albanian costume. The painting came into the possession of the museum in 2009 by agreement with its owner, Professor James Pettifer, of St Cross College, Oxford University.

Beside the palace and separated by the crocus meadow from the present-day monastery in 1886, Prince Nikola built a **court chapel** on the foundations of the central church of the original 15th-century Crnojević Monastery. Some remnants of this early monastery are still visible and the place continues to be known quaintly as *cipur* (derived from the Greek word *kipuria* meaning 'vegetable plot'). It was to this chapel that the remains of King Nikola and his Queen Milena were finally returned with great ceremony in 1989. Now it is known as the **Royal Mausoleum** (*adult/child €3/1.50*) and for the people of Montenegro the memory of this relatively recent event symbolises the end of communism.

National Museum and Art Gallery of Montenegro (Narodni muzej Crne Gore)

(*Vladin Dom, Novice Cerovića 7;* \ *041 230310; www.mnmuseum.org; adult/child €3/1.50 for each museum*) Founded in 1989, the National Museum of Montenegro (sometimes called the Historical Museum) and the Art Gallery of Montenegro are situated in the old government house, Vladin Dom, and broadly cover the social, economic, political, military and cultural heritage of Montenegro. The **National Museum** includes a comprehensive display of weaponry, both Montenegrin and trophy, and a section devoted to the country's heroic World War II resistance to fascism. The **Art Gallery** is composed of five collections: the Arts of Yugoslav Nations and Ethnic Groups; the collection of Icons; Montenegrin Fine Art; the Milica Sarić-Vukmanović Memorial Collection – including works by foreign artists such as Renoir, Picasso, Chagal and Salvador Dalí; and a collection of copies of frescoes. This museum is where you will find the Plava Kapela (Blue Chapel), recently designated as a showplace for *Bogorodica Filermosa* (*the Madonna of Philermos*), the enigmatic and much-travelled icon (see box, opposite). More recent is the modern extension dedicated to the late Montenegrin artist, Miodrag Dado Đurić, which showcases contemporary art. There is currently no gift shop.

Museum of Njegoš at Biljarda

(\ *041 230310; adult/child €3/1.50*) This museum contains memorabilia of Petar II Petrović Njegoš, including a small armoury and the original manuscript of *The Mountain Wreath*. There is also an adjacent pavilion displaying a large World War I Austrian relief map of Montenegro. A new lapidarium opened in 2012 in the courtyard, with a number of medieval tombstones (*stećci*).

Ethnographic Museum of Montenegro (*trg Kralja Nikola;* \ *041 230310; adult/child €3/1.50*) The smallest of the museums houses textiles, folk costumes and musical instruments. It is presently located in the building of the former Serbian Embassy (Central Square, diagonally opposite the Palace of King Nikola). Some good gifts and reproduction ornaments are for sale at the entrance.

AROUND CETINJE

From the turn-off to **Dobrsko Selo** (signed to Belveder restaurant), 2km along the road leading from Cetinje to Podgorica and starting directly below the restaurant, a rocky donkey track can be followed on foot down the valley to **Rijeka Crnojevića** (taking approximately four hours one way). Along it are awesome views of Skadar Lake and the mountains beyond. Early spring brings wild crocuses, visible through the still lingering traces of the winter snow, and the breeze carries the scent of smouldering olive wood. A story in these parts tells how a poor housewife, taking pity on a thirsty St Peter, gave him a drink of her preciously preserved blackberry juice, whereupon the saint blessed the blackberries that they might grow through the relentless karst and produce enough fruit and pollen for the bees to make honey.

Several other trails are waymarked, but be warned that distances aren't always accurately quoted. In the village of Dobrsko you will find a small church dedicated to the Dormition of the Virgin. **Dobrska Celija** (m *067 440332*) is an off-shoot of Cetinje Monastery and it is said that it was here that Njegoš founded the first national country school. The building dates from the 15th century and was restored in 1993.

In the same area there is an intriguing and extensive cave system named **Lipska Cave**. The 3,512m so far explored are made up of wide passages leading to vast galleries that feature underground springs and lakes. Reputedly it was an Englishman, as long ago as 1839, who first ventured to any depth in this pot-hole. At the Belveder restaurant (page 83), the owner's son remembers years back visiting the cave with his grandfather. At the time of writing the cave is gated but not locked, but please be warned that entry is entirely at your own risk; it should be attempted only by properly equipped speleologists.

LOVĆEN NATIONAL PARK

No longer black, the mountain is bone-grey,
Limestone, melting in the rain,
Sagging into the face of a skull.

Jeffrey Henning, The Curse of Crna Gora, 1986
Used with the permission of the author

Covering 6,400ha, Lovćen National Park lies to the southwest of Cetinje and is dominated by the twin peaks of Mt Lovćen. The approach road from Cetinje to the tomb forms a 20km series of serpentines, each curve disclosing a yet more sensational view. The landscape is predominantly barren and harsh but there are sparse clusters of pine, hornbeam, birch, beech, juniper, sycamore, even wild rose.

At the summit of Stirnovik, at 1,749m the higher of the two, is a telecommunications facility, and approach to it is prohibited. Jezerski vrh, at 1,657m, is most dramatically surmounted by the **mausoleum of Petar II Petrović Njegoš** (page 92). From the parking area, there's a five-minute walk along a long flight of steps to the mausoleum itself. Montenegrins regard the magnificent summit of Jezerski and its precious resting place as their Mt Olympus: a symbol to Njegoš's people and a message to all comers that the heart of Montenegro is

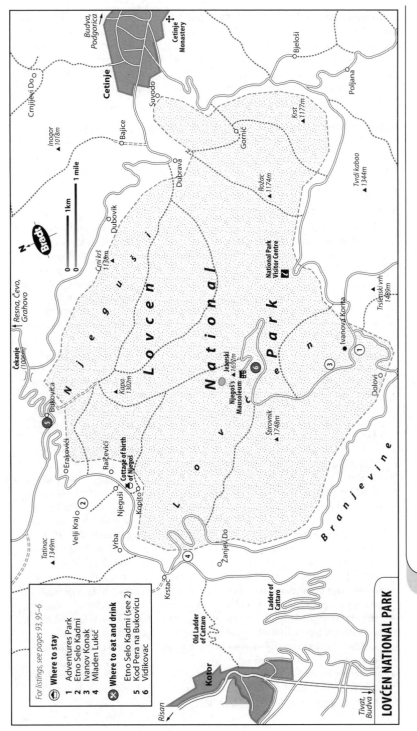

For listings, see pages 93, 95–6

Where to stay

1 Adventures Park
2 Etno Selo Kadmi
3 Ivanov Konak
4 Mladen Lukić

Where to eat and drink

5 Etno Selo Kadmi (see 2)
6 Kod Pera na Bukovicu
   Vidikovac

LOVĆEN NATIONAL PARK

Risan

Tivat,
Budva

Kotor

Old Ladder
of Cattaro

Ladder of
Cattaro

Krstac

Branjevine

Tatinac
▲ *1349m*

Velji Kraj ○ ②

Vrba

Njeguši

Kopito ○

Cottage of birth
of Njegoš

Rajčevići ○

○ Erakovići

Bukovica ⑤

○ Žanjev Do

Dolovi ○

Ivanova Korita ●
                  ①

③

⑥

Štirovnik
▲ *1748m*

Njegoš's
Mausoleum ⛩

Jezerski
▲ *1659m*

Kapa
1302m ▲

Trslenski vrh
▲ *1489m*

National Park
Visitor Centre ℹ

L o v ć e n   N a t i o n a l   P a r k

Crni krš
1138m ▲

N j e g u š i

Inogor
▲ *1018m*

Crnijevi Do ○

Čekanje
(1006m)

Resna, Čevo,
Grahovo

N

Bradt

0   1km
0   1 mile

Bajice ○

Dubrava ○

Dubovik ○

Suvodo ○

Gornič ○

Rožac
▲ *1174m*

Tvrdi kabao
▲ *1344m*

Krst
▲ *1177m*

Poljana ○

Bjeloši ○

Cetinje
Monastery ✝

Cetinje

Budva,
Podgorica

ever unassailable. In World War II the Italian army tried to destroy it with artillery but in time-honoured tradition Mt Lovćen and Njegoš survived unscathed. Each Montenegrin sees in this man a personification of all that he or she holds sacred.

Beyond the mausoleum itself, a short, very slippery (even in dry weather) pathway leads to a rotunda, a symbolic threshing floor with a 360° view. It is claimed that on a very clear day one can make out the Italian coast – but no-one is known to have done so.

Getting there There are no public transport connections within Lovćen National Park. The nearest bus station is Cetinje, so if you don't plan to visit either the mausoleum or the Adventure Park at Ivanova Korita as part of a tour group (or to travel by car or by bike), the alternative will have to be either taxi or on foot.

PETAR II PETROVIĆ NJEGOŠ

Little Montenegro paradoxically breeds the giants of Europe, and it is no surprise that basketball is a national sport. It seems entirely appropriate, too, that the spirit of the republic's most revered titan, Petar II Petrović Njegoš (1813–51), should be set high upon their own Olympus. In 1969 when a young Prince Nikola Petrović, Njegoš's descendant, first set foot in Montenegro, he felt himself compelled forthwith to ascend the ancient Lovćen way from the sea to the summit tomb. History has it that when Njegoš was asked how long it takes from Kotor to Cetinje, he replied 'for a friend it takes five hours and for an enemy a lifetime'.

The poet-prince Njegoš was the last of the *vladikas*, the prince-bishops who had ruled since 1696. By all accounts his physical stature (he is said to have stood 6ft 8in/2.03m) was matched by his intellect. Above all, and from the very beginning of his tenure at the tender age of 17, he was to demonstrate a unique insight and understanding of his people and their history, and his particular genius has come to epitomise the aspirations of Montenegro, elevating him in his nation's eyes to divine hero status.

His education began at the monastery of Cetinje, which throughout the Petrović dynasty also served as a school, and continued at Savina on the Gulf of Kotor. But his real mentor was the Serbian poet Simo Milutinović, who fired his enthusiasm for the great European poets, from Horace to Milton. Njegoš himself then went on in his brief life to compose some of the finest poetry in the Serbian language. His most famous verse play, *The Mountain Wreath*, is based on a historically factual and brutal incident: a rationale for the 1702 ultimatum which, on the orders of Danilo – the first *vladika* – was offered to renegade Montenegrins who had remained in the central plain near Žabljak Crnojevići and had out of expediency become Muslims. A choice was given that either they reconvert to Christianity or face death. In the ensuing confrontation, a bloody episode which later became known as the Montenegrin Vespers, many were slaughtered but, Njegoš reasoned, this was the price to pay for defection to the enemy. The point at which the end justifies the means is the essence of his play: 'we are bound each to each by our natural impieties', he wrote.

Before he had even reached the age of 40, Njegoš had succumbed to tuberculosis. In spite of the brevity of his rule, he remains today undeniably Montenegro's most illustrious figurehead.

The main road, ul Lovćenska, leading from Cetinje to the national park and on to the summit of Mt Lovćen, is in the northwest of the town. To find it, take the westward road past the old Italian embassy building and follow signposts to Ivanova Korita which, at 1,261m, is 14km from Cetinje. It should be noted that during periods of heavy snow the next 7km of road leading from this small settlement to the mausoleum may become blocked.

A minor, **scenic route** linking Krstac (poised high above Kotor) to Ivanova Korita is frequently impassable with snow cover between November and April, when a 4x4 is essential.

A **taxi from Cetinje to the mausoleum**, with waiting time, will cost upwards of €30. From the car park 461 steps lead to the mausoleum. There is no disabled access and some of the steps are crumbling.

It takes between four and five hours to **walk from Cetinje** to the mausoleum by road, with obvious short cuts a little less. From Bukovica, some 3km southeast of Njeguši (see pages 95–6) there is a posted trail climbing to the summit. It's mostly though forest so not too hot in summer. Allow about three hours to reach the top – and keep an eye out for snakes.

Park information The National Park Visitor Centre (✆ *041 761128;* m *069 328858;* e *jpnpcg@t-com.me; www.nparkovi.me/sajt/np-lovcen; €2;* ⊕ *May–Oct 09.00–17.00*) on the Cetinje–Ivanova Korita road has information and a guide service by arrangement (in groups). It also has hiking maps and some other related material for sale.

A national park **entrance fee** of €2 may be levied at Bjeloši, on the Cetinje–Ivanova Korita road, and another entrance point is planned for visitors coming from Krstac. On certain dates, such as World Environment Day on 5 June, there is no charge.

Where to stay   *Map, page 91.*

Wild camping is not permitted in the park but facilities are in place at the Adventures Park in Ivanova Korita (below).

Like the other national parks, Lovćen will eventually have a dedicated **motorhome park** (*www.nparkovi.me*) offering 30 spaces, each with connections for electricity, fresh water and waste water. Cash will be available from an on-site ATM.

⌂ **Ivanov Konak** (7 rooms) Ivanova Korita; ✆041 233700; e odmaraliste@t-com.me; www. ivanovkonak.com. Built in 2011 in a delightful rural setting in the foothills of the real black mountain, Ivanov Konak has 2 dbl rooms & 5 suites with terraces. Internet, satellite TV, minibar. Elegant restaurant (€€–€€€). Great for hiking: marked trails depart in several directions from near its entrance. **€€€**

⋏ **Adventures Park** Lovćen (5 bungalows, camping) Ivanova Korita; m 069 543156; e info@ avanturistickipark.com; http://avanturistickipark. com. As well as fully equipped **bungalows** (*€40 pp per night, max 4 ppl*) there is a **campsite** (*tents €3–5 per night*).

Where to eat and drink   *Map, page 91.*

There's a restaurant at the Ivanov Konak guesthouse (above).

⋏ **Restoran Vidikovac** ⊕ *08.00–20.00.* Beside the car park at the mausoleum itself, Vidikovac has an outside terrace & a splendid view, serving

drinks & decent light meals. There is quite a good gift shop alongside, with a reasonable selection of postcards. **€€**

The royal prince, later to be King Nikola Petrović (1841–1921), and his wife Milena had three sons and nine daughters. The girls, all well schooled and 'finished' in St Petersburg, had the confidence and the understanding of the nuances of court life to hold their own among the stars of European aristocracy. Of the nine, five married into regal households. In 1883 Zorka, the eldest, married the pretender to the Serbian throne, Petar Karađorđević, to whom Nikola had granted asylum in Cetinje. She bore him five children but died before her husband was installed on the throne in a bloody coup instigated by the sinister intelligence organisation, 'The Black Hand'. In 1889 Milica married Grand Prince Petar Nikolajevich Romanov of Russia and in the same year another Russian Romanov, Duke Dorde Maximilianovich of Leichtenberg, swept away Princess Anastasia (Stane), though that marriage did not last and in 1906 she married for the second time, on this occasion to Grand Prince Nikolaj Nikolajevich. In 1896 Jelena, once the teenage rebel, settled down contentedly with Crown Prince Victor Emmanuel of Italy, while Ana married Franz Joseph von Battenburg, kin of the British Mountbatten family. The latter marriage and that between the heir to the Montenegrin throne, Danilo, and Princess Jutta Mecklenburg-Strelitz contributed to the establishment of diplomatic relations between Cetinje and Berlin. In the sepia family groupings on the royal bedchamber wall in Cetinje it is interesting to identify the players, splendidly decked out; and hardly surprising that Prince Nikola earned the nickname of the father-in-law of Europe.

What to see and do

Mausoleum of Petar II Petrović Njegoš (m *069 050024;* €4; ⊕ *08.00–21.00*). At the entrance to the tomb, opened to the public on 28 July 1974 by Comrade-President Milatović of the Socialist Republic of Montenegro, stand two stylised Montenegrin caryatids in Jablanica marble, each weighing 7.5 tonnes. The mausoleum was dedicated by Duke Danilo in 1855 in a church built by Njegoš himself.

In the forecourt of this complex couples may dress up in very attractive national costume and be photographed for around €5. A similar price will buy you a short guidebook in several languages, hence very few pages in each, which was published in 1985.

Adventures Park Lovćen (m *069 543156;* e *info@avanturistickipark.com; http:// avanturistickipark.com;* ⊕ *Jun–mid-Sep 10.00–18.00 daily; mid-Apr–end May & Sep–late Oct w/ends 12.00–18.00 & w/days on request; from €18 for over 14s; €12 for 8–13s; €8 for under 8s*) A series of aerial walkways, zip-lines, cargo nets and hanging log poles, the adventures park presents different challenges depending on age and fitness. Equipment, including safety helmets, is provided; qualified instructors supervise. You can go paintballing too, and mountain bikes are for rent – there are three main trails, each from two to six hours' riding time. Irresistible.

Hiking Aside from the access trail from Cetinje (see *Getting there*, page 92), marked long-distance trails depart in several directions from Jezerski vrh: north to Njeguši (4hrs); southeast towards Budva (Podmaine Monastery) (4½hrs); and west to Kotor (5½hrs). For details of the routes, get hold of a copy of Rudolf Abraham's *The Mountains of Montenegro* (page 326).

CETINJE TO NJEGUŠI An easy 19km route links Cetinje to Njeguši, the asphalt road twisting through a meagre rocky landscape, dry-stone walls indicating that someone has at least laid claim to parts of it. Ignore a right turn snaking away to Čevo, Trešnejevo and ultimately noble Grahovo (or another day take it to enjoy a singular bike ride).

Some 3km short of Njeguši in the hamlet of **Bukovica** is an unspoilt picture-book inn (see page 96).

Approximately 200m east of the inn a farm track leads to a marked trail which climbs southwards to the summit of Jezerski and the mausoleum (see opposite).

Beyond Bukovica, the road southwest continues, encircling Mt Lovćen in the direction of Kotor, through a wild highland of karst, granite and scrub; punctuated here and there by the distinctive pale blue of iris, a determined plant that appears to flourish even in the most barren soil. Now it isn't far to the old Austrian frontier and the dizzying escarpment that descends dramatically to the sea below.

NJEGUŠI The village that gave birth to the Petrović dynasty is little more than a cluster of stone cottages bordering the byway. In one of these, a simple barn-like building, Njegoš was born (*entry adult/child €2/1*). Njeguši is noted for its air-dried ham, versions of which can be found all over Montenegro, though here, where the Mediterranean breezes ruffle the cool of the high plateau, they do it best. Many houses are in the business; ask to see the hams suspended from the rafters where they are left for a minimum of 12 months. To buy a whole one will cost (tourist price) say €35, but there are two or three rustic restaurants where you can indulge inexpensively in a platter of the product, sliced prosciutto style (there's also a smoked mutton alternative to the ham – an acquired taste; see page 55) and accompanied by some chunks of local cheese, a Balkan version of the Italian *caciocavello* and also a village speciality. Washed down with a bottle or two of Vranac (the ubiquitous red wine that embodies Montenegro; see page 55) and the purest of ice-cold mountain water, this should make you most content and prepared for a stunning view of the Boka Kotorska – Gulf of Kotor – from **Krstac**, 2km further on. At 960m, Krstac is midway between Kotor and Cetinje, about 22km from each. A short stroll through the adjacent pine forest leads to a splendid panorama of the Boka Kotorska and Mt Orjen.

Getting there There is no public transport but the village is a regular tour stop in high season. A **taxi** from Cetinje will cost approximately €15.

Where to stay *Map, page 91.*

Etno Selo Kadmi (10 cabins) m 067 486733, 067 665471; e mladenadija@live.com; http://mojposlovniadresar.com/reklame_cetinje/ etno_kadmi/kadmi.html. A slightly quirky place but with a warm welcome, easily visible from the road through the town centre. You'll spot the well-spaced cabins from afar & be greeted by a collection of garden gnomes, but the remainder of the property is pleasingly bucolic. Milo the chef & his family make horticulture a feature & each unit has its own little garden. Price inc an excellent big b/fast with cheese, ham, bacon & eggs. The restaurant (🕐 *24hrs;* €€) offers generous portions of regional dishes. Horseriding, archery, bike rental, guided tours from €30 pp negotiable. Good for families; popular with touring cyclists. €

Near Krstac

Mladen Lukić (7 rooms) Krstac; m 069 050814. This friendly family live part of the time in Kotor (Dobrota 14, Kotor) & have a country chalet near the top of the Ladder of Cattaro. They will sometimes let bedrooms or even the entire property (6 dbl & 1 sgl, 2 bathrooms). There are good views from the terrace, with fresh air & silence, but in summer be prepared for some interruptions to the water supply. €

�҂ Where to eat and drink *Map, page 91.*

As well as Etno Selo Kadmi (page 95), there are a few restaurants along the main road near Njeguši, serving mostly ham and cheese.

✗ **Restoran Ivmi** ✆041 239801. Snacks & drinks. They speak some English. €€
✗ **Restoran Sveta Planina** ✆041 239715. Nice vine-covered terrace, slightly more ambitious menu, reasonable English. Also has 1 room with bath to let, inc b/fast. €€
✗ **Restoran Zora** ✆041 239702; m 069 515038; ⊕ 07.00–23.00. Friendly & cheerful atmosphere, a bit of English, snacks & drinks. Share a table with the villagers. Rooms offered. €€

In Bukovica
✗ **Kod Pera na Bukovicu** Bukovica ✆041 760055; http://kodpera.com; ⊕ 07.00–22.00. Until a few years ago, 2 grumpy Dalmatians stood guard, fortunately chained to their kennels. Now their son has taken on the responsibility. The same family has been serving local food & drink in this establishment for 130 years; choose between a traditional public bar inside or a terrace just across the road & overlooking a green valley. There's no accommodation available at the moment, but they have ambitions to open eco-chalets. No CCs. €€

Other practicalities There's a small **post office** (⊕ *07.00–14.00*) in the centre of the village.

CETINJE TO PODGORICA

A short ascent east out of Cetinje leads to a choice between a road south to **Budva** and another which continues east in the direction of **Podgorica** (50km). Choosing the latter, each twist and turn of the way reveals new far-reaching vistas, each appearing more incredible than the one before: fold upon fold of mountain unfurling to gauze before ultimately dissolving into ether: 'a scene so magnificent and so impressive that it is worth all the journey from England just to have looked at it', wrote Edith Durham in *Through the Lands of the Serb* in 1903. Certainly the route remains unchanged; it is regrettable only that the journey from England has not yet been completely untangled.

That it would be worth twice the effort cannot be overstated. In contrast to the horizontal view, far below the stony canyon yields lush, untrodden pastures, sweet, green and beckoning. Soon there is a first glimpse of the opalescent **Skadar Lake** – at 390km^2 the largest lake in the Balkans – and finally the vast **Plain of Zeta**, the tall chimney of the KAP aluminium plant (now Russian-owned) and to its left and north the sprawl of Podgorica.

RIJEKA CRNOJEVIĆA Approximately 10km after leaving Cetinje an asphalt lane cuts south through the scrubby stonelands to the hamlet of Rijeka Crnojevića, where the river of the same name flows beneath an ancient triple-arched bridge before swirling away to the lake beyond. More often visited from Skadar Lake (see page 230), it also makes a pleasant detour here, and affords the opportunity to visit one of the region's finest restaurants, Stari Most.

⌂ Where to stay *Map, page 78.*
⌂ **Villa Oktoih** (3 dbl, 3 suites) Rijeka Crnojevića; m 069 323000. Slick, modern place with balcony, jacuzzi, wellness centre, river views, & enviable central location near the old bridge. English spoken. €€€€€

⌂ **Panorama-Gazivoda** (6 rooms) ✆020 712037. Some 5km east along the road to Podgorica, this hotel/restaurant enjoys superb views from a belvedere overlooking the head of the lake & a panoply of peaks inc twin summits known locally as Sophia Loren. It is fairly recently built & its dbl bedrooms share the view (rooms 2 & 5 are best). Rooms are spotless & efficient but the tap water is not for drinking. There are ceiling fans & AC but even in Aug it is silent at night except for the grasshoppers, & it's nice to sleep with the windows open to be woken by birdsong. The staff speak good German but minimal English & are economical with their charm. There's parking between the hotel & the precipice. €€€ (inc excellent b/fast), €€€€ (HB)

🏠 **Dragan Pajkovič Guest House** (1 suite) Rijeka Crnojevića; e enquiries@ undiscoveredmontenegro.com. Near old bridge. Balcony, river views, restaurant, AC, TV, use of kitchen. Serbian only, but can book through Undiscovered Montenegro, who speak English. €€

✗ Where to eat and drink *Map, page 78.*

✗ **Stari Most** (Old Bridge) Beside the bridge in the centre of the village; ☏041 239505; e starimost-ndj@t-com.me; ⏲ daily, from noon 'till the last guest has been served'. Nikola Jovanović, ex-footballer, is proprietor of this 'restaurant for those with reservations'. There is no need for any reservation about the fish, which comes directly from the river or the lake & is as fresh as the immaculate white tablecloths, the fluffy, newly baked corn bread & the sparkling mountain water. Delicious soup, a stock from carp, eel & trout, precedes either carp or trout, home-smoked, or whatever the latest catch comprises, fried or grilled. Everything is locally sourced, inc olives from the historic groves of Bar & wine from vineyards at Ceklin which, were you to stand on tiptoe, you would be able to see. Tables are set out on the terrace, an invitation to while away a pastoral afternoon, with only the whisper of a breeze momentarily shimmying across the glassy image of the blossom-framed bridge to nudge the patiently attendant boats. Take time to reflect that a century past, this sleepy nostalgic village was mooted as a tiny Montenegrin Monte Carlo (as today they speak prophetically of Tivat & its glamorous Port Montenegro). Picture how it was: a summer resort for the royal court within easy reach of Cetinje; how they would come to boat, fish & parade on the little waterfront; & where, long before, in the late 15th century the world's second printing press stood close by on Obod hill, until it was moved to Cetinje Monastery (page 85). €€€€

✗ **Konoba Mostina** Also beside the bridge; m 069 843317; e dusko@mostina.me; www.mostina.me. Cheerful spot with riverfront terrace, serving carp & eel from Skadar; run by 4 brothers. €€€

✱ ✗ **Poslednja Luka** Potpočivalo. For a simple cosy meal, try this friendly little locals' local, on the left-hand side of the road between Rijeka Crnojevića & the Panorama-Gazivoda. Everything from the bread to the trout is super-fresh, & the ambience is good. €€

Other practicalities There's a **visitor centre** (☏ *041 879103; e np-skadarlake@ t-com.me; www.nparkovi.me; ⏲ Jun–15 Oct 08.00–18.00, closed in winter*) built in the form of pile dwellings (settlements built on poles in or near water) displaying the history of Rijeka Crnojevića and its former importance as a crossroads of caravan and water routes, as well as descriptions of navigation and fishing on the lake.

Kayaking For kayak tours contact Undiscovered Montenegro, based in Virpazar (page 228), who have a BCU-qualified kayak coach. They also run hiking and other tours and have a truly wonderful guesthouse (page 228).

BEYOND RIJEKA CRNOJEVIĆA The route clearly leads on again uphill without crossing the bridge, whose arches historically were used as a gallows by those who controlled the town, whether Montenegrin or Turk. After 10km you will rejoin the original road from Cetinje to Podgorica, but shortly after leaving Rijeka – as it is simply called by the locals – on the left-hand side of the road is the hotel/restaurant Panorama-Gazivoda (see opposite).

Podgorica is now a further 15km.

As the mountains push back to pudding-basin hills speckled with juniper and stunted oak, it is easy to picture some future golf course here on the outskirts of the city – something which is very much a gleam in the eye of many a prospective developer. At the time of writing nothing solid has properly reached the drawing board, let alone got beyond it. Watch this space …

The Podgorica–Cetinje highway is a bit of a racetrack, as the police have noticed. You will see large signs with pictures of clouds and the message *'Ne! Brže od Života – Sky Forever'*, which roughly translates as 'Don't Speed from Life – the Sky is Forever'. The statement has a particular emotional resonance because it was on this road that one of Montenegro's best-loved young singers was killed. It poignantly relates to a lyric he sang.

PODGORICA

Podgorica is an easy town to navigate but today, in common with other European cities emerging from the mantle of communism, it bears the scars of collective government. Drab concrete blocks and endless washing-lined balconies are in stark juxtaposition with the snow glistening on distant mountain tops, leafy parks and the cheerfulness and conviviality of its people. Within these dismal grey cubes, homes are immaculate and welcoming. 'We do always seem to manage, somehow, though sometimes I can't imagine how,' an inhabitant agrees. Appearances matter in this city. In the evening, when Slobode – Freedom Street – becomes pedestrianised, it seems that all Podgorica has come out to enjoy the *passeggiata*. Pretty girls in labels frequent boutiques and coffee bars; the latest and chicest mobile telephone is as much a designer statement as an essential means of communication.

This must be one of the only capital cities in the world still without McDonald's (not for want of trying on the latter's part, it might be added – the company are even said to have lobbied the US Embassy in Podgorica, though to the country's great credit, such attempts have so far failed). Who needs it when there is an excellent hamburger, chicken and hot-dog outlet on Vučedolska, the street forming the southwest side of the central square (trg Ivana Milutinovića, since Independence renamed trg Republike)? And on a narrow cross street where cars jam the pavement, lovers arm in arm circle a row of sparkling ring shops. In Montenegro 20-somethings, both boy and girl, still speak of marriage as the ideal, even if someone special has not yet come along.

The striking **Millennium Bridge** (Most Milenijum) over the Morača River, on the north side of Nova Varoš, has become a symbol of the city. Also known as Novi Most (New Bridge), it was designed by Podgorica engineer Mladen Ulićević. The structure is supported by 12 cables attached asymmetrically to a pylon soaring to 57m, with 24 further cables acting as counterweights. The bridge incorporates four lanes of traffic and two pedestrian walkways, linking Bulevar Ivana Crnojevića and ul 13 July. It was opened on 13 July 2005, in honour of Montenegro's National Day.

At the traffic lights by the bridge, a sun-browned Romany child, no more than five years old, sponge in one hand, cigarette in the other, flings herself up at a windscreen: *'Ne – ne – ne'*; she wipes it anyway, sort of, and retires with a dismissive drag on her fag. The cars range from sleek BMWs to rusty old Jaguars. The Montenegrin has a wry sense of humour, a decade ago they used to say their tourist slogan ought to read: 'Come to Montenegro: your car is here already.' There are lots of rules too, not always taken very seriously; sometimes it feels safer to cross the road on the red man as at least you then have some idea where the traffic is coming from.

For much of the year the 186,000 inhabitants of Podgorica enjoy a comfortable Mediterranean climate, but in July and August the mercury can hover around a sweltering 40°C. At such times the propinquity of both the coast and the mountains is much appreciated.

HISTORY Through its long and tempestuous history the land where Podgorica lies has undergone many transformations. The area was first documented in the 1st century AD as **Doklea** (Duklija). The metroplex formed by the Illyrian Docleati and Labeati tribes was conquered by the Romans who established a town (Birziminium) as a trading centre at the confluence of the Ribnica and Morača rivers, for the caravan route linking Skadar (Škodra) in Albania to Neroni (now Vid, near Metković in Croatia). Archaeological excavations have uncovered remnants of a 6km Roman aqueduct which led from the springs of Ribnica towards today's town, indicating the size and wealth of Birziminium. Its fate after the fall of the Roman Empire remains unknown, but the region is believed to have been struck by a disastrous earthquake in the 6th century AD and subsequently ravaged by the barbarian Avari and Slav tribes. Many clashes followed between the southern Slavs and the Byzantines.

In the 10th century 'the town where the rivers joined' was known as Ribnica. The first mention of it as Podgorica was in 1326. The name means 'Beneath the **Gorica Hill**' – and that hill remains a landmark, located north of the city by the road to Kolašin and Belgrade. Beneath it sits a small park sheltering the Church of Sv Đorđe (St George), believed to date from the 12th century. The hill, handy for bearings, is matched by its sister, Ljubović, slightly smaller and to the south. By this time the Ottoman sultans were already sizing up the Balkans and soon it was battle upon brutal battle until the valley and the town of Podgorica were lost. The Turks held the city for the following 400 years, developing it as both a stronghold and a trading centre. After the Berlin Congress of 1878 the area was ceded to Montenegro. Bismarck is reported to have remarked rather rudely: 'The Balkans is not worth the bones of a single Pomeranian grenadier.' His successors clearly thought otherwise. In 1916 Podgorica was occupied by the Austrians and in World War II first by the Italians and subsequently by the Germans.

During World War II Podgorica was essentially wiped out by repeated bombardment and only a small part of the earlier city can be seen on the south bank of the **Ribnica River**, a tributary of the Morača which has driven a passage through the karst limestone from the mountains near Durmitor. This is the old Muslim quarter known as Stara Varoš where, across from the parliament building and close to the main bridge, Most Blaža Jovanovića, there are ruins of an Ottoman fortress, some surviving houses and two mosques. A significant date in the country's more recent history is 13 July, because it was on that day in 1941 that the Partisan uprising against the Fascist occupation began.

After the war, in spite of economic constraint, reconstruction began with urgency and within no time a grid was in place; a monument to Socialist Realism. On 13 July 1948 the city was declared the administrative capital of Montenegro and renamed Titograd, in honour of the wartime hero Josip Broz Tito who had become president of the Federation of Yugoslavia, reflecting his special affiliation with the people of Montenegro who had supported him so valiantly in the bitter Partisan struggle. The name reverted to Podgorica in 1992.

GETTING THERE AND AWAY
By air For details of flights to Podgorica, see pages 34–5.

Golubovci (Podgorica) Airport Podgorica Airport underwent a complete face-lift in 2006 and is now fairly modern and airy, though facilities are still somewhat

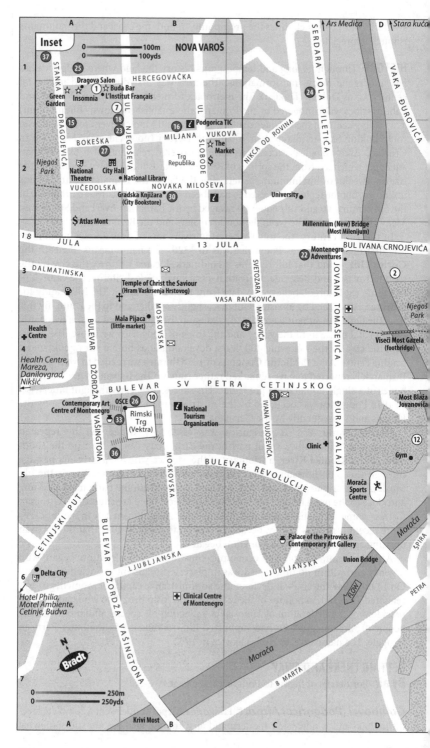

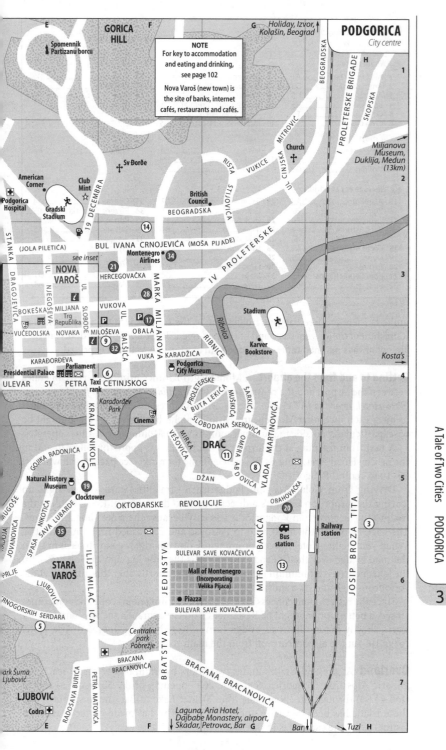

PODGORICA
City centre

NOTE
For key to accommodation
and eating and drinking,
see page 102

Nova Varoš (new town) is
the site of banks, internet
cafés, restaurants and cafés.

Holiday, Izvor,
Kolašin, Beograd

Spomennik
Partizanu borcu

GORICA
HILL

Sv Đorđe

American
Corner

Club
Mint

Podgorica
Hospital

Gradski
Stadium

British
Council

Miljanova
Museum,
Duklija, Medun
(13km)

Church

BEOGRADSKA

RISTA STIJOVICA

VUKICE

UL CINJSKA MITROVIĆ

I PROLETERSKE BRIGADE

SKOPSKA

19 DECEMBRA

BEOGRADSKA

(14)

(JOLA PILETIĆA)

BUL IVANA CRNOJEVIĆA (MOŠA PIJADE)

see inset

Montenegro
Airlines

(34)

NOVA
VAROŠ

(21)

HERCEGOVAČKA

MARKA MILJANOVA

IV PROLETERSKE

STANKA

DRAGOLJEVICA

NJEGOŠEVA

BOKEŠKA

MILJANA
Trg
Republika

(28)

VUKOVA

UL SLOBODE

(P)

OBALA

(P) (17)

Ribnica

Stadium

VUČEDOLSKA

NOVAKA

MILOŠEVA

(i)

(9)

(32)

BALŠIĆA

VUKA KARADŽIĆA

RIBNICE

Karver
Bookstore

Kosta's

KARAĐORĐEVA

Parliament

Presidential Palace

Taxi
rank

(6)

Podgorica
City Museum

ULEVAR SV PETRA

CETINJSKOG

V PROLETERSKE

BUTA LEKIĆA

ŠARKIĆA

MUŠIKICA

Karađorđev
Park

Cinema

MIRKA VEŠOVIĆA

SLOBODANA ŠKEROVIĆA

DRAČ

(11)

OMERA AB DOVICA

VLADA MARTINOVIĆA

KRALJA NIKOLE

GOJIKA RADONJIĆA

(4)

Natural History
Museum

(19)

Clocktower

DŽAN

(8)

(⊠)

A Tale of Two Cities   PODGORICA

JOVANOVIĆA

SPASA SAVA LUBARDE

(35)

OKTOBARSKE

REVOLUCIJE

ORAHOVAČKA

(20)

Railway
station

(3)

PRLJE

DRUGOŠE

(⊠)

STARA
VAROŠ

ILIJE MILAČ IČA

BULEVAR SAVE KOVAČEVIĆA

JEDINSTVA

MITRA BAKIĆA

Bus
station

(13)

JOSIP BROZA TITA

LJUBOVIĆ

CRNOGORSKIH SERDARA

(5)

Mall of Montenegro
(Incorporating
Velika Pijaca)

Piazza

Centralni
park
Pobrežje

BRATSTVA

BRACANA
BRACANOVIĆA

BULEVAR SAVE KOVAČEVIĆA

RADOSAVA BURIĆA

PETRA MATOVIĆA

BRACANA BRACANOVIĆA

ark Šuma
Ljubović

LJUBOVIĆ

Codra

Laguna, Aria Hotel,
Dajbabe Monastery, airport,
Skadar, Petrovac, Bar

Bar

Tuzi

3

101

ALAMEDA FREE LIBRARY

PODGORICA *City centre*
For listings, see pages 105–8

🛏️ **Where to stay**

1	Alexander Lux	A1	7	Eminent	A1
2	Ambasador	D3	8	Europa	G5
3	Aurel	H5	9	Kerber	F4
4	Bojatours	E5	10	Montenegro, Premier	
5	City	E6		Best Western	B4
6	Crna Gora	F4	11	Montenegro Hostel	G5

12	Podgorica	D5
13	Terminus	G6
14	Ziya	F3

Off map

Ambiente	A6	Izvor	G1	Philia	A6
Aria	F7	Kosta's	H4		
Holiday	G1	Laguna	F7		

✖️ **Where to eat and drink**

15	Alan Ford	A2	23	Greenwich	A2	33	Opera	A4
16	Bocun	B2	24	Gurman	C1	34	Pizzeria Calabria	F3
17	Caballero	F3	25	Highland	A1	35	Pod Volat	E6
	Café Astoria	(see	26	Il Giardino	B4	36	Salvador Dali	A5
	Delta City, D6)		27	Kaktus	A2	37	Sempre	A1
18	Corto Maltese	A2	28	Lanterna	F3		Ziya	(see 14)
19	Dvor	E5	29	Leonardo	C4			
20	Express	G5	30	Lupo di Mare	B2	**Off map**		
21	Four Leprechauns	F3	31	Maša	C4		Stara kuća	D1
22	Fufluns	C3	32	Nero	F4		Mareza	A4

limited. There are free baggage trolleys but, at the time of writing, no pay phones. Refreshment options are basic and not always open. There are **car-hire** desks but they are not always manned unless someone with a prior reservation is expected.

Getting to and from the airport A Montenegro Airlines **minibus** service operates between the airport and the central square (*trg Republike – 5mins on foot from Crna Gora Hotel, near the JAT & Montenegro Airlines offices; €3 one way*). It is scheduled to meet each incoming Montenegro Airlines flight, but having a Plan B might be wise, particularly outside the summer months when Montenegro Airlines operates.

A **taxi** from the rank at the airport to midtown costs approximately €20 and to the nearby Hotel Aria about €4. If you telephone for a taxi (see page 104) it will cost €5–10 to central Podgorica.

Driving from Golubovci into Podgorica is straightforward – turn right on leaving the airport area and it's a direct road into the centre of town. Finding the road to the airport from Podgorica is less easy because there are almost no signs. The trick is to take the main road to Petrovac and Bar, called Bratstva–Jedinstva. When you see the Hotel Lovćen prominently on your right, you will be 4km from the road bridge over the Cijevna River. Here is the only big sign to Golubovci, on the left, and to the aluminium factory on the right. Shortly after this, turn left at the 'Aerodrom' sign and it's a shortish straight road.

Since the refreshment concession at the airport is limited in scope and sometimes closed, a better option might be Restaurant Kod Crnagora, on the left coming from town, shortly before the road bridge turn-off; or the well-appointed Aria Hotel (page 105) at the airport turn-off from the main road.

Overland At present it takes under two hours by train, bus or car to reach the Dinaric Alps from Podgorica. Since the 2005 opening of the Sozina road tunnel (toll €3.50) through the mountains from Skadar Lake to Bar, the road journey to the Adriatic has been halved to under one hour. This has made it much easier for visitors using the car ferries in Bar.

By bus and rail All tickets may be purchased at the stations prior to departure. Otherwise you can pay on board: on the train for a supplement, or on the bus for a slightly lower price than at the terminal. A ticket purchased at the bus station costs an extra €1 but ensures you a seat.

Buses connect to all the main towns throughout the country. Services are regular, for example up to 22 services daily to Kotor and every 15–25 minutes to Cetinje and Budva. Out of high season, service may be more sporadic.

Buses cost around €2.50 to Cetinje, €7 to Herceg Novi, €6.50 to Žabljak, €3 to Nikšić, €7 to Kotor, €5 to Kolašin, €7 to Pljevlja, €6.50 to Bijelo Polje, €5 to Budva, €7 to Bar and €7 to Ulcinj, all one way.

There is also a long-distance service to and from large cities in other Balkan countries, including daily bus services to Sarajevo, Novi Sad and Belgrade, and less frequently to Skopje, Istanbul and elsewhere, which then connect to the international network.

A bus timetable for departures from Podgorica can be found at www.visit-montenegro.com/transport-bus.htm, but it is always wise to check with the **bus station** [101 G6] (*Mitra Bakića br 5;* \ *020 620430*) in advance of travel.

The **railway station** [101 H5] is at trg Goloočkih Žrtava 7 (\ *020 441211/212/209; www.zcg-prevoz.me;* ☺ *05.00–23.00*). The main railway runs from Bar on the coast to Belgrade in Serbia for a total length of 476km, comprising Bar–Gostun 175km and Gostun–Belgrade 301km (with 8.9km travelling through Bosnia–Herzegovina); see page 203. The ride north from Podgorica is a treat, carving at 110km/h through the very heart of this magnificent untamed land, soaring with the eagles high above the canyons and gorges of Morača and Tara. The so-called business train, at a slightly higher fare, seems the best way to go – though the 'Montenegrin' train depicted in the James Bond film *Casino Royale* it certainly isn't (see page 38).

Currently there is no passenger service operating on either the Podgorica–Nikšić or the Podgorica–Škodra lines.

Examples of standard one-way ticket prices from Podgorica are Bar €2.40, Kolašin €3.20 and Belgrade €19.

You can find some information on arrivals and departures at www.visit-montenegro.com, and the Railways of Montenegro website (*www.zcg-prevoz.me*) has a national timetable, but as with the buses it is advisable to check with the station prior to travel.

ORIENTATION Podgorica was divided by the Turks into two parts, now known as Nova Varoš, which today includes the principal government buildings, the shopping streets around the central square and the theatre; and Stara Varoš, on the opposite bank of the Ribnica. The town is now growing in a westerly direction and a major new *Hram* (Orthodox temple) dedicated to Christ the Saviour (*Hristovog Vaskrsenja*) is nearing completion in this quarter, with the small market (*mala pijaca*) beside it and across the street from the Best Western Premier Hotel.

GETTING AROUND With Gorica Hill to the north and Ljubović in the south, it is not hard to navigate this town. Although it is growing in area, Podgorica remains a pleasant town to explore **on foot**.

The airport lies only minutes away to the south by **taxi**, and the **bus** and **train stations**, to the east of the city, are conveniently side by side, within walking distance (15 minutes to trg Republike) or a short taxi ride (€2–3) from the centre.

Drivers will find secure paid **parking** alongside Crna Gora Hotel on Bulevar Sv Petra Cetinjskog; otherwise try the Central Square (trg Republike) [100 B2].

Taxis There are several ranks around the city, including one on Slobode between the Crna Gora Hotel and the post office [100 E4]. Most drivers have mobile phones and business cards and if you are in town for any length of time it is recommended to deal solely with a driver you can understand and trust, and who knows where you are staying. Metered cabs are identified by their lit rooftop signs and will charge about €0.50/km. Beyond the city limits, however, fares are negotiable according to distance, and it is sensible to establish a fare in advance, for example with the help of hotel reception. A taxi to Podgorica airport should cost about €5–10; to Čilipi Airport about €90; and to Budva about €25. Beware: airport taxis waiting to take passengers to town *may* ask the unwary for a fare of €20. It's much better to telephone for one of the taxis listed below; there is a wide range of options. Most taxi companies provide a 24-hour service. Tips of 5–10% will suffice.

🚖 **Alo Taxi** ☎ 19700 (yellow car)
🚖 **Bel Taxi** ☎ 19600
🚖 **City Taxi** 19711
* 🚖 **HIT Taxi** ☎ 19725
🚖 **IN Taxi** 19755
🚖 **Plus Taxi** ☎ 19712

🚖 **Podgorica Taxi** ☎ 19704
* 🚖 **Red Taxi** ☎ 19714
🚖 **Sava Taxi** ☎ 19723 (green & white)
🚖 **Taxi Bum** 19703
🚖 **Taxi de Lux** ☎ 19706
🚖 **Taxi Gold** ☎ 19805

Car hire Car rental can be arranged through the tourist office or your hotel, or you can call direct in advance (certainly in high season). There are several car-rental desks at the airport, but they are manned only when they are expecting a passenger who has pre-booked.

🚖 **Delta Rent-a-Car** Gojka Radonjića 31; ☎ 020 625114; www.rentacar-delta.com. 5–10% discount for Montenegro Airlines passengers. Clio, Jeep, etc. Min age 23, min licence 3 years. Visa & MasterCard accepted. Also at Golubovci Airport, m 067 259800.

🚖 **Efel Rent-a-car** ul Jerevanska 8; ☎ 020 641044; e efelint1@t-com.me. Corolla, etc; delivery extra; chauffeurs available.

🚖 **Kompas Hertz** trg B Vučinić bb; ☎ 020 602680; e kompasrat@t-com.me. VW Polo, Ford Mondeo, etc. All AC but insurance not inc. Also at Golubovci Airport ☎ 081 244117.

* 🚖 **Meridian** bul Džordža Vašingtona 85; ☎ 020 234944; e meridian@t-com.me; www.

meridian-rentacar.com. The manager, Dejan Perić, is helpful & pleasant, & they are happy to pick up or drop off. Also at Podgorica Airport, m 069 316666, & Dubrovnik Airport, m +381 069 078557.

🚖 **Perfekt** Cetinjski put bb, zgrada Vektra; ☎ 020 205065; e perfectgroup@t-com.me; www. perfectgroup.co.me (Montenegrin only). VW Golf manual, Ford Transit, etc. Min age 22.

🚖 **Razvršje** Bracana Bracanovica 40c; ☎ 020 647222; e razvrsje@t-com.me; www. razvrsjerentacar.me

🚖 **Rokšped** J Broza Tito 67; ☎ 020 445555; e rentacar@roksped.com; www.roksped.com. VW Polo, Passat, etc. Visa accepted.

Tourist information and tour operators
Tourist information
🔲 **National Tourism Organisation of Montenegro** [100 B4] bul Sv Petra Cetinjskog 130; ☎ 077 100001; e info@montenegro.travel; www.montenegro.travel. 24hr tourist information line ☎ 1300.

🔲 **Podgorica Tourist Information Centre** [100 B2] Slobode 47; ☎ 020 667535; e info@ podgorica.travel; www.podgorica.travel; ⏰ Jun–

Oct 08.00–20.00 Mon–Fri, 09.00–13.00 Sat, Nov–May 08.00–16.00 Mon–Fri. Centrally located & helpful office with maps, literature & information on rental cars, excursions & more.

Tour operators
Montenegro Adventures [100 D3] Jovana Tomaševića 35; ☎ 020 208000; m 069 315601; e info@montenegro-adventures.com; www.

montenegro-adventures.com; ⊕ 08.00–20.00 Mon–Fri, 09.00–15.00 Sat. Highly efficient & knowledgeable. All tourist arrangements, coastal & mountains; sports activities & trekking. Transport & accommodation in more remote areas; business conferences arranged; MICE a speciality. They will go to endless trouble to fulfil personal requirements. Diagonally across the street from the Millennium Bridge.

Montenegro Airlines [101 F3] bul Ivana Crnojevića 55; ☎ 020 664411; www. montenegroairlines.com; ⊕ 08.00–20.00 Mon–Fri, 08.00–14.00 Sat.

🏠 **WHERE TO STAY** *Map, pages 100–1.*
Podgorica hotels are almost all quite expensive.

🏠 **Montenegro, Premier Best Western** (41 rooms, 7 suites) Svetog Petra Cetinjskog 145; ☎ 020 406500; e montenegro@bestwestern-ce. com; www.bestwestern-ce.com/montenegro. A comfortable, shiny hotel that opened in mid-2006, in the business district. All rooms with high-speed internet access, satellite TV, AC, room safe & minibar. Some of the sgl rooms are smoking, so specify if you want a non-smoking sgl. Bar, dining room & bistro, conference facilities, garage (*€15 per day*), car hire. CCs accepted. €€€€€

🏠 **Podgorica** (36 rooms, 8 suites) ul Svetlane Kane Radević 1; ☎ 020 402500; www. hotelpodgorica.co.me. Built in 1967 but fully refurbished in 2005, the former sister hotel to the Crna Gora is now an extremely comfortable private hotel, on the banks of the River Morača. All rooms have AC, TV, room safe, internet access & bath; some with terrace. B/fast inc. 24hr room service. Restaurant (€€€€€), bar & nightclub, conference facilities. Shop, hairdresser, rent-a-car & travel agent. Casino features roulette (*stakes €0.50–5*) & poker. Women should take care not to crash into the mirrored wall in the ladies! CCs accepted. €€€€€

🏠 **Alexander Lux** (6 rooms, 8 apts) Hercegovačka 12; ☎ 020 664510; e hotelalexandarlux@t-com.me; www.alexandar-lux.com. Central location. AC, TV, Wi-Fi; apts with fitted kitchens. Fitness centre, conference room, airport transfers. €€€€

🏠 **Ambasador** (3 rooms, 6 suites) Vaka Djurovica br 5; ☎ 020 272233; http://hotel-ambasador-podgorica.montenegro365.com/. Beside the Morača River & near the Millennium Bridge. Rooms have AC, cable TV, internet access, minibar. Avoid room 101 adjacent to noisy generator. Sauna, bar & very nice, peaceful terrace restaurant (€€€) with river view. Parking tricky & tight; better to use car park above hotel. €€€€

✱ 🏠 **Aria** (10 dbl, 3 quad apts) Mahala bb, 800m from Golubovci Airport; ☎ 020 872570/572; www.hotelaria.me. Well-appointed hotel, opened in 2010, with attractive minimalist wood & stone décor. AC, LCD TV, room safe, minibar, free Wi-Fi, mini gym, conference room, bar & restaurant, garden, parking. CCs accepted. Children aged 6 & under stay free. €€€€

🏠 **Aurel** (55 rooms) bul Josipa Broz Tita bb; ☎ 078 113333; e info@hotel-aurel.com; www. hotel-aurel.com. 1km from city centre in newly built business zone. Stylish, spacious rooms with AC, TV, Wi-Fi. Restaurant & bar. €€€€

🏠 **Bojatours** (20 rooms) ul Kralja Nikole 10; ☎ 020 623349; e autoboja@t-com.me; www. bojatours.me. Rooms, inc 2 sgl & 1 suite with enormous terrace, all have satellite TV, AC, minibar, safe-deposit box & Wi-Fi. Restaurant, sauna, fitness centre. Very well appointed. €€€€

🏠 **City** (80 rooms) Crnogorskih serdara 5; ☎ 020 441500; e recepcija@cityhotelmn.com; www. cityhotelmn.com. 500m from the town centre, on the edge of the old Muslim quarter, this was formerly named after the Ljubović hill to the south of town. Built in 1983 & thoroughly renovated in 2008, it is now a most comfortable & efficient business hotel. AC, TV, gym, parking. Summer garden with café at the back. Credit cards accepted. €€€€

🏠 **Crna Gora** (142 rooms, 7 suites) bul Sv Petra Cetinjskog 2; ☎ 020 443443; e recepcija@ hotelcg.com; www.hotelcg.com. A comfortable hotel with an Edwardian atmosphere, although it was actually opened in 1953. It was traditionally the best large hotel in Podgorica & remains up to scratch for business travellers, though comprehensive redevelopment is at the planning stage but not yet settled. All rooms come with minibar & satellite TV. On-site casino (⊕ 20.00–04.00), Manija disco (⊕ 21.00–05.00), 4 large conference rooms with 750 seats. There is also a pleasant outside terrace bar on the boulevard. The hotel showcases some good examples of modern Montenegrin art inc works by Vojslav Stanić. The street-level hotel car park is supervised & offers secure parking; useful for non-guests as well as residents. CCs accepted. €€€€

🏠 **Kosta's** (22 suites) bul Pete Proleterske Brigade bb; 📞020 610000; e hotelkostasprodaja@ hotmail.com; www.hotelkostas.com. About 850m from town centre. Rooms have stereo CD, satellite TV, internet access, in-room kitchens, room service. Restaurant, bar & meeting room; massage centre. Parking. €€€€

🏠 **Ziya** (25 rooms, 3 suites) Beogradska 10; 📞020 230690; e reception@hotelziya.me; www. hotel-ziya.me. Boutique hotel in central location, with AC, TV, Wi-Fi, parking. Spa, wellness centre & smart Lebanese restaurant (opposite). €€€€

🏠 **Europa** (26 rooms, 2 suites) Orahovačka br 16 at Oktobarske Revolucije; 📞020 623444; e shole@t-com.me; www.hotelevropa.co.me. A short walk from bus & train stations. All rooms – 12 sgl, 12 dbl & 2 trpl – inc internet access, AC, satellite TV, telephone & room service. Restaurant & café with 2 terraces, serving local dishes. Parking for 20 vehicles. CCs accepted. €€€–€€€€

🏠 **Kerber** (20 rooms) ul Novaka Miloševa 6; 📞020 405405; e info@hotelkerber.me; http:// hotelkerber.me. Good-value B&B, oddly but peacefully situated at the inside end of a central shopping arcade. Satellite TV, AC, minibar, direct-line room phones & internet access. Restaurant, bar. CCs accepted. €€€–€€€€

🏠 **Ambiente** (14 rooms) Cetinjski put 34; 📞020 235535; e ambiente@t-com.me. Small, functional motel 10mins from town in the direction of Cetinje. Restaurant (🕐 07.00–23.00). AC. Parking. CCs accepted. €€€

✱ 🏠 **Eminent** (6 rooms & 7 suites) Njegoševa 25; 📞020 664545; e eminent@t-com.me; www. eminent.co.me. Recommended as an unpretentious, fair-value hotel with a central location; popular with foreign visitors. With satellite TV, internet, open-air pool, AC, minibar, restaurant. Sgls, dbls & trpls. Children 3–12 50%; one under-3 stays free. Pets allowed. CCs accepted. €€€

🏠 **Holiday** (20 rooms) I Proleterska 11; 📞020 611411; e recepcija@hotelholidaypg. com; www.hotelholidaypg.com. A useful, clean & simple stop out of town on the way north, with a local ambience. TV, AC, minibar. Bar & children's playground. €€€

🏠 **Laguna** (20 rooms) Vojislavljevica 72, 📞020 641777; e info@hotel-laguna.me; www.hotel-laguna.me. Good-value & well-reviewed hotel on southwest edge of city near Delta City shopping mall. Rooms with wooden furniture, AC, TV, Wi-Fi. Terrace; restaurant with €6 daily menu. Parking. CCs accepted. €€€

🏠 **Philia** (12 rooms, 3 suites) Cetinjski put bb; 📞020 262510; e info@philiahotel.com; www. philiahotel.com; 5km from downtown Podgorica on road to Cetinje, 500m from Delta City. A hospitable & efficient business-friendly, family-owned hotel with garden. Cable TV, AC, room service, Wi-Fi, safe deposits, car hire & laundry services. Parking, airport shuttle. All CCs accepted. €€€

🏠 **Terminus** (16 rooms) trg Goolotočkih Žrtava; 📞020 622752; m 067 611302; www. terminushotel.me. Opposite the railway station, a brand new, understated hotel, small & low-rise but so clean you could eat off the floor. Very welcoming staff. €€€

🏠 **Izvor** (15 rooms, 5 'hostel rooms') Smokovac bb; m 067 364760; e info@hostelizvor.me; www. hostelizvor.me. A convenient if simple stop, 7km north of Podgorica on the road to Belgrade & Kolašin. Hotel-hostel with dbl/tpl rooms (€10–15 pp) & shared rooms with 4+ beds (€7–10 pp). Restaurant with local cuisine. €€

🏠 **Montenegro Hostel** (1 room; 8 dorm beds) Dječevića 25; m 069 255501; e montenegrohostel@gmail.com; www. montenegrohostel.com. Under same ownership as hostels in Kotor & Budva, 100m from bus & rail station on 2nd floor of left-hand house; can be tricky to find after dark but good map on website or telephone ahead. Twin room sharing bathroom €13–15 pp. 2 4-bed dorms (1 en suite, 1 sharing bathroom) €7–13 pp. Helpful reception/manager. Common room with TV & kitchen, free Wi-Fi, AC, secure lockers, washing machine/dryer. Tours, boat trips & rafting can be arranged. €€

✗ **WHERE TO EAT AND DRINK** *Map, pages 100–1.*
There are many coffee shops and small cafés in the streets running off the central square, but it is difficult to escape the ubiquitous pizza.

In town

✗ Ziya Beogradska 10; ☎020 230690; www. hotel-ziya.me. Upmarket restaurant in boutique hotel of same name (opposite), serving good Lebanese dishes. €€€€€

✗ Maša bul Sv Petra Cetinjskog 31, in the Maša shopping centre; ☎020 224460; ⊕ 07.00–24.00. Montenegrin & Italian cuisine with a strong fish bias. Large terrace & a sophisticated upstairs dining room. €€€€

✗ Opera Rimski trg 59, Poslovni Centar Kruševac; ☎020 205110; m 068 407844; ⊕ 08.00–24.00 Mon–Thu; 08.00–02.00 Fri–Sat. A popular local choice, with soft lighting & good atmosphere. French cuisine; shrimps with tomato & garlic; steak with pistachio & celeriac. €€€€

✗ Salvador Dali bul Džordža Vašingtona 87; ☎020 234567; www.dali.co.me. Well on its way to achieving its ambition to be one of Podgorica's top restaurants. Good international food, attentive service. €€€€

✳ ✗ Sempre Stanka Dragojevića 14; ⊕ 12.00–23.00. Definitely an expatriate Italian favourite, especially for those attracted to what is probably the only Montenegrin source of egg-white omelettes & low-fat cappuccino. There are some good things with more cholesterol, too, inc homemade pasta. CCs accepted. €€€€

✗ Caballero Marka Miljanova 17; ⊕ 07.00–24.00. A series of interconnecting dining rooms serving predictable grills & pasta to an acceptable standard. €€€

✗ Dvor Kralja Nikole 36; ☎020 622265; e restoran.dvor@gmail.com. An atmospheric, good restaurant in a 1630 house, said to be the oldest in Podgorica, specialising in traditional local grills & salads. On some evenings there is live music. €€€

✗ Lanterna Marka Miljanova 41; ⊕ 10.00–23.00. Good pizzas & traditional Montenegrin dishes. €€€

✳ ✗ Leonardo Between Vasa Raičkoviča & Svetozara Markovića; ☎020 242902; ⊕ 08.00–24.00. Tucked away in a square behind bul Sv Petra Cetinjskog. Good & moderately priced Italian food in a sophisticated ambience with AC. Local & Italian wines. Private booths for 4–6 diners, warm welcome, good English. CCs accepted. €€€

✗ Lupo di Mare trg Republike 22; ⊕ 08.00–24.00. Chef Francesco Ruggeri cooks fish in the Sicilian way: catch of the day, risotto, carpaccio & octopus, washed down with local, Italian or French wine. €€€

✳ ✗ Pizzeria Calabria Nr corner of Marka Miljanova & bul Ivana Crnojevića; ⊕ 08.00–24.00. Considered one of the best pizzerias; even ex-Prime Minister Đukanović has been seen eating here with his bodyguards (though how it is hard to say, as you need a candle to read the menu). Pizzas from the wood-burning ovens are thin & crispy, & avoid both heavy toppings & abundant tinned mushrooms. Good service. Quite atmospheric. €€€

✗ Pod Volat trg Vojvode Bećir Bega Osmanagića; ⊕ 08.00–23.00 daily. Popular restaurant with good reasonably priced local dishes on the old town square, near the clocktower. €€€

✗ Stara kuća Iva Andrića 5; m 069 030204; ⊕ 10.00–24.00 Mon–Sat. Rustic interior & traditional Montenegrin dishes near Gorica hill. Live music some nights. €€€

✗ Café Astoria Delta City shopping mall; www. podgorica.astoriamontenegro.com; ⊕ b/fast through lunch & dinner. Minimalist, trendy & popular with 'ladies who lunch'. Same ownership as boutique hotels in Budva & Kotor. Delicious salads. €€

✗ Express trg Golootočkih Žrtava; ⊕ 08.00–20.00 daily. Cheapie spot by the bus station with surprisingly good food, inc stews & salads. €€

✗ Il Giardino Rimski trg 28, Kruševac; m 069 313313; ⊕ 08.00–24.00 Mon–Fri, 10.00–24.00 Sat–Sun. Large terrace in the square as well as downstairs dining room, with decent Italian food at moderate prices. English menus & good spoken English. €€

✳ ✗ Gurman Jola Piletića 27. Inexpensive take-away, with mouth-watering hot sandwiches made to order. €

Cafés

▯ Corto Maltese Njegoševa 21; ⊕ 08.00–24.00. Café named after comic strip of the same name; snacks served.

▯ Kaktus Njegoševa 47; ⊕ 08.00–01.00. Small café/bar, popular with locals; live music some evenings.

▯ Nero Vuka Karadžića 7; ⊕ 08.00–24.00 Mon–Sat. Café/bar with wooden interior & live jazz.

Outside Podgorica

✗ Mareza Mareški put bb; ☎020 511031; e plantaze@t-com.me; http://plantaze.com/cg/#/

Mareza; ⊕ 10.00–24.00 Tue–Sun. 5km NW of city centre, next to a trout farm, a notably good restaurant &, although owned by the vineyard, with a very cosy atmosphere. It's good for sampling local dishes at moderate prices; try *teleca corba* (veal soup); *popeci na podgoricki nacin* (veal rolled & stuffed with ham & deep fried; lighter than it sounds). Ask for Vranac Monte Cheval premier reserve 1994, said to be available only at Plantaze's own restaurants & a wine to be taken seriously (especially if you are paying the bill). €€€

BARS AND NIGHTLIFE *Map, pages 100–1.*

Nightlife in Podgorica is for the most part centred on the dozens of wine bars, clubs and discos in the vicinity of the central trg Republike. The overall scene here and in the coastal towns is hot and impressive. It's not unrealistic to suggest Montenegro is earning itself the title of the Ibiza of the eastern Mediterranean. As in every capital city, such places come and go in popularity if not in presence; DJs are personalities and what's hot varies from month to month. For a visitor, a good clue is to follow your ears. Listed here are a few – of many – current favourites:

♀ **Alan Ford** Stanka Dragojevića 10; ⊕ 08.00–01.00. Small café/bar themed around the cult 1970s comic strip of the same name, which has iconic status across the former Yugoslavia.
♀ **Bocun** trg Republike 27; ⊕ 08.00–02.00 Mon–Sat. Wine bar with large selection of local & international wines.
☆ **Buda Bar** [100 A1] Stanka Dragojevića 26; ⊕ 08.00–03.00. This popular spot is open all day with a disco in the evening. Asian décor not reflected in the music.
☆ **Club Mint** [101 E2] 19 Decembra 5; ⊕ 22.00–05.00 Thu–Sat. Located in the south stand of the city soccer stadium; all-night late-week revelry.
☆ **Crno Gora Casino** [101 F4] bul Sv Petra Cetinjskog; ☎020 634823; ⊕ 24hrs. In hotel of the same name. A small glitzy room dominated by chandeliers.
♀ **Four Leprechauns** Hercegovačka 71; ⊕ 08.00–01.00. Busy Irish bar serving draught

Guinness. Like the Irish pub in Budva Old Town, popular with expatriates.
♀ **Fufluns** 13 Jula bb; m 068 480600; ⊕ Mon–Sat 08.00–01.00. Wine bar with wide range of local & international wines; also a restaurant.
☆ **Green Garden** [100 A2] Stanka Dragojevića 26; ⊕ 22.00–03.00. Hugely popular disco especially at w/end, with plenty of turbo folk.
♀ **Greenwich** Njegoševa 27; ⊕ 08.00–02.00. Cool & glam; jazz, blues & some live acts. CCs accepted.
♀ **Highland** Hercegovačka 3; m 067 577731; ⊕ 08.00–01.00. A tilt to Scotland on a street of bars & cafés; lots of malts; karaoke.
☆ **Insomnia** [100 A1] Stanka Dragojevića; ⊕ 22.00–03.00. Next door to Green Garden & often bursting at the seams; Balkan rock.
☆ **The Market** [100 B2] trg Republike bb; ⊕ 22.00–03.00. Disco-chic, techno, ex-YU classics & sometimes a band. Usually heaving.

ENTERTAINMENT AND CULTURAL CENTRES
Entertainment
National Theatre [100 A2] Stanka Dragojevića 18, adjacent to the City Hall; ☎020 664074; box office m 078 111075; www.cnp.me. Box office ⊕ 09.00–13.00 Mon–Sat & from curtain-up when a performance is scheduled. Plays & concerts.
Strike Bowling [101 G6] Mall of Montenegro, Bratstva i Jedinstva 85; m 067 523899. 12 bowling lanes, 4 pool tables, café.
Cineplexx [100 A6] Delta City shopping mall, Cetinjski put bb; ☎020 414424; www.cineplexx. me; 6-screen multiplex showing English-language

films with Montenegrin subtitles as well as Balkan movies. CCs accepted.

Cultural centres
American Corner [101 E2] Vaka Đurovića 12; ☎020 667065; e amcorner@t-com.me; http:// podgorica.usembassy.gov/american_corners3. html; ⊕ 11.00–18.00 Mon–Fri. US magazines & newspapers.

British Council [101 G2] Ulcinjska 8; ☎020 618410; e pginfo@britishcouncil.me; www. britishcouncil.me; ⏱ 10.00–12.00 Mon–Thu. Promotes English-language events, books & publications.

Contemporary Art Centre of Montenegro [100 A4] Kruševac bb; ☎020 243914; www.csucg. co.me

L'Institut Français [100 A1] Njegoševa 26; ☎020 667000; e contact@ccf.c.me; www. ambafrance-me.org; ⏱ 08.00–18.00 Mon–Fri. French courses & cultural events.

SPORTS AND OTHER ACTIVITIES In addition to the options below, you could try ballooning (page 63), and trout fishing on the Ribnica, Morača and Cijevna rivers (pages 66–7).

Soko Gym Mall of Montenegro, Bratstva i Jedinstva 85; m 069 406069; http://soko-gym. com; ⏱ 07.00–23.00 Mon–Sat, 09.00–20.00 Sun

Gradski Stadion [101 E2] Vaka Đurovića; ☎020 664294. Football stadium where the national as well as the local team play. Tickets under €10 are considerably less expensive than the equivalent in Britain.

🚁 **Montenegro Charter Company** bul Svetog Petyra Cetinjskog 92; m 067 220195; e info@montenegrocharter.com; www. montenegrocharter.com. Helicopter tours.

🧗 **Outdoor Club Podgorica** e ocp@ montenegroclimbing.net; www. montenegroclimbing.net. Grassroots organisation promoting climbing & mountaineering in Montenegro's outstandingly beautiful mountain areas, inc the crags around Podgorica, as well as Kučka krajina, Durmitor & elsewhere.

🧗 **Planinarski klub Gorica** m 069 606148; e planinargorica@t-com.me; http://pkgorica.me. Local hiking club.

🚣 **Rafting Montenegro** m 069 070997; e info@raftingmontenegro.com; www. raftingmontenegro.com. Day trips (or longer) to raft on the Tara River. Various trips inc full day with b/fast & lunch (€40/28 adults/12 & under) & 3-day trips (€200). Also jeep safaris & hiking tours.

🚲 **Tempo Rent-a-Bike** Bratstva i Jedinstva 57; ☎020 290690 or contact through tourist office; e tempobike@t-com.me; www.tempo.co.me; ⏱ 09.00–21.00 Mon–Sat. Mountain-bike rental.

🎾 **Tennis Club AS** ul D Kokoti 1; m 069 570547; e tkas@t-com.me; www.tkas.me

🎾 **Tennis Club Eminent** m 067 247394; e tkeminent@gmail.com; www.tkeminent.me

SHOPPING The main shopping streets are Njegoševa, Slobode and Hercegovačka. On the Slobode corner of the Crna Gora Hotel you will still sometimes find Montenegro's only street shoeshine man. Locals will probably tip him 50 cents or less; you should give him €1–2. Your shoes will sparkle.

In 2008 Crna Gora's first grand retail mall, **Delta City** [100 A6] (*Cetinjski put bb; m 068 878637; www.deltacity.me; ⏱ 10.00–22.00 daily*), opened for business at the junction of the Cetinje and Nikšić roads, in the expanding western quarter of town. A full complement of long-awaited international stores is represented, including Marks & Spencer, Zara, Nine West, Guess, Tommy Hilfiger, Monsoon and Office, along with a six-screen multiplex cinema (*Cineplexx; www.cineplexx. me*), Montenegro's first hypermarket, and masses of parking.

Competing with this complex, a second mall, **Mall of Montenegro** [101 G6] (*Bratstva i Jedinstva 85; www.mallofmontenegro.com; ⏱ 09.00–22.00*), was opened in 2010. Constructed on the site of the old market, *Velika Pijaca* (page 111), to the east of the road leading to Bar and Skadar, it too includes a wide range of fashion stores and a hypermarket, as well as a bowling alley and a fitness centre. The complex has also incorporated a 'green market', where the locally produced (and often organic) milk, meat, fruit and vegetables of which Montenegro is so justly proud are a feature.

Books and computers

Computer Repairs, Tagor Svetozara Markoviéa 18; ☏020 238431; www.tagor.co.me; ⏲ 07.00–15.00

Gradska Knjižara (City Bookstore) [100 B2] trg Republike 40; ☏020 210375; www.novaknjiga.com; ⏲ 08.00–22.00 Mon–Sat. Some English-language books. Also in Mall of Montenegro [101 G6].

iCentar Radoja Dakića bb (City kvart 2-1); ☏020 290532; e servis@icentar.me; www.icentar.me

⏲ 09.00–21.00 Mon–Sat. Apple Mac repairs & authorised seller.

Karver Bookstore [101 G4] Obala Ribnice, Cvijetin brijeg bb; ☏020 600625; www.karver.org; ⏲ 09.00–22.00 Mon–Sat. Bookshop located in former Turkish bathhouse.

Mamut Bookstore [100 A6] Delta City, Cetinjski put bb; ⏲ 10.00–22.00. Used to be midtown in Hercegovačka; helpful assistants.

OTHER PRACTICALITIES Many banks and internet cafés are located in the new town area, Nova Varoš [101 E3].

Banks

$ **Atlasmont Banka** Vaka Đurovića bb; www.atlasmontbanka.com; ⏲ 08.00–16.00 Mon–Fri, 08.00–13.00 Sat

$ **Hipotekarna Banka** Josipa Broza Tita 67, Stari Aerodrom; www.hb.co.me; ⏲ 08.00–20.00 Mon–Fri, 08.00–13.00 Sat

$ **Montenegrobanka** bul Stanka Dragojevića 46; bul Revolucije br 1; www.nlb.me; ⏲ 08.00–20.00 Mon–Fri, 08.00–13.00 Sat

$ **Podgorička Banka** ul Novaka Miloševa br 8a; www.pgbanka.com; ⏲ 09.00–17.00 Mon–Fri

Business visitor information

American Chamber of Commerce Rimski trg 4/V, Telenor Bldg; ☏020 621328; e info@amcham.me; www.amcham.me

Centralna Banka Crne Gore (CBCG) bul Svetog Petra Cetinjskog 6; www.cb-mn.org

Ministry of Finance Stanka Dragojevića 2; www.mif.gov.me/en/ministry

Ministry of Foreign Affairs & European Integration Stanka Dragojevića 2; ☏020 246357; www.mvpei.gov.me/en/ministry

Ministry of Sustainable Development & Tourism www.mrt.gov.me/en/ministry

Ministry of Economy Rimski trg 46; www.mek.gov.me/en/ministry

Ministry of Transport & Maritime Affairs Rimski trg 46; www.minsaob.gov.me/en/ministry

Montenegro Chamber of Economy Novaka Miloševa 29/II; ☏020 230545; www.privrednakomora.me

Opština (Town Hall) Njegoševa 13; www.podgorica.me

Prime Minister's Office Jovana Tomaševića bb; ☏020 242530

English-speaking school

QSI International School of Montenegro Donja Gorica bb, 81000 Podgorica; ☏020 641734; e montenegro@qsi.org; www.qsi.org/schoolpages/mtg/home/. 10mins from centre of Podgorica on road to Cetinje. A new purpose-built building with large classrooms, plenty of natural light, & a grassy play area. International curriculum taught in English; ages 3–18.

Hairdressers

Dragova Salon [100 A1] Hercegovačka. Stylist Marija does great work for a very small number of euros. She doesn't speak English.

Zoran Several branches inc Bratstva i Jedinstva 51 & Njegoševa 29; www.frizerzoran.me

Internet

Most hotels have Wi-Fi, usually free, as do many cafés & bars. There are also several free Wi-Fi hotspots, including trg Republika and part of Njegoševa; look for the 'MAIN-CITY-FREE' network. Internet cafés open & close but are invariably cheap.

Net Centar ul Vučedolska 13, across from the National Theatre; ☏020 403444/5; ⏲ 09.00–20.00 Mon–Fri, 09.00–14.00 Sat

Planet Telecom bul Sv Petra Cetinjskog 3; ☏020 202655; ⏲ 09.00–20.00

WWW Club Bokeška 3; m 069 452069; ⏲ 08.00–02.00 daily

Medical facilities

ARS Medica [off 100 C1] Gavro Vuković; ☏020 227227; e arsmedica@t-com.me; www.arsmedica.co.me. General.

✚ **Clinical Centre of Montenegro** [100 B6]
Ljubljanska bb; ✆020 412412; www.kccg.me
✚ **Codra** [101 E7] www.codrahospital.
com Radosava Burića, ✆020 648335.
Montenegro's first private hospital.
✚ **Health Centre** [100 A4] ✆020 265322/3;
emergency: ✆020 665513
✚ **Podgorica Hospital** [101 E2] ✆020 225125
or 243726

Pharmacies
✚ **Montefarm Kruševac** bul Svetog Petra
Cetinjskog; ✆020 241441
✚ **Montefarm Podgorica** Slobode 26; ✆020
230798

Post offices
✉ **Slobode 1** [101 E4] Across the street from
Crna Gora Hotel; www.postacg.me; ⏲ 07.00–
20.00 Mon–Sat
✉ **Moskovska 32** [100 B4] An alternative small
post office, close to several amenities.

Sources of local information for visitors/expatriates
Daily News Montenegro www.
dailynewsmontenegro.com. Online magazine.
Internations www.internations.org/expats/
members/montenegro/podgorica. Global network
& online guide for the international community;
information exchange for foreigners living in
Podgorica; membership required.
Narodna Biblioteka Radosav Ljumović
(National Library) [100 A2] Vaka Đurovića bb;
✆020 664217; e info@nbp.me; www.nbp.me;
⏲ 07.00–20.00 Mon–Fri, 07.00–15.00 Sat
Podgorica www.podgorica.me. Local government
website (with English version), especially useful for
things like local bus timetables & healthcare.
Podgorica In Your Pocket PgIYP, c/o Marko
Mirović, Goričani bb, 81304 Golubovci; e Podgorica
@inyourpocket.com; www.inyourpocket.com.
Excellent English-language booklet, updated every
6mths, with listings & helpful info. Complimentary
& available from larger hotels, tourist offices, etc,
or download online.

WHAT TO SEE
Daily market [101 G6] Beside the Mall of Montenegro on Bratstva i Jedinstva, in the direction of Virpazar and Skadar Lake, there is a colourful and extensive daily market (*Velika Pijaca*) stocked with produce from surrounding villages. It's well worth a visit even if you're not intending to do any food preparation while in Podgorica.

Museums
Palace of the Petrovićs and Contemporary Art Gallery [100 C6] (*On Ljubljanska in Kruševac, to the west of Sportski Centar Morača;* ✆ *020 243513;* e *csucg@t-com.me;* ⏲ *07.00–14.00 & 17.00–21.00 Mon–Fri, 10.00–13.00 Sat; entry free*) The mansion resembles the Royal Palace in Cetinje. Built towards the end of the 19th century it is sadly now the only public building in Podgorica which reflects that era. The father of King Nikola, Grand Duke Mirko Petrović Njegoš, lived here after leading the Montenegrin army in the 1858 battle of Grahovo, one of its most famed victories against the Turks (see pages 242–3). Today the museum contains decorations, paintings and sculptures from around the world, some of which belonged to the royal family. It also houses a collection of 20th-century works by Balkan artists, a number of them Montenegrin.

Podgorica City Museum (Muzej Grada Podgorice) [101 F4] (Historical and Ethnographic Museum of the District of Podgorica) (*ul Marka Miljanova 4;* ✆ *020 242543;* e *pgmuzej@t-com.me;* ⏲ *12.00–20.00 Tue–Fri, 09.00–14.00 Sat–Sun; entry adult/child €5/1*) A well-curated and displayed archaeological and cultural collection showing the history of the region including pre-Christian bronzes, Hellenistic and Roman artefacts, icons, printed works, and regional versions of national costume and jewellery. A significant art collection is incorporated.

Natural History Museum [101 E5] (*trg Nikola Kovačevića 7, behind the clocktower in Stara Varoš;* \ *020 633184;* e *prmuzej@t-com.me; www.pmcg.co.me;* ⊕ *09.00–12.00 Mon–Fri; entry free*) Established in 1995, the museum and institute are devoted to 'the protection of nature', and to the ongoing study of it. The collection is made up of 11 sections: algae, mosses, fungi, ferns and flowering plants, invertebrates, insects, amphibians, reptiles, birds, mammals, and Palaeozoic specimens.

AROUND PODGORICA

MONASTERY OF DAJBABE [map 78] This curious cavern monastery was founded in 1897 by Father Simeon Popović who, inspired by the natural vaulting, painted the irregular face of the rock comprehensively with religious imagery. Unfortunately, humidity has resulted in some loss of definition; even so the effect he created makes a visit to the little church a singular experience.

Getting there Some 4km southwest of Podgorica, off the Virpazar–Petrovac road; take Bratstva i Jedinstva out of the city in the direction of Skadar Lake and the airport. The monastery is signed right near the large KAP aluminium works.

DUKLIJA [map 78] This extensive excavation is the site of the ancient city of Duklija (Latin *Doclea*). It is believed to have been settled originally by the Illyrians at the convergence of three rivers – Morača, Zeta and Širalija – to provide a natural protective moat. It subsequently became one of the first Illyrian towns to be conquered by the Romans and it has been claimed that the Emperor Diocletian (AD284–304) was born here. When Sir Arthur Evans excavated the site between 1875 and 1882, an early necropolis was uncovered, proof that at one time Duklija maintained a population numbering between 8,000 and 10,000, with a 10km sewer system. Ruins of the town centre suggest there was a grandiose forum and basilica, ornate with marble and stucco. Large stones lie half buried in the soft turf: the luxury of a bygone era, now just a forlorn reminder scattered in the empty pasture of today. Much work remains to be done and in all probability you will have the place to yourself.

Getting there About 3km northwest of Podgorica, take the secondary road to Danilovgrad. From there turn right in the direction of Spuž, crossing the Zeta River, and then right again on a minor road towards Cerovice and Durkovici, crossing the tributary Širalija and the railway line to Nikšić.

MEDUN Around 13km northeast of Podgorica, on the road to Vrbka and Orahovo and lying on the Kukla Plain, Medun dates from the 4th century BC and from the very beginning was a fortressed city. Cyclopean stones are all that remains of its massive walls today. Ruined Gothic basilica columns, sarcophagi and traces of a bridge across the River Morača can also be seen. Founded by the Illyrian Labeati and Medeati tribes, who called it Meteon, it finally fell to the Romans in AD167 after a battle in which they captured the last Illyrian King, Gentije, and his family. Contested repeatedly over the centuries, it was taken in 1456 by the Turks in their relentless drive through eastern Europe. It is an intriguing site and holds many secrets yet to be revealed. There are, for example, reliefs that would appear to bear evidence of a snake cult. This, perhaps, has a connection with coastal finds linked to the ancient myth concerning Cadmus and Harmonia and their metamorphosis into serpents (see page 112).

Though there is still plenty of excavation waiting to be done, Medun receives more attention than Duklija because in recent history it was home to the Montenegrin hero Duke Marko Miljanov, whose **museum** (📞 *020 719247*; e *pgmuzej@t-com.me*; 🕐 *08.00–14.00 Tue–Sun*) stands halfway up the hill. The duke was leader of the romantic Kuči tribe, whose lands stretch to the Albanian border. He was a renowned warrior, so it's perhaps a little surprising that in 1901 at the age of 68 he died of natural causes. More surprising though was that he was an autodidact who learned to read only as an adult, yet he became a respected writer and philosopher. His edict:

it is important to think before you act; to be first a hero in the mind; it is finer to defend others from yourself than yourself from others.

There is a good statue of the duke in Karađorđev Park, Podgorica, east of the Crna Gora Hotel. He and his wife are now buried in the acropolis in front of the small church, normally locked but with shutters through which you can inspect the bare interior, which stands at the top of the hill. It is well worth scrambling through the undergrowth to the top of the steep fortress – if only for awesome 360° views: the Kučka Mountains to the northeast; to the south, all the coastal mountains stretched out for your singular delectation, from Rumija to Lovćen and a distant Orjen to the west, and below it all fields of tall grass, a hologram in eau-de-Nil.

The museum is full of fascinating treasures, well worth a visit even if you cannot read the Cyrillic labelling (at the time of writing the curator is monolingual too). The costumes, both Montenegrin and Albanian, could surely inspire some latter-day designer.

TUZI Around 10km due southeast of Podgorica, Tuzi lies in the middle of the plain, an unremarkable expanse of withered grass stretching to the border with Albania at Božaj–Hani i Hotit, 15km beyond. This straggly settlement emits an air of impermanence common to many border towns, but in fact the bustling little marketplace has been here since Roman times, when it was already an established stop on the route connecting Škodra (Skadar/Scutari) with cities to the north and west. It is understood that a number of ancient roads crossed the territory that was to become Montenegro.

Getting there Buses go to Tuzi from Podgorica several times daily. Bus lines 41 and 42 are the most regular, but you can also get 44 and 45. For timetables, see www.podgorica.me/saobracaj-0, Prigradske linije.

Where to stay and eat

🏠 **Hotel Liria** (22 rooms) 📞020 875700; www.liriahotel.com. Opposite the bus station, rooms have AC, TV, Wi-Fi. Restaurant, nice terrace. Parking. English spoken. €€€

✕ **Restaurant Nijagara** Cijevna bb Kuće Rakića; 🕐 10.00–23.00 daily. Attractively situated by waterfalls on the River Cijevna, 6km from the centre of Tuzi, & very popular with Podgorica people, especially during the summer. Turn right off Tuzi road in the direction of Albania, just before the river bridge. €€€

INTO ALBANIA With a second border post opened at Sukobin further south near Ulcinj, it is now feasible to make a round trip from Podgorica to Škodra in Albania, without retracing one's steps (see page 304). Note, however, that the passenger railway link between Škodra and Podgorica has been suspended for some time and it now transports freight only.

From the border at Božaj it is now possible with a 4x4 or a good mountain bike to traverse the Vermosh Gorge in Albania and eventually reach Grnčar, Gusinje and Plav (see page 284). Note, however, that this route is not for the faint-hearted: it involves negotiating a riverbed and other obstacles, and is out of the question in wintertime. Improvements to the road surface have been rumoured to be 'imminent' for some time, but for the time being, while the journey through the Vermosh cuts the distance between Gusinje and Podgorica from 200km to 80km, it is likely to take rather longer.

4

Bay of Kotorska

HERCEG NOVI

This sunny city is splendidly sheltered from the extremes of the elements by lofty **Mt Orjen** (1,893m) rising above, and two lush green arms of land reaching out to each other across the bay. To the west, the Prevlaka Peninsula (see box, page 120) only emerged from years in limbo under UN occupancy in early 2003, while the eastern promontory constitutes the beautiful and as yet relatively underdeveloped Luštica Peninsula. Between the two, the sentinel island of **Mamula** was in Austro-Hungarian times a fortress and later, in World War II, served as a prison camp. Now the walls are guardian only to the wild *agave*, the century plant.

In recent years Herceg Novi's monuments have become overgrown with wisteria, wild rose and ivy. The city is renowned for its flowers, for the many exotic plants brought back from different corners of the world by its sea captains. In springtime a sweet cocktail of orange blossom, honeysuckle and jasmine permeates every cranny. (They will tell you wryly that it is a Dalmatian tradition that if you steal a cutting it will thrive when you replant it, but that if you ask for a cutting it will grow more slowly.)

During the last decade the population of Herceg Novi has rapidly expanded, with many Serbian refugees from Croatia and Bosnia establishing residence and the town, which formerly had a majority of Catholics and a significant Croatian minority, now has a Serbian Orthodox majority. But the overriding spirit of the people inured to transition has remained remarkably robust.

Perhaps it is the very beauty of the place that has encouraged its inhabitants to adopt a positive role in its upkeep. The absence of litter and the maintenance of the public spaces are conspicuous. The intrinsic beauty of its setting has surely influenced the artistic aspect that has developed. Among others, leading Montenegrin painter Vojslav Stanić has his home and studio here and, although the art academy has recently transferred to Cetinje, the town hosts regular exhibitions.

With its equable Mediterranean climate, this is a resort for all seasons but in high summer it gets quite crowded. Blossoming spring and golden autumn are surely to be preferred.

HISTORY From the very beginning, sovereignty over this territory has been highly valued because of its strategic position at the mouth of the Boka Kotorska (the Gulf of Kotor), and after its foundation in 1382 by Tvrtko I, ruler of Bosnia, the 'City of Stairways' changed hands with grim regularity. The name comes from *herceg* (duke) Stjepan Vukšić, who fortified the town in the middle of the 15th century, though to little avail, for in 1483 it was seized by the Turks who occupied it in effect for the following 200 years. The Turks' occupation was temporarily lost in 1538 after a

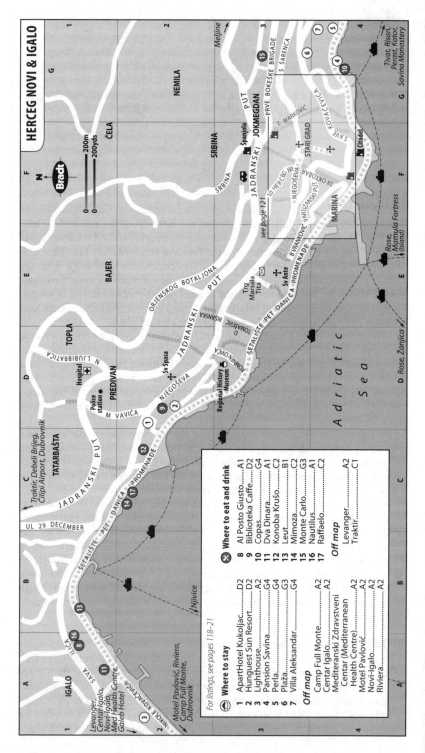

HERCEG NOVI & IGALO

see page 121

For listings, see pages 118–21

Where to stay

1 ApartHotel Kukoljac.............D2
2 Hunguest Sun Resort............D2
3 Lighthouse............................A2
4 Pansion Savina......................G4
5 Perla......................................G4
6 Plaža......................................G3
7 Villa Aleksandar....................G4

Off map

   Camp Full Monte...................A2
   Centar Igalo..........................A2
   Mediteranski Zdravstveni
   Centar (Mediterranean
   Health Centre).....................A2
   Motel Pavlović.......................A2
   Novi-Igalo..............................A2
   Riviera...................................A2

Where to eat and drink

8 Al Posto Giusto....................A1
9 Biblioteka Caffe....................D2
10 Copas...................................G4
11 Dva Dinara...........................A1
12 Konoba Krušo.......................C2
13 Leut......................................B1
14 Mimoza.................................C2
15 Monte Carlo..........................G3
16 Nautilus................................A1
17 Raffaelo................................C2

Off map

   Levanger...............................A2
   Traktir...................................C1

116

Spanish-reinforced Venetian attack, to be regained a year later under Khair ed-din Barbarossa (the corsair who in 1533 had become grand admiral of the Ottoman fleet). In 1687 the Turks were finally expelled by a Venetian force supported by the Montenegrins, the Maltese knights and the papal fleet. Thereafter Venice held the town until the republic's downfall in 1797, after which it became a pawn between the powers involved in the Napoleonic wars, ruled by Austria (1797–1806), Russia (1806–07), France (1807–13), then Britain and Montenegro, each for a few months only. In 1814, along with the rest of the Dalmatian coast, it became part of the Austro-Hungarian Empire and remained so until the end of World War I.

GETTING THERE AND AWAY Herceg Novi lies 50km from Dubrovnik city, 30km from Dubrovnik's Čilipi Airport, 23km from Tivat (where the airport is 4km east of town), and 112km from the capital, Podgorica. A taxi to/from either Tivat or Čilipi airport will set you back around €35–40 each way.

Southwards from **Dubrovnik** the Adriatic Highway (route E80) winds through rolling scrubby hills dotted with cypress and mulberry with the long bare escarpment of Snije Žnica shielding the northern valley visible to the left. After the frontier controls at **Debeli Brjeg**, the border of the old Republic of Dubrovnik, the route gradually descends to the fertile plain of Sutorina, where ruins of a Roman settlement have been found, and to the sparkling sea beneath the terraced gardens of Herceg Novi.

By bus The bus station [116 F3] (*ul dr Jova Bijelića br 1;* \ *031 321225*) is at the top of the town and there are services to most destinations on the coast, some vehicles taking the long road round the Boka Kotorska via Risan, Perast and Kotor; others crossing the narrows by ferry and cutting the time it takes to reach Tivat and beyond.

To **Podgorica**, there is a roughly half-hourly service, sometimes a bus, other times a minibus. The journey takes 3–3½ hours, €9 one way (plus €1 if purchased in advance).

To **Dubrovnik**, there are usually three buses a day (€12, plus €1 for each bag carried in the hold) and they will let you off on the main road outside Čilipi Airport if you warn them in advance – although this will entail a 500m walk to the terminal.

For information on other destinations, the schedules of which are subject to unpredictable change, consult **Autosaobracj AJ** (*Trebinjska 48 Igalo;* \ *031 336006*); or the **bus station.** There is also a page in English on the city website (*www.hercegnovi.cc*), giving details of some routes and times. For travel from Croatia, see pages 35–6.

GETTING AROUND As with most Montenegrin cities, Herceg Novi is best explored **on foot**, but getting from the sea to the top of the town involves lots of steps, which are almost impossible to avoid. Indeed this is known as the 'town of stairs'. And beware the marble paving stones in the old quarter, which can be treacherous when wet.

The seafront walkway extends all the way from below Savina monastery to Igalo (approximately 7km), a very pleasant walk with plenty to catch the eye – though in April 2014 part of it was being repaved. In summer, there is a **mini-tram** which chugs along the length of the seafront.

Drivers should be aware that the central part of the town has a one-way system. **Parking** within the city is always difficult and it's often easier to find a legal roadside parking space east of the bus station and walk down. The central part of town is divided into two zones and parking is charged accordingly: zone 2 costs €0.40 per hour or €4.00 per day; zone 1 costs €0.50 per hour with no daily rate. Charges apply 07.00–21.00 Monday to Saturday; Sundays are free. Payment can be made either at a kiosk or by SMS.

Car hire

* 🚗 **Budget** Njegoševa 90; ✆031 321000; e budget@t-com.me. Reasonable prices for Opel Astra for 7-day rental, unlimited mileage; Amex, Diners Club, MasterCard, Visa accepted. Pleasant, efficient & hooked into the Budget system; 1-way rentals to 3rd countries are possible.

🚗 **Europcar** Njegoševa 87b; ✆031 321999; e matkovic@t-com.me. Fiat Punto, VW Sharan, etc. Chauffeur-driven option available.

🚗 **In Montenegro** Šetalište Pet Danica 34/6; ✆031 321195; e info@inmontenegro.com. Renault Clio, Megane Grandtour, etc. Free delivery up to 25km. Visa accepted.

🚗 **Simplyrentacar** ✆031 321519; m 068 634774; e simplyrentacar@gmail.com. CCs accepted.

Taxis There's a taxi rank at the bus station [116 F3] (✆ *031 321399*). Also try:

🚗 **More Taxi** ✆19730
🚗 **Novi Taxi** ✆19767

TOURIST INFORMATION AND TOUR OPERATORS

Tourist information

ℹ️ **Tourist office/information centre** Jova Đabovića 12; ✆031 350820; e info@hercegnovi.travel; www.hercegnovi.travel; ⊕ 08.00–14.00 Mon–Sat. On a stairway midway between bus station & Njegoševa, signed from latter. Helpful & experienced staff but their stock of brochures is limited.

Tour operators

* **Black Mountain Adventure Travel** e info@montenegroholiday.com; www.montenegroholiday.com. Internet-based company run by a young English couple who set it up in 2005 to organise adventure travel, inc hiking, mountain biking, kayaking, rafting, canyoning &

sailing on the Boka Kotorska, as well as bespoke itineraries, accommodation & transfers. UK registered, with knowledgeable local guides. Their enthusiasm is infectious & they know their stuff.

Gorbis Travel & Service Njegoševa 66; ✆031 324423; e office.hn@gorbis.com; www.gorbis.com. One of a chain providing a full range of domestic & international travel.

Trend Travel [121 E2] trg Hercega Stjepana 4 (also known as trg Belavista); ✆031 321639; m 069 570027; e trendtravel@t-com.me; www.trendtravelmontenegro.com. Helpful agency offering excursions to Ostrog Monastery, Skadar Lake, Dubrovnik & elsewhere; organising rafting & other activities; & arranging transfers & accommodation.

🏠 WHERE TO STAY

Near the border

Off map, page 116.

🏠 **Motel Pavlović** (8 rooms); ✆031 688224. Fairly basic motel on the main road leading from the Croatian border to Herceg Novi. TV, AC, no English spoken, but German & some Italian. €€€

⋀ **Camp Full Monte** m 067 899208; e holidays@full-monte.com; www.full-monte.com. Take the first left turn after crossing the border on the Adriatic Highway, signed to Prijevor, & follow the signs. Very popular clothing-optional eco-campsite, thoughtfully designed on the

peaceful slopes of Mt Orjen. Environmentally sound in every detail, the camp is largely self-sufficient & beautifully maintained. It's a 15min drive from nearest beach (Njivice, with designated naturist section), or cool off in the small mountain stream on the property. Built & run by a British couple, Steve & Denise, who offer some free bed & food to volunteers for specific projects: rebuilding stone walls, organic gardening, etc. €10 pp per night with own tent; fully equipped tent hire €15–25 pp inc continental b/fast. ⊕ Closed in winter. €–€€

In Herceg Novi

Maps, pages 116, 121.

⌂ **Hunguest Sun Resort** (230 rooms) ul Sv Bubala; ☎031 355022; e hotelsunresort@ hunguesthotels.com; www.hunguesthotels.hu. Refurbished in 2006, a park of Hungarian-owned hotels stretching for 400m, comprising 3 hotels & 4 apt buildings, all with AC & most with sea views. 3 restaurants & several bars, own beach, wellness centre, jacuzzis, solarium, 2 pools. Package deals available for stays of 4 nights or more. €€€€

✳ ⌂ **Perla** (16 rooms & 4 suites) Šetalište Pet Danica; ☎031 345700; e perla@t-com.me; www.perla.me. A delightful, cool hotel with sophisticated atmosphere, good food & good English, where everything works. It is signposted from the east of the city, just below the Savina Monastery complex, on the western outskirts of Meljine, a 15min stroll from the town centre. All rooms come with fridge, minibar, satellite TV, AC & internet access. Book ahead to get what you want: rooms with sea views cost the same as those without & are much nicer, if slightly noisier; the next-door annexe is extremely similar but a bit cheaper & for free Wi-Fi you'll need to take your laptop to the main hotel. Restaurant (€€€€) on the edge of the Boka; cross the small road for b/fast & dinner beside the water. Plenty of sun-loungers & umbrellas on a pleasant stone-fronted swimming area. Gym. Transfers & excursions arranged (€50 to Čilipi Airport). Car hire. Limited parking. All CCs accepted. €€€–€€€€

⌂ **Plaža** (286 rooms) ul Sava Kovačeviča 58; ☎031 346151; e vektraboka@t-com-me; www. bokaturist.com. A large old state hotel that's changed ownership but not personality, though reconstruction is slowly proceeding. On the beach with good sea views but distinctly shabby & a bit severe. CCs accepted. €€€–€€€€

⌂ **Villa Aleksandar** (16 rooms) ul Save Kovačevića 64; ☎031 345806; e hotel.aleksander@t-com.me; www.

hotelvilaaleksandar.com. 300m from the beach, with free chairs & umbrellas. Rooms have sea views, balconies, AC, cable TV, telephone. Aquarius Restaurant (€€€); bar & pool. Good English & a warm welcome. Sgl supplement 30%. Children under 2 free, up to 12 yrs 30% discount, 50% for 2nd child sharing a room (FB €9 per day extra). €€€–€€€€

⌂ **ApartHotel Kukoljac** (23 apts) Njegoševa 111a; ☎031 321719; e vilakukoljac@gmail.com; www.vilakukoljac.com. Bright & fairly spacious accommodation, all with AC, TV & kitchen; some (higher rent) with sea views. Private beach. Visa & MasterCard accepted. €€€

⌂ **Aurora** (6 rooms; 3 suites) Šetalište Pet Danica 42; m 069 021600; e info@aurorahotel. me; www.aurorahotel.me. New small hotel at foot of steps down from old town. Conference room, cinema & coffee bar. AC, TV & Wi-Fi. €€€

⌂ **Pansion Savina** (21 apts) Šetalište Pet Danica 99; m 064 1605365; e kancelarija@savina. rs; www.savina.rs. Attractive apt-hotel beside the Perla with a café & a sunbathing area. AC, TV. €€€

⌂ **Škver Apartments** (8 apts) Vasa Ćukovića bb; m 067 284224; e jelenasiriski@hotmail. com; www.skver-apartments.com. Stylish, wood-furnished apts (all dbl), all with AC. Admiral Restaurant. €€€

⌂ **Villa Palma** (4 rooms) Šetalište Pet Danica 62A; ☎031 345797; e momo@villapalma.me; http://villapalma.me. At the quieter end of the walkway. Restaurant (see Copas, below) with rooms. AC, TV. Sea view, a tiny beach & terraces. CCs accepted. €€€

✳ ⌂ **Apartments Mediterano** (27 beds) Partizanski put; m 069 897048; e martinettila@yahoo.com; www.facebook.com/ ApartmentsMediterano. Excellent new hostel, in a renovated 100-year-old building, opened in 2014. Six rooms, 3 with 3 beds & 3 with 6 beds, on 2 floors, each with communal lounge, kitchen, etc. Nice leafy terrace. Central location, halfway down Partizanska. Lovely owners & a very welcome new budget choice in Herceg Novi. €–€€

Private villas Enquire at the helpful local tourist office, which has a long list of private accommodation, either rooms with a bath in private houses or villas (*sobe*, the equivalent of British B&Bs; see page 54) or apartments for short-term rental. You will see many *sobe* signs along the coastal highway. They are almost always clean and welcoming as well as being inexpensive, though less so on the coast in high summer. Think in terms of €10–25 per person in season.

✖ WHERE TO EAT AND DRINK
Near the border
Off map, page 116.
There is a Lukoil mini-market/petrol station shortly after the Croatian border. It features good clean toilets, a café (*no food served, sandwiches available summer only*) & an economical opportunity to pick up basic supplies. Helpful staff with good English.

✖ **Traktir** 800m from the Croatian border, on the road to Herceg Novi in Sutorina; ⏲ 10.00–23.00. The name of this restaurant, opened in 2010, means 'road house' in Azerbaijan. Good English & a warm welcome. Attractively decorated with a pleasant tree-lined terrace & a wood-fired rotisserie for speciality dishes: whole lamb or suckling pig. Russian, Azerbaijani & Montenegrin food. Visa & MasterCard accepted. €€€

In Herceg Novi
Maps, pages 116 & 121.
In Herceg Novi there are dozens of restaurants & cafés to choose from, the majority along the Šetalište Pet Danica (the sea-facing promenade), or within the squares of the Stari Grad (Old Town). Simply take a stroll & choose one that takes your fancy.

✖ **Admiral** Šetalište Pet Danica bb; ☎031 323265; m 069 149144. Housed in a former customs house, this is a lively spot with some evening entertainment in season. There's a roof terrace overlooking the marina & boats. Adriatic influenced menu specialising in seafood. €€€€
✖ **Copas** Šetalište Pet Danica bb; ☎031 345797; http://villapalma.me. On its own private beach

with a big terrace overlooking the sea. Family-run (also rooms to let; see Villa Palma, page 119). €€€
✖ **Dva Dinara** Šetalište Pet Danica; ⏲ 08.00–23.00. Relaxed *konoba*-style place offering decent food with a Serbian accent & good value. AC. English spoken. No CCs. €€€
✳ ✖ **Konoba Feral** Šetalište Pet Danica 47; ☎031 322232. ⏲ 09.00–24.00. Probably the best prepared of the usual fishy *konoba* menu, facing the harbour. Atmospheric & usually packed. CCs accepted. €€€
✖ **Mimoza** Šetalište Pet Danica bb; ☎031 322893; www.mimoza.me; ⏲ summer 07.00–02.00, winter 07.00–24.00. On the 1st floor beside the beach at Igalo, near the Health Institute. Good English & very good seafood. €€€
✖ **Monte Carlo Vidikovac** Dubrava, Manastirska 4; ☎031 345277; ⏲ 07.00–23.00. On hillside above Savina Monastery complex, with panoramic views over town & sea. (Vidikovac loosely translates as 'viewpoint'.) €€€
✖ **Portofino** trg Belavista; ⏲ 09.00 until customers go home. A renowned meeting place for locals & expatriates with good bistro food in season, drinks only in winter. Run by brothers Miki & Zelko who speak good English. There are generally English newspapers (only a week old) by the bar. €€€
✖ **Gradska Kafana** Njegoševa 31. For drinks & pastries in the town centre with a super terrace overlooking the sea. No CCs. €€
✳ ✖ **Pod lozom** trg N Djurkovića bb; ☎031 322800. Friendly & relaxed with tables in covered area outside. Good-value & very tasty Montenegrin dishes. The updater's favourite place to eat in Herceg Novi. Visa & MasterCard accepted. €€

THE PREVLAKA PENINSULA

The Prevlaka Peninsula, the disputed border area between Montenegro and Croatia, was for some years the home of UNMOP (the UN Observers' Mission in Prevlaka), the UN's smallest peacekeeping force and the only one never to have suffered casualties. On 8 October 2002 the UN Secretary-General announced, to the great disappointment of the garrison, that it would be withdrawn in December of that year. Prevlaka was technically Croatian territory. Montenegro said it needed the peninsula to ensure the security of the Boka Kotorska; Croatia disagreed.

Relative harmony has now been achieved, with Prevlaka remaining Croatian and Montenegro in control of the surrounding waters – satisfactory for everybody but the blue berets, one feels.

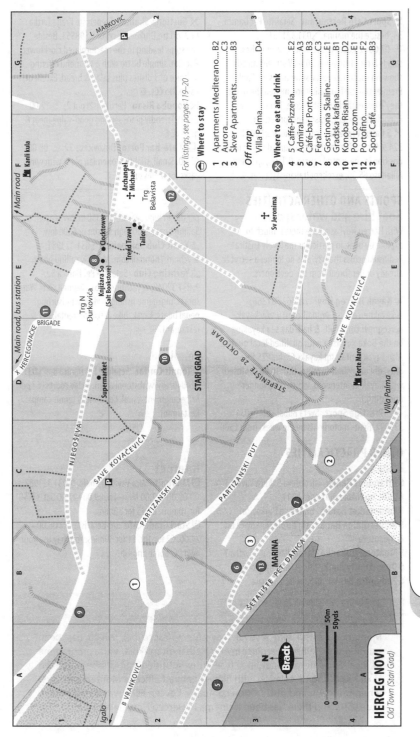

HERCEG NOVI
Old Town (Stari Grad)

For listings, see pages 119–20

Where to stay
1. Apartments Mediterano....B2
2. Aurora..........................C3
3. Skver Apartments...........B3

Off map
Villa Palma.......................D4

Where to eat and drink
4. 5 Caffé-Pizzeria.............E2
5. Admiral........................A3
6. Café-bar Porto...............B3
7. Feral...........................C3
8. Gostinona Skaline...........E1
9. Gradska kafana..............B1
10. Konoba Risan................D2
11. Pod Lozom....................E1
12. Portofino.....................F2
13. Sport Café....................B3

✘ **Sport Café Restaurant** Šetalište Pet Danica 34, beside the marina; ☏ 031 321161; ⏱ 07.00–23.00. Pizza, burgers, sandwiches, salads & nice fruit juice; 20+ TV screens mostly showing sporting events, sometimes inc English Premier League football; if you missed the match, they'll generally know the score. Terrace or AC. Friendly & efficient, reasonable prices. €€

✘ **5 Caffé-Pizzeria** trg N Đurkovića; ☏ 031 324264; e caffepizzeriapetica@gmail.com. Sunny position in the central square. B/fasts; spaghetti Milanese €5.80; excellent Italian-style ices. €

✘ **Gostiona Skaline** Stepenište Kralja Tvrtka br 2, off trg Đurkovića; m 069 598553. Beside the steps leading to the machicolated clocktower. Popular, simple bistro with a set menu offering a choice of 3 dishes plus salad & bread. Excellent value. No CCs. €

✘ **Konoba Risan** Partizanski put 2; ⏱ 12.00–23.00. Friendly place serving good-value meat & grills. €€

🍷 **Café-Bar Porto** Đukovićeva 22; ⏱ 08.00–02.00. Small, slightly Bohemian place with wine casks for tables outside. €

SPORTS AND OTHER ACTIVITIES
Boat hire and water sports

With Herceg Novi as a base there is much to explore by boat, in particular the lovely Luštica Peninsula across the bay, alas no longer a secret & already under threat from the developers.

🛶 **Kayak Herceg Novi** m 067 531366; e kayakhercegnovi@gmail.com; www.kayak-hercegnovi.com. Full- & half-day sea kayaking on the Boka Kotorska with qualified local guides. Also kayak rental: sgl kayaks €5/hr, €25 for 8hrs; dbl only slightly more. (Not to be confused with Kayak Montenegro, which is no longer operating.)

🚤 **Prestige Sport** Sveta Bubala bb; ☏ 031 323092. Rents motorboats by the week, from €500

per day in high season, or €350 in low season. Sailing boats €400 high season or €300 low.

⚓ **Yacht Club Spinnaker** ☏ 031 323981; e ychnm@hotmail.com. Motor & sailing boats.

⚓ **Yachting Club** Šetalište Pet Danica 32; ☏ 031 32040; e yachtingclub32@gmail.com. Water sports, big-game fishing, diving, windsurfing, pedal boats; kayak, bike & scooter rental; bar & restaurant.

Tennis

🎾 **Tennis Centar** Šetalište Pet Danica 8a; ☏ 031 324040; www.sbstennis.com. 4 clay courts (*€7 per hr*), equipment rental. Coaching & tennis camps. Restaurant.

OTHER PRACTICALITIES
Banks

$ **Atlasmont Banka** Njegoševa 5; Mića Vavića 3
$ **CKB** trg Nikole Đurkovića br 11
$ **Euromarket Banka** trg Nikole Đurkovića
$ **Komercijalna Banka** trg Nikole Đurkovića bb & Njegoševa 40
$ **Montenegrobanka** Stepenište Kralja Tvrtka 1
$ **Opportunity Bank** Nikole Đurkovića br 26
$ **Podgorica Banka** ul Sava Ilića 5, Igalo

Internet

🖥 **Mikrobit** Mića Vavića 3, Igalo; ☏ 031 321987; ⏱ 08.00–22.00 Mon–Fri, 09.00–22.00 Sat. €0.50 for 10mins, €1.25 for 30mins.

🖥 **Stari Grade Café** trg Belavista, ⏱ 08.00–24.00. €2 for 1hr, €1 for 30mins. You may use your own PC. Some English.

HERCEG NOVI FILM FESTIVAL

Montenegro's top film festival (*www.hercegfest.co.me*), which has been running since 1987, takes place in August in the Kanli kula, with a programme of local and international films (the latter subtitled, not dubbed). Herceg Novi has a long association with film – the head office of Montenegro's first film production and distribution company, Lovćen Film, was based here in the 1950s, and there has been a cinema in Herceg Novi since around 1920.

Pharmacies

✚ **Montefarm** Stepenište 28 Oktobra 1; ☎031 322848; & Nikole Ljubibratića 1; ☎031 325353
✚ **Stari Grad** ul 28 Oktobra br 1; ☎031 343153
✚ **Veselin** Njegoševa bb; ☎031 321712; ⏰ 08.00–20.00
✚ **Vujović** ul Spasića Mašare br 1; ☎031 322011

Other

✉ **Post office** [116 E3] Njegoševa br 31; r Igalo, ul Sava Ilića 1a (near seafront); ⏰ 07.30–20.00 Mon–Sat

Bookshop [121 E1] Knjižara So (Salt Bookstore) trg Nikole Đurkovića 3 (to right of steps leading up to clocktower); e knjizaraso@gmail.com; www. knjizaraso.com (Montenegrin only). Good up-to-date stock of local books, a few in English. Owner Neda is knowledgeable about the mountains.
✳ **Tailor/seamstress** [121 E2] Olja, trg Belavista (opposite church entrance); m 069 087937. Alterations or dressmaking (*€10 for a simple skirt or blouse*). Works fast.

WHAT TO SEE Remnants of the city's stormy past make an exciting jigsaw for visitors and the full extent of the old wall-fortified city warrants thorough investigation on foot. The steps are excellent exercise, too, so you may be killing two birds with one stone.

Standing high on a hilltop overlooking the bay, the best-preserved building is the **Fortress Španjola** [116 F3], started in 1538 by – not unexpectedly – the Spaniards. It was later finished by the Turks who left the inscription above the gate:

> This tower is erected by the sultans on the orders of Suliman, son of Suliman, the powerful and honourable knight. May he live long and attain happiness and fortune. Let the poets who arrive by road look on these works and exclaim at such beauty.

Not quite as succinct as Shelley's *Ozymandias* but not a bad try. The Montenegrins prefer to remember its Spanish provenance.

Rising above the town in the east are the ruins of the notorious **Kanli kula** (Bloody Tower) [121 F1] which served both as a defence fort and a prison for those who resisted the Turks. Traces of prisoners' messages and drawings are still visible on the walls – they too are not as succinct as Shelley but they get their message across.

The lower seaward-facing wall, **Forte Mare** [121 D4], was rebuilt under the Venetians; but note the Bosnian coat of arms (see *Šćepan Polje*, page 247) above the gate, Porta di Mare, leading to the sea. Today, coming from the east, one enters the town through the Forte Mare.

Also from the Venetian period is the Catholic parish **Church of St Jerome (Sv Jeronima)** [121 F3], whose altarpiece has the Virgin Mary with the saint rather thoughtfully depicted in a Herceg Novi setting (note a similar artistic licence in the St Ivan altarpiece in Budva, page 176). Several other churches from this time seem likely to have been built on sites previously occupied by mosques.

The entrance to the innermost section of the **old quarter** is beneath a machicolated tower built in 1667, 20 years before the departure of the Turks. Nowadays it holds a clock and is a symbol of the town. Beyond, in the centre of the pretty Belavista Square, is the small and beautifully proportioned **Church of the Archangel Michael (Sv Archangela Mihaila)** [121 F2], built in 1900 in Serbo-Byzantine style. On a warm evening soothing incense-infused prayer drifts from its open door, curling around the tables neatly grouped outside the cafés close by.

WEST OF HERCEG NOVI

TOPLA AND IGALO A 7km promenade, until the mid-20th century a railway line, joins Herceg Novi to Topla and Igalo to the west. Topla means 'warmth', so-called because it is purported to have the mildest climate in the Boka Kotorska. This is enhanced by pleasant beaches with a shallow sea particularly suitable for small children. In Venetian times it was a centre in itself and in the 19th century boasted its own merchant navy. Today, a carnival celebrating the blossoming of the bright yellow mimosa in February is one of the most colourful coastal festivals.

Walk down the slope to the east of Ivo Andrić Mansion, 'Writers' Club', on Njegoševa, to discover the **Regional History Museum** (**Zavičajni muzej**; see opposite) and its once lovely botanical garden.

🏠 Where to stay *Off map, page 116.*

As an alternative to a hotel in this area, consider staying at one of Igalo's health facilities (below).

🏠 **Riviera** Njivice; ☎031 356000; e rivierahotel@t-com.me; www.rivierahotelhn. com. West of Igalo in the direction of Prevlaka Peninsula, this attractive 4-star hotel beside the sea is valuable addition to the local hotel community. Large open pool. Bar & restaurant, with b/fast & dinner buffet. €€€€€

🏠 **Lighthouse** (60 rooms) ul Norveška 2; ☎031 331615; www.hotellighthouse.me. The former Metalurg was renovated in 2011, with AC, TV, restaurant, bar & a dive centre. HB €€€

🏠 **Novi Igalo** (28 rooms, 56 apts) Obala bb. Opened in 2010. TVs, fridges & safes in rooms; Wi-Fi in public areas. Restaurant serving Mediterranean cuisine. Private beach at 200m with free sun-loungers & umbrellas. €€€

Health facilities The silt from the seabed in this area has since ancient times been known for its special therapeutic qualities. As well as several hotels, Igalo hosts a major facility to utilise this resource in a large Scandinavian-style mineral spa and centre for thalassotherapy. The institute is under medical supervision and is open year-round. Any number of treatments (rheumatic, neurological, coronary rehabilitation, etc) are available, on either a residential or a day-visit basis. Prices are extremely reasonable in comparison with other European spas. This may be therapy on an industrial scale but standards are said to be very good. At the moment there are few British or American patients; most are Scandinavian, German, Russian or Polish. The **Galeb** mansion, once the residence of President Tito, is now part of this complex.

You can stay in the following health facilities:

✳ 🏠 **Mediteranski Zdravstveni Centar (Mediterranean Health Centre)**
(752 rooms & suites) Sava Ilića 5, 85347 Igalo; ☎031 658833; www.igalospa.com. Teaching affiliate of Podgorica Medical School, part of the University of Montenegro. 52 doctors, 93 registered nurses & 178 physiotherapists. Most rooms have sea-facing balconies, AC, TV & direct-dial telephones. Restaurant, bar, beauty centre, room service, tennis, gym, bowling, indoor pool, physiotherapy, hydrotherapy, cosmetic & aesthetic surgery,

acupuncture, alternative medicine, dentistry. Conference hall. 'Light' medical programme (3 therapies daily) €25 pp per day; 'basic' programme (5 therapies daily) €32. CCs accepted. HB low/high season €€€/€€€€; sgl rooms & suites €€€€

🏠 **Centar Igalo** (253 rooms) Sava Ilića 7; ☎031 332442 (reception), 031 332014 (sales); e centar-igalo@t-com.me; www.centar-igalo. com. Adjacent to the Mediterranean Health Centre & convenient for treatments. AC restaurant & summer terrace. Wi-Fi. €€€

✗ Where to eat and drink *Map, page 116.*

✗ **Konoba Krušo** Šetalište Pet Danica, Topla; ☎031 323238; e kruso@t-com.me; www.

konobakruso.me. On a quayside next to & connected with Raffaelo; terrace & beach with lounge chairs. Dock for boat tie-up. Menu concentrates on specialities of the region. Live music in season. €€€€

* ✕ **Leut** Njegoševa br 166, Sutorina; ✆031 670157. Atmospheric family-owned fish restaurant right beside the sea on the road to Dubrovnik. They have their own boat, as well as an airy covered terrace behind a big green hedge. Visa accepted. €€€€

* ✕ **Raffaelo** Šetalište Pet Danica, Topla; ✆031 323238. Café connected to Konoba Krušo. No CCs. €€€€

✕ **Al Posto Giusto** Nikole Kovačevića 6, Igalo; ✆031 331071; ⏰ 07.00–01.00. Translates to mean 'the Right Place' which it will be for you, particularly if you prefer your pizza cooked in a wood-fired oven. Terrace. Same ownership as Optimist in Tivat (page 158). €€€

✕ **Biblioteka Caffe** This library-themed coffee shop/bar is also a cool spot for an aperitif. No terrace. €€€

✕ **Levanger** Obala Nikole Kovačevića 24, Igalo. Low-key place with inside dining room (AC) that appeals to locals: more of a middle-aged crowd. Though they have an English menu, they don't speak it. Good for its type. €€€

✕ **Nautilus** Nikole Kovačevića 9, Igalo; ✆031 331883. Two family-owned branches quite close together; the one at this address has been there since 1970, is more ambitious, with a café downstairs & a decent restaurant upstairs, AC with good sea views. CCs accepted. €€€

Sports and other activities There is a **tennis club** in Igalo (m 068 042416), which offers individual and group classes, as well as courts to rent (€5–12 per hour).

Other practicalities Topla has a **bank**, Komercijalna Banka (*Šetalište Pet Danica, Poslovni centar Galeb*).

What to see

Regional History Museum (Zavičajni muzej) [116 D3] (⏰ 09.00–20.00 Mon–Sat; entry €2)
Built in the Baroque style 150 years ago as the home of the Komnenovića family, the Regional History Museum houses a collection dating from the Neolithic period through to the present day. This includes a comprehensive ethnographical history of the area, exhibits relating to the National War of Liberation, and a marvellous display of iconography with examples of the Dimitrijević–Rafailović School of the Boka. There's also a permanent art collection featuring works of local artists such as Vojo Stanić. If the bell isn't answered, wander around the back and look in the windows; you might find someone. Some English is spoken.

The museum's once lovely **botanical garden** at Mirka Komnenovića 9 is also worth a visit.

EAST OF HERCEG NOVI

SAVINA MONASTERY To the east of Herceg Novi, a short stroll down an oak-shaded pathway leads to the monastery where Njegoš received his early education. (If you're driving yourself, you'll find the vehicular access from the main road is just before Melinje.) Serenely set in woodland above the bay, the sanctuary is composed of a small and a larger Church of the Assumption of the Virgin, the cloister and a second little church on the hill above dedicated to **Sv Sava Nemanja**; appointed first archbishop of the Serbian Orthodox Church in 1219, he was to become their most revered saint.

It is unclear how early there was a religious presence in this lovely Boka location but it is believed that some church existed here as early as the 11th century. The present monastery dates from 1693 when monks, fleeing after the destruction of the Tvrdoš Monastery near Trebinje (Herzegovina), brought their treasury here for protection; today it forms a large part of the valuable collection that is now on display. Most treasured is a crystal and silver cross believed to have belonged to Sv Sava Nemanja himself, but you will also find a silver model of the original monastery at Tvrdoš (1685), a chalice (1650), a 16th-century book of rules for monks and a gospel from 1685. Among the paintings is a large collection of icons, many from the respected Dimitrijević–Rafailović School of the Boka (see box, page 25). The ornate clerical vestments include a blue silk robe belonging to the Justinian family, who ruled the Greek island of Chios from 1363 to 1565.

The latest research has shown more about ecclesiastical life at Savina in the mid-15th century and it seems that it was then that the two smaller churches were built. In the small **Church of the Assumption of the Virgin** older frescoes have been discovered under the layers of later painting. They are examples of the youthful work of Lovro Dobičević of Kotor (c1455). In style they are a compromise, presumably designed to satisfy the Eastern ideas supported by the monks and their benefactors as well as the more Western inclinations of the painter himself. Recently discovered Turkish documentation confirms that the church was erected on an endowment from Bosnian Herceg Šćepan. Compare the paintings here with examples of Dobičević's mature work in Dubrovnik, his painting of *Gospe od Škrpjela* on the island of that name opposite Perast, and the *Immago Pietatis* in the cathedral at Kotor.

The larger of the two churches, also dedicated to the Virgin, was built at the end of the 18th century by Nikola Foretić of Korčula (Croatia), employing in the carved detail the exquisitely hued stone for which his native island is famed. The result is a successful combination of Byzantine and Baroque. Within the church the iconostasis is the work of master painter Simeon Lazović and his son Aleksej of Bijelo Polje (north Montenegro). It too is essentially Byzantine in detail but also indicates a degree of Venetian influence. Look closely.

If you have transport, **Podi**, a few kilometres north on the back road from Meljine to Kameno, is another 'must see'. The perfectly proportioned cruciform Church of Sv Sergije and Sv Vakha is an enigma; so far no clues have been found to its origin. Clearly a visible inscription, '760', is a red herring. Argument over its real date ranges between the 13th and 15th centuries. What is undeniable is its beauty. Inside is an 1804 iconostasis, but you will be lucky to see it unless your visit coincides with a service.

THE ORJEN MASSIF The great mountain rises over 1,600m directly to the rear of Herceg Novi, making it relatively easy to access some not too strenuous hiking in the vicinity. Even setting out on foot from the town itself, it is not long before one reaches the countryside. That said, it is the higher elevations where the most rewarding trails are to be found, beyond the village of Kameno on the peaks of Subra and Orjen. There's a **mountain hut** at Vratlo (*1,160m; for opening times, contact Planinarski klub 'Subra'; e subra@t-com.me; www.pksubra.me; €10 pp in dorm*).

From Herceg Novi and the Orjen Massif, a well-signposted long-distance footpath known as the **Montenegrin Coast Transversal** (Primorska Planinarska Transferzala or 'PPT' for short) continues all the way to Bar, a distance of some 182km.

The local *Guide to the Orjen Massif* and Rudolf Abraham's *The Mountains of Montenegro* (see *Appendix 3*, page 326) are useful for planning and following routes, or contact Black Mountain Adventure (*www.montenegroholiday.com*) to arrange a guided visit.

THE BOKA KOTORSKA

The grandest of Montenegro's deep-blue inlets, the stunning Boka ('inlet') Kotorska is renowned for its spectacular scenery and cultural heritage, including the UNESCO-listed old city of Kotor. While its inner bays largely lack real beaches, the Boka holds plenty of potential for divers. And foodies will find here a couple of Montenegro's best restaurants.

The entire length of the Boka Kotorska is 15 nautical miles or 28km, stretching from Meljine, just east of Herceg Novi, to Kotor. The road, which follows the northern coastline through Bijela, Risan, Perast and Dobrota, covers the same journey in a little over 40km of beautiful scenery.

HISTORY In the 4th century BC the Greeks founded the town of Risan here (and Budva further down the coast). The Romans, after defeating the Illyrian tribes, settled in the 2nd century AD, renaming the coast Dalmatia. By the 5th century, after the Roman Empire had divided, the Boka remained under Western influence while the rest of the land became part of Byzantium. But by the end of the 6th century the southern Slavs had taken all the territory inland and the Dalmatian coast into the bargain. Although from the early 15th century until 1797 the Republic of Venice was a significant presence in this inner part of the Boka and left such an indelible mark, the region has always essentially been the domain of its indigenous seafarers, acclaimed over the centuries for their mastery of all matters maritime.

MELJINE TO KAMENARI

Meljine On the eastern outskirts of Herceg Novi, Meljine marks the entrance to the Boka Kotorska. To the east, the gulfside road runs wends its way through several further small villages towards Kamenari, a staging post for the narrow Verige channel.

Where to stay and eat

RR (20 rooms) Meljine bb; \031 348123; e hotel.rr@t-com.me; www.rr-hotel.com. An attractive small hotel in an old stone sea-captain's mansion, RR is a little bit removed from the action but right on the water with lovely bay views & a beach of small pebbles. Rooms, 13 with sea views, have AC & TV. Children's playground, parking. Nice terrace restaurant. HB available. €€€

Oaza (24 rooms) Meljine bb; \031 348237. On the coast road to the west of town, 60m from the sea. Restaurant; parking; simple rooms with shower & WC. €€

ZELENIKA If you were planning a visit to Montenegro by private yacht, this is the port where you might choose to register your intentions (**Port Authority**; \ 031 678024; *all year*).

Once the terminal station of a narrow-gauge railway line to Dubrovnik, Zelenika also boasted the first hotel on the Boka, the Plaža, which opened here in 1902. King Nikola himself figured among the luminaries on the guest list. The service was said to be of such high order, with 'boats, cars and even donkeys to hand – that the book of complaints became a book of commendation'. Maybe today's hoteliers could take some tips.

Where to stay and eat.

In addition to the following, there are water-polo clubs, a bar and a restaurant with beach facilities reserved for patrons on the beach, Zelenika Plaža.

4

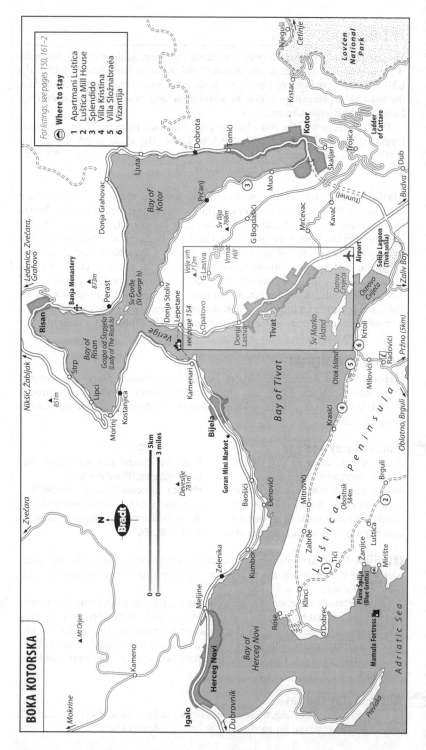

BOKA KOTORSKA

For listings, see pages 150, 161–2

Where to stay
1. Apartmani Luština
2. Luština Mill House
3. Splendido
4. Villa Kristina
5. Villa Složnabraća
6. Vizantija

N

Bradt

5km
3 miles
0
0

Lovćen National Park

Njeguši → Cetinje

Krstac → Ladder of Cattaro

Kotor

Škaljari
Trojica
Dub → Budva
Tunnel
Kavač
Mrčevac
G Bogdašići
Muo
Sv Ilija ▲768m
Prčanj
Ljuta

Bay of Kotor

Dobrota
Tomići

Donja Grahovac

Banja Monastery
873m ▲
Perast
Sv Đorđe (St George Is)
Gospa od Škrpjela (Lady of The Rock Is)

Risan

Bay of Risan

Strp
Lipci
851m ▲
Morinj
Kostanjica

Donja Stoliv
Lepetane
Verige
Kamenari

Bijela

Donja Lastva
Tivat

see page 154

Velje vrh ▲712m
G Lastva
Opatovo
Vrmac Hill
Ostrvo Cvijeća
Sv Marko Island
Ostrvo Cvijeća

Airport

Solila Lagoon (Tivat solila)
Zaliv Bay

Bay of Tivat

Krtoli
Radovići
Pržno (5km)

Milovići
Otok Island
Krasići
Mitrovići

Oblatno, Brguli

6
5
4

Ledenice, Zvečara, Grahovo →
Donja Grahovac

Nikšić, Žabljak →

Zvečara →

Mokrine →

Kameno

Mt Orjen ▲

Devesilje ▲781m

Goran Mini Market

Baošići
Đenovići
Zelenika
Kumbor
Meljine

Herceg Novi

Igalo
Dubrovnik →

Bay of Herceg Novi

Rose
Dobrec
Klinci
Žanjice

Plava Spilja (Blue Grotto)
Mamula Fortress
Mirište
Prevlaka

L u š t i c a   P e n i n s u l a

Obostnik ▲584m
Zabrđe
Tići
Luštica
Brguli

1
2

Adriatic Sea

Hotel Palace (8 rooms) Sunčana Obala bb; ☏031 678102. Free Wi-Fi; garden with internet café; sea views; restaurant. €€€

Apartments Bianca (14 apts) Zelenika bb; m 068 118801. All apts have kitchen, balcony, AC, satellite TV & free Wi-Fi. Gym access. Bar/lounge, plus terrace. Parking. €€

Haus Helena (2 apts) Sasović bb; e office@ montenegro-zelenika.com; www.montenegro-zelenika.com. 1km from the coast, these 2 apts with kitchens sleep 6 & 8 respectively. Garden, parking. €€€–€

Gostiona (Inn) Tažex Maraska Sunčana obala bb; ☏031 678225. Inexpensive grills, soups, etc. €€

KUMBOR, ĐENOVIĆI AND BAOŠIĆI

In **Kumbor** village, 6km east of Herceg Novi, the remains of a 17th-century Turkish fort are still detectable on the cape, and in **Đenovići** a Greek settlement, Stoli, existed in ancient times. **Baošići** also dates from early times and a plaque denotes where French novelist Pierre Loti stayed in 1880. He came as a naval officer, fell in love and later wrote a short story about it called 'Pascale Ivanović'.

Where to stay and eat A number of houses on the bay road have rooms to let; look out for *sobe* signs. Several apartments are listed with contact details and prices at www.apartmani-kumbor.info.

32 Kumbar (4 apts) nr Kumbor; ☏031 684505. There are good reports of apts overlooking the water here, each with AC, TV, shower, lavatory, fridge & cooker with equipment, plus front-door parking. €€

Max (22 rooms) Baošići; ☏031 674448; e hotelmax@t-com.me; www. hotelmaxhercegnovi.co.me. Off the main road, a fairly simple establishment without much English but with its own beach. AC, TV, minibar; restaurant. €€–€€€

Xanadu (39 rooms, 17 suites) Kumbor; ☏031 684748; e info@hotelxanadu.me; www. hotelxanadu.me. Beside the coast road, this nice hotel had pretentions but rather quickly fell into a state of some disrepair. However, at the time of writing it was being refurbished. Restaurant, bar, TV, AC, internet, pool, sauna & parking. A tunnel under the road leads to the private beach. The bus from Dubrovnik will set you down nearby if requested, but take care on the road: there isn't a walkway. €€€–€€€€

Camping Đardin (☏031 674365) & **Camping Magnolija** (m 067 506281) are two well-organised campsites near both the main road & the sea in Đenovići. **Camping Vujisić** is a third alternative in Baošići.

Olimpija Restaurant Kumbor; ☏031 580235; ⏰ 08.00–23.00. Just past the Xanadu hotel, decent food, flowery terrace & fountain & Mediterranean music make this family-run place one of the best eating stops on the main road. Mother runs the kitchen & sons are front of house. Also 3 simple rooms (€). €€€

Amaro Kumbor; ☏031 684746. Beside the village, this pleasant, monolingual pizzeria has tables practically paddling in the water. It basically serves pizza, pancakes & ice cream. Don't be misled by the sign claiming grills & fish; they don't keep a chef these days. €

Other practicalities There is a **post office** in Đenovići, on the lower, small road close to the bay (⏰ 07.00–14.00 Mon–Fri, 07.00–noon Sat).

BIJELA Bijela is notable for its sizeable dockyard whose function is the repair and maintenance of both foreign and domestic ships. It is one of Montenegro's largest and most profitable commercial enterprises. Also in Bijela, the **Church of the Mother of Christ** was reconstructed in 1824 incorporating the remains of the apse from its Romanesque predecessor. From the surviving 13th-century frescoes, one portraying a bishop, it appears that the church at that time had cathedral status.

But by and large you might as well stay on the main road. And if you do and you are in need of supplies consider pausing at the tiny mini-market, **Goran**, on the north side of the highway. It is a delight and a perfect example of the pride these small shopkeepers take in their work. Every item, prices carefully marked, has its place – almost like a doll's shop – it seems a shame to move a banana. If you buy some meat or cheese and bread, one of the attendant ladies will assume you want a sandwich. Service with a smile, whatever the hour. It's open early until late.

Where to stay and eat.

🏠 **Azzurro** (21 rooms) On the waterfront; ✆031 671606; e azzurro@t-com.me. Probably the pick of the rather uncompetitive Bijela bunch, with AC, TV, internet, & Wi-Fi throughout. Restaurant & bar, private beach. Friendly & efficient, they can organise water sports or car hire (inc airport pick-ups). Monitored parking. CCs accepted. **€€€–€€€€**

🏠 **Delfin** (114 rooms, 8 apts) Bijela Beach; ✆031 683400; e hoteldelfin@t-com.me; www.hotel-delfin.net. Most likely to appeal to businessmen who have to visit the neighbouring Bijela shipyard. Restaurant, bar, TV, AC, fitness centre, pool & water sports. Built in 1985, refurbished in 2003. CCs accepted. **€€€**

🏠 **Jadranska Straža** (8 rooms, 3 apts) Just off main coastal road; ✆031 671610; e jadranskastraza@t-me.com. In a pleasant, peaceful & only slightly shabby old villa, 300m from its own beach. AC, minibar, TV & terrace. Bar, restaurant & conference room. Hotel proceeds are used to support a local orphanage. **€€€**

🏠 **Vila Mireli** (19 rooms) ✆031 671242. Small, simple & also beside the shipyard. AC & TV. Beach access & parking. **€€**

✳ **Λ Camping Zloković** On main road on the Kamenari side of Bijela; ✆031 341028; e uroszlo@t-com.me; ⏲ all year. Clean, attractive, quiet & good value, with sites beside the water for tents & caravans. Uroš Zlotković is a most capable & hospitable host who has been in the business a long time &, as president of the Camping Association of Montenegro (CTU), has sound knowledge of campsites throughout the country. €7 per tent per day, €20 per day to rent a caravan for 3.

KAMENARI TO KOSTANJICA Kamenari gets its name from the lustrous red marble quarried since Roman times on the slopes nearby. Many squares in Venice have been paved with this marble, and it was used for the pedestal beneath Augustinčić's red monument beside the United Nations building in New York City.

And it is here that you must beg, borrow, steal or, as a last resort, rent a boat to slide through the narrowest channel in the Boka, **Verige**. Here in 1624 a chain was deployed across the gap to prevent history repeating itself, following a raid by North African pirates who had crept through one night and captured 400 prisoners for slaves. At this point, where the two shores all but touch, the strait is 300m wide and 30m deep, but think twice before you attempt to swim it: there are currents. But come traveller – and above all – see. This is no Norwegian fjord; this is Wagner: Gothic, *Sturm und Drang*. Mile-high mountains hemmed with Venetian palaces

SWIMMING IN THE BOKA KOTORSKA

Beneath the gulf, as well as mineral springs and caves, there obviously lie wrecks, amphora and treasure undiscovered. The Boka has been subject to the ravages of time, man-made in the form of great sea battles and piracy, and natural in its historical earthquakes. It is tempting to plunge in and explore. However, it is important to bear in mind that, especially with regard to the innermost reaches of the Boka, where the surface of the water often barely stirs, one is essentially swimming in a harbour, with all that implies.

rise vertically from the mirrored deep. And slightly askew Perast, unbowed though now a wraith, stands guard *in perpetuum*.

From Kamenari the road circles the two bays, Risan and Kotor, respectively. For a more direct route to Kotor or to Tivat, rejoin the Adriatic Highway eastward by taking the five-minute **ferry** from **Kamenari** to **Lepetane** (\ *031 673522; www.ferry.co.me; €4.50 per regular-sized car, €2 per motorbike, €1 per bicycle; buy ticket on quayside before you embark; foot passengers free*). Three ferries run in both directions 05.00– midnight, with one an hour in each direction midnight–05.00. It must surely contend for the title 'most beautiful ferry ride in the world'. Try it under a full moon.

The large church perched on top of a rocky headland to the west is **Sv Nedjelja** (Holy Sunday) but the author, try as she might, has never been able to find a way up to reach it. In season the ferry area is a squeegee merchant hang-out. Keep your doors locked. For Lepetane, see pages 151–2.

Keeping to the west, the longer shore route emerges from Verige revealing the two wide bays spread like butterfly wings; at their head **Perast** and her teardrop islets, one the silent Monastery of St George, the other Our Lady of the Rock (Gospa od Škrpjela). The way passes through **Kostanjica**, named after its encircling chestnut trees. And on to Morinj.

🛏 Where to stay

🏨 **Vila Kostanjica** (7 suites) 5km beyond ferry towards Morinj; \032 373232. Rebuilt in 2011, the hotel enjoys exceptional views but is on a road that can at times be noisy. Cable TV, minibar, AC. Restaurant Kaštel & bar (€€€). €€€

⛺ **Camping Vasiljević** Kamenari, behind the sea, between the hotels Park & Delfin (both signed from the main road); \031 683447

MORINJ In the 19th century this tiny village possessed 13 ocean-going vessels. Today there are only the fishermen, barefoot, blackened and canny. Turn off the engine and hear the wind rustling the willow fronds. But listen further for the tattling of a mountain brook, spilling round little dams to ponds teeming with trout; and taking good care for the ducks and the geese, lots of them, follow a winding trail lined with mimosa and camellia and leading ultimately to the old mill **Restaurant Čatovića Mlini** (below).

🛏 Where to stay

* ⛺ **Autocamp Naluka** m 069 346346; www.montenegro.com/accommodation/ morinj/Autocamp_Naluka.html; ⏰ Jun–Aug. Just before Čatovića Mlini & on the left coming from the ferry, this simple but super site is adjacent to the restaurant grounds. It is set in a mandarin orchard through which the ice-cold Morinj mountain stream flows & forms a natural refrigerator (tie your goods – &, of course, the wine – tightly in a plastic bag & suspend it by a string). The site has for several years running been awarded the distinction of

'cleanest campsite in Montenegro'. Certainly Duško Milinović is a very committed patron who cultivates a substantial vegetable plot, inc the sweetest of tomatoes. There are communal showers & toilets with solar heating & a large, open-sided barn offering shelter for those under canvas in the event of a storm. English & Norwegian spoken. Market & post office at 60m for all supplies except meat, for which you must usually go to Risan. €2.50/1 adult/child, €2 per car, €3 per tent, €1.50 for electricity, €0.66 tax.

🍴 Where to eat and drink

🍴 **Konoba Čatovića Mlini** \032 373030; e lazarc@t-com.me; www.catovicamlini.me;

⏰ 11.00–23.00. Dreaming of risotto, cold & black with ink from squid; warm shrimp risotto

& icy Sauvignon, Montenegrin grown? This place is for you. Despite increasing competition this charming pastoral inn still has the edge. It is to be commended not simply for its delicious food but also for the charming family who have owned the property for over 200 years, after whom it is named & who will ensure your happiness. Various home-produced products are available, inc wine. (As a matter of tiny interest perhaps to some, this is still one of the very few places in Montenegro that offers artificial sweeteners.) CCs accepted. See advert, 2nd colour section. €€€€€

MORINJ TO RISAN It would be easy to linger, enchanted by sweeping views across the Boka, its islands, and the surrounding mountains, but continue you should. The road passes beneath steep granite and, as long as there has been some rain lately, a sudden magnificent waterfall (*scpot*) plunging 30m into the sea below.

In the village of **Lipci** there are cave drawings (well signed off the main road) purporting to be 8th century BC. Turn up a narrow cemented road beside a white house with a basketball hoop to where the road becomes unpaved. After 300m follow the marked rocky path uphill (watch where you tread) to a small cave and see if you can see them. A torch might help.

Just beyond Lipci is the beginning of the long-awaited new road to **Grahovo**, **Nikšić** and ultimately **Žabljak**, affording spectacular views as the road ascends high above the gulf. Completed in December 2010, this route considerably cuts the time it takes to reach Durmitor National Park from the coast, giving access to the superlative hiking opportunities and winter skiing facilities in the far north of the country. Although a fast road, caution should still be exercised with regard to tight mountain hairpins. The distance from the Boka Kotorska to Žabljak via this road is approximately 152km; allow three hours in fair conditions.

Further along the road towards Risan is the small village of **Strp**. If you want to stop here try the well-rated:

Apartments Stella del Mare (7 apts) m 067 845710. Newly furnished apts have AC, kitchenette, balconies, nice views of Boka & use of a private beach. €€€.

RISAN At the innermost point of the bay is **Risan**, believed to be the oldest settlement in the Boka and founded by the Greeks c400BC. Today the seafront is dominated by the concrete blocks of the old Hotel Risan, which obscures the view of the Boka.

History The name Risan comes from the Illyrian tribe Rizonti, and at one time the whole Gulf of Kotor was named after them. Queen Teuta (Queen of Illyria, defeated by the Romans in 229BC) is thought to have taken refuge here. Her pirates in their galleys were attacking and robbing Roman ships in the Adriatic and from the plundered gold and silver they were coining money in the image of their queen.

Risan is the only town in the Boka whose inhabitants were never seamen, and Montenegrins connect this fact to Queen Teuta's curse. The story is that after at last being conquered by the Roman legionnaires, she climbed a steep cliff above the sea where she saw her harbour filled with Roman ships. Before she threw herself to her death she laid a curse upon the town: that it might never again be a port for ships. And as if her curse had been fulfilled, Risan never again had its own fleet. The story certainly has the ingredients for a lovely opera.

But many legends are associated with the town's origins. One is based on the story of Cadmus and Harmonia, who myth says were ultimately transformed into serpents. Caves and other finds have borne out the belief that some form of snake cult existed (see page 112). The Greek poets Callimachus and Apollonius of Rhodes mention heroes settling on the 'black deep Illyrian River where the graves of Harmonia and Cadmus are located' and this has been taken by some to refer to the Gulf of Kotor.

There is not much left to show from the Roman period, although Risan was mentioned by Pliny and it is known that as Risinium it enjoyed great status in the 1st and 2nd centuries AD when it was attached to the province of Dalmatia. Some years ago, a wide area of Roman **mosaic flooring** dating from the 2nd century AD was uncovered close to the sea (see below). One section depicts Hypnos the god of sleep, elegantly reclined.

During Roman times Risan had more than 10,000 inhabitants; today there are only 1,500. Sacked by the Saracens in AD865, the early city is said to have been comprehensively destroyed by an earthquake, date unknown. Some remains are visible in the water at the edge of the bay. Local people claim that on a stormy night the bells of the church which sank beneath the sea can be heard to toll, as vanished bells are apt to do. Sir Arthur Evans dug here from 1882 to 1885 and nowadays Jovan Martinović, a local archaeologist, works here during the summer. His instincts tell him there are wonders still to find, maybe an amphitheatre on the hillside.

For some time the town was ruled by the southern Slav Zetans and in 1451 passed to the Republic of Ragusa (Dubrovnik). Together with Herceg Novi, in 1539 it was occupied by the Turks until 1687 when it came under the authority of Venice. The notable icon school of Dimitrijević–Rafailović was at work during the 17th and 18th centuries.

Where to stay and eat Hotel Teuta is closed while people make up their minds what do with it. It is not much of a loss and if you need a bed you will do better in a *soba*.

Apartments Konoba Stari Ure (2 apts) Gabela 14, Risan Beach. Clean, centrally located apts with AC, balcony, parking & free Wi-Fi.

Atmospheric stone-walled *konoba* downstairs. €€€

Other practicalities

Post office opp old Hotel Teuta; 08.00–14.30 Mon–Sat.

Shops A small number of small food shops in the town are useful for picnic supplies.

What to see

Risan Mosaic (*Rimski Mosaic;* 032 322886; *www.risanmosaics.me;* Jun–1 Nov 08.00–20.00; May 09.00–17.00; winter visits by appointment; entry €2, under 12 free, group visit €1 pp; admission inc audio guide & map of Risan) The beautiful site harbouring Roman **mosaic flooring** dating from the 2nd century AD was until a few years ago sadly neglected, with a rickety leaking roof and a token barbed wire fence. However, there is now a newly built **visitors' centre**, with a tourist information desk.

The mosaics cover the floors of four rooms in the west part of the villa and another two in the east. The western floors are made of local grey-and-black stone incorporating the motif of a *labys* Cretan battle axe. The eastern floors are more colourful, with floral patterns surrounding a depiction of Hypnos, the Greek god of dreams, as a young winged boy reclining on a pillow in what must have been the master bedroom. Traces of other rooms include sea creatures such as cuttlefish and squid, also geometric patterns. The mosaics have suffered somewhat since their discovery in 1930, both from souvenir hunters and from the 1979 earthquake, but they still deserve a visit. A few steps west of the mosaic collection and immediately below the gates to Vaso Cuković specialist hospital, a pleasant, small park has recently been restored.

Getting there Travel southeast from Risan towards Kotor and you'll find it on the left of the main street with an inconspicuous sign to the 'Mozaicim: Rimski Mosaic'.

Above Risan Climb the serpentines above the town for Queen Teuta's final view and then press west through the foothills of **Mt Orjen**. Up here you will find pastures unexplored and you can see, far below, glimpses of impossibly unattainable Elysian valleys that it seems might vanish in a blink. A word of warning to those who might wish to come down from those hills after dark: the safest route winds through many hairpin bends and it is all too easy to take a wrong turn and find yourself suddenly on a narrow unpaved track, facing in the wrong direction, with Risan still far below. Since the opening of the new road leading north from Lipci (see page 132) – a few kilometres west of this historical town – you might feel happier to take in the similar, though marginally less dramatic, view from a lay-by there.

High above the town is **Crkvice**, believed to be subject to the highest annual rainfall in Europe. This is hard to believe in summer months when it can be dry enough for forest fires. The region is riddled with barely explored karst caves, intriguing for adequately equipped speleologists. Caving in Montenegro is in its infancy and who can say what treasure lies hidden.

PERAST Continuing beside the gulf in the direction of Kotor the road turns south, passing on the left the **Banja Monastery** (actually a convent). A sister will happily unlock the pretty church for you. One of their number studied at Maldon in England, with Father Sephronimus. Originally from the Middle Ages, Banja was rebuilt in 1720 after destruction by the Turks.

The town of **Perast**, the jewel in the crown, is only a short distance further. Standing proud between the two bays of the inner Boka and with a unique vantage point on the Verige channel (see page 127), Perast commanded a most valuable strategic position and, with those safe harbours large enough to accommodate a mighty navy, a highly desirable one.

Today, once-proud mansions are strung along the waterfront, dusty balustrades, tracery laced with ivy, exotic gardens tousled by time where fig and oleander hold lonely vigil. The elegant balconied **Bujović Palace** now houses the **Muzej Grada Perasta** (page 136).

The grand Venetian **Church of Sv Nikola**, designed by Giuseppe Beati but never finished, remains part of the silhouette of Perast. Only the apse stands, along with its 55m belfry – the tallest in the Boka – the construction of which cost the enormous sum of 55,000 ducats. An inscription commemorates the glorious defeat of the Turks in the battle of Perast in 1654: '*Christianae Reipublicae Triumphanti*'.

Plaques mark the naval school of Captain Martinović (1663–1716) and the house where Admiral Zmajević (1680–1735) was born. Matija Zmajević grew to command the Russian Baltic fleet in its victories over the Swedish navy. High above town the ruins of the palace built by his brother, Archbishop Andrija Zmajević, rest against the church of **Our Lady of the Rosary**, whose octagonal belltower completes the distinctive tableau of Perast viewed from across the bay.

History The name Perast derives from the Illyrian Pirusta tribe. Before the arrival of the Venetians, Perast consisted of a handful of corsairs, with more ships than men and a toughness to match their cousins on the Zetan plain.

They were in frequent contention with Kotor, under whose protection they fell, and during the 14th century even assisted Venice in attacking that city. In 1420 both towns became part of the Venetian Republic. After an infamous incident in 1535 on the island of **St George (Sv Đorđe)** in which a group of Perastins murdered the Kotor-appointed Benedictine abbot during Sunday mass, they succeeded in simultaneously freeing themselves from the dominance of their larger neighbour and getting the whole town excommunicated. Somehow, and probably aided by the ministrations of the Venetians, this all came out in the wash.

The city was now on the brink of its 15 minutes of fame. The Venetian cloak fitted well and beneath it a magnificent merchant fleet grew exponentially. Palaces and churches were built in harmony, to create the lovely Baroque tableau we now see suspended in dignified silence. With minimal defences, consisting of only the small 16th-century fortress of **Sveti Kritž**, the town kept its head above the tide of Islam. As a measure of their brave conduct at the battle of Lepanto in 1571 the Perastins earned the honour of guarding the Venetian *gonfalon* (standard) in time of battle. Their maritime skills became the stuff of legend.

At the beginning of the 18th century, Peter the Great of Russia dispatched a number of his noblemen for tutelage at the naval academy under the famed Captain Marko Martinović. And so the town prospered for a further 200 years until, with the withering of the Venetian Republic, it too lost its importance and faded to the muffled monument we find today.

Where to stay Perast's hotels and restaurants are strung out along the street which loops down along the waterfront from the main coast road and back up again.

🏠 **Hotel Conte** (14 apts) ☎032 373687; www. hotel-conte.com. At the east end of the waterfront road, apts sleeping 2 or 4 ppl have sea view & kitchens, plus AC, LCD TV, PC & internet. Jacuzzi, reception safe. 10% discount with Amex. Newest apts are in a separate building. Nautilus Restaurant (see below). CCs accepted. €€€€

🏠 **Hotel Per Astra** (11 suites) ☎032 373608; e perastra@t-com.me; www.perastra.me. Newly opened, beside the sea & pine woods. Terrace with bay views, restaurant. Spa, wellness & fitness rooms. Swimming pool. Wi-Fi. Conference room. €€€€

🏠 **Villa Perast** (3 apts) Perast; UK m (+44) 07931 561044; e villaperast@gmail.com; www. villaperast.com. Beautifully renovated, Australian-owned apts with AC & balcony; 2 with kitchen. €€€€

🏠 **Admiral** (8 rooms, 5-apt annexe) Obala Marko Martinovića; ☎032 373556; e hoteladmiral@t-com.me. Some rooms have balconies; all have sea views, TV, Wi-Fi, AC, minibar & room safes. An additional 5 apts near the church have similar facilities. Restaurant with terrace. Parking. €€€–€€€€

✕ **Where to eat and drink**

✕ **Nautilus Restaurant** opposite Hotel Conte (above); ☎032 373687. On the water, with 3 terraces & splendid views, Nautilus has a varied menu & 150 wines. A little more expensive than the branch at Herceg Novi. CCs accepted. €€€€

✕ **Konoba Otok Bronza** ⏰ 09.00–24.00. In a vine-shaded 15th-century house on the waterfront/high street. They concentrate on fairly decent seafood. €€€

✱ ✕ **Konoba Školji** ☎032 373653; e skolji@t-com.me; ⏰ 10.00–24.00 Apr–Nov. Another waterside terrace, with a nice terrace, a happy family atmosphere & an Italian bias in the kitchen. Probably the best in Perast. Specialities inc lamb cooked under the *sač* (€14) & a fish platter for 2 (€40). Grandfather's national dress decorates the *konoba*. Also 4 apts (€€€) that can be rented in various combinations, with satellite TV, internet access & free Wi-Fi. €€€

Other practicalities

✉ **Post office** ⏰ 08.00–14.00 Mon–Sat. On the bay at the east end of town.

What to see

Muzej Grada Perasta (*Obala Marka Martinovića;* ☎ *032 373519; www. muzejperast.me;* ⏰ *08.00–19.00 Mon–Sat, 09.00–14.00 Sun; entry adult/child €2.50/1*), located in the **Bujović Palace**, is a town museum filled with maritime nostalgia: weapons, charts, banners, portraits of the nobles, seascapes and richly decorated costumes glittering in the fusty rooms. At the water's edge and commanding a marvellous view of the bay, the little islands and Verige, the palace and its contents together provide a richly atmospheric experience. Not to be missed; allow plenty of time.

Islands in the bay Across the water two tiny islets floating silently form a hypnotic scene.

Shrouded by cypress trees the **Benedictine Monastery of St George** (Sv Đorđe) is balanced on a natural reef. It is the final resting place of dozens of sea captains, among them the gallant Marko Martinović.

Our Lady of the Rock (*Gospa od Škrpjela*) is an exquisite anomaly which grew, perhaps, out of remorse for the heinous act perpetrated on St George (see page 135). Around a small crag (*škripio* in the Dalmatian dialect) local people started to build another island. It began with the hulls of scuttled ships and was reinforced by stones, carried boatload after boatload, to form a base for a votive chapel which in 1630 they dedicated to the intercession of the Mother of Christ. By 1725 the original chapel had been enlarged by the addition of a sanctuary with a distinctive octagonal dome. In the small square in front of the church they arranged a so-called 'place of reconciliation', the idea being that quarrelling parties in local disputes might work out fair solutions in the shade of the church and so avoid the Venetian courts. The stone benches are a reminder of the personal and community dramas that must have been enacted here.

The interior of the church forms a prodigious homage to the work of Tripo Kokolja (1661–1713), a self-taught local artist, no fewer than 68 of whose paintings cover the walls and ceiling, portraying Old and New Testament events. Above the altar of white Carrara marble hangs an icon of the *Madonna and Child* by Lovro Marinov Dobričević of Kotor (15th century) – compare this with his frescoes at Savina (pages 125–6). On each side of the altar are marble figures: St John the Evangelist on the left and St Roch on the right, by Venetian sculptor Francesco Gai (1783). The painting of St Roch to the right of the altar is attributed to Tiepolo and the four large canvases that decorate the dome are from the 17th-century school of Genoa.

At the back of the church the 'keeper's lodge' holds a small **museum** (not to be missed): two floors devoted to the turbulent history of Perast, a vivid assembly of

ON THE SUBJECT OF CHURCHES

To help avoid confusion it should be mentioned just how close a relationship there is in these regions between the Catholic and the Serbian Orthodox faiths. Before the 11th century their saints were shared and many churches, like Sv Luka in Kotor, have two altars side by side, or in some cases even one in common and similar prayers. Each mass is simply celebrated at a separate time.

Every year at dusk on 22 July the rite of 'scattering stones' is re-enacted at **Our Lady of the Rock** in a colourful procession of brightly decorated boats tied together and accompanied by music and folk-singing. A second ritual, in which a rooster – in the absence of Ottoman invaders – is set adrift and subsequently despatched in a great volley of fire, is no longer encouraged (but nevertheless features in the current tourism literature).

wonderful paintings of stormy seas, dramatic exploits and heroic struggles; pieces of Greek and Roman amphora from the seabed; pottery shards and stone weapons from 3500BC discovered in the cave (*špilja*) above Perast; an early hand-powered iron screw with two transmissions that served to propel the St George Monastery boat; and best of all a delicate, embroidered icon, the labour of one Jacinta Kunić, in which she sewed her own golden hair on to the heads of the Madonna and Child. It took her 20 years to complete, by which time those hairs were grey.

An adjoining room holds a veritable antique shop of artefacts dedicated over the centuries in gratitude for delivery from danger: everything from sea-rusted pirate-proof locks to latter-day protection – twisted car bumpers.

Whether by chance or design the completed island has taken the outline of a galleon. A visit here is pause for thought that for all the gorgeous churches on the mainland endowed by rich merchants and ship owners, Our Lady of the Rock represents a distillation of the spiritual conscience of the ordinary seamen of Perast.

Getting there Small passenger boats make the journey over to the islands and back, including 30 minutes on the islands (m *069 089726; €5 pp, min 3 ppl*). Between April and October, boats wait for passengers at the small jetty by the museum; outside this period, call the number above to arrange a visit.

PERAST TO KOTOR Beyond Perast, a number of small settlements are beautifully placed along the narrow shore leading to the walled city of Kotor, respectively: Dražin Vrt, Orahovac, Ljuta and Dobrota.

Ljuta The 18th-century church of **St Eustace** has painted walls and ceiling, a treasury of trophies captured from the Turks (no heads) and a collection of Dobrota lacework – a local speciality. It's also home to a well-known restaurant:

✗ *Where to eat and drink*

✗ **Stari Mlini** (The Old Mill) Ljuta bb; ☏ 032 333555; www.starimlini.com; ⏲ 10.00–24.00. A well-signed & well-regarded restaurant on the coast road. The mill dates from 1670 & was built at the source of the River Ljuta. It has been owned by the Đurica family since 1976 & serves a wide range of fish & other local produce. Most of the tables are in the garden. Language is not a problem & there's parking for cars & boats. €€€€€

Dobrota Never can there have been a more handsome suburb. The shores stretching some 10km almost to the gates of Kotor are chequered with ancient churches, patrician mansions and summer houses. It is well worth detouring along the waterside road. The leaning palace of Radomir Dabinović is only one of many. Its Venetian belltower is especially attractive.

At nearby **Tomići,** the Baroque church of **Sv Matija** is keeper of a *Madonna* by Giovanni Bellini. It seems likely there are other Italian painters hiding in these churches: you will simply have to go in search. The story is the same; as sail gave way to steam the power and wealth of this area simply melted away into the Boka mist.

🏠 *Where to stay*

🏠 **Forza Mare** (10 rooms) Kriva ul Dobrota; 📞032 333500; e hotelforzamare@t-com. me; www.forzamare.com. An extremely well-appointed new hotel, whose rooms all have a different décor (Africa, China, Dubai, etc), as well as AC, cable TV & internet. Sauna, wellness & spa centres, outdoor pool & private beach. Restaurant & terrace. CCs accepted. €€€€€

🏠 **Palazzo Radomiri** (10 rooms) Dobrota 220; 📞032 333172; e info@palazzoradomiri.com; www.palazzoradomiri.com. For generations this was the mansion of a shipping family. Today, it has elegant & individually furnished rooms with stone walls & extensive views over the bay towards Ljuta. Satellite TV, AC & internet; laundry service. Restaurant (*HB in high season*), sauna, swimming pool, small fitness studio & mooring facilities. Visa & MasterCard accepted. €€€€

🏠 **Silver Moon Apartments** (32 apts) Sveta Vrača 12; 📞032 308577; e gihkotor02@t-com. me; www.silver-moon.me. Well-furnished, modern apts in Dobrota have AC, TV, internet, bay views. Something of a one-stop shop for business travellers with conference rooms, technical equipment, secretarial services & foreign-exchange desk. Also beauty salon, car rental, gift shop, laundry service, luggage store & safe boxes. Spa & wellness centre. Moon Restaurant (📞*032 330322;* €€€), with Wi-Fi; bistro & cocktail bar. Room rate inc use of gym, sauna & internet. €€€–€€€€

🏠 **Amfora** (12 suites) Orahovac bb; m 069 900588; e hotelamfora@t-com.me; www.amfora-hotel.com. New contemporary hotel in a peaceful seaside setting near Dobrota, with a private beach. Rooms have sea or mountain views, with AC, satellite TV, internet, minibar & room safe. Sauna, jacuzzi & gym. Restaurant & beach café. CCs. €€€

🏠 **Marija II** (18 rooms) 📞032 335307; e hotelmarija@t-com.me; www.hotelmarija.me. Overlooking the sea, a recently built & slightly cheaper version of Marija I in Kotor Old Town. Supervised parking. €€€

🏠 **Vila Panonija** (7 apts) Dobrota 1; 📞032 334893; e vilapanonija@t-com.me; www.vilapanonija.com; ⊕ all year. Waterside apts with minibars, safe deposit boxes, satellite TV & AC. Restaurant & bar. €€€

🏠 **Apartments Daković** (3 apts) Dražin Vrt; m 069 456772; www.cipa-booking.me. 2km from Perast, 12km from Kotor, 2-, 3- & 4-bed apts with private beach. €€

🏠 **Spasić i Mašera Youth Hostel** (118 rooms, 7 apts) Just off main road; 📞032 330258; e sdomkotor@t-com.me; www.hostelkotor.com. Up an unsigned lane away from the Boka, 50m SW of the ambulance station, the hostel has a bar & restaurant with satellite TV, internet & some sports facilities. Dbl & trpl rooms are available with private bath or shared bath. HB (*€2 supplement*) & FB available. €€–€

🍴 *Where to eat and drink*

* ✗ **Restoran Ellas** Dobrota 85, donji put-obala; 📞032 335115; e elas@t-com.me; www.restoranelas.com. From Kotor, take 1st turning left, signed Dobrota, then right at T-junction & follow signs. One of the best restaurants in Montenegro (& a new off-shoot has just opened in Kotor Old Town); it sounds Greek but isn't. Ground-floor dining room with AC; terrace above with lovely watery view. Long menu but very good food; lots of fish (everything from whitebait to lobster); even the french fries are exceptional. Credit cards accepted. €€€€

✗ **Dobrotski Dvori** 2km north of Kotor Old Town; 📞032 330840. Popular local bistro that also has rooms (€€). €€€

✗ **Tiha Noć** Dobrota 151; ⊕ 07.00–24.00. Simple surroundings beside the sea, but the welcome is warm & the food good; covered terrace. They are justifiably proud of their spit-roasted lamb. Visa accepted. €€€

✗ **Caffé del Mare** Dobrota; ⊕ 08.00–11.00 (summer 08.00–01.00). Lovely views across the bay to Muo & mountains. Serves fish & sandwiches. Visa & MasterCard accepted. €€

During early summer 2009 a joint underwater exploration and mapping survey was conducted in the Boka Kotorska by the Malta-based RPM Nautical Foundation, the Underwater Dive Training De-mining Centre in Bijela, archaeologist Vilma Kovačević from the Institute for Cultural Heritage Protection in Kotor and the Montenegro Ministry of Culture.

Within only a few weeks the research vessel *Hercules*, employing state-of-the-art investigative equipment, had made several remarkable discoveries, notably the apparent remains of a Roman ship bearing a cargo of ceramic tiles. In the same area a scattered collection of amphorae indicated the likelihood of another ship, its date so far a matter of speculation. The wreck of a German submarine believed to have been sunk in World War I was also spotted.

For the present time, to protect against unauthorised exploitation of the sites, their exact location is a closely guarded secret and plans are in place to enclose the wrecks in expensive protective steel cages.

In 2010 a joint Montenegrin/British team funded by various charities – including the Headley Trust – and by the Montenegrin Ministry of Culture, and led by Mladen Zagarčanin of Bar Museum, Dr Lucy Blue of Southampton University and Charles LeQuesne of RPS Group, carried out an initial two-week survey of underwater ruined columns in Maljevik Bay and the harbour site in Bigovica Bay. The only previously published reference to these ruins, so far as we can establish, is in previous editions of this book, which spoke of 'an unidentified settlement underwater' off Maljevik Beach (see page 202).

✗ **Golden Bar Fish Restaurant** ⏰ 07.00–01.00. Very attractive location overlooking Boka. Wide terrace, BBQ, beach facilities with sunbeds & umbrellas, swimming area & dock for boats. Cash only. €€

Other practicalities
✉ **Post office** In Dobrota on the waterfront; ⏰ 08.00–14.30 Mon–Sat.
Shopping Centar Kamelija, trg Mata Petrovića; www.kamelija.me; ⏰ 07.00–22.00. Immediately north of Kotor on the coast road to Dobrota. Inc wellness centre, pharmacy, ATM, children's playground, restaurants & cafés, & car parking.

KOTOR

In the furthest recess of the Boka at the very foot of majestic Mt Lovćen lies Kotor:

> In the winter the sea freezes and in the morning the first rays of sun melt the ice, turning the water into a thin layer of very light fog. Boats then seem to sail on the clouds, as if in a painting by the extraordinary Montenegrin artist Vojo (Vojslav) Stanić.

But Italian writer Nicolò Carnimeo, in *Montenegro, A Timeless Voyage,* is describing the shortest midwinter days when the sun barely reaches the top of the mountain. In spring or in autumn, the most beautiful seasons throughout Montenegro, the city is held spellbound while the sun slips minute by minute down the jagged face of rock, bathing granite and marble in a honeyed glow. By now Jovan Martinović, archaeologist, polymath and respected citizen of Kotor, is viewing this daily pageant from the sea wall across the bay. Each morning he rises at 04.00 and, carrying his fishing rod, strides west beyond Prčanj.

Behind the mighty 20m ramparts that shield Kotor from the waterfront, the vegetable and fish market, and the harbour bustle, the medieval city is labyrinthine but small enough that it is impossible to be lost – just frequently confused. The streets are mostly unnamed, though a few are known informally. For example, Pusti me da prođem (Let Me Pass Street) which speaks for itself. The city's irregular squares are known by their original designations: trg od Brašna (Square of Flour), trg od Oružja (Square of Milk), and so on. Cats scuttle everywhere but the absolute monarch is Mićun ('the Big One'). See him strutting his stuff in front of St Tryphon Cathedral. But do not speak to him: like sentries everywhere he will ignore you.

Kotor is listed by UNESCO as a World Heritage Site.

HISTORY The special character of Kotor has been determined by its history. It was always a place of mixture, a marriage of styles: western European and Byzantine, reflected even in the building blocks themselves with their varying textures and many marbled hues. Jovan Martinović feels it: 'the stone speaks to you – touch it – run your hand over its story'; like writer Jan Morris caressing her standing boulders in the hills of Wales or Alain de Botton, in *The Art of Travel*, finding it hard to resist an impulse to kiss the crumbling bricks of a beautiful house in Amsterdam. These are intuitive responses.

Tales abound of Kotor's beginnings: the romantic notion of the nymph Alkimi (mother to Jason of the Golden Fleece) guiding the nameless founder to a plateau by the sea where there is an abundant spring of fresh water, is one of them. They speak of a matter of minutes every month when, high on the cliff, the new moon appears beneath a natural bridge in the rock, suspended like a hammock: 'Oh look,' they will say, 'Alkimi is there in her golden boat, still watching over her beautiful town Kotor.'

Be that as it may, there was a settlement here in Byzantine times known as Dekaderon. In the Middle Ages it entered the constitution of the Slavonic Zeta and Raška whose rulers had residences here. At that time the town enjoyed a considerable degree of autonomy and from 1391 to 1420 Kotor, with its surrounding land, was an independent city-republic with its own elected prince, senate and lesser councils; it even minted its own coins. With the Ottoman threat ever present, in 1420 the city placed itself under the protection of Venice. In all the city has exchanged rulers and occupiers 14 times (including a brief occupation by Britain in 1813 during the Napoleonic Wars) but never, insist its inhabitants, was it taken by force of arms: 'On 21 November 1944, the Germans simply withdrew.' It has, however, suffered three major earthquakes, in 1563, 1667 and 1979, and an outbreak of the plague in 1572.

GETTING THERE There are several buses a day to Kotor from Podgorica, Budva, Herceg Novi and Tivat, and minibuses to Muo, Stoliv, Prčanj and Lepetane. The journey from Podgorica takes about two hours (€7), from Budva about one hour (€3) and from Tivat about 45 minutes (€2). All these timings are dependent on traffic, which can be very heavy around the coast in holiday season. There is currently no direct service from Cetinje via the Ladder of Cattaro and Njeguši. To get here from Cetinje by public transport one must travel via Budva.

The **bus station** [off map 142 B4] (✆ *032 325809*; *left luggage* ⊕ *09.00–21.00*) is to the east of the city where the roads to Tivat and Budva divide, a five-minute walk south from the main gate to the old city.

GETTING AROUND No vehicular traffic is allowed within the city gates. Bear this in mind when considering accommodation, transport of baggage, etc. There is secure and fairly inexpensive paid **parking** [142 A2] beside the bay, opposite the main western gate, and across the little Škurda River close to the northern entrance. Note that marble paving stones are slippery when wet.

Car hire
🚗 **Baron Gautsch** Markov rte bb, Stoliv; 📞032 338121; e info@kotorrentacar.com; www. kotorrentacar.com. Peugeot 206, Opel Corsa, etc.
🚗 **Dakris** 📞032 303032; e dakris@t-com.me; www.dakriscompany.com
🚗 **Ineska** 📞032 330063; e info@ineska.net; www.ineska.net
🚗 **Loading** 📞032 332222; e loading@t-com. me; www.montenegro.com. CCs accepted.

🚗 **Maremonti** Dobrota 63; m 067 227293; e maremonti@gmail.com. Chauffeur service available. CCs accepted.

Taxis
🚗 **Đir** 📞9737 (24hrs)
🚗 **Red** 📞19719 (24hrs); www.redtaxikotor.com

TOURIST INFORMATION AND TOUR OPERATORS
Tourist information
ℹ️ **Tourist information centre** [142 B2] Kiosk just outside main gate of the old city; 📞032 325947, 032 325950; e tokotor@t-com.me; www. tokotor.me; 🕐 08.00–14.00.

Tour operators
Adventure Montenegro Stari Grad 375; m 069 049733; e adventuremontenegro@ t-com.me; www.adventuremontenegro.com. All sorts of tours, inc hiking, kayaking, rafting &

speedboat cruising. They can also be contacted through Konoba Cesarica (see *Where to eat and drink* , below).
Forza Cattaro Travel Agency Stari Grad 432; 📞032 304068; e forza.cattaro@t-com.me; 🕐 winter 08.00–16.00 Mon–Sat, summer 08.00–22.00. Beside the main city gate.
Vizin Travel Sq of Weapons; 📞032 302548. Airport transfers, car rental & yacht rental. East of main gate.

⌂ WHERE TO STAY *Map, page 142.*
It's worth noting that hotels within the city walls can be very noisy in the evening from local bars, but are pretty silent after 24.00, or 01.00 during festivals.

✳ ⌂ **Astoria** (6 rooms, 3 suites) Stari Grad 322; 📞032 302720; www.astoriamontenegro.com. Elegant, award-winning boutique hotel, sibling of the Astoria in Budva, built in the shell of the 14th-century Buća Palace. Rooms with AC, minibar, cable TV, room safe. Free internet. Sophisticated & luxurious, with a restaurant & bar to match. €€€€€
✳ ⌂ **Vardar** (24 rooms) trg od Oružja, Stari Grad 476; 📞032 325084; e info@hotelvardar.com; www.hotelvardar.com. Most attractive inside & out with a pretty terrace facing the Square of Weapons. Free Wi-Fi & rooms with TV & AC. Small gym. Turkish bath & sauna. Highly respected restaurant (Galion, see below) outside the city walls at Šuranj serves national cuisine with an emphasis on seafood. 24hr room service. Children up to 10 free, 10–15 half price. CCs accepted. €€€€€

⌂ **Boutique Hotel Hippocampus** (7 rooms) Stari Grad 489; m 078 106160; e hotel. hippocampus@gmail.com; http:// hotelhippocampus.com. Newly opened, award-winning boutique 4-star in renovated 17th-century Venetian palazzo, tucked away in the old town beside the 12th-century church of St Anne. Original stone walls combined with Nepalese stone, oak floors, wooden ceilings, antique & designer furniture. AC, TV, elevator, Wi-Fi, restaurant. Free transfers to/from Tivat airport. €€€€
⌂ **Cattaro** (17 rooms, 1 suite) Stari Grad 232; 📞032 311000; e cattarohotel@t-com.me; www. cattarohotel.com. This impressive hotel on the main square is adapted from 3 old city buildings: the former palazzo of a senior Venetian official from the late 18th century; Napoleon's Theatre,

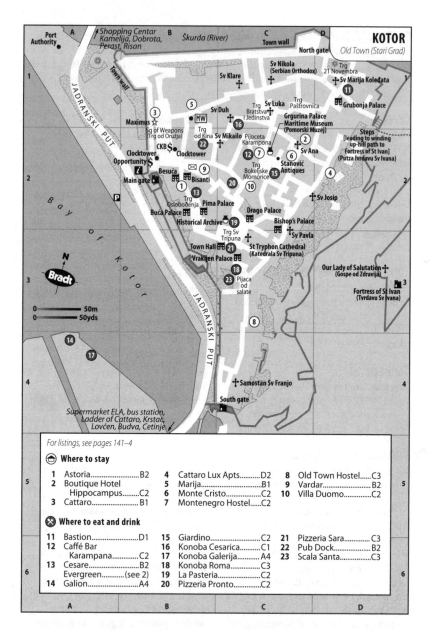

For listings, see pages 141–4

Where to stay

1	Astoria...........................B2	4	Cattaro Lux Apts...........D2	8	Old Town Hostel......C3
2	Boutique Hotel	5	Marija............................B1	9	Vardar..........................B2
	Hippocampus.........C2	6	Monte Cristo.................C2	10	Villa Duomo...............C2
3	Cattaro........................B1	7	Montenegro Hostel......C2		

Where to eat and drink

11	Bastion........................D1	15	Giardino........................C2	21	Pizzeria Sara..............C3
12	Caffé Bar	16	Konoba Cesarica...........C1	22	Pub Dock.....................B2
	Karampana..............C2	17	Konoba Galerija............A4	23	Scala Santa.................C3
13	Cesare..........................B2	18	Konoba Roma................C3		
	Evergreen............(see 2)	19	La Pasteria....................C2		
14	Galion..........................A4	20	Pizzeria Pronto.............C2		

built in 1810; & the premises of the town guards. All rooms have TV, minibar, safe & a view of the square. Lifts. Royal restaurant, piano bar & conference room. A sign by the front door forbids guests to enter with dogs or ice cream; sadly, the sign announcing that pistols were banned has gone. CCs accepted. (The adjacent nightclub, Maximus, is the 'in' place & hugely popular. Other

visitors should be reassured; it is thoroughly sound-proofed. In winter there is a sports bar here.) €€€€

🏠 **Cattaro Lux Apartments** (4 apts) ul 29 Novembra 409; m 679 140501. Opulent, stone-walled apts at the edge of the old town, near the base of the walk up to the fortress of St Ivan. AC, Wi-Fi, TV. €€€€

🏠 **Hotel Monte Cristo** (8 rooms) ✆ 032 322458, 032 322459; e office@ montecristo.co.me; www.hotelmontecristo. me. Luxurious boutique hotel opened in 2011 in the former residency of the Bishop of Kotor, a building dating from the 14th century. It features Luna Rossa restaurant (€€€), with balcony & terrace seating, serving modern Mediterranean cuisine. €€€€

* 🏠 **Marija** (17 rooms) Stari Grad 449; ✆ 032 325062; e recepcija@hotelmarija.me; hwww.hotelmarija.me; ⏰ all year. One of Montenegro's first private hotels & still one of the nicest, located in an old but thoroughly modernised mansion & run by owner-manager Vojin Radanović. All rooms come with AC, minibar, TV & free Wi-Fi. Everything works. Also has a bar & restaurant serving pleasant b/fasts with local eggs, jam & honey. No parking but porterage available. Wake to the church bells (Catholic Sv Klare in the neighbouring square is notably unlocked in winter). There's now a new Marija II at Dobrota (page 138), a few hundred metres outside the city walls. CCs accepted. €€€€

🏠 **Villa Duomo** (13 suites) Stari Grad 385; ✆ 032 323111; www.villaduomo.com. Large (33m²) suites/apts with views to St Tryphon's Cathedral have plasma TV, DVD, internet, minibar, AC & dbl glazing (welcome on noisy Kotor evenings). 7 suites have jacuzzis. The furniture has been chosen to complement the renaissance palazzo architecture. €€€€

* 🏠 **Montenegro Hostel** Museum Sq (trg od Muzeja); m 069 270510; e montenegrohostel@ gmail.com; www.montenegrohostel.com. Excellent hostel within old town. 2-, 4- & 6-bed dorms with kitchens, bathrooms, free Wi-Fi (& 1 computer for general use), TV, AC. Also common room & washing machine/dryer (€4). Dinner available for guests Jul–Sep (€). Good range of tours offered. A very efficient & useful base for budget travellers; sister hostels in Podgorica & Budva. €7–15 pp per night. €

🏠 **Old Town Hostel** (10 rooms) Stari Grad 284; e info@hostel-kotor.me; www.hostel-kotor.me. Newly opened hostel within old town near South Gate, in renovated 13th-century building. 2-, 3-, 4-, 6-, 8- & 10-bed rooms. Wi-Fi, lockers, AC. B/fast (€). €

✖ **WHERE TO EAT AND DRINK** *Map, page 142.*
Restaurants

✖ **Scala Santa** Stari Grad, Pijaca od Salate, in southern corner of old town (turn right by cathedral); m 069 295833; www.scala-santa.com. Very good *konoba* restaurant but near to London prices. Specialities inc risotto, soup & veal, all served in a cosy, rustic setting. There's a big log fire in winter. No CCs. €€€€€

* ✖ **Bastion** Stari Grad 517; ✆ 032 322116; m 068 517460; http://bastion123.com; ⏰ 10.00–24.00. Traditional-style restaurant close to north gate; large choice of very fresh fish (mussels, squid, St Pierre, turbot, octopus & local specialities). €€€€

* ✖ **Galion** Šuranj bb; ✆ 032 311300; e galion@t-com.me; www.hotelvardar.com. On the water's edge, 5min stroll from the gates of the Old City, a superior & sophisticated fish restaurant owned by the Vardar Hotel with a splendid view of the Boka & mountains. Cover €2. CCs accepted. €€€€

✖ **Konoba Cesarica** Stari Grad 375, kod Muzičke Škole; m 069 049733; www. adventuremontenegro.com; ⏰ 09.00–23.00. Dalmatian food, mostly fish, served up in a crypt-like atmosphere. B/fast. Fish & chips €8. Owned by Adventure Montenegro. CCs accepted. €€€

✖ **Konoba Galerija** Šuranj bb; m 068 825956; ⏰ 11.00–23.00. Good, attractive restaurant with a terrace specialising in seafood & grills, near Galion (see above). €€€

✖ **Konoba Roma** Stari Grad, Pijaca od salate; m 069 545261; ⏰ 09.00–01.00. Friendly *konoba* on this square near the South Gate, with lower prices than the neighbouring Scala Santa. €€€

✖ **La Pasteria** Stari Grad, trg Sv Tripuna. Friendly Italian restaurant with a big terrace opposite the cathedral. CCs accepted. €€€

✖ **Cesare** Facing Buća Palace; ✆ 032 325913; ⏰ 07.00–24.00 Mon–Sat, 08.00–24.00 Sun. Sophisticated & comfortable coffee shop & bar. Cocktails & good selection of ice cream. Terrace & inside tables. CCs accepted. €€

✖ **Giardino** Stari Grad 350; ⏰ winter 08.00– 24.00 daily; summer 08.00–02.00. Small, bustling & welcoming, restaurant that's family-run & popular with all ages. Limited English. Traditional, good-value menu: pasta, pizza, wide variety of seafood & meat dishes. Typical Kotor dessert *krempita* (similar to mille feuilles). They also rent apts. CCs accepted. €€

❋ ✗ **Pizzeria Pronto** Behind Vardar Hotel; ⊕ 09.00–11.00 Sun–Thu, 09.00–01.00 Fri–Sat. Best pizza in town. Tiny restaurant with half-a-dozen tables under a vaulted ceiling, on narrow street between Vardar & Villa Duomo. Popular, low key, good value. Take-away available. €€

✗ **Pizzeria Sara** trg Sv Tripuna. Pleasant open-air café for snacks & ice creams. €€

Bars and nightlife

♀ **Caffè Bar Karampana** Karampana (Sq of Water Pump); ⊕ 07.00–01.00. Behind Maritime Museum. Free internet. Ethno-Balkan & commercial music.

♀ **Evergreen** Stari Grad, Pjaca od Cirkula; ⊕ 10.00–24.00. Jazz bar with live music, near Montenegro Hostel.

♀ **Pub Dock** Pijaca od Kina (Sq of the Cinema); ⊕ 08.00–22.00, closes later in season. Opposite Church of Our Lady of Angels cinema & beside lapidarium of Sv Mihaila. Resembles an English pub with 2 long bars & a smoking area. Draft beers & Guinness; no food.

☆ **Maximus** [142 B1] Stari Grad, Sq of Weapons 232; www.discomaximus.com; ⊕ 23.00–05.00. Up steps beyond the Cattaro Hotel, one of the hottest clubs on the coast, especially in summer, with local & international attractions. Entrance fee for live shows.

SPORTS AND OTHER ACTIVITIES

Boat trips and hire There are plenty of small boats available all along the coast for group or individual hire at negotiable prices.

Yacht rental is available in summer and many chartered yachts berth in Kotor. The passenger boarding formalities in Montenegro are said to be easier than in neighbouring countries.

⚠ **BWA Yachting Montenegro** m 069 024327; e info@bwayachting.com; www.bwayachting. com. Sailing & motorboats.

⚠ **Marina** Kotor Marina; ☏ 032 325578. 87 boats.

⚠ **Marsenic Boat Hire** Šuranj bb, close to Galion restaurant; m 069 649749. Boat & yacht rental.

⚠ **MCC (Montenegro Charter Company)** Kotor Marina; ☏ 032 322462; head office bul Sv Petra Cetinjskog 92, Podgorica; ☏ 020 220195; e info@montenegrocharter.com; www. montenegrocharter.com. Rentals, Sat–Sat, of new Sun Odyssey 54 & 45 & various Elan sailing boats with 6–10 beds; Jeanneau Prestige motorboat; Nautitech 47 & Lagoon 440 catamarans. Inc all sorts of electronic kit as well as dinghies. It also

has a sailing school. Skippers & hostesses can be hired. Knowledgeable & efficient, they will arrange airport transfers. English, Italian & German spoken. CCs accepted.

⚠ **Monte Marine Yachting** Kotor Marina; ☏ 032 302380; e info@yachtmm.com; www.yachtmm. com. Yachts & catamarans.

⚠ **Montenegro-For-Sail** e yachtmontyb@ gmail.com; www.montenegro4sail.com. Run by a British couple who offer day sailing & sunset cruises in the Boka Kotorska aboard their 44ft sailing ketch, Monty B.

Port Authority ☏ 032 325414; e uckauprava@ t-com.me; www.luckauprava.me; ⊕ all year

SHOPPING An excellent market operates in front of the ramparts selling fresh fruit and vegetables from local villages at reasonable prices. Saturday is the main market day. Expect to find eggs, seasonal fruit (in spring look out for delicious kumquats – Fortunella), a wide variety of fish and meat, olive oil, homemade wine, flowers and plants, along with clothing items such as socks and gloves.

There's a supermarket (⊕ 06.00–23.00) with an ATM a few minutes' walk southeast from the old city, on the road towards the bus station. It's excellently stocked with all the things you'd expect.

Antiques shopping Stanović trg Bokeljske Mornarice, next to the Maritime Museum. Good collection of old prints, postcards & miscellaneous

bric-à-brac. The helpful owner dispenses advice in good English.

The Tobacco Shop Behind Vardar Hotel; ⊕ winter 07.00–23.00, summer 07.00–01.00. One of the few places in Montenegro where you can buy English-language newspapers, albeit the choice is restricted to the *Financial Times* & the *International New York Times*.

OTHER PRACTICALITIES One of Montenegro's few **public lavatories** is in the little street opposite the Marija Hotel, just off trg od Kina [142 B1] (⊕ *06.00–20.00*).

Banks
$ **Atlasmont Banka** Tabačina bb
$ **CKB** Benovo 584
$ **Hipotekarna Banka** Stari grad br 368
$ **Komercijalna Banka** trg od Oružja bb
$ **Montenegrobanka** trg od Oružja bb
$ **Nikšićka Banka** trg od Oružja bb
$ **Opportunity Bank** Stari grad br 431

Internet
Laptop users should note that all of the old city of Kotor is a Wi-Fi area, & most hotels also provide free Wi-Fi.

🖥 **Café Forza** Stari Grad 432, to the right of the main gate; ☎082 304352; ⊕ 07.00–24.00. €1 for 30mins; printing €0.50 per page.

Medical facilities
⊞ **Health Centre** ☎032 325633

Pharmacies
✚ **Galen** ☎032 304212
✚ **Montefarm–Stari grad** ☎032 325215
✚ **Salvija** ☎032 325109

Other
✉ **Post office** [142 B2] Southeast of Sq of Weapons (trg od Oružja); ☎032 322362; ⊕ 07.30–19.30 Mon–Fri. There is a 2nd post office west of the old city, opposite Fjord Hotel.

WHAT TO SEE The town is triangular in form, with three gates. The main one leading from the quay is Renaissance (mid-16th century). The northern gate, with a suspension bridge spanning the bubbling Škurda rivulet, was built in 1540 and commemorates victory the previous year over Khair ed-din Barbarossa when, with a fleet of 200 ships and 60,000 men, he unsuccessfully besieged the town.

The third, south gate, was cunningly composed of three ingenious parts which included a drawbridge where at high tide the Grudić spring forms a brackish pool. Alkimi should have thought of this. This gate was an important one because it lent access to the steep ascent to Montenegro and the interior lands. For more on this see page 143.

The old city remains encircled by walls. At 4.5km in length they are twice the length of those at Dubrovnik and rise spectacularly to the crest of the rocky hillside behind the tight-knit buildings and harbour. Originally built in Byzantine times, they were considerably reinforced under the Venetians when Kotor became one of the best fortified towns on the Adriatic.

Above the city To take in the whole picture, exit by the north gate of the old town, leaving the Škurda River on the left, and take the uphill way east by **St Mary's Church** (**Sv Marija Koleđata**, [142 D2], page 148). Guided by butterflies you may now climb a winding path punctuated by several flights of steps cut from the rock – 1,350 sounds a lot of steps but you will be pausing at every turn to review the scene – to the topmost point (260m) and the now pacific **Fortress of Sv Ivan** [142 D3]. Halfway to the brow you will pass the tiny 16th-century **Chapel of Our Lady of Salvation** (Gospe od Zdravlja) [142 D3], built by the survivors of the plague. It will probably be locked, but you can peer through the gate into the dark interior.

At the ruined, ramshackle fortress at the top, the vistas are in juxtaposition: westward and far below is the jumble of urban roofs, the audible pulse of activity around the little port and its humming market. The gorge to the east falls away steeply and with it the centuries; a bee idling among the wild cyclamen and somewhere unseen beneath the rock face, the contented clucking of chickens.

Behind the fortress you can see, a little way below, the deserted **St George's Church (Sv Đorđe)**, and the pathway that was the original Ladder of Cattaro snaking its way up the mountainside. There are some red waymarkings indicating a route to the church and a gentle downhill route to join the course of the Ladder of Cattaro (page 148) and down to Kotor. When the Ladder reaches Kotor, follow the path back to the River Gates and you will see, on the right-hand side, the spring where the Škurda River emerges.

Allow at least 1½ hours for the round trip and take something to drink.

Rumour was that Austrian investors had plans to construct a cable-car between Kotor and Njegoš's mausoleum with an intermediate station at the Fortress of St Ivan. This intention may please some but dismay others, and in any case seems to have faded. From summer 2014 visitors are likely to find a small coin-operated telescope at the top.

The lower city The Square of Weapons (trg od Oružja) [142 B2] just within the main gate is the largest of the squares, with several pavement cafés set around it. To the left is the never-completed Renaissance ducal palace and next to it, at the far north corner and built by the French in 1810, what used to be one of the oldest theatres in Yugoslavia, now converted into the Cattaro Hotel. Opposite the gate is a medieval pillory and behind it the clocktower built at the very start of the 17th century, with the clock itself added in 1810. A narrow street from the south side of the main square passes between two mansions, the 17th-century **Bisanti** on the left and 18th-century **Besuća** opposite [142 B2], into a small square dominated by the Renaissance **Pima Palace** [142 B2] with its long Baroque balustrade.

St Tryphon's Cathedral (Katedrala Sv Tripuna) [142 C3] (entry €1.50; ⏲ daily) From this small square, a further narrow street enters the square of St Tryphon's Cathedral, the best-known landmark in Kotor. It was consecrated in 1166, five-and-a-half centuries before London's St Paul's, three centuries before the discovery of America and 254 years before the Venetians settled in Kotor. Montenegro is justly proud of it.

In spite of reconstruction over the centuries, the cathedral remains an outstanding example of Romanesque architecture. After the catastrophic earthquake of 1667 destroyed the west front, replacement belltowers in warm Korčula stone added a Baroque aspect. They are connected by a wide balustraded arch spanning the porch, surmounted with a distinctive rose window. To the right of the main entrance is the sarcophagus of Andrea Saracenis, who built the earlier church, and of his wife Maria, with a 9th-century inscription. But the central feature of the lofty interior is the ciborium of the high altar, a masterpiece of Romanesque Gothic workmanship. Four columns of red Kamenari marble support a three-tier octagonal construction crowned by an angel. Scenes depicting the life of St Tryphon are carved on each tier. In the apse and in the vaults of the nave look for traces of recently uncovered frescoes. Their 14th-century origin is proven, but it is unclear whether the Byzantine-influenced painters were Greek or Serbian. Originally all the walls were covered with frescoes.

Tradition has it that St Tryphon was a gooseherd in Phrygia, martyred as a young boy for his refusal to make an offering in front of the statue of the Roman emperor. (We British remember him as the patron saint of gardeners.) His bones were brought from Constantinople in the 9th century. Now they are kept in the 14th-century reliquary chapel where there is a frieze of white Carrara marble, the work of 18th-century Venetian sculptor Francesco Cabianca, quite exquisite in its detail, even to the nails in the hooves of the horses. (See a different example of his work in the multicoloured Baroque altar of the Franciscan **Church of Sv Klare** not far to the west.) But most stirring is a large wooden crucifix, its image not quickly forgotten and mystifying in that its provenance is another unknown. It is said to have Austrian characteristics and to resemble similar figures found in Venice, Trieste and Split. Like the detail in the hooves of Cabianca's horses, the finer points of this sculpture are brilliantly defined, in the facial pain expressed from every angle and in the clenched toes.

During excavations in 1987 the existence of an earlier church was confirmed. The rotunda of this is partly beneath the sacristy and partly in the street between it and the 14th-century bishopric (in whose courtyard Martinović as a boy would steal oranges). This early church dates from the 9th century, so is of the same vintage as the first guild of Boka seamen (*Bokeška mornarica*), a mutual benefit union which still retains its ancient traditions, its songs and its own version of the wonderful *kolo* wheel dance. See them in action in their formal dress at the ceremony marking the martyrdom of St Tryphon in the first week of February; or buy a CD of their lilting music (*Bokeljski mornari*) – cheapest at the kiosk at the main gate.

Elsewhere in the lower city Close to the cathedral, the 16th-century **Drago Palace** [142 C2] is identifiable by its distinguishing Gothic window features; it was originally a 12th-century mansion demolished by masonry from the falling cathedral in the 1667 earthquake.

Further on, the Baroque **Grgurina Palace** holds the **Maritime Museum** (**Pomorski muzej**) [142 C2] (*trg Bokeljske 391;* ✎ *032 304720; www. museummaritimum.com;* ⊕ *Jul–Sep 08.00–23.00 Mon–Fri, 10.00–16.00 Sat–Sun; Apr–Jul & Sep–Oct 08.00–18.00 Mon–Fri, 09.00–13.00 Sat–Sun; Oct–Apr 09.00–17.00 Mon–Fri, 09.00–12.00 Sat–Sun; entry (inc audio guide) adult/child €4/1*). With a wider display than its Perast equivalent, the Maritime Museum serves to remind how inseparable are the Boka and the sea, and illustrates a seafaring fraternity that has survived since the 9th century. In the 18th century over 400 ships from the Bay of Kotor sailed the seas of the world, in addition to the 300 vessels plying local waters. The museum has a splendid collection of paintings recalling great sea battles, charts, weaponry, furniture and costumes along with the fascinating minutiae of marine history.

It is also interesting to find a selection of English earthenware and learn that it was high fashion in 19th-century Kotor. There are many local peculiarities of national dress, one rather jarringly representing a black-veiled bride. A showcase of bottles brightly decorated and inscribed – 'remember me', 'for my true love' – is left to speculation: were these in the absence of photographs, for keepsakes or floating talismans, or were they for tossing to the ocean when all hope was gone? No doubt there is someone who knows the answer.

Outside again there is much to explore. Within the twisting pink-paved streets much is still under restoration (echoes of 'New York would be beautiful if only they would finish it'). Do not overlook the pretty **Church of St Luke (Sv Luka)** [142 C1], facing the town hall and built in 1195. Originally Catholic, it transferred to the Orthodox Church in 1657 and now serves both.

Near the north gate, the Bastion Restaurant and the route to the heights above the city, is **Sv Marija** [142 D1]. The pink-and-white stone church you see is essentially 14th century but again it is an example of a church built over a predecessor, which in this case is said to have been the first Episcopal church of Kotor. Within the last few years remnants have been found here of a 6th-century baptistry from the time of the Byzantine Emperor Justinian. (From the earliest Middle Ages St Marija was always considered a protector and one may find her church in most medieval towns.) Some 17th-century Serbo-Byzantine-influenced frescoes have also been uncovered. During the cleaning of a crucifix in 1984, three coins were found dating it to c1374. Rebecca West described the sculpture in 1940:

> the crucifix of a suffering Christ with a crown of real thorns and hair made of shavings, which is ascribed to Michaelangelo by a learned monk of the seventeenth century, who must have been a great liar.

In the last century the church was dedicated to Berta Hosanna, a nun – there are relatively few of them in the Serbian Orthodox Church – beatified 75 years ago for her participation in the 16th-century fight against Barbarossa. Scenes from her life feature in bas-relief on the great door of the church and her sarcophagus lies within.

BEYOND KOTOR

LADDER OF CATTARO To ascend the wall of rock to the pre-1916 frontier, to Njeguši and to Cetinje beyond, the thrilling road makes a series of ever more impossible hairpins – only matched by the ancient zig-zag mule track known as the Ladder of Cattaro (Cattaro being the Italian name for Kotor). As Edith Durham explained in 1904, until 1879 this:

> was the only path into Montenegro … making of the road was for a long while dreaded by the Montenegrins who argued that a road that will serve for a cart will also serve for artillery.

The views at each of the 25 ascending turns become ever more spectacular until after 20km you reach **Krstac**, on the edge of **Lovćen National Park**, where you will wish to linger and take in the stunning view of the entire gulf. (There is an agreeable pit stop at **Konoba Krstac**, situated just beyond the summit of the road, where local ham, cheeses and grills are served on a terrace.) Cetinje (pages 79–90) lies 25km ahead.

Getting there To find the asphalt road which is today known as the Ladder of Cattaro, leave Kotor port in an easterly direction, passing the south gate of the old city. At the first junction you may either go straight up the hill to the left on a small road, or follow the main road right, leaving a supermarket on your left. At the second junction follow the Budva road for 2km before turning left steeply uphill. Note that when you meet oncoming traffic it is sometimes a tight squeeze.

KOTOR TO BUDVA There are three routes you can take to Budva, all of them rather confusingly signed.

In 1941 the staff of the British Legation in Belgrade, including wives and undercover SOE officers, was evacuated by road to the Bay of Kotor, where they were to be picked up by either an RAF flying boat or an RN submarine. Unfortunately, the Italian occupying force got there first and was in attendance when HMS *Regent* surfaced.

The Italians observed diplomatic protocol impeccably, sending two of their officers to the *Regent* to guarantee the safety of the RN officer who had landed to finalise arrangements. But no-one had told the Luftwaffe, who sent three Stuka dive bombers to attack the *Regent*. Fortunately they missed but the *Regent* crash-dived with her Italian visitors on board and shipped them off to Malta, leaving the real and pretend diplomats on shore with the submariner.

The happy ending to the story is that everyone continued to observe the niceties and all the marooned officers were duly flown to their intended destinations in no time.

Direct route For the most direct road (21km), through the tunnel (1,637m) in the direction of Tivat Airport, bear left after leaving Kotor (the extreme right-hand fork takes you by a slow route over Vrmac Hill to Tivat), then beyond the tunnel turn left beneath the ridge of Lovćen National Park and across the **Grbalj Plain**. Like the Cetinje–Podgorica road, this is a bit of a racetrack, further complicated by the fact that it is a garden road with smallholdings on each side and plenty of signs offering local produce, like honey, for sale. There are more often than not police speed checks in operation along this route.

As you near Budva, you'll pass close to Jaz Beach; for details, see page 177.

Where to eat near Tivat Airport

✕ **Konoba Velji Mlin** Radanovići; m 067 644460, 069 788392; ⊕ 12.00–24.00. Unless you keep your eyes skinned you could easily miss this *konoba*, situated before Jaz Beach; look out for a blue metal bridge, on the left in the direction of Budva. From the road it looks little more than a shack but it is an appealing place, just 2 or 3 tables inside & a few more beside the little trout stream, & a talented chef who slow-cooks in the traditional country way, using pots with special lids to hold glowing coals, rather like an upside-down barbecue. The method is called cooking *ispod sač* ('beneath the cover'). When meat is prepared with vegetables in this manner the result is charcoal-flavoured but, with the moisture intact, it yields a delicious natural sauce. Dishes, composed only of local ingredients, inc local lamb & veal, sea or river fish & soft Grbalj cheese with fennel & fresh-baked bread. No CCs. €€€

✕ **Restoran Šebelj** Lastva Grbaljska; ☎ 033 463544; e restoran@sebelj.com; www.sebelj.com; ⊕ 08.00–24.00. On the other side of the road to Konoba Velji Mlin, the Šebelj has specialities that include grills, seafood & traditional dishes, as well as meals cooked *ispod sač*, & several vegetarian options. They also have 3 1st-floor rooms to let, all with AC & terrace (€€). No CCs. €€€

Route through the Lovćen foothills There is a corkscrew alternative to the fast road linking Kotor with Budva, twisting above it and through the Lovćen foothills. That is the region Hubert Butler describes (see page x). If you have time to spare, take this route and see the traditional villages of Šisići and Gorovići. During the restoration of Podlastva Monastery after the 1979 earthquake, evidence of a 6th-century Christian church was uncovered.

Route via Tivat A third route to Budva travels round the inner Bay of Kotor via Prčanj to Tivat, 14km away. (For details, see following section.) This road is very narrow, which can make passing other vehicles tricky at times. Look out for cosy *konobe* (taverns) in this area. Usually they will also serve light meals – delicious local ham and cheese, sandwiches and so on – which are sometimes accompanied by the lilting tunes of the *Bokeljski mornari* (see page 147) in the evening. This is a treat because in general Montenegro, oddly, does not have a great musical tradition. (In the mountains the old ballads were traditionally accompanied by the *gusle* – a one-stringed fiddle.) Along the way you will notice how each group of houses will have its own tiny stone harbour or landing place, with nets and floats laid out to dry in the sun. Keep an eye open towards the grassy slope above for a tall house with three clearly defined dormer windows: the home of three legendary sisters, each in love, so the story goes, with the same errant sea wolf and each watching day after day for his return. Eventually one died and the other two walled up her window; the same fate later befell the second and now there remains only one window unblocked.

MUO Some 2.5km north of Kotor is the hamlet of Muo. Nearby is **Vila Kavač**, a four-bedroom rental villa with views towards Sv Marko Island. Contact as Vila Prčanj, page 151. (**€€€**).

PRČANJ The village of Prčanj has a church, **Rođenje Bogorodice** (**Birth of Our Lady**), which is out of all proportion to its thousand inhabitants and took 120 years to build. Second in size only to the cathedral at Dubrovnik, it bears witness to the prosperity of this tiny place in 1789 at the time of its inception, when it was the home port to 30 ocean-going vessels. Designed by Venetian Bernardino Maccarucci, the church displays a collection of painting and sculpture worthy of its size, including works by Piazzetta, Tiepolo, Balestra and numerous domestic artists. In the sacristy there is a silver cup that once belonged to Lord Byron who, it is rumoured, enjoyed a romantic tryst with a lady of Prčanj; not at all beyond the bounds of possibility.

For two centuries from 1625 the sailors from here ran an early mail service through the Mediterranean which, bearing in mind the number of pirates at large, can have been no mean task. But the village is most proud of Captain Ivo Visin who, in 1852, set out aboard a 300-tonne brigantine, the *Splendido*, to circumnavigate the globe 'with ten guns and a crew of eleven'. Stories of his adventures are woven into village folklore: the mutinies and the pirates; the faithful ship-boy and the riches accrued; and how on his homecoming seven years later, without so much as stopping at his house, he climbed barefoot to the church to give thanks to the Virgin. For his troubles he earned the white flag with the black eagle, the highest Austrian naval decoration, which he received from Emperor Franz Joseph himself and which now occupies pride of place next to Lord Byron's cup. And Splendido is now a favoured hotel name.

⌂ Where to stay and eat

✱ ⌂ **Splendido** (43 rooms) Naselje Glavati bb; ✆032 301700; e rezervacije@splendido-hotel. com; www.splendido-hotel.com. Although this is the innermost stretch of the Boka, the Splendido has a peaceful bayside position where the private pebble beach is carefully maintained & the water looks translucent. Lovely swimming pool with beguiling views over the Boka to the mountains, seawater jacuzzi. Rooms have safe-deposit boxes,

AC, cable TV, internet connection, minibars, though some readers have complained that those on the top floor are too small to make comfortable dbls. Restaurant, incorporating bar & snack bar. CCs accepted. **€€€€€**
✱ ⌂ **Bokeljski Dvori** (10 rooms) Glavati bb; ✆032 336113/4; e bokeljskidvor@t-com.me; www.hotelbokeljskidvori.com. On the coast road from Kotor to Tivat, overlooking the bay

above **The ancient seaport of Ulcinj is as bustling as ever, full of warm hospitality** (NTOM) pages 212–18

below **This view of the Budva Riviera features Sveti Stefan in the foreground** (B/S) pages 165–97

left   The Church of St Luke, Kotor, was built in 1195. Although it was originally Catholic, it transferred to the Orthodox Church in 1657 and now serves both (NF/AWL) pages 147–8

below   Founded in 1252, the pristine Morača Monastery sits beside an orchard, where the Svetigora waterfall plunges into the ravine below (MM/S) page 298

bottom   The Sv Trojica Monastery in Pljevlja, originating from the early 16th century, lies on a hillside to the north of the centre (D/S) pages 268–9

right   A mosaic Orthodox Serbian icon of St Peter from Cetinje in old town Budva (VZ/S) pages 174–6

below right   Picturesque Savina Monastery lies to the east of the sunny city of Herceg Novi (S3P/S) pages 125–6

below left   Ostrog is Montenegro's most atmospheric monastery, miraculously carved into the side of a cliff (SS) page 235

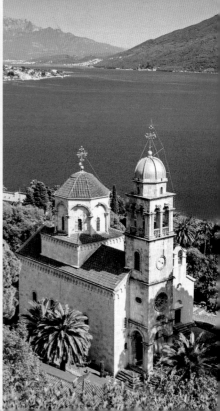

above The Kolo-oro national dance involves a routine in which one circle of men is elevated by another standing on their shoulders (NTOM) page 251

left A fisherman checks his nets in one of the numerous small fishing villages along the coast (NTOM)

below left An accordion player in Virpazar, a traditional fishing village on the edge of Skadar Lake (WP/A) pages 227–9

below A grove of olive trees, some of the 500,000 trees growing in Montenegro's coastal areas (PK/S)

above **The vegetable and fish market in Kotor, shielded by 20m ramparts** (MV/S) page 144

above right **Tobacco leaves drying in Montenegro** (O/S)

below right **Local lace for sale in Petrovac na Moru** (WB/AWL) pages 191–7

The diverse terrain and climate in Montenegro means that, despite its small size, it is home to a large variety of birds and mammals.

above **Purple heron (*Ardea purpurea*)**
(DVDN/MP/FLPA) page 6

left **Dalmatian pelican (*Pelecanus crispus*)**
(I/FLPA) page 6

below left **Eurasian lynx (*Lynx lynx*)**
(FIO/FIO/FLPA) page 5

below **Grey wolf (*Canis lupus*)**
(FIO/FIO/FLPA) page 5

above   **At 1,465km, Žabljak is a natural base for winter sports and a tourist hub** (S3P/S) pages 251–6

below   **Created in 1952, Biogradska Gora was Montenegro's first national park** (O/S) pages 271–4

left Climbing on the cliffs above the Morača River is not for the faint hearted (NTOM) pages 299–300

below left Rafting on the Tara River is a wonderfully exhilarating experience (VP/S) page 245

below right Mountain biking around Mt Bjelasica is best undertaken in the summer months (NTOM) page 274

to Dobrota & the mountains. Small & intimate 3-star run by Dragoljub Četković with his wife & son. Atmospheric, cheerful & friendly; all rooms AC, 6 with partial Boka views. Restaurant (€€€) with extensive menu inc national specialities & bar. Parking. HB & FB also available. **€€€**

🏠 **Vila Prčanj** (3 rooms & 4 apts) ✆020 642495; m 067 000044; e monte.vila@hotmail.com; www.montevila.com. On the sea in the centre of town, simple but attractive rooms with AC, TV & mini fridge. Private beach. Under the same ownership is Vila Kavač, back near Muo. **€€€**

🏠 **Galia** (8 dbl, 4 sgl) ✆032 336215; e hotelgalia@t-com.me; www.garnihotelgalia. com. Clean but simple rooms have Wi-Fi, TV, AC,

safe, minibar. Balconies & terrace with bay views. Restaurant for hotel guests only. Parking. B&B, HB & FB available. **€€–€€€**

✱ ✗ **Konoba Lanterna** ✆032 337396; m 069 045227; www.kotorbay.info/firma-Konoba-Lanterna-884.htm; ⏱ summer 10.00–24.00, winter 10.00–24.00 Mon–Fri, evening only Sat–Sun. Family-run taverna with welcoming atmosphere & typical Boka décor. Seafood, meat & pancakes washed down with local wine from the barrel. Owner Ester Knejović makes pastries & tasty petits fours. Live music at w/ends with Boka musicians. Also a couple of apts for rent (€€). No CCs. **€€**

STOLIV From the straggling village of Gornji Stoliv, there are footpaths climbing the north face of Vrmac Hill.

🏠 Where to stay and eat

🏠 **Castello di Boca** (30 rooms) ✆032 338250; e mail@castellodiboca.com; www.castellodiboca. com. Rooms with AC, TV & balconies. To feed the inner artist, there's a quayside restaurant that exhibits works from Bosnia, Serbia, Russia & Ukraine, & rooms are decorated with paintings by Balkan artists. There's also an art gallery & painting classes; weekly Montenegrin food & wine tastings; & folk evenings (check future programme when booking). Russian & English spoken. HB €46; under 12s 50% reduction. **€€€€**

⛺ **Autokamp** ✆032 336551. Just beside the mini-market is a handwritten sign saying 'Autokamp'. This refers to a small field just across the road from the bay where a charming but monolingual elderly couple will be delighted to let you pitch your tent for €2, park your caravan for €3 or your car or motorbike for €1. Grandma will also ply you with homemade goodies.

✗ **Caffe Centar** Boarding house menu: soup, main course, salad, dessert & bread €5.50. **€**

Other practicalities
✉ **Post office** ⏱ 08.00–14.30 Mon–Fri

LEPETANE The beautiful shore road to Tivat continues with lyrical views across to Perast and along the Verige narrows to the ferry port of Lepetane, opposite Kamenari, whose name derives from the Venetian slang *putane* for whores. By the dock there are one or two nice little cafés with tables and chairs outside to enjoy the nautical activity. In front of the 18th-century church is the village shop – whose owner speaks no English but has plenty of the universal language of goodwill – which is a useful place for picnic supplies.

Getting around A number of **buses** cover the route between Lepetane and Tivat each day, both those connecting to Herceg Novi via the ferry and local kombi buses travelling between Tivat and Kotor, by the gulf road.

For **ferry** details see *Kamenari to Kostanjica*, pages 130–1.

Tourist information
🗺 **Tourist office** Lepetane rd, by turn-off to Donja Lastva village; m 069 435496; ⏱ summer only.

⌂ Where to stay and eat *Map, page 154.*

Near Lepetane is the **Lovćen Motel and Autokamp,** but it proved unwelcoming and cannot be recommended. Instead try:

⌂ **Apartments Vila Antonia** (8 apts) Lepetane village; 📞 032 686035; ⊕ 09.00–14.00 & 17.00–20.00; ℮ montenegro.apartments@ gmail.com; www.apartmentsantonia.com. Built in 2010, just 20m from the bay, apts behind & above the coastal road have balconies with bay views – so watch ferries come & go from Kamenari. AC, multichannel TV, internet & – in some – washing machines. Own water supply so no shortages in high season. Owners Karolina & Zlatko Vucinović also own a local computer shop. €€

⌂ **Konoba Restoran Tivat** (6 rooms) 📞 032 684717. Conveniently located near a (marked) bus stop on the Lepetane bayside road, some 3km south of the ferry. A lovely little place with nice views, though the road can be noisy. Home cooking. Also B&B (€€). No CCs. No English spoken. €

DONJA LASTVA In the little square of this bayside village, Sv Roko church faces an art gallery café and a fish restaurant.

It takes about 15 minutes to walk from the waterside lower village into the town of Tivat. Or you could stay awhile. From the village, a minor road climbs to the upper village of **Gornja Lastva** (page 160), which gives access to paths beyond for hiking on **Vrmac Hill** (pages 160–1).

⌂ Where to stay and eat Both the **Zlatno Sidro** hotel and restaurant and the **Sky Blue** hotel were closed at the time of writing, with no signs of reopening soon.

⌂ **Hotel Perper** (9 apts) Donja Lastva bb; 📞 032 684904; m 068 031004; ℮ hotelperper@ live.com; www.hotelperper.com. Usefully positioned 2km from Tivat centre, 5km from Lepetane ferry terminal, 4km from Tivat airport & 50m from the sea. All apts have sea view balcony, kitchen, living room (3 extra beds possible), AC, cable TV, Wi-Fi, minibar & safe. Parking, bar & garden restaurant (€€€). €€€

✗ **Giardino** opp church; m 069 435496; ⊕ 10.00–01.00. A fish restaurant with a nice Boka ambience. Ask the amiable proprietor Zoran for the catch of the day; it will be well prepared & reasonably priced. Service can be slow but it's all part of the scene. Tables inside have the appropriate fish-net décor & there's a log fire when it's chilly. Or you can sit outside on the leafy square. No CCs. €€€

⊑ **Mar & Mar** opp church; ⊕ 17.00–24.00. Art gallery café.

TIVAT

Like Herceg Novi, south-facing Tivat is a garden city, each family cultivating its own *dvori* (yard) with roses in abundance. Often it is referred to as the youngest town in the Boka and there is no substantive evidence of urban life before the Middle Ages when, to enjoy the benefits of its milder climate, the noblemen of Kotor began to build second homes here, strange as that may seem today considering Kotor is barely 14km away. It is a reminder that distance, like everything else, is relative and long ago 'over the hill' could be far away. Certainly in winter it is sunnier in Tivat, and subtropical palms, magnolias, oleanders and bougainvillea grow in profusion. The town park blooms with exotic plants brought home by gulf sailors but little else is left to show from those earlier days.

In the town, the 14th-century **St Antun's Church** has an inscription mentioning Tvrtko I of Bosnia who, in that century, founded Herceg Novi. Near the water a **defence tower** still stands, a marker to the Buća family's once-huge estate.

PORTO MONTENEGRO Forty-odd years ago when its airport was modernised to receive large aircraft, Tivat, with its surrounding sandy beaches, enjoyed a surge in tourism and several new hotels appeared. However, it was not to last and, with political tensions growing in the region, visitor numbers soon fell back, leaving the pretty little town a shadow of its former self. And so it might have stayed had it not been for the vision of Canadian financier Peter Munk and his fellow investors who, early in the new millennium, identified immense potential in an abandoned military shipyard with an especially deep natural harbour. The master plan they subsequently devised was to centre around a grand marina comprising 600 berths, to include ample facilities for 'mega yachts'. On shore a community would be constructed, made up of waterfront residences, shops and a nautical museum, all set in landscaped parkland.

The project became known as **Porto Montenegro**. The complex offers 250 berths ranging from 12m to 150m, with a further 240 berths planned by May 2015, and has the potential to build this up to 850. The existing residences, grouped around the waterfront, each have private pools, courtyards and covered parking. All residential owners have the option to take up a long-term berth lease.

A quayside restaurant and a swimming pool are among the latest additions to Porto Montenegro. Munk is supporting various institutions in the town and is a sponsor of the local soccer team, known as Arsenal (echoing the name applied to the original shipyard area). The fears of cynics have been allayed and the massive development hasn't drowned the unique charm of little Tivat. The yachtocracy have already come, seen and conquered.

BAY OF TIVAT A thin chain of islets floats in the south of Tivat's bay. On **Ostrvo Cvijeća** (the Island of Flowers – also, somewhat confusingly, known as **Prevlaka**, though it has no connection with the peninsula on the Croatian border that bears the same name) are the partially excavated ruins of a 13th-century Benedictine monastery, which is dedicated to St Michael the Archangel (Sv Arhangela Mihailo), and, beneath these, of an earlier church believed to be circa 9th century. The monastery was from 1219 the seat of the Zeta metropolinate, until its mid-15th century destruction by the Venetians. Bar archaeologist Mladen Zagarčanin has been working laboriously at this site for some time. The island was once a tourist settlement and has lately sheltered refugees from neighbouring countries.

Sv Marko (also known as **Stradioti**) operated as a Club Med in the rosier 1970s, but this has been closed for some time. On tiny **Otok** (also known as **Gospa od Milosti** – Our Lady of Grace) there are the remains of a 15th-century Franciscan monastery. It is also believed to have been built on the site of a previous church. At the time of writing, there were no organised boat trips to the islands, but you could enquire at the tourist office to see if any are running.

GETTING THERE AND AWAY

By air For details of flights to Tivat, see pages 34–6.

Tivat Airport The airport (☎ *032 670960; www.montenegroairports.com*), a fairly modern, airy building, is 4km south of the town. There's a tourist information machine and a kiosk at departures, free baggage trolleys, and a Costa coffee café, with a baby-changing facility and a disabled toilet combined. Useful for arriving passengers is an ATM, but there's no exchange desk. Montenegro Airlines has an office here (☎ *032 670500*).

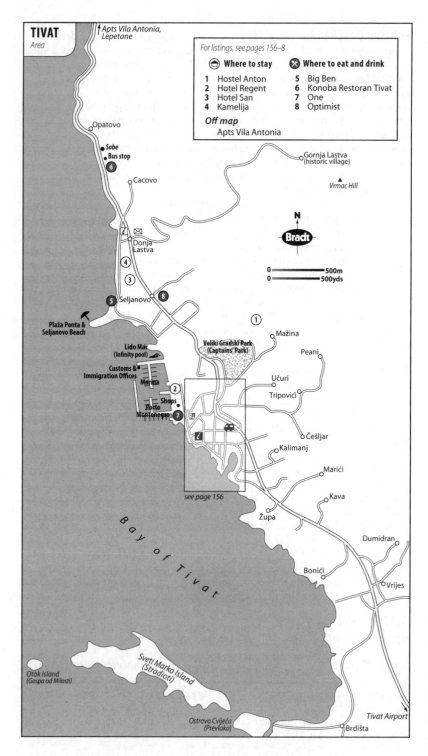

TIVAT
Area

For listings, see pages 156–8

🏠 Where to stay
1 Hostel Anton
2 Hotel Regent
3 Hotel San
4 Kamelija
Off map
Apts Vila Antonia

✖ Where to eat and drink
5 Big Ben
6 Konoba Restoran Tivat
7 One
8 Optimist

↑ Apts Vila Antonia,
Lepetane

Opatovo

Sobe
● Bus stop
⑥

○ Cacovo

Gornja Lastva
(historic village)

▲ Vrmac Hill

N

Bradt

0 ————— 500m
0 ————— 500yds

Donja
Lastva

④

③

⑤ Seljanovo   ⑧

Plaža Ponta &
Seljanovo Beach

Lido Mar
(Infinity pool)

Customs &
Immigration Offices

Marina

Porto
Montenegro

②
Shops
⑦

Veliki Gradski Park
(Captains' Park)

①

Mažina ○

Peani ○

Učuri ○

Tripovići ○

Češljar ○

Kalimanj ○

Marići ○

Kava ○

Župa ○

see page 156

B a y   o f   T i v a t

Dumidran ○

Boniči ○

Vrijes ○

Otok Island
(Gospa od Milosti)

Sveti Marko Island
(Stradioti)

Ostrovo Cvijeća
(Prevlaka)

Tivat Airport ↗

○ Brdišta

154

Car-hire desks at the airport are usually manned only when a passenger with a reservation is expected. Airport parking from 06.30–21.00 costs around €1 per hour.

Getting into town A **bus** connection (*€1 one way*) between Tivat Airport and town operates about once an hour in each direction.

A **taxi** from midtown to the airport should not cost much over €5. Calling one of the taxi services (see below) will result in a much lower bill than hailing a cab at the airport entrance, which is likely to set you back about double this.

Getting to Budva from the airport A Montenegro Airlines **minibus** service operates between the airport and Budva bus station (*€3 one way*). It is scheduled to meet each incoming Montenegro Airlines flight, but don't rely on it, particularly outside the summer months when there are no local Montenegro Airlines flights.

By bus The **bus station** [156 C3] (*ul Palih Boraca bb;* ✆ *032 674262*) is in the middle of town with good services to destinations throughout the country and beyond. Timetables are only selectively displayed and each bus company has its own booth (⊕ *06.00–20.00*). Prices vary slightly over competitive routes but the ticket sellers do not speak English and it's probably best and certainly easiest to take pot-luck unless you have a tame interpreter.

The fare to Belgrade (12–13hrs) is €18.50. There are half-a-dozen buses a day to and from Herceg Novi (€3) and an hourly service to Budva (€2). At the ticket office they can show you a handwritten current timetable. The national services are augmented by a local independent company with at least ten small buses a day serving the immediate Boka region – Lepetane, Prčanj, Kotor, etc.

Car hire

🚗 **Avis Tivat Airport** ✆032 673448; www. avisworld.com. 1-way rentals can be arranged. Specialises in Opel, mostly diesels.

🚗 **Europcar** Tivat Airport; m 068 848402; e tivat@europcar.me; www.europcar.me. International 1-way may be possible. Min age 21 & 2 years' driving experience.

🚗 **In Rent-a-Car** ✆031 345700; www. inmontenegro.com. Fiat, Renault Twingo, Renault Grand, etc. Free delivery anywhere in Montenegro, baby seat & mobile phone inc.

🚗 **Kompas Rent-a-Car** Tivat Airport; ✆020 244117, m 069 423800

🚗 **Meridian Rent A Car** Tivat Airport; m 069 060525; online reservation www.meridian-rentacar.com

🚗 **Sixt Rent-a-car** Tivat Airport; ✆033 453100; e office@sixt.co.me; www.sixt.co.me. Also Porto Montenegro.

GETTING AROUND Central Tivat is relatively compact and most spots within the town can be reached **on foot**.

Taxis

✳ 🚗 **Auto taxi** ✆032 671517; m 069 341517. Đuretić Duško is a reliable taxi driver (mention the Bradt guide).

🚗 **Đir taxi** ✆19777

🚗 **Red taxi** ✆19729

TOURIST INFORMATION

ℹ **Tourist information centre** [156 B3] Palih Boraca 8; ✆032 671324; e totivat@t-com. me; www.tivat.travel; ⊕ summer 08.00–20.00

Mon–Sat, 08.00–12.00 Sun, winter 08.00–15.00 Mon–Fri, 08.00–14.00 Sat. A particularly helpful & knowledgeable office supplying good details

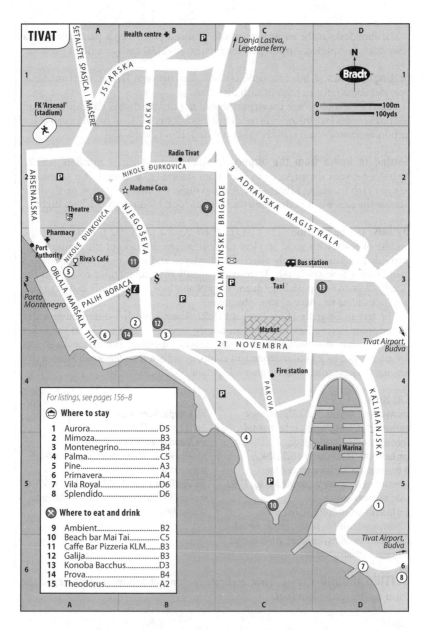

Map labels:

TIVAT

Health centre ✚

Donja Lastva,
Lepetane ferry

N

Bradt

0 — 100m
0 — 100yds

FK 'Arsenal'
(stadium)

Radio Tivat

NIKOLE ĐURKOVIĆA

☆ Madame Coco

Theatre

Pharmacy

Port
Authority

Riva's Café

Bus station

Taxi

Market

21 NOVEMBRA

Fire station

Porto
Montenegro

Tivat Airport,
Budva

Kalimanj Marina

Tivat Airport,
Budva

For listings, see pages 156–8

🛏 **Where to stay**
1   Aurora............................D5
2   Mimoza..........................B3
3   Montenegrino.................B4
4   Palma.............................C5
5   Pine................................A3
6   Primavera.......................A4
7   Vila Royal......................D6
8   Splendido.......................D6

🍴 **Where to eat and drink**
9   Ambient.........................B2
10   Beach bar Mai Tai...........C5
11   Caffe Bar Pizzeria KLM....B3
12   Galija.............................B3
13   Konoba Bacchus.............D3
14   Prova.............................B4
15   Theodorus......................A2

---

of hotels, restaurants & local beaches. As well as providing maps & brochures, they also have some local handicrafts for sale & a good selection of information on local hiking.

Regional kiosks, in Donja Lastva & on the Luštica Peninsula at Krašići & Radovići, operate seasonally only.

🏠 **WHERE TO STAY** *Maps, above and page 156.*
Like the other coastal towns, Tivat experiences occasional water-supply problems during the high season, July to August.

⌂ Hotel Regent (86 rooms) Porto Montenegro; ☎ 032 660660; e reservations. pm@regenthotels.com; www.regenthotels. com. Brand spanking new waterfront luxury accommodation, set to open in Aug 2014. The 5-storey, terracotta-roofed building incorporates designs inspired by Venetian Renaissance masters, while still rooted in the traditions of local architecture. Each room is set to boast awe-inspiring views of the Boka Kotorska & surrounding mountains. €€€€€

⌂ Primavera (3 rooms, 6 suites) Maršala Tita 15; ☎ 032 674830; e hotel.primavera.tivat@gmail. com; www.primavera.co.me. Facing the sea, rooms have AC, TV, Wi-Fi, safe, laundry service, minibar, balcony & bay view. Bar & restaurant (20% food discount for residents). Parking. Pets allowed. Free transfer from Tivat airport; Dubrovnik or Podgorica airport transfer €35. €€€€

⌂ Hotel San (19 rooms) Seljanovo bb, 2km from Donja Lastva; ☎ 032 675017; e recepcija@ hotelsan.me; www.hotelsan.me. Quiet location 10m from the sea; balconies. Garden & restaurant with traditional Montenegrin cuisine. €€€

✳ ⌂ Montenegrino (10 rooms) ul 21 Novembra 27; ☎ 032 674900; e montenegrino@ t-com.me; http://hotelmontenegrino.com. A warm & efficient welcome. AC, satellite TV (CNN available), Wi-Fi, safe, minibar, laundry service, terrace. Unpretentious restaurant with national cuisine (€€€). They will arrange anything from boats & rafts to motorbikes. All CCs except Diners. €€€

⌂ Palma (122 rooms, 8 suites) Šetalište Iva Vizina; ☎ 032 672288; e primorjesales@t-com. me; ⊕ all year. There's a touch of nostalgia about this old bayfront place with distinctive blue shutters; it must have been a bit of a destination in its own right once upon a time. Some rooms with minibars, AC, satellite TV, fridge; half with sea view. Suites have 4 beds. Conference hall with 60 seats. Internet. Restaurant Marzamin (€€€), across the street, is part of the hotel & serves above-avg food. CCs accepted. 50% sgl supplement; children under 2 free; 2–12 30% discount. HB €€€

✳ ⌂ Splendido (8 rooms & 4 suites) Kalimanjska bb; ☎ 032 301700; e rezervacije@ splendido-hotel.com; www.splendido-hotel.com. Comfortable & friendly hotel 50m from beach, though the rooms are sparsely furnished. AC, satellite TV, minibar. Laundry service. Internet at reception. Good-quality restaurant (€€€) with terrace & varied menu; also a café-pizzeria (€€) on the promenade itself. Parking. Their recommended taxi driver will drive you to or from Tivat Airport for €5. CCs accepted. €€€

⌂ Vila Royal (6 rooms, 6 suites) Kalimanjska bb; ☎ 032 675310; e villaroyal@t-com.me. A smart little boutique hotel, 20m from beach. AC, satellite TV, minibar. Restaurant & bar. Pets allowed. €€€

⌂ Aurora (30 rooms) Kalimanjska bb; ☎ 032 671259; e aurora@t-com.me. East of Kalimanj marina, & with a local ambience, but not much English. AC, TV, room fridge. Fair-sized garden with a variety of plants. €€

⌂ Hostel Anton (16 rooms) Mazina bb; m 069 261182; e hostelanton09@gmail.com; http://hostelanton.com. 3km from Tivat Airport; 700m from bus station. Beds in 6- & 10-bed dorms, or dbl/twin rooms. AC, lockers, common room, washing machine, laundry service, parking. Garden with fruit trees & BBQ area, free b/fast & use of Wi-Fi, TV, DVD library, kitchen, iron, linen & hairdryer. Reasonably priced evening meal available in season. 3 nights for 2, Oct–May. Cash only – on arrival. Dorm bed €11; dbl/twin €27. €€

⌂ Kamelija (120 rooms) Seljanovo bb, 2km on bayside road to Donja Lastva; ☎ 032 684588; www.htpmimoza.me. Old-style, state-owned place opposite a stone beach. A few further rooms available in adjacent Vile Park. Pool, tennis & basketball courts, restaurant & bar. €€

⌂ Mimoza (72 rooms) Njegoševa bb; ☎ 032 672393; www.htpmimoza.me. Typical old-style state hotel in city centre, 20m from beach, & clean but plain. Restaurant & bar. €€

⌂ Pine (26 rooms) Obala Pine bb; ☎ 032 671255; www.htpmimoza.me. State-owned & pretty basic, albeit near the sea in city centre. AC, telephone & minibar. Tavern & restaurant. €€

✗ WHERE TO EAT AND DRINK *Maps, opposite and page 154.*

Restaurants

✗ One Porto Montenegro; m 067 486045; e one@jettyone.com. Cool white marina's-edge

restaurant opening on to terrace with glam sofas for posing; stylish light menu. *Forbes* magazine has described One as providing 'the country's only serious wine list outside the Aman'; we assume it refers to a selection of whites & reds from the usual Western suspects along with some stars from Croatia & Montenegro. €€€€

✗ **Optimist** Seljanova bb. Restaurant on 1st floor above a bakery & supermarket on the Adriatic Highway, between Donja Lastva & Tivat centre. Pizzeria & Mediterranean food, & catch-of-the-day fish. Same ownership as Al Posto Giusto in Herceg Novi. €€€€

✗ **Konoba Bacchus** Palih boraca bb; m 069 042688. One of Tivat's best restaurants, with fish & grilled meat specialities. Free transport from Porto Montenegro. €€€

✗ **Prova** Šetalište Iva Vizina 1; ✆032 671468; www.prova.co.me; ⏰ 08.00–24.00. Restaurant lounge bar. Owned by HTP Primorje, the Montenegrin company that ran the old traditional state hotels, this is one of the nicest restaurants in town, & reflects the all-abiding seafaring history of the place. Prova translates as 'prow' of a ship; hence the design. The promenade here is named for the noble Ivo Visin, captain of the *Splendido* (see page 150). The elegant terrace overlooks the bay. Innovative menu for lunch & dinner, but the old-fashioned 'gourmet' b/fast of sausages, eggs, carrot salad, aubergine chutney, cheese, grilled mushrooms & yoghurt, all for under €5 should not be overlooked. W/end music; good English spoken. CCs accepted. €€€

✗ **Theodorus** trg od Kulture. Cocktail bar, garden & inside restaurant; a decent varied menu, popular with expatriates as well as locals. €€€

✗ **Ambient** ul II Dalmatinske 7; ✆032 671434; www.ambienttivat.com. Secluded terrace & polished ambience, popular with locals & expatriates. Mediterranean food; pizza & pasta. Pianist plays every evening 20.00–23.00. €€–€€€

✗ **Big Ben** Seljanovo bb; m 068 054588. Near the Kamelija Hotel on the bayside road, a relaxed café/pizzeria that's a favourite of local expatriates, with a few dbl/trpl/quadruple rooms available (€€€). €€

✗ **Caffe Bar Pizzeria KLM** Njegoševa 10, opposite the tourist office; ✆032 672112; www.klmtivat.com. A cheerful, uncomplicated corner café with a pleasant terrace where they will make you feel welcome in good English & pleasantly serve you reasonable food, inc burgers, pasta, salads, pancakes & an English b/fast. €€

✗ **Galija** Moše Pijade 9. Friendly pizza & pasta place with booths & above-avg pizza. No CCs. €€

Bars and nightlife

♀ **Beach bar Mai Tai** Water's edge between Palma Hotel & Kalimanj Marina, this well deserves a mention. A lovely sunset spot to linger – mostly outside but some cover – over a fresh limonata or even something stronger in company with locals of all ages. Nice staff.

☆ **Madame Coco** A few steps east of Porto Montenegro; m 069 244662; ⏰ 22.30–05.00. DJs, w/end events, karaoke nights, generous prizes.

SPORTS AND OTHER ACTIVITIES In addition to the following, sports facilities are being developed at Porto Montenegro (see opposite).

Diving

↝ **Diving school** D C Neptun-Mimosa, next to the Kamelija Hotel on the bayside road; m 069 044225. Run by brothers Boris & Igor & recommended by a reader who also likes the Big Ben bar almost next door.

Tennis

⚲ **Tennis club** ul Seljanovo bb; m 069 340260

Yachting

Porto Montenegro has become an official port of entry into Montenegro & vessels are able to purchase a vignette allowing unlimited use of the country's

navigable waters for periods varying from a week to a year. The new marina is a 10min boat ride from the Azalea Maritime Training Centre at Bijela.

✱ △ **Avel Yachting** Luke Tomanovica bb; ✆032 672703; e info@avel-yachting.com; www.avel-yachting.com. Charter (*day charters from €450, week-long from €3,000*), guardiennage, maintenance, repairs, sales & brokerage. Office 3min walk from Porto Montenegro, Jetty 1.

△ **Marina** [156 D5] Kalimanj Marina ✆032 671039. 330 berths, owned by the town.

△ **MMS, Montenegro Marine Services d.o.o** m 069 845613; e montenegromarineservices.

com; www.montenegromarineservices.com. Yacht management, boatyard services, winter berthing; brokerage, charters, yacht deliveries.
△ **MRM d.o.o** trg od Kulture 7; ✆032 540344; www.mrm-maritime.me. Yacht support services. Yacht agency & full concierge service.

Porto Montenegro See pages 153 and below.
△ **Yacht Guardiennage Montenegro d.o.o** bul Ivana Crnojevića 63, Podgorica; www. yachtservices.com. Various monthly packages available from Anglo/Australian/Dutch team.

SHOPPING There's a fruit and vegetable market (*zelena pijaca*), and a fish market (Ribarnica Montefish) [156 C3] in trg Magnolija, in front of the town hall and off 21 Novembra. For more general supplies, head to the large Voli supermarket on the Adriatic Highway at the main Tivat–Kotor crossroads, adjacent to Vuk petrol station.

At **Porto Montenegro** [off map 156 A3], you'll find a selection of shops, including a branch of the Podgorica bookstore, Narodna Knjiga (*www.narodna-knjiga.me*), a furniture store, a chandlery and a handful of designer boutiques.

Cvjećara Gardenija trg Magnolija, beside the green market. Flower shop.

Đurđa Florist 100m from Porto Montenegro, 50m from Theodorus restaurant. 'Your friendly flower shop' they say in English & they offer free delivery.

OTHER PRACTICALITIES
Banks
ATM machines can be found across from the promenade on Maršala Tita & across from the tourist information office on Palih boraca.

$ **Atlasmont Banka** ul Nikola Đurkovića
$ **CKB** ul Palih boraca bb
$ **Hipotekarna Banka** ul Palih boraca bb
$ **Montenegrobanka** ul Palih boraca 10
$ **Podgorička Banka** Moše Pijade 5

Internet & phone
🖴 **Sunrise Wireless Internet Club** trg Magnolija, opposite the main post office
T-Mobile Corner of Palih boraca & Maršala Tita. Telephone shop.
Telenor ul II Dalmatinske bb, trg Magnolija; ✆032 674327; 🕐 09.00–21.00 Mon–Sat. Telephone shop opposite the town hall. Sells Montenegro SIM cards.

Pharmacies
✚ **Mansa** ul Dalmatinska 2; ✆032 673397
✚ **Montefarm** Obala M Tita bb; ✆032 672373
✚ **Poen** ✆21 Novembra bb; ✆032 674929

Other
Fiko 2 Boraca bb. Hairdresser: cutting, colouring, highlights, blow dry.
Knightsbridge School ✆032 672655; e enquiries@knightsbridgeschools.com; www. knightsbridgeschools.com. At present housed within the Porto Montenegro complex, the school has pupils aged 3–11. Plans are ultimately to have facilities in place for ages 3–18, & to move to a dedicated building in Tivat town. Summer camp programme: 5-day sessions €450 (*transportation from Budva, Kotor & Herceg Novi available for additional fee*) for full details ✆067 814239; e kscamp@knightsbridgeschools.com; www. kscamp.org.
✉ **Post office** [156 C3] Palih boraca bb; 🕐 07.00–19.00 Mon–Sat. Opposite town hall.

WHAT TO SEE AND DO
Porto Montenegro [off map 156 A3] (✆ *032 660700 or 032 674660*; e *info@ portomontenegro.com*; *www.portomontenegro.com*). It's the intention of the team at the helm of the new marina and its surrounding community to promote the amenity as a 'year-round home port'. Even if the competitive palaces of the floating rich are berthed for all to gaze upon, the overall effect makes a pretty picture.

At the time of writing, facilities at the complex include the five-star Hotel Regent (page 157), a chic restaurant, One (page 157), a deli, a wood-fired pizzeria, and various shops. A naval heritage museum features such diverse subjects as a submarine recovered from the Boka and a set of historic correspondence from the Montenegrin royal family.

Sports facilities (*membership enquiries* ╲*032 660744;* e *vtanjga@portomontenegro. com;* ⊕ *06.00–22.00 Mon–Thu, 06.00–23.00 Fri–Sat, 06.00–20.00 Sun*) include a 65m bayside infinity pool, squash and tennis courts, a fitness facility, yoga and pilates, an extensive spa and wellness centre and a bowling alley. The port also has on-site customs and immigration, as well as Wi-Fi, laundry facilities, round-the-clock security and a school, Knightsbridge School International (KSI) (*www.ksi-montenegro.com*).

Vrmac Hill   In the 12th century, high on leafy **Vrmac Hill** at the rear of the city, the Slavs built a settlement known as **Pasiglav**. For whatever reason, perhaps the plague, by the 17th century it had died out and all that remains are a few stones overgrown with weeds. It is nice to find that elsewhere on the same hill life goes on, if only in a small way, in the tiny and bucolic 14th-century village of **Gornja Lastva**. Maybe from the beginning there was something healthier about its aspect; certainly its inhabitants are reputed to live to a great age, though this is hard to

---

WALKING IN VRMAC

Just above Gornja Lastva the tarmac road ends. Continue on foot up the rocky track, filling your water bottles beside the way at the spring serving the village well. Walk 2km up an easy uphill track through trees and wild flowers with blue, yellow and red/brown butterflies for company. After 4–5km you will come to a large circular clearing with two paths joining from the left. Continuing on the original track for another 60m you will see a small footpath going down to the right. Some 35m down the path lie the remains of Pasiglav, overgrown and barely recognisable, waiting for the archaeologists. Even to the layman a church is identifiable.

The main track – an old military road which has survived remarkably well in most parts – continues on all the way to the Austro-Hungarian Grlica fortress at Vrmac. About 2km past Pasiglav you will come to a prominent Partisan memorial commemorating the deaths of six fighters in August 1944, and in due course you will emerge on to the crest, walking through beechwoods and bracken with amazing views on both sides to the Boka, the Adriatic and Mt Lovćen.

This walk can be approached from the other end by turning right off the Kotor–Budva slow road (see *Route via Tivat*, page 150), just opposite the turning to Njeguši and Cetinje. It is signed to Vrmac, a narrow uphill road through gorse bushes and wildflowers, leading to the old Austro-Hungarian fortress and indeed to several World War II fortifications as well.

A useful map called *Vrmac – Hiking Paradise* (2005 edition) is obtainable from the tourism office in Tivat, and costs €2.

GETTING TO GORNJA LASTVA   There is no bus service to Gornja Lastva but you can park a car by the road. A taxi up to Gornja Lastva from Tivat will cost about €9–12 each way. If you are planning to hike on Vrmac Hill you would have to arrange a pick-up time in advance.

prove because only a handful are still full-time residents of the dozen or so dry-stone dwellings tucked into the fold beneath another **Sv Marija Church**. This 17th-century Sv Marija has her hands full as guardian of several Italian paintings, one of which, portraying the Virgin with her saints, is claimed to be from the school of Tiepolo. Perhaps it is no bad thing that it is often difficult to see inside these churches, with access often depending on the presence of the priest who could well be away shepherding his flock. As Jovan Martinović would say, 'it is always the problem of the key – always the key'. (For information on getting to Gornja Lastva, and on walking on Vrmac Hill, see box opposite.)

In August, on the first Saturday of the month, the village celebrates its festival. The little square and its two threshing floors are decked with flags and as many as 200 people come up from town to join the party and share the delicious homemade mulberry *rakija*.

Traditionally each house consisted of a ground floor where the wine and farm equipment were kept and an upper floor inhabited by the family. An attic on top was considered the very height of luxury. Most would have a walled garden area and a trellis to support the vine. Olive oil would be prepared in autumn for storage in never-washed ancient crocks, the remaining stones and pulp burned as winter fuel.

LUŠTICA PENINSULA

The peninsula of Luštica consists of around 40km² of *maquis* and meadowland, blue-flowering rosemary and wild pomegranate. Beyond the bay on the seaward side, the coast is serrated with hidden coves and conceals the cobalt vault of Plava Špilja (Blue Grotto).

As you set off, you'll cross the saltpans close to the shallow **Solila Lagoon** (**Tivatska solila**) formed by tidal seawater which has been recognised, along with other Montenegrin coastal regions, as an important stopover on the Adriatic Flyway (see page 63). The appellation relates to migrating and wintering birds, a significant proportion of them endangered species. Among others, the area is popular with waders, common crane, snipe, osprey and pygmy cormorant.

The road leading west and following Luštica's northern coastline passes through a growing number of settlements.

The peninsula is crisscrossed by small roads, largely signpost-free, and fringed by dense vegetation. Every now and then you suddenly emerge in an unspoilt cove with picture-book views. Sadly, however, this is one of the areas where the property developers are moving in and already there are clusters of new houses.

NORTHWEST TO ROSE

Getting there From Kotor, the most direct route to Budva travels through a tunnel and emerges close to Tivat Airport and thence on to the main Tivat–Budva road (about 16km). Almost opposite this junction is a tarmac road running across the Solila salt flats to the Luštica Peninsula.

Tourist information There is a seasonal tourist kiosk at Radovići.

Where to stay *Map, page 128.*

Luštica Mill House (3 rooms) Nr Marovici; m 065 513 5659; e kaminskijas@gmail.com; www.lusticahouse.com. Beautifully restored old stone olive mill house with en-suite dbl rooms.

€700–€1,500 per wk, depending on season. **€€€–€€€€**

Anderba (8 rooms) Krašići bb; \032 673027; e hotelanderba@t-com.me; ⊕ all year. Just 10m

4

from the beach in Krašići, 11km from Tivat, 9km from Rose. AC, satellite TV, safe deposit at reception. Bar & rooftop terrace restaurant (🕐 *08.00–late*). Stone sunbathing area, swimming jetty beneath. Conference room & parking. CCs accepted. **€€€**

🏠 **Vizantija** (Byzantium) (12 rooms) Kaluđerovina bb; 📞032 680020; www.vizantija. com. 10m from the beach & 9km from Tivat. AC, TV, minibar, terrace, sea view. Restaurant & terrace. Heated indoor pool, sauna, fitness room & massage. Private beach with free use of sun-loungers & umbrellas; dedicated children's bathing area separated from open sea. Cruising in hotel yacht (*6–8 persons*). Shooting excursions organised in season. Under 3s stay free; 3–12 reduced prices. **€€€**

✳ 🏠 **Villa Kristina** (4 apts) Bjelila bb; 📱 068 012098; e office@villakristina.me; www.

villakristina.me. Restaurant (🕐 *08.00–24.00; daily Boka menu;* **€€€**) with well-appointed apts for 2–4 ppl in a 17th-century vernacular stone building, located in an idyllic, off-the-beaten-track, tiny sheltered harbour. King-size beds, terraces, Wi-Fi, room safe, minibar. AC & TV in rooms & living room. Room service available. Sun-loungers & umbrellas. Gay-friendly. Parking. CCs accepted. **€€€**

🏠 **Apartmani Luštica** (2 apts) www. apartmanilustica.com. Modern, nicely designed apts, sleeping up to 5 & 3 ppl, in the villages of Mardari & Brguli respectively Priced at €55–75 & €25–45 depending on season. Baby cots available. **€€–€€€**

🏠 **Villa Složnabraéa** (17 rooms) Bjelila bb; 📞032 679749; e idavor@t-com.me. AC, restaurant, boat trips organised, night-fishing excursions. **€€–€€€**

✗ **Where to eat and drink**   As well as the hotel restaurants above, two individual places stand out:

✳ ✗ **Restaurant Vino Santo** Obala Đuraševića, Krtoli; 📱 067 851662; www.vinosanto.me; 🕐 12.00–24.00. This elegant restaurant has splendid sea views & one of Montenegro's best chefs, specialising in fish with a French flavour. Patron Dragan Peričić, having worked in Paris, is much happier talking to you in French than in English. CCs accepted. **€€€€€**

✗ **Konoba Maestral** Obala Đuraševića bb, Krtoli; 📱 068 045102; http://konobamaestral.wix. com/fishrestaurant. 🕐 10.00–24.00. On the beach with a good view of the islands in the bay. Good fish & shellfish & an attached windsurfing school. Sun-loungers & beach umbrellas for guests only. Some live music events in season. **€€€**

ROSE   At the western end of the promontory, follow the signs down the winding road to the sea and to the still-unspoilt village harbour of Rose (pronounced as if it were pink wine).

The village rises directly from the shingle beach, each group of cottages served by its sloping jetty. The little **church of Sv Gospe od Karmena (Presentation of the Virgin)** is thought to date from the 12th century and then to have been reconstructed in 1880. If only considering its strategic position near the mouth of the Boka, it's easy to see that Rose is a settlement with a long history. There are tales of Saracen raids as far back as the 9th century. Little or no archaeological research has been attempted here.

Getting there   Rose is easily accessible by boat and a popular trip from Herceg Novi; in the height of the season there are usually three boats a day crossing the bay. There's car parking at the foot of the hill.

🏠 **Where to stay and eat**   Beautifully asleep in winter, when you can't even get a cup of coffee, Rose has several nice little restaurants that spring to life in June. Of the cluster of café-restaurants perched along the harbour wall, **Adriatic** (📞 031 687020) is marginally the smartest. It and **Konoba Aragosta** both serve nice cold beer, Vranac and some newly landed fishy offerings. Both provide postprandial sun-loungers.

⌂ Apartments Male Rose (6 apts) Small Rose Beach (Rose poluotok, meaning 'peninsula'); m 069 451691. Over the hill from Rose, in the next small cove, & a 10min walk from parking. Each apt has its own entrance. Secluded & very quiet indeed; private jetty for boats. €€€€

⌂ Forte Rose (15 thatched apts) m 067 377311; e info@forterose.me; www.forterose. me; ⊕ 1 May–31 Oct. The views & the ambience of this simple place are memorable. Its quite sophisticated rooms with AC & plasma TV have been built around the perimeter of an old Austro-Hungarian fortress on the tip of the peninsula. Delightfully peaceful at night. An open-air bar beneath a cypress tree forms the central feature. Tavern & restaurant serve Luštica-sourced *pršut*, cheese & olive oil from trees behind the village, plus BBQ grilled fish. Wi-Fi. They have a beach bar, their own yacht for rent, also bicycles, & can arrange scuba diving. 10-day art colony event in Jun. CCs accepted. Apts from €45 per night. €€€€

What to see A short sunset boat ride from Rose takes you to the hidden cove of **Dobreč**, which is accessible only by sea. The beach is a mix of pebbles and rock and its pristine waters claim to be the purest in Montenegro, making for great snorkelling. There is a café on the beach, so you may toast your adventurous spirit with another beer. Try the egg-like sea urchin. All fresh water comes from a spring in the rocks. Those who maintain this place are determined that it should remain unsullied.

RETURNING THROUGH THE PENINSULA To make a circuit of Luštica travelling east after retracing your steps back up the windy road from Rose, look for the road that meanders more or less through the centre of the peninsula.

Žanjice and Mirište beaches Off this road there are turns leading to one or two attractive coves. One is **Žanjice**, a wide pebble beach set against a backdrop of olive trees and with several bars and restaurants, including **Cuba Libre** (m *069 462103*) and **Porto Žanjice**. There are sun-loungers, umbrellas, kayaks, pedaloes, catamarans, jet skis and windsurfing boards for hire. A lifeguard is on duty 10.00–17.00. Another similar but somewhat smaller beach is **Mirište**, also with sun-loungers and umbrellas for hire. Both these beaches can get pretty crowded in high summer. They can be reached by rental boats and excursions from Herceg Novi, Igalo and Tivat.

From Žanjice and Mirište it is possible by boat to visit the **Plava Špilja** (Blue Grotto). Cliffs rise 40m above the two entrances of the cave and the eerie cobalt effect created within is the result of bright sun-rays refracted through the opening by an exceptionally blue sea.

The tiny **Vavedenje Island**, lying just off the Austro-Hungarian fortress of Arza on the south coast, can also be reached by boat from these beaches, though like the small islands off the coast of Tivat it is confusingly sometimes called something else – Žanjic Island. Its 700m² is almost completely taken up by a fortified monastery complex known as Our Lady of Mirište. The Church of the Presentation of the Virgin reveals traces of fresco painting and is thought to date from at least the 16th century when records tell it was called Sv Marija de Sagnic. Visiting such places in this country never fails to fascinate, and makes the visitor long to discover more detail.

Trašte Bay Further east and in prime position on the spectacularly peacock-blue Trašte Bay is **Oblatno,** its **Almara Beach Club** currently the coolest spot on the peninsula.

In contrast, way across the wide bay in the even more beautiful horseshoe inlet of **Pržno** (not to be confused with the other Pržno beside Sveti Stefan), 300m of sandy beach is encircled by pine, *garrigue* and olive groves. The idyllic Robinson Crusoe effect is rather spoilt though by a building site, which is all that remains of the ugly, high-rise hotel that used to stand there.

Where to stay and eat

✕ **Almara Beach Club** Oblatno; ℮ info@almara. me; www.almara.me. Arrive by boat (moorings await), or by land. Some 11 nautical miles from Budva or 22km by road, it feels far further. However, there is Wi-Fi for those who must keep in touch with reality. Private tented daybeds cost €25; & there are various styles of sun-lounger & umbrellas for €5–15, dependent on the position. There are young & trendy evening beach parties with DJs. In the restaurant, chef Francesco Ruggiero is in charge, with his zippy Adriatic menu. Exotic cocktails from the bar can be delivered to your sunbed. €€€

It is in Trašte Bay that investors Orascom are pursuing an ambitious scheme for what, if built, would prove to be the largest tourist development yet launched in Montenegro. It would involve a new marina, hotels, a town and the country's long-overdue first 18-hole golf course. The lawyers have still to iron out various land-rights issues and the project has yet to be given the final go-ahead. If their plans materialise it will undoubtedly change the face of Luštica forever.

Bigova Returning to the road that leads from the Tivat–Budva (Adriatic) highway and crosses the Solila Saltpans, if you turn east on a signed road that skirts the edge of the Grbalji plain and then bear south you can reach the charming seaside village of **Bigova.** (The south coast of Grbalji can be accessed by more than one turning from the Adriatic Highway.) In ancient times Bigova Bay held a renowned Greek settlement known as Grispoli. Today, it is a close-knit fishing fraternity with a particularly narrow main street, tricky to negotiate in your rental car when headed for its highly regarded waterside *konoba*.

Where to eat and drink

✕ **Grispolis** ☏ 032 363251; www.grispolis.me; ⏲ 11.00–'till our last customer leaves', closed mid-Jan & Feb. It's in a nice old stone building with vine- & wisteria-shaded terraces on two levels. The best table has the inlet on three sides. The old-fashioned dining room is presided over by a commanding portrait of owner Nikola Lazarević's father. It's filled with ghosts, one of them still alive. Local beer is €1.50; 70cl imported Jacob's Creek €25; choose your fish from the morning's catch. €€€–€€€€

Little Bigova With its patched family fishing boats, its orange and lemon trees and its daily fish market (⏲ 07.00–22.00), Little Bigova today feels like a lovely step back in time. Alas the tranquillity is unlikely to last: foreigners are buying up the cottages, building new ones on the hillside, adding pools and designer flourishes; the road from Tivatska Solila is newly paved; and there are rumours of medicinal qualities in the creek mud. Visit soon, before someone thinks of building a spa.

5

The Budva Riviera

BUDVA

Historians are generally agreed that Budva and Risan represent the oldest settlements on the Montenegrin littoral. And like Risan, Budva is associated with legendary King Cadmus of Thebes and his spouse Harmonia. Various versions of the legend tell how they came to build the city, produced a late baby, Illyrius, and then, for one reason or another, were turned by Zeus into blue-spotted serpents, after which they vanished into:

> a sweet-smelling grove nearby and since then as favourites of the gods they have enjoyed eternal bliss among the roses and golden pomegranates, constantly refreshed by scented sea-breezes. Groves like this, which later became shrines honouring Cadmus and Harmonia, are found all around Budva.

That is how Dragoslav Srejović describes it in his essay, *Ancient Budva in Myth and History*. Favourites of the gods maybe – but the presence of snakes in the grass must have put rather a dampener on eternal life in Elysium.

The newer part of Budva, with wide boulevards, cheerful flowerbeds and open views, has a sunny disposition, with a string of beaches to its credit, stretching in both directions – Jaz, **Mogren**, **Slovenska**, **Bečići**, **Rafailovići**, **Kamenovo** and **Pržno** – and it is easy to understand Budva's popularity as a seaside resort. In August the whole of the Slovenska Beach pullulates with bodies and the summer nightlife scene is intense; with the bars and clubs jumping it isn't hard to imagine the Budva Riviera rivalling Ibiza for action in the future.

There are several beaches accessible by foot from the town: **Slovenska** (sand) and its promenade, which is lined with bars and restaurants, extends almost to the boundaries of Budva; **Ričardova Glava** (also known as Gradske/Town Beach) links Stari Grad and the Avala Hotel, and from Avala Hotel an attractive undercliff walkway curves around to reveal the first of **Mogren's** two coves (100m long, coarse sand and some pebbles). In summer there are changing cabins, showers and a lifeguard, as well as a section with sun-loungers to rent. It's a good spot for small children. A bridge leads through a gap in the rock to Mogren 2. In winter it's a pleasant wild place to stroll around, within easy reach of the city.

HISTORY In all probability it was the Greeks who founded Budva, and if Sophocles was right the Illyrians were somewhere in on the act. By the mid-2nd century BC the Romans were in occupation and when the empire was split the border between it and Byzantium was drawn through the centre of Budva. In AD535 the city became entirely Byzantine and stayed that way until it was sacked

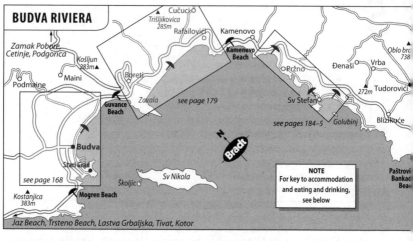

BUDVA RIVIERA

Zamak Pobore,
Cetinje, Podgorica

Košljun
383m

Zavala   *see page 179*

Guvance
Beach

Podmaine   Maini

Boreti

Trišljikovica
285m   Cucuci

Rafailovici

Kamenovo

Kamenovo
Beach

Pržno

Denaši   Vrba

Oblo brc
738

272m   Tudorovici

Sv Stefan

see pages 184–5   Golubinj

Blizikuce

Budva

Stari Grad

see page 168

Školjic

Sv Nikola

Kostanjica
383m   Mogren Beach

NOTE
For key to accommodation
and eating and drinking,
see below

Paštrovi
Bankac
Bea

Jaz Beach, Trsteno Beach, Lastva Grbaljska, Tivat, Kotor

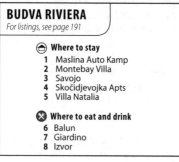

BUDVA RIVIERA
For listings, see page 191

Where to stay
1 Maslina Auto Kamp
2 Montebay Villa
3 Savojo
4 Skočidjevojka Apts
5 Villa Natalia

Where to eat and drink
6 Balun
7 Giardino
8 Izvor

by the Saracens in AD841. During the 20th century, excavations for the construction of the Avala Hotel in the close vicinity of the old city revealed a rich **Roman necropolis** and below it a **Hellenic** one, a treasure trove of gold and silver jewellery, glass and ceramics.

After the debacle at the Saracens' hands, the city became, through various transitions, Slavonic – until in 1443 it acceded to Venice, becoming the republic's southernmost outpost in the Adriatic. It remained with them for almost four centuries. Over this period the old town basically acquired the appearance it retains today. After the demise of Venice its fate was similar to that of the other towns along the coast until 1918, when it became part of Montenegro.

GETTING THERE AND AWAY From Tivat to Budva is 23km by road.

By car Depart from Tivat by the east road, passing to the left of the airport after 4km before joining the Kotor road to continue across the long scrubland of the **Grbalj Plain**. For potential places to stop along this, the coastal route to Tivat Airport, see page 149, and *West of Budva*, page 177.

By bus Budva is in effect the hub of the Montenegrin coastline and it is reasonably easy to get here by **bus** from just about any corner of the country. There are several buses a day from Podgorica (€5), Tivat (€2) and Herceg Novi (€4.50); and at least three from Ulcinj and Cetinje. Sometimes the bus may be a kombi/mini. **Olimpia Express** (*trg Sunca br 2;* ✆ *033 451567*) operates an hourly bus service between Budva and Sveti Stefan (€1) and five or so a day between Budva and Petrovac (€1.50).

A Montenegro Airlines **minibus** service operates between Tivat Airport and Budva bus station (*€3 one way*). It is scheduled to meet each incoming Montenegro Airlines flight, but outside the summer months it's best not to rely on it.

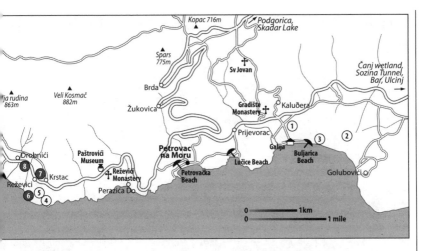

By taxi A taxi to Tivat will cost about €15, Podgorica €40, Dubrovnik €90.

GETTING AROUND

By bus The **bus station** [168 C1] (☏ *033 456000*) is off Popa Jola Zeca, close to the junction with Prva Proleterski, 1km north of the old town, and 20 minutes' walk from the seafront. It boasts a large soft-play room, useful for those travelling with young children, and there is also a left-luggage facility.

The Olimpia Express service between Sv Stefan, Budva and Petrovac (see above) makes numerous stops both within town (Jadranski put) and along the beaches, and the current timetable is posted at some of these. Buses go about half hourly in summer and hourly in winter, and the fare is €2.50 per stretch – whether to Sv Stefan or to Petrovac. A useful stop is on the main road at the eastern end of town, in front of the soccer stadium opposite the Rabello Pizzeria. Olimpia also organises excursions.

Taxis There are taxi ranks at the bus station [168 C1], by JAT Airways office on ul Mediteranska, and at Slovenska Plaža. Taxis are metered (*€1 plus €0.80/km*). A taxi from the bus station to the old town should cost about €5 but it is advisable to check this with the driver beforehand. Reliable are:

✳ 🚕 **Terrae Taxis m** 067 248899

Car and scooter hire Expect to pay from €35 per day depending on the season. There is convenient and plentiful parking in the northwest of town, off Mediteranska and close to the old town (Stari Grad); €1 per hour.

A number of places on Slovenska Plaža rent bikes and Vespas, from around €10 per day, or €50 per week.

🚗 **Bon Voyage** Bečići; **m** 067 350333; www.bonvoyage-rentacar.com
🚗 **Budget** Slovenska obala 14; ☏ 033 459720; **m** 069 422244. Opels €40–147 per day for weekly rental.

✳ 🚗 **Destra Rent-a-car** [168 D3] Jadranski put bb; ☏ 033 453130. Beside the Rabello Pizzera & Bar. Reasonable English.
🚗 **Kompas Hertz** ul Mediteranska 7; ☏ 033 456467. VW Polo €70 per day or €300 per week; Ford Mondeo €100 per day or €425 per week, all AC but insurance not inc.

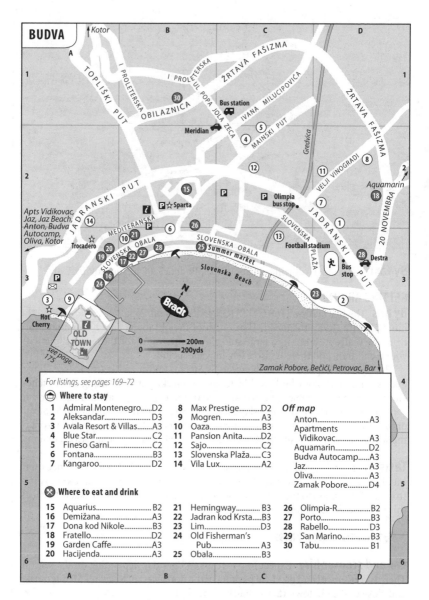

For listings, see pages 169–72

Where to stay

1	Admiral Montenegro......D2	8	Max Prestige............D2
2	Aleksandar........................D3	9	Mogren.....................A3
3	Avala Resort & Villas......A3	10	Oaza........................B3
4	Blue Star............................C2	11	Pansion Anita.........D2
5	Fineso Garni......................C2	12	Sajo.........................C2
6	Fontana..............................B3	13	Slovenska Plaža......C3
7	Kangaroo............................D2	14	Vila Lux..................A2

Off map

Anton.............................A3
Apartments
  Vidikovac....................A3
Aquamarin..................D2
Budva Autocamp.........A3
Jaz................................A3
Oliva.............................A3
Zamak Pobore..........D4

Where to eat and drink

15	Aquarius...................B2	21	Hemingway.............B3	26	Olimpia-R................B2
16	Demižana..................A3	22	Jadran kod Krsta.....B3	27	Porto......................B3
17	Dona kod Nikole.........B3	23	Lim...........................D3	28	Rabello....................D3
18	Fratello.....................D2	24	Old Fisherman's	29	San Marino...............B3
19	Garden Caffe...............A3		Pub..........................A3	30	Tabu.......................B1
20	Hacijenda.................A3	25	Obala.......................B3		

🚗 **Lucky Car** 📱 067 503379; www.luckycar.me
🚗 **Meridian** [168 B2] Mediteranski Sportski Centar,
Popa Jola Zeca bb; 📞 033 454105; e meridian@
t-com.me; www.meridian-rentacar.com. Hyundai
€35 up. Also at Tivat Airport (📱 *069 060525*)

🚗 **Sixt** Hotel Avala, Mediteranska 2; 📱 067
645207, www.sixt.co.me
🚗 **Terrae Car** Mediteranska bb; 📞 033 19717;
www.terraecar.com

TOURIST INFORMATION AND TOUR OPERATORS
Tourist information
🛈 **Tourist Organisation of Budva** [168 B2]
Mediteranska 8/6; 📞 033 402814–16;

e info@budva.travel; www.budva.travel. Located
conveniently on Mediteranska, near the corner of
22 Novembra, & close to numerous restaurants &

Slovenska Beach. In the summer months, there is also an information kiosk in the Old Town.

Tour operators

* **Adria d.m.c** Popa Jola Zeca bb; \033 455181; e adriaex@t-com.me; www.adriaex. com. English, German, French, Italian & Russian spoken. Offers a comprehensive service for all local & international travel requirements. Individual or group; tailor-made programmes; MICE; destination management. Excellent local knowledge & very professional standards.

Apolotours Zgrada Zanatski Centar, Topliški put bb; \033 454841; e apolotours@t-com.me; www. apolotours.me. Manager Nada Radanović.

Mijović Travel Zanatski Centar, Topliški put; \033 452168; www.mijovic-travel.com. Specialises in day trips, inc 1-day visits into Albania.

🏠 **WHERE TO STAY** *Maps, opposite and page 175.*

As well as hotels, there is an increasing amount of accommodation available in private houses; expect to pay €15–25 per person, per day in season. For availability enquire at the tourist office (see above).

Hotels

* 🏠 **Astoria** (12 rooms) Njegoševa 4, Stari Grad; \033 451110; e hotelastoria@t-com.me; www.astoriamontenegro.com. Opened 2007 in the old city (near west gate & Avala). Super VIP roof terrace & private dining room. AC, satellite TV, room safe, minibar, whirlpool baths. 1 child under 13 free in parents' room. Restaurant & bar. €€€€€

🏠 **Avala Resort & Villas** (220 rooms, 6 suites, 67 1- & 2-bed villas) Mediteranska 2; \033 441000; e avalasales@t-com.me; www. avalaresort.com. Beside the old city & beaches, under the same ownership as the Bianca in Kolašin (page 295), the Avala architecturally resembles a Frank Lloyd Wright building. Dbl & sgl rooms have stylish glass-walled 'long bar' minibar, satellite TV, AC & balcony. Indoor & outdoor pools, inc most attractive infinity pool. Wi-Fi free of charge in bar & lobby. 24hr internet café. Hairdressing salon, spa. Safe deposit boxes. Conference hall. Restaurants, nightclub (⏰ 22.00–05.00), casino (⏰ 21.00–05.00, stakes €0.50–10). CCs accepted. Children under 2 free; €10 per child sharing parents' room. €€€€€ (HB €€€€/€€€€€ low/high season)

* 🏠 **Max Prestige** (11 rooms, 8 apts) Žrtve fašizma bb; \033 458330; e maxprestige@t-com. me; www.hotelmaxprestige.com. An attractive hotel that works well. All rooms have AC, cable TV, safe boxes, telephones, internet access; most with balcony. Restaurant & bar; outdoor pool; fitness centre, jacuzzi & sauna, all free to guests. Babysitting available by off-duty receptionists. Secure parking. CCs accepted. €€€€

* 🏠 **Admiral Montenegro** (29 dbl, 3 suites) Jadranski put bb; \033 459263; e info@ hoteladmiralbudva.com; www.hoteladmiralbudva. com; ⏰ all year. Near Slovenska Beach, 1km from Budva. Rooms have AC, cable TV, internet, hairdryer, minibar. Laundry service. Outdoor swimming pool, private beach, restaurant, bar & coffee bar, terrace, garden, parking. €€€ (HB €€€€)

🏠 **Aleksandar** (75 rooms, 123 apts) Slovenska Obala bb; \033 402456; www. hgbudvanskarivijera.com. Small simple rooms around a courtyard with balcony, minibar, cable TV; better appointed apts with kitchens. AC €4 per day. Hairdresser, babysitting, restaurant, snack bar, bar & terrace. Also good seawater pool, beach & parking. Same management as Slovenska Plaža (below). €€€ (HB €€€ high, €€ low season)

🏠 **Aquamarin** (6 rooms, 19 suites) Podkošljun bb, near Slovenska Plaža; \033 460269; www. aquamarin-hotel.com. All rooms with sea view, balcony, satellite TV, AC, minibar, internet access. Bar, restaurant, room service, laundry service, babysitting, garden, outdoor pool. CCs accepted. B&B €€€ (HB €€€€)

🏠 **Blue Star** (20 rooms & 4 apts) Mainski put bb; \033 773777; e reservations@ montenegrostars.com; www.montenegrostars. com; ⏰ all year. Comfortable & well appointed. All with minibar, room safe, TV & AC. Internet access, spa, fitness room & beauty salon. Lift. Restaurant, café, bar. Pets allowed. Visa/ MasterCard ATM in lobby. Guests may use all facilities at hotels Splendid & Montenegro

(Bečići) without charge. Diners Club & MasterCard accepted. €€€

⌂ **Kangaroo** (24 apts) Jadranski put bb; \033 458653; www.kangaroo.co.me. 250m from beach. AC, fridge, minibar, cable TV. Room & laundry service. Restaurant. Internet access. CCs accepted. €€€

⌂ **Mogren** (45 dbl, 4 suites) Mediteranska 1, beside Stari Grad; \033 451102; e hotelmogren@t-com.me; www.mogrenhotel. com; ⊕ all year. 100m from beach, a privatised hotel that retains its tired state-hotel ambience. AC, room safe, telephone, minibar, TV & terrace. Parking. Conference hall. Visa accepted. €€€

⌂ **Oaza** Slovenska Obala 27; \033 402608; e oazabudva@t-com.me; www.oaza.co.me. AC, Wi-Fi, TV, balcony, restaurant, parking, close to beach. €€€

⌂ **Sajo** (12 rooms, 6 studios, 8 suites) Jadranski put bb; \033 460243; www.sajohotel.com; ⊕ all year. 300m from the sea. All with telephone, cable TV, AC, internet, minibar, lift. Restaurant, 2 bars, sauna, fitness centre, roof terrace, secure parking. Pets allowed. CCs accepted. €€€

⌂ **Slovenska Plaža** (762 rooms, 249 apts) trg Sloboda 1; \033 402456; www. hgbudvanskarivijera.com; ⊕ summer only. Vast socialist-era tourist village 30m from the beach & 500m from the old town. All rooms have cable TV & balcony; apts with 2–8 beds also have kitchen & dining room. AC €4 pp per day. Tennis & water sports, volleyball, basketball. Shops, doctor & dentist, playground. CCs accepted. €€€

⌂ **Apartments Vidikovac** (4 apts) Vidikovac bb; m 069 185522; e vidikovac@mail.ru; www. vidikovac.me. Modern apts just west of the old town with good views. €€€

⌂ **Vila Balkan** (5 suites) Vuka Karadžića 2; \033 403564; e info@vilabalkan.me; www. vilabalkan.me. On the edge of the old city. Suites, all with harbour view, AC, cable TV, internet, laundry service & kitchenette, sleep up to 5. No CCs. Restaurant (€€€€€) with large terrace, under separate management, takes CCs. €€€

⌂ **Zamak Pobore** (80 rooms) Pobori bb, Poštanski fah; \033 464601; www.hotelzamak. com. 10km towards Cetinje on a hill behind Budva. AC, cable TV, minibar, internet, some disabled facilities. Bar & restaurant. Terrace, garden & parking. €€€

⌂ **Fineso Garni** (17 rooms) Mainski put bb \033 454120; e hotelfineso@t-com.me; www. hotelfineso.com. AC, safe, cable TV, minibar. Internet, bar, restaurant, parking. €€

✳ ⌂ **Hotel-Restaurant Fontana** (9 rooms) Slovenska obala 23; \033 452153; e fontana. lekic@t-com.me. A quiet location in pleasant gardens, 50m from beach. Balcony, AC, safe deposit boxes, TV. Friendly owner & staff. Parking. €€ (HB €€€)

⌂ **Vila Lux** (22 rooms) Jadranski put bb; \033 455950; www.vilalux.com. Simply furnished with AC, cable TV, internet corner, minibar. Bar & restaurant. Parking. €€

⌂ **Pansion Anita** (28 rooms) Velji Vinogradi bb; \033 458611; e hotelanita@t-com.me; www.hotelanita.me. AC, cable TV, internet, restaurant. Cheap, clean & fairly cheerful. They also have apts, as well as the Hotel Anita at Bečići (page 182). €

Hostels

⌂ **Montenegro Hostel** Vuca Karadžica, Stari Grad; m 069 039751; e montenegrohostel@ gmail.com; www.montenegrohostel.com. Opened 2011, with modernised interiors in typical vernacular buildings in the centre of old town, close to beach. 1min walk from tourist information centre; next door to Prestige Boutique (Bosnian owner, Gordana Knežević is also a clothes designer; she runs 2 other hostels – one in Kotor, page 143; another in Podgorica, page 106). Brightly colour co-ordinated & well-appointed dorms & rooms with dedicated kitchens & bathrooms. Common room on each floor. Free Wi-Fi. AC, in-room lockers, cable TV. Good local transport information; tours & transfers can be arranged. In all, a highly organised budget-travel facility – Gordana can even recommend a cut-price taxi service. CCs accepted. High season: private dbl €25 pp; private trpl €20 pp; 8-room dorm €16 pp. €–€€

Campsites
(see also Jaz Beach, page 177)

⋏ **Anton** (30 units) Majinskii put bb near Slovenska Beach, at Velji Vinogradi; \086 457157

⋏ **Budva Autocamp** (30 units) Majinskii put 33a, Velji Vinogradi; \033 458923; e vaslijarucovic@t-com.me

⋏ **Oliva** (30 camping units & facilities) Jadranski put 63, about 200m from beach; \086 458841

✕ WHERE TO EAT AND DRINK *Maps, pages 168, 175.*

There is a wide selection of restaurants, particularly in the old quarter; in Budva one is never more than a few steps from a pizza. Booking is seldom necessary and it is worth wandering around to see what catches your mood. Prices don't vary much (with rare exceptions) up or down. In summer you might encounter a small, seasonal **McDonald's** – the only one in Montenegro – operated from a mobile site (which once tried its luck in Podgorica, and failed) on Slovenska Beach.

✕ **Demižana** Slovenska obala 3; ⏱ 12.00–24.00. Nice terrace, typical ambience, good fish, attentive service, expensive. €€€€€

✱ ✕ **Dona kod Nikole** Gradska Marina; ⏱ 09.00–24.00. Traditional dishes & excellent fresh fish in a friendly atmosphere. Deservedly popular. €€€€

✱ ✕ **Jadran kod Krsta** Slovenska obala 10; ☎ 033 451028; ⏱ 09.00–01.00. Really fresh fish in a warm ambience with attentive service supervised by owner Krsto Niklanović, who clearly understands how to run a thoroughly good restaurant (as well as the local Rotary Club). A favourite of the locals & you will see why. Don't miss the light garlic sauce. CCs accepted. €€€€

✕ **Obala** Slovenska obala; ☎ 086 402782. Beside the beach, 220m from Stari Grad. Large open terrace; good English; Visa & MasterCard accepted. €€€€

✕ **Olimpia-R** Slovenska obala bb; ☎ 033 451629; www.en.restoranolimp-budva.com. Large terrace by the sea. Good English. CCs accepted. €€€€

✕ **Aquarius** Zmajeva br 6; ☎ 033 402716; e aquarius@budvaonline.cim; www.budva.com/aquarius; ⏱ 09.00–01.00. With a small terrace, this is actually the above-avg restaurant of a small hotel. Specialises in fish. €€€

✕ **Bound** Cara Dušana. In a vine-covered courtyard decorated with Warhol-type pictures of Monroe & Hepburn. Good simple steaks (beef & tuna) & pasta & a very good wine list. €€€

✱ ✕ **Konoba Galeb** Vrzdak 11 Stari Grad; ☎ 086 456546; ⏱ 11.00–02.00. Long-established, atmospheric restaurant in a quiet alley with a pleasant garden & the usual fish & grills well prepared. €€€

✕ **Hemingway** Slovenska obala 11; ☎ 033 452400; ⏱ summer 08.00–01.00; winter 11.00–23.00. A friendly place in a conservatory that opens to a terrace in summer, buzzy & popular with locals. Extensive menu at reasonable prices with generous helpings. Salads, pancakes (savoury

or sweet), shrimp risotto, etc. Draft beer, but a big mark-up on wine – often cheaper by glass than bottle. €€€

✕ **Hot Moon** trg Kanjos & Njegoševa 32; m 069 332682; ⏱ all day in summer, evenings only off-season. Cocktails & Mexican cooking in a nice garden with a good view of the churches. €€€

✕ **Konoba Knez** ul Pero Ičagić, Stari Grad; m 069 475025; ⏱ 12.00–01.00. Small, with 2 or 3 outside tables & no more than this inside. Fish soup, prawns, catch of the day. Moderate prices: 1 dish frequently enough for 2. €€€

✕ **Konoba Feral** trg Palmi Stari Grad; ⏱ 11.00–01.00. Low-ceilinged, intimate & full of atmosphere; ('feral' means 'the light on a boat'). Wisteria terrace in summer. Catch their own fish. MasterCard & Visa. €€€

✕ **Konoba Stari Grad** Njegoševa 14; www.konobastarigrad.me; ⏱ 11.00–01.00. Stylish, laid-back & very popular. Rear opens on to beachside private terrace under the old walls, with smart chairs & tables & matching umbrellas. Soft local or other European music every evening in season. Set menu available. Children's playground alongside. Good English. CCs accepted. €€€

✱ ✕ **Lim** Slovenska obala; ⏱ 10.00–24.00. Friendly good-value place which comes highly recommended. Grills, pasta dishes, etc. €€€

✕ **Porto** Gradska Luka bb; m 033 451598; www.restoranporto.com; ⏱ 09.00–01.00. Features fish, black risotto, steak. Extensive wine list. Good English. Visa accepted. €€€

✕ **San Marino** Slovenska obala 21; ⏱ 09.00–01.00. Italian cuisine & pizza, with an emphasis on fish – they have their own boat. They hope to evolve into a hotel. Diners Club & MasterCard accepted. €€€

✕ **Shanghai** Vojvodanska 22; ⏱ 11.00–24.00. http://kineskirestoran.me. Chinese food, the speciality of chicken & almonds prepared by Chinese cooks. Not a lot of charm but the food is pretty good. Diners, Visa & MasterCard. €€€

5

✘ **Juice Bar** Vranjak 13, Stari Grad; ☎033 457023; www.juicebar.me. Freshly squeezed juices, sandwiches, pasta, salads. '& best of all,' writes Siân Pritchard Jones, 'real English tea comes in a teapot'. Anglo/Canadian owners. €€

✘ **Fratello** 29 Novembra bb; ⏱ 09.00–24.00. On the main ring road, unpretentious with good, inexpensive grills & other dishes. €€

✘ **Garden Caffe** ul Mediteranska bb; m 067 590659. Near car park behind Mogren Hotel. Pizza, weekly BBQ, live music some nights, candle-lit leafy garden. €€

✘ **Old Fisherman's Pub** Slovenska obala bb; ⏱ 07.00–24.00. Beside Stari Grad & the harbour, the location is better than the food. Burgers, English b/fast, wood-fired pizzas. Free Wi-Fi. No CCs. €€

✳ ✘ **Rabello** Jadranski put bb; ⏱ 08.00–01.00. Good simple Italian food & some of the best pizza in town; modest prices; English spoken. Connection with Destra car rental (page 167), so useful pick-up point for vehicle. Convenient for Olimpia (coastal) bus stop. €€

✘ **Tabu** Proleterska bb; ☎069 100900; ⏱ 07.00–23.00. Above the town centre, a large bar & restaurant serving a range of food; cheerful & friendly. €€

✘ **Pizzeria Lav** Iva Mikovića, Stari Grad; ⏱ 08.00–24.00. Good variety of toppings; thin & crispy base. €

✘ **Pizzeria Picasso** trg Palmi bb, Stari grad. One of the better pizzerias, with a nice terrace. €

ENTERTAINMENT AND NIGHTLIFE Budva itself, and the area around it, is home to various nightclubs, discos and casinos, a reflection of the area's popularity as a holiday resort. It's quieter in winter, when the young of Budva tend to migrate to Kotor or Tivat for nightlife. Bars usually close at around 01.00 while nightclubs tend to stay open as long as there are people in them – often from 22.00 till 05.00 or 06.00. They generally charge admission only when they have a live show; prices vary from about €3–8.

Bars, pubs and cafés

♀ **Astoria** Njegoševa bb; ⏱ 08.00–01.00. A good place for coffee & cocktails is the café of the hotel of the same name (page 169).

♀ **Casper** Dušana 10; ⏱ 10.00–02.00. Café-bar with pleasant pine-shaded terraces in the old town, & a decent range of fairly laid-back, chilled out, jazz- & r'n'b-infused music.

✳ ♀ **Chest O'Shea's** Small sq off ul Vuka Karadžića, Stari Grad bb; m 069 579468; ⏱ 10.00–01.00. Matey & cheerful English & Irish expatriate hangout. Snug & welcoming, serves Guinness (*a pint is €7, €5.50 when big game on TV*) & very cheap draft beer. English papers off the internet are sporadically available. Several sports TVs are generally on & they will retune on request. Irish stew on St Patrick's day: 'the guy who cooked it wasn't Irish, neither was the stew – but what the heck – this is Montenegro'. €€

♀ **El Mundo** Stari grad; ⏱ 20.00–02.00. Open-air bar near the marina, with Latin music & good cocktails.

✘ **Hacijenda** Mediteranska bb; ⏱ 08.00–02.00. Eatery by day, cocktail bar & live music venue by night. Latin flavour, as the name suggests.

♀ **Korkavado** trg Slikara; ⏱ 08.00–01.00. Popular café on this square in the old town, with plenty of tables outside providing the perfect place to sit & watch the world go by.

♀ **The Prince English Pub** Vranjak Br 8 in the old town. Has a Serbian owner who speaks English, a Montenegrin barman who does not, & serves no English beer or any food – but it is well signposted.

Nightclubs

☆ **Hot Cherry** [168 A3] Avala Resort & Villas; ⏱ 22.00–05.00. Popular disco; DJ playlists inc house, techno & funk.

✳ ☆ **Miami, Rafaelo & Trocadero Red** Nr Slovenska Beach; ⏱ 22.00–05.00. All noisy, lively & recommended by the young.

☆ **Perla** Mediteranska bb; www.perlabudva.com; ⏱ Mon 12.00–03.00; Tue–Sun 10.00–01.00. Restaurant, cocktail bar & live music venue. W/end singers, Balkan performers; Tue salsa party.

☆ **Sparta** [168 B2] Mediteranska bb; m 069 914914; www.clubsparta.net; ⏱ 22.00–05.00. Exclusive club with capacity for 600.

✳ ☆ **Top Hill** Topliski put bb; m 067 478888; www.tophill.me; ⏱ 23.00–05.00. Situated above the city, overlooking the sea. Claims to be biggest outdoor disco in Montenegro.

✳ ☆ **Trocadero** [168 A3] Mediteranska 4, m 069 069086; www.trocaderobudva.com (Montenegrin only); ⏰ 23.00–05.00

FESTIVALS During the August **Cinemania** film festival, there is a nightly film shown at 22.00 on a big outdoor screen by the pool at Slovenska Plaža hotel.
The week-long Budva International Carnival is held at the start of May.

SPORTS ACTIVITIES
Beach volleyball
Mediteranski Sportski Centar Eastern end of Jadranski put

Boat trips & water sports
There are always a number of boats (with skippers) for hire – pleasure cruising, taxi, fishing – moored along the dockside at the west end of Slovenska Plaža. They are in competition with each other & prices are usually negotiable. Always establish a firm figure in advance. Mid-season they will be asking €15–20 per hr. See also *Fishing*.

Diving
꙰ **MAC** See *Paragliding*, page 174.

Waterskiing
🎿 **Aqua Ski** m 069 554485. €8 for 30mins, €29 for 3hrs.

Boat and yacht charters
⚠ **Dukley Marina** Stari Grad; ☎ 033 451059; e info@dukleymarina.com; www.dukleymarina.com. Berths for 300 boats up to 25m.
⚠ **Flying Inflatable Boat** Aeroklub ZMAJ. In the middle of Bečići Beach in front of the St Toma.
⚠ **MennYacht** Marina Stari Grad bb; ☎ 033 452540; e montenegro@mennyacht.com; www.mennyacht.com/montenegro. Luxury yachts with crew.
⚠ **MIFIS** m 069 521082; e mifisworld@t-com.me; www.mifisworld.com

Fishing
🚣 **Big Game Montenegro** m 067 317717; www.biggamemontenegro.com
🚣 **Montimare Shop** Stari Grad; e montimare@t-com.me. For fishing tackle; also diving permits.

PARAGLIDING

Given the terrain, it is hardly surprising that this sport has, quite literally, taken off in Montenegro. It all began at the end of the 1980s, and the first official competition was organised in 1993 by the Yugoslav Federal Aviation Administration in the Budva area, with a launch from Barjići, close to the Austro-Hungarian fortress of Kosmač, which has a 760m drop to Bečići Beach. As well as MAC (above), there are now half-a-dozen paragliding clubs in operation: Fenix (Mojkovac), Budućnost (Podgorica), Soko (Budva), Fram (Nikšić), Dragon (Ulcinj) and Dynamic (Bijelo Polje), having in total 20 or so fully qualified pilots.

The mountainsides above the coast dropping steeply to the glittering Adriatic can provide a magnificent experience and in summer tourists in coastal regions can be airborne after only 15 minutes' drive from their hotel. Those staying at Sveti Stefan, Miločer or Bečići can take off from Brajići and fly over the Budva Riviera; over Bar and Sutomore, taking off from the Sutorman Mountain; or over the stunning Boka Kotorska and Herceg Novi with a launch from Orjen or Vrmac (550m). It is also possible to glide from Mt Lovćen, taking off from 1,660m and landing at sea level.

In winter, paragliding and skiing can be combined at the Bjelasica resort near Kolašin and at Durmitor near Žabljak.

Hiking and biking

🚴 **Adria DMC** ☎033 455181; e adriaex@t-com. me; www.adriaex.com

🚴 **MAC** See below.

🚴 **MN Holidays** ☎033 402522; e mnholidays@ t-com.me; www.mn-holidays.com

Paragliding

✈ MAC m 067 580664; e montenegrofly@ hotmail.co.uk; www.montenegrofly.com. Englishman Robin Brown is based in Lapčići, a village 9km up the hill, on the road to Cetinje & Lovćen. He offers lessons, flights (both solo & tandem), guided hiking, mountain biking & diving. There is also accommodation at Mac Lodge, 20mins inland from Budva (*6 en-suite rooms; lounge with satellite TV & internet. Guide price, inc airport transfers, €465 pp B&B in twin room per week*).

✈ Paragliding Club Soko (Eagle) m 069 600211. Tuition available.

Tennis

⛹ **Tennis club** ul Dositejeva 26; ☎033 451131

⛹ **Tennis complex** ☎033 451304. 14 concrete courts.

OTHER PRACTICALITIES

Banks

$ **Atlasmont Banka** Slovenska Obala br 13

$ **CKB** Mediteranska br 7

$ **Komercijalna Banka** Mediteranska 17

$ **NLB Montenegro Banka** Mediteranska br 2

$ **Opportunity Bank** ul 22 Novembra bb

$ **Podgorička Banka** Mediteranska bb

Internet In summer there are several tented internet sites near the beach.

✳ 📶 **Internet 'Stefan'** Mediteranski Sportski Centar, central Budva; ⏲ 10.00–23.00. €1 per half hr, €2 per hr, €3 per 2hrs.

📶 **PC Centar** Mediteranska 4; ☎033 457212

📶 **Quasar** Slovenska obala bb; ☎033 401730

📶 **Santa Marija** Poslovni centar; ☎033 403424; ⏲ 08.00–24.00. €1 per hr. Near traffic light, turn left entering Budva from west; not especially welcoming to tourists.

Medical facilities

✚ **Health-care centre** trg Sunca 6; ⏲ 24hrs

Pharmacies

✚ **Althaea** ul Jadranski put bb; ☎033 455000

✚ **Meditas** ul 13 Jul bb; ☎033 452454

✚ **Montefarm** ul Popa Jova Zeca bb; ☎033 451944

✚ **Stari Grad** trg Pjesnika; ☎033 453705. Only pharmacy in old city.

✚ **Uniprom** Mediteranska 17; ☎033 452155

Church services

✝ **Sv Trojica (Holy Trinity)** [175 B4] Stari Grad; ⏲ winter 08.00–12.00, 16.00–19.00; summer 08.00–12.00, 17.00–20.00; Orthodox service 09.00 Sun.

✝ **Sv Ivan** [175 C4] Stari Grad; Catholic mass 10.00 Sun.

Other

Daca Cosmetic Salon [168 D3] Aleksandar Hotel, Slovenska obala; m 068 528020; e daca_ so@yahoo.com. Nails (*manicure €10, pedicure €15*), massage (*€25/hr*), waxing, treatment for problem feet a speciality.

✉ **Post office** [168 A3] Mediteranska 8, to the rear of Avala Hotel; ⏲ 07.00–20.00 Mon–Sat

WHAT TO SEE

Stari Grad (Old Town) At one time the Stari Grad was similar geographically to Sveti Stefan across the wider bay (see pages 186–9): a clenched fist joined to the shore by a short isthmus. From today's walkway one can picture how it must have looked. Since the cataclysmic earthquake in 1979 the ancient enclave has been meticulously restored, *almost* to that borderline where, to the eye at least, real slides into replication. But to say that would be unfair, because the stones are still the same and their reassembly has been a labour of painstaking devotion, a refusal to permit a natural invader to destroy a city where since time immemorial human enemies have failed. Now the little alleys and squares brim with boutiques, art galleries,

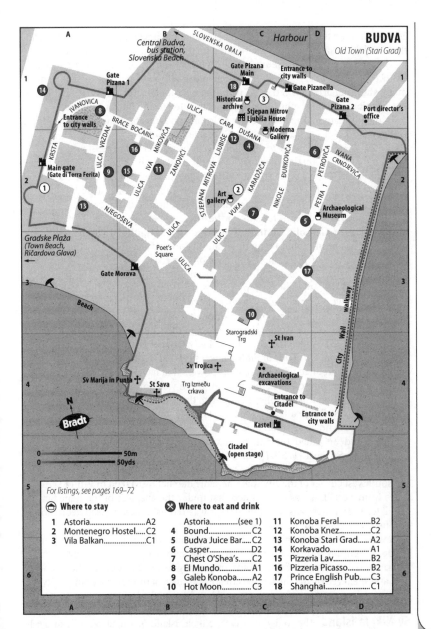

A   B   SLOVENSKA OBALA   C   Harbour   D

Central Budva, bus station, Slovenska Beach

Gate Pizana Main

Entrance to city walls

Gate Pizanella

⑭

Gate Pizana 1

⑱

Gate Pizana 2

Historical archive

③

Stjepan Mitrov Ljubiša House

Port director's office

IVANOVICA

⑧

Entrance to city walls

BRACE BOČARIĆ

ULICA

CARA DUŠANA

Moderna Gallery

KRSTA

ULICA VRZDAK

⑯

ULICA IVA MIKOVIĆA

ZANOVIĆI

STJEPANA MITROVA LJUBIŠE

VUKA KARADŽIĆA

NIKOLE ĐURKOVIĆA

PETRA I PETROVIĆA

IVANA CRNOJEVIĆA

⑥

Main gate (Gate di Terra Ferita)

①

⑨

⑮

⑪

Art gallery

②

⑦

⑤

Archaeological Museum

⑬

NJEGOŠEVA

ULICA

ULICA A

Poet's Square

ULICA

⑰

Gradske Plaža (Town Beach, Ričardova Glava)

Gate Morava

Beach

⑩

Starogradski Trg

St Ivan

City Wall walkway

Sv Trojica ✝

Sv Marija in Punta ✝

St Sava ✝

Trg Između crkava

Archaeological excavations

Entrance to Citadel

Entrance to city walls

Bradt

Kastel

N

0   50m
0   50yds

Citadel (open stage)

For listings, see pages 169–72

🛏 Where to stay

1 Astoria...................A2
2 Montenegro Hostel.....C2
3 Vila Balkan.................C1

🍴 Where to eat and drink

Astoria..............(see 1)		11	Konoba Feral...............B2
4	Bound.....................C2	12	Konoba Knez................C2
5	Budva Juice Bar.....C2	13	Konoba Stari Grad......A2
6	Casper.....................D2	14	Korkavado...................A1
7	Chest O'Shea's........C2	15	Pizzeria Lav..................B2
8	El Mundo..............A1	16	Pizzeria Picasso...........B2
9	Galeb Konoba........A2	17	Prince English Pub......C3
10	Hot Moon...............C3	18	Shanghai.....................C1

konobe and pizzerias, fish restaurants galore with prominently displayed menus: a Mexican, a Chinese – even an English pub of sorts.

A massive fortress protects the wide main square, its huge ramparts not simply historical monuments but serving also as a backcloth for summer-long theatrical events, poetry and music. The **Citadel** [175 C4] (⊕ *May–Oct 08.00–24.00; entry €2, under 10 free*) includes a museum and art gallery. The art gallery contains Balkan and other 20th-century painters; part of it forms an annex to the Archaeological Museum (see below). From the top there is a panoramic view of all Budva and across to the vertiginous cliff of Sv Nikola Island and beyond to Sveti Stefan. Beside the Citadel is a small street market selling pictures, sweaters, hats and socks.

The **Archaeological Museum** [175 D2] (*Petra I Petrovića;* e *muzejibd@t-com.me;* ◷ *09.00–22.00 Tue–Fri, 10.00–17.00 Sat–Sun*), although modest in size, exhibits many stunning artefacts retrieved from the necropolis after the 1979 earthquake. An additional ethnographic department is devoted to the Budva environs.

In the intimate setting of the house of Jovan and Dragana Vahović, the **Moderna Gallery** [175 C2] (*ul Cara Dušana 19;* e *galerijabd@t-com.me;* ◷ *08.00–14.00 & 16.00–22.00 Mon–Sat; entry to museum & gallery €2, children & pensioners €1, €1.50 for groups of 5 or more*) demonstrates how local artists have found inspiration in their surroundings. Beside it is the **Stjepan Mitrov Ljubiša House** [175 C2] (✆ *033 452060;* ◷ *08.00–14.00 & 19.00–22.00; entry free*) which celebrates one of Budva's greatest philosophers (1824–78); it has a small museum and hosts cultural events.

All of Budva's Old Town feels like a theatrical backdrop, and centre stage is the honey-coloured **Catholic Church of Sv Ivan** [175 C4], until 1828 the seat of the diocese. It has been rebuilt many times and its origins are unclear; what is known is that it was one of the earliest churches on the coast, possibly dating from the 9th century when it is believed to have been circular in design. The prominent belltower and the adjacent bishop's palace are 19th-century Gothic Revival. On entering, the eye is immediately drawn to the bright mosaic altarpiece by Ivo Dulčić of Dubrovnik; a delightful recent acquisition, it shows Jesus being introduced to the people of Budva (notice similar licence taken in the Church of St Jerome at Herceg Novi – page 123). Above the altar in the **Lady Chapel** is a precious and beautiful 12th-century icon, *Our Lady of Budva*, always carried in procession on 24 June, the saint's day, and credited with miraculous powers that have saved the town from the plague and from pirates, to name but two. If the welcoming parish priest is about you may hear his mobile telephone ringing to the tune of *Auld Lang Syne*. Opposite, the Orthodox **Sv Trojica** (Holy Trinity) [175 B4], built in 1804, is decorated with paintings by Nicholaos Aspioti of Corfu.

This could be called the square of churches. To the southwest is the small 14th-century **Sv Sava** [175 B4], for a long period dually Orthodox and Catholic. Subsequently during the Austrian occupation it served as an arsenal. Beside it on the southwest corner of the city wall, the sadly derelict **Sv Marija in Punta** [175 B4] dates from AD840. It was consecrated first under the auspices of the Benedictines and later the Franciscans, until in 1807 it was requisitioned by Napoleon's forces and used as a stable for their horses.

A walk to the east along the seaward fortifications provides a good view over the harbour teeming with small craft. During the summer months the port assumes international status with full customs and immigration facilities. To the landward side and sheltered by the thick wall is the reassurance of immutable domesticity, *rus in urbe*, neat vegetable rows, geese, scrabbling hens and a lazy cat.

Sv Nikola Island

The wedge that is Sv Nikola Island is a nautical mile away; in summertime boats run to and fro continuously from almost any area of the city. Paths climb through the greenery to the summit for excellent views of the **Budva Riviera** and the olive-covered hills beneath the spurs of Lovćen. Legend has it that some of the old tombs around the Church of St Nikola are the graves of crusaders who died in an epidemic when they paused in Budva on their way back from the Holy Land. Even Our Lady was not infallible. Though uninhabited, the island the locals call Hawaii has a **summer restaurant** serving fish, vegetarian dishes and local cuisine. Beach equipment is on hand and the sapphire sea is a paradise for snorkellers. At low tide, at least in theory, it is possible to wade by way of a sandbank known as **Tunj**, which connects with **Slovenska Beach** (although the author remains cynical about this); how you return is another matter and a boat in attendance is advised. Many swim it – but do remember that most Montenegrins are natural athletes.

Summer market Lining the pathway behind Slovenska Plaža there is a seasonal open-air market selling everything from souvenirs to books, CDs/DVDs, toys, clothes and shoes. Quality ranges from handmade to mass produced.

WEST OF BUDVA

Some 4km from Budva, as the road dips down into a valley, there's a sign to the left to **Jaz Beach**. In summer there are boats available here for transport to less accessible coves (you will see signs all along the coast indicating *krstarenje* – boat rides). In 2007 an enormous outdoor stage was constructed for a sell-out performance by the Rolling Stones, and since then it has featured various top artists including Madonna and Lennie Kravitz.

WHERE TO STAY AND EAT

Beach Hotel Poseidon (60 rooms) Plaža Jaz bb; ✆033 463134; e info@poseidon-jaz.com; www.poseidon-jaz.com. Nicely positioned on the beach, this has rooms with AC, fridge, TV & balcony. Parking, Wi-Fi, restaurant. Children under 2 free; HB (*€7 supplement*) & FB available. Free transfers from Tivat airport, as well as transfers from Dubrovnik or Podgorica airports for a fee. Visa & MasterCard. **€€€–€€€€**

Hotel Odissey (18 rooms) Jadranski put bb; ✆033 463707; e info@hotelodissey.com; www.hotelodissey.com. The hotel is clean, convenient & practical, though without much atmosphere. It has some private balconies, AC, minibar, cable TV, in-room safe, free Wi-Fi & a restaurant (⏰ 07.00–24.00). B/fast is €5. It's clean, convenient & practical, though without much

atmosphere. The mountain-view room at the rear is probably preferable. **€€€**

✗ **Savina** ✆033 465130; e jaz@t-com.me; www.restoransavina.com. For a couple of decades owner Željko Marović has presided over this vine-covered terrace, a nice spot for seaside dining, offering reasonably priced plates such as octopus & scampi with smoked ham & cheese. 8 studio rooms are also available (TV, balcony, cooking facilities, hairdryer, 2 sunbeds & umbrella €10; children under 12 free, b/fast inc). **€€–€€€€**

▲ **Jaz** (100 units) Right by Jaz Beach; ✆033 451699. Facilities here are not great, but following the closure of Camp Jaz Hostel in nearby Lastva Grbaljska in summer 2014, this remains the only budget option for travellers.

Beyond Jaz, **Trsteno Beach** is small and sandy and the sea is very shallow, suitable for young children. The downside is that there are very loud (pop music) beach bars at both ends. Nevertheless, at the end of the day the bar to the east is a nice place for a sunset beer. Park above the beach and walk down. You could walk all the way from Jaz Beach but it would be quite a hike, or you could arrange to be taken by

SEND US YOUR SNAPS!

We'd love to follow your adventures using our Montenegro guide – why not send us your photos and stories via Twitter (@BradtGuides) and Instagram (@bradtguides) using the hashtag #montenegro. Alternatively, you can upload your photos directly to the gallery on the Montenegro destination page via our website (www.bradtguides.com).

boat. There are many taxi boats for hire by the dock at Budva. Be sure to negotiate a price first. Easiest, in season, is by Olimpia Express bus (\ *033 451567*), which has a service between these two beaches and Budva several times daily.

SOUTH ALONG THE COAST

Proceeding south from Budva, the small 15th-century burial chapel of the last Duke of Paštrovići is visible on the headland above Guvance Beach (sand, bounded by rock). The Paštrovići were a powerful clan that once controlled this part of the littoral. Here the road branches left to **Cetinje**, a route which, while not quite equalling the Ladder of Cattaro (page 148) for drama, still offers stunning views.

After 2km the Cetinje road leads to **Maini**, a village that was the starting point of a bizarre twist in Montenegrin history. It was here that Šćepan Mali ('Stephen the Little'), an 18th-century pretender to the princedom, first appeared in the guise of a monk specialising in homoeopathic medicine and claiming to be the overthrown Tsar Peter III of Russia. Rather surprisingly he manoeuvred himself into becoming ruler of Crna Gora for the following seven years, and by all accounts quite an efficient one. Perhaps there is a lesson to be learnt. His role was only curtailed when he was murdered by his barber. Read all about him in Sebag Montefiore's *Potemkin, Prince of Princes* (page 325). Pretending, it seems, was all the rage at that time.

That said, more recently, in June 2011 in fact, the Montenegrin newspaper *Vijesti* carried reports of a 21st-century pretender, one Stephen Chernetić, a 51-year-old journalist and culinary critic 'living in Turin and Belgrade [who] claims to be a Montenegrin prince, heir to the Crnojević dynasty, and sometimes bestows titles on his attendants'. Despite his conviction, it relates, he has never tried to establish contact with officials in Montenegro and 'does not wish anything from them'. According to Chernetić, as quoted in *Montenegro Today* (19 June 2011): 'he is technically Crown Prince of Montenegro, Serbia, Albania and Macedonia. His family comes from [the] Byzantine family Comneni and is descendant of Montenegrin historic leading family Crnojević. He feels that the Montenegrin coat of arms dates from the Crnojević family but that there is now more attention paid to the dynasty of Petrović'.

Around 2km from Maini is the **Monastery of Podostrog** and the former seat of Montenegrin bishops. This is where Prince-Bishop Danilo, founder of the Petrović dynasty, of whom Njegoš wrote in his *Mountain Wreath*, died. Njegoš also wrote about Stephen the Little in *Lazni car Šćepan Mali*. The monastery began as a small church in the 12th century but was considerably expanded in the 18th. Nearby is the **Monastery of Podmaine** with 18th-century frescoes by Rafail Dimitrijević of Risan and an iconostasis by Nicholaos Aspioti of Corfu.

Pass, on the right, a memorial to the beginning, in 1941, of Tito's uprising against the Italian fascists. Near to the top of the ridge to the right (east) is the ruined 19th-century Austro-Hungarian fortress of **Kosmač**, to and around which there are hiking possibilities offering exceptional views. For access to the fortress there is a footpath that leads over the Paštrovića Gora (hill), all the way down to Rafailovići and on to Petrovac. This footpath gives more great views of the sea and is safe for tourists. It is not a posted path, but since it is parallel to the old Austro-Hungarian tarmac road you shouldn't get lost. A number of other **Budva Riviera hikes** are described in a useful free booklet, *Pješačimo* (*Let's Walk*), produced by Centar za Podsticanje Razivoja Turizma, and should be available from the tourist office.

The highway on the coast meanwhile continues past several beach communities, including Boreti, Bečići, Kamenovo and Pržno.

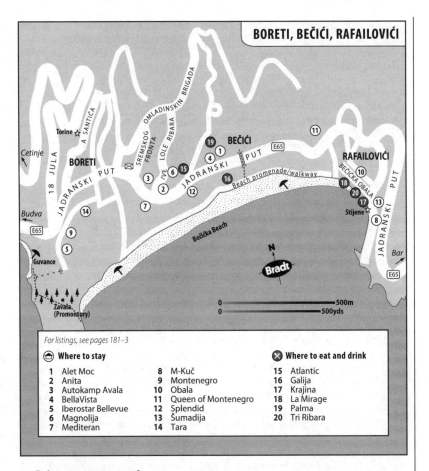

BORETI, BEČIĆI, RAFAILOVIĆI

For listings, see pages 181–3

Where to stay

1	Alet Moc	8	M-Kuč
2	Anita	9	Montenegro
3	Autokamp Avala	10	Obala
4	BellaVista	11	Queen of Montenegro
5	Iberostar Bellevue	12	Splendid
6	Magnolija	13	Šumadija
7	Mediteran	14	Tara

Where to eat and drink

15	Atlantic		
16	Galija		
17	Krajina		
18	La Mirage		
19	Palma		
20	Tri Ribara		

BEČIĆI AND RAFAILOVIĆI **Bečići's** long beach and calm sea have established it as a good place for both children's holidays and beach games. Besides the full range of water sports, there are facilities for tennis, paragliding and even an international beach soccer tournament. The many hotels are concentrated in one big complex by the beach, the pine woods behind the town in solemn retreat from all this rampant enterprise. What Bečići does have is one of Montenegro's finest fish restaurants – **Tri Ribara** (page 183) – though arguably that is in next-door **Rafailovići**, a little village that melds into Bečići.

Rafailovići has a few old villas, now dominated by apartment blocks, but remains relatively unspoilt. It retains its Italian ambience, with a narrow, fine-sand, child-friendly beach and quite a few small boats in a mini-port.

Note that while it is possible to drive into Rafailovići from the coastal highway running above, the roads down to the waterfront are extremely narrow and tend to become congested in season. Parking in the village is limited. A pleasant seaside walkway can be followed eastward and via a lighted tunnel (185m) through the cliff to adjacent **Kamenovo Beach** (page 183).

Getting there and around The Olimpia Express **bus** linking seaside towns between Budva and Petrovac comes through in both directions several times a day,

Louise Schofield and Sean Kingsley

Montenegro, nestling along the eastern Adriatic coastline, is simply enchanting. Alongside stunning landscapes of dense forest, undulating mountains and well-sheltered smugglers' coves, Illyrian hill-forts, enclosed medieval towns and Baroque palaces illuminate a land that time – and certainly globalisation – has long left to its own devices.

Little imagination is needed to call to mind the fantastic Illyrian backdrop in Shakespeare's *Twelfth Night*. Even a scholar of Arthur Evans' repute was strongly 'touched' by this region, waxing lyrical about the stupendous scenery, which he described as an 'earthly fairyland'. Decades before excavating Knossos, it was while sailing along the northern borders of this eastern Adriatic coastline that Evans started contemplating perplexing subterranean 'boomings'.

The country is both a dream and a source of nightmare for the archaeologist. One is hard pressed to think of any other European country whose archaeological landscape remains so enigmatically *terra incognita*. Because Montenegro has for centuries comprised the periphery of empires and nations, historically its cultural heritage has tended to be neglected. In terms of potential, however, it is overripe for the picking. Currently only 25 archaeologists operate in the country, of which 70% are prehistorians.

The adjacent edge of this double-edged sword is the consequent worrying absence of enforced political legislation capable of protecting the country's ancient cultural heritage. Not surprisingly, complete ancient settlements have simply disappeared in recent times. This is the case with Risan, an Illyrian settlement that evolved into a medium-sized Hellenistic and Roman town, which has a rich history. In the Risan that Arthur Evans surveyed in the 1870s, Roman roads, an aqueduct and a Hellenistic grave were still visible across the landscape. A field with coins strewn across its surface enabled Evans to identify the town as a source minting issues under Prince Ballaeos. During excavations at depths of some 3m Evans 'layed bare the basement floors of houses and the pavements of narrow streets, while Roman remains, inscriptions, coins, pottery and glass abound'.

Budva, a bustling medieval coast town straight out of an improbable Hollywood film backdrop, is situated on a picturesque promontory, with a double harbour on either side. Although it has experienced a similar fate to Risan, rescue archaeology seems to have been more successful in documenting the vanishing past. Hellenistic and Roman Budva is largely sealed under a maze of narrow stone-flagged streets and small squares, but traces of its monumental past emerge as you wander its alleys, with columns, architrave blocks and funerary markers scattered in dark corners, in the shadows of pizza shops.

Today the Budva necropolis finds are scattered among various museums in the former Yugoslav countries, and some have found their way into private hands.

and half-hourly during the summer, operating until late in the evening. Check with your hotel for a current timetable, or you should find the timetable posted on the main bus stops. In summer there's a **miniature train** that runs the length of the beach walkway.

There is an area by the beach for parking mobile camper vans and caravans – at least there was at the time of writing.

This internationally important town is almost completely unknown outside the former Yugoslavia.

The country enjoys good recreational diving facilities, but unlike adjoining countries only one shipwreck is catalogued in A J Parker's *Ancient Shipwrecks of the Mediterranean and the Roman Provinces* (Oxford). By contrast, Italy boasts 428 wrecks, Croatia 92 and a recent report on the western Black Sea coast of Bulgaria lists over 80 wrecks.

The Montenegro anomaly is clearly an artificial pattern. The region is located along a key shipping lane that links the Near East, Asia Minor and Greece with Italy and the heart of the Roman Empire. A survey completed by the authors [in June 2003] confirmed an abundance of shipwrecks, with 20 sites (formerly unknown internationally) emerging from discussions with museum staff, personnel at the Institute for the Protection of Culture and Heritage of Serbia, and dive instructors, and through the detection and examination of pottery recovered from the sea.

Local archaeologists retain immense pride in their cultural heritage and continue to protect and document the country's archaeology with the limited resources available. Perast Museum houses extremely important inscriptions from the Risan region, as well as shipwreck finds; a new museum, with a Roman street tastefully incorporated into its basement, [opened in 2006] in an elegant old town house in Budva; at Stari Bar, the 'medieval Pompeii of Montenegro', local artisans work with great dedication and a small United States Agency for International Development (USAID) grant to sensitively conserve a site that really ought to be a UNESCO World Heritage Site. Down on the coast a rich collection of sculpture, pottery and armour is displayed in the newly renovated King Nikola I Museum, an opulent royal palace built in 1885.

The archaeology of Montenegro currently stands at a critical crossroads. Social reform and economic development are pushing the country away from the political disruptions and associated insecurities of the 20th century and setting it on a road towards European Union membership. For the first time in decades the country now holds the potential for overseas investment, development, and for the initiation of international scientific projects. On the other hand, without formal recognition of Montenegro's cultural heritage at governmental level, and associated legislative protection, there can be little doubt that its coastal archaeology will be eradicated in a short period of time.

This article is abridged from a feature in Minerva, *the International Review of Ancient Art and Archaeology,* November/December 2003 issue. *It is reproduced with kind permission. For further news on Montenegrin marine archaeology, see box on page 139.*

Where to stay   *Map, page 179.*

Queen of Montenegro (220 rooms, 24 apts) Narodnog fronta bb; 033 662662; e hotel@queenofmontenegro.com; www. queenofmontenegro.com. A well-appointed & comfortable hotel with great views, set in landscaped gardens back from & above the beach, with direct access to the beach by private bridge. All rooms with balcony, AC, minibar, flat-screen cable TV, room safe. Indoor & outdoor pools, restaurant, cocktail & snack bars, gift shop, 24hr casino, conference hall; parking. Internet access €2 per 15mins. A popular choice through British travel agents. Hot rocks massage at the beach, but note there are charges for hotel beach chairs & umbrellas in season (*€7 pp/day when booked through hotel, more if purchased on the beach*). CCs accepted. HB €15 pp extra. Low–high season €€€€–€€€€€ (sgl €€€–€€€€)

🏠 **Splendid** (332 rooms, 6 for disabled guests, 21 suites) ☎033 773777; e reservations@montenegrostars.com; www.montenegrostars.com. Before the reopening of Sveti Stafan & Miločer (pages 186–9), this was arguably the most luxurious hotel in Montenegro in terms of both facilities & staff. Set in gardens beside the beach, its rooms have 42m² balconies & sea views, plus flat-screen TV, internet access, minibar, safe. 4 restaurants, 4 bars. Free to guests are sauna, spa, jacuzzi, gym, solarium, indoor & outdoor pools, golf driving range, private beach. Hairdresser, kids & teens clubs, daily live entertainment, shops, car rental desk, business centre, extensive conference centre, ballroom, garage. Popular with w/enders from Italy. CCs accepted. Sgl supplement €30. Low–high season €€€€–€€€€€ (HB €€€€€)

🏠 **Mediteran** (222 rooms, 2 suites) ☎033 424009; e maestral@t-com.me; www.hotelmediteran.info; ⏱ 1 Apr–31 Dec. All rooms with minibar, safe, satellite TV, most with sea view. Restaurant, disco & English pub. Aqua park, indoor & outdoor pools, solarium, fitness centre, wellness & thalassotherapy centre, jacuzzi, garden & TV lounge. Hairdresser/beauty salon, shops, 24hr room service, 100m from private beach. Tennis & volleyball. Garage parking. High season charge for gym, beach, chairs & umbrellas. Visa & Diners Club accepted; ATM in lobby. €€€€ (HB €€€–€€€€ low–high season)

🏠 **Tara** (295 rooms) ☎033 404196; www.hoteltara.me. AC, lift, terrace, room safe, satellite TV, hairdryer, minibar, laundry service, internet, bar, restaurant, nightclub, fitness & beauty salon, internet café, pool & private beach. Conference room & parking. Bosnian owned. €€€€

🏠 **Alet Moc** (131 rooms, 69 suites) On the Bečići rd; ☎033 471808; e vektra.moc@vektra.co.me; www.vektra.co.me; ⏱ 1 May–1 Oct. Dbls & trpls with shower & lavatory; suites with kitchenette; all have sea views. Restaurant, terrace, basketball, volleyball, handball. €€€

🏠 **Hotel BellaVista** (9 rooms, 9 suites, 22 apts) Marina Bečića 2; ☎033 471377;

e bellavista@t-com.me; www.bellavista.me. AC, cable TV, minibar, internet access, balcony; bar, restaurant, terrace, gym, jacuzzi, sauna; all facilities free to guests. B/fast inc. CCs accepted. €€€

🏠 **Hotel Iberostar Bellevue** (578 rooms) ☎033 425100; e reservations@iberostar.co.me; www.iberostar.com. All rooms have sea view, AC, cable TV, minibar, in-room safe, laundry service. Restaurant, bar & internet café, lift, boutique. Spa, fitness & beauty salon, plus outdoor & indoor swimming pools. Parking. The hotel has a private beach but this can get very crowded despite the fact that in season hotel guests are charged for the privilege of using it (*€6 sunbed & umbrella*). Diners credit card accepted. €€€

🏠 **Hotel Magnolija** (24 rooms) Boreti bb; ☎033 471606; e hotelmagnolija@t-com.me. Slightly inland, up the road opposite the Splendid & turn right. Most rooms with balcony, AC, minibar, TV. Swimming pool. CCs accepted. €€€

🏠 **Hotel Montenegro** (168 rooms, 4 suites) 20m from the beach; ☎033 773773; e reservations@montenegrostars.co.me; www.montenegrostars.com; ⏱ Apr–Nov. All with AC, minibar, balcony, cable TV, room safe, internet access; most with sea view. 3 restaurants & 4 bars; all meals served buffet-style. Nightclub, beer garden, children's playground. Garden with live music. Foreign-exchange office, laundry, hairdresser, shop & conference centre. Indoor & outdoor pools, gym, sauna & jacuzzi, all free to guests, as are facilities at Splendid (above) & Blue Star in Budva (page 169). CCs accepted. €€€

🏠 **Hotel Anita** (25 rooms) Jadranski put bb; ☎033 471777; http://hotelanita.me; ⏱ summer only. All with AC, TV, balcony, fridge & kitchen. Beside busy main road but has an underground garage. Same ownership as Pansion Anita in old town. CCs accepted. Friendly. €€€

✳ 🏠 **Hotel Šumadija** (111 rooms) Pastrovska 2, Rafailovići; ☎033 471003; www.recreatours.co.rs. AC, cable TV, minibar, lift. Restaurant, beer terrace & parking. Simple but recommended. €€

🏠 **M-Kuč** (42 rooms) Rafailovići; ☎033 471180; e hotelkuc@aol.com; www.hotel-kuc.com. Slightly threadbare rooms & a bit institutional, but everyone gets a generous balcony overlooking the sea. Lift, AC, minibar, cable TV, internet bar, restaurant, indoor pool, laundry service, parking. Quietly positioned. €€

⌂ **Obala** (54 rooms) Bečićka plaža 25, Rafailovići; ☎033 471045; e info@hotelobala.me; www.hotelobala.me; ⊕ 1 Apr–1 Nov. AC, satellite TV, minibar, internet bar, shop, beauty salon, restaurant, parking, outdoor pool. €€

Ⓐ **Autokamp Avala** (300 pitches) Across the highway from the Splendid; ☎033 453941. Campsite in an orchard 200m from the beach. Restaurant & terrace. Simple facilities. €

✖ Where to eat and drink *Map, page 179.*

Restaurants

✳ ✖ **Tri Ribara** Bečićka plaža 35, Rafailovići; ☎033 471050; ⊕ 08.00–24.00. Owned by a fishing family, in a simple stone house, with sheltered terrace beside the water. Excellent fresh fish at fair prices. Choose from a selection of the day's catch brought to your table. Intensely flavoured seafood broth. Justifiably wide reputation makes booking advisable. They also have a few small apts (€€) to rent in conjunction with La Mirage (see below). €€€€

✖ **Atlantic** ul Marina Bačića 1; ☎033 471380; http://domatlantic.com. ⊕ 12.00–23.00 only. By the turning to the Queen of Montenegro Hotel, a small casual restaurant with a reasonable balance of fish & meat choices. Also rooms with AC, some with sea views (€€€). €€€

✖ **Palma** ul Narodnog fronta 6. Popular alternative for local hotel guests, a family restaurant with Montenegrin & Serbian specialities. Covered terrace. No CCs. Sometimes rooms or apt for rent; contact them for availability & price. €€€

✖ **Restaurant Galija** Below the Queen of Montenegro. Fish, grills & cocktails on the beach. €€€

✖ **Krajina** East of Tri Ribara, Rafailovići; ⊕ summer only. Nice family-run bistro & bar. Perfect spot for a sundowner. €€

✖ **La Mirage** Almost beside Tri Ribara, Rafailovići; ☎033 471061, 033 471061. Run by the same family as the Tri Ribara, but with a menu at the Knickerbocker Glory end of the spectrum, plus pizzas & salads & a pretty good b/fast. Their rooms (€€) are neat & clean with sea views (no lift), well-equipped kitchens, AC, TV & Wi-Fi, but parking can be a bit of a problem. No CCs. €€

Entertainment & nightlife

☆ **Stara Crna Gora** Boreti, Bečići; also Torine; both ⊕ 22.00–05.00

☆ **Stijene** Rafailovići. Beside beach. More of a DJ lounge than a club, with quite stylish outdoor drinking & a pizza-&-omelette type of snack menu.

Other practicalities

Giant water slide Midway along the beach at Hotel Mediteran. €0.30 for 1 ride, €5 for 24.
Mini-market Close to camping & post office

✉ **Post office** Main highway opposite Splendid; ⊕ 07.00–20.00

PRŽNO AND KAMENOVO Pržno is still a delightful little port that largely retains its identity, despite the imposition in the last few years of a major hotel/resort on its traditional picture-postcard aspect. With luck, extensive parkland surrounding the newly restored Sveti Stefan–Miločer estate and forming an eastern border to the village may discourage further development. The craggy island in the bay was once a sailors' quarantine post.

Kamenovo is a comparatively quiet and hotel-free beach and has nice views of Sveti Nikola and Sveti Stefan. There are four beach bars (⊕ *summer only*), the quietest of which is at the Budva end. Raffish Zoff fish restaurant in the far eastern corner can get crowded at weekends, but it is a nice spot, beer in hand, to watch the sun go down. This end of the wide beach can be reached by steps down from Pržno.

Kamenovo and Pržno beaches both have regulated parking in season, at rising prices; Pržno for a full day in summer should be in the region of €10 (free if you're staying at the Maestral Hotel).

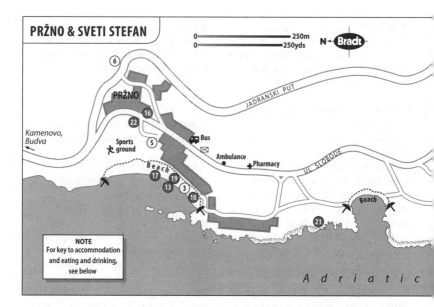

PRŽNO & SVETI STEFAN

0 ————— 250m
0 ————— 250yds N → **Bradt**

PRŽNO

JADRANSKI PUT

Kamenovo,
Budva

Sports
ground

Bus

Ambulance
Pharmacy

UI. SLOBODE

Beach

Beach

NOTE
For key to accommodation
and eating and drinking,
see below

A d r i a t i c

Getting there and away The Mediteran Express **bus** service linking Budva with Petrovac (*check for timetable at bus stop behind Maestral Hotel*) passes through several times daily, with a more frequent service during the summer months.

Pržno **taxi** service, located behind Maestral Hotel (see below), offers fares to Budva (€10), Petrovac (€15), Cetinje (€40), Kotor (€40) and various day trips, eg: four persons to Dubrovnik (€220), four to Cetinje, Podgorica and Ostrog (€140), etc.

Car hire
🚗 **Krisma Motors** Maestral Hotel; m 069 308698. Ford Fiesta €50 per day for 1–6 days, €40 for 16–30 days, €35 for longer; Mustang €120, €90 & €80 respectively. Limited mileage under 16 days. Min age 22. Chauffeurs available. CCs accepted.

Where to stay *Map, above.*
🏠 **Maestral Hotel** (180 rooms, 9 suites) Pržno bb; ☎ 033 410100; e hotel@maestral.info; www.maestral.info. Owned by the Slovenian HIT organisation, which has brought the hotel up to a good but expensive international standard. Sea view rooms with bath, minibar, AC, safe, TV & balcony. Restaurants & bars. Also indoor & outdoor infinity pools, private beach, children's pool & playgrounds, sauna, jacuzzi, bikes to rent, solarium, tennis, beauty parlour & health spa. Internet access €10 per day. Entertainment centre & casino (🕐 *18.00–05.00 Mon–Fri, 12.00–05.00 Sat–Sun*) offering roulette, blackjack, *chemin de fer, punto banco* & slots. CCs accepted; travellers' cheques changed at 4%. The hotel newsstand has an eclectic selection of English-language magazines inc *My Hair, Time, Cosmopolitan, Men's*

Health & Euro-Truck Weekly. Low–high season
€€€€–€€€€€

❊ 🏠 **Residence** (30 rooms, 22 apts) Jadranski put; ☎ 033 427100; e reservations@ hecmontenegro.com; www.residencemontenegro. com. Although the address is strictly Miločer, this is on the coast road just above turn-off to Pržno. A modern & extremely well-appointed hotel opened in 2008, with free use of the Maestral Hotel beach. AC, cable TV, room safe, minibar, balcony. Non-smoking rooms. Wi-Fi throughout, restaurant & bar, 2 conference rooms. Spa & beauty centre. Rooftop pool & terrace with fine views. Bike rental. Free shuttle to beaches. Evening entertainment – folklore, oriental, etc. 8-seater minibus for excursions. Gay-friendly. The Residence also runs a hotel school in conjunction with the Hotel

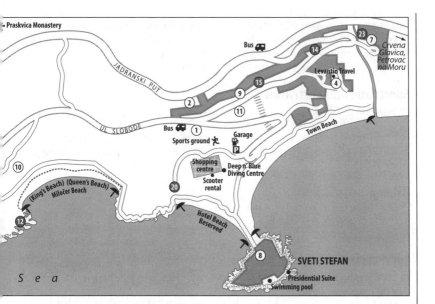

Education Centre in Pljevlja & Algonquin College, Canada. CCs accepted. (Note, if booked direct they will inc dinner gratis, ie: HB). €€€€

* 🏠 **Guest House Kazanegra** (5 rooms) Obala 30 (overlooking the cove & below the large Maestral Hotel) 📞033 468407; m 069 081147; e blanila@ t-com.me; www.kazanegra.com. In a prime location overlooking the sea, all rooms are dbl with bath & AC, cable TV, safe & internet access. Good English. Proprietor Diki Kazanegra also runs Adria DMC travel agency in Budva (📞033 455181), very good fixers who arrange imaginative personalised tours on sea & land, fish picnics, transfers from local airports, car & bike rental, etc. €€€

🍴 **Where to eat and drink** *Map, above.*

* 🍴 **Blanche** Obala 11; m 067 311391; ⊕ 11.00–24.00. Sandro Mitrović's elegant & appropriately uncoloured establishment, perched over the sea at the end of town. Its menu is imaginative, its setting delightful & its welcome warm. Sicilian specialities. €€€€

* 🍴 **Gastro Club Mitrović** ul Stefana Mitrovića br 17; e gastroclub@t-com.me. Owned & run by Vuko Mitrović, who used to cook at Sveti Stefan & now runs a cookery school in conjunction with the restaurant. Menus are eclectic with a fishy bias & sometimes feature visiting chefs who are also making school presentations. Wife Eva provides B&B accommodation at the same address (e

sindimm@yahoo.com; €€€) in season. AC, cable TV, internet, parking. Visa accepted. €€€€
🍴 **Konoba Langust** Obala 34; ⊕ 11.00–24.00. Fresh fish by the sea, delicious soup. 3 linked

terraces in summer. Takes MasterCard. €€€€
✕ Restaurant 'R' ul Stefana Mitovića br 37.
Well-cooked Mediterranean food in a pleasing
atmosphere. A bit expensive but worth it. €€€€

✕ Konoba More Obala 18; ⏰ 11.00–23.00.
Good fish in a pleasant atmosphere by the beach.
No CCs. €€€
✕ Mlin Obala bb. Pizzeria. €€€

Sports and other activities
Big-game fishing
There are boats offering fishing trips of all varieties;
negotiate your own conditions. Try
m 069 027944, or **Srdjan Kuljaca** Budva;
m 067 317717.

Diving
⤳ **Pro Dive Hydrotech** At Maestral Hotel;
m 069 013985; e rm2@t-com.me; ⏰ May–1
Oct. Offers everything for divers, from training to
excursions & equipment.

Other practicalities
✉ **Post office** Behind Maestral Hotel, near
stone archway to Miločer & Sv Stefan Hotel
complex; ⏰ 08.00–14.00

SVETI STEFAN Soon after leaving Pržno, the road southeast runs above the island
of Sveti Stefan, with its cluster of pink roofs and the sandbar linking it to the shore:
a beckoning siren in the deep blue sea.

Until 50 years ago this was simply a pretty little fishing village, eye-catchingly
placed. Then someone had the cunning idea of transforming it all into a unique and
luxurious hotel. Connected by honeysuckled alleys, crooked mossy slopes and steps,
the cottages were converted into intimate suites, with the tiny, original 15th-century
church of St Stephen preserved, a reminder of its previous incarnation. A small pool
was sunk into the south-facing corner and a wide terrace laid out looking westward
to the pewter peaks of Lovćen, providing a grand-circle view of extravagant sunsets.

A singular setting in Tito's Yugoslavia, soon it became a showpiece with *Vuittons*
of glitterati sailing in. And so it continued, until the regional problems in the final
decade of the 20th century left the island sanctuary a forgotten dream. Nonetheless,
like the old London Windmill, it never closed. Never, that is, until 2007, when
a major restoration of the entire property was initiated, including work on a
substantial tract of mainland grounds, and a further hotel was incorporated. By
2011 it was up and running once again.

Until not long ago there was little more than a cluster of fishermen's cottages
in the vicinity of Sveti Stefan, but such an attractive prospect inevitably lured the
developers and today there is, in effect, a second Sveti Stefan village overlooking
the island and extending downhill to the easterly beach. Happily, so far at least, the
settlement has retained its pulchritude.

Getting there and away The Olimpia Express **bus** service connects Sveti Stefan
with Budva and Petrovac. An hourly service operates in summer, less frequently in
winter. Times are posted on the main bus stops along the coastal road.

Getting around Scooters are available to rent at Rent-a-Motor (m *067 317717,
069 027944*).

Tour operator
✱ 🖪 **Levantin Travel** Vukice Mitrović br 3; ☎ 033
468086; m 069 028436; e levantin@t-com.me.
Offers a range of hotel & private accommodation,

travel tickets, car hire & excursions. Helpful,
experienced staff, who speak good English.

Where to stay *Map, pages 184–5.*

⌂ **Sveti Stefan** (50 units) ☎033 420000; e amansvetistefan@amanresorts.com; www. amanresorts.com. Unmistakable even from high on the road that descends the mountain, hairpin after hairpin, to the coast, this tiny island has long served as a symbol of Montenegro herself. Now the renovations are complete, it represents a more valuable treasure than ever before. Each accommodation option is unique, offering all the peace & privacy you could desire while being only a matter of steps away from the central piazza (featuring a traditional taverna & bakery – either of these an option for b/fast or lunch – along with an antipasti bar, cigar room & *enoteca*). Beauty treatments & massage available in-room or at dedicated 'spa cottages' dotted around the property. Wi-Fi, 2 pools, gym, restaurant &, maybe best of all, an infinity terrace providing the tableau of mountains, sea, sunsets & stars. From €700–€2,500 for the most superior suite with secluded pool. CCs accepted. Round trip transfers from Tivat Airport inc. €€€€€+

⌂ **Villa Miločer** (8 suites) Contact as for Sveti Stefan, above. Two coves away & diagonally across the channel from Sveti Stefan, Miločer may make it difficult for Aman junkies to make a choice. At a glance the 2 properties could not appear to be more different, but here (as on the island) it is the interiors that give away the brand. Miločer was also historically one of the finest hotels in Montenegro & it too has undergone a full-scale renovation. The mansion, with its lovely wisteria-clad loggia, was originally the summer property of the Karađorđevićs, the royal family of Yugoslavia. Framed on 3 sides by stately parkland, the overwhelming impression is one of symmetry, with neat lawns & its own spacious beach. Inside, creams & browns predominate; with parquet flooring, fireplaces, loggia daybed, an intimate 7-table dining room, a living room for afternoon tea or cocktails, Wi-Fi & impeccable service. Suites – inc 2 'garden' suites – €800–900. CCs accepted. Round trip transfers from Tivat Airport inc. €€€€€+

✻ ⌂ **Villa Montenegro** (5 rooms, 6 suites, presidential suite) Vukice Mitrović 2; ☎033 468802; e info@villa-montenegro.com; www. villa-montenegro.com; ⊕ all year. Unique small hotel, built to a very high standard on the hillside in burgeoning Sveti Stefan village. Panoramic sea views, Turkish bath, sauna & jacuzzi, lift, infinity pool & fitness centre. AC, plasma TV, safe box & minibar. 24hr room service. Stylish international restaurant. Garage. High security & great discretion. CCs accepted. Free transfers to Čilipi & local airports. €€€€€

⌂ **Romanov** (20 rooms, 4 suites) ul Šumet bb; ☎033 468471; e hotelromanov@t-com. me; www.hotelromanov.com. Well appointed & hospitable, slightly back from & above the beach. Most rooms with sea views; AC, cable TV, minibar, internet. Laundry & babysitting services, pets allowed. Restaurant & coffee shop. CCs accepted. €€€€

⌂ **Azimut** (17 rooms & apts) Šumet bb; ☎033 468992; e info@hotel-azimut.com; www. hotel-azimut.com. Modern, but rather lacking in atmosphere. All rooms have balcony, sea views, AC, cable TV & minibar. Discounts for children. CCs accepted. €€€

⌂ **Levantin Apartments** (25 apts) Vukice Mitrović. Adjacent to travel agent (opposite) & run by the same family. Attractive, well-appointed rooms & apts. Popular with English visitors; book well ahead. Visa accepted. €€€

⌂ **Vila Drago** (6 rooms, 2 apts) ul Slobode 32; m 069 032050; petardss@t-com.me; www. viladrago.com. Small hotel run for 40 years by the charming & helpful Radenović family, overlooking Sveti Stefan & adjacent bays. Comfortable large rooms with balconies, as well as self-catering apts. Cool terrace restaurant (see below). No CCs. €€€

⌂ **Hotel Adrović** (22 apts) Jadranski put bb, on main road beside Sveti Stefan turn-off; ☎033 468507; www.hoteladrovic.com. Young, happy staff infect this hotel with a holiday-party feel. Apts, each with 2–5 dbls, extend down the cliff beneath, all with AC, cable TV, terraces with sea view. Larger apts have kitchens. 24hr café & restaurant. No internet. No CCs. €€

✻ ⋏ **Crvena Glavica** (2,200 units) 1km east of Sveti Stefan; ☎033 468070; m 069 776716 (Sonja); ⊕ Jun–Sep. Campsite with lovely meadowland setting among pines, olives, bougainvillea & lots of wild roses; extending along a wide declivity above its own small coves. €2.50 pp per day, plus tent €3.50, caravan €4, car €2.50, electricity €3.50, fridge €3. Lockers. Beach restaurant: grills, fish. Facilities are quite basic, but recommended.

✕ Where to eat and drink *Map, pages 184–5.*

Ul Slobode

The steps up from the Sveti Stefan Hotel lead to ul Slobode, which has several quite good restaurants, all serving the usual mix of grills, pasta & pizzas at similar prices & most with terraces with broad views.

✕ **Drago** Vila Drago, ul Slobode 32; ☎033 468477; http://viladrago.com. ⊕ summer only. Similar food & welcome to Kentera but on a shadier vine-covered terrace. No CCs. €€€

✕ **Famelja Kentera** ul Slobode br 24; m 069 231922. Perhaps the best of the bunch, just uphill from the top of the steps. Nice terrace & a warm welcome. Italian style comfort cooking with such dishes as steak gorgonzola & chicken parmigiano. You can order special dishes a day in advance & they will deliver locally. No CCs. €€€

✕ **Šumet** ul Slobode br 13; ☎086 468152; www. svetistefan-sumet.me. Open-sided terrace but no views. Food & ambience more local in style, but good English. No CCs. €€€

⊑ **Café Café** ul Slobode. Cakes & desserts.

Mainland

There are a further 3 dining venues at Villa Miločer, in the Aman mainland property:

✕ **The Queen's Chair** Kraljičina stolica; ⊕ dinner only. This restaurant is perched clifftop on the western boundary & commands splendid views over the bay of Budva. Mediterranean food with an Italian accent. CCs accepted. €€€€

* ✕ **The Olive Tree** Maslina drvo; ⊕ b/fast, lunch & dinner. Informal brasserie. Close to Sveti Stefan island causeway, indoor & outdoor seating overlooking the beach. Delicious burgers, steaks & seafood cooked on wood-fired grills & rotisserie. Open to non-residents & offering some of the tastiest dishes in the area, served with panache at not exorbitant prices. CCs accepted. €€€

⊑ **The Beach Café** In the cove next to Miločer; ⊕ all day. Alfresco & shaded by cypress trees; snacks.

Sports and other activities The Aman hotels – Sveti Stefan and Villa Miločer – can offer personalised guided excursions throughout Montenegro. Many activities

THE PAŠTROVIĆI

The once semi-autonomous Paštrovići lands comprise the central littoral from Budva in the west to beyond Petrovac in the east, rising into the foothills of the Crmnica Mountains. With a language of its own, some words of which are still in use (see *Months*, page 319), and discrete traditions, the eponymous clan is fascinating and little known outside the region.

It was first recorded in the 14th century as a dukedom and legend has it that sometime in the 15th century the intrepid Paštrovići succeeded in sinking the Turkish fleet in the vicinity of what is now known as Jaz Beach, using the proceeds to build a fortress on Sveti Stefan. From this base they were well placed to engage in fresh forays against their enemies. On secluded Drobni Pijesak Beach near Petrovac they held their annual parliamentary sessions, elected their leaders and convened meetings to resolve tribal disputes, large or small. Such an assembly was called *Bankada*, and since 1999 the Paštrovići have renewed the tradition. Every 28 June representatives of the 12 clans gather at Drobni Pijesak Beach to choose four judges, two dukes and 12 landowners. The assembly then reviews the previous 12 months to ensure that traditional customs and religious practices have been maintained as far as possible, along with historical monuments, the natural habitat and civil rights.

Close to the Reževići Monastery (beside the Petrovac road) is the site of the first Paštrovići school, founded in 1856 by Dimitrije Pirazić. The building has been restored and now acts as an **ethnographic museum, art gallery and library** can be arranged, including birdwatching, biking, big-game fishing, diving, sailing and private tastings of regional wines. You can also try:

⚓ Big Game Montenegro Fishing m 067 317717; www.biggamemontenegro.com. 8hr fishing trips on the *Galex Fish* start in the early morning; equipment & instruction provided. Normal passenger no is 4; more by arrangement.

🤿 Diving Deep 'n' Blue Diving Centre m 069 030003; e deepblue@t-com.me. All levels, PADI-specialised courses, night dives, underwater photography & shipwrecks. All equipment provided. Excursions twice daily to a variety of diving sites up & down the coast.

Other practicalities

Car park Adjacent to public beach east of the island, €2 per hr. But a tip – especially in winter when on-street parking in upper Sveti Stefan is more readily available, & if you don't mind a flight of steps – is to park for free higher up on the winding approach road down to the island.

Local paintings A few local artists display paintings for sale beneath the olive trees just above the parking lot. Among them is Vladimir Jakovljević; asking price €50–4,000, but negotiable.

THE PAŠTROVIĆI HILLS They will tell you that somewhere in these Paštrovići hills, among the wild-flowering pomegranate, is hidden the mythical Elysium where Cadmus and Harmonia, changed by Zeus into serpents, are destined to remain forever. You are unlikely to run into them. There are two types of venomous snake in Montenegro, and as elsewhere both will do their best to slither out of your path (see page 5). But the scarlet pomegranates are everywhere.

This district also has a concentration of ecclesiastical buildings as great as anywhere in Montenegro. It seems that every headland is topped by, at the very

dedicated solely to the clan (e *sdomrezevicimn@t-com.me;* ⊕ *summer 08.00–12.00 & 16.00–22.00 Mon–Fri, winter 08.00–14.00; admission free but donations welcome*).

The cliff-top setting of the museum and the monastery complex, dotted with cypress and olive trees, reflects the villages of the Marche and Abruzzo across the sea and underlines the strong Italian influence that has permeated this coast for centuries. A wealth of detail is arranged for viewing within the little museum: domestic utensils, agricultural implements; costumes – violet coloured for a bridal robe; a *bauo*, her wedding chest, her dowry neatly listed in a *nota*; a *faculet*, the clan name for their traditional white head-shawl, worn with skirt, jacket and apron. These *nota* are so detailed that it has been possible to base fashion histories on them. Everyday clothes used to be made out of local materials such as wool, linen, hemp and even brushwood, which was soaked in the sea for the month of July then rubbed and rolled until it became fibrous. It must have been a relief when industrially produced cloth became available.

Some replicas of unique garments are on sale: knee socks – *kalcete* – at €30; a beautiful linen shirt – *komes* – at €45; a costumed doll – *lutka* – at €30.

The home cooking is delicious and if you have the opportunity to eat in a traditional household you might be given *polpete* (meatballs) flavoured with the local wild sage (*tušt*) that grows beside the sea. Alan Davidson, in his *Oxford Companion to Food*, mentions that this variety of sage (*salvia*) is considered the finest. *Šucenica* (wild chicory) is also a springtime ingredient in the Paštrovići kitchen.

least, a chapel. Monasteries abound and days can be passed exploring them, though gaining admission to the smaller ones can be a hit-and-miss adventure, and difficult to plan in advance.

Praskvica Monastery A short climb on foot above Miločer (also accessible by car) is the Praskvica complex, the monastery where the Paštrovići children learned to read and write. In March the pathway is bounded by peach blossom – from which, in the local dialect, it gets its name. Even the water which gushes from a nearby spring smells of the fruit.

The larger church is dedicated to Sv Nikola, protector of travellers and sailors, and was built in 1847 on the foundations of another, endowed in 1413 by Balsa III, ruler of Zeta, and of which part of the north wall is still visible. Note the Gothic frescoes, with images of Stefan Nemanjić, his son Sava, and Christ between the prophets Solomon and David; also a 19th-century iconostasis by Nicholaos Aspioti of Corfu. The smaller church of Sv Trojica (Holy Trinity) dates from much earlier (origin unknown). Its walls are covered with frescoes by the Serbian 17th-century painter Radul.

Duljevo Monastery Restored in 1995, Duljevo perches on a mountain plateau to the northeast (access by a minor road above Kamenovo). It was built in the 14th century by Emperor Dušan the Mighty of Serbia and served as a subordinate to the Dečane Monastery (Kosovo). Wall paintings in the church depicting sumptuously robed saints, holding sceptres and wearing Western-style crowns, have no apparent analogy. An abandoned *konak* (monks' sleeping quarters) is typical of old Paštrovići houses, with thick walls and narrow windows.

Reževići and Gradište monasteries Two other significant monasteries are to be found southwards on the Adriatic Highway. One, **Reževići**, less than a couple of kilometres along the main road west of Petrovac, positively encourages visitors. It is said that in years gone by the local people would always leave a jug of wine under a tree so travellers could refresh themselves on their journey. Now the monks sell hand-pressed olive oil and honey. On feast days there is local cheese and smoked ham; if you pick the right time it could very nicely take care of lunch. The monastery is said to date from the 13th century but has been restored several times. Until 1907 it received regular subsidies from the Russian court. Dmitrije Perazić, a member of the Reževići tribe, was the archimandrite at the beginning of the 19th century, ordained by Prince-Bishop Daniel in person in 1810. Perazić spent the subsequent 40 years in Russia and it was because of this that the church received such beneficence. The church has 17th-century frescoes.

The second, the **Gradište Monastery**, lies on an outcrop at the foot of Pelištice mountain, commanding a fine view of the long Buljarica Beach (page 199). The complex has three churches. Sv Nikola has 17th-century frescoes representing scenes of the Old and New Testaments and several Serbian rulers, painted by Father Strahinja from Budimlje. The iconostasis is by Vasilije Rafailović of Risan. The church of Sv Sava dates from the 16th century; and the third and smallest, dedicated to the Virgin, has frescoes from 1620, also by Strahinja, as well as busts representing the Nemanjić family. After the buildings were looted by the Turks they were restored but were again burnt in World War II by Italian troops and have only recently been renovated. Drive up off the main road around a kilometre east of Petrovac until you reach a well-marked parking area, then walk on up a steep and slightly slippery slope for about 300m.

REŽEVIĆI This compact little village is just off the main road, halfway between Sveti Stefan and Petrovac. However, the name Reževići is somewhat confusingly also applied to a significant part of the surrounding area, including a monastery just west of Petrovac (see above). It has a nice place to stay nearby and a couple of worthwhile restaurants. The village itself is also home to respected Montenegrin painter, Savo Pavlović.

Where to stay and eat *Map, page 167.*

Villa Natalia (10 apts) Skočidjevojka bb; m 065 2003473; www.skocidjevojka.net. New apts halfway between Sveti Stefan & Petrovac. AC, TV, kitchen, balcony with sea view. €€€

Gostionica Paštrovića dvori (9 rooms) Blizikuće; 033 451472. Excellent northward outlook to the island of Sveti Stefan. Well-signed access up a steep lane left off the Adriatic Highway, coming from Sveti Stefan. AC, cable TV, internet, laundry service, pets allowed. 10% discount if you eat at their rustic restaurant (€€€), decorated by artwork of larger-than-life patron, Željko Niklanović, who is also a musician. All fresh organic produce is sourced from the village of Tudorovići further up the mountain. €€

✷ **Apartments Skočidjevojka** (5 apts) Skočidjevojka bb; 033 468043; m 069 324781; e marcop@t-com.me; www.skocidjevojka.com. Self-catering 4-bed & studio apts, well positioned on a high bluff 5km west of Petrovac & 5km east of Sveti Stefan (from the west, the turn-off left, 300m beyond a petrol station, requires caution). The name, meaning 'Maiden's Leap', refers to a young girl who jumped off the cliff to protect her honour.

Surrounded by rich Mediterranean vegetation, the house has beautiful views seaward & to the wild mountains rising behind. Owner-managed by Marko & Sandra Pribilović, an old Paštrovići family. They speak excellent English & a variety of other languages, inc German & Italian, & are highly knowledgeable on Montenegro & its customs. Apts have fridge & hotplate, Wi-Fi, AC, TV & sea views; top-floor apt boasts a sunset view to rival that from the terrace at Sveti Stefan. There's a mini gym & a good-sized new pool. A footpath leads down to a secluded rocky swimming area. Getting in & out can be a bit tricky in rough weather but there are several other attractive coves nearby. Book well ahead. Room-only, B&B or with delicious meals by arrangement (*€10 pp*). Marko can organise

customised guided tours (*Paštrovići Museum & Reževići Monastery 1km*). €

✷ ✗ **Izvor** Rijeka Reževića; 033 468316; m 069 038011; ⊕ 11.00–22.00. Below & just off the Adriatic Highway, beside a small brook on its way to the sea; be prepared for a sharp right turn when coming from Petrovac. Steak & fish. Distinctly good food & service, pleasant & sophisticated in a rural setting. €€€€

✷ ✗ **Balun** m 067 473213; ⊕ b/fast–about 19.00, or by special arrangement. Hard to find but well worth the effort. From Reževići village, follow the narrow road downhill on foot until, just beside the small church, there is a left turn on to a footpath. Continue down this track & through woodland until you reach the beach, clamber over a few rocks to the right, & you're there (10mins from the church). To avoid the final stony approach, you may branch off a little before the beach, pass through a green gate & down a narrow path through shrubbery & the vegetable garden, arriving at the rear of the terrace. The beach-club style restaurant is run by a personable young couple with good English. You can eat grills, freshly caught fish or pasta, & drink all the obvious things, inc notably good coffee, while lounging in an idyllic cove. Sun-lounger rental €2.50; umbrella €1.50. (You could make your walk to Balun an attractive round trip by returning via Skočidjevojka, see above: after leaving the restaurant turn east up another narrow path & follow it to the cliff top. From there, go north to rejoin the Adriatic Highway back down to the village of Reževići.) €€€

✗ **Giardino** Reževići bb, Krstac. Good food in a nice garden setting. €€€

✗ **Narcis** Krstac; 033 468313. Pleasant, traditionally decorated restaurant with a few rooms to let. Turn inland off Sveti Stefan to Petrovac road. Visa accepted. €€€

PETROVAC NA MORU In earlier editions of this guide, Petrovac-on-Sea was described as one of those largely unspoilt small resorts travel writers are tempted to

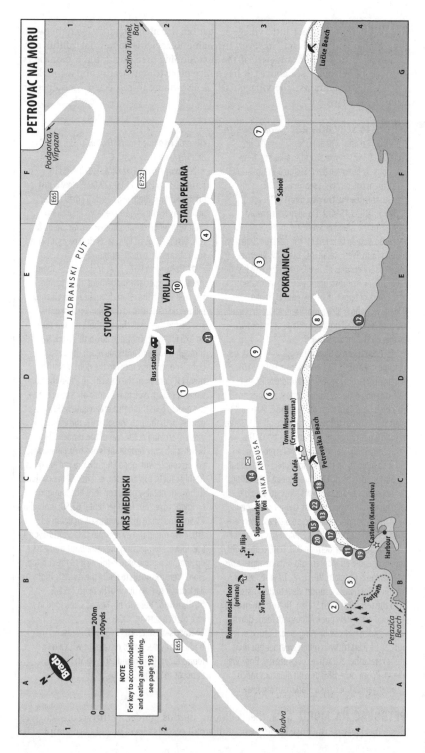

PETROVAC NA MORU

NOTE
For key to accommodation
and eating and drinking,
see page 193

0 ——— 200m
0 ——— 200yds

Bradt

N

Podgorica,
Virpazar

E65

Sozina Tunnel,
Bar

JADRANSKI PUT

E752

STUPOVI

KRŠ MEDINSKI

NERIN

VRULJA

STARA PEKARA

Bus station

(1)

(10)

(4)

(21)

(3)

POKRAJNICA

School

(7)

(9)

(8)

(12)

(6)

Roman mosaic floor
(private)

Sv Ilija

Supermarket
Voli

NIKA ANDUSA

(14)

Sv Tome

Town Museum
(Crvena komuna)

Cuba Café

Petrovačka Beach

Castello (Kastel Lastva)

Harbour

Footpath

Perazića
Beach

(20)

(15)

(17)

(22)

(13)

(18)

(11)

(19)

(5)

(2)

Budva

E65

Lučice Beach

192

omit, in the selfish hope that it should stay exactly as it is. Well, we wrote about it – and it hasn't. While the majority of hotels are restricted to the extremities and north of the sickle of coarse sand, more recent density of construction, particularly in the western corner, sadly demonstrates – to quote *Condé Nast Traveller* magazine – 'scant civic responsibility'.

But the pretty little prom is still lined with greenery and flowers, the offshore breeze rosemary-scented. And although nowadays most of the fishermen's seafront cottages and their gardens serve as restaurants, a small museum, a marginally larger bookshop and a sprinkling of boutiques, there remains a real charm and intimacy to the place. Out of season – admittedly one that is increasing in length – in winter, life here becomes very tranquil.

OPERATION HYDRA: THE SOE IN PERAZIĆA DO

Between Sveti Stefan and Petrovac is an interesting cove called Perazića do. Sheltered by thickly wooded cliffs dropping into the sea, the pocket handkerchief of sand would be notably secluded were it not for a sizeable 1970s hotel tucked into the left-hand corner, currently derelict but being rebuilt, and a scattering of villas above.

It was certainly secluded on a moonless night in January 1942 when it formed the stage for one of the more optimistic but unsuccessful SOE operations of World War II. A party of three under the leadership of Major Terence Atherton, a former journalist who had spent ten years in Belgrade, and including Corporal O'Donovan with his wireless set and a Royal Yugoslav Air Force officer, came silently ashore by small boat from the submarine HMS *Thorn* with 2,000 gold sovereigns and 1,000,000 lire and instructions to make contact with Tito's Partisans in the Podgorica region. This was Operation Hydra.

After some adventures Atherton met Tito but, partly because of the presence of the air force officer, was suspected of being a spy for the Chetniks. After a few fruitless weeks Atherton and O'Donovan left Tito and shortly afterwards they disappeared, as of course did their money. A disloyal Partisan was subsequently seen with Atherton's boots and binoculars, but the bodies and the money were never recovered and the disloyal Partisan was himself later executed for events unconnected with Operation Hydra. No SOE mission was again entrusted with such a rash sum of money and the planning of later operations was very different. By the time of Operation Typical, led by Bill Deakin, the SOE had learnt its lessons on how to work with Tito (see box, page 17).

The Budva Riviera SOUTH ALONG THE COAST

5

Getting there and away At least one bus a day between Herceg Novi and Ulcinj passes through Petrovac, where it is possible to be let off. The **bus station** [192 D2] (*Stupovi bb;* ✆ *033 461510*), a rather ramshackle affair that keeps irregular hours, is located in the north, off the road leading from the coastal highway to the centre of the town, along with a summer-only tourist information kiosk, a café and mini-market.

In summer, the Olimpia Express bus connects Petrovac with Budva (€2.50) at half-hourly intervals, until late; a less frequent service operates out of season but the exact times should be posted at the bus station. There is also a Mediteran bus service between the two towns. For up-to-the-minute guidance, ask at your hotel or the tourist office.

To catch a bus to a non-local coastal destination in summer, it is best to travel first to Budva from where there are regular connections to most other towns, both seaside and inland, and from where you can be sure of obtaining a seat. While it is possible to pick up a through bus in Petrovac, note that timetables are subject to change.

Getting around Petrovac, Lučice and even beyond the big Buljarica Beach (page 199) are easily, indeed best, negotiated **on foot**. The walk downhill from the bus station to your destination in the town should not take more than 20 minutes; uphill, with luggage, back to the bus station, a little longer.

Parking in the centre of Petrovac in August costs €2–2.50.

A reliable **taxi** service for excursions and journeys further afield is:

✱ 🚘 **Stefan Drascović** 📱 *069 444506*. Speaks good English & is knowledgeable about

the country; fares for excursions & trips are negotiable.

In summer there are **boat transfers** operating between Petrovac harbour and Buljarica. Taxi boats can be hired for longer journeys. Fares and waiting time should be arranged in advance of hiring.

Tourist information
🇮 **Tourist office** [192 D2] Stupovi bb; e info@ petrovacnamoru.net; www.petrovacnamoru.net;

⏱ summer only 08.00–20.00. Resembles a sailing boat, so it's easy to spot.

🏠 Where to stay   *Map, page 192.*
Hotels
🏠 **Monte Casa** (63 rooms & suites) Obala bb; ✆ 033 426900; e reception@montecasa.co.me; www.montecasa.com. In front of Danica Hotel at far western end of town, the former Hotel 4th July (though it never really opened with this name) caters especially for the Russian market. Harbour & sea views. AC, cable TV, lift, shop, minibar, babysitting service. Spa, indoor & outdoor pools, beauty salon, wellness centre & fitness coaching. Nightclub & casino. CCs accepted. €€€€
🏠 **Del Mar** (14 apts) Brežine bb; m 067 207470; e info@hoteldelmar.me; www.hoteldelmar.me. New hotel with luxury apts. AC, TV, Wi-Fi. Bar & restaurant, pool, private parking. €€€€
🏠 **Palas** (167 rooms, 4 suites) In town; ✆ 033 421100; e hotelpalas@t-com.me; www.

hgbudvanskarivijera.com. Just 17m from the beach, one of the better state-owned hotels is currently leased to the French company FRAM. Sgl & dbl rooms. Indoor & outdoor sea-water pools, bowling alley, sauna & gym. 3 bars, sun terrace, TV lounge, restaurant, hairdresser. Internet café in basement (⏱ 08.00–23.00; €4 per hr). CCs accepted. €€€€ (HB Jun–Sep €€€€, May & Oct €€€)
🏠 **Rivijera** (49 rooms, 42 apts) East end of town; ✆ 033 422100; www.hotel-rivijera-montenegro.com; ⏱ May–Oct. 50m from the beach, refurbished to a good standard & used by British tour companies. AC, cable TV, room safe, minibar & balcony. Shop. Cement tennis court, water sports, outdoor pool surrounded by spacious lawns & jacuzzi. Sunshine Club for children. 2

restaurants & bar, some evening entertainment in season. CCs accepted. €€€€ (HB low–high season €€€–€€€€)

⌂ **Vile Oliva** (304 rooms, 137 apts) Towards east side of town; ☎033 461194; e vileoliva@ t-com.me; www.vileoliva.com; ⊕ 20 May–20 Oct. In a park, unsurprisingly surrounded by olive trees, 50m from beach. All with AC (*extra €4 pp per day*), cable TV. Good swimming pool. Pets allowed. Restaurant & bar. CCs accepted. Rooms €€€, apts €€€€

⌂ **Đurić** (16 rooms, 4 apts) Naselje Brežine bb; ☎033 461814; e office@hoteldjuric.com; www.hoteldjuric.com; ⊕ 1 May–1 Sep. On a quiet side road 200m back from the beach, low-rise & attractive. All with AC, internet, cable TV. Restaurant. Visa accepted. €€€

⌂ **Renome** (15 rooms) Brežine bb; ☎033 462237; ⊕ 1 May–31 Oct. Friendly, family-run place on eastern outskirts of town, near school & path to Lučice. AC, cable TV, internet bar, laundry service, minibar. Bar & restaurant but no sea view. €€€

✳ ⌂ **'W' Grand** (50 rooms) Brežine bb; ☎033 461703; e wgrand@t-com.me; www. wgrandpetrovac.com. A welcoming & efficient hotel, set back 300m from the sea but with sea views. Under same ownership as Café Ponte (page 96). All with cable TV, AC, fridge & cooker, internet access, hairdryer & terrace. Lifts. Sauna & gym. Roof-top restaurant with big terrace. Conference room. Parking. Good value for money. CCs accepted. €€€

⌂ **Castellastva** (171 rooms) Town centre; ☎033 461418; e hotelcastellastva@t-com.me; www.hgbudvanskarivijera.com; ⊕ 1 May–1 Oct. Still a state hotel, but on short-term private lease, this hotel is a bit dingy but fair value for money. Shouldn't be confused with the harbour-wall nightclub, Castello. AC, cable TV, restaurant & bar. Water sports. No CCs. €€ (HB Jul–Aug €€€, Jun & Sep–Oct €€)

⌂ **Danica** (16 rooms,14 apts) Nika Andjusa bb; ☎033 462304; e pinusverde@t-com.me; www.hoteldanica.net; ⊕ summer only. Beside pine woods, 100m from the beach, the Danica has sadly given up its old name (remembered only in its email address), & is under Russian management. Now rather overshadowed by bulky buildings nearby, but still used by some British tour companies. All rooms have cable TV, AC, room safes & minibars; apts are self-catering. Jogging path, restaurant, bar, sauna, heating & fitness centre. English spoken. Pets allowed. No CCs. €€ (HB €€€)

Self-catering

A recommended agency for all holiday rentals of houses, rooms & apts in the Petrovac area is:

✳ **Mornar-Petrovac** Nerin bb; ☎033 461410; e mornar@t-com.me; www.mornartravel.com. Their slogan is: 'We tell the truth' – & they tell it in English.

✗ Where to eat and drink   *Map, page 192.*

There's a certain similarity in terms of both menu and ambience in most of Petrovac's restaurants. As well as the establishments listed below, there's a string of little restaurants by the flowerbeds in front of the water. Delicious Montenegrin ice cream in dozens of flavours can also be found at various outlets along the promenade; the one nearest to the harbour is the best (alas they all give up selling ice cream in the winter).

✗ **Ambassador** Obala bb, near the jetty; ☎033 462050, 033 426900; ⊕ 11.00–24.00. A good waterside terrace, this Russian-owned & styled off-shoot of the Monte Casa Hotel is one of the self-consciously smarter places in town & certainly one of the most expensive. CCs accepted. €€€€

✗ **Konoba Mediterraneo** Obala 17. Another in the line of fishy beachfront restaurants. Good food; the seafood platter comes highly recommended. €€€

✗ **Fortuna** Obala bb. A good, unpretentious fish restaurant on the seafront with a big terrace beside the beach. Landlord Miki's English is limited but he will give you an extra warm welcome if you can convincingly claim to be a Notts County supporter, & he might even serve you some wine from his father's vineyard (an eminently drinkable version of Beaujolais Nouveau). Deservedly popular with the locals, in winter it has the atmosphere of a village pub (before the smoking ban). No CCs. €€€

✷ ✕ Konoba Bonaca Set back slightly from the seafront to keep the rent & prices down; this & the vine-covered terrace also result in a more local atmosphere. They have their own fishing boat & you will eat well for a reasonable price. €€€

✕ Odiseja Beside the water. One of the slightly larger & more professional fish places. Good English, decent food & prices. €€€

✷ ✕ Orada Beside the harbour. The affable patron, Srdjan, speaks English, Italian & Russian & serves straightforward food at moderate prices. Excellent veal soup & above avg *pršut*. Large-screen satellite TV shows BBC, CNN & appropriate big matches. Terrace. €€€

✕ Restoran Castio Obala 16. They too have their own fishing boat & you can eat & drink in a pleasant atmosphere. €€€

✕ Restoran Sutjeska Obala bb, right beside the beach. Some say it's named after the major Partisan battle of 1943 (see box, page 312), others that it is just the name of a river valley. It serves

the usual things, quite nicely presented. No CCs. €€€

✕ Café Ponte Easternmost corner of Petrovac Beach; ☉ summer only 08.00–24.00. In prime position, great location for a sunset drink. The usual pizzas. Beyond the bar is a terrace on the rocks, with free sun-loungers. A lovely cool spot on a hot day, especially when the waves wash over. Enter through a short cave-like tunnel in the cliff. No CCs. €€

✕ Restoran Pod Lozom Brežine; ☉ 07.00–23.00. Back from the sea, above a mini-market on the road between the supermarket & Hotel 'W' Grand. Less of a holiday atmosphere than many; slightly more of a functional local eating place with local cuisine. Simple menu, good value, very popular. No CCs. €€

✕ Gril-Rasta Beside the post office & just up from the supermarket; ☉ till late. Great take-away fast-food joint. €

Entertainment and nightlife There are several nightclubs beside the sea in Petrovac, including:

✷ ☆ Cuba Café [192 C3] With jazz
☆ Beach Night Club [192 E4] At Café Ponte (see above).

☆ Castello [192 B4] A good disco hidden inside the old Venetian fort on the harbour point. No relation to the hotel with a similar name.

Sports and other activities
⚲ Tennis Contact Marko Kaloštro; ☏ 033 468133; m 069 402416

Other practicalities
Banks
$ Atlasmont Banka has a teller window in the Hotel Palas; **CKB** has one outside the Voli supermarket (below).

Medical facilities
✚ First-aid station ☏ 033 461055
✚ Specialist medical practice Mensana; ☏ 033 461851
✚ Pharmacy Montefarm; ☏ 033 402112

Supermarket
Voli supermarket [192 C3] ☏ 033 461411; ☉ 06.00–10.00. Between turn-off from the main coastal road & the beach, is well stocked with essentials, inc wine & fresh vegetables, & with an ATM. Some free parking in front & in a small lot diagonally opposite.

What to see The walled harbour is guarded by a 16th-century Venetian fortress, **Kaštel Lastva** [192 B4], once simply an admonition to pirates and waves alike. The waves, even on the calmest day, still thunder and spit at the jagged rock beyond, only now the Kaštel has become Castello, a nightclub. Out in the bay two outcrops, **Katić** and **Sv Nedelja**, are each crowned with a chapel marking a sailor's gratitude for salvation from the perils of the sea.

Starting just beside the good small swimming beach in Perazića do (see box, page 193), a pedestrian tunnel cutting through the rock has traditionally linked this beach with a lovely cliff-edge path that passes through tall pines and beechwood before descending into **Petrovac**. Until summer 2006 this walkway was at least as pretty as the little path around Cap Ferrat in the south of France, but for several years the tunnel has been closed because of work on the **Hotel As**. This once-spectacular hotel with its own beach and jetty is at last undergoing reconstruction after an extended wait for the bulldozers. It is to be hoped its Russian owners will restore it to its former glory. However, it was said to be reopening back in 2008, so don't hold your breath. Meanwhile, the once lovely path through the trees to Petrovac has been spoilt by fly-tipping.

In the west of the town, parallel to the seafront, you will find **Sv Ilija Church** [192 B3], dating from the 15th century. Further up the hill is **Sv Tome** [192 B3], close to which among a small grove of olive trees lie the remains of a **Roman villa** and baths, including some detailed mosaic flooring [192 B3], alas in a poor state of preservation. These are believed to date from the 4th century AD. To find it, follow the sign, *kasnoanticki mozaik,* to the church and turn sharp right. The area was excavated in 2007 by Mladen Zagarčanin, an archaeologist from Stari Bar. Sadly, the author has since been dismayed to find considerable new construction activity in progress very close to the site.

The Town Museum (Spomen dom 'Crvena komuna') [192 C3] (*Obala bb, midway along the waterfront street;* \ *033 402877;* e *crvenakom@t-com.me; www. crvenakomuna.webs.com;* ✆ *08.00–11.00 & 18.00–23.00; entry free*) The museum houses exhibitions of modern art and electoral mementos. And its name, 'Crvena komuna', means 'Red Commune', which comes from the communist local election victory in 1919.

Beaches The narrow strand that forms **Petrovačka Beach** [192 C4] is delightful, especially so in spring and autumn; in summer, be warned, it can become very, very crowded. From the eastern end of the town a pleasant ten-minute stroll takes you over the wooded headland, 500m to the southeast to a neighbouring cove called **Lučice** [192 C4] (where the beach may be less busy – though not in July and August), or you may drive to this cove, passing by Petrovac School (limited beach parking €0.50). Close to hand are one or two seasonal snack bars.

Beyond Lučice the paved footpath continues for about 20 minutes over a further headland to the majestic sweep of Buljarica Beach (page 199). In summer small boats ferry passengers between Petrovac harbour and Buljarica Beach (about €2 each way).

We'd love to follow your adventures using our *Montenegro* guide – why not send us your photos and stories via Twitter (@BradtGuides) and Instagram (@bradtguides) using the hashtag #montenegro. Alternatively, you can upload your photos directly to the gallery on the Montenegro destination page via our website (*www.bradtguides.com*).

The Budva Riviera   SOUTH ALONG THE COAST

5

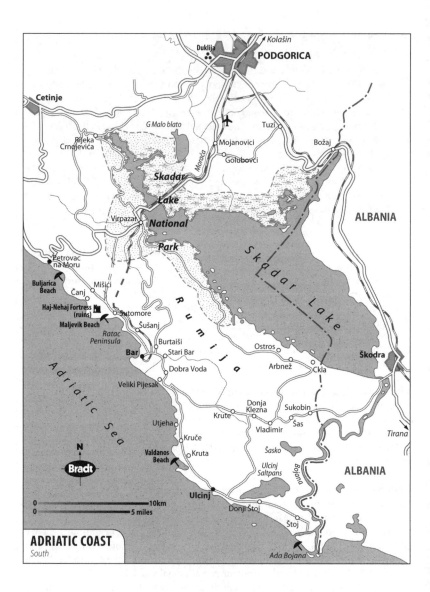

ADRIATIC COAST
South

6

Haj-Nehaj

Just east of Petrovac, the old E80, a good but slow road which in heavy snow can become impassable, runs northeast over the mountains to **Virpazar** at the head of Skadar Lake, and beyond to Podgorica. The journey to both these destinations was considerably shortened by the opening of a road in 2005 through the **Sozina Tunnel**, beneath Sozina Mountain (971m), part of the Rumija Massif. Once the lofty fortress of Haj-Nehaj marked the old division between East and West, Islam and Christianity; now it marks the entrance to this deep tunnel (4,189m in length), which unites the coast with the wide plain of Zeta. The tunnel toll for a regular-sized car is €2.50. I'm not sure I'd try it on a bike.

SOUTHEAST FROM PETROVAC

BULJARICA BEACH The coastal road from Petrovac continues southeast in the direction of **Bar**, **Ulcinj** and ultimately **Albania**. As you pass Gradište Monastery perched on a hilltop to the left – it too a fortress, commanding a magnificent eastward view – there is a turn-off right to Buljarica Beach and the long fertile plain known in the past as the breadbasket of Montenegro. Even this long strand stretching for 2.5km can become quite crowded in summer. If you don't fancy company, strike out for the far eastern end. The needle-shaped rock rising from the sea in front of Buljarica Beach is called Mravinjak, which translates as 'anthill'.

The Buljarica plain, as part of the Adriatic Flyway and in common with much of the Montenegrin littoral, is a significant stopover for migrating birds – a good reason to remember the binoculars.

Getting there and away In the absence of public transport to the beach itself, and unless you have a vehicle, the easiest access is either on foot or by boat. The **walk** over the headland from Petrovac takes about half an hour; note that the sign on the track beyond the steps leading down from Petrovac footpath ('Naluško polje 7km 3hr') is incorrect. In season you can take a **boat** from Petrovac harbour (€2 each way).

Otherwise Bar–Budva **buses** pass on the main highway several times daily and you will then have a 15-minute walk along the approach road to the beach.

Where to stay and eat

⌂ **Montebay Villa** (4 rooms, 3 suites) Buljarica 2; ☏ 033 461766; e montebay-villa@t-com.me; www.montebayvilla.com. In a secluded location, 100m from the farthest eastern corner of Buljarica Beach, Montebay is far from other habitation (wait till you see the stars – the celestial lot) with wide sea views. Coming from Petrovac & shortly before the main turning to the beach, take very small asphalt lane seaward, signed 'Golubovići'; ignore all turn-offs until after several km you arrive at

6

a place called Kolač, & a short driveway uphill to the hotel. There is another route from nearer Čanj but it's easy to miss it. TV & internet, swimming pool; €5 boat transfer to cove inaccessible by road. Indoor/outdoor restaurant & bar (€€€€), candlelit in the evening, with a French-trained chef & featuring locally sourced organic produce. It's also open to non-residents (booking advised). Standard room €150 Jun–mid-Sep min 3 nights; 30% extra for less than 3; child under 2 free; discount for under 12s; airport transfers arranged. French & English spoken. €€€€–€€€€€

🏠 **Galija** (12 rooms) On Buljarica Beach; ☎ 033 461717; m 069 513494. Ranko & Dado Rakićević are the owners of this popular tavern (€€) serving fish caught from their own boat. AC; quite simple rooms, some of them rather small but most with balcony & sea view. Internet & ample parking behind the building. Friendly & hospitable. €€–€€€

🏠 **Hotel Savojo** (30 rooms) On Buljarica Beach ☎ 033 461876; m 067 221442; e savojo@gmail. com; www.hotelsavojo.com. Step from the terrace bar/restaurant (€€€) on to the sandy/pebbly beach. Rooms with balcony & sea view, plus AC, cable TV, Wi-Fi & fridge. Beach chairs & umbrellas. Secure parking. €€

⚓ **Camping Auto-Camp** (200 spaces) Buljarica Beach; ☎ 033 461212. €7 for car, tent & 2 ppl, plus €2 tax; €10 if it's a caravan. Rent on-site caravan for 4, €15 plus tax. Showers & cooking facilities. €

✴ ⚓ **Maslina Auto-Kamp** 200m off the main Petrovac–Bar road & 200m from the beach; ☎ 033 461215; m 068 602040; e info@campingmaslina. com; www.campingmaslina.com; ⊕ all year. An efficient facility & a good base for touring the southeast coast. Owner-manager is helpful & speaks good English. €3/1.50 per adult/child, €3 per car, €3 per tent, €7 per mobile home, €2 electricity. Wi-Fi. 10 caravans for rent, booked in advance in high season. €

✕ **Nobel Konoba** A little above the highway, just past the Buljarica turning, around 400m from the beach; m 069 040663, 069 251640; http:// nobel.petrovacnamoru.net. Local atmosphere. National cuisine. Also 9 rooms available (€€). No CCs. €€

ČANJ AND BEYOND The Bar road rolls on through arid craggy rock and pockets of dense *maquis*. At Mišići turn down towards the sea for Čanj and its lovely sandy beach. Basically this is an unreconstructed resort in pretty surroundings, popular with school groups from neighbouring countries and a useful stop for the budget traveller, although litter collection is not a priority. One could probably find a room in a house in Mišići village for under €10. Return-trip coaches between Čanj and Bar cost €10 but the service is a franchise and doesn't adhere to a regular timetable. Enquire locally for details.

To the west of Čanj is **Kraljeva**, a quiet inlet accessible only by boat. Queen Milena is reputed to have favoured it for secluded bathing during her stays at the Royal Palace in Bar; hence its informal name, Queen's Beach.

The **Sozina Tunnel** road continues southeast, soon passing beneath the tenebrous silhouette of the ruined Turkish citadel **Haj-Nehaj** – 'Fear and Fear Not'. This was the area known as *Kufin*, the 18th-century border separating the then Venetian-held Paštrovići lands from the Ottomans. Early in that century the plague had broken out in this corner of the Balkans and while the Turks took little action to curb the spread, believing only the infidel would be infected, the Venetian government made efforts to improve hygiene and control the outbreak. Beyond this point there is a perceptible change and the houses, scattered among the hillside olive groves, take on a more Eastern appearance, their roofs steeper and tent-like running from a short ridge, their windows smaller and sometimes only at the second-floor level. Among the trees a slim minaret signals the presence of a mosque.

🏠 **Where to stay and eat**

🏠 **Vila Milica** (8 apts) 100m from the beach, Čanj; m 069 320210, 069 675338; e vilamilica@ yahoo.com; www.canj-montenegro.com. At the time of writing, probably the nicest option in town. Its apts sleep 1–5 ppl, with terraces & sea or mountain views. Contact Vaso Novaković. €€

🏠 **Vila Montenegro** (100 rooms) Beogradska bb, Čanj; 📞 030 377051; e vila-montenegro@ t-com.me; www.hotel-vila-montenegro.me. 50m from sea. Restaurant, bar, tours available. €€

🏠 **Hotel-Pansion Adria II** (7 rooms) 80m from sea, Čanj; 📞 030 350340; e adriacom@t-com.

me; www.adriatours.co.me. Rather plain but serviceable rooms, under same ownership as the Adria in Bar. €€

🏠 **Galeb** (19 rooms) Beogradska bb, Čanj; 📞 030 377046; e hotelgalebcanj@gmail. com; www.hotelgaleb.com; ⏲ summer only. Most rooms with sea view. TV, shared kitchen. Restaurant. €–€€

SUTOMORE The little town of Sutomore is a seaside resort, and indeed it is the sea that welcomes the railway, and the new road, as they emerge from the long **Sozina Tunnel** that plunges through the mountain soon after Skadar Lake and links Belgrade and Podgorica with the coast.

Sutomore itself is jolly, old-fashioned and a bit down-market. Ice cream cones are €0.20 on the prom. There is a nice sandy beach (but you can hardly see it in summer) and the snorkelling is good.

Getting there and around The **bus station** (📞 030 373128), car park and a tourist information kiosk, along with a taxi rank, are all to be found on the main highway, above and about 800m west of town. Several times daily, **buses** connect Sutomore with Bar (€2) and Ulcinj, and in the other direction with Budva (€4), Tivat, Kotor and Herceg Novi. There is also a railway station, a few minutes' walk north of the centre of town.

Most **trains** connecting Bar with Podgorica stop here. There is also a local service between Sutomore and those two stations, twice daily – morning and evening. The fare to Podgorica is around €2. For timetables call 📞 030 301692, or see the Railways in Montenegro website (www.zcg-prevoz.me).

🏠 **Where to stay** The hotels are mostly low-priced, but none of them is especially inspiring.

🏠 **Korali** (330 rooms) By the sea; 📞 030 373720; e prodaja.trendkorali@t-com.me; www.trendkorali-montenegro.com. Large hotel complex about 1km from bus station, right on the beach. €€€

🏠 **Mirela** (20 rooms, 2 suites) Miroška 2; 📞 030 374737; e info@hotel-mirela.de; www. hotel-mirela.info (German only). Situated beneath Haj Nehaj & convenient for Sozina Tunnel. AC & TV. German spoken but minimal English. €€€

🏠 **Sirena Marta** (20 rooms) 6 S Kovačevića; 📞 030 373319; e sirenamarta@t-com.me; www. sirenamarta.com; ⏲ Jun–Sep. 150m from the bus station, 200m from the beach, a simple hotel/pension & pizzeria with local atmosphere. TV, AC & kitchenette. Parking. No English spoken. €€€

🏠 **Sozina** (32 rooms) ob Iva Novakovića bb; 📞 030 373302, 069 689056; e reservations@ hpkorali.com. All rooms with sea views. Restaurant, snack bar, parking; nightclub facing the beach. Local ambience, not much English. €€

🏠 **Stari Grad** (7 rooms) Iva Novakovića bb; 📞 069 553599; e mladen.mne@gmail.com; www. apartmanistarigrad.me. Small restaurant/pansion with simple rooms/apts, close to railway station. €€

🏠 **Sveti Nikola** (24 rooms) Cara Lazara 140; 📞 030 372301; e hotelsvetlana@t-com.me; www.sveti-nikola.me; ⏲ summer only. AC, TV. Restaurant, pool, parking. €€

🏠 **Svetlana** (12 rooms) Haj Neglect bb; 📞 030 373790; e hotelsvetlana@t-com.me; www. vladka-company.com. Under same ownership as Sveti Nikola (above). Rather plain with brightly painted rooms, at Haj Nehaj end of town: a useful stop when heading south, or through the tunnel. Restaurant. €€€

🏠 **Vila Izvor** (12 rooms) Iva Novakovića bb; e vilaizvor.me@gmail.com; http://vilaizvor.me. Rooms above well-known restaurant/pizzeria of same name, with AC & Wi-Fi. HB/FB available. HB €€

6

✕ Where to eat and drink

✕ **Izvor** Iva Novakovića; vilaizvor.me@gmail.com; http://vilaizvor.me. Quite a local landmark, up 2 flights of stairs (leading ultimately to the main road), overlooking the beach. Local dishes. Rooms available. €€€

* ✕ **Pirat** ob Iva Novakovića, facing the sea; 📞030 373427. The ambience is hospitable & relaxed, the cooking splendid. Try the sea bass or the bream, the fish soup or the chateaubriand. All cooking is on a wood-fired grill. Moderately priced. €€€

What to see around Sutomore To the west of town the 14th-century, rough-hewn stone church of **Sv Tekla** provides once more an example of the humble practicality of twin altars permitting both Catholic and Orthodox worship.

Extensive ruins of an early Benedictine monastery can be investigated on the **Ratac Peninsula, southeast of Sutomore**. Archives date it from 1247 but some sections appear more ancient. In the 16th century it was ravaged by the Turks.

Maljevik Beach, a couple of kilometres to the west, is a most attractive small bay of sand and shingle, sheltered by pines – good for picnicking. There is free parking here and a little tram conveys passengers between the beach and Sutomore. There's a beach bar and fixed umbrellas for shade. Below Crni Rt (Black Cape) to the west there is interesting snorkelling; swim around to view unidentified ruined columns underwater.

BAR

Modern Bar is primarily a terminus both for the railway linking it with Podgorica, the north of the country and Belgrade, and for ferry connections to Bari and Ancona in Italy, as well as to Albania. Beyond that role, and overshadowed by its drab utilitarian architecture, the town once appeared to have little else to offer. But now a revival is well under way, the entire dock area has been renovated, the museum has been restored to its former palatial glory, trees are blossoming and a smartish new hotel has opened in the place of the old Topolica.

In 1885, a **palace** was built for King Nikola I in the same style as Prince Danilo's Blue Palace in Cetinje. The main purpose of this port-side residence was for the reception of official guests arriving by sea. It is set in a garden and today provides a home for the **Historical and Archaeological Museum** (pages 206–7). The propinquity of a number of important sites, not least Stari Bar (Old Bar), combined with the energy of the local experts, has yielded the valuable collection now on display. Nearby are the remains of a *trikonhos*, a **triangular 6th-century church** from the Justinian period. Fragments of decorative ceramics and graves have been found in the vicinity.

GETTING THERE AND AWAY The **railway** (📞 *030 301615, 030 301619*) and **bus stations** (📞 *030 346141*) are not too far apart, about 2km southeast on the edge of town, but rather too far to walk from the ferry port if you are encumbered with heavy baggage. A metered **taxi** to either should cost you around €5. Roads in and out of the termini are wide and easy to follow and there is rarely any real congestion.

By train Bar is the end of the railway line from Belgrade and Podgorica. There are several trains daily to Podgorica in each direction (€2.40–3.60 one way), as well as several to Nikšić and Bijelo Polje, and two a day to Belgrade (with one continuing to Subotica). For timetables, see www.zcg-prevoz.me.

The (faster) business train is recommended, slightly more expensive but proportionally more comfortable and usually including a buffet car. (For details of the thrilling journey, see box, above). Alas, at the time of writing both the line and the rolling stock are showing their age and are in need of modernisation.

By bus There are several Red line bus connections a day to Ulcinj, Budva, Tivat, Kotor, Herceg Novi and Podgorica. One-way fares cost about €5 to Podgorica, and around €4 to Ulcinj and Budva.

By taxi A taxi ride from Bar to Ulcinj should cost €15–20. There are taxi ranks at the ferry port, the train and bus stations and by the park in Topolica.

🚕 **Euro radio taxi** ☏19701; ⏱ 24hrs
🚕 **Kuk Taxi** ☏19744

By ferry The ferry port is 300m from the centre. The modern passenger terminal has nice clean lavatories and a small post office that also sells souvenirs and reasonable postcards. Good English is spoken. If you have to wait for a ferry, consider investing around €2 in an umbrella and beach chair on the well-kept pebble beach 400m north of the harbour. If you swim too, keep your mouth shut. There is a children's playground on the beach, along with some fast-food outlets. There's no ice cream available in winter months.

Haj-Nehaj BAR

6

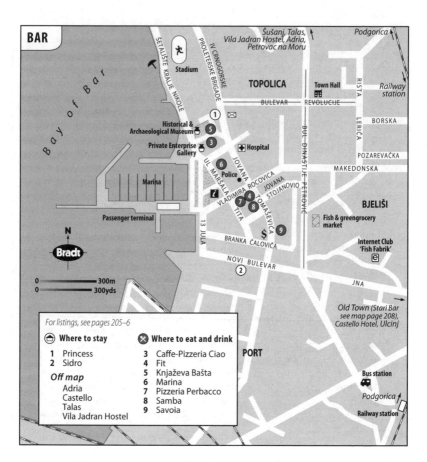

The sizeable **marina** is on Maršala Tita, north of the ferry port. For details of yacht charter and sales, see page 206.

Bar–Bari and Bar–Ancona Ferry connections with Bari in Italy run most days of the week.

Montenegro Lines Putnički Terminal, Obala 13 jula bb; ℡030 303469, 030 312366; e online@ barplov.com; www.montenegrolines.net. The *Sveti Stefan* & the *Sveti Stefan II* make 2–7 trips per week depending on the season, with departures either late in the evening or around midday. Crossings take about 7hrs on the day trips & 10hrs on the overnight. Cabins are available with en-suite or shared bathroom, with prices one-way Bar–Bari ranging from €67–210 in high season to €56–180 low. Aircraft-type seats €50–55; deck tickets €44–48. Cars are free with 4 passengers, or €68–78 with 1.

Car hire

🚗 **Danmil** Obala 19 jula-putnički; ℡030 313719; e danmil@t-com.me
🚗 **Delltex Rent-a-Car** ℡030 313200; m 067 303555
🚗 **Grmožur** IV Crnogorske brigade 34; ℡030 314301; e grmozur@t-com.me

🚗 **Kompas Rent-a-Car** Jovana Tomaševića 24; ℡030 602680
🚗 **Meridien** Jovana Tomaševića 30; ℡030 314000; www.meridian-rentacar.com
🚗 **Taurus** ul Rista Lekića D12; ℡030 318170; e tuljan@t-com.me

TOURIST INFORMATION There are numerous tourist agencies in the vicinity of the port, many of them clustered around Vladimira Rolovića.

Z Tourist information centre Obala 13 Jula; \030 311633; e tobar@t-com.me; www.bar.travel; ⊕ Jun–Sep 08.00–21.00 daily, Oct–May 08.00–16.00 Mon–Sat. Helpful staff will go to enormous lengths to help you with any travel questions, especially valuable in a gateway town. The office sells a small selection of souvenirs, postcards & booklets.

WHERE TO STAY *Map, opposite.*

Princess (135 rooms) Jovana Tomaševića 59; \030 300100; e reservations@atlashotelsgroup.com; www.hotelprincess.me. Following privatisation & refurbishment, this 4-star hotel, formerly a state establishment called the Topolica, is now the best, as well as the most expensive, place to stay in Bar, but it is lacking in soul. Most rooms have a balcony overlooking the sea or pine trees, with AC, satellite & cable TV, internet, minibar & safe. Restaurant & bar. Pleasant & spacious pool area. Spa & tennis court. Laundry service. It claims to have facilities for wheelchairs but these will need to be verified before booking. Conference facilities. Credit cards accepted. €€€€–€€€€€

Castello (45 rooms) Ilino bb; \030 350501; e castellobabovic@t-com.me; www.hotelcastellobabovic.com (Montenegrin only). Rooms with balconies, satellite TV, internet access; some with minibar. Restaurant, café-bar, gym & sauna. Conference room. Free private beach some 1km away. €€€

Sidro (93 rooms) Obala 13 jul bb; \030 312425, 030 311146; e sidro@lukabar.me; www.hotelsidro.com. Owned by the Port of Bar & about 200m from ferry terminal. Dbl & trpl rooms all have bathrooms, heating, telephones & balconies; newer & somewhat better rooms have AC, TV & minibar. 2 terraces, restaurant with satellite TV & tavern. €€–€€€

Vila Jadran Hostel (20 rooms) Rista Lekića, Šušanj; \030 373048; m 069 023364; e vilajadran@hotmail.com; http://vilajadran.freshcreator.com. On the western edge of town, 2km from rail/bus stations (can arrange free pick-up), this well-equipped guesthouse/hostel close to the beach was renovated in 2011 & is well reviewed. Dbls, trpls & quads from €12 pp. Satellite TV, Wi-Fi, balconies, kitchens with fridge, hairdryer in bathrooms, laundry facilities. B/fast buffet €4. Parking. Front desk open 24hrs. CCs accepted. €€

Adria (31 rooms, 2 apts) Šušanj; \030 350340; e adriacom@t-com.me; www.adriatours.co.me; ⊕ summer only. On western edge of Bar, 400m from the sea, 2-, 3- & 4-bedded rooms, each with terrace, TV & refrigerator; some with AC. There are 2 annexes with apts. Fitness club, terrace, parking, restaurant. Free transfer to beach. €

Talas (27 rooms, 4 apts) J Jovanovića Zmaja 6, Šušanj; \030 317697; www.talastours.com. Rooms & apts with TV & kitchenette. Restaurant. €

WHERE TO EAT AND DRINK *Map, opposite.*

Bar is relatively short of restaurants, but there are plenty of cafés and bars in the central area.

✕ Samba Jovana Tomaševića 41, 1st floor; \030 312025; e restoransamba@gmail.com; ⊕ 09.00–24.00. Half inside & half on a big terrace with mountain views. Popular with locals. Visa accepted. €€€€

✕ Knjaževa Bašta Dvorac Kralja Nikole; \030 312601; e nirwana@t-com.me; www.knjazeva-basta.com (Montenegrin only); ⊕ 12.00–23.00. Montenegrin/Adriatic menu (porcini or prawn risotto, spaghetti with clams, steak in gorgonzola sauce) in what was an early elegant conservatory/greenhouse given as a present to Nikola by Italian King Victor Emmanuel & erected on the edge of the park encircling the palace. Little more than a few cork trees remains of the subtropical gardens that originally flourished here. Hookah pipes. CCs accepted. €€€

✕ Savoia Jovana Tomaševića 16; 030 311214; www.restoransavoia.me. Serves Italian-accented food & cakes in a friendly setting. €€€

✕ Kaldrma Stari Bar \030 341744; e kaldrmarestoran@t-com.me; www.kaldrma.me; ⊕ 11.00–22.00. Interior has a good atmosphere, & a couple of rickety tables extend on to the narrow Stari Bar street. Authentic & friendly, with good food. €€

✗ **Marina** Gat 5, obala 13 jula; ☎ 030 317785. Convenient for the ferry terminal, with adequate food. €€

✗ **Pizzeria Perbacco** Vladimira Rolovića; ☎ 030 550312; ⏰ 07.00–24.00. Centrally located pizzeria with terrace. CCs accepted. €€

✗ **Konoba Špilja** Stari Bar; ⏰ 08.00–23.00. Atmospheric little place serving a good range of traditional dishes. €€

🍴 **Caffe-Pizzeria Ciao** Šet Kralja Nikole. Wooden cottage on 2 floors next to the Historical & Archaeological Museum; coffee & sandwiches. Useful pit stop before or after museum visit. Friendly staff. €

♀ **Fit** Jovana Tomaševića 42. Self-styled *pivnica*, or beer hall, with good simple food in a robust local atmosphere. No CCs.

SPORTS AND OTHER ACTIVITIES
Beach volleyball
Port of Bar Volleyball Club ul Obala 13 jula bb; ☎ 030 312213

Climbing
⚡ **Ahil** m 067 555320; e lijavukotic@hotmail.com

Diving
🤿 **DC Scuba Quest** m 069 495604; e info@divemontenegro.com; www.divemontenegro.com

Yacht charter and sales
△ **Bar Marina** Obala 13 Jula bb; ☎ 030 315166; e marinabar@marinabar.org. www.marinabar.org. Capacity for 900 boats.

△ **OMC Yachting** Obala 13 jula bb, Marina Sv Nikola; ☎ 030 313911; m 069 030602; e omc@t-com.me; www.omcmarina.com. For sail or motor charters, service or purchase. Prices very competitive in comparison with most other European companies.

Port Authority www.luckauprava.me

OTHER PRACTICALITIES Bar is a user-friendly city. Most services are centrally located and easy to find.

Banks
$ **Atlasmont** Jovana Tomaševića
$ **CKB** Maršala Tita br 7
$ **Hipotekarna Banka** Vladimira Rolovića bb
$ **Komercijalna Banka** Obala Kralja Nikole bb
$ **Montenegrobanka A D** Branka Čatovića 13

Medical facilities
✚ **General hospital** Podgrad bb, Stari Bar; ☎ 030 313428
✚ **Health centre** Jovana Tomaševića 42; ☎ 030 311001; 24hr emergency unit, ☎ 124

Pharmacies
✚ **Belladona** Makedonska 15; ☎ 030 314689
✚ **Montefarm** Rista Lekića; ☎ 030 311021
✚ **Topolica 1** Jovana Tomaševića 42; ☎ 030 312946

✚ **Topolica 2** Vladimira Rolovića bb; ☎ 030 315328

Other
Voli hypermarket 20min walk from the port in the direction of Stari Bar (just off Novi bul). Useful for picking up supplies for the ferry; good budget restaurant on upper floor.

🖥 **Internet Club 'Fish Fabrik'** (fish factory) Pop Dukljanin 11, behind Caffé Madera, 5min walk from central square; m 067 265361; ⏰ 12.00–20.00 Tue–Fri, 11.00–21.00 Sat–Sun. 8 computers available; copy & scanning service; €1 per hr, €0.50 per 30mins. Russian, German & English spoken.

✉ **Post office** Off Jovana Tomaševića; ⏰ 07.00–20.00 Mon–Sat

WHAT TO SEE
Historical and Archaeological Museum (Zavičajni muzej) (*Šet Kralja Nikole*; ☎ *030 314079*; e *jpkcbar@t-com.me*; *http://kulturnicentarbar.me*; ⏰ *08.00–*

22.00 daily; entry €1) Major restoration work on the former Town Museum, housed in King Nikola's former southern palace, was completed in 2010 and it is well worth visiting. Engineer Josip Slade, who was responsible for so much late 19th-century design in Montenegro, was architect of the original building, which the King later presented to his daughter Zorka on her marriage with Petar Karađorđević.

The skilfully curated collection covers not only the prehistory and history of the Bar municipality (established as recently as 1959) but includes an ethnological section on the upper floor. On the ground floor the archaeological finds displayed chronologically are precisely explained in both Montenegrin and English and feature important items originating from the town and its surrounds, from Hellenist through Roman, medieval and Turkish eras.

On the next floor the liberation movement of Bar against the Turks in 1878 is celebrated in an array of flags, and political and economical changes within Bar in the first decades of the 20th century are described. Focused on the same era, the upper floor depicts the style of King Nikola and his court, with lots of regal red and gold upholstery and drapes, and furniture fit for a king. There are ivory dressing-table pieces that once belonged to Crown Princess Milića-Yutta and porcelain dishes with the initials of King Nikola. There is also a section showing typical examples of male and female costume, peculiar to individual parts of the municipal region; a proud 19th-century Montenegrin army flag and a tattered Turkish one of the same vintage; and a lovely beach photograph of the royal family all covered up against the strong Bar sunshine.

In another room a section is devoted to the 1908 construction of the narrow-gauge railway that ran from Bar to Virpazar on Skadar Lake. It was the first to be built in Montenegro and stretched for 43km. In addition to two passenger cars and an engine at either end there was, of course, a special royal salon. Hikers on the slopes of the Rumija Massif above Skadar Lake can still find the original tunnel, 1,969m in length. The old railway continued in operation until 1959.

Also illustrated is the erection in 1904 on Volujica headland, east of Bar harbour, of the first radio-telegraph station in the Balkans. Transmitting via a station in Bari on the Italian coast, it was able to communicate with anywhere in the world. Alas after only a decade it was destroyed by Austrian ammunition.

It is also recorded, as a matter of interest, that 30 years later, in November 1944, Radio Cetinje was able to announce the liberation of the capital, auguring ultimate victory for Josip Tito and the brave Partisans.

The palace guardhouse is now a gift shop with museum-related items, postcards and local literature. In theory it's open at the same times as the museum.

Stari Bar (Old Bar) (*08.00–22.00; adult/child €1/0.50)* On the summit of Londža Hill, inaccessible from all but one side and wreathed above by the Rumija, Sutorman and Sozin mountains, the situation of this ancient walled city is spectacular, and clearly it must have held considerable status.

Getting there The old city is 5km east of Bar itself. To visit by car from the west, it is possible to avoid entering the modern city by following the ring road in the direction of Ulcinj – bear right after the bridge over the railway and turn left at the sign for Stari Bar. The final approach is narrow and steep. Parking just below is recommended.

Coming from the ferry port you could do it on foot, heading east at the bus station until you reach the ring road and then following the directions above. In hot weather you might prefer to take a cab; expect to pay around €6.

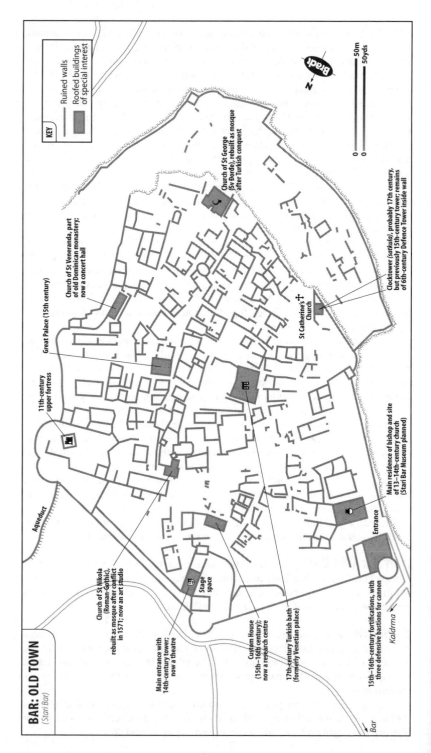

BAR: OLD TOWN
(Stari Bar)

KEY

Ruined walls

Roofed buildings of special interest

Church of St Veneranda, part of old Dominican monastery; now a concert hall

Church of St George (Sv Đorđe), rebuilt as mosque after Turkish conquest

Great Palace (15th century)

Clocktower (*sarkula*), probably 17th century, but previously 15th-century tower; remains of 6th-century Defence Tower inside wall

11th-century upper fortress

St Catherine's Church

Aqueduct

Church of St Nikola (Roman-Gothic), rebuilt as mosque after conflict in 1571; now an art studio

Main entrance with 14th-century tower; now a theatre

Main residence of bishop and site of 13–14th-century church (Stari Bar Museum planned)

Stage space

Custom House (15th–16th century); now a research centre

17th-century Turkish bath (formerly Venetian palace)

Entrance

15th–16th-century fortifications, with three defensive bastions for cannon

Kaldrma

Bar

N

Bladi

0   50m
0   50yds

208

History Recent finds of pottery and metal have confirmed occupancy as early as 800BC and there is a small museum just inside the main gate. Archaeologists working at the site explain that evidence of rough *gradina* masonry indicates it must at that time have been a primitive hill fort, presumably inhabited by some Illyrian tribe but one not as yet identified. What is certain is that the settlement was destroyed during the 3rd century BC at a time when the Romans were conquering much of the east Adriatic coast. All indications are that the Romans chose not to settle on this Illyrian site but rather to build an urban centre nearer to the sea. Traces of Roman culture – amphorae, ceramics and rustic houses from much later (3rd–5th century AD) – have already been discovered, lending substance to this theory.

In the 6th century, Byzantine Emperor Justinian built a new and heavily fortified town on the hill. Evidence of this is in the oval defence tower and traces of a paleo-Byzantine church, described as 'at the top of a rock, known to have been called Vidikovac or Londža, which commands a fine view'.

At the time of Emperor Constantine VII in the 10th century, Stari Bar was referred to as Antinbaris (opposite to Bari, Italy) and by the beginning of the 11th century it had become part of Duklija or Zeta, the first Slavonic littoral state. Soon it came to be recognised as one of the most important economical, political and cultural centres of the Adriatic. In 1089 under the auspices of Turkey, Bar became the semi-autonomous seat of the archbishop. It was subjugated by Venice in 1443 and retaken by the Turks in 1571. In 1878 it acceded to Montenegro.

The site today The oldest part of the existing town was built by Justinian II and it is thought that parts date back to the 5th century. Diggings in 1952 uncovered Slovenian ceramics from the 7th–9th centuries AD. The well-preserved 11th-century upper fortress was used as a prison in World War II. In this part of town are the foundations of the Romanesque **Church of St George (Sv Đorđe)**, the patron saint of Bar. The church was rebuilt in the 17th century as the Sultan Ahmet Mosque and in 1882 was demolished in a gunpowder explosion. Under its walls there are traces of even earlier 6th-century foundations, with 5th/6th-century mosaics and 9th-century reliefs. (Beware: near the church is an unplumbed well only partially covered by a giant stone, within which an echo repeats, it is claimed, no fewer than 18 times; the volume must be vast.)

Within the site, there are two other better-preserved 14th-century churches, **St Veneranda** and **St Catherine**, and there is also a well-preserved 17th-century Turkish bath demonstrating a sophisticated steam-circulation system. It is interesting to observe how these buildings reveal their various histories of adaptation; a mix of Mediterranean and Balkan elements.

The west part of the town was fortified during the 14th and 15th centuries and the defences were augmented by the Venetians in the 16th century. In this area you will see the ruin of **Sv Nikola's Church**, once part of a Franciscan monastery whose walls show remains of Serbo-Byzantine frescoes. The west defence tower encircled a small 11th- or maybe 12th-century church; nearby is what was probably the bishop's palace. North of the upper fortress is a well-preserved 17th-century **aqueduct**.

Perhaps the best advice to the layman visitor to this extraordinary site is simply to clamber through the ruins, wild flowers peeping between the ancient stones, to gaze up to lofty Rumija, the mountain unmoved by centuries or earthquakes, and dream of Illyria. Better still, carry with you a copy of Mladen Zagarčanin's excellent *The Old Town Of Bar; A Guide Through The Centuries*, published in English or Montenegrin and available either from the ticket office at the site entrance or from the Historical and Archaeological Museum in the newer Bar (pages 206–7).

Market Below the gates of Stari Bar there is a colourful market on Friday mornings.

'The oldest tree in Europe' These are the lands of the olive, the slopes all about stippled with their shimmering leaves. An olive tree can survive longer than the city it supports. Near Stari Bar there is one that is said to have lived for two millennia; it is a showpiece and claimed to be the oldest tree in Europe (see also box, pages 8–9). Certainly it has a colossal girth and is dusty and fatigued, its ancient branches arthritically twisted – beginning to show its age, one might say. You will find it just below and to the east as you descend from Stari Bar; turn hard left at the first intersection. Alternatively, it is well signed (*stara maslina*) just off the Bar ring road.

Bigovica marine archaeological site From undersea finds of amphorae and coins – both Hellenistic and Roman – and from other pottery shards, there has been speculation that sheltered Bigovica Bay, a little south of the port of Bar, may have served as a winter harbour from as far back as the 3rd century BC, perhaps until the 16th century AD. Remains of a small ship's hull, as yet undated, have also been detected in the silt. A team of marine archaeologists from Southampton University – along with Montenegrins and others and under the auspices of the Montenegro Ministry of Culture – have been conducting research in the area since 2010. At the time of writing, this is one of two protected marine sites in Montenegro (the other off the coast of Risan; pages 132–3) and as such any visiting divers in the area who are not part of the authorised team must leave the seabed undisturbed. There has been evidence of looting in the past.

THE ROAD TO ULCINJ

Heading south from Bar, in the suburb of **Čeluga,** there's a convenient **post office** (🕐 *08.00–14.30*) on the south side of the main road.

VELIKI PIJESAK AND DOBRA VODA At **Veliki Pijesak**, on the beach approximately 10km south of Bar, archaeologist Mladen Zagarčanin from Stari Bar has recently excavated the remains of a church that he believes dates from as early as the 4th century. If he's right it may be the oldest church uncovered in what was the Roman province of Dalmatia.

Continuing on the Adriatic Highway high above the shore, pass a left fork to the Albanian border at Sukobin (and the Kalamper restaurant, see below) and through the lower village of **Dobra Voda**. The road crosses bridge after bridge over rivers hurrying to the sea: Bušat, Šmošić, Cola Glava, Meret, Sintin, Šprenik, Ujtin Potok – and many more – *sweet water* all of them, as Montenegrins call spring water.

Continuing on, a sign will indicate '**Maslina Plaža**'. There's no need to go and look unless it is frenetic beach activity you are after. The short seafront is awash with disco, fast-food and casino action. There's a decent pebbly beach and lovely sea. The sea at least is tranquil, as, in winter, are the deserted kiosks.

🏠 **Where to stay**

🏠 **Ruža Vjetrova** (17 rooms, 4 suites) Veliki Pijesak; 📞030 306000; e rezervacija@ruzavjetrova. me; www.ruzavjetrova.me. A small resort hotel of stylish design on its own beach, with lovely sea views. The name means 'wind rose' & refers to the flower-like pattern of cardinal points on the seaman's compass. AC, minibar, safe, internet, jacuzzi bath, kitchenettes in suites, restaurant. Parking. Beach bar, sunbeds & umbrellas free. Playground, tennis & volleyball. Mini zoo. Special packages. €€€€

🏠 **Kalamper** (15 apts) Veliki Pijesak; 📞030 364335; e kalamper-hotel@t-com.me; www. apartmentskalamper.com. Apt hotel in the lower village, set back from the beach. AC, cable TV, safe, kitchenette, balconies & roof terrace with sea views. Fish restaurant. Parking with video security. Private beach with free loungers & umbrellas. €€€–€€€€

✖ Where to eat and drink

✱ ✖ **Kalamper** Dobra Voda; 📞030 361281; www.kalamper.com. Same ownership as hotel (above). Turn left from the main Bar–Ulcinj road (6km approx from Bar) at sign to Sukobin (Albanian border); restaurant is a further 5km, though alas the 'gorgeous views over wide rugged coastline' described in previous editions are becoming rather obscured by new construction below. Locally sourced fish & veg. Seafood risotto, homemade loza. Try the spiced cheese pâté, very good with toast. That & the veal broth make a perfect light lunch. Sunny terrace with pool & changing rooms, loungers & umbrellas beside a pretty orange grove. Excellent spot to break a hot journey, take a dip & relax. They have reason to be proud of the good water (*dobra voda*) from this area; there are dozens of springs tumbling down to the sea. Visa & MasterCard accepted. €€€

Shopping Next door to the Kalamper restaurant is a small convenience store. Small it may be, but it seems to have anything you might need in the basic provision line, with each item individually hand-priced; lovely.

UTJEHA Some 12km beyond Bar, this once-peaceful fishing village is situated where olive trees stretched down almost to the sea. In recent years, though, it has been transformed, with an artificial beach, busy sea-front street, and a rather overcrowded campsite. Unfortunately, too, the turquoise waters and rocky points of this pretty strip of coast, once accessible to all (with varying degrees of difficulty), are now largely the preserve of guests at the hotels that have been built here.

🏠 Where to stay and eat

🏠 **Apartments Utjeha** (5 apts) ul Maršal; 📞069 546851; e info@utjeha.me; www.utjeha. me. New, 4-star, luxurious, EU ecolabel-certified carbon-neutral apts under German management. English spoken. Excursions & car rental available. Several other local properties under same ownership. €280–995 per week. Security deposit payable on arrival. €€€–€€€€

🏠 **Hotel Vidikovac** (20 rooms) 📞030 458253; e michaela2@volny.cz; 🕐 all year. Only slightly set back from the through road, but most of the bedrooms face seaward. Minibar, AC & TV. Restaurant (€€€) & plenty of parking. Small open-air pool; evening live music. They have their own well & generator, but not much English. At the side of the hotel a path runs down to the beach, 300m away. MasterCard accepted. €€€

⛺ **Campsite Oliva** (25–30 pitches) ul Borska 18, 20m from sea; 📞030 319258; m 069 331150; e olive-utjeha@t-com.me; www.oliva.co.me; 🕐 Apr–Nov. Down at Utjeha Beach among the pine & olive trees. 4 toilet cabins, 4 bathrooms with hot water, 4 outdoor showers. Jul–Aug €3 per adult, €1.50 per child, €2.50–€3.50 tent; €2 per car, €6 per camper van, plus electricity €2; rates slightly lower outside these months. They can also offer a small number of apts & rooms (€€), all with AC but simply furnished. Taxi boats call at the beach for trips to small coves, Bar or Ulcinj. €

AROUND UTJEHA From Utjeha the higher ridges begin to retreat, giving way to more gently rolling hills of scrub interspersed with cultivation and orchards with kiwi, oranges and lemons. There's plenty of wildlife too – hares, rabbits and an occasional boar. And if you turn off the road, there's no sound but a chorus of birds. Turn off you should if you are riding a bicycle; it is far safer and infinitely more enjoyable to pick your way through the lanes. You can find your way back to Bar, for instance, if you turn inland at **Kruta** (4km from Ulcinj). You may get lost, you may even have to retrace your route, but does it matter? Howard Boyd writes:

> one thing which I think you would only notice when cycling is the mulberry spring. On the back road from Old Bar to Ulcinj [via Kruta] we stopped in the shade of a tree by a spring and found that the ground and the seat were covered in white mulberries. We passed several more such juxtapositions, all at road junctions, and decided it must be a deliberate feature for serving travellers. The mulberries were absolutely delicious and as well as the windfalls the branches themselves were weighed down with fresh fruit.

The writer goes on to warn cyclists to beware of road tunnels, in particular unlit ones. If necessary, he says, it might be safer to dismount and walk. Either way be sure to wear fluorescent marking; encounters with trucks are potentially lethal. Better still just stick with those back roads.

Continuing south by the main road, you will soon be on the outskirts of Ulcinj. In a lay-by near to **Kruče** there is a tourist information kiosk but they speak no English and have no information; it is not an official municipality outlet. Turn right at the first sign to Ulcinj and you will soon arrive at the **bus station** on your left and the **Hotel London** (page 216) on the right, where you will be able to find some leaflets on the town.

ULCINJ

As just one indication of how close Ulcinj is to its eastern neighbour, the population is 85–90% Albanian, most of them Muslim. In Albanian the name is Ulqin, and not unexpectedly that language is much in use in these parts.

Mrs Will Gordon tells a tale from the winter of 1916, when news was coming through of the Serbian retreat south, of two wounded British tommies chatting in a London hospital, one commenting:

> Oh I knows about Albania. Them's Albinos there, people wot 'ave white 'air and pink eyes. Then they go and marry the Montenegro folk, who're black and their kids are called Dalmatians – because they're spotted black and white.

The city is as bustling as ever, that never changes, but over the last few years Ulcinj has been in a somewhat transitional phase, with a number of the old state hotels either undergoing extensive renovation or seeking buyers; the streets readjusting to altered names; rumours abounding as to the future of the vast Velika Plaža (Big Beach) to the east of the city (where it is understood the government seeks to enter into a long-term lease agreement with an international company to provide a major tourist facility); and barely beneath the surface is an air of concerned anticipation.

Above all, Ulcinj welcomes her visitors. Hospitality to travellers is embedded in the hearts of Montenegrins and nowhere is it more evident than in these eastern corners of the country. Ulcinj Day is celebrated on the first Saturday in April.

HISTORY Ulcinj is another ancient seaport. Believed to have been founded by the Greeks in the 5th century BC, there is also likelihood of an early Illyrian presence. As in Stari Bar, there are traces of immense Cyclopean walls still visible in the old citadel. In the 2nd century BC, when the Romans took the town, it became known

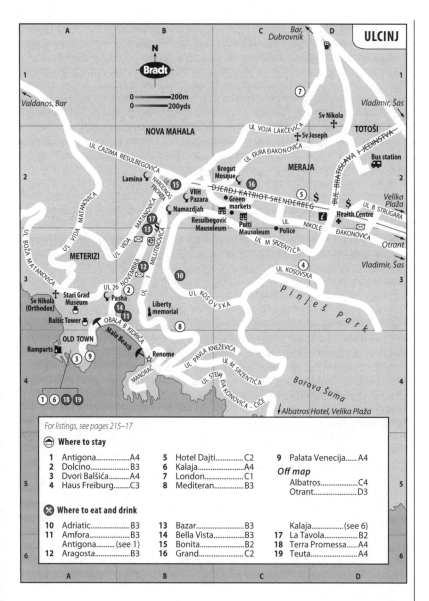

Bar, Dubrovnik

Valdanos, Bar

N

Bradt

0 — 200m
0 — 200yds

Vladimir, Šas

NOVA MAHALA

Sv Nikola

UL VOJA LAKČEVIĆA

Sv Joseph

TOTOŠI

UL ĐURA ĐAKONOVIĆA

MERAJA

Bus station

Velika Plaža

UL CAZIMA RESULBEGOVIĆA

Bregut Mosque

Lamina

⑮

VRH Pazara

Namazdjah

ĐERĐJ KATRIOT SKENDERBEG

⑯

⑤

$

$

UL B STRUGARA

Green markets

UL NIKOLE ĐAKONOVIĆA

Health Centre

Resulbegović Mausoleum

Pulti Mausoleum

Police

Otrant

METERIZI

UL VIDA MATANOVIĆA

UL BOŽA MATANOVIĆA

UL VIDA

UL MILUTINOVIĆA

UL M SRZENTIĆA

⑫

⑩

UL 26 NOVEMBRA

② Pasha

UL KOSOVSKA

④

Vladimir, Šas

Sv Nikola (Orthodox)

Stari Grad Museum

⑭ ⑪

UL I

UL KOSOVSKA

P i n j e š   p a r k

Balšić Tower

OBALA B KIDRIČA

Liberty memorial

Ramparts

OLD TOWN

③ ⑨

Mala Beach

Renome

⑧

UL PAVLA KNEŽEVIĆA

UL M SRZENTIĆA

Borova Šuma

MANDRAĆ

UL STEVA ĐA KONOVIĆA - ČIĆE

① ⑥ ⑱ ⑲

Albatros Hotel, Velika Plaža

For listings, see pages 215–17

Where to stay

1	Antigona	A4	5	Hotel Dajti	C2	9	Palata Venecija
2	Dolcino	B3	6	Kalaja	A4		
3	Dvori Balšića	A4	7	London	C1	*Off map*	
4	Haus Freiburg	C3	8	Mediteran	B3	Albatros	C4
						Otrant	D3

9 Palata Venecija...... A4

Where to eat and drink

10	Adriatic	B3	13	Bazar	B3		Kalaja	(see 6)
11	Amfora	B3	14	Bella Vista	B3	17	La Tavola	B2
	Antigona	(see 1)	15	Bonita	B2	18	Terra Promessa	A4
12	Aragosta	B3	16	Grand	C2	19	Teuta	A4

as Olcinium and a section of their refortification can be distinguished from the Illyrio-Greek by the rustication of the walls.

After the division of the Roman Empire, Ulcinj became part of the Byzantine province of Prevalis and the population converted to Christianity. From medieval times, and quite likely earlier, it was regarded as an important trading and maritime centre and it established city autonomy within the Slavonic state of Raška.

The **Balšić Tower** [213 A3] in the upper part of the Old Town was built by the Zetans in the late 14th century. In 1405 the Venetians conquered the town and ruled until overthrown in 1571 by the Ottomans, in whose domain it remained for over 300 years, during which time its far-reaching reputation as a lair of pirates was established.

Initially, this band of buccaneers comprised about 400 North African and Maltese corsairs, but before long many others were involved: Albanians, Turks and a certain number of Serbs. Romantic stories are legion. At first they used small galleys but they progressed to galleons built in the local shipyard. Their leaders, who achieved notoriety throughout the eastern Mediterranean, included the Karamindžoja brothers, Lika Ceni, Ali Hodža and Uluč Alija. With the objective of causing maximum confusion, their galleons would frequently change flags at sea. After a successful attack the pirates would celebrate with a roistering party on Pinješ Hill on the Mala Plaža (Small Beach), boiling oriental *halvah* in great cauldrons stirred with an oar. Oars were used to divvy up the plundered treasure, derived especially from Venetian, but also Austro-Hungarian, Greek and sometimes even Turkish ships.

When Lika Ceni destroyed a ship full of pilgrims *en route* to Mecca, the sultan put a large reward on his head. Then he put an even bigger reward on the head of a Greek pirate called Lembo. Lika vanquished Lembo, pocketed the reward and was given the title of captain by the sultan.

A flourishing black slave trade arose through the port of Tripoli and involved the export of North African adults and children, some as young as two or three years old, who were either sold on or put to work on their owners' lands or ships. There were over a hundred slave houses in Ulcinj, with the main square serving as the local slave market. It can still be seen in the old town.

It has been claimed that in 1571 the Spanish writer Cervantes was at first imprisoned in the vaults alongside the market, after he was wounded in the battle of Lepanto and captured by the pirates. There may be some poetic licence in this detail; as at Sveti Stefan any number of luminaries *may* have slept here.

Some North Africans came to Ulcinj not as slaves but of their own volition. Ritual dances would be performed on a part of Pinješ Hill known as **Arabian Field** (*Arapsko polje*). They danced to an amalgam of Balkan and African music, which in time developed into the exotic Šaravelji, a version of which is still around. A few families of African descent remain today.

In the 17th century a Jewish dissident named Sabetha Seti (1626–76) caused turmoil throughout the Turkish Empire with his evangelising, which attracted thousands of followers. He was eventually captured and exiled to Ulcinj in 1666, where he died quietly ten years later. He was buried in the courtyard of a Muslim house which, along with two Jewish altars in the Balšić Tower, is still preserved as a mausoleum.

After the Congress of Berlin in 1878, borders between Montenegro and the Ottoman Empire were redrawn, with Ulcinj becoming a part of Crna Gora. Although prepared to cede Plav, Gusinje and the Albanian villages of Grude, Hoti and Kastrati, Turkey still desperately wanted to retain Ulcinj. Ultimately Montenegro, supported by the British prime minister, Gladstone, and others from western Europe, resisted and on 30 November 1880 the town was officially annexed to the principality.

GETTING THERE

By bus The **bus station** [213 D2] (*Totoši bb;* ✎ *030 413225*) is at the top of the town in Totoši, not far off the Adriatic Highway linking the town with Bar. Ulcinj has good bus links and is the last stop on the airport bus route from Dubrovnik. There is at least one bus a day in the early morning in each direction (journey time roughly five hours), with an extra service some days during the summer.

There are regular buses connecting the town with Bar (€3) and other coastal towns, as well as with Podgorica, and there are services to Albania, Serbia and Kosovo. For timetables see www.busstation-ulcinj-montenegro.com.

Frequent kombi-buses operate between Ulcinj and Škodra in Albania via the border crossing at Sukobin–Muricani (Muriqan). From Škodra there are bus connections to Tirana.

By train If bus timings don't fit very well, you can take a bus to Bar and transfer to the train. The onward journey to Podgorica should take under an hour. There is a scheduled rail service between Bar and Podgorica and on to Kolašin, Bijelo Polje and Belgrade in Serbia (see box, page 203), and in addition local trains operating within Montenegro.

GETTING AROUND Ulcinj town is compact and its sites are easily, indeed best, covered **on foot**. Note that some street names are subject to frequent change (eg: Bulevar Maršala Tita is regularly referred to as Gjergj Kastrioti Skënderbeu – or in some cases Djerdj Katriot Skenderbeg).

If you are **driving** note that the one-way section where 26 Novembra (29 on some maps and also known as Hafiz Ali Ulqinaku) joins Obala Borisa Kidriča in front of Mala Plaža is generally ignored. Also watch out for under-age – and over-age – tearaway motorcyclists on the pavement on the seafront road.

On a summer afternoon there is a fair degree of anarchy in the bay too, with jet skis and waterskiers weaving in and out among the bathers. On dry land there are lots of street sweepers doing what they're meant to, very well indeed.

Car hire
🚗 **Kompas Hertz** Ivana Milutinovića; ✆030 423513
🚗 **Real Estate & Co** 26 Novembra; ✆030 421609; e realestate@t-com.me; www. realestate-travel.com. Min age 23. Also rent boats. MasterCard accepted. (See also under *Where to stay* & *Sports and other activities* for their other specialities).

Taxis
🚗 **Auto Taxi** ✆067 527678
🚗 **De Luxe Radio Taxi** ✆19766
🚗 **Radio Taxi Kalija** ✆19761
🚗 **Smart Group Taxi** ✆19788
🚗 **Taxi station** ✆19706

TOURIST INFORMATION AND TOUR OPERATORS
Tourist information
🛈 **Tourism Organisation Ulcinj** [213 D2] bul Djerdj Katriot Skenderbeg bb; ✆030 412333; e info@ulcinj.travel; www.ulcinj.travel

Tour operators
Dulcinea Ali Ulqinaku; ✆030 422193; http:// dulcineabooking.com. Accommodation, rentals, excursions, diving, fishing, etc.
Dina Skënderbeu; ✆030 411238; www.dinatravel. com. Accommodation, excursions, flights.

WHERE TO STAY *Map, page 213.*
As well as the places listed below, there are also several places to stay at Velika Plaža (see pages 219–20).

🏠 **Dvori Balšića & Palata Venecija** (62 beds in suites sleeping 2, 4 or 6) Stari Grad, on a bluff looking down at the harbour; ✆030 421609; e realestate@t-com.me; www.hotel-dvoribalsica-montenegro.com, www.hotel-palatavenezia-montenegro.com. Family-owned, well-appointed & attractive neighbouring hotels with splendid views, but be warned: you have to park your car at the bottom of a long series of steps & the only access is on foot. Get the hotel to help with the luggage unless you are feeling fit or travelling light. Spacious, comfortable, imaginatively furnished suites with AC & TV. Restaurant, bar & wine cellar. B/fast on the terrace. MasterCard accepted. €€€€

✷ ⌂ **Haus Freiburg** (9 rooms) Kosovska bb, Pinješ; ☎030 403008; e villafreiburg@gmail.com; www.hotelhausfreiburg.me; ⊕ all year. Up the hill behind the town with pine woods at the back & a good view in front, a new & very well-equipped hotel with restaurant & bar. Charming owner Karin Mehmet – not surprisingly – comes from Freiburg. AC, cable TV, free Wi-Fi, safe, minibar. Secluded pool, balconies, garage parking. Non-residents welcome to use all facilities. English & German spoken. Part of Bed & Bike scheme (pages 64–6). Out of season rooms half price. CCs accepted. **€€€–€€€€**

⌂ **Otrant** (240 rooms) Velika Plaža bb; ☎030 401801; www.hotelotrant.me. Large resort-style hotel with colourful rooms, right on beach. AC, restaurant, pools, sauna. **€€€–€€€€**

⌂ **Albatros** (175 beds, some self-catering apts) ul Steva Đakovića bb; ☎030 423263; e hoteli-albatros@t-com.me; www.albatros-hotels.com. On the south headland, in a pine wood 50m from the beach, 1km from the town centre, the Albatros is getting dated but is just about adequate. All rooms with shower, WC, balcony & sea view. Private beach, naturist beach, tennis court, billiards, table tennis, water sports, sauna. CCs accepted. **€€€**

✷ ⌂ **Dolcino** (15 rooms & 2 suites) ul Hafiz Ali Ulqinaku; ☎030 422288; e dolcino@t-com.me; www.hoteldolcino.com. An efficient, attractively furnished hotel opened in 2006. All rooms with cable TV, AC, minibar & internet, balcony.

Restaurant & bar with contemporary European menu. Conference room. Internet café across street. Good English. Visa & MasterCard accepted. **€€€**

⌂ **Hotel Dajti** (12 rooms) bul Maršala Tita bb; ☎030 413088. AC, internet, TV, minibar, balcony. **€€€**

⌂ **Mediteran** (134 rooms) Mujo Ulqinaku bb (also Ivana Milutinovića), 100m from Mala Plaža (Small Beach); ☎030 403124; e sales@hotel-mediteran.com; www.hotel-mediteran.com. Privatised & renovated under American/Albanian ownership. Sea & old town views, balcony, fridge, TV, AC. Restaurant & terrace bar. Fitness room, spa. Conference room. Free Wi-Fi. Special w/end packages. **€€€**

⌂ **Kalaja** (9 rooms & 2 self-catering studios) Stari Grad bb; ☎030 421435; m 069 037076; www.kalaja-ulqin.com. Intimate budget family hotel, hidden in the middle of the old city, owned by the Bushati family. AC & TV. Restaurant (see below). **€€**

⌂ **London** bul V Frasheri bb; ☎030 412425; m 069 031601. Simple hotel, convenient for bus station. TV, AC, no CCs. **€€**

⌂ **Restaurant-Gasthaus Antigona** (13 rooms) Stari Grad bb; m 069 220792; e antigonabushati@yahoo.com. www.antigonaulcinj.webs.com. Fairly simple rooms with sea views, & shower en suite. Terrace with fish restaurant (see below). **€**

✗ **WHERE TO EAT AND DRINK** *Map, page 213.*
Restaurants
In town

✗ **Aragosta** Ivana Milutinovića bb; m 069 692008, 069 332528; ⊕ 10.00–24.00. Highly regarded by the locals & certainly one of the best restaurants in town. Some English. MasterCard & Visa accepted. Close to Pinješ Park, where the pirates liked to celebrate. **€€€€**

✷ ✗ **Grand** Maršala Tita bb, 1st floor; ☎030 411326; ⊕ 15.00–01.00 Tue–Sun (earlier in season). Swiss-trained owner divides his time between Ulcinj & Zermatt. Good English. Relatively international cuisine 'from beef Wellington to *spaghetti alla vongole*'. AC & new décor. W/end piano bar. **€€€€**

✗ **Antigona** Stari Grad bb; m 069 220792; www.antigonaulcinj.webs.com. Seafood restaurant with terrace overlooking the sea &

lovely sunset views. Rooms available (see above). Has its own fishing boats. **€€€**

✷ ✗ **Bazar** Iljav Čauši, corner of Hafiz Ali Ulqinaku, 1st floor; ☎030 421639. Concentrates on fish & does it well. Run by 3 brothers, 2 of whom fish in Bojana. Welcoming owner creates a hospitable atmosphere. CCs accepted. **€€€**

✗ **Bella Vista** Cafo Begu Sq, ul Hafiz Ali Ulqinaku; ☎030 402088; www.bella-vista.me; ⊕ 08.00–24.00. Family restaurant in a convenient central location specialising in grilled fish & pizza. Also rooms (**€€€**): not the cheapest, but with AC, cable TV, fridge, no internet. CCs accepted. **€€€**

✗ **Bonita** 26 Novembra; ⊕ 08.00–24.00. Duplex eating: a pleasant open gallery on upper floor, plus pavement café. Mediterranean cuisine. No CCs. **€€€**

✕ Kalaja Stari Grad bb; ✆030 421435; **m** 069 037076; www.kalaja-ulqin.com. Mediterranean restaurant featuring shellfish & pasta, hidden in centre of old town, part of intimate budget family hotel (see above). €€€

✕ Teuta Stari Grad bb; vlasnik Šazi Ninanbegović ✆030 421442; www.restaurant-teuta.com; ⏰ 09.00–24.00. Up on the hill with a big terrace & fine views. Also rooms (€€). No CCs. €€€

✕ Amfora ul 26 Novembra Pristan, Mala plaža. Fish specialities. €€

✕ La Tavola restaurant-pizzeria 26 Novembra bb; **m** 069 102010; ⏰ 08.00–24.00. B/fast, daily lunch specials, summer terrace, friendly staff. English, Italian & Albanian spoken. No CCs. €€

✕ Terra Promessa Stari Grad bb. Popular restaurant with sea view. €€

✱ 🍨 Ice-cream parlour ul Hafiz Ali Ulqinaku, next door to Hotel Dolcino.

Above Pinješ Park

Along Kosovska, above Pinješ Park, an increasing number of new buildings are springing up, many containing small restaurants & often with rooms &/or apts for rent above them. All are a bit of a climb up from the centre of town & the beach, but the views compensate & the street is quiet at night:

✕ Adriatic Kosovska bb. Restaurant offering BBQ grills, & with a few rooms for rent (€€). €€

Entertainment and nightlife
☆ **Disco FAMA** Plazhi i vogel
☆ **Renome Night Club** [213 B4] Mala Beach, eastern end of seafront

SPORTS AND OTHER ACTIVITIES
Diving
✱ 🤿 Club D'Olcinium **m** 067 314100; **e** info@ uldiving.com; www.uldiving.com. Specialises in undersea archaeology & wreck diving. Equipment rental & tuition. Individual dives €15–20, diving course inc equipment €200.

Kitesurfing
Kitesurf Club D'Olcinium **m** 069 330492; **e** info@kitesurfclub.me; http://kitesurfclub.me

SHOPPING The citizens of Ulcinj have always been good merchants and the enormous *zelena pijaca,* the green market [213 C2], off Bulevar Maršala Tita, is a sensory treat. From outlying villages men and women dressed to varying degree traditionally (blue jeans now a most likely adjunct) will have been at their positions since dawn, a profusion of produce carefully spread out on broad tables: jewel-like olives, displayed by size and colour; misshapen tomatoes and a medley of carrots, onions, courgettes and brightly coloured peppers; suspicious-looking fungi for the brave, and game bagged in the nearby hills; great heaps of plums and an abundance of farm-fresh cheeses, each with its own unique flavour and their vendors competing for you to taste the difference.

OTHER PRACTICALITIES
Banks
There are ATMs at the eastern end of Obala Borisa Kidriča facing Mala Plaža (Small Beach), at the northern end of 26 Novembra, & 3 ATMs in Maršala Tita.

$ **Atlasmont Banka** 26 Novembra
$ **CKB** Maršala Tita
$ **Komercijalna Banka** 26 Novembra bb
$ **Montenegrobanka** 26 Novembra bb
$ **Opportunity Bank** Maršala Tita

Internet
There are more internet cafés in Ulcinj than in most other towns in Montenegro: probably on account of the large Albanian, either expatriate or vacationing, presence. The majority of these facilities can be found in & around Maršala Tita. Prices are low & sometimes negotiable.

🖥 **Begu Internet caffe** [213 B3] 26 Novembra; ⏰ 10.30–late. Lots of computers; €0.20 low season, higher in summer.

Internet café Shtypshkronja Rr Maršala Tita;
030 401144. €1 per hr.
(Also on Maršala Tita: internet cafés 'Azemina'; Vojo
Lakćević; 'Rinia')
Internet café Cyber Club West corner of
Mala Plaža
Internet caffe Mimi Đura Đakonovića 11;
m 069 351999; ⏱ 09.00–24.00. Low season
€0.50 per hr; high season €1 per hr.

Medical facilities
⊞ **Health Centre** [213 D2] 030 412424

Pharmacies
✚ **Montefarm** Maršala Tita; 030 412858
✚ **Viola** Maršala Tita; 030 412523

Other
✉ **Post office** [213 B3] 26 Novembra;
⏱ 08.00–12.00 & 17.00–20.00, Mon–Fri 08.00–
12.00 Sat. In the middle of 26 Novembra on the
west side, diagonally opposite Bella Vista.

WHAT TO SEE

Old city The old fortified city stands on a promontory to the northwest and can be entered either from the harbour below or through the main gate above. The upper section holds an excellent, ethnographic and archaeological **museum complex**: **Stari Grad Museum** [213 A3] (030 421419; e leart@t-com.me; ⏱ 09.00–13.00 & 16.00–21.00 Tue–Sun). Incorporating a 14th-century church-mosque, its contents represent the municipality in general. It displays two Bronze Age axes, an interesting lapidary collection, both Ionic and Turkish, and many artefacts from past urban life. It also includes finds from Šas/Svač (see pages 221–2). Several narrow paths lead to the lower level where there is now a hotel.

New town The newer town and bazaar-like shopping streets stretch uphill behind the sandy **Mala Plaža** (Small Beach) [213 B4]. The general atmosphere is one of bustle, interrupted only by the insistent invocations of the *muezzin*. Near the beach is the **Pasha Mosque** [213 A3], built in 1719 by Klič Alija of Constantinople. The hammam, the only one of its kind in Montenegro, was later turned into a public bath. Facing the sea, the ruins of the old **sailors' mosque**, which had been serving as a car park, are scheduled for excavation.

The Orthodox **Cathedral of Sv Nikola** [213 A3] stands just west of the old town on the site of a 15th-century monastery. After the Turks invaded, it was converted into a mosque. It was rebuilt as a church in 1890, in honour of the Montenegrins who died in the wars of 1878. Its interesting iconostasis is of Russian origin.

A church at the very top of the new town, near the main road from Bar, is also dedicated to **Sv Nikola** [213 D1] and was erected towards the end of the Ottoman rule. Notice a peculiarity: the Turkish authorities would not allow any building, particularly from another religion, to be as high as the minarets of the mosques. For that reason the floor of the church is below ground level.

Opposite the old town, a headland masked by stone pines curves neatly to enclose the little bay. The cliff behind it discloses, to the east, several attractive rocky coves dropping steeply to the sea. One of these is reserved for female naturists and has a reputation for enhancing fertility, which might or might not be a beneficial addition.

Otherwise the area offers good deep-water bathing and snorkelling close to the town.

AROUND ULCINJ

VALDANOS This is a deep, horseshoe-shaped, white-shingled bay 6km west of Ulcinj. It was here that the pirates were finally outwitted and suffered ignoble defeat by Pasha Mahmoud Bushati's trim Albanian fleet. Surely there must be gold lying somewhere out there beneath those clear blue waters. Swim in the pellucid bay, or picnic under the olive trees that encircle it.

VELIKA PLAŽA From the southeast headland of Ulcinj, by the Albatros Hotel, it is possible to walk east beside the sea to **Velika Plaža** (Big Beach) in about an hour. However, as a reader has pointed out, it is a fairly rugged route, first through woods and then involving clambering over some rocky terrain. Perhaps most would prefer the option of an inexpensive taxi ride from Ulcinj town to Velika Plaža, costing approximately €3. However you reach it, the Big Beach is an amazing 12.5km long, stretching east to the Bojana River and the Albanian border, and over 50m wide. It's enjoyed Blue Flag status since 2003.

The sand is soft and fine and, as at Igalo in Herceg Novi, reputed to be especially rich in healthy minerals, notably iodine here. But maddeningly (for some), because of the uniformity of the plain, the sea is very shallow, ideal for tiny children and the elderly but a very long haul for anyone wishing to swim in anything approaching waist-deep water.

Behind the *maquis* and pine that border the silver sand, which stretches away into the hazy distance, are flat fields of watermelon, another speciality of Ulcinj, and beyond them the **Ulcinj Saltpans** and marshes (not always that safe), haven to a wide variety of birdlife. Efforts are in force to target poachers, and proper shooting/hunting licences may be obtained on a daily or seasonal basis (enquiries to the Ulcinj Tourist Board).

From a tourist perspective, Velika Plaža has remained relatively undeveloped, but in 2008 a Dutch design company, Van den Oever, Zaaijer & Partners, won a competition to develop the area into an eco-friendly tourist complex. At the start of this beach you cross the **Milena Canal** (named after the wife of King Nikola). Here you will find an unusual method of catching fish. The banks are lined with long flexible willow rods supporting wide nets which are hauled up when a shoal of mullet, bass or lamprey swim over them. These devices, known locally as *kalamera*, from the Albanian 'to take in passing', might take all the fun out of fishing but are nevertheless ingenious. At the far end of the beach is the **Bojana River**. The technique is employed there too and the result is an ongoing supply of super-fresh fish.

The marshy land of **Štoj**, between Ulcinj and Bojana, is a popular hunting area, with wild duck, goose, woodcock, quail and partridge. Many birds are protected and in summer flocks of flamingo can be seen in this area. In common with other Montenegrin coastal flatlands this plays an important role in the Adriatic Flyway (see page 63) and is an excellent place for birdwatching. As a result, relationships between the hunters and the twitchers are not especially harmonious.

Line-fishing possibilities in the area include sea bass, mullet, bream and dentex, while sport-fishing includes shark, rays and conger and moray eels. Molluscs, lobster and crab are harvested and enormous quantities of shrimp, normally rare in the Adriatic, are netted here.

Zoganj lying north of Štoj is a well-regarded small wine-growing area.

Where to stay

All along Velika Plaža are cafés, campsites, *sobe*, etc.

Petriti (18 rooms, 8 apts) bul Teuta bb; ☏030 413664; e info@hotel.petriti.com; www.hotelpetriti.com. Modern hotel, situated on the road between Ulcinj & Velika Plaža. AC, minibar, satellite TV. Restaurant & bar. Parking. HB & FB available. **€€€**

Eldorado (9 rooms) bul Teuta bb, Velika Plaža bb; \030 455172; m 069 031617; e nora1934@hotmail.com; http://apartmans-eldorado.weebly.com. Family hotel with kindly owner on main road to Ada Bojana, 200m from beach. AC. 4 rooms with kitchen. MasterCard & Visa accepted. €

Å Tropicana (100 pitches) m 067 515477; www.tropicanabeach.co.me. 5km east of Ulcinj, close to the Imperijal Hotel on Velika Plaža. Pitches at €10 per day Oct–Mar; €12 Apr–Sep. Includes toilet & showers, but bring your own tent or caravan. Also 6 rooms (€€) & restaurant (€€). Internet café, disabled toilet. Information on rare indigenous plants, & likely nearby spots to find them. See also *Where to eat and drink*.

✗ Where to eat and drink

✗ Antique Velika Plaža at Donje Štoj, 3km beyond Ulcinj; m 067 527991. Good atmosphere & a high reputation among the locals. Off the main road & unsigned; turn right at intersection to Velika Plaža where the main road continues to Ada Bojana. No CCs. €€€

✗ Hollegro Copacabana Beach, 6km from Ulcinj; \030 421481. Beach bar & restaurant; toilets & showers; lifeguard on duty 08.00–18.00. €€€

✗ Tropicana Beach See Tropicana above. Beach bar & restaurant. Umbrellas & chairs €5; toilets & showers; lifeguard on duty ◷ 08.00–18.00. €€

ADA BOJANA The Bojana River marks the border with Albania. In 1858 the schooner *Merito* sank at the mouth of the river, where it appears from charts of that time that there was a small delta. With the gradual build up of sand around the wreck, this grew in size to form today's **Ada Bojana** (Bojana Island), which is joined to the mainland by a bridge. The island is now devoted to naturism and is still a very popular place in high summer.

The *maestral* breezes which blow onshore in this area are particularly favourable for windsurfing (for which there is a well-equipped school on hand) and also ensure that even the hottest days are never sultry. Once upon a time any number of activities were laid on; the old adverts make horseriding look very uncomfortable.

The banks of the Bojana are of particular interest to botanists, with some rare species to be found.

⌂ Where to stay

As an alternative to a hotel, some of the area's private houses can be rented overnight. They have minimal facilities and heavy vegetation but are peaceful beyond words.

⌂ Hotel Olympic & Hotel Bellevue (132 rooms & 329 rooms) \030 412382 (Olympic), 030 412610 (Bellevue); e ulrivjera@t-com.me; www.ulcinjska-rivijera.com. Large, concrete resort-style hotels with AC, both on the beach. Olympic 4km from Ulcinj. The Bellevue was renovated in 2012. €€€–€€€€

⌂ Hotel Ada Bojana (296 cabins, rooms & villas) \030 411351; e ulrivjera@t-com.me; www.ulcinjska-rivijera.com. Under same ownership as Olympic & Bellevue, a naturist resort where accommodation inc 46 wooden bungalows. Clothing required in restaurant & bar; nudity not necessarily required on beach 100m away. Some English spoken but good German, the language of most foreign guests. No CCs. €€€

✗ Where to eat and drink

Beside the bridge over the river is an impressively long row of similar-looking wooden restaurants with almost identical menus. They all serve fish, much but not all of it from the river, plus a few token bits of meat for the carnivores. They are all built over the river on stilts, somewhat reminiscent of southeast Asia, and they all seem to get on with each other. They all cater for tourists and speak good English. Just try and decide which chef is on form that day.

✘ **Miško** m 069 324346; www.restoranmisko.
com; ◷ 08.00–24.00. Family-run place that
claims to be the oldest & is slightly more expensive
than some of the others. Bar designed to resemble
a capsized ship with all bottles upside-down.
Contact them for a taxi boat to pick you up from
somewhere else on the coast & return you after

dinner, or for a cruise to where the river forms a
delta. €€€
✘ **Restoran Riblja Čorba kod Marka** ✆030
405040; m 069 400504. Has a reputation for being
at or near the top of the Ada Bojana list. Family
run. Menu features some game in season (mallard,
quail, woodcock). No CCs. €€€

THE ALBANIAN BORDER REGION

The roads described in the following section are in less frequent use than most in
Montenegro. This particularly applies during the winter months, when low-lying
areas are subject to flooding and driving conditions can be hazardous. The roads
are best travelled in a group, but if that is not practicable you should at least ensure
your vehicle is thoroughly roadworthy before setting out. (*Note: for automobile
rescue, traffic information, roadside assistance, towing:* ✆ *19807 or 020 234999; www.
amscg.org; šlepslužba (tow trucks);* ✆ *122 for police/emergency.*)

ŠASKO LAKE (ŠASKO JEZERO) Šasko Lake is connected to the **Bojana River** and so
also to the sea, by a narrow canal. In summer the lake is 3.5km by 1.5km in area but
when the rains come it swells to half as much again. It is teeming with fish, the majority
from the carp family, but there are delicious crayfish too and some immigrant sea
species such as mullet, perch and bass. Eight metres at its deepest, close to the shore
it is very shallow and, as at Štoj, the surrounding marshes offer good duck shooting
for those so disposed; poachers are often an easier target. But the region is largely
undisturbed wilderness, a paradise for ornithologists and also an excellent location
for observing the autumn migration of songbirds (see pages 63–4).

Getting there From Ulcinj, the road strikes east just before the petrol station
on the southern edge of town, in the direction of **Vladimir** (18km). When you
arrive at this town, instead of continuing to the border you can choose a small road
bearing right to **Šasko jezero** (Šasko Lake).

Šas On a northern ridge above the lake you will find the ruins of a medieval wall
with two entrances, one at the rear and one for the descent to the lake. Fortified
originally in Illyrian times, this is all that is left of the city of **Svač** – or, as it is
more commonly known these days, **Šas**. The Romans were later to build a road
connecting Olcinium (Ulcinj) and Škodra (Skadar/Scutari) which passed through
here, and in 1067 the city is mentioned as the episcopal town of Zeta. In 1242 it
was razed by the Mongols, then afterwards rebuilt, only to be once again devastated
in the 16th century by the Ottomans. From that time it never rose again. Annals
record that it was a 'magnificent city, with as many churches as days of the year'.
Myth always has some historical validity and it has been suggested the hyperbole
might have grown from the fact that many of the mansions in such an important
city could have been built to include individual chapels. Whatever the case, in
the 14th century the image of its awesome renaissance fortress featured on coins
minted in Svač (see Stari Grad Museum, Ulcinj, page 218). Now all that remains is
a heap of stones on a silent hillside.

In a valley a little to the west the untroubled village of **Donja Klezna** replays
each pastoral day in very much the same manner as when the splendid city was its
neighbour.

Getting there The ruins are unsupervised and a ten-minute hike from the road below. Leave the rustic soccer pitch by the top left-hand corner and follow a rocky path in the direction of the single broken wall silhouetted against the sky on the crest of the hill. The final 200m is a bit of a scramble but well worth it, magically evocative at dusk with the *muezzin* calling.

✖ Where to eat and drink

✖ **Restaurant Shasi** East of the ruins; m 069 592873. To find it, follow the road to Šasko Lake (see *Getting there*, above) until a wooden sign leads up a track through blackberries & wild lupin towards the lake. 3 floors high, the rambling stone house is perched on a hillock. Just as well: in winter the river bursts from its banks, the lake rises & their pretty garden becomes a water meadow. The Albanian Catholic family offer a warm welcome & delicious regional dishes. Well worth a visit & not just because there is little competition. Sequestered & atmospheric, 2km from the border, the road ahead a cul-de-sac. 'Do not forget us,' they say. Rooms also available (€€). €€€

ALONG SKADAR LAKE Even if your plan is to cross the border at Sukobin, it is worthwhile making a detour north beside Skadar Lake, perhaps venturing into the national park. In Vladimir turn north to **Brajše** where the road climbs high to the **Štegvaš Pass** on **Mt Taraboš**, scene of a terrible battle between the Montenegrins and the Turks during the bitter six-month siege of Scutari (winter 1912/13). As Mrs Will Gordon reports in her journal of 1916, *A Woman in the Balkans*:

> In the midst of all the carnage came a woman looking for her only son. She found him, mangled and dying, caught in the barbed wire. 'Alright my son,' she exclaimed. 'It is good, for it is all for Montenegro, all for Montenegro!'

Here, a few hundred metres from Albania, you will have a spectacular view: the huge expanse of Skadar Lake to the north and west, Škodra to the east, and south to the Bojana delta and the sea. Follow a stony path east for 200m along the edge of the escarpment for an even better look.

Just south of the pass, and sharing much of the view, is:

🏠 **Restoran Panorama** (4 rooms) 030 750021; m 069 850466; e restoran_panorama@hotmail.com; ⏰ all year 09.00–23.00 daily. New en-suite rooms at this established restaurant have AC, & 3 have balconies. In the restaurant (€€), a set menu at under €10 inc soup, salad, fish & dessert. B/fast €5. €€–€€€

Ostros From the viewpoint it is possible to follow this route on down to Skadar Lake, where it continues parallel with the southern edge of the lake, passing through **Ostros** with its colourful bazaar (main market day Thursday) and the medieval ruins of the **Monastery and Church of Prečista Krajinska**. The significance of the church lies in the suggestion that it was the earliest Slav monument in Montenegro. The first mention of it was in the 10th-century chronicle of a certain Father Dukljanin, as having been founded by Dukljian King Jovan Vladimir, about whom legend tells an immoderate tale of star-crossed love with Kosara, beautiful daughter of King Samuilo of Macedonia. All too brief a relationship, it ended in tears, the way these stories should, with the murdered Vladimir finally joined in the grave by the bereft Kosara. No-one will be able to tell you where to look for the remains of the church but you can find them 1km east of the village, not far down a side road leading towards the lake. Investigating them requires some scrambling through brambles and over makeshift stick barriers. It appears the ruins now serve as some kind of animal pen.

✗ Where to eat and drink Ostros is a nice little town with several cafés for refreshment.

✗ Café Ostros The furthest west on the main street, serving good cheese, bread & beer. Don't ask for ham, though; they don't do it. €

Ckla

A further diversion, turning northeast on a small unsigned road just outside the settlement of **Arbnež,** could bring you down to the very edge of the lake and the well-maintained harbour of **Ckla** a stone's throw, literally, from Zogaj in Albania. Half a century ago it was an official customs post between the two countries. Now it lies empty and apparently unused. Besides a locked wooden hut at the water's edge and a ruined ivy-clad building 400m back up the scrubby hill, nothing. A good spot for a quiet swim on a hot day.

Ostros to Godinje

To travel on west you must retrace your route back to the higher road, then after Ostros, chestnut woods, bracken underfoot, fields of tobacco, fig trees, orchards with mules, cows in Alice bands, a tortoise in the road, maybe. The way becomes single track with few passing places, and all the while the pacific lake far below, dissolving into the misty distance, every shade of grey. **Murići** is another nice place to bathe but you will need to take a lane downhill to reach the beach; **Đuravci** and its tiny school (do the children gaze in wonder at their view?); **Dračevica** with its lovely walled church, its cypress trees; **Seoca** (see *Skadar Lake National Park*, below). And finally the geometric vineyards that mark the beginning of the **Crmnička nahija** region and the old stone houses of **Godinje,** each with its traditional wine cellar. Godinje was partially destroyed by the devastating earthquake of 1979, and has been largely abandoned ever since. If you have called ahead you could visit the *konoba* of vintner Miodrag Leković (m *069 476591, 067 308664*) and sample his product straight from the barrel.

In 1907 an early Miss World Beauty Pageant was staged in London. As the story goes, it was King Nikola himself who persuaded a young inhabitant of Godinje village, one Milena Delibašić, to travel against her father's wishes to London to represent Montenegro in the competition. The short of it was she won and was crowned Miss World, after which she returned forthwith to her tiny mountain village and married, as she had been destined to do, a young chap from the Lakovica clan. When later asked why she had not embraced the opportunities and riches that could surely have been hers, she replied with true Montenegrin éclat, 'I went to London to represent the beauty of my country: I came back to my country because it is my home.'

Next stop is **Virpazar** at the head of the lake, gateway to Skadar Lake National Park and at the junction for the main road to Podgorica.

SKADAR LAKE NATIONAL PARK

Bordered to the east by Albania, **Skadar Lake** is enclosed on three sides by Montenegrin mountains. One of the largest lakes in Europe – some 43km long, sometimes as much as 14km wide and with an average depth of 7m – roughly two-thirds of its waters are in Montenegro and one-third in Albania. Of the lake's 168km coastline, 110.5km lies in Montenegro and 57.5km in Albania. No-one really knows if the lake was always here. Records from a millennium ago refer only to rivers. Strange stuff, karst.

Skadar Lake became a national park in 1983, covering 400km², and in 1996 was added to the RAMSAR list of Wetlands of International Importance. The surface

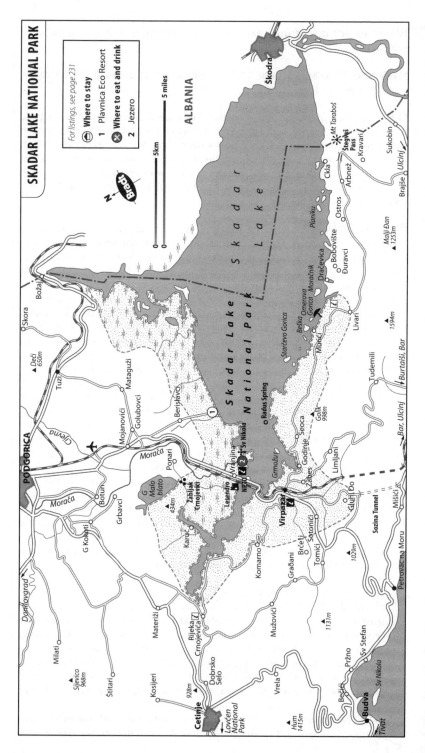

SKADAR LAKE NATIONAL PARK

For listings, see page 231

Where to stay
1 Plavnica Eco Resort

Where to eat and drink
2 Jezero

ALBANIA

Skadar Lake

Skadar Lake National Park

0   5km
0   5 miles

N

Beach

Podgorica

Cetinje

Lovćen National Park

Budva

Tivat

Škodra

area of the lake ranges from 370km² in summer to 540km² in the winter. It is host to 40 different kinds of fish and is one of the biggest bird preserves in Europe.

The lake varies in size considerably over the course of the year. In the rainy season it is full and blue and in the summer it appears silver, shimmering in the sun while the mountains of Albania appear to hover in the distance above its surface. It is fed not only by its various rivers but also by 50 active springs in the karst floor (known as *oke* – 'eyes') which provide a continuous source of pristine water, something of a clean swimming pool effect. The most famous, **Radus**, is very deep indeed – some claim as much as 90m – and certainly below sea level. It is located not too far offshore from the village of Seoca on the south shore. Around such places the canny fishermen know their catch will be plentiful. The dominant species found close to the underwater springs is bleak.

Little islets are sprinkled near Skadar's western shores, many supporting diminutive solitary monasteries. Not far from Radus is **Grmožur**, the onomatopoeic defence built in 1843 by the Turks on a stony island in the bay of Godinje and later converted to an Alcatraz by King Nikola I. History has it that no-one who was able to swim could be banished here and that included custodians. If someone did succeed in escaping, his gaoler was then condemned to serve out the balance of his sentence in his place. Two made it, we are told, cheekily using the great prison door as a raft.

At the lake's northwestern extremity is the nostalgic village of **Rijeka Crnojevića**, once the glamorous summer refuge of the court of King Nikola. What a difference a century makes …

FISH The lake is primarily fed from rivers hosting a salmonoid family of fish – marble trout, endemic trout and rainbow trout. As well as carp and their bleak brethren (along with a varying proportion of common rudd, South European roach, white chubb, common nase and Mediterranean shad), saltwater fish that can appear by way of the short stretch of the Bojana River may vary from sea eels even to the occasional bass (we are reliably told that Adriatic sturgeon, grey mullet, sea bass, European flounder, eel and sea lamprey have all put in an appearance in the lake).

BIRDLIFE The surrounding reed-filled swamps are an important habitat of aquatic birds. As a rough breakdown, the bird count of 270 bird species includes some 73 species that are migrating and nesting, 18 that regularly transit during autumn and spring, 45 regular winter guests, 12 species that visit during summer without nesting and 90-odd that reside on Skadar Lake from time to time.

Among these are some rarely found elsewhere in Europe, such as the Dalmatian pelican and black ibis. The pelican is traditionally the fisherman's foe and, who knows, perhaps that is part of the reason sightings of them are now so rare. Pygmy cormorant and glossy ibis, however, are far from uncommon. On **Omerova Gorica**, one of the many small islands, there is a colony of 40 grey heron nesting among the laurel trees. It is said heron will normally avoid laurel but of late the greys have even been joined by a contingent of the purple variety.

Special protected areas have been established, namely Panceva Oka and Manastirska Tapija, where globally endangered bird species have found peace and isolation for nesting. Mixed colonies have been identified there, including pygmy and great black cormorants, great and little white egrets and grey herons.

VISITING THE NATIONAL PARK (*adult €4 1-day ticket; €8 3-day ticket; student €1; child under 7 free; fishing permit €5/day; tickets & information from National Park*

6

Visitor Centre, page 228) The gateway to Skadar Lake National Park is at Virpazar (opposite) Watercolour artists should come equipped; the painterly peaks have arranged themselves so beautifully around the mirrored lake, the greatest in the Balkans. Waterlilies bloom on the lake's surface, and *kesoranja* (something between a water chestnut and an artichoke) grow in abundance.

Tourist information and tour operators See also page 228.

Tourist call centre ☎1300 (24hrs)

OTHER PRACTICALITIES
Police ☎122

AROUND THE LAKE Midway down the west side of the lake, **Murići Beach** is an idyllic swimming place, with bleached pebbles and translucent water beside a hamlet set aside by time. There is a **vacation resort** here (m *069 688288, 067 822205; http://nacionalnipark-izletistemurici.com; with several log cabins, a shower block, a campsite & a simple restaurant; €*) and it is also possible to organise kayaking (contact Undiscovered Montenegro, page 228).

To the northeast of Murići Beach is **Beška Island**, with its tiny 15th-century church of **Sv Đorđe**, where you may see little owls, or flocks of rock doves circling overhead.

On tiny **Starčevo Gorica** there is a 14th-century monastery. Here the resident monk was once an electrical engineer; now he is a hermit. Visit by all means but do not disturb him: 'If I had wanted that I would not be here.'

Strange to reflect how this gentle place was for centuries the scene of so much bloody warfare. They say the worst insult you can pay a Montenegrin is to suggest that his ancestors must have died in their beds.

Excursions on the lake The best way to arrange an excursion on the lake – whether by **kayak** or in a traditional flat-bottomed **gondola** (*čun*) – is to contact Undiscovered Montenegro or 'Milica' (see *Tour operators*, page 228).

Alternatively, strike a private deal with a local fisherman, but expect to hire the owner along with his boat. Besides anything else, he knows where the border is, which is important since foreigners straying over unannounced can arouse hostility on the part of the authorities, among others. Skadar Lake has seen its share of smugglers, bearing cargoes of cigarettes, petroleum or refugees, and the police keep watch on unidentified traffic.

Fishing Should you wish to fish, arrangements can be made through the national parks office at Virpazar or Vranjina (see above). Otherwise, the warden may come to you when he sees you fishing and collect the dues in that way. The licence will cost €5 per day. The closed fishing season is 15 March–30 April.

Birdwatching Birding expeditions from dedicated towers, platforms and hides can be organised through the visitor centre. They are also possible from small boats, although these may require two days' advance notice.

Hiking and biking There are a number of hiking and biking trails in the area around the lake, some marked, some not. Maps are available from the visitor centre, and you can also arrange hikes through local agencies such as Undiscovered Montenegro.

Wine and food tours Skadar Lake Ethno-Gastronomic Route (`020 510125;` e *info@cstimontenegro.org;* *www.ethnogastro-balkan.net*) is an excellent, enthusiastic project to highlight local food (honey, cheese, etc) and wine of the Skadar region, with a great list of recipes. Note that enquiries go to the office in Podgorica, not direct to local producers. Undiscovered Montenegro also offer local wine and food tours.

VIRPAZAR The little town of Virpazar serves as the main harbour on the Montenegrin side of Skadar Lake and for many is the gateway to Skadar Lake National Park. Until the beginning of the last century, it represented the strategic border with the Ottoman occupied lands. Here was the centre of one of the leading tribes of Crna Gora – the *Tsernica nahia* – and it was in this area that the contentious Montenegrin Vespers was implemented (see box, page 92).

A few years ago Virpazar had a downcast air. Today the ghosts have gone and the place is blooming, streets swept, cats reposed in warm car-roof siesta and honey for sale at the Friday market in the maple-leafed square.

Getting there and away The lakeside town is on the main road connecting Podgorica with the Sozina Tunnel and the Montenegrin littoral.

Podgorica's airport at Golubovci is roughly halfway between the Montenegrin capital and Virpazar, and the introduction of Ryanair's new route to Podgorica from the UK makes Virpazar and Skadar Lake particularly quick and easy to get to.

All local **trains** between Bar and Podgorica stop here, and in summer there is a connection several times a day. The fare from either town is in the region of €1.50.

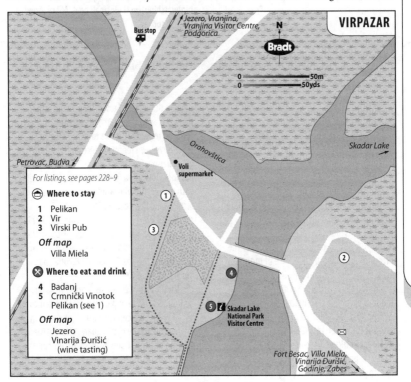

There are around three **buses** a day to and from Virpazar, running between Podgorica, Bar and Ulcinj.

Tourist information and tour operators

Tourist information

Z Skadar Lake National Park Visitor Centres By the old bridge, & at Vranjina, midway across the causeway from Virpazar, on Sozina–Podgorica road; ☎ 020 711104, 020 879103; e np-skadarlake@t-com.me, npcg.marketing@t-com.me; www.npskadarlake.org; ⊕ Jun–15 Oct 08.00–18.00 daily, 16 Oct–31 May 08.00–16.00 Mon–Fri. Tickets for the national park can be bought at either of the 2 visitor centres. Literature, maps & information, inc advice on which boat cruises are operating at any given time. Birdwatching expeditions. Small museum with flora & fauna exhibits, ethnic room. Gift shop with local crafts, pottery, selection of books, toys, souvenirs.

A lakeside restaurant, Konoba Badanj (see opposite), is alongside the Virpazar centre, as is an *enoteca* (wine store; opposite). Parking is available at both centres.

Tour operators

❉ Undiscovered Montenegro Virpazar; m 069 402364; e enquiries@undiscoveredmontenegro.com; www.undiscoveredmontenegro.com. Run by English couple Ben & Emma Heywood, who have made Virpazar their home since 2008 & know the Skadar region like the back of their hands. The first tour operator in the area dedicated to encouraging ecotourism, they are doing a huge amount for the region by using local suppliers & family-run businesses & focusing on sustainability & local culture. Small groups. Kayaking trips with fully qualified BCU kayak coach; boat trips; birdwatching trips; hiking excursions; wine tours & yoga holidays. English, German, French & Serbian spoken. Also offer rooms in the beautiful Villa Miela (below).

❉ ⚠ *Milica* Virpazar; m 067 755355, 068 702376; e dabanovicj@t-com.me. Friendly, reliable & knowledgeable local husband-&-wife team operating eco-friendly tours of the lake (inc birdwatching) on their small boat, *Milica*. Good English spoken.

🏠 Where to stay *Map, page 227.*

There's also a useful list of accommodation, including private rooms, at www.lake-skadar.com/accommodation.

❉ 🏠 Villa Miela (4 rooms) Just outside Virpazar; m 069 402364; e enquiries@undiscoveredmontenegro.com; www.undiscoveredmontenegro.com. Wonderful old stone villa, about 20mins' walk southeast of Virpazar, beautifully renovated by Ben & Emma Heywood. The house sleeps 8–10 guests, all in en-suite bedrooms. Large shared kitchen & open-plan living room with TV, DVD, etc. Enormous terrace with hot tub, loungers & BBQ, & panoramic views over the surrounding landscape. Free use of mountain bikes. Jun–Sep: 7-night stay inc self-catering accommodation, a welcome dinner, & 4 standard excursions/activities with lunch, from €575 pp; Oct–May dbl room €80 per night. 20% discount for under 14s. €€€€

🏠 Hotel Pelikan (8 rooms) Virpazar; ☎ 020 711107; e pelikanzec@t-com.me; www.pelikan-zec.com. A simple but attractively old-fashioned

hotel in the centre of town. Proprietors wait to meet bus arrivals in search of potential customers. Terraced restaurant, boats to rent. However, there have been reports of hiccoughs in staff/guest liaison, & a recent incident of unwanted advances towards a female guest on a boat trip, with the result that it would be inappropriate to recommend this hotel. €€€

🏠 Hotel Vir (22 rooms) Virpazar; ☎ 020 711120; e reservations@atlashotelsgroup; http://hotelvir.me. Formerly called 13 July. Beside the lake, rooms have bath & terrace. Restaurant & coffee bar. Not much English. €€€

🏠 Virski Pub (20 rooms & apts) Virpazar; m 069 594347; e virpazar.smestaj@gmai.com; ⊕ all year. A welcome new budget choice in town, right on the main square. Clean & friendly, offering dbl/trpl rooms & apts with en-suite bathrooms. €

� Where to eat and drink *Maps, page 224, 227.*

✗ **Jezero** Ground floor of visitor centre, Vranjina; ⊕ 10.00–22.00. National cuisine. Nicely appointed with great views over the lake. Owned by Plantaze vineyard so some interesting wines, but tiresome background music. €€€

∗ ✗ **Konoba Badanj** Virpazar; ⊕ 08.00–24.00. Next to visitor centre. Excellent, well-priced food in a relaxed lakeside setting with pretty views. Specialises in good local fish – inc some lovely grilled trout on the updater's visit. Tables indoors & on a vine-covered terrace beside the water. €€€

✗ **Pelikan** Details as for Hotel Pelikan (opposite page). Garden restaurant; lake specialities. €€€

⏛ **Crmnički Vinotok** Virpazar; ⊕ summer 10.00–22.00, winter 08.00–12.00. Local specialities such as smoked & dried carp with olive oil. €€

⏛ **Vinarija Đurišić** Zabes, 1km outside Virpazar; m 067 781111. Wine tastings, arranged by appointment. €€

Shopping

Enoteca **(wine store)** National Park Visitor Centre, Virpazar. Offers a comprehensive selection of local wines.

Voli supermarket At the entrance to the town from the main road.

What to see and do The ruins of **Fort Besac** stand on the top of **Besac Hill** directly above the town. Built by the Turks following the fall of Donja Zeta in 1478, it was in 1702 the scene of yet another bloodbath between Montenegrin and Turk. Virpazar changed hands many times, clearly its position on the lake of considerable strategic value.

Between the 20th-century world wars the fort served as the town police station and when World War II brought further conflict to the little town the Italians used it as a prison, after which it was abandoned. The large bronze monument on Karić rock at the foot of the hill, showing a Montenegrin warrior bearing weapons and flags, was put in place in 1964 over the remains of what is claimed to have been a watchtower of Bishop Prince Njegoš. The monument is a reminder both of the Battle of Besac and of the people of Crmnica (this region) who lost their lives in World War II.

AROUND VIRPAZAR Near Virpazar, where the road and rail causeway crosses the northwest corner of the lake, and where in April cream-and-gold waterlilies are in Monet-like profusion, the whiskered tern anchors her nest daintily on a floating leaf and the frogs hawk night and day in constant reminder that spring is a busy season.

Close to the **Virpazar–Vranjina** causeway are the prominent ruins of the stronghold **Lesendro**. Stories as to its provenance conflict but it is clear that it changed hands between Turk and Montenegrin more than once. Today only the sanguine-flowering Judas tree stands guard.

At the north end of the causeway, beneath the mammary peaks of the two **Vranjina** hills (a distinctive landmark, visible from far away – see them even as you descend from Cetinje), is the recently restored Orthodox **Monastery of Sv Nikola**, the oldest on the lake.

On the same tranquil belvedere are the remains of a half-completed house. It was built by King Nikola for his black-eyed tomboy daughter, Jelena: a fifth girl, whom he feared would remain a spinster. In the event she went on to marry the Prince of Naples, Victor Emmanuel, and soon became Queen of Italy. Today the house stands an empty shell.

Karuč The scruffy lake-edge fishing village of Karuč is not far from Virpazar. Reached along a minor road, its huts and dwellings spread haphazardly over the muddy banks of a reedy inlet, willow trailing among the little boats bumping patiently below, and goats, pigs and fowl of all varieties sharing equal rights with all comers.

The first passenger steamboat for cruising on Skadar Lake, and frequently referred to as **King Nikola's boat,** was built in Škodra, Albania, in 1914. It was in fact named *Skenderbeg* after the Albanian hero. It was sunk on 12 February 1942, during World War II, and now lies at 11m depth off the banks of Karuč.

� **Where to eat and drink** Karuč seems a rather extraordinary place to site a **restaurant,** even an inexpensive makeshift summer one, open-sided to the lake. And yet it grows on you.

✗ **Konoba Čudo Neviđeno** ⏱ 10.00–23.00. Whatever they have on the fire, meat or fish, tastes fine enough, the familiar Vranac is what you want to drink, & for those of a romantic disposition soon nothing could seem sweeter. Time will oblige & turn away, until you are ready to resume reality. €€

Žabljak Crnojevići
Near the mouth of the **Morača River**, within the borders of the national park, stands an outcrop crowned by the ruins of 15th-century Žabljak Crnojevići. These ruins were the capital of the first southern Slav state of Zeta before Ivan Crnojević and his people were driven by the Turks up the river which now bears his name, to Rijeka Crnojevića and thereafter in 1482 to Cetinje. It seems likely, though not yet proved, that this Žabljak fortress was built on previous Roman foundations. When the Zetans fled they torched their city behind them, but large parts of the walls, ramparts and towers remain, together with the machicolated main gate and the water cistern.

Because it is unprotected from both tourists and pilgrims, as well as the weather, the old town is decaying, but it remains a most impressive site in its own right as well as offering spectacular views over the lake and the adjoining countryside. Chances are you will have the place to yourself. Although the Montenegrin Ministry of Culture has focused on it as a site of major national importance, and a preliminary assessment was drawn up in 2005 under the auspices of the European Commission/Council of Europe Joint Programme on the 'Architectural and Archaeological Heritage of South East Europe', this has yet to be translated into a significant conservation plan.

Getting there If the water level in the lake is unusually high, Žabljak Crnojevići is an island, but almost always it can be reached by car along tarmac roads by turning west from the road to Podgorica at the only traffic light in the sprawling town of **Golubovci** and then following this smaller road, crossing two bridges, for 12km.

Rijeka Crnojevića
Heading west along the lake road from Virpazar brings you to the small village of Rijeka Crnojevića, which is also easily accessed from Cetinje. Close to the old bridge in the centre of the village are two restaurants, including one of the area's finest, Stari Most. The village also boasts a visitor centre, and is the starting point for kayak tours. For details, see pages 96–7.

Sotonići
At Sotonići, on the western Crmnica slopes of the old pre-tunnel road to Petrovac, there is a useful stopping place beside the road (see below).

By the church to the east just below the road you may encounter a queue at the spring, children dispatched to collect the family water.

Further on another turn west, with some fumbling through rambling lanes and by pretty cottage gardens, will bring you to **Brčeli** and the church of Sv Nikola, where impostor Šćepan Mali was buried after he was murdered by his servant (see page 178).

A wide tract of land west of the lake, below the northern entrance to the Sozina Tunnel, had been destined to become the site for the **Skadar Lake Golf and Country Club.** The project, like many other Montenegrin developers dreams, appears to have stalled.

Keep an eye open for turtles, which are common in the Skadar region.

✗ Where to eat and drink

✗ **Restaurant Voda u Kršu** (literally 'water from the crags') Sotonići; ☏020 712713; m 069 376876; www.vodaukrsu.com; ⊕ 10.00–22.00. Like so many others it features 'national food' but here the produce comes from these hills, the wine too, & there is a terrace where you might catch that fleeting moment when the last blush of sunset is fading from the crests of faraway Komovi. No CCs. €€

Plavnica Travelling in the direction of Podgorica, then turning right (southeast) in **Golubovci** beside a prominent white war memorial on a road signed to **Plavnica**, will bring you to a **recreation complex.** The access road is long and straight and although it leads no further than the inlet, it has historical significance in that a century ago Plavnica functioned as an important commercial port on the lake, with a tramway linking it to the towns of the Zetan plain. From there freight would be transported to and from Virpazar by barge. Virpazar in turn connected to the seaport of Bar by a mountain road or, after 1908, by a narrow-gauge railway which was the first of its kind in the country. As for the mountain road, it is now as long and steep and winding as then. The difference today is tarmac. It makes a good but tiring bike ride, with dramatic views at every turn as you climb through the majestic karst cliffs of the Rumija Massif to the lonely pass at Sutorman, and a rewarding freewheel down to the coastal plain. Do not attempt this road in bad weather, and it's probably best avoided late at night. It is subject to frequent mini-landslides, with fallen rocks to negotiate and kilometre upon kilometre without any sign of habitation.

✗ Where to stay and eat *Map, page 224.*

🏠 **Plavnica Eco Resort** (4 apts) ☏020 443700; www.plavnica.me. 2.8ha of landscaped riverside gardens with a marina, regular nightly music & entertainment in season, a large swimming pool built around a panoramic restaurant-boat & 2 shore restaurants with cocktail bars. The complex also has well-equipped apts, each with AC, TV & some with kitchenette, minibar & internet access. Plenty of secure parking. Marina berth for 30 days €100; hourly rentals: kayak €3–4, canoe €4, pedalo €6, catamaran €5, catamaran for 10 ppl €70. €€€€–€€€€€

6

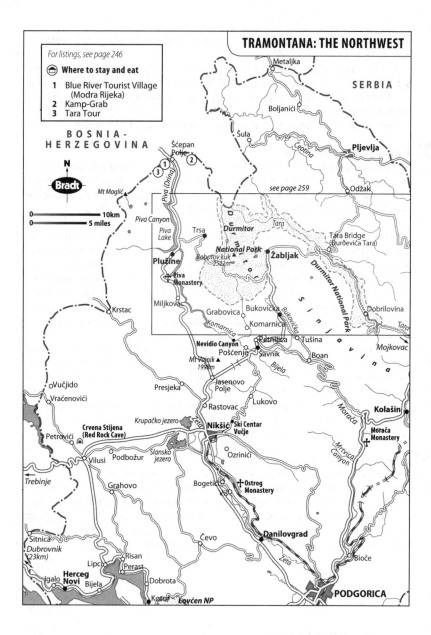

For listings, see page 246

Where to stay and eat

1 Blue River Tourist Village
   (Modra Rijeka)
2 Kamp-Grab
3 Tara Tour

BOSNIA-
HERZEGOVINA

N

Bradt

SERBIA

Metaljka

Boljanići

Šula

Pljevlja

Šćepan
Polje

Odžak

Mt Maglić

Piva (Drina)

0 _____ 10km
0 _____ 5 miles

Piva Canyon

Piva
Lake

Trsa

Durmitor

Tara

see page 259

Plužine

Piva
Monastery

Bobotov kuk
2523m

National Park

Žabljak

Tara Bridge
(Đurđevića Tara)

Durmitor National Park

Miljkova

Grabovica

Bukovička

Dobrilovina

Krstac

Komarnica

Komarnica

Bukovička

Tara

Nevidio Canyon

Retništa

Tušina

Sinjavina

Mojkovac

Mt Vojnik ▲
1998m

Poščenje

Savnik

Boan

Presjeka

Jasenovo
Polje

Bijela

oVučjido

Vraćenovići

Rastovac

Lukovo

Morača

Kolašin

Krupačko jezero

Zeta

Nikšić

Ski Centar
Vučje

Morača
Monastery

Crvena Stijena
(Red Rock Cave)

Mrtvica
Canyon

Petrovići

Vilusi

Podbožur

Slansko
jezero

Ozrinići

Trebinje

Grahovo

Bogetić

Ostrog
Monastery

Viš

Sitnica
Dubrovnik
(23km)

Čevo

Danilovgrad

Risan

Bioče

Lipci

Perast

Herceg
Novi

Igalo

Bijela

Dobrota

Zeta

Kotor

Lovćen NP

PODGORICA

7

Tramontana

PODGORICA TO NIKŠIĆ

Leaving Podgorica by highway 762, northwest towards Nikšić, the road travels through the fertile **Bjelopavlići** with any number of smallholdings on either side. Unemployment over the last decade of the 20th century encouraged individual initiative and many enterprises began in a small way by producing vegetables, fruit, milk and honey to sell at market. With a renewed sense of economic optimism such enterprise is visibly on the increase. In winter you will see necklaces of dried figs on sale at the roadside.

DANILOVGRAD Surrounded by thick woodland, Danilovgrad is some 17km northwest of Podgorica. The town developed from Petar II Petrović Njegoš's concept of its potential in a growing Montenegro, to be an ideal setting for a 19th-century capital to replace Cetinje. In his dream it would eventually connect, via widened Zeta and Morača rivers and Skadar Lake, with Škodra. After Njegoš's premature death, Prince Danilo extended the idea, establishing a new large bazaar on the banks of the Zeta. Gradually a settlement began to grow and following Danilo's assassination at Kotor in 1861 Prince Nikola, who succeeded him, had sophisticated urban plans drawn up. Unfortunately, the vicissitudes of Balkan history overtook the project and Danilovgrad was destined to remain a rather well laid-out minor town, overshadowed by Podgorica and Nikšić.

There is good trout fishing potential in the River Zeta. The Bjelopavlići Valley is also renowned for its **honey**. Buy it from stalls at Bogetići near Ostrog or elsewhere in the Danilovgrad area.

Getting there and away The good Podgorica–Nikšić highway passes Danilovgrad on the southwest side of the River Zeta. The smaller road that it replaced in general follows the northeast bank of the river.

There is a good bus service between Podgorica, Danilovgrad and Nikšić; fares are about €3 one way. For details contact the **bus station** in Danilovgrad (✆ *020 811711*).

Danilovgrad is the only intermediate station on the railway line from Podgorica to Nikšić, though for some time this line has only been used for freight.

For **taxis**, try **Taxi Maxi** (✆ *020 811812*).

Tourist information
🛈 Tourist Organisation of Danilovgrad Sava Burić 2; ✆ 020 816015; e info@danilovgrad.travel; www.tod.co.me

🏠 Where to stay

🏠 **Perjanik** (14 rooms, 2 apts) ☎020 813130; e hotelperjanik@t-com.me; www.perjanik.me. On the main Podgorica–Nikšić road, 3km from Danilovgrad & 20km from Podgorica, this well-regarded 4-star is popular with business travellers. Facilities include Wi-Fi, satellite TV, terraces, children's playground. Restaurant offers a wide variety of food & wine. €€€

🏠 **Pejović** (10 rooms) Ćurilac bb, Crikvenica; ☎020 810866. 4km from Danilovgrad on main highway to Podgorica. Simple rooms with AC, TV. 24hr restaurant (€€) with local ambience & menu. Laundry service. €€

✕ Where to eat and drink

The number of restaurants and cafés in the vicinity of the Ostrog Monastery (see opposite) is on the increase. Two good ones are in **Bogetići**, the first village after the turn-off from the highway:

✕ **Konoba Bogetići** m 069 222885; www. konoba.co.me. Local & national specialities inc lamb cooked in milk, Njeguši smoked ham, *raštan* (sea kale), etc, in rustic setting; can get crowded when a coach tour is in. €€€

✕ **Konoba Kolibe** m 067 888189; www. kolibe.me. Rustic setting near river; nice smells of wood fire; national specialities: smoked ham with melon, trout, eel & barbecued lamb. Can also be crowded with Ostrog tourists. They also have 5 rustic wooden chalet-style bungalows & 8 rooms (€€€). €€€

Nightlife If you want to sample Danilovgrad nightlife, your only choice is Discotheque Inter (*Baja Sekulića;* e *gigap123@hotmail.com*).

Other practicalities

Banks

$ **CKB** Baja Sekulića 22; ☎020 812532
$ **Podgorička Banka** Radosava Burića bb; ☎020 812704

Medical facilities

➕ **Hospital** ☎020 812106

Pharmacies

➕ **Montefarm** ul Baja Sekulića bb; ☎020 810175
➕ **Zdravlje** ul Novice Škerovića bb; ☎020 811220

Other

🎣 **Fishing** Contact SFA Trabuco; e ribolovici@t-com.me
🖥 **Internet café Zabave** West of central sq, opposite sculpture garden
✉ **Post office** ul Baja Sekulića bb; ☎020 811256; ⊕ 07.00–20.00 Mon–Sat

What to see Between the town square and a lovely stone bridge over the river is the **Danilovgrad Art Colony and Cultural Centre** (e *colonja@t-com.me; www.vajarska-kolonija.co.me;* ⊕ *10.00–15.00 Mon–Fri*), with some good modern sculptures in the local white marble, some on show in the gardens.

A small but interesting **Historical Museum and Library** (*Rsojevica, on the outskirts of town;* ☎ *020 812629;* e *ubzp@t-com.me;* ⊕ *08.00–16.00 Mon–Fri; entry free*), housed in the old palace of King Nikola, has an eclectic collection of archaeological finds, both Roman and medieval, militaria including World War II, maps, books and photographs.

Around Danilovgrad The Bjelopavlići Valley surrounding the town has some of the most beautiful **bridges** in Montenegro. Don't miss the creeper-covered stone bridge just north of Viš.

At **Gradini Martinići**, 5km from Danilovgrad on the old road to Podgorica, you can see the ruins of a Roman city, fortress and churches, presumed to have been some outpost of nearby Duklija (see pages 12 and 112); intriguing.

Ostrog Monastery The monastery was built – somehow – in the 17th century, by Vasilije Jovanović, Metropolitan of Western Herzegovina. Later he was to become Sv Vasilije (St Basil), and he never left. The saint's darkened bones may be visited in their sepulchral chapel, watched over by a black-robed, pigtailed monk. This chapel and another higher up, linked by a series of caves, narrow passageways and staircases, are decorated with paintings by the Serbian master artist Radul. The atmosphere is intense. Believer or not, tread softly. Beside the monastery is the *konak* (night quarters), a peaceful resting place for pilgrims and visitors alike, offering dormitory beds (separate men's and women's; €).

St Vasilije is credited as a healer and there are countless stories of miracles. Cracks and crevices are filled with coins and folded notes beseeching help. In the Orthodox Church such financial offerings are discouraged, but the desperate ignore this. In a draughty corner, on a high wooden balustraded ledge, a vine grows strongly. They will tell you that no other vine has been known to thrive in such a disadvantaged position. It is also claimed there has never been an accident on the approach road. Unfortunately the same cannot be said for the main road beyond.

Getting there If you're travelling by car, take a small road to the right, 15km beyond Danilovgrad at a crossroads near the crest of the hill, signed to Ostrog Monastery. This narrow road wends its way through beech, juniper and oak, becoming more precipitous and alpine by the minute. To maximise the effect take the road early in the day, or at dusk. In March the mists spiral ethereally from the valley floor and the woods are filled with violets and snowdrops. Maybe a great crusader eagle will sweep across the ravine bearing a rabbit to its mountain grave.

It is best to park at the lower **Church of the Holy Trinity**, built in 1820 within an existing garden and vineyard, and for the final half hour's climb take the pilgrims' path through the trees. You may fill your water bottle at the spring, reputed to have holy properties, behind the lower church. In summer there will be wild cyclamen to line the way, round and round and upward, ever upward (vehicular access is equally possible but parking at the top limited). As you turn the final bend the sight of the white monastery, lodged in the perpendicular rock, with hundreds of metres sheer rock above and below, is spectacular.

It is possible, if not entirely straightforward, to use public transport to reach the monastery on your way to Nikšić. Take the Podgorica–Nikšić bus and ask to be dropped off at the Ostrog turning. There you will find taxis waiting to take pilgrims to the monastery. Negotiate a rate for the round trip to the monastery plus waiting time – and your onward journey as well, unless you want to take your chances on stopping a passing bus after your detour. The complete trip (Danilovgrad–Ostrog–Nikšić), including two hours' waiting time, should cost €20–25.

For Nikšić, return to the main crossroad and turn right on the E762.

NIKŠIĆ

Modern Nikšić, Montenegro's Birmingham, dates from the end of the 19th century and is now the country's second-largest town, known in all quarters for its eponymous and palatable beer. After the break-up of the old Republic of Yugoslavia, Nikšić suffered under the same straitened circumstances as the other inland towns in Montenegro, caused by a major fall in business and tourist revenue. But with the advent of the new millennium, the easing of Balkan tensions and Montenegro's definitive independence, the situation is becoming rosier. At the end of the 1990s the Belgian group Interbrew acquired a major share in the brewery, becoming the largest single foreign investor in Crna Gora at that time and setting the way for others to follow. The general outlook now is optimistic and as elsewhere there is an expectant buzz about the place.

HISTORY Soon after the expulsion of the Turks in 1877 Sir Arthur Evans, the British archaeologist, visited this area. He was intrigued by the place, knowing it had been inhabited since ancient times, that earliest records referred to it as Anderva and that it had passed through many hands. Evans deduced that there had been a Roman settlement here, dating from the late Classical period and founded between the 3rd and 4th centuries, when it appears to have marked the intersection of at least two important military and trade routes linking it to neighbouring and distant territories. The Roman town was demolished by repeated incursions from numerous barbarian tribes, ultimately the Goths, who then fortified themselves against Byzantium in the late 5th century. The Gothic city became known as **Anagastum** after its military leader, Anagast. It was later subject to frequent dispute between the Byzantines and the Slavs and by the 14th century that name had been adapted to **Onogošt**. The Slavs, however, considering themselves to be the rightful occupants, simultaneously and informally began to refer to the town as **Nikšić**, after the local tribe or clan. In the 15th century, when the Turks became the occupiers, they built a fortress on the Gothic and medieval foundations and called it **Bedem**.

GETTING THERE There are various **bus lines** linking the city with Podgorica (€3) and the coast (€6). **Buses** from Podgorica are every 15 minutes from approximately 08.00 to midnight; from Budva there are 12 buses a day and some ten from Kotor. The new bus station (*Gojka Garčevića;* ✆ *040 213018; left luggage €1*) is five minutes from the town centre.

Although a **railway** line connects Podgorica with Nikšić, at the time of writing there is no passenger service between the two places, only freight; this line has opened and closed a few times in recent years. In the past there were two trains daily leaving Podgorica at 06.45 and 14.55, reaching the end of the line at Nikšić via Danilovgrad, with return journeys starting at 04.00 and 12.15. To see whether this service has surprisingly restarted (as has been promised for some years) contact the railway station (✆ *040 214480*).

GETTING AROUND Nikšić has a bustling main street with plenty of cafés along Njegoševa, leading northeast from the bus and railway stations. There's **parking** just north of trg Slobode, off Njegoševa.

Taxi companies include Maxi Trade (✆ *040 200300*) and Nik Taxi (✆ *19733*). **Car hire** is available from Holand Auto (*Strasevina bb;* ✆ *040 253347*).

TOURIST INFORMATION
🆔 **Tourist office** Ivana Milutinovića 10, 81400 Nikšić; ✆ 040 213262; e info@niksic.travel; www. niksic.travel.

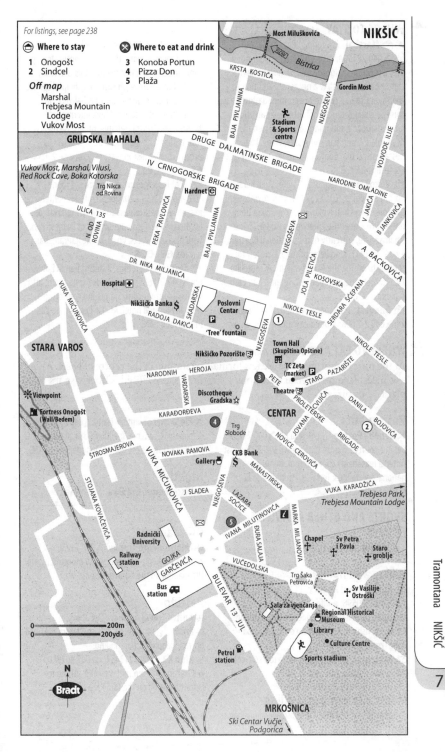

For listings, see page 238

🛏 **Where to stay**
1 Onogošt
2 Sindcel

Off map
   Marshal
   Trebjesa Mountain
   Lodge
   Vukov Most

❌ **Where to eat and drink**
3 Konoba Portun
4 Pizza Don
5 Plaža

Most Miluškovića

Bistrica

KRSTA KOSTIĆA

Gordin Most

BAJA PIVLJANINA

NJEGOŠEVA

Stadium & Sports centre

VOJVODE ILIJE

GRUDSKA MAHALA

DRUGE DALMATINSKE BRIGADE

NARODNE OMLADINE

*Vukov Most, Marshal, Vilusi,
Red Rock Cave, Boka Kotorska*

IV CRNOGORSKE BRIGADE

Trg Nikca od Rovina

Hardnet @

V JAKICA

B JANKOVIĆA

ULICA 135

PEKA PAVLOVIĆA

BAJA PIVLJANINA

NJEGOŠEVA

A BACKOVIĆA

N OD ROVINA

DR NIKA MILJANIĆA

JOLA PILETIĆA

KOSOVSKA

SERDARA ŠĆEPANA

Hospital ✚

SKADARSKA

NIKOLE TESLE

NIKOLE TESLE

VUKA MIĆUNOVIĆA

Nikšićka Banka $

Poslovni Centar

RADOJA DAKIĆA

P

'Tree' fountain

NJEGOŠEVA

①

Town Hall (Skupština Opštine)

PAZARIŠTE

STARA VAROS

NARODNIH HEROJA

VARDARSKA

Nikšićko Pozorište 🎭

TC Zeta (market)

P STARO

DANILA

☀ Viewpoint

Fortress Onogošt (Wall/Bedem)

KARAĐORĐEVA

Discotheque Gradska ☆

③ PETE

Theatre 🎭

PROLETERSKE

JOVANA

BOJOVIĆA

CENTAR

④ Trg Slobode

NOVICE CEROVIĆA

BRIGADE

②

ŠTROSMAJEROVA

NOVAKA RAMOVA

Gallery 🎨

CKB Bank $

MANASTIRSKA

VUKA KARADŽIĆA

*Trebjesa Park,
Trebjesa Mountain Lodge*

STOJANA KOVAČEVIĆA

VUKA MIĆUNOVIĆA

J SLADEA

NJEGOŠEVA

LAZARA SOČICE

IVANA MILUTINOVIĆA

⑤

MARKA MILJANOVA

ℹ

Chapel ✝

Sv Petra i Pavla ✝

Staro groblje ✝

Radnički University

ĐURA SALAJA

Railway station

GOJKA GARČEVIĆA

Bus station 🚌

VUČEDOLSKA

BULEVAR 13 JUL

Trg Šaka Petrovića

Sala za vjenčanja

Sv Vasilije Ostroški ✝

Regional Historical Museum

Library

0 —— 200m
0 —— 200yds

● Culture Centre

Petrol station ⛽

Sports stadium

N

Bradt

MRKOŠNICA

*Ski Centar Vučje,
Podgorica* ▼

⌂ WHERE TO STAY *Map, page 237.*

✳ ⌂ **Marshal** (16 rooms) Partizanski put bb; ☎040 223504; e reception@marshalgroup.me; www.marshalgroup.me. 3km from town centre on road north & a necessary addition to the town's sparse choice of accommodation, this is a clean & functional businessman's hotel, located above a shopping complex. Friendly staff. AC, cable TV, minibar, room safe, Wi-Fi, jacuzzi. Restaurant & bar. Conference room, parking. CCs accepted. €€€€

⌂ **Vukov Most** (9 rooms, 1 suite) Vuka Karadžića bb, Kapino polje; ☎040 257131; e vukovmost@t-com.me; www.hotelvukovmost.com. 2km from town centre, near the eponymous bridge (& near a small airfield, currently non-operational but from where, in 1941, King Peter of Yugoslavia left the country to escape the Axis invasion). AC, satellite TV, internet, safe, minibar, restaurant & bar. Garden & parking. €€€€

⌂ **Onogošt** (189 rooms & 3 suites) ul Njegoševa 24; ☎040 243608; e onogost@gmail.com; www.

htponogost.me. Centrally located, round the corner from Slobode Square. Though a slightly gloomy monument to socialist realism, this is actually a comfortable hotel with extremely helpful service. Spacious rooms with bath, TV & balcony; lift. Bar, restaurant & casino. Shop, internet café & hairdresser. B/fast is reliable; otherwise meals resembling school dinners are available. CCs accepted. 20% discount for stays of over 2 days. €€€ (FB €€€€)

⌂ **Trebjesa Mountain Lodge** (8 rooms) Trebjesa bb; ☎077 200060; e info@hoteltrebjesa.me; www.hoteltrebjesa.me. Newly renovated. Located in the dense pinewoods of Trebjesa Park, with pleasant walks. Wi-Fi, TV. Restaurant, bar, terrace. €€–€€€

⌂ **Sindcel** (11 rooms, 2 suites) Danila Bojovića bb; ☎040 213655; e sindcelnk@gmail.com; http://sindcel.blogspot.com. Simple but comfortable, centrally located hotel. AC, TV. Restaurant, bar, fitness room. €€

✗ WHERE TO EAT AND DRINK *Map, page 237.*

At the time of writing there are few formal restaurants in the centre of Nišić. Arkade – a nice place for special occasions – has now sadly closed. Otherwise it's pizza, pizza … or pizza.

Restaurants

✗ **Konoba Portun** Njegoševa bb; ☎040 212336. Set in a courtyard close to the town hall & Onogošt Hotel, a reasonably cheerful spot, featuring national specialities. Terraces. Parking. Visa & MasterCard accepted. €€

✗ **Plaža** Ivana Milutinovića 10; ☎040 213262; e toniksic@t-com.me. Traditional Balkan cuisine. €€
✗ **Pizza Don** West side of Slobode Square. €€

Nightlife

☆ **Discotheque Gradska** Njegoševa bb

SPORTS AND OTHER ACTIVITIES

Fishing
⌇ **SFA Nikšić** ☎040 241417

Hiking and biking
🚲 **Anitra Travel Agency** PC 'Atrium', Njegoševa 12; ☎040 200598; e info@anitra.me; www.tara-grab.com. Rafting, hiking, biking, climbing, kayaking, fishing. Also have an office in Šćepan Polje (m 069 101002).
🚲 **Skytours** ☎040 212266; e skytours@t-com.me; www.skytoursmn.com

Mountaineering and skiing
⛷ **Javorak** m 067 560170; e psdjavorak@yahoo.com

Off-roading
🚙 **Montenegro Trophy** ☎040 212509; e monttrophy@t-com.me; www.monttrophy.me. Off-roading on the Krnovo Plateau.

Rafting
🛶 **Anitra Travel Agency** See above.
🛶 **Fram** ☎040 200530; e fram@t-com.me. Also off-road jeeping & paragliding.
🛶 **Klub K2** ☎040 213431; m 067 401880; e K2rafting@t-com.me; www.K2-rafting.me. Extreme rafting on the Tara River.

OTHER PRACTICALITIES

Banks
$ **Atlasmont Banka** ul Serdara Šćepana S/70
$ **CKB** Njegoševa br 23
$ **Hipotekarna Banka** Njegoševa 16
$ **Komercijalna Banka** Njegoševa 23
$ **Montenegrobanka** Karađorđeva 10
$ **Nikšićka Banka** ul Radoja Dakića br 2; also Njegoševa 16 & Krug Željezare
$ **Opportunity Bank** trg Slobode 22
$ **Podgorička Banka** trg Slobode 3

Medical facilities
✚ **General hospital** ☏040 244216
✚ **Pulmonary Institute Brezovik** ☏040 371099

Pharmacies
✚ **Iković** ul Narodnih heroja br 18; ☏040 213216
✚ **Latković** ul Pete Proleterske br 11; ☏040 213455
✚ **Remedia** Vardarska br 3; ☏040 213022

Other
Gradska Knjižara (City Books) Karađorđeva 2; ⊕ 10.00–20.00 Mon–Sat
✳ 🖳 **Internet café Hardnet** 6 Crnogorske bb. All sorts of laptop assistance; very helpful.
✉ **Post office** trg S Kovačevića br 3; ⊕ 07.00–20.00

WHAT TO SEE AND DO Near the railway station on the west side of the city, a large section of the old walls and fortress has been restored to create a venue for cultural events, a theatre and a platform for the city orchestra. Look for the first street within these walls; it has an attractive row of cottages apparently hardly changed since the 16th century.

King Nikola's once-elegant **Royal Palace**, built in 1900 and, like the residence at Topolica in Bar, a carbon copy of Prince Danilo's Blue Palace in Cetinje, is now the **Regional Historical Museum** (*trg Šaka Petrovića;* ☏ *040 212977; e czk-nk@t-com.me;* ⊕ *08.00–12.00 & 17.00–20.00 Tue–Sun; adult/child €1/0.50*). Its archaeological and ethnographical collection includes exhibits relating to the prehistoric Red Rock Cave site (see pages 240–2). Between this and the large Orthodox temple dedicated to **Sv Vasilije Ostroški** (see also page 235), built at the same time but upon 13th-century foundations, there is an ancient graveyard with *stećci* (see box, page 261) and nearby the medieval church of **Sv Petra i Pavla** (St Peter and St Paul).

The last decades of the 19th century saw the creation of a new town, and a comprehensive plan was drawn up at the instigation of King Nikola by the engineer Josip Slade. He envisaged a grid of wide avenues crossed by smaller streets leading to an inner-city square (**trg Slobode** or Freedom Square) in which the plan provided for a harmonious arrangement of smaller plebeian dwellings on two floors. These now house an assortment of shops and cafés. Situated behind the Onogošt Hotel, the square is the hub of the early evening *passeggiata*.

From this time too, and not far from town (near Pandurića, on the old road to Podgorica), the **Tsar's Bridge**, with its 16 arches of stone, spans the **River Zeta**. Designed by the ever-diligent engineer Josip Slade, it is so named because it was funded by an extravagant gift from the Russian emperor. Nikšić is fortunate in having an extensive green area within the city limits. **Trebjesa** ('natural landscape') **Park** is to the southeast of King Nikola's palace, thickly wooded and rising up a hill from which to look down on the town.

Ski Centar Vučje This sports recreation centre (**m** *067 319719; e* vucje.niksic@ gmail.com; *www.vucje.me*) can be reached by taking the old road south from the bus station in the direction of Podgorica, passing a flea market, and after 6km turning northeast for Lukovo. The small ski centre lies some 14km further on, in the direction of Šavnik, 1,300m up on the slopes of the Kmovo Plateau. There are three ski lifts varying in length from 1,000m to 120m and a total of seven ski runs or paths, mostly better suited to novices or children. A day pass for adult/child is €10/5. Pony rides for children. There are seasonal bus connections with town, leaving from the front of the Onogošt Hotel between 08.00 and 09.20, returning between 15.15 and 16.30.

Where to stay

Ski Centar Motel (7 rooms, 9 apts); m 067 319719; e vucje.niksic@gmail.com; www. vucje.me. Equipment can be rented. Restaurant in season (€€). Sgl occupancy +20%; children up to 12 less 50% sharing parents' room. FB & HB inc ski pass. €€–€€€

Red Rock Cave To the west, near the Herzegovina border at **Crvena Stijena**, is the thrilling Red Rock Cave, where the oldest traces of Neanderthal man in Montenegro

A PARTISAN RESCUE MISSION BY SOE

By 22 August 1944 the war in northern Europe was going quite well for the Allies, with successes in France as well as in Russia. The story in Yugoslavia was rather different, with the beleaguered Partisan forces under constant German attack. The Partisan Second Division in Montenegro was under particular pressure, severely outnumbered and outgunned by Nazi troops and struggling to protect an increasingly large column of wounded.

Transporting the stretcher cases, who were only those physically incapable of walking, was a mammoth task in the Durmitor region. Many of the stretcher bearers were young women, sometimes covering 20km a day but at others managing only 500m when a deep ravine and a river lay on the route. The risk of the Partisans being overrun and slaughtered by the German Army was real and growing. Progress was slow and manpower was being absorbed by medical duties. Some of the surviving wounded had been travelling for four months with minimal skilled attention or drugs. Malnutrition and infection were standard, typhus and malaria not uncommon.

SOE personnel travelling with the Partisans included two seconded RAF officers, Flt Lt Philip Lawson and Flt Lt Thomas Mathias. They agreed with RAF HQ in Italy that the only hope was an airlift. But first they would have to construct a temporary airstrip in the mountains, long enough to take Dakotas. Lawson was sent ahead of the column, together with a British Army Major, a Partisan engineer and a few couriers, to reconnoitre a site. They were clever or lucky enough to find one near the hamlet of Brezna. The ground was not ideal, being on a slight slope covered by a wheat field, with fences and trenches across it. But the advance party mobilised the population of the five nearest villages who came willingly from miles around to scythe their unripe crops, destroy their fences, fill in their ditches and clear the ground of rocks by carrying them away in wooden buckets.

Two Spitfires came over and dropped message bags to confirm that Dakotas, both British and American, were on their way. White parachute canopies were put out as markers and grass fires lit to show wind direction, which by the grace of God was down the slight slope so the visitors were able to land up the gradient and into the wind. Very shortly waves of Allied aircraft arrived, Dakotas to carry the wounded and Spitfires and Mustangs to protect the Dakotas.

Incredibly, more than 900 wounded were evacuated, with Wing Cdr James Polson as senior medical officer to supervise the evacuation. By the last take-off the Germans were less than 8km away and a few hours later they had occupied Brezna.

have been found. Archaeologists have worked through 31 strata and are still digging, though at the time of writing work appears to be suspended. Other significant caves are located in Morača and Piva canyons, as well as near Risan in the Boka Kotorska and Gusinje in the east, and there is a vast cave complex east of Bijelo Polje (see pages 274–7). Much remains to be discovered and one cannot stress enough what potential interest this extraordinary little country holds in store historically.

Getting there Finding the cave can be a serious initiative test: take the main road west from the city in the direction of **Vilusi** (30km) and Trebinje. At Vilusi turn right (north) on a small road to **Broćanac-Grahovski** and **Vraćenovići** and after 13km make a left turn in the direction of **Petrovići**. The cave is near the **Trebišnjica River** and almost on the border. Follow the road until it ends, just past a large walled estate on the right, and park on the grass. Head straight on towards a cliff

To find the airstrip, take Route 762 almost due north of Nikšić in the direction of Plužine. Halfway there, in the village of Bajovo Polje, turn right to the hamlet of Donja Brezna. On the edge of the straggle of houses, look for one which bears a Cyrillic memorial on its wall. In translation the plaque reads:

In August 1944 an airfield of the National Liberation Army (NOV) was constructed on this field from which 700 wounded partisans were transported to Italy for medical treatment.

Veterans' Association of Plužine

The original plaque somewhat understates the number involved and makes no mention of who planned the airstrip or who flew the aircraft. But it was put up in 1961, when political realities were different.

Look out for a gentle slope about 760m long without any looming mountains that might interrupt the flight of a Dakota. That's where it happened.

Philip Lawson was 23 when he laid out the airstrip. In 1940 he had gone up to Oxford but left almost at once to join the forces, qualifying first as a bomber pilot, flying transport planes in North Africa and serving with 223 Bomber Squadron in Sicily. After the fall of Rome an interview with Fitzroy Maclean in Viš led to a posting in Montenegro with the Partisan Second Division with whom he remained until February 1945. Subsequently he returned to the RAF and 500 Squadron, and was engaged on night intruder operations until the end of the war, when he went back to Balliol.

Note: The above account first appeared in the second edition of this guide, printed in 2005, and was the first published report of the rescue. In 2008 it was reprinted in the third edition and duly caught the imagination of the then British Ambassador in Podgorica. He brought it to the attention of the Montenegrin Government and the UN Office in Montenegro. The happy ending to the story is that on 3 September 2009 the Montenegrin Minister of Defence, the Ambassador, the UN Coordinator and, most importantly, Philip Lawson, attended a ceremony and flypast at Brezna to pay tribute to those who participated in the extraordinary rescue and to unveil a new plaque commemorating the event.

which is, indeed, of reddish rock. You will soon reach an area which is fenced off, but the gate is not locked. Walk along a short path past signs warning you of the risk of falling in, until you come to a steep ladder leading down to a muddy pool with bats wheeling around the cave entrance. This is where sensible people stop unless and until they can find a guide.

North of the cave and still close to the border, on the road that connects Vraćenovići with Vrbica, is the monumental 19th-century battlefield of **Vučji do**. A detachment flag riddled with Turkish bullets is displayed in the state museum in Cetinje (page 87). It holds great significance for Montenegrins.

TOWARDS RISAN AND THE BOKA KOTORSKA

Much of the route linking Nikšić with the Boka Kotorska (65km) is covered by a new road opened at the end of 2010. It leaves Nikšić in the westward direction of Vilusi and Trebinje. To view the beautiful Roman **Moštanica Bridge** (*Most na Moštanici*), turn left after approximately 7km, as signed, then where this road divides bear left on to an unsigned track. The five-arched cobble-stoned bridge is believed to be 3rd century. It lies in pastoral land not far from a small farmhouse with rather grand gates. One wonders if there was also a Roman settlement here. In a nearby field there is evidence of *stećci* (see box, page 261).

Returning to the main route, the road to the coast passes high above – and with fine views over – lakes **Slansko** and **Krupačko**. It then continues through scrubby moorland, arid and stony (a nameless café – advertising *Bavaria* beer – is a pit hardly worth the stop, were it not for a World War I and II memorial across from it), before bearing left at Vilusi and gradually descending towards the Adriatic. At the start of the downward journey, travelling through Arcadian countryside, with glimpses to picture-book valleys far below, the descent becomes steeper from the **Krivošije** region in the foothills of the **Orjen Massif** and in summer the land becomes drier and drier, with patches of *garrigue* struggling through the karst, and more karst. It's hard to believe, but *Encyclopedia Britannica* confirms that Crkvice's claims to the highest levels of precipitation in Europe are accurate. Care should be exercised when driving, even more so on a bike, as most of the tunnels are as yet unlit. The views of the Boka from Queen Teuta's suicide cliff, while not quite matching in drama those from the Ladder of Cattaro, are splendid nonetheless.

GRAHOVO Some 25km from Nikšić, at **Podbožur**, make a left turn (southwest) on a small road to **Grahovo**. Ignore the right turn after 4km and another one after a further 5km. For the next 8km the road swings through remote woodland and *maquis*-covered hills before descending into Grahovo, a dusty, melancholy little town that's never really recovered from serious earthquake damage in 1979. (Buses from Nikšić are infrequent but you might negotiate a lift in an independent minibus.) There's also a shorter (unasphalted) route to Grahovo, turning from the main road just before **Dragalj**.

Leave your vehicle by the small café/shop on the right of the linden-lined street and climb the grassy bank to the west to view the colossal rectangular battlefield, a soccer pitch for giants, where on May Day 1858 Montenegro scored an important victory over her long-time Turkish foe and, in so doing, secured international recognition and the return of much of her territory in the Nikšić region.

To put it in perspective take the steps up to the top of the large war memorial. It reflects several conflicts – Serbian, Montenegrin, Yugoslav Partisan – and is sadly neglected. But looking out over the field of the original battle of Grahovo, the lie of the land cannot have changed. One can still sense the battle, feel the adrenalin. Time and again it is so at these great theatres of war, the vibrations are there in the ether. Was there perhaps a dash of sport to the event? After all, Montenegrins will wryly recall the apocryphal battle when, having captured all the Turkish weapons, they felt obliged to return some so that action might recommence. They will tell you that when Montenegrins have no-one left to fight, they will fight each other; hence the long, long history of tribal blood feuds and *izmirenje* (reconciliation). Above all, as Italian 19th-century traveller Antonio Martini wrote:

> [his] racial pride and an excessive sense of his own bravery together with chivalrous ideas inculcated since childhood, instil into a Montenegrin's appearance and gait a sense of elevation and dignity that make him stand out in the eyes of a foreigner.

This reference could equally be applied to the women (see *Jelica Mašković*, page 293).

NIKŠIĆ TO PLUŽINE AND THE BOSNIAN BORDER

The Podgorica–Nikšić highway leads on to Plužine and the northwest of the country. Nikšić to Plužine is 60km and a further 20km will bring you to the border with Bosnia at Šćepan Polje.

BACK ROADS AND BYWAYS: CETINJE TO GRAHOVO

Note: *For important practical hints on tackling Montenegro's back roads and byways, see box, page 50.*

A long and lonely road twists through a wild karst landscape to link **Cetinje** with the neglected but historic town of **Grahovo**, a distance of about 60km. It is asphalt all the way but there are no facilities for refreshments or for petrol *en route*. If you do not have your own transport, you might be able to pick up a local Iminibus from Cetinje bus station, serving the scattering of outlying communities. But the stalwart characters who remain in these isolated regions are largely self-sufficient and any service will be infrequent.

Leave Cetinje by the road to the west through Lovćen National Park, in the direction of Njeguši and Kotor, but at Čekanje fork right (north) at a sign to Resna. (A police car often patrols this junction and you may be asked to show your papers, so make sure you have them with you.) Turn left at Resna, in the direction of Grab and Tršnjevo. Now, above and below, there is barren rock on every side. Even on a sunny August day the outlook seems bleak. It comes as a surprise therefore when, after a few kilometres, a bend reveals a grassy valley, fruit trees and an immaculate smallholding, the reinstated national flag fluttering proudly from its wall. As the journey goes on these fertile pockets become ever more prevalent, a field with a mare and her foal; a farmer, bucket in hand, striding purposefully towards a precious spring channelled gratefully into a tiny reservoir; a row of beehives; sunflowers, and then in the middle of nowhere in particular, a deserted post office, its letterbox shining yellow.

Finally, after winding around a series of wide punch bowls and by groves of a red-leafed shrub which, infuriatingly, the author is unable to identify, the road reaches the outskirts of poor, forgotten Grahovo. 'Only the nature is beautiful,' regretted Father Luka back at the monastery. About this, he is correct.

7

From the outskirts of Nikšić the road reaches high ground above the Zeta Valley and follows a ridge northward through pasture and beechwood, with the pewter **Golija escarpment** away to the west and the distant ribbon of the Komarnica River to the east shimmying through the green glen leading to the Piva. Near the village of **Miljkovać** you can find the defiant **Doli Memorial**, erected in remembrance of 500 elderly men, women and children, civilians executed by the Axis in an act of reprisal in June 1943. The monument shows three lifted arms, man, woman and child; arms that embody labour, love and life.

This should be a reasonable route at any time of the year, bearing in mind that once into the mountains any side trips should be restricted to the summer months. More remote districts such as Šavnik can be cut off from the external world for much of the winter. At the best of times a 4x4 is the sensible option for more extensive adventures.

PLUŽINE

The little town of Plužine, where many families were displaced as a result of conflict in neighbouring countries, currently has few conventional facilities for tourists. Most visitors are attracted to the area by the Piva Canyon and Piva Lake, or the Piva Monastery.

GETTING THERE There is a **bus station** (✆ *040 271239*) and five buses daily to Plužine from Podgorica (€7) and from Nikšić (€3.50). One bus in the middle of the night passes through Plužine on the way from Bosnia to Herceg Novi.

TOURIST INFORMATION
🄯 **Tourist office** ul Baja Pivljanina bb; ✆040 270068; e topluzine@t-com.me; www.pluzine. travel.

🏠 **WHERE TO STAY AND EAT** The old village is situated behind an upper, unpaved parking area and in front of the old state-run Hotel Piva. Families who have come back to the town have now either returned to their lands or are settled locally in new purpose-built apartments, and the Piva, where they temporarily lodged, has been tidied up. Local **ethno villages** – traditional wooden or stone cottages in a beautiful, rustic setting – offer hearty local cuisine, and **camping** is usually possible as well. Some are include here; for others, see the tourist office website (*www. pluzine.travel/page.php?scat=32*). A room in a farmhouse could be an agreeable alternative but foreign languages are not a local speciality.

🏠 **Ecovillage Jugoslavia** (7 bungalows, camping) Crkvićko polje, Piva bb; m 069 615431; e ekoseloyu@t-com.me; www.ekoseloyu. com. Fully equipped bungalows with private bathrooms, sleeping 2–4, in beautiful rural surroundings. Restaurant serving national cuisine. Campsite available. Parking. Horseriding can be arranged; plus rafting, boat cruises on Piva Lake & biking. €€

🏠 **Etno Selo (Ethno Village) Izlazak** (8 cabins, 1 cottage) 13km outside Plužine on the road to Nikšić; m 069 635412 (English spoken), 069 476277; e nvnvg@t-com.me; www.etno-selo-izlazak.me. In unspoilt countryside on the edge of the Piva Canyon; cabins sleep 2–4 ppl. Small children's playground, ethno museum, restaurant (€€) which prepares everything from scratch, inc the bread. They also organise boat rides on Piva Lake, jeep safaris & rafting on the Tara. €–€€

🏠 **Etno Selo Montenegro** (10 bungalows, camping) Brezna, Piva; m 067 209049; e etnoselo. mn@gmail.com; www.etno-selo.me. Owners

Mico & Radonja Blagović provide a variety of stone & wooden bungalows/cabins, surrounded by meadows or forest, by the Piva Canyon, & with a rustic restaurant (€) in beautiful tranquil surroundings. 'Disneyland Cottage' with adjacent playground good for those travelling with kids. Secluded 'Love Cottages' aimed at couples on a romantic break. They also have a campsite & organise rafting (*€25 pp*), lake boating & jeep safaris. €–€€

🏠 **Eko Selo Milogora** (5 huts) Piva village, off the road to Žabljak; m 068 522410 (minimal English); e milogoratrsa@yahoo.com. Simple accommodation in healthy rural surroundings with plenty of free advice on outdoor pursuits & reasonable home cooking (€€) featuring local lamb. €

🏠 **Piva** (20 rooms) ul Baja Pivljanina bb; ☎040 271132. A bit tatty but quite adequate for a night or 2 in a town where accommodation is still scarce. Rooms with 2 sgls seem generally in better shape than dbls. Restaurant & bar; good lake views. €

✗ **Carine Sočica** Across from Piva Hotel; ☎040 271133. Pretty country restaurant named after Lazar Sočica, duke of this commune at the time of

the kingdom. Informally it is known as 'the pub where the boy said no to the king'. The story goes like this: no-one was supposed to answer the king in the negative but once, when dining here, Nikola enquired of the waiter if the soup was salted. 'No,' replied the boy, 'would you like me to add some?' (Presumably 'yes, but very little' would have been the wiser response.) The menu is limited but lamb & trout from the Piva are specialities – & of course the Vranac, as full-blooded as ever. The dining room is log-fire cosy, but by early Apr one would instead opt for a table on the terrace looking out on an ungrazed meadow of wild flowers & almond blossom. If you look contented the patron might bring you a plate of walnuts fresh from the garden. They also offer combined Piva tours to the monastery & boating on the lake, plus a 2-course lunch. €€

✗ **Zvono** Plužine; m 069 471893 (English spoken); www.zvono.me. Lakeside restaurant serving national cuisine. Rooms available (€€), as well as tours & excursions. Homemade mead. €€

✗ **Café Bar Ciro** Plužine turn-off from the main road, just before the EKO petrol station. Fine for light meals; something of a local pub. €

SPORTS AND OTHER ACTIVITIES
Fishing
🎣 **SFA Bajo Pivljanin** m 069 990762

Rafting
🚣 **Rafting Eko Piva** m 069 070997; e info@ raftingmontenegro.com; www.raftingmontenegro.com. Rafting on Tara River; cruising on Piva Lake; canyoning in Nevidio, Škurda, Mrtvica; mountaineering Durmitor & Komovi. Transport & accommodation can be arranged.

🚣 **Tara Tour** m 069 086106; e taratour@t-com.me; www.tara-tour.com. Based in Plužine. Wooden & rubber rafts. Reputed to offer the most serious rafting; €70 for half a day's whitewater rafting, inc b/fast & lunch.

🚣 **Rafting Tara** Šćepan Polje; m 069 216506; www.rafting-tara.me.

OTHER PRACTICALITIES
➕ **Pharmacy** Montefarm ☎040 270001
✉ **Post office** Njegoševa bb

WHAT TO SEE Turn left as you exit the Carine Sočica tavern and follow a short lane round the corner to find **Marshal Tito's 1942 headquarters** for the Partisan Brigade: an old stone farmhouse, its shingled roof typical of the region and topped with a thatching of rush. There is talk of a future museum. Meantime try asking in nearby cottages for a key. A few years ago it was an extraordinary time-locked place, its rooms and contents apparently resting undisturbed during the 65-year interim, but at the time of writing there were disturbing barbed-wire signs that it might be reverting to a private dwelling without due regard for its history. Interestingly, it is in this neighbourhood that the British SOE operative

Atherton and his team were last reported alive (see box on the submarine landing at Petrovac in 1942, page 193).

AROUND PLUŽINE

If you fly into Montenegro's principal airport, Podgorica, from Belgrade or anywhere north, you share the view of the imperial eagle – *Aquila heliaca* – of the extraordinary hinterland of this tiny country, the strangely faceted pinnacles, the crushed-velvet plateaux and the shadowy abysses of the gorges slicing through them: Piva, Durmitor, Tara, Komovi, Prokletije.

Remember the words of Gladstone: 'Do not forget glorious immortal Montenegro.' What a shame he never saw this spellbinding picture show. The expressive features of the landscape have been composed by the peculiar properties of this honeycomb of limestone known as karst.

> rivers burst abruptly from underground or spring fully-fledged from walls of rock, torrent foaming through gorges, only to vanish as unexpectedly into gaping holes and reappear miles further on

was how Cuddon described it.

Superior knowledge of their terrain has given the indigenes huge advantage over would-be invaders. It is not hard to figure out why those Austrians at Cetinje in 1916 commanded the construction of that highly detailed relief model we can still see at Biljarda (page 86). Today the characteristic topography – alp and plateau perforated by sinkholes and caves, the underground channels and cascading white water – are increasingly the focus of recreational activity, not just from enthusiasts of traditional trekking, on foot and horseback, mountaineering and skiing, but also of those searching for newer conquests in the form of so-called extreme sports: rafting, canyoning, bungee jumping, hang-gliding, snowboarding and para-skiing.

WHERE TO STAY *Map, page 232.*

🏠 **Blue River Tourist Village (Modra Rijeka)** (20 chalets) m 069 027154; www.monteriver.com; ☺ all year. Nice riverside location, 300m from confluence of Tara & Piva rivers, & near border crossing with Bosnia & Herzegovina. Rooms with bathrooms in wooden chalets. Locally grown food served. 1- to 3-day rafting packages (☺ *Jun–Oct*) inc all meals, equipment & board; min age 14. €€

⋏ **Camp Grab** (4 bungalows, 9 rooms, camping) 9km from Šćepan Polje; ☏ 040 200598; m 069 101002; info@anitra.me; www.tara-grab.com; ☺ May–Oct. On the Tara River. Bungalows with en-suite/shared bathroom, rooms & campsite surrounded by oak & beech trees. Catering, BBQ, camp fire, log rafting, fishing & canyoning organised. HB/FB only. €€

⋏ **Tara Tour** (8 chalets, camping) Nr Šćepan Polje; m 069 086106; e taratour@t-com.me; www.tara-tour.com. The rafting company also has a campsite & some small chalets with basic ablutions & a simple restaurant (€). €

PIVA CANYON The Piva Dam and hydro-electric power station were constructed in 1975, 10km from the confluence of the Piva and Tara rivers which flow on over the border into Bosnia under the alias of the Drina. The dam comes at the narrowest part of the Piva Canyon, where the width of the riverbed does not exceed 25m. At this juncture the canyon is 100m high with exceptionally steep sides.

HIKING AROUND PIVA LAKE (PIVSKO JEZERO) It is possible to drive in a westerly direction around and above Piva Lake, then hike from there. Some 2–3km beyond the dam the asphalt road becomes loose gravel and further on a reasonably maintained stony track. At the head of the lake, where the **River Vrbnica** feeds in, park by the timber-yard.

Beyond this you can walk 300m to a modest settlement: a deserted school, a couple of smallholdings and some medieval ivy-clad tombstones among woodland above the river. From here it is possible to hike gently uphill in a southwesterly direction and, leaving the river to your right, through deep woods to remote lush green fields beyond. Any deep wooded cluster of roofs picked out in the distance is a self-sufficient community. In these parts there is no telephone, no television and no water other than the spring. There are few firs or pines, mostly the trees within this canyon are deciduous – beech, maple and lime. Bearing in a northwesterly direction it is possible to discover, beneath the towering crag of the ruined medieval fortress **Talban**, two limpid pools, the **Stabanska Lakes**. This is only a short distance from the border with the Sutjeska National Park in Bosnia–Herzegovina (see page 311).

Another route climbs a steep gravel road northwest above the river. It leads through short tunnels on and up. Watch out for an occasional truck on this route to who knows where, stirring up blinding dust as it hurtles past. The sides of the mountain are perpendicular and dwarfing as you ascend, but seem to gain no height. 'Every ledge in the valley is as exposed as the shelf of a china cupboard' was the way Rebecca West put it. Think of those valiant Partisans, only a matter of months after she wrote those words.

Following this track and bearing left and northwest could eventually bring you, with no little fumbling, to trout-filled **Lake Trnovačko** in the lonely valley between **Mt Maglić** and **Mt Volujak**, again close by the Bosnian border. From here it is said to be possible, by way of **Mratinje** village, to regain the main Nikšić–Plužine–Šćepan Polje road.

There are no maps and no markers. It should be emphasised that both these expeditions involve un-posted trails and wilderness and therefore, to be sensible, a knowledgeable local companion-guide is strongly advised. But the adventurous will probably survive.

ŠĆEPAN POLJE At the border, **Šćepan Polje** is surmounted by the remains of the medieval **Soko Fortress**, its church and graveyard. The stronghold was first mentioned in 1419 as the seat of **Herceg** (duke) **Sandalj Hranić**. In 1435 the residence was inherited by his nephew **Herceg Stjepan Vukčić Kosača**, Duke of Hum, ruler of the Bosnian state including what became known as Herceg Novi. During the time he lived in this place he extended his territory even further. Šćepan Polje today, however, comprises just a few houses and a few rafting outposts.

PIVA MONASTERY The Piva Monastery rests a little out of place on a bare slope by the village of **Goransko**. Once the church stood firm at the source of the **Piva River** but when plans were under way for the hydro-electric dam which would flood the gorge, its value as a national treasure prompted the decision to relocate it with its associated premises – a monk's house, bakery and even the enclosing wall – to higher ground 8km away, an undertaking which took from 1969 until 1982.

The **monastery church**, dedicated to the Dormition of the Mother of God – in the Orthodox Church, the passing of the Virgin from earthly life, the equivalent of the Assumption in the Western Church – was constructed between 1573 and 1586 and was the most important church to be built in the country during the period of Turkish domination. The removal of the interior has been handled with immense care and the frescoes appear quite intact. One icon defaced in an 18th-century Turkish attack, an original example of iconoclasm, has been left purposely unrestored.

The main part within was decorated by unknown Greek hands in the early 17th century. The upper parts of the narthex were the work of Father Strahinja of Budimlje (from near the town that is today called Berane) and the lower zones, in a more sophisticated manner by Kir Kozma, were begun in 1626. He is credited too with the outstanding carved and gold-plated iconostasis dating from 1638 which highlights the interior. But also of significance are the two-sided icons in the choir, representing the cycle of festivals. These were painted by Father Longin of Peć in the 16th century. He was inspired by the finest traditions of Byzantine 14th-century painting and his use of colour influenced future Serb artists.

Piva Monastery is also notable for its sumptuous furnishings: the chandelier, episcopal seat and its beautiful inlaid interior door. The treasury holds a wealth of interest, in particular illuminated manuscripts, a silver-plated manuscript of the 1588 gospel, a chalice from 1590 and a cross from 1623; as well as a 1495 psalter from the early Obud (Cetinje) printing press.

Delightful Father Stefan welcomes visitors but speaks little English. His little cairn terrier Karuša – Old Bitch – will bite your ankles until you seek refuge within the church, to which she fully understands she is not admitted.

In Goransko is **Restoran Pivsko oko** (✆ *040 271905;* €€), which does a fair job of local cooking.

NIKŠIĆ TO ŽABLJAK

About 18km north of Nikšić, turn east off the Plužine road at **Jasenovo Polje**. The way to Šavnik passes through a tunnel beneath **Mt Vojnik** near the village of **Kruševica**. This road, leading ultimately to the Durmitor Massif, was somewhat improved in 2011, with 28km in the vicinity of Šavnik rebuilt. It has now become the preferred winter route from the Boka Kotorska to the most challenging skiing to be found in the country.

Stop at the observation point for a view over the **Drobnjak Valley** encircled by Durmitor, Vojnik and Ivica peaks. Walk up the nearby hill, **Krnovska Glavica**, for an even grander view east to the distant crenellations of Sinjajevina and southeast to the Moračka and Lola mountains. The village of **Gradac**, as you drop down to Šavnik town, has an icy spring that locals swear provides the 'coldest water in the region'. From Gradac Hill there is another fine view to the confluence of the Bijela, Bukovica and Pridvorica rivers.

Among these hills if you find yourself, as you inevitably will, seeking to confirm directions, chances are it will be from some elegant black cat of a lady laboriously tilling a wayside field. She will bound to meet you and before you have a chance to speak, throw her arms about you in a bear hug, beseeching you to return to her home for refreshment: herb tea, *rakija*, water. Whatever she has she will want to share with you. The warmth and hospitality of these indigent mountain souls will move you beyond words.

Never can one forget that Crna Gora remains a patriarchal society, a truth underlined in the mountain settlements. The Montenegrins themselves tell a story about a man descending Durmitor, riding his mule and with his wife walking beside him. He meets a friend who calls out: 'Hey Marko, where are you going?' 'I'm taking my wife to the hospital,' he replies.

ŠAVNIK Šavnik, halfway between Nikšić and Žabljak, is the least-developed municipality in Montenegro and one of the most spectacular, its slopes threaded with rivers and waterfalls. The winter snows frequently cut the area off for weeks and children from the outlying countryside may have to walk as far as 10km to school. The majority of smaller roads are unmetalled and even at the best of times a 4x4 is the optimal vehicle. In spite of this it is a thriving small community, boasting one of the biggest dairy farms in the country.

Getting there There are two **buses** a day to Šavnik from Podgorica, one scheduled to leave at 06.00, and at least five a day from Nikšić, continuing on to Žabljak. Timings are subject to change and should always be checked at the tourist office prior to travel.

Tourist information
⛿ Tourist office ☏040 266066; e info@
savnik-travel; www.savnik.travel

🏠 **Where to stay** Accommodation options are limited in Šavnik, so you may prefer to look for something in Pošćenje (see below) or in Žabljak, some 45km further on (pages 254–5).

Šavnik
🏠 **Hotel** (20 rooms) Šavnik; ☏040 266131. This shabby hotel may not be your choice for an overnight sojourn but for a drink or a snack it is better than fine, & it has no competition. A flask of Krstač wine for 3 ppl, cold & dry, will set you back around €2. There is nowhere to sit other than the dingy dining-room but you will be waited upon with the solicitude of the Savoy. €€

Pošćenje
Some 7km west of Šavnik, close to the mysterious & barely accessible Nevidio Canyon (page 250), are

two further options, both offering rafting trips in the canyon & elsewhere:

🏠 **Etno selo Nevidio** (6 cottages) m 069 735103; www.etnoselo-nevidio.com. Traditional wood & stone chalet-style cottages (2 sizes available, one quite large). Restaurant with national cuisine. Canyoning, rafting, sports climbing, hiking, cycling & other activities on offer. €–€€
⛺ **Ethnovillage & Campsite Jatak** m 069 010045; http://jatak.me. Great location close to the canyon. 1- or 2-day rafting trips. 50% discount under 6 years; 30% under 12s. €

BACK ROADS AND BYWAYS: MORAČA MONASTERY TO ŠAVNIK

Note: For important practical hints on tackling Montenegro's back roads and byways, see box, page 50.

Beyond **Morača Monastery** (page 298) the main road north in the direction of Durmitor turns right to Kolašin. Instead consider turning left (northwest), signed Boan and Šavnik. It will lead you through a pass between Kapa Moračka and the Sinjajevina with the Morača River in the valley far below. About 10–15km are unpaved, and be prepared to dodge the fallen rocks. At the major bifurcation in the stony road turn right (north) to travel on until the road becomes asphalt once more (shortly after the makeshift basketball court comprised of a roadway and a tree). At dusk the author came upon a solitary little boy waiting hopefully by the wayside with one small cup of delicious wild raspberries to sell. Perhaps he will be there still. Our euro will certainly have been an encouragement.

Other practicalities

$ Bank Nikšića Banka; opposite Hotel Šavnik   ✉ **Post office** ☎ 040 266220
✚ Pharmacy Montefarm; ☎ 040 266112

ŠAVNIK TO ŽABLJAK There are two routes from Šavnik to Žabljak (40km). One starts out north over the **Bukovička Gora** and straddles the rivers **Komarnica** and **Bukovička**, passing through **Mijetičak** and a hilly terrain, scene of several 19th-century sanguinary engagements with the Turks. The other road turns east through the Bukovička River valley; at **Boan** (12km from Šavnik) you head north through the village of **Tušina**. Both these ways join up just short of Bukovička village (11km from Šavnik). You then travel on towards Žabljak, passing on the right and to the east the rolling highlands of **Sinjajevina** (sometimes called simply Sinjavina). With no road into its heart, this wilderness offers some interesting **hiking** but it is an infinite and lonely quarter, with paths here being notoriously difficult to find until they were cleared recently – so remember your compass. There are only volunteer rescue organisations and little or no mobile telephone coverage. (The Regional Travel Office in Kolašin – page 294 – has an excellent free *Hiking Guide to the Mountains of Sinjavina*.)

Keep an eye open for *stećci*, strange Manichaean gravestones dating from the 14th and 15th centuries and found in Montenegro, Serbia and Herzegovina (see box, page 261). On the plain beneath the **Durmitor Massif** there are clusters of them, some barely standing and askew, others long fallen awry. Sometimes one can make out a carved symbol representing maybe a moon, an animal or traces of ornate edging. Little is known about these tombs or the significance of their positioning, although the theory that they were once linked to the Bogomils has been shown to be highly improbable. The Durmitor region has not so far been thoroughly researched archaeologically but enough evidence has been found to prove habitation from the Stone Age through Illyrian, Roman, Goth, Hun, Avar and Celt to the present Slav population. Indications have also been noted of a Roman road which crossed this region, linking it with the Adriatic coast and the interior of the Balkan Peninsula. A Roman bridge spans the Bukovička near Šavnik and the remains of another can be seen from the lower banks of the Tara.

DURMITOR

North from Šavnik it is possible to drive in the direction of **Komarnica** village below the foothills of the Durmitor Massif. The road passes the tiny villages of **Petnijica** and **Pošćenje**, the latter bordering two quiet lakes. (For places to stay near Pošćenje, see page 249.)

From Komarnica, which in the Middle Ages gave its name to the whole region, the way leads downstream to the mysterious and inaccessible **Nevidio Canyon**, where the river runs through a ravine 4.5km long with waterfalls cascading more than 100m and the canyon walls sometimes only 2–3m apart. It is called *nevidio* ('invisible') because even from far above, standing at its edge, you cannot see the foaming water in the gulch beneath. The canyon was only fully explored by specially equipped climbers from Nikšić in 1965.

Upstream you can follow the deeply forested **Dragišnica Valley**, overshadowed by the precipitous cliffs of **Boljske Grede**, where chamois forage meagre sustenance among the barren limestone and where eagles nest high above. Retracing your steps south towards the village of Petnijica there is a fork for **Grabovica** and the source of the Grabovica River which, passing through more rocky pasture of sheep and cattle, like the Komarnica, vanishes and reappears several times before finally sliding into a waterfall to join the other river.

As you approach the sprawling settlement of Žabljak, on the Durmitor Plain at the edge of the national park, and survey the majestic turrets of the Durmitor rising from the plain, it is striking how their juxtaposition mirrors the great Crnogorsko national dance, the Kolo-oro: a routine in which one circle of men is elevated by another standing on their shoulders. These people, giants already, raised to double their height, surely resemble the mountain massifs themselves. When the Turks were in the vicinity the dance would be executed in elegant silence: a *gluvi ples* deaf dance, so the enemy would not be aware of their presence. The traditional musical instrument of the mountain people was the one-string fiddle known as the *gusle*. This would normally accompany narration – epic poetry such as Njegoš's *Mountain Wreath*, but also traditional ballads. Performances would take place on the threshing floors.

ŽABLJAK The tourist centre of the Durmitor National Park is the town of Žabljak, at 1,465m a natural base for hiking and mountaineering, as well as for winter sports: skiing, snowboarding and cross-country skiing in the national park.

Until 100 years ago Žabljak was a tiny trading post known as Hanovi ('Inns'). Only at the beginning of the 20th century did it begin to develop as a tourist centre. Durmitor had its earliest winter visitors in 1933 and in the following years its peaks were one by one summited. The first facility for mountaineers, the **Durmitor Hotel**, opened in 1940 but was soon commandeered as a Partisan military hospital. During World War II most of Žabljak was destroyed by fire, so much of the existing town is no more than 60 years old. As such the buildings are of little interest but in the uplands among the black pine, the houses are generally of stone and quite beautiful with their steeply pitched roofs of thatch almost reaching to the ground – although even these are gradually being replaced by tiling. *Katuni* is the word for the distinctive tall tent-like wooden huts used by the shepherds and their families during the summer months in the higher grazing pastures. Second homes in effect, but created out of expediency.

On a rise behind Žabljak Hotel and the central square (trg Durmitorski ratnia) is a significant pyramid-shaped monument to the victims of fascism in World War II, a staggering 2,400 of them.

For tourists, Žabljak has perfect temperatures in summer; little or no humidity; warm sun and gentle breezes. Winter snow is guaranteed.

Getting there In the past the Durmitor region has never been particularly easy to reach, which has in many ways been part of its charm. In summer the roads are fine but in winter it can be another matter. To counteract the effort of winter access, expenses incurred in wintersports activities had intentionally been kept low. However, since late 2010, when rebuilding work on the Risan–Nikšić–Šavnik–Žabljak road was completed, the journey has been considerably eased.

By train The closest **railway** connections are to Mojkovac and Kolašin, both on the Belgrade–Podgorica–Bar line (for details, see pages 37 and 203). From either, the cost of a taxi (likely to take close to two hours in winter conditions) is considerable (at least €40), though better from Mojkovac.

By bus There is a **bus** station [252 F3] (*5min walk from central square on route to Šavnik;* ✎ *052 261318*) but timings do not always fit. From Podgorica there are two

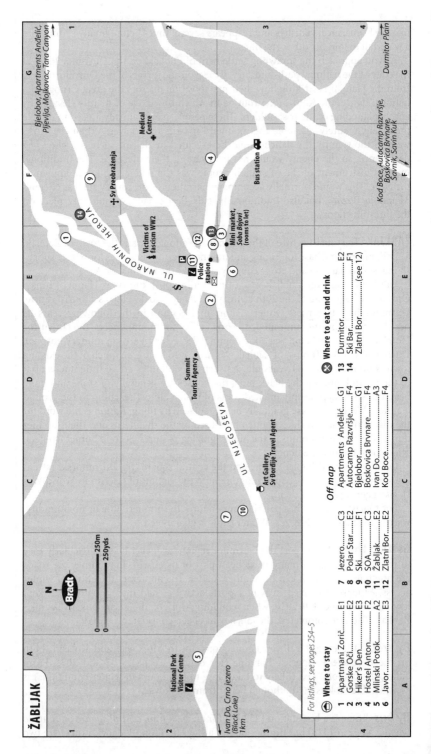

ŽABLJAK

N
Bradt

0 ——— 250m
0 ——— 250yds

*Ivan Do, Crno jezero
(Black Lake)
1km*

*Bjelobor, Apartments Anđelić,
Pljevlja, Mojkovac, Tara Canyon*

National Park
Visitor Centre ℹ️

Art Gallery,
Sv Đorđije Travel Agent 🔊

Summit
Tourist Agency ●

UL NJEGOŠEVA

UL NARODNIH HEROJA

† Sv Preobraženja

Victims of
fascism WW2 †

Medical
Centre +

Police
station ●
✉

Mini market,
Soba Bojovi
(rooms to let)

🚌 Bus station

*Kod Boce, Autocamp Razvršje,
Boškovica Brvnare,
Savnik, Savin Kuk*

Durmitor Plain

For listings, see pages 254–5

🛏 Where to stay

1	Apartmani Zorić	E1
2	Gorske Oči	E2
3	Hiker's Den	E3
4	Hostel Anton	F2
5	Mlinski Potok	A2
6	Javor	E3

7	Jezero	C3
8	Polar Star	E2
9	Ski	F1
10	SOA	C3
11	Žabljak	E2
12	Zlatni Bor	E3

Off map

Apartments Anđelić	G1
Autocamp Razvršje	F4
Bjelobor	G1
Boškovica Brvnare	F4
Ivan Do	A3
Kod Boce	F4

✖ Where to eat and drink

13	Durmitor	E2
14	Ski Bar	F1
	Zlatni Bor	(see 12)

252

buses daily, one leaving early and a second in early afternoon, travelling via Nikšić and Šavnik (*€9; 3–4hrs*). There are also infrequent buses from Tivat on the coast (*€10; 5hrs*), and several through the day from Nikšić and Šavnik. There are also shared minibuses, arranged informally. In winter, delays are to be expected.

By car The traditional route into Durmitor was along the main Belgrade–Podgorica highway, turning west at Mojkovac (pages 270–1). Since 2010, however, there has been an alternative route from Risan via Nikšić and Šavnik, reducing the distance to the Boka Kotorska to 145km.

Getting around Žabljak is easily navigable **on foot**. Locals are friendly and helpful; street names are rarely used, more a case of indicating the direction.

4x4s are sometimes available for rental privately and you can enquire at either the tourist office or the national park office, but you should check the insurance situation.

Tourist information and tour operators

Tourist information

🄱 **Durmitor National Park Office & Visitor Centre** [252 A2] ul Jovana Cvijića; ☎052 360228; e npdurmitor@t-com.me; www.nparkovi.me; ⊕ 09.00–17.00 Mon–Sat; park entry €3 pp, children under 7 free, car park €2. The new centre is some 2km from the centre of Žabljak, 700m from Black Lake parking lot, a pleasant tree-lined 20- to 30-min walk. It is easy to spot with its blue roof; access is via a short flight of steps.

With some information available on all Montenegrin national parks, the centre supports a collection of preserved insects & animals endemic to Durmitor & Tara Canyon, along with a small ethnographical & historical exhibition (*entry €1*); a video projection room seating 30, & a souvenir shop.

Details of sport fishing & licences for lakes & rivers can be obtained here, as can information on hiking, caving & other activities in the region.

Wintersports information covers alpine & cross-country skiing, snowboarding, sledging/motor sledge & paragliding.

Boat rental on Black Lake is €10 per hr. National park guide service €20 per day. Camping on designated sites is €5 per night for a large tent.

A useful independent website & overview describing the park & its facilities, road access & more is www.durmitorcg.wordpress.com.

🄱 **Tourist office** [252 E2] trg Durmitorski Ratnika, in a log cabin beside the central car park; ☎052 361802; e info@zabljak.travel; www. zabljak.travel; ⊕ officially: winter 08.00–20.00 Mon–Fri, 08.00–16.00 Sat–Sun; summer 08.00–23.00 daily; but in practice there is nearly always someone in this user-friendly office until quite late in the evening. The staff, who are themselves enthusiastic skiers & mountain guides, speak good English as well as being helpful & knowledgeable, & they stock a good range of leaflets.

A **mountain rescue service** (☎*040 256084; 052 361407, or 112;* m *067 673367*) is available, but as anywhere in the world it relies on the bravery of a small group of individuals whose services shouldn't be called upon lightly.

Friends of Tara River Society ☎052 261726

Tour operators

Miro-Tara Sv Sava 37, Žabljak; m 069 311032; e office@mirotara.com; www.miro-tara.com. 1–3-day rafting trips, jeep touring, horseriding, fishing, lodging, cabins, camping & transfers.

Sv Đorđije (St George) Travel Agents [252 C3] Jovana Cvijića 47; ☎052 361367; m 069 074367; e tasaint@t-com.me. Director Milanka Blagojević speaks good English & is knowledgeable about everything in town, inc rooms & apts; married to Miko, an artist who does surrealist paintings & sculptures in wood & bronze. Rafting.

✱ **Summit Tourist Agency** [252 D2] Njegoševa bb; m 069 016502; e info@summit.co.me; www. summit.co.me. Excellent English. Rafting, trekking, canyoning, mountain biking. Jeep safaris – high plateau circular drive through stunning scenery of the massif visiting summer pasture villages, wild flowers, mountain lakes, ravines & canyons, with lunch stop at mountain lodge.

Žabljak Holidays e info@zabljak holidays.com; www.zabljak holidays.com. UK-based operator with an emphasis on sustainable tourism. Rafting, skiing, hiking, mountaineering.

Where to stay *Map, page 252.*

The high season for skiing around Žabljak runs from about 20 December to 20 March. Accommodation listed here is all in or close to the town. For further options within the national park, including mountain huts, see pages 257–8.

Hotels

SOA (8 rooms, 10 suites) On road to national park office & Crno jezero; 052 360115; e info@hotelsoa.com; www.hotelsoa.com. New upmarket hotel with AC, TV, Wi-Fi, restaurant, lounge bar, wine bar. €€€€

Ski (28 rooms) Narodnih heroja bb; 052 361038; e skihotel@t-com.me; www.skihotelzabljak.com. A relatively new (2010) hotel opposite the Planinka with an ex-Yugoslav ski champion as proprietor. Same family owns the Ski Bar. Satellite TV, free Wi-Fi, but the standard rooms are uncomfortably small & it is literally quite difficult to get around the bed. Some have no view but a wall. Superior rooms are bigger. No lift. Bar & restaurant but out of season the menu is very limited. Sauna & indoor pool. Visa & MasterCard accepted. €€€–€€€€

Žabljak (15 rooms, 11 apts) trg Durmitorskih Ratnika 1; 077 400190; www.hmdurmitor.com. Newly built & very swish-looking boutique hotel. TV, Wi-Fi, jacuzzi, spa, café-bar. Parking. €€€–€€€€

Gorske Oči (32 rooms) ul Božidara Žugića bb; 052 361118; e hotelgorskeoci@t-com.me; www.hotelgorskeoci.me. Quite a new hotel with a slightly stark décor but pleasant & business-like service. TV, fridge, fitness centre, billiards, Wi-Fi, bar & restaurant. Not much English. CCs accepted. Children under 2 stay free, up to 12 half price. €€€

✱ **Javor** (6 rooms, 2 apts) Božidara Žugića br 8; 052 361337; e vladoprof@hotmail.com; www.durmitor.in; ⊕ all year. Very nice & intimate with plenty of hot water; TV. Apts are in next-door house. Restaurant & bar; good straightforward local food; seasonal game inc pheasant. Locals in the evening give a village-pub feel. All sorts of tours & activities can be arranged, & transfers to ski slopes. CCs accepted. €€€ (FB €€€)

Jezera (61 rooms, 7 suites) 052 360205; e hmdurmitor@hotmail.com. Indoor pool, sauna, solarium, billiards. Restaurant & bar. €€€

Polar Star (8 rooms, 6 apts, 8 bungalows) Borje bb, 2km outside town on route to Tara Bridge; m 067 609444; e polarstar@polarstar.me; www.polarstar.me. Newly opened hotel in a semi-alpine style that could be an attractive option. TV, DVD, parking. Not always English speakers at reception. Restaurant & wine bar. Children's playground. Under 7s stay free. €€€

Apartmani Zorič ul Narodnih heroja 11; m 069 646665; e apartmanizoric@gmail.com; www.apartmani-durmitorzabljak.com (Montenegrin only). In central Žabljak, close to the Ski Bar, with mountain views. Central heating. €€

Apartments Anđelić Marka Miljanova 2; 069 898240; e andjelic.zarko@gmail.com. On north side of town. €€

Autocamp Razvršje (8 apts, camping) 2km from bus station off road to Šavnik (also brown-signed Durmitor); 052 361383; m 067 444477; e misorazvrsje@t-com.me, razvrsje@yahoo.com. Peaceful, rustic setting on the outskirts of Žabljak with wide views across plain to mountains beyond. Well-appointed & comfortable apt accommodation in newly constructed small villas. Also a campsite; camping & sports equipment available for rent. Very good facilities. Can arrange rafting, mountain biking, skiing & various excursions. Telephone & they will collect you. Group discount available. €€

Bjelobor (24 rooms) Tmajevici bb; 052 361635; e bjelobor@t-com.me; www.hotelbjelobor.com. Functional hotel under same ownership as Zlatni Bor. TV. Restaurant & snack bar. €€

Boskovica Brvnare (1 apt) Motički Gaj bb. €€

Zlatni Bor (15 apts) Cmajevci bb; 052 361535; e bjelobor@t-com.me; www.hotelbjelobor.com. Simple wood-furnished apts with AC. Part of popular restaurant of same name. €€

Hostels

Hiker's Den Hostel (4-, 5- & 6-bed dorms) ul Božidara Žugića bb; m 067 854433; e hikersden@live.com; www.hostelzabljak.com. Small, centrally located hostel with dorms (*beds from €11 pp*) & en-suite sgls/dbls. €–€€

Hostel Anton Marka Miljanova 2; 069 898240; e hostel.anton09@gmail.com; http://hostelanton.com/tag/zabljak/. New (2012) hostel under same ownership as Hostel Anton in Tivat. €–€€

Private houses

This is a town of landladies. The avg cost for a room with bath in high season is €10. One that is simple & monolingual but homely & spotless, with hand-embroidered duvet covers, is run by Mrs Miluša Bojović (*Božidara Žugića 39, opp Durmitor Restaurant & over Toni mini-market;* \052 361806; m *069 258087*).

Campsites

There are several campsites within easy reach of Žabljak, & there is also camping at Autocamp Razvršje (opposite). For other campsites within the national park, see pages 257–8. Expect to pay around €5 for a large tent, €3 for a small one.

* **Ⅹ Ivan Do** Near national park office at Black Lake; m 069 041749; e info@autocamp-ivando. com; www.autocamp-ivando.com. Excellent, long-established campsite just outside town in a lovely open setting on the hiking trail to Lokvice. Used by the updater for years! Bungalows available. Has its own well. €2 pp; €2 tent; €1.50 car; €5 camper van; €3 electricity. Adjacent to Mlinski Potok (below).

Ⅹ Kod Boce m 069 223218; e novak. vojinovic@t-com.me; www.kampkodboce.me. South of town before Motički Gaj there are 2 campsites next to each other. Small wooden cabins €7; free use of kitchen. Can also organise rafting.

Ⅹ Mlinski Potok Near national park office at Black Lake; e minakamp@gmail.com. Rafting, kayaks & transfers arranged.

✗ Where to eat and drink *Map, page 252.*

As well as those listed below, there are a couple of inexpensive eateries/bars in the central square, near the tourist office: **Caffe Bar Stara Varoš** and **Restoran Duga**. For restaurants within the national park, see page 260.

✗ Zlatni Bor Cmajevci bb; www.hotelbjelobor. com. National cuisine, nice terrace. Rooms available. €€

✗ Durmitor Restaurant Božidara Žugića bb in town centre. Small restaurant with terrace for b/fasts & light meals; bacon & eggs, hamburgers. Clean, & decent home cooking. €

♀ Ski Bar ul Narodnih Heroja. Run by a family of serious skiers, a focal point & jolly evening gathering place. Popular with locals.

Other practicalities

Banks

$ **Atlasmont Banka** ul Narodnih Heroja bb
$ **Investbanka** ul Narodnih Heroja 1
$ **Komercijalna Banka** trg Durmitorskih Ratnika br 1

Internet

🄴 **Start** \051 261467
🄴 **Top Goal** \051 281957
🄴 **WWW** ul Svetog Sava; \051 361353

Health

✚ **Medical Centre** [252 F2] off ul Njegoševa; \052 361504
✚ **Pharmacy** Montefarm; trg Durmitorskih Ratnika bb; \051 260130

Other

Petrol station [252 F3] Šavnik rd, just beyond bus station; ⏱ 06.00–22.00
✉ **Post office** [252 E2] trg Durmitorskih Ratnika 1; ⏱ 07.00–20.00 Mon–Sat. Visa & MasterCard. Telephone SIM cards.

What to see and do Žabljak is a natural base for both hiking and winter sports: skiing, snowboarding and cross-country skiing; if you wish to skate, at present you must bring your own equipment. Rather surprisingly, at the time of writing there are no riding stables in Žabljak or Durmitor National Park, although some individual establishments and camps in the region can provide horses. For information and details, see *Tourist information and tour operators* (page 253) and *What to see and do* in the national park (pages 260–3).

Lots of tracks leading out of the town and into the interior, to view *katuni* and agricultural community life, are now tarmac in part – and there's usually a turning place when it runs out. One such easy and attractive route is to follow the road uphill behind Ski Bar.

DURMITOR NATIONAL PARK (*entry €3, under 7 free*) The 39,000ha Durmitor National Park has magnificent mountains, alpine lakes and high pastures. It is bordered by two deep canyons, the **Tara** to the east and the **Piva** to the west. As a summer resort it offers endless opportunities for nature lovers, hikers and mountaineers. The area received national park status in 1978 and since 1980 Durmitor National Park and the Canyon of the River Tara have jointly been listed by UNESCO as a site of natural and cultural heritage.

Geography The Durmitor range has 27 peaks reaching over 2,200m and in all there are 48 peaks over 2,000m, the majority of them accessible without the use of special equipment (but cirques and couloirs are there as well to challenge the alpinist). They encircle five canyons and 18 glacial lakes, among which, surrounded by a dense forest of pine, **Crno jezero** (**Black Lake**) is the best known. Two lakes actually make up the placid Crno jezero: Veliko, with a maximum depth 24.5m, and Malo jezero, a surprising 49.1m deep. The two sections are joined by a stony pass which, when the water level is high, is partially submerged by a stream (*struja*).

SOE AND THE PARTISANS

The Durmitor Massif rises abruptly to the west of the Jezerska Plateau. This plain was the dropping zone of the British–Canadian SOE contingent on 28 May 1943. In an operation code named Typical, SOE Captain Bill (later Sir William) Deakin (see box, page 17) and Canadian Captain Bill Stuart, Signals Sergeants Rose and Wroughton, Marine Sergeant Campbell (bodyguard) and Canadian–Croat interpreter Starčević parachuted on to this plain in the midst of a major German offensive against the Partisans. After a three-hour march they met with Tito at the Black Lake and established the first British Military Mission attached to Tito's headquarters. Subsequently the group moved on with the Partisans and, at what is now Sutjeska National Park (northwest of Plužine and beyond Talban Fortress), Deakin and Tito were wounded by the same bomb, Tito in the shoulder and Deakin in the leg. Stuart was killed as was Tito's dog, Tiger. Deakin stayed on as the mission commander until he was eventually succeeded by Fitzroy Maclean in September 1943. (See page 18; it is easy to see why Deakin called his engrossing book *The Embattled Mountain*.)

To inspect the original drop zone, leave Žabljak in an easterly direction and after approximately 11km make a right turn south. At Njegovuđa there is a memorial plaque to mark the first military air base on territory liberated after World War II. Continue south to an intersection where a westerly road will return you to Žabljak (50km in total). The plain, still a bleak area, is a network of small roads but with the Durmitor mountains such an obvious landmark you are unlikely to get lost. Keep a lookout for *stećci* (see box, page 261); at Nova Kovići there are a dozen good examples.

Note: The prominent memorial in Cyrillic at the crossroads in the middle of the Durmitor Plain, where the road to Šavnik branches off, is not Partisan-related but records a family of five and their home destroyed by lightning. Traces of the house and its chimney are visible beneath a carpet of grass and wild flowers.

There are 748 springs of pure mountain water, and forests in which trees are more than 100 years old (though finding a reliable spring when trekking is much more limited than you might expect from this figure).

Close to the Durmitor Massif is the **Tara River** (156km), the longest in Montenegro. Its crystal-clear water is equally enchanting whether it is tripping through the plains or hurtling through the magnificent canyon. The canyon (93km) is the longest and deepest in Europe, reaching at points 1,300 sheer metres. Black pine trees (*crna poda*) grow at impossible angles from its sides, some of them as tall as 50m and several hundred years old; waterfalls seem to appear from nowhere, tumbling to the river below. If you are camping overnight on the banks you might discover its community of bats. You are less likely to discover the *Durmitor zvončić* (Durmitor bell), a flower unique to the mountain.

Flora and fauna Bears and wolves are uncommon in Durmitor but might be seen on the periphery and in the wilderness of Sinjajevina. Chamois are found on the higher slopes, along with the more familiar hare and fox; other residents include marten, deer and boar. Not unexpectedly, squirrels are the most numerous species of wildlife, and trout are the most usual fish in the fast-flowing rivers and lakes, but there are also many less usual ones. Besides frogs, in pools and lakes there are some rare protected amphibians of particular scientific interest.

Among some 168 different bird species are grouse, grey mountain eagle, white-headed vulture, falcon and crossbill. Expect your walks to be accompanied by a choir of songbirds. The region also boasts 130 types of butterfly.

In the highlands of Durmitor there is spruce, mountain pine (called *klek* by the local people), beech, birch, maple and aspen. On the lower slopes and in the valleys you will see oak, ash, elm, dogwood, hazel and juniper; meadows Liberty-printed with gentian, hawkweed, sage, wild thyme, violet, clove pinks and everywhere white and yellow saxifrage clinging to the rocks. From late May till October you will not have to look far to find sweet-tasting wild strawberries; like the blueberries they grow in abundance here. And in moist areas you can also discover various edible fungi – and a number of inedible ones (take local advice on these and exercise caution). There is much of specialist interest for the botanist, including some 150 medicinal herbs (see box, pages 8–9).

There are some very knowledgeable locals – consult the park office or your hotel.

Park information See *Durmitor National Park Office and Visitor Centre*, page 253, which includes details of **mountain rescue**.

🏠 **Where to stay** *Map, page 259.*
All the accommodation listed in and around Žabljak (pages 254–5) is convenient for access to the national park, but the following lie within the national park itself.

Hotels
🏠 **Hotel Ravnjak** (6 rooms, 3 bungalows, camping) **m** 069 434849; **e** info@ravnjak-hotel. com; www.ravnjak-hotel.com. President Tito's former hunting lodge, now a hotel, is further down Tara Canyon, 18km from Žabljak on the way to Mojkovac. Also convenient for visits to Biogradska National Park. For details see page 270. €–€€

Mountain huts
There are two types of mountain hut in Durmitor National Park: staffed huts (the Škrka and Sušica huts), usually open Jun–Oct, & small basic unstaffed mountain shelters (Lokvice & Velika Kalica), usually open all year (no facilities – bring your own sleeping bags & mats, & of course be prepared to cook your own food). You can also camp at Lokvice & a couple of other designated places.

To book at the Sušica or Škrka huts, call ☎ 051 360228 or 052 361802. Information as to availability can be obtained from either Durmitor National Park office or at the tourist office in Žabljak (see page 253). Also check out www. durmitorcg.wordpress.com.

🏠 **Škrka Hostel** (30 beds) On a plateau between the large & small Škrčko lakes at 1,723m. €5.

🏠 **Planinski Dom Sušica** (18 rooms, 55 tent sites) Sušica Canyon; ☎ 051 261346, 051 360228; ⊕ May–Oct. 30km from Žabljak. Camping is permitted in designated places beside this attractive mountain hut. No service at the hut but it is in good condition & usually open to general public – always check first. Bring all food & equipment. €

🏠 **Lokvice Cottage** (8 beds, camping) At 1,800m. Camping permitted around hut. This is the best base for exploring central Durmitor on foot. Gratis.

🏠 **Velika Kalica Hut** (15 beds) At 2,020m. Very remote at the head of high cirque & less useful than Lokvice. Gratis.

Camping

In addition to three campsites just outside Žabljak (see page 255), & the option to camp at some of

---

BACK ROADS AND BYWAYS: ŽABLJAK TO THE PIVA CANYON

Note: *For important practical hints on tackling Montenegro's back roads and byways, see box, page 50.*

This is a route only realistically feasible with your own wheels, either a car or a bike, but it includes a spectacular descent to the Piva Canyon, in itself worth the hire of a vehicle. The full length of this road has recently been paved.

Leave Žabljak on Vučedolska with the bus station to your right, travelling in the direction of Šavnik and Nikšić. Continue for approximately 5km to a right-hand sign indicating west to Plužine (49km) and Trsa (38km). Take this route, which gradually climbs to a saddle over the wasted foothills of the Durmitor Massif, with Bobotov kuk (2,522m) rising to the right and soon the strangely pleated north face of Todorov Do looming on the left, a distant assembly of *katuni* in the valley far below. The road traverses the pass at Dobri Do; and after a further 9km reaches a second pass – Prijespa – where a poignant rocky outcrop is surmounted by a memorial, a homage to an alpinist, Danilo Petrović, who died in 2005 in an avalanche on the Matterhorn in Switzerland. Aged 48 and one of Montenegro's most prominent mountaineers, he had previously expressed the wish that should he be killed while climbing he would choose to be buried on his beloved Durmitor, near to the Prijespa Pass. At the foot of the monument, carefully wrapped against the elements, there is a bottle of Vranac and a stack of paper cups. An inscription requests the unknown traveller to drink a glass of wine to Danilo's spirit. He was a descendant of Duke Željko Petrović from the Montenegrin royal family and his friends arranged to have the surrounding road paved.

After this the route leads on beneath a massive cave on the right, passing dry-stone walls and beautifully handmade fencing and then through golden beechwoods to Pišče, a little church on the right looking rather British with its long windows. Then Lice and on to Trsa, another rather forlorn little place: Milogora *nacional restoran*, an empty campsite and a post office. That's about the sum of it. Turn left for Plužine, through more beechwoods and then the thrilling corkscrew descent to Piva, arguably one of the hairiest roads in Montenegro, and that is saying something. The driver must resist the temptation to snatch a glance at the spectacular views from every corner to the lake vertically below. On a bike, be sure of those brakes.

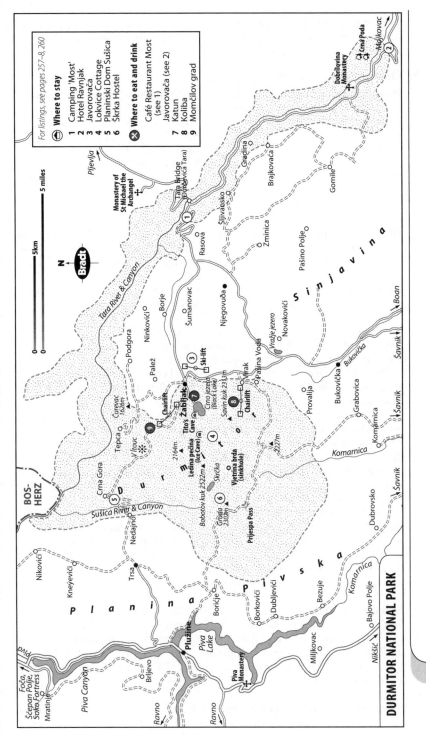

DURMITOR NATIONAL PARK

For listings, see pages 257–8, 260

Where to stay
1 Camping 'Most'
2 Hotel Ravnjak
3 Javorovača
4 Lokvice Cottage
5 Planinski Dom Sušica
6 Škrka Hostel

Where to eat and drink
   Café Restaurant Most (see 1)
   Javorovača (see 2)
7 Katun
8 Koliba
9 Momčilov grad

the mountain huts, Durmitor National Park will in time have a dedicated **motorhome park**. This will have spaces for 30 vehicles, inc connections for electricity, fresh water & waste water, plus an on-site ATM. For details visit www.nparkovi.me.

✕ Where to eat and drink *Map, page 259.*

✕ **Momčilov grad** Mali Štuoc; ☎077 400190; www.hmdurmitor.com/en/restaurant; ⏲ Jun–Aug. Situated at the top of Stoić ski-lift with wide views over the plain way below. Accessible & well-signed by road from Black Lake. Owned by Hotel Žabljak. Varied menu. €€€

✕ **Javorovača** Javorovača, by ski resort; ☎052 361104; http://restoranpansionjavorovaca.weebly.com. Local specialities, well prepared at reasonable prices. Chalet-like with a cosy interior inc open fireplace. Also pansion with 10 rooms. €€

✕ **Katun** Obala Crno jezero, on Black Lake. Highland specialities inc lamb & local cheese dishes. Moderate prices. €€

✕ **Koliba ('Cabin')** 1,600m up Savin kuk, beside the ski lift; ☎051 366599. Drinks & simple traditional dishes. €€

What to see and do It is beyond the scope of a book such as this to detail the huge network of trekking, biking, climbing and mountaineering routes, but below are some suggestions. It is also worth consulting the helpful tourist office in Žabljak.

Caves and sinkholes Because of the karst formation, Durmitor can claim 200 caves and sinkholes (pot-holes) so far discovered, many of them located in the river canyons, and some can be presumed to shelter traces of prehistoric man. Ask at the park office for directions to **Tito's Cave**, where Tito stored his supplies during World War II and which for several months served as his headquarters. It is near the junction between the two halves of the Black Lake.

The most notable caves include the awesome **Ledina pećina** (Ice Cave), on the north face of **Bobotov kuk**, and the sinkhole near **Vjetrina brda** in the south, so far explored to a depth of 905m.

If you decide to make the long and quite arduous trip, and choose to enter and view Ledina Pećina's impressive stalagmites – some over 3m high and the width of a man's waist – and stalactites (remember the childhood line: 'Mites grow up and tights go down'), dress warmly, even during summer. The hike to the cave – one of the most popular and best marked – is graded medium difficulty and takes about seven hours round trip from Žabljak, stops excluded. A guide can also be hired if you prefer; ask at the visitor centre or one of the tour operators.

You will need to be fit: the final steep uphill clamber, beneath the peak of **Obla Glava** (2,100m), involves negotiating rocks, scree and frequently patches of snow, which can remain at these heights until August. Access to the cave involves a tricky, steepish descent which can be slippery. An ice axe would not go amiss at this point if there's snow. Nevertheless, the extraordinary cave is undeniably *vaut le détour*. And is just one of the many wonders of Montenegro.

Fishing There is an abundance of fish in the Tara River, plenty both for you and for the otters that live on its banks. Daily permits issued from 1 May–1 October cost €15 per day on the Tara River or €10 for Crno or Vražje lakes (maximum catch three fish). These may be obtained from the National Park Office and Visitor Centre (page 253). Alternatively, contact **SFA Crno jezero** (m *067 559555;* e *andjelic.m@t-com.me*).

Hiking and mountaineering Durmitor is Montenegro's best-known and most accessible hiking area, with clear, well-marked trails through truly spectacular scenery. There are over 60km of posted paths interweaving the peaks of **Bobotov kuk** (at 2,523m generally listed as the highest summit in Montenegro, though Maja Kolata in Prokletije Massif is actually 2,528m), **Savin kuk** (2,313m), **Crvena kuk** (2,175m), **Medjed** (2,287m) and **Planinica** (2,330m) and the **Sušica Canyon**. Along dozens of climbing and hiking trails you can find many caves (see opposite).

The walk to Ledina pećina (see opposite) is one of the most popular, but plenty of other easy hikes in the national park are as or even more scenic. These include the hike to the summit of Bobotov kuk (but it's a very, very long day out if you start in Žabljak); the walk around Crno jezero (Black Lake); and the hike to **Savin kuk**. For the latter, take the chairlift from the bus stop at **Virak** to **Sv Sava's Spring**, considered to have healing properties, and in ten minutes you can walk to **Kulina** peak for a splendid view. King Nikola would ride up here on horseback (he brought his own). A second chairlift rises from near the national park office building and the Black Lake to **Mali Štuoc**.

However, if you really want to see the best of what this magnificent area offers for hiking, pack a tent (and map) and head into the heart of the mountains at Lokvice (around 2½ hours from Žabljak). From here you can make several outstanding one-day excursions, including climbing Bobotov kuk. A long and fairly demanding day out, even from this point, this involves some scrambling just before the spectacular summit with its jaw-dropping views over the surrounding mountain scenery.

Further information

Map Durmitor & the Tara Canyon; available from national park office

Guidebook *The Mountains of Montenegro*, Rudolf Abraham's comprehensive guidebook

STEĆCI

On open moorland throughout the north of Montenegro (eg: Durmitor Plain, Novakovići, Sinjajevina and in Šćepan Polje), as well as in Bosnia–Herzegovina, Serbia and Macedonia, these granite 'tombstones' dating from the late 14th–15th centuries can be found in groups of a dozen or so. Strictly speaking they are monuments rather than tombs: some upright, others apparently toppled, roughly carved in low relief or decorated with foliar friezes; sometimes depicting a figure or two, an animal or what might appear to represent a hunting victory. Others might show the sun or moon. Uniformly their style is naive and their origin not fully understood other than that they derive from one of the various dualist heresies of the period: Manichaeism or something very similar. These cults explained the perversity of nature and life as the result of an ongoing struggle between the equally potent forces of Good and Evil. Arguably such beliefs were, from the start, deeply rooted in superstition, and over the centuries these *stećci* became objects of ritual, attributed with special and magical powers, in a similar way to Stonehenge or the chalk giant of Cerne Abbas. For example there was a belief that to touch one of these stones would cause lightning to strike.

One can relate only from personal experience but, crossing the wide Njegovuđa Plateau beneath the Durmitor Massif at dusk on a March evening, a huddle of *stećci*, spotted beckoning from the skyline, certainly succeeded in summoning up an instant monumental storm, out of which, as if to order, galloped two bareback huntsmen, nostrils aflare, long rifles afore. The author thought it sensible to regain her vehicle.

(page 326), contains detailed descriptions of trekking routes in Durmitor National Park lasting several days, & inc variety of side trips that are possible within one day from a base at Lokvice.

Guide Batrić Grbović m 067 673367. A guide for climbing & hiking.
Mountaineering Association of Montenegro ul Jovana Cvijića 4, Nikšić; 020 622220; e info@pscg.me; www.pscg.me

Mountain biking With the benefit of a decent mountain bike it is possible to make an exceptional round trip of the piedmont area of the massif at altitudes of 1,500m.

Skiing Durmitor enjoys about 120 days of snow a year between December and April. At its highest reaches there is even the possibility of bikini skiing in summer on the short (200–300m) snowfield of **Debeli Namet**, near **Kalica** (*namet* is the Montenegrin word for 'eternal snow').

In winter, surprisingly, there is so far no organised lake skating (bring your own skates, but not in hand luggage) and the full potential of downhill skiing has not yet been exploited. Skiboarding is rapidly becoming popular.

Besides the two chairlifts at **Savin kuk**, there are so far three drag lifts: **Javorovača**, **Petrova Strana** and **Jablan Bara**, plus two nursery ones. Pistes are graded by alpine standards and range between intermediate red and easy blue, with one very challenging black possibility. The trail from Savin kuk is 3,500m long; that from Štuoc is shorter at 2,630m, but harder. The Javorovača trail is only 800m long. There are also cross-country tracks between 3km and 12km long.

RAFTING ON THE TARA

Once upon a time, rafting expeditions involved lovely old log rafts, not unlike the great black pines that a century ago would have been tied together to travel, beneath their agile steersman, 600km over the rapids of the Tara, the Drina, the Sava and finally the Danube, to be sold in Belgrade. There are still some log rafts built by the river but these days the rubber variety are more frequent. These recreational trips run for one, two or three days and can involve overnight camping in rudimentary shelters or under the stars with a big fire. All food, barbecue, party and drink are provided. The experience is magical if sometimes chilly. It is all too easy to get wet and all too hard to dry off once the sun has gone down. The rapids are not too challenging and those in search of a white-fright experience will have to be compensated with the lazy pleasure of gliding over limpid water and gazing up at the forbidding pine-punctured walls of the canyon towering above and from which there is often no (immediate) escape. The final section of the three-day trips carries the biggest and most rapid thrills.

The journey generally begins at **Sljivansko**, 3km upriver from the dizzy bridge. After passing beneath this, near the hamlet of **Leveri** ('guardsmen' in Turkish) watch out on the banks for the foundations of a Roman bridge. This was the river crossing on the **via Anagnasti** which ran from the coast over Durmitor Plain to Pljevlja and beyond (a connecting Roman bridge still spans the **Bukovica** near Šavnik). From a natural stopping place, where the **Leverska Rijeka** flows into the Tara, a short walk through deep grass will take you to a stone monument: a sacrificial altar to the god Mitra. Near the bank are two tombstones, one bearing traces of a hunting scene.

Ski pass, equipment rental and instruction (some English spoken) are a bargain – approximate prices as follows: ski pass €7 for one day, €40 for a week, €60 for ten days or €100 for the season; baby lift €3.50 for one day, €15 for a week, €25 for ten days or €80 for the season; rental of skis plus boots €5 for one day, €20 for a week; ski school €5 for one lesson, €20 for seven.

≋ Ski Centre Durmitor ✆ 052 361144; www. durmitor.com

≋ VZ Sport ✆ 052 360253

≋ Žabljak Ski Club Božidara Žugića 27; ✆ 052 261421

White-water rafting The mighty **Tara Canyon**, the deepest in Europe, stretches for 80km at an average depth of 1,100m. Its drama is heightened by the verticality of the walls. **Rafting** the rapids has been comprehensively assessed on this river and is a wonderfully exhilarating experience, whether by kayak, rubber boat or elaborately handcrafted wooden vessel.

Rafting trips are organised throughout the summer months. These can easily be arranged directly with private companies (see below), through many of the hotels, the tourist information centre in Žabljak (✆ *052 361802*) or the national park office (✆ *052 360228*).

Rates are around €40 for a half day (approximately 2½ hours), €60–100 per day, €70–160 for two days and one night, €200 for three days and two nights.

Rafting companies have proliferated lately. Among the more established are:

⊁ Eco Piva m 069 070997; www. raftingmontenegro.com

⊁ Kamp i rafting Kljajevića Luka m 069 809188; e kljajevicaluka-rafting@t-com.me; http://tara-rafting.info/?page_id=145.

⊁ Miro-Tara See page 253.

⊁ Tara Tour See page 245.

⊁ Summit See page 253.

✳ ⊁ Vila Jelka m 069 400094; e vilajelka@ t-com.me; www.vilajelka.co.me. Recommended, but they have only rubber rafts.

⊁ Žabljak Holidays See page 253.

ŽABLJAK TO PLJEVLJA

Leave Žabljak to the east, crossing the plain (SOE drop zone; see box, page 256) in the direction of Tara and Pljevlja (37km from Žabljak). At about 23km the road divides, one way leading south down the Tara Canyon towards Mojkovac, Kolašin and Podgorica, the other crossing the vertiginous **Tara Bridge** (Đurđvića Tara), poised 150m above the river, and heading north towards Pljevlja. No Samaritan telephones here, just two sobering monuments. One is in memory of Lazar Jauković, the engineer who bravely detonated its fifth arch on the left bank in 1942 to prevent the passage of enemy forces and died for his efforts; the bridge had only been completed a year before and through Jauković's skill the rest of it remained intact and could be reconstructed in 1946 according to the original plans. The other is the bust, erected by his mother, of a handsome young Partisan hero killed in April 1941.

At the west side of the bridge is **Café Restoran Most** (*outside tables look down the canyon, inside rustic & amicable; cook speaks good English;* €€) and **Camping 'Most'** (m *069 311032;* €).

Alongside the campsite, in the garden of a little house, there are a number of very beautiful lilac trees, full of blossom in mid-May. The housewife hanging out her washing caught sight of us pausing by the fence to smell the flowers and immediately ran inside to fetch her secateurs and cut us an enormous bouquet. The price, a hug. This is yet another example of the warm spirit and generosity so often encountered in the still impoverished Montenegrin mountains.

The main road bears uphill to the north; a drinking fountain is on the canyon side of the road just beyond the bridge. In the mountains the local people can tell you where the water is safe to drink and to fill your water bottles. To view the recently and beautifully restored diminutive **Monastery of St Michael the Archangel**, originally from the 14th century, after approximately 2km take a small road left parallel with the gorge – the road is to **Levertara** but it may not be signed – and descend a steep stony track (2km) to the sylvan plateau of **Bruljici**, above the east bank of the river. (Access to the interior of the church is difficult, and there is presently no priest's house. Ask at **Holy Trinity Monastery** in Pljevlja.)

Return to the main road and continue hard uphill and through dense pine forests, faintly sinister with serried rank upon rank of black pine (the dense **Ljubišnja Forest** is also host to a unique spruce community, *Picetum abieti montenegrium*). This territory is known to shelter wolves which, not unexpectedly, are most visible in January (though you are still highly unlikely to see one). There is a bounty of €15 for killing one. Brown bear are rare and protected; there are thought to be only around 100 in the whole of Montenegro and maybe just half-a-dozen in the Durmitor region. In winter wild boar have been known to attack hunters but they may be shot; a hunting licence is required; check at the Durmitor Park office, page 253.

Continuing north, the road makes a long descent into open and feral land and the valley of the prolific **Čeotina River**, its grayling, trout and char plentiful perhaps because so few are around to hook them; then onward to the city of Pljevlja.

8

Eastern Highlands

PLJEVLJA

The forgotten city of Pljevlja is Montenegro's third-largest municipality. Balkan unrest in the 1990s exacted a particularly heavy toll on the northern and eastern extremities of the country and it is a task for them to catch up with the rapid improvement all too obvious in the coastal regions. Pljevlja struggles with an outdated infrastructure and, in spite of representing a strong mining and thermo-power resource and a once-strong timber and wood-conversion industry, and in addition to providing a robust agricultural contribution to the general economy, the town is threatened with a degree of insolvency. For the people of Pljevlja, good times will surely come around again. But they could be forgiven for wondering when.

Antiquated industrial equipment gives rise to winter pollution and the skies are often overcast although according to records the town has the lowest precipitation in Montenegro. Yet despite the economic gloom the mood is up-beat. The charismatic mayor is committed and energetic. There is a thriving cultural life with a well-regarded orchestra, an art gallery and also a museum of humour and satire. They need that. Meanwhile, for the enlightened traveller a wealth of historical and cultural treasure awaits.

The Pljevlja region produces delicious cheese.

HISTORY There is ample evidence of 20,000 years of human presence in the area. Many thousands of flint, stone, bone and iron artefacts, terracotta vessels, jewellery, tools and weapons from the Bronze and Iron ages have been excavated at **archaeological sites** within the widespread municipality, at such places as Gospića, Milišine, Potkapine, Zenica and Gotovuša. The Romans occupied from the 1st to the 4th centuries AD and a considerable number of valuable objects and stone monuments have been found in the few necropolises so far examined at **Municipium S**, a Roman town discovered in **Komini**, 3km from the centre. Its full name has not yet been established, only that its first letter was an 'S'. One priceless example of treasure that lay buried there is a Roman cage cup of peacock blue **Diatreton** glass. It is now carefully wrapped in a cardboard box and stored in a strong room at the unsatisfactory museum.

After the arrival of the Slavs sometime late in the 9th century, the town became known as Breznica. The name Pljevlja was first mentioned in 1430, deriving from the Serbian word for 'chaff' – which according to legend would drift on the wind from the threshing floors of the huge estates of the monastery of the Holy Trinity, causing grain to grow where it alighted. In 1373 the area came under the control of Bosnian ruler Tvrtko I. The Ottomans conquered it in 1462 and renamed the town

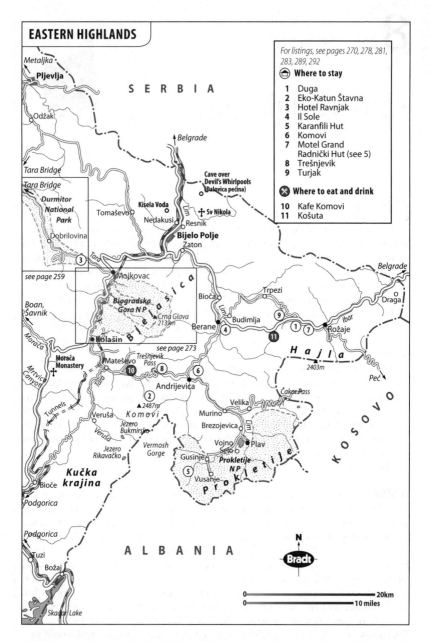

EASTERN HIGHLANDS

For listings, see pages 270, 278, 281, 283, 289, 292

⌂ **Where to stay**

1 Duga
2 Eko-Katun Štavna
3 Hotel Ravnjak
4 Il Sole
5 Karanfili Hut
6 Komovi
7 Motel Grand
   Radnički Hut (see 5)
8 Trešnjevik
9 Turjak

✖ **Where to eat and drink**

10 Kafe Komovi
11 Košuta

Tašhlidže ('rocky place' in Turkish) or Kamenica in Serbian, and from 1575 to 1833 it became the seat of the regional Sanjak-Bey.

After the 1878 Berlin Congress the Austro-Hungarians inherited it and stayed until 1913 when Pljevlja became part of Montenegro for the first time. With some justification, the town sees itself as a fusion of the Christian and Islamic spirits, a hat it wears well. During World War II first the Italians, followed by the Germans, occupied the town. The famous battle of Pljevlja took place on the night of 1 December 1941, when 4,000 Montenegrin Partisans equipped variously with hunting weapons attacked the Italian-held fortress. The memorial to the 214 Partisans killed stands on **Strazica Hill**. Pljevlja Day is celebrated on 20 November, with a number of literary and artistic events staged.

GETTING THERE AND AROUND   There is a good **bus** service connecting Pljevlja with other parts of the country. During the summer the bus station (*ul Miloša Tošića bb;* ☎ *052 323114, 087 281040*) is open 24 hours a day but in winter service is reduced and in bad weather delays are to be expected. From Podgorica the journey should take around 4½ hours (€7); from Tivat it will be more in the region of six hours (€9).

From Mojkovac on the Belgrade–Podgorica–Bar **railway** it is possible to catch a bus on to Pljevlja but the timings are unlikely to fit neatly; a taxi from Mojkovac could cost €50 or more.

By **road**, leave the Podgorica–Belgrade highway at Mojkovac and head northwest towards Tara Bridge (page 263). From northern Serbia, Pljevlja is best accessed from the east via Prijepolje (37km further up the same highway) then crossing the border near Jabuka. The old slow easterly road linking Pljevlja with Bijelo Polje has been much improved. It travels mainly through agricultural land and small settlements; pleasant enough but by no means one of Crna Gora's most colourful routes. It is, however, a useful alternative for cyclists.

Taxi services in town are run by In Exclusive (☎ *19732*), Stilo (☎ *19789*) and Flash (☎ *19732*).

TOURIST INFORMATION
🛈 **Tourist office**   Kralja Petra 1 br 43; ☎ 052 300148; e topljevlja@t-com.me; www.pljevlja. travel

🏠 WHERE TO STAY
🏠 **Gold**   (9 rooms & 2 apts) Marka Miljanova; ☎ 052 323102; e goldpv@t-com.me; http:// pvportal.me/2012/06/hotel-gold-pljevlja. Comfortable & welcoming. Bar, restaurant, TV, billiards. Parking. €€€

✳ 🏠 **Oaza**   (6 rooms, 1 suite) ul Ratnih Vojni Invalida bb; ☎ 052 353049; e hoteloaza@t-com. me. Sometimes spelt Oazza to avoid confusion with similar site in Serbia. Modern, efficient hotel in a new quarter, a useful addition. On the outskirts of town turn east on Prijepolje rd by an Eko petrol station. AC, Wi-Fi, cable TV (receives BBC World Service), a suite that could sleep 4 for a reasonable €80. 24hr reception; good restaurant & bar (🕐 07.00–23.00). Warm welcome though little English spoken. €€€

🏠 **Pljevlja**   (40 rooms, 2 self-catering suites) ul Kralja Petra 1 bb; ☎ 052 323140; e hotelpljevlja@ gmail.com; www.hotelpljevlja.com. Old state hotel amenities & comfort but cheap & central. Bar, restaurant, terrace. Parking. €€ (HB/FB €€€)

🏠 **Delta**   (9 rooms); ul 1 Decembra br 17; ☎ 052 356022; e hoteldeltapv@t-com.me; www.hoteldelta-pv.com. Centrally located, fairly small & simple. Restaurant, buffet b/fast. €€

🏠 **Franca**   (20 rooms) ul Mila Tošića bb; m 067 617532. Ist floor of modern building in central location. AC, TV, restaurant, bar, Wi-Fi. Parking. €€

🏠 **Taša**   (8 rooms, 2 apts) Pet učitelja bb; m 068 839999; www.restorantasa.me. Small place southeast of Hussein Pasha mosque. Restaurant, TV, Wi-Fi; apts have AC & kitchenette. €€

✗ WHERE TO EAT AND DRINK
✗ **Čevabdznica 4**   Pleasant & inexpensive little restaurant on the outskirts of Pljevlja, on the left side of the road leading west to Gradac. €€

✗ **Milet Bašta**   Prvog Decembra bb; m 052 554332. National cuisine. Very popular with the locals. Large & tends to be rather crowded. Generous helpings at modest prices. €€

✗ **Taša** Pet učitelja bb; www.restorantasa.me.
Southeast of Hussein Pasha mosque. Grills, fish.
See also *Where to stay* above. €€
✗ **Tri Džedžira** (The Three Top Hats, also
called Tri Sesira (Three Hats)) ul Njegoševa br
26; ✆052 352005. Good local restaurant with a

cheerful ambience, set on a residential hillside
among Turkish-style houses & gardens. Try the
beef broth, selection of 3 local cheeses (a house
speciality) with lettuce, cucumber & tomato
salad, smoked ham, beef & grilled lamb; menu in
Cyrillic only. €€

OTHER PRACTICALITIES
Banks
$ **CKB** [142 B2] ul Velimira Jakica br 2
$ **Montenegrobanka** ul Tršova 6
$ **Opportunity Bank** [142 B2] ul Kralja Petra br 1
$ **Pljevaljska Banka** ul Kralja Petra br 27

Medical facilities
✚ **General hospital** ✆052 281883

Pharmacies
✚ **Montefarm** ul Tršova br 19; ✆052 21139
✚ **Popović** ul Kralja Petra 1 br 27; ✆052 472183

Other
✉ **Post office** ul Velimira Jakica br 2
🎣 **Fishing SFA Lipljen** m 069 220943

WHAT TO SEE The town today comprises a clump of late Socialist architecture centred around the harmoniously proportioned Hussein Pasha Mosque and fringed by attractive old Turkish-style houses and their gardens, sloping uphill towards the Holy Trinity Monastery.

Regional Museum (Zavičajni muzej) (*trg 13 jula bb;* ✆ *052 322002;* e *info@ muzejpljevlja.com, muzejpv@t-com.me; http://muzejpljevlja.com;* ⊕ *11.00–14.00 & 18.00–20.00 Mon–Fri*) In dire need of new premises, the museum is currently co-located with the public library in the Hall of Culture, one of the drab buildings across from the mosque. Although little is currently exhibited, the museum holds a collection of ancient finds including Copper and Bronze Age items from a site at **Medena stijena** in the Ćeotina River canyon; a considerable amount of jewellery and the beautiful Diatreton cage cup from the necropolises at Municipium S, **Komini**; and a number of rare regional costumes and historical records from the Balkan wars and World Wars I and II. Modest director Radoman-Risto Manojlović (who speaks little English) and his small team are doing a grand job under the most difficult circumstances, but few foreign visitors find them.

Hussein Pasha Mosque The mosque was built towards the end of the 16th century by the man whose name it bears. He came from the nearby village of **Boljanić** and was son-in-law of Mahmoud Pasha Sokolović, architect of the old bridge at Mostar. The mosque is to a square plan with a low dome and a minaret next to it, rising to 42m. The interior is luxuriantly decorated throughout in deep oriental colours and intricate patterns. A number of old manuscripts and printed books in Arabic and Turkish are retained including a valuable 16th-century Koran scripted in Arabic.

Sv Trojica (Holy Trinity) Monastery Situated in attractive parkland, the monastery lies on a hillside a little to the north of the centre. There is speculation that it was built, as are so many religious structures in Montenegro, on earlier foundations, but the church we see originates from the early 16th century with the narthex and the dome added in 1592. That year Father Strahinja from **Budimlje** (in nearby Berane) painted the frescoes in the narthex, followed in 1595 by those in the nave. These are interesting in that not only do they depict the Resurrection, but there is also an extensive portrayal of the Nemanjić genealogy, a departure from the normal tradition of wall painting in this period. A spacious outer narthex was added in 1875 and the iconostasis also dates from this time. The monastery protects a notably venerable treasury and library including a fragment of the 1495 *Manual of Rituals* from Crnojević's original printing press at Obud.

There was, in the 16th and 17th centuries, a monastic scriptorium in which the renowned Gavrilos produced the most beautiful books of his time. The miniatures in his 1646 psalter were the work of Jovan Kir Kozma, considered the greatest Slav painter of the 17th century.

A waterfall cascades emotively from the rock beside the church, separating it from its beautiful wooden balustraded residential quarters (*konak*). Together the property encloses three sides of a stone square, most attractively viewed from the oblique angle of its approach-way. The last major restoration work on this church took place in the 1920s when it was rededicated in dual celebration of the date in 1912 when the Turks were finally sent packing and of the subsequent eviction of the Austro-Hungarians.

AROUND PLJEVLJA Within the wider area covered by the municipality of Pljevlja, as well as the excavation so far achieved at Municipium S, there are a number of identified necropolises, ruined churches, hill forts and medieval towns such as **Kukanj** and **Kožnik**. This region was for centuries bisected by major routes, both east–west and north–south.

The road that follows the sparkling Ćeotina River westward in the direction of Gradac, towards the Bosnian border, emerges from the city into enchanting countryside and it is easy to find a happy spot to picnic. And picnic it must be for on this route there is neither restaurant nor café.

Municipium S, Komini The intriguing, partially investigated remains of the Roman settlement at **Komini** – estimated 1st–4th century AD and considered to be second only in importance to Duklija in the south – are well signed from the main Tara Bridge–Pljevlja highway on the southern outskirts of the city (51km from Žabljak). The last 3km section can be tricky, however. After passing a prominent red-and-white striped factory chimney, take the first turn westward, following the lane for 250m into the village. The archaeological site lies beneath a small rise on the right. Walk between the houses to reach the line of monumental white slabs on a low grassy ridge. The stones bear engravings and pictures in low relief.

PLJEVLJA TO MOJKOVAC

Driving south, the road from the Tara Bridge follows the canyon upstream for 44km to Mojkovac. Look out for Sljivansko, where many rafting trips commence. After 20km, at Dobrilovina on the east side of the river, is the **Monastery of St George (Sv Đorđe)**, dating from the 16th century but destroyed many times during the 18th and 19th centuries. In a nearby cave there was the only school of that period for the whole region. On the west side of the river a forest path leads through woodland to **Lake Zabojsko** on the lower slopes of **Mt Sinjajevina** – a good picnic stop. Very close is **Crna Poda**, a forest of black pines said to be 400 years old – mere infants compared with those old olives at Bar. In April the stony roadsides are garnished with the purple of wild iris. Around 8km further down the gorge is **Bistrica**, where the river of the same name joins the Tara and from where you could launch a kayak or canoe to travel downstream. Because of many obstacles in the river, these are the only craft suitable for navigating this upper part.

WHERE TO STAY AND EAT *Map, page 266.*

🏠 **Hotel Ravnjak** (6 rooms, 3 bungalows, camping) near Bistrica, 18km from Mojkovac; m 069 434849; e info@ravnjak-hotel.com; www. ravnjak-hotel.com. Former hunting residence of President Tito, now a hotel & restaurant. Simple but comfortable chalet-style accommodation in rooms (*€7.50 pp*) or bungalows (*€17.50 pp*) with wood panelling, restaurant with terrace. Campsite (*€5.50 tent, €14.50 caravan*). Mountain biking, rafting, kayaking, hiking, canyoning & other activities offered. Serbian, English, Russian, Dutch spoken. B/fast €2.50. See also page 257. **€–€€**

MOJKOVAC Mojkovac is a small crossroad town on the main Podgorica–Belgrade highway, the turn-off point to Durmitor and Žabljak, as well as a convenient station on the Bar–Belgrade railway line and a useful stop to pick up supplies for expeditions to the two adjacent national parks, Durmitor and Biogradska.

Mojkovac used to be a major mining town for silver, zinc, coal and lead. (Efforts continue to clean up the inevitable resulting pollution, but it is still advisable not to drink the water – boiled or otherwise.)

The countryside encircling this little town is beautiful, fertile and varied. Somehow, perhaps because of so much drama on offer nearby – Tara Gorge, Durmitor, Bjelasica, Biogradska Gora – it has come to be overlooked, a place on the way to somewhere else. This is a pity because one could happily spend a week here, hiking the hills and thick forests and not encounter another soul. And yet, unlike so many other desirable spots in Montenegro, it is just so easily accessible, by bus or train.

History Mojkovac was an important Balkan caravan stop and a market centre for metal trading. In the 14th century King Uros established the first Serbian mint here. The silver coins were called *krstasti perperi* and are much valued by collectors.

The place is remembered for the World War I battle of Mojkovac in 1916. In freezing January conditions the Montenegrins, under the command of Duke Janko Vukotić, engaged in the bloodiest of fights, mostly hand-to-hand and with fixed bayonets, with twice their number of Austro-Hungarians. In spite of this the Montenegrins were the victors. The most recent battle of Mojkovac was in April 1944 when the Sandžak Brigade won another famous Montenegrin victory against the odds, this time over the Fascists.

About 5km away by the **Rudnica River** there are still visible traces of a medieval town known as **Brskovo**.

Getting there and away Mojkovac is on the **railway** line between Belgrade and Bar. At the time of writing two trains a day in each direction stop here (*railway station:* ☏ *050 472130*). For an up-to-date timetable visit the Railways of Montenegro website (*www.zcg-prevoz.me*).

Buses connecting the far east of the country – Gusinje, Plav and Rožaje with Kolašin, Podgorica and the coast – also stop at the bus station here (*trg Ljubomira Bakoča bb, north end of town, near central square;* ☏ *050 472247*), as do numerous independent kombi-buses. At the time of writing there is, however, no **bus** connection with Žabljak, Durmitor or the far west of the country.

A useful local **taxi** firm is Halo Taxi ☏ *19747*).

Tourist information

🛈 **Tourist office** Serdara Janka Vukotića bb; ☏ 050 472428; e tomojkovac@gmail.com; www. mojkovac.travel.

Where to stay and eat There was never much in the way of accommodation but now, with three much-needed and reliable new hotels opening over the course of the last decade or so, perhaps things will look up.

🏠 **Dulović** (7 rooms) trg Lubomira Bakoča; 📞050 472615; m 067 631654; e hoteldulovic@ t-com.me; www.hoteldulovic.me. Internet access, TV, minibar. Restaurant & bar. Friendly reception. No CCs. €€

🏠 **Palas** (30 rooms) Kolašin rd, on outskirts of Mojkovac; 📞050 472508; e hotelpalasmojkovac@ t-com.me. TV & some rooms with minibars. Restaurant, disco, gym, sauna, conference room, laundry service, children's playground & use of internet at reception. No CCs. €€

🏠 **Motel Krstac** (12 rooms) Stevanovac, 4km north of Mojkovac on Bijelo Polje rd; 📞050 795003; e motelkrstac@hotmail.com; www.motelkrstac. com (Montenegrin only). Bright & cheerful. Restaurant (€€) with English menu but no spoken English. Good views over the valley. €

South of Mojkovac
Map, page 273.
There are a number of simple restaurants & refreshment stops by the Tara River between Mojkovac & Kolašin:

✗ **Dobra Voda** Sjerogošte; m 069 233000; ⊕ 24hrs. Overlooks river; near to entrance of Biogradska Gora National Park. €€
✗ **Restoran Raj** Tables set under the trees by the river. No English. €€
✳ ✗ **Terasa na Tari** Kod Brana; m 069 655749. English menu. Terrace overlooking rapids & swinging bridge leading to footpath & parkland. Currently closed following a fire in 2014. No CCs. €€
✗ **Kamp Rakocevića** Fairly peaceful, opportunity to stretch your legs by the waterfall below the terrace. They will make you an adequate *pršut* sandwich, but the choice is limited. No English. €

Other practicalities
Banks
$ **Atlasmont Banka** ul Mališe Damjanovića bb
$ **Montenegrobanka** trg Ljubomira Bakoča bb

Other
🪂 **Paragliding klub Fenix** Vojislava Šćepanovića bb; 📞050 472290

➕ **Pharmacy** Montefarm, ul Valjevska bb; 📞050 470088
✉ **Post office** trg Ljubomira Bakoča bb, opposite Hotel Dulović; ⊕ 08.00–14.30 with a break 09.30–10.00 (these short breaks are common in rural post offices)

BEYOND MOJKOVAC Around 5km beyond Mojkovac, the Belgrade highway turns east to meet the **Lepešnica**, a tributary of the ebullient River **Lim**, which bubbles on through Bijelo Polje and Berane.

BIOGRADSKA GORA NATIONAL PARK

The 5,400ha Biogradska Gora National Park (*€3 pp; children under 7 free*) covers the northwestern part of the **Bjelasica Massif**, from the Tara River to the summit. An isolated area, of which some 30% is primeval forest, it has been to a degree protected since 1878, the date when the Turks were finally evicted from the region. Thereafter the tract of land became known as Prince Nikola Petrović's preserve. Some of the park's trees reach a height of 60m and some are as old as 500 years.

GEOGRAPHY The park's five glittering glacial lakes – Biogradska, Pešica, two by the name of Ursulovačka (one Great and one Small) and Šiško – are known as 'mountain eyes', revealed one by one as you pass through the tall fir forests. Reflected in the waters, the huge trees seem even higher, and the intensity and depth of colour of the eponymous Biogradska Lake is in part due to these reflections. The three highest Biogradska peaks – **Crna Glava** (2,139m), **Zekova Glava** (2,117m) and **Troglava** (2,072m) – together form a protective shield around the great forest and the emerald of Biogradska Lake. It is impossible not to be impressed by how neatly nature arranges the vase without human intervention.

FLORA AND FAUNA Since 1952, when it was officially accredited with national park status – the first in Montenegro – the region has been under strict preservation control. No artificial intervention is permitted – no pruning, no planting, no removal of dead wood unless hazardous and no introduction of new species of flora or fauna – allowing natural evolution in every respect. As a consequence it is rapidly inviting considerable scientific interest, in no way detracting from the pleasure which it offers the casual visitor.

Over 2,000 plant species are said to be represented, 86 tree types, numerous fungi, dozens of butterflies, and birds including the majestic crusader eagle. Protected fauna include roe deer, red deer, large grouse, brown bear, grey eagle and golden eagle.

An excellent little guidebook, giving plenty of information for the interested layman, is available from the park office. The director of the park tells a Montenegrin tale of how the local people, no longer allowed unrestricted cattle-grazing rights within the park boundaries, have taken to muffling their cows' bells with straw.

GETTING THERE The entrance to the national park is at **Kraljeva Kola**, by a dedicated bridge east over the Tara River from the main Mojkovac–Kolašin road, 5km from Mojkovac and 15km from Kolašin. From there it's a further 4km along a minor road to the national park office and lake itself.

Buses from Mojkovac and Kolašin will stop at the turn-off to the national park if asked, though they don't go up the road to the national park office and lake. Taxis can be arranged from Mojkovac and Kolašin. Note that minibuses are often arranged for groups staying in Mojkovac and Kolašin, so ask around if that's where you're based.

TOURIST INFORMATION

ℹ **Biogradska Gora National Park Office**
[295 B3] Kolašin; www.nparkovi.me (see page 294).

ℹ **Kolašin Tourist Office** [295 B2] See page 294.

🏠 **WHERE TO STAY AND EAT** *Map, opposite.*

Hotels

🏠 **Jelovica** (8 rooms) Between Biogradska Gora & the Komovi Mountains; book through Montenegro Adventures; 📞020 229635; e info@montenegro-adventures.com; www.montenegro-adventures.com. A remote countryside hotel. Private shower, restaurant, disco. Biking & hiking tours, horseriding, jeep safaris, paragliding, rafting. HB **€€**

🏠 **Biogradska Jezero Visitor Centre** (8 huts, camping) 17km from Kolašin, by the lake; 📞020 865625 (same as Kolašin office); e npbiogradskagora@t-com.me; www.nparkovi.me; ⊕ 1 May–30 Oct. Situated inside the park, it has twin-bedded log huts at €20 pp per night, or €3–5 for your tent depending on its size. Rowing boats for rent (*€8 per hr for 3 ppl*); lake fishing permits €20 per day. Nearby National Park gift shop sells postcards & local crafts (⊕ *08.30–21.30*).

Camping

In Jul 2011 Biogradska Gora opened the first Montenegrin dedicated site for motorhomes. There are spaces for 30 vehicles, each with connection to electricity, fresh water & waste-water disposal. Cash can be withdrawn from an on-site ATM.

There is also a restaurant with a terrace overlooking the lake. It's rather solemn & in season often busy with excursion groups who have not been given a choice of venue (**€€**).

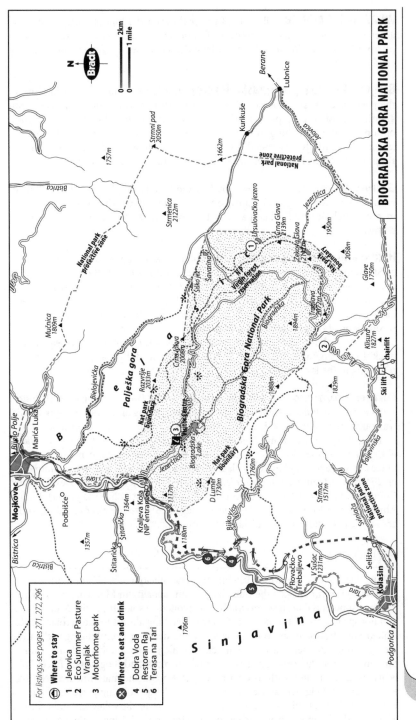

BIOGRADSKA GORA NATIONAL PARK

For listings, see pages 271, 272, 296

Where to stay
1 Jelovica
2 Eco Summer Pasture Vranjak
3 Motorhome park

Where to eat and drink
4 Dobra Voda
5 Restoran Raj
6 Terasa na Tari

WHAT TO SEE AND DO All parts of the park, even the highest peaks, are easily accessible to the reasonably energetic. To idle by the reflective Biogradska Lake, a mirror of Thoreau's Walden Pond in Massachusetts, is an altogether more relaxing exercise.

Biogradska Lake (Biogradska jezero) The largest and most enchanting of the park's five lakes is Biogradska (altitude 1,094m, length 1,100m, average depth 4.5m). Accessible by asphalt road and with parking close by, it is also a good option for visitors wishing to take things a little easy. A pedestrian path encircles it, with thoughtfully positioned rest benches, and a long wooden bridge spans the **Biogradska River**. In summer this bridge is lost in luxuriant greenery.

Getting there The 4km access road to the lake is supplemented by 40km of earthen roads allowing heavy-duty tourist vehicles, mountain bicycles and hikers to cross Bjelasica and other parts of the park. These roads are intersected by pathways.

Hiking and mountain biking A strenuous trek from Mojkovac to the summit of **Strmenica** ('Steep Slope'), the second highest point on Mt Bjelasica at 2,122m but just outside the Biogradska borders, takes ten hours return and has views over the national park and two of its lakes: Šiško and Biogradska. As the peak has snow cover for six months of the year, without special equipment the hike is recommended only in June, July and August.

A good workout for those with mountain bikes is to follow the unsealed farm track from Biogradska Lake up to Katun Lalević dolovi and beyond, before returning to the lake.

Further information In 2002 the estimable *Green Path Trekking Map: Bjelasica, Komovi and Biogradska National Park*, including hiking and mountain-bike trails, was published by the OSCE with support from Naturefriends International, the Norwegian government and Siemens. Nothing so detailed existed before and it is highly recommended. It's available (but not invariably) from national tourist offices in the region and in Podgorica, and costs €2. A useful and newer *Mountains of Bjelasica Mountaineering Guide*, sponsored by the Austrian Development Cooperation, is available free from the Regional Tourist Office (page 294). Rudolf Abraham's *The Mountains of Montenegro* (page 326) gives details of a hiking route across the national park and Bjelasica to Komovi.

BIJELO POLJE

While Pljevlja has the wider catchment area, Bijelo Polje (27km northeast of Mojkovac) is in urban size the third-largest municipality in Montenegro. Nowhere has tourist potential been so miserably unexploited, despite its plenitude of mineral and hot springs, its vast pastoral front lawn stretching almost to the Serbian border (Bijelo Polje translates as 'White Plain', a name deriving from long ago when the area is said to have been carpeted with chamomile), its mountains and caves and its proximity to the ski areas and state parks of Durmitor and Biogradska. Bijelo Polje is also well connected, with its own railway station on the main line between Bar, Podgorica and Belgrade, as well as providing a useful stopping place on the main Podgorica–Belgrade highway. From ancient times the fertile valley and mild climate encouraged all-comers. It was ideal for growing crops, raising cattle, bee-keeping and hunting. The caravan routes from the Adriatic to the north and east enabled its inhabitants to trade and in return to obtain salt, one commodity they lacked.

HISTORY The town of Bijelo Polje is believed to have been founded by the Serbian Nemanjićs in the 12th century when the **Church of St Peter and Paul** was built. This church became, in 1321, the episcopal seat. Here, as in Pljevlja, there was a scriptorium and some examples of its work remain, including the Miroslav Ljevo Gospel, named after the Nemanjić duke benefactor of the church. Inscribed in Cyrillic on parchment, this is regarded as one of the finest illuminated manuscripts in the country.

It is surprising anything survived the 15th-century Turkish sacking of the town. The Turks destroyed the church and drove out the monks, who took what they could for safe keeping to the 14th-century **Church of Sv Nikola**, on the opposite side of the River Lim, which was easier to protect. This church still contains a sizeable library, including historical detail recorded by the monks. Two hundred years later, when it was decided to construct another church, and to avoid further incurring Ottoman wrath, a remote site was chosen above the Bistrica River. That church too was named Sv Nikola. In 1741 the Turks rebuilt St Peter and Paul as a mosque. It is said that they brought the stone they needed in one day and one night and that it remained a mosque until 1912, when they were evicted. A few years later, beneath layers of plaster, an exquisite fresco by an unknown painter was discovered. It depicts the original church resting in the hand of its protector. From this a reconstruction was initiated and the building was finally consecrated in 1962. Elements of the belltower, however, do not belie its previous incarnation as a mosque.

Bijelo Polje's population today is 49% Muslim and 49% Orthodox, and there is a flourishing mosque one street away from the Church of St Peter and Paul.

GETTING THERE AND AWAY Bijelo Polje is on the main highway linking Podgorica with Belgrade, and on the Bar–Belgrade railway line. The **railway station** (✆ *050 478560*) is beside the main road some 2km on the northern outskirts of town. There are four trains daily going to Bar, and one each to Podgorica, Belgrade and Subotica; for timetables visit the Railways of Montenegro website (*www.zcg-prevoz.me*).

There are about seven **bus** connections a day with Podgorica (€7.50), and others to the coast, and the eastern corner of the country, as well as one through bus a day to Belgrade. Podgorica buses start from the **bus station** (✆ *050 432219*) at around 06.00. Some bus timetables are listed at www.autobusni-kolodvor.com.

Taxi companies around town:

🚖 **Auto Taxi** ✆19760
🚖 **De Luxe Taxi** ✆19716
🚖 **Gradski Taxi** ✆19797
🚖 **Plavi Taxi** ✆19757
🚖 **Roller Taxi** ✆19735

TOURIST INFORMATION
ℹ️ **Bijelo Polje Tourist Office** Nedjeljka Merdovića bb; ✆050 484795; e tobp@t-com.me; www.tobijelopolje.me. You can also seek travel advice from the tourist office in Kolašin (✆*020 864254; tokolasin@t-com.me; www.tokolasin.me*).

WHERE TO STAY
🏠 **Bijela Rada** (57 rooms) ul Slobode; ✆050 432908; e g-prab@yahoo.com. Uninspired & not very welcoming; expensive for what it offers. **€€€**

🏠 **Durmitor** (17 rooms) Rakonje bb, Kancelarija; ✆050 488111; e durmitorbp@t-com. me. The hotel is pretty basic & a bit noisy, between

8

the main road & the railway line, but hospitable. AC, TV. Laundry service. One of the town's better restaurants (€€€). Decent b/fast, popular with locals; don't miss the *priganice* with honey. English spoken. CCs accepted. €€

⌂ **MB Dvori** (10 rooms) Main Belgrade–Podgorica road (travelling from the south don't follow signs to centre of town or you'll miss this hotel); ☎ 050 488571; e mbdvori@t-com.me. Quite new & well appointed, quieter at the back, a useful addition to the town. Decent pizzeria/restaurant (€€€). €€

⌂ **Royal** (10 rooms) Main Belgrade–Podgorica road, closer to town; ☎ 050 431900. A comfortable new hotel with a local atmosphere; right now the best hotel in town. Minimal English unless the delightful son of the house, Duško, is home from school. Well-equipped spacious bedrooms (all on 1st floor; no lift). Dbl glazing, AC, TV with English movie channel, decent bathroom with proper hairdryer. No need to remove shoes; this is a Serbian house. Large restaurant (€€€) popular with the locals, all of whom chain-smoke. Parking in front can become congested. CCs accepted. €€

✗ WHERE TO EAT AND DRINK

✗ **Kisela Vode** 5km north of town by the Kisela Vode springs; ☎ 050 478506. Traditional northern Montenegrin country cooking; delicious buckwheat pancakes with soft cow's milk cheese are a speciality. Garden seating. €€

✗ **Redjina** 6 Omladinska bb, in town centre; ☎ 050 31599. Cheerful small place serving ham, cheese, pizza, snacks & main meals; or you may simply order a bottle of wine. Very welcoming owner. €€

SPORTS AND OTHER ACTIVITIES
Biking and hiking
🚲 **RAMS** ☎ 050 432374; e rams@t-com.me

Fishing
🎣 **SFA Sinjavac** m 067 328777

Paragliding
🪂 **Paragliding klub Dynamic** 3rd Januara a/3; ☎ 050 476557; e paramonte@t-com.me. Help & support for visiting paragliders. Transport & guidance; lessons; tandem flights arranged.

Rafting
🛶 **Durmitor** ☎ 050 488111; e durmitorbp@t-com.me

OTHER PRACTICALITIES
Banks
$ **Atlasmont Banka** Tomaša Žižića 18
$ **CKB** Živka Žižića 14
$ **Montenegrobanka** ul Slobode 6
$ **Nikšića Banka** Muha Dizdarevića bb
$ **Opportunity Bank** 3 Januara br 1

Other
➕ **General hospital** ☎ 050 432411
➕ **Pharmacy** Montefarm, ul Slobode bb; ☎ 050 432040
Market day On Sat (towards railway station)
✉ **Post office** ul Tomaša Žižića br 2; ⏰ 07.00–20.00 Mon–Sat

WHAT TO SEE
Town Museum (Zavičajni muzej) (*Radnička bb;* ☎ *050 431579;* ⏰ *08.00–16.00 Mon–Fri; entry €1*) Bijelo Polje's museum contains local archaeological artefacts and folk objects as well as World War II memorabilia. It's worth a visit.

Around Bijelo Polje North of town take the small road that follows the east bank of the River Lim, crossing the plain to the point where it is joined by the sparkling **River Bistrica** ('Bright Water'), which tumbles down from the remote **Đalovića Gorge**. At **Lozna Luka** the attractive stone bridge over the Bistrica is the oldest monument from the Turkish period. Continuing east on this minor road, look for another and quite different **Sv Nikola Church** (approximately 20km from Bijelo Polje). On the south side of the river, it rests on a small hillock. The place is called **Podvrh** but there is nothing to tell you so. It is quite difficult to find, but beautifully bucolic and worth the effort. Alas you are unlikely to locate the key. Built in the troubled 17th century, its concealed position was purposely chosen.

The road soon deteriorates and were you to follow the gorge on up a rough track (4x4, mountain bike or foot) near the spring of Bistrica you would arrive at one of the entrances to the awesome **Pećina nad Vrazjim Firovima** ('Cave over Devil's Whirlpools') also known as **Đalovića Pećina** – not yet fully explored; so far 12km of the cave has been surveyed. At present it is open only to speleologists.

Around 5km north of the centre of Bijelo Polje (26km from the Serbian border) are the **Kisela Voda** springs, rich in minerals. You may fill your bottles at no cost. The rustic restaurant nearby has the same name.

BIJELO POLJE TO BERANE Leave Bijelo Polje in a southerly direction and where the road divides, turn left (east and subsequently south), following the twists of the lilting River Lim through lovely rugged countryside. Roughly 7km south of Bijelo Polje, near the village of Ribervina and among the plum orchards, look out for the newly reconstructed tiny church of **Sv Jovan** (9th–11th century). It sits on the hill beside a small post office (⊕ *07.00–13.30 Mon–Sat*); no queue and a good place to buy stamps – if the postmistress isn't still chatting up the gravedigger.

Following the Lim all the way, pass by the small town of **Bioča**, with its big mosque still under construction at the time of writing. From here it's a further 12km or so to Berane.

BERANE

Berane, 32km from Bijelo Polje, is often referred to by local people by its former name, **Ivangrad**. It is ironic that poor Berane should wear on its closest hilltop a huge monument to freedom, for in recent times the city has experienced economic problems. In common with neighbouring border towns, towards the end of the 1990s it took its full share of responsibility for refugees escaping conflict in nearby states. As a result, some facilities – such as hotels that provided temporary shelter for the dispossessed – have been slow to reopen and are still out of action.

These things should not deter the open-eyed traveller though; this town deserves a closer look.

HISTORY The town was ostensibly founded by the Turks in 1862, but there is already ample evidence of settlements long before: Neolithic, Bronze Age, Celt, Illyrian, Roman, Byzantine, Slav – take your pick (an appropriate term in view of the wealth of accidental finds in the surrounding area).

A nice Montenegrin tale features a young boy, Milutin Babović of the Vasojevići clan, and tells of how, on 7 April 1862 after victory over the Turks at the battle of Rudes, near Berane, he carried the news on foot to Prince Nikola at Cetinje, covering 100km in eight hours. As a result the Prince nicknamed him 'Telegraph' and hired him as a permanent 'postman'. A subsequent story relates that Telegraph was one evening instructed to carry a dispatch to Cattaro. As the Prince was coming from dinner he was surprised to encounter Babović apparently still in the passageway. 'You had better be on your way, Telegraph,' said the Prince. 'But I have already returned,' replied the boy.

GETTING THERE AND AROUND Berane is on the bus route connecting Rožaje (€1.60) and Podgorica (€6). There are about a dozen **buses** in each direction daily starting at 05.10 and finishing at about 20.30 (*bus station: ul Dušana Vujoševića bb;* ☏*051 234828*). To check departures from Podgorica visit www.autobusni-kolodvor. com. Some long-distance buses make a refreshment break in or near Berane; for instance, at the time of writing, the once daily connection from Peć in Kosovo stops here at around 13.30.

There is no railway station. For a **taxi** service contact Limtaxi (☏ *19595*).

TOURIST INFORMATION
🖪 **Tourist organisation** Mojsije Zečevića bb; ☏051 236664; e toberane@t-com.me; www. toberane.me

🏠 WHERE TO STAY *Map, page 266.*

🏠 **Il Sole** (26 rooms) ul Polimska 71; ☏051 231270; e hotelilsole@t-com.me. Just 30m from the River Lim, & 500m from the centre of Berane in the direction of Andrijevica, the relatively new Il Sole has set the standard for Berane hotels. Comfortable modern décor. Gym, sauna, massage, conference room, internet access. Children under

2 stay free; up to 12, half price. Also runs the Etna restaurant (see below). **€€€**

🏠 **S** (10 rooms) Mitropolita Pajsije; ☏051 232031. Comfortable & hospitable place, centrally located on road leading from the bus station. TV, free Wi-Fi, laundry service. Pets allowed. Restaurant & bar. CCs accepted. Limited parking. **€€**

🍴 WHERE TO EAT AND DRINK There are several cheerful **café-bistros** in the vicinity of the bazaar serving simple snacky food.

✳ 🍴 **Dva Jelena** ('Two stags') Svetosavska bb; m 067 853693. Good, friendly, family-run restaurant close to the west bank of the Lim. Jelena Pesić will welcome you warmly, albeit in Montenegrin. Veal, fish & traditional Montenegrin dishes with an Italian twist. No CCs. **€€€**

🍴 **Etna** Polimska 78a; ☏051 233776. Attentive service & above-avg food with an Italian emphasis. Smart ambience. A subsidiary of, & just across the road from, Il Sole hotel (above). **€€€**

OTHER PRACTICALITIES
Banks
$ **Atlasmont Banka** trg 21 jula bb
$ **CKB** 21 jula bb
$ **Opportunity Bank** Mojsija Zečevića 22

Medical facilities
➕ **General hospital** ☏051 230614

Pharmacies
➕ **Apoteke Centar** ul Mojsije Zečevića; ☏051 233033
➕ **Montefarm** ul Mojsije Zečevića; ☏051 231079

Other
✉ **Post office** ul IV Crnogorska brigade 5; ⊕ 07.00–20.00
🎣 **Fishing SFA Lim** m 067 544966; e obadovicz@t-com.me

WHAT TO SEE AND DO Berane is centred on the west bank of the river, its streets radiating from the main square. However, it is the mountain backdrop to the town that at once captures the visitor's attention. To get your bearings, climb the low **Jasikovac Hill** on the east side of the river. Its summit, once a Turkish fortress, has since 1977 been the guardian of a rather stark monument to freedom (*slobode*). Forty slabs of stone surround a gigantic 18m obelisk representing a bullet. The stones are engraved to depict the history of adversity this region has withstood, bearing an axiomatic reflection, 'Better a grave than a slave', and concluding with a marmoreal statement by Njegoš: 'Who would teach others to be gallant, were it not for their martyrs?'

Polimski muzej (*Miloša Mališića 3;* ✆ *051 234276;* e *polimskimuzej@t-com. me; www.polimskimuzej.me;* ◷ *09.00–21.00 Tue–Sun; €1*). Especially when the weather is inclement, Berane's mountain setting, with its strange carbon-copy rock formations, can all appear very stagey, so this is an appropriate time to seek refuge in the excellent museum. Completely reworked a few years ago, the exhibition covers a wide region, embracing Berane, Plav, Andrijevica, Rožaje and Bijelo Polje. Numismatic, heraldic and photographic displays feature within the historical, ethnographic and archaeological collections. Look out for the 14th-century chain-link vest serendipitously recovered from the Lim.

In a street adjacent to the museum there is a lively **bazaar**.

Đurđevi Stopovi (Pillars of St George) Monastery

Close to a disused military airport on a slope a little to the north of town is this 13th-century monastery. In 1219 Sv Sava (Nemanjić) established the Budimiljan Episcopy here (since then it has been partially burnt and half destroyed five times but there is still quite a lot to see). Note the bishop's throne; its built-in ceiling has recently been increased in height; the newest bishop is another Montenegrin giant, 2m tall, and they were concerned for his head. The beautiful glass chandelier is also a fairly recent acquisition and a deviation from the more austere style of lighting normally encountered in northern Montenegrin churches. It was chosen by Father Nikodem who, sadly, died aged only 57 in spring 2002. Another martyr, he had been in prison twice for smuggling literature – ten years in total. A very good man, they will tell you. During the Turkish occupation the lead was taken from the roof to make bullets and in World War I the monastery was requisitioned by the Austro-Hungarians to stable their horses. A few early frescoes have been uncovered (possibly from the brush of Strahinja of Budimlje), certainly since Edith Durham passed by in 1903 ('Inside no trace of wall painting remains ... all is forlorn and melancholy'). Incorporated into the wall is a Byzantine gravestone discovered in Budimlje (see below).

Sudikovo Monastery

As you look down from Jasikovac Hill it is interesting to speculate on ancient settlements. The topography, with three similar pyramidal outcrops, is curious. One of them, over the east bank of the Lim and a little to the north, bears all that remains of Sudikovo Monastery. When or by whom it was built is still a question, but it is considered to have been of sufficient importance that at least one of the Serbian emperors was crowned here. What is well recorded is the scriptorium that was installed and which survived until 1738, at which time the Turks razed the entire complex and its contents.

To visit (2½ hours round trip on foot), set out from opposite the disused Berane Hotel, follow the east bank of the Lim initially along a suburban street of attractive Turkish houses, turn uphill to go widely around two sides of a large paper mill, thereafter follow a small track over a bridge and past a garbage dump, then through rural smallholdings. Keep the riverbank as a point of reference. Above the remains at this spectacular spot at the entrance of **Tivranska Gorge** is **Budimlje** village, where the church painter Father Strahinja was born. Recent finds in this village have lent credence to the importance of the area.

Skiing **Lokve Ski Centre** (*beside Mt Cmiljevica, 15km east of town on road to Novi Pazar;* m *067 465834;* e *htpberane@t-com.me*) Recently reopened. Ski-lift and runs for varying levels of experience, including slalom run. No website but contact tourist office in Berane for up-to-date information, including accommodation at the ski centre.

BEYOND BERANE

BERANE TO ANDRIJEVICA Southwest from Berane, the route again takes up with the River Lim and follows it south through **Gornje Polimje** to **Andrijevica**, 16km from Berane, where it is joined by the **Zlorečica** and **Kraštica** rivers on the narrow **Radunovac Plateau**.

ANDRIJEVICA From a traveller's viewpoint the particular significance of the oversized village of Andrijevica is as a gateway to the Komovi, yet another breaking wave in the seemingly infinite ocean of rock that constitutes Crna Gora's share of the Dinaric Alps. But it's more than simply a junction of roads.

Founded in the 12th century by the Nemanjićs, the stronghold was eventually destroyed by the Turks but in more recent centuries grew to prominence again. It is particularly associated with the Montenegrin Basojević clan who, in a country where heroism is the benchmark, were noted for their exceptional valour against all opponents. In many respects these doughty mountain men resemble the traditional Scottish Highlander. As Carnimeo puts it:

> Great bravery and pride made the Balkan tribes akin to the Scottish clans. Even their clothing was strangely similar because of their *strouka*, a fringed wool cloak like the British plaid.

In the 19th century, *vladika* Petar II Petrović Njegoš laid the foundation of the **Church of St Andrew**, to be built of hewn stone in the same manner as an original 12th-century church inevitably demolished in the wars with the Turks. It was completed in 1887 and is now the oldest building standing. Nearby is a garden of juniper, lime and acacia, a memorial to the warriors of battles in 1912–21 (for these people it never ceased) and for all who died between 1941 and 1945.

This little town, so easily passed by, also forms the corner of Montenegro's inconvenient pocket with Kosovo to the east and Albania to the south. For these geographical reasons Andrijevica became host to a significant number of refugees. Its lovely position at the confluence of three rivers and its historical associations mean that it should have a good tourist future.

Getting there The **bus** connecting Gusinje and Plav with Berane, Mojkovac, Kolašin and Podgorica stops here five times daily between 07.00 and 20.50, but do check times with the tourist office. There are no trains.

If you're coming by **car** or **bike** from Podgorica or Kolašin you can take a shorter and more attractive route via Mateševo and over the pass (with wonderful views of the Komovi peaks) at Trešnjevik.

Tourist information
🖿 **Andrijevica Tourist Office** Branka Deletića
bb; ☎051 243113; e toandrijevica@gmail.com;
www.toandrijevica.me

Where to stay and eat *Map, page 266.*

✻ ⌂ **Komovi** (43 rooms) Branka Deletića bb
on central sq; ☏051 243016; e hotelkomovi@
gmail.com; www.hotelkomovi.com. The only
proper hotel in the immediate area is family-
run by Slobodan Guberinić & son Marko (who
speaks fluent English), & warmly welcoming. It
has retained much of the dark panelling of its
state-owned days, but also has local artefacts
& cheerful touches. Clean & functional with
satellite TV & Wi-Fi. Good bathrooms with decent
hairdryer. Conference hall, pretty garden with
tree-shaded seating, & bar & restaurant serving
local specialities. Traditional cosy sit-around
hearth in corner of restaurant where a triptych

hangs, the work of respected Serbian artist Mileć
od Hačve, who was inspired to paint it when
he passed through in 1981. Tennis & volleyball.
Parking. They will arrange rafting & other local
tours. Big reductions for children. CCs accepted.
€€€

✕ **Restoran Most** m 069 563791. This charming
restaurant on the outskirts of town, just before
side road that leads through the Komovi to Kolašin,
has a good selection of grills, fish & meat, as well
as a terrace on the river & some accommodation (*3
basic rooms, B&B* €). The name refers to the bridge
over the River Kraštica. **€€€**

Other practicalities There is sadly not yet much in the way of facilities for visitors
but the town does include a **post office** (⊕ *07.00–20.00 Mon–Sat*), a **chemist** (☏*051
230680*) and a branch of **Atlasmont Banka** (☏*051 243487*); the address for all three
is Branka Deletića bb.

Cycling routes There is an increasingly well-developed network of cycling
trails in this part of Montenegro, both on- and off-road, ranging in length
and difficulty from a few hours to several days. Brochures with maps and route
descriptions of cycle trails in the Andrijevica area can be picked up from the
tourist office, or downloaded from www.northernexposure.me/wp-content/
uploads/2013/11/2013-11-19_150618.pdf   and   www.toplav.me/wp-content/
uploads/2013/09/Andrijevica-brosura-EN-WEB.pdf.

Two of the shorter, easier routes (marked AN01 and AN02, 7km and 16km
respectively) stay almost entirely on asphalt; more rewarding is the ride up to the
pass at Trešnjevik, and from there up to the pastures at Štavna, below the Komovi
peaks.

The 'big' route in this area is the challenging **TT3**, covering some 305km with
8,900m of ascent and taking around seven days to complete.

A detailed brochure with maps is available from local tourist offices, or download
a copy from www.toplav.me/wp-content/uploads/2013/09/bro%C5%A1ura-tt3-
eng2.pdf.

BERANE TO ROŽAJE East of Berane lies another lovely valley drive towards Rožaje
(30km from Berane), through fields overgrown with deep grass and quilted with
red and yellow poppies, heliotrope, buttercup and gentian (gentian is protected
throughout Montenegro and may not be picked, but is not as uncommon as that
implies). The locals will tell you this is the sunniest region in former Yugoslavia, or
perhaps second only to the Croatian islands. You will see groups of women, heads
covered, busy in the fields.

ROŽAJE

Enfolded by dark jade mountains, little Rožaje is a gemstone, well known
throughout the Balkans for the richness of its evergreens. This is in part because
the town has long adopted an ecological principle that for each tree felled, two

should be planted. Late in April the high escarpment that forms the mighty **Hajla** (2,400m) is still white-rimmed. Beyond and behind lie the mighty **Čakor Pass** and the **Rugova Gorge**, through which the battered Second Serbian Army was forced to retreat in the winter of 1915/16 to Albania and then to Corfu. (For an account of crossing the pass by bike, see the box on pages 286–7.) Kosovo is only 38km away but this does not feel like a border town.

The town itself is assembled around the little **River Ibar**, which flows down the valley beneath the Ganića kula, a rebuilt Turkish tower originating from the early 19th century, at which time it would have served as a traditionally fortified residence used to shelter citizens from their enemies.

The contemporary town consists of a mix of unexceptional recent architecture with a fair number of mellowed and intricate Turko-Balkan houses. The latter represent a perfect example of the genre seen in a more diluted form in the vernacular of Bar. A typical dwelling comprises a wide umbrella-like tiled roof surmounting an upper storey, often with a decorative bay-window feature, the ground floor taller with small windows or no windows at all. Frequently there is a dominant central chimney. Of the two mosques, the 19th-century one echoes the same harmonious style whereas the older, dating from the 17th century, was reconstructed in the 1960s and did not preserve its original design.

Rožaje is almost 90% Muslim. The women hard at work in the surrounding fields are gathering *kopriva* (nettles), but not for soup. Here a local speciality is *pita od kopriva* (cheese and nettle pie). In Rožaje everything you eat will be locally grown, and often organic. This is a naturally healthy place: no-one is overweight, few are rich and the inhabitants are known for their longevity – especially the women, they will add. There is a special sense of well-being and community about the place.

HISTORY Rožaje was founded as a Turkish fortress in 1683 but, if only from its geographical position, earlier habitation can be assumed. Indeed, remnants of walls at the edge of town on **Brezovac Hill** are thought to be Illyrian, while foundations of a church in the valley, excavated at the beginning of the last century, were established as dating from the Nemanjić period when it is suggested that the place may have been known as Ružica, though details are opaque.

Rožaje has an especially hospitable reputation and a long tradition of caring for the disadvantaged. When the Serbian Army was in retreat in December 1915, some of them passed through Rožaje. The local populace, though already poor themselves, fed and clothed the despairing soldiers. In recognition of this humanity, a street in Belgrade is named after the town. In a cruel twist, the pursuing Austro-Hungarians subjected the local people to three terrible years of deprivation, which are still referred to as 'the hungry years' and which only ended with the Armistice and the withdrawal of the occupying forces.

GETTING THERE There are regular **buses** to and from Podgorica via Berane (*bus station:* \ *051 271115*). The journey takes about five hours and should cost €9–10. One bus per day travels to and from Prizren in Kosovo, via Peć. For a timetable of departures from Podgorica visit www.autobusni-kolodvor.com, or speak to the tourist office in the centre of town (see below).

GETTING AROUND 4x4s are recommended in this area as many of the outlying roads are unpaved and the hills are steep. The town, though growing fast, is still easily negotiable **on foot**. A **mountain bike** would be useful for adventures, with minimum impact on the unplundered nature all around.

TOURIST INFORMATION
🛈 **Tourist office** ul Maršala Tita; ☎051 270158;
e info@rozaje.travel; www.rozaje.travel

WHERE TO STAY AND EAT At 1,450m on Hajla there is a mountain refuge with 20 beds. It can be reached by 4x4, but it is better to go on foot (all enquiries through the tourist office).

In town
🏠 **Rožaje** (33 rooms) ul Maršala Tita bb, town centre; ☎051 240100; www.hotelrozaje.montenegro.com. Ambitiously & expensively remodelled in 2007, by 2011 they had no guests & had closed the 700-seat restaurant. The atmosphere now is failed bling. Pool, lift, TV, AC, laundry service, sauna, massage, Turkish bath, casino, nightclub & bar. €€€
✕ **Restoran Milenijum** ul Maršala Tita bb. A capably organised restaurant also serving any guests from the Rožaje Hotel. €€€

Out of town
Map, page 266.
✱ 🏠 **Duga** (7 rooms) Rasadnik, 6km from town towards Berane; ☎051 278266. The recently added pension at this restaurant is traditional, comfortable & friendly, with internet, AC & TV. Definitely the best place to stay in the immediate area. The restaurant itself (€€€) features local dishes, well prepared, & a friendly English-speaking patron who was at one time mayor of Rožaje. No CCs. €€
🏠 **Motel Grand** (22 rooms) Kalače, 5km from town towards Berane; m 069 465539; e beko-rozaje@hotmail.com. A bit of a truck stop but adequate in an area short of alternatives. Small & basic bedrooms with showers. Restaurant has limited menu & a very loud TV. Cash only. €€
✕ **Košuta** In a hamlet called Naselje Kalace, 8km from Rožaje on the road towards Berane; m 069 217066. Opened in 2011. National cuisine. No English menu & no English spoken, but clean, simple & friendly. €€

SPORTS AND OTHER ACTIVITIES
Fishing
🎣 **SFA Ibar** ☎051 272130

Mountaineering
⚲ **Jelencica** m 067 332090; e omkok@t-com.me

OTHER PRACTICALITIES
Banks
$ **Atlasmont Banka** ul Maršala Tita br 1
$ **CKB** ul Maršala Tita 42
$ **Montenegrobanka** ul Maršala Tita 45A

Other
➕ **Pharmacy** Montefarm, ul Maršala Tita br 50; ☎051 271111; ⊕ Mon–Fri
✉ **Post office** ul 13 jul bb; ⊕ 07.00–20.00 Mon–Sat

WHAT TO SEE
Ethnographical Museum (*trg 9th Crnogorski Brigade bb; m 067 566864; ⊕ 08.00–15.00 Mon–Fri, or by arrangement; adult/child €1/0.50*). The permanent exhibition was not completed at the time of writing, but the collection is largely made up of textiles and costume, household items and examples of local crafts.

Arts and crafts Recreation and the arts are emphasised in Rožaje and the **Cultural Centre** is the town's focal point with its theatre, public library and reading room, its programme for young writers and its group of 12 'academic artists', with a gallery mounting 10–12 exhibitions each year. Rožaje does not enjoy the same reputation for painting as Herceg Novi and Cetinje, but it deserves to be mentioned in the same breath. The works of painters on long-term exhibition in the Cultural Centre all deserve attention. Father and son, Čatović and Ismet Hadžić, each have unique styles and they make one think there must be a special local artistic gene.

Not surprisingly, hand-crafted wood is a local art form. Search out the boards and bowls made of hornbeam which add a subtle woody tang to the cheese and yoghurt for which they are designed.

Astonishingly, this little town also has its own hugely active and ambitious **folk dancing** troupe and choir, with a special emphasis on youth. The participating children are as young as seven or eight.

Rožaje also hosts an annual **Days of Mushrooms and Medicinal Herbs** (Dani gljiva i ljekovitog bilja), which runs for a week in July. Around 700 species of fungi, of which at least six species are endemic, have been identified around the town.

AROUND ROŽAJE

Ibar River Canyon Northeast of town on the road to the border at Špiljani, the Ibar River, which has its source in Hajla Mountain, runs through a precipitous canyon, 500m deep. Extreme sports such as rafting at this location are in their infancy and you will need to enquire at the tourist office.

Hiking and cycling The area's enormous potential as a winter and summer travel destination remains virtually unexploited. The upside of this is hills and mountains providing an infinite variety of **trails** for hiking, biking or climbing, all of which can be appreciated in comparative solitude with the added benefit of an abundance of springs, so it is claimed that no-one need ever carry water. Several local mountain guides await your custom; contact the tourist office for details.

ROŽAJE TO ANDRIJEVICA AND PLAV Unless it is your intention to go over the border into Kosovo – Peć is only 50km away – you must now retrace the way to Berane (where the road north leads back to Mojkovac) and Andrijevica, at the crossroads of this neglected eastern corner of Montenegro. From there, continue either over the Trešnjevik Pass to Kolašin or along the River Lim all the way to Plav. The pastoral panorama is every bit as nice viewed for a second time, but in the opposite direction.

CROSSING THE VERMOSH (VRMOŠA) GORGE Only a narrow Albanian seam – the **Vermosh Gorge** that runs **across the finger-like northern tip of Albania** – separates the Plav region from Podgorica and coastal Montenegro. Once a great caravan route traversed the gorge, bartering its way from Dubrovnik, Kotor and Skadar (Škodra) and on to Constantinople; now, part of it has reopened. But the route is unsuitable unless you are well prepared, either with a 4x4 or a mountain bicycle. Very little of the remainder of the road is asphalt and the rest is very rough and stony, and in places – notably at its eastern extremity – suicidally steep. Be prepared for punctures. But the good news is that it cuts the overall distance from Gusinje to Podgorica from 200km to 80km (see page 305).

PLAV

The cheerful River Lim will have been your guide all the way from Andrijevica to Plav, for this is where it came from – out of the bright blue lake (Plavsko jezero) that gives the town its name. On every horizon there are mountains. This area has been inhabited since the earliest times, and there are stories of drawings in remote caves, but it was the Ottomans who left the most obvious imprint.

The town extends upwards, with the quiet lake, a neat oval 2km by 1km, at its feet and the oldest landmarks nearest to the top of the rise. Of these the **Kula**

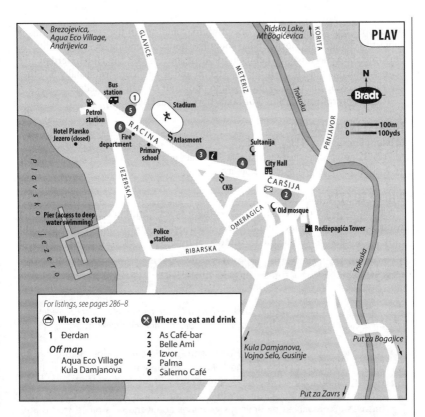

For listings, see pages 286–8

Where to stay

1 Đerdan

Off map
  Aqua Eco Village
  Kula Damjanova

Where to eat and drink

2 As Café-bar
3 Belle Ami
4 Izvor
5 Palma
6 Salerno Café

Redžepagića (**Redžepagića Tower**) is the most imposing. Built in the 17th century by one of the most prominent Muslim families, it served as a communal dwelling as well as a defence tower. In detail it resembles, in essence, a Turko-Balkan house, but with a taller and much more solid base.

Two mosques stand a few streets apart; the older, shingled with an attractive wooden gazebo at its entrance and surrounded by a garden, is one of the oldest Turkish buildings in the town. All the buildings at that time were made of wood. The new mosque is known as **Sultanija**.

The rustic Orthodox **Church of Sv Trojica** (**Holy Trinity Church**), like **Sv Nikola** at **Podvrh** near Bijelo Polje, was built in the 16th century on 13th-century foundations. It is almost hidden among woodland on a hillside at **Brezojevica**, 3.5km north of Plav beside the Andrijevica road, its wooden belltower a little way apart.

Some 20% of the population of Plav is Orthodox and 80% Muslim. The majority of the 2,000 refugees who were sheltered here for several years and occupied the main lakeside hotel (now closed) have now been resettled but it is taking time for the little town to get its breath back.

Friday is market day. In May, there is a **rafting regatta** along the River Lim, from its source in Plav Lake to its confluence with the Milesevka River. A **blueberry festival** is held at the end of July.

GETTING THERE AND AROUND The **bus station** (*Racina bb;* \ *051 251371*) is on the left as you enter town from Andrijevica, opposite the out-of-action lakefront hotel. Buses connect from Podgorica (€10); in summer there are three daily in each direction – one in the morning, one at midday and one in the evening, but this is subject to change. The journey takes about five hours depending on road conditions. For timetables check www.autobusni-kolodvor.com, or visit the **Hotel Đerdan** (see below), which is not far from the bus station and where there will usually be other travellers passing through, enabling you to pool your current knowledge.

There is no **railway** station. For **taxis**, try **City Taxi** (✆ *19787*).

TOURIST INFORMATION

🛈 **Tourist Organisation of Plav** Racina bb; ✆ 051 250151; e toplav@t-com.me; www.toplav. me. A relatively new office run by the municipality; located in a log cabin within the cultural centre complex.

🏠 WHERE TO STAY *Map, page 285.*

These days few tourists reach Plav and there is very little hotel accommodation available. In summer the small hotels listed below tend to fill up quickly, and early booking is recommended. Another option is to seek accommodation in a

---

CYCLING ČAKOR – FROM MONTENEGRO INTO KOSOVO, 2004

Stuart Candy

Note: *Since this trip, taken in 2004, cycling in Montenegro has become considerably more common and straightforward; the Čakor Pass, however, remains closed.*

The Čakor Pass promised to be one of the trickiest rides Montenegro had to offer. At its highest point, around 1,900m, this mountain road to Kosovo has a border crossing. However, while we had obtained advance permission to cross it from UNMIK and KFOR, the international force in charge of the Kosovo side, this was accompanied by ominous warnings about the risks of ice storms and hypothermia, unmade roads and various other perils. Our appetite for adventure duly whetted, we pressed on, reasonably confident that it couldn't possibly be that bad. The journey was part of a two-week trek exploring the tourism potential of the remote Prokletije ('Forbidden') mountain range, where the borders of Montenegro, Kosovo and Albania meet. It is here that an international Peace Park is slowly being dreamed into existence, and the Čakor Pass is in the heart of this spectacular region.

At a crossroads in the Montenegrin village of Murino, the way to the Kosovan town of Peć (called Peja in Albanian) is still signposted, but this road has not been in regular use for years. Our party of eight intrepid souls embarked on the 1,000m ascent with warnings from the villagers ringing in our ears that not only was the road impassable, but bandits roamed the mountains. Just over halfway up, the tarmac surface came to an abrupt end and we proceeded on the stony track uphill. My chain broke; a dark omen for any cyclist. We encountered two women who again grimly made reference to the bandits a few kilometres up the way. Carrying on fearlessly in that direction, we found not bandits but yet more locals, who helpfully assured us that the bandits were just a bit further on. Meanwhile, as the track rolled out beneath us, we rose to see some of the most spectacular views of the trip, overlooking the valley of tranquil farmland and hay bales, stands of evergreen trees, and the jagged peaks of Albania to the southeast. A shepherd, calmly tending his flock against this sweeping backdrop, told us we had just a few kilometres to the top of the pass. But where were the promised bandits?

private home. In any case, a knowledge of Montenegrin or a good phrasebook is an advantage. Contact the local tourist office for help booking any of these.

The **Hotel Plavsko Jezero** is still empty pending sale and redevelopment at the time of writing, as it has been for several years. With its waterside position it has potential, which will be greater if and when the United States Agency for International Development (USAID) project to clean up the lake and build a new jetty is complete. However, they are rumoured to be losing their enthusiasm for the task.

Hotels

⌂ **Aqua Eco Village** (10 rooms, 3 bungalows) Brezojevica bb, 3km outside Plav on the road to Gusinje; m 069 889759. 3-bed rooms as well as bungalows; conference room; children's playground. Lakeside position, so boat hire, rafting on River Ljuča & fishing. National cuisine cooking lessons. If this hotel is full they can usually arrange accommodation in a local home. The bus between Plav & Gusinje conveniently stops nearby; the hotel can give you the best info on the timetable. Summer only. €€

⌂ **Kula Damjanova** (85 beds) Vojno selo, on the lake, about 1km outside town; ☏ 051 255350 e kuladamjanova@yahoo.com; www. kuladamjanova.com. A wood-&-stone ethno

At the top of the pass, there was a cheerful group of boys with purple grins, who had spent the day picking and eating blueberries. There was also a pair of camouflage-uniformed Montenegrin border guards in a 4x4. They hadn't heard anything about our planned ride and apologetically explained that they would need to radio their superior for permission to let us cross. While they took care of business, we drank in the cool mountain water and the stunning views in all directions.

To our relief, they agreed to escort us down the other side of the mountain, taking the car while we followed on bikes. Although technically still in Montenegro, this verdant mountainside served as a Kosovo buffer zone through which no tourists had passed for at least five years. One or two small houses clung to the slope, and coming downhill we passed one person, a citizen of this no-man's-land, leading his horse back up along the track. At one time this road had been paved, but apparently it was torn up in order to counter criminal activity in the borderland that came with the tragic war in Kosovo in the 1990s. At the bottom, signposts indicated that we were about to cross into the KFOR-patrolled area, and the Montenegrin guards took their leave of our party and wished us well. Now in a narrow valley with sheer rock faces on both sides, there were large concrete slabs and deep craters strategically placed in the middle of the road, which told us why it had been impossible for vehicles to use the route. Anything larger than a bicycle simply would not have got through. However, we rolled on through this silent valley as the sun set, and were grateful for a warm welcome and meal with friends at the Kosovan village of Drelaj shortly after dark.

The Čakor Pass was indeed one of the more challenging parts of the two-week trek. Since some of our party had road bikes, when more robust mountain bikes would have been preferable, and a few were carrying heavy panniers, it would have been nearly impossible had we tackled the pass in the opposite direction. It was also certainly one of the most memorable stages in terms of sheer natural beauty and isolation. However, the episode highlighted the fact that in this part of the world, the danger now exists mainly inside people's minds, a sad legacy of recent history.

resort with a rustic interior, slightly reminiscent of a holiday camp. Popular with children (by the busload) in school holidays. Sgl, dbl & trpl rooms. Restaurant. Sauna, sports facilities, handy for lake & mountain pursuits. TV, internet, conference room. No CCs. €€

⌂ **Hotel Đerdan** (16 beds) Near town centre; 📞051 252503. €6 per bed in shared room of 3 or so beds; if you are lucky, the other beds will be empty; otherwise splurge & take the lot. B/fast inc. Goodish fish dinners. Take your shoes off at the door, bring your own towels & soap. Hospitable; laundry facilities possible. €

Mountain refuges and camping

The incredibly beautiful mountains around the Montenegro/Kosovo/Albania borders are home to a variety of mountain huts, campsites & places to park a sleeping bag. They are without exception inexpensive, somewhat lacking in creature comforts & very seldom patronised by western

Europeans. They can be irresistible to lovers of nature with a sense of adventure & personal flexibility. Such a person will meet friendship & good humour.

On Visitor Mountain northwest of Plav there are two **hunting lodges** (*25 places; bring your own sleeping bag; access by car then on foot*). Some shepherds will also rent you a bed (or a bed space) in their huts. The system is not well organised or easily accessible at long range, but the tourist office (see above) or one of the following should be able to point you in the right direction. Otherwise you could seek advice from Mensur Markisić who works in the mayor's office & speaks English.

Montenegro Adventures (page 30)
Black Mountain Adventure Travel (page 31)
Jelka Tours (page 294)
Mountaineering Association of Montenegro (page 327)

✕ WHERE TO EAT AND DRINK Map, page 285.

✕ **Belle Ami Pizzeria Restoran** ul Racina bb; 📞051 252727. Probably beats the competition but that's a modest achievement. Ask here for help with private house accommodation. €€
✕ **Izvor** Racina bb. A local's local. €

✕ **Palma** By bus station; no tel. Serves grills. €
⊑ **Salerno Café** ul Racina bb; 📞051 251666. €€
⊑ **As Café-bar** ul Čaršija bb; 📞051 252907. Good cappuccino. €

SPORTS AND OTHER ACTIVITIES
Fishing

Lake Plav (Plavsko jezero) & the Lim & Ljuča rivers are teeming with many types of fish, such as pike, trout, grayling, char & chub.

↩ **SFA Plavsko jezero** e omarb@t-com.me. Lake & river fishing for trout, black sea salmon, pike, chub, barbel, grayling, huchen. Club will give you advice on licences, guides, boats, etc.

OTHER PRACTICALITIES
Banks

$ **Atlasmont Banka** ul Racina bb
$ **CKB** ul Čaršija bb

Internet

🄴 **Charlie** ul Čaršija bb; €1 for 1st hr, then pro rata.
🄴 **Internet Caffe** ul Racina bb. Same price.

Other

✚ **Pharmacy** Montefarm; ul Čaršija bb; 📞051 255150; ⏱ 07.00–15.00 Mon–Fri
✉ **Post office** ul Meteriz bb. Also on Čaršija, opposite old mosque.

WHAT TO SEE AND DO Lake Plav (Plavsko jezero) offers plenty of opportunities for fishing (see above) and swimming. At present the nicest swimming is in the middle of the lake: the River Ljuča flows in from the south and the River Lim flows out.

The special joys of Plav lie in its ravishingly beautiful surroundings. About 18km east on the slopes of **Mt Bogićevica**, accessible on foot, by bike or 4x4, the glacial **Ridsko Lake** is concealed by juniper and spruce. Legend has it those who bathe here naked will become more beautiful. Take care; the rocks surrounding this lake are very slippery.

The closest mountain to Lake Plav is **Visitor** (2,211m) to the west. It too offers a lonely lake: Visitorsko Lake. More exposed, in winter this lake freezes over but it is best known for its floating island. The story holds that the island used to be a raft constructed by cowherds who wanted to protect their beasts from wild animals. Because the raft was well fertilised, it gradually became covered with grass which eventually became a layer of peat. There are several hiking routes on Visitor, the easiest being from the north side of the mountain.

SOUTH OF PLAV

South of Plav the asphalt road continues west along the course of the **Ljuča River**. Quite unlike the Lim, it is a placid river given to dawdling. It picks up silt and drags it to the lake. For this reason wicker has been woven in endless bands to support each bank. The result is known as *plot* and has a lovely appearance with the willows weeping above. After 11km, at **Gusinje**, the river assumes its maiden name, the Vruja. It springs from the mountains beyond.

GUSINJE Gusinje is a nostalgic town; once a continuous caravanserai rolled along its wide cobbled street. In the 14th century a settlement grew up with inns and shops, then gradually larger houses of stone were added. Curiously, the few of these buildings that remain bear a likeness in style to their equivalent on the Dalmatian coast, a memento of the dispersal of people and taste. By the 19th century Gusinje was large and prosperous and much more important than Plav. But by the end of that century, when the Turks had lost the **Gornje Polimje** region to Montenegro, the roles had been reversed and Plav had become the administrative centre. However, nothing could take away Gusinje's view of the glorious **Prokletije**, rising even higher than Durmitor and shared with Albania. Today, Gusinje is effectively the gateway to Montenegro's youngest national park, **Prokletije**.

Where to stay

Hotels
Gusinjska kula (9 rooms) Čaršijska 2; 051 256651; e gusinjskakula@gmail.com; http://gusinjskakula.com. 19th-century stone tower-house restaurant & accommodation. €€

Rosi (16 rooms) 051 256646; e hotelrosigusinje@hotmail.com; www.hotelrosigusinje.webs.com. Renovated in 2009 by its new Albanian owners, the Gjonbalaj family. Rooms are very small but clean & the beds quite comfortable. Satellite TV, Wi-Fi. Restaurant. Supermarket on ground floor. Owner, who spent 20 years in Tennessee, speaks English, Italian & Spanish. No CCs. €€

Motel Galerija (5 rooms) 500m from town centre, by the bridge from Plav; 051 256493. Basic but clean & serviceable. €

Camping and mountain huts
Map, page 266.
To stay at any of the mountain huts, it is important to make arrangements in advance.

Eventually, space should be made available for 30 **motorhomes** on the edge of the Prokletije National Park (€10). It is anticipated that each site will have connections for electricity, fresh water & waste-water disposal, and that there will be an ATM machine nearby.

Karanfili Hut (2 huts, 100 tent pitches) Grbaje Valley, 7km from Gusinje; 051 251612; e micoprascevic@hotmail.com. 2 furnished huts with 3 & 6 beds. €5 pp. Owned by the Karanfili Mountain Club in Gusinje.

Radnički Hut e info@pk-radnicki.in.rs; www.pk-radnicki.in.rs. Similar facilities to Karanfili. Owned by the Radnički Mountaineering Club in Belgrade.

Ropojanski Zastan Very basic 'hut' in Ropojana Valley on the Montenegro–Albania border. Enquire at one of the huts above about a key.

✕ Where to eat and drink

✕ **Krojet** Ali Pasha Springs, 1km south of Gusinje on road to Vusanje; m 069 467656. Housed in the formerly well-known Vodenica (watermill), Krojet offers traditional dishes in an idyllic setting, evocative of a Victorian watercolour: a wide rippling water meadow, hedged by mulberry & willow, where the cows wade shin-deep. Ali Pasha was the Turkish commandant of an odd autonomous enclave from 1878 until he was assassinated in 1912, at which point the territory reverted to Montenegro. €€

✱ ✕ **Napolis** Bedluci bb; Plav rd on the edge of town; ☎ 051 256732. As you can guess, a pizzeria/ Italian restaurant, but the pizzas, cooked in a wood-fired oven, are thin crust & delicious. The menu has a few words of English, the waiter less, but he is affable & efficient & you are likely to get good food at a modest price. €€

✕ **Primorka** ul Čaršijska bb. Pleasant atmosphere, decent food, low prices. €€

PROKLETIJE NATIONAL PARK In August 2009 these mountains and their surrounding valleys became Montenegro's fifth national park, home to Montenegro's highest mountain, Maja Kolata (2,528m), which lies on the Albanian border. So far there is no visitor centre and no director has been appointed, but plans are in place and in the meantime this sequestered place has official protection.

From the Grbaja Valley, which runs south from Gusinje, the view to the towering semicircle of peaks is Wagnerian and hypnotising. The Prokletije Massif ('Accursed mountains'), so named because it was traditionally perceived as an unassailable wilderness, has been described as 'the amphitheatre of the gods' and it is easy to imagine Wotan himself skulking among the summits and to picture Valhalla ablaze beyond. It is a sight worth any detour.

🏠 **Where to stay and eat** Overnight camping as part of a hiking trip within the national park can be arranged (see *Hiking* below), but for other options see under *Gusinje* (page 289).

Hiking Towards the head of the Grbaja Valley there is a small, immaculate and well-equipped refuge. Reminiscent of an English village cricket pavilion, it forms the base camp of an exclusive but informal alpine hiking association. The association is a highly experienced, compact group who are able to act as guides. Their English is minimal but with a shot of *rakija* the prospect from their terrace to the wonderful **Prokletije** is enough in itself. You must take your boots off at the door (as in most mountain huts): these men are house-proud. For more details, contact the president of the association, Rifat Mulić (*home* ☎ *051 156535*). Note that there are no beds here, but camping trips can be arranged.

Above Grbaja, on the slopes of Popalija Mountain at 1,790m, there is a rock carving depicting a wolf and a child that is considered to be from the Neolithic period. It is however notoriously difficult to find – although one of these mountain men might well be persuaded to lead you to the site. Conversely, the route to nearby Vološnica, a viewpoint at 1,879m with jaw-dropping views out over the Grbaja Valley to the Karanfili peaks, is easy to find and well marked. Allow a good 4hrs return, starting from near the Karanfili hut.

This and other walks in the Grbaja and Ropojana valleys are described in Rudolf Abraham's book *The Mountains of Montenegro* (see page 326).

On a summer afternoon I came upon two sun-ripened sisters who, having set up their seasonal premises beside the valley stream, were quietly going about their housekeeping. They naturally greeted me as an honoured guest: embraces, *rakija*, fresh soft cheese, warm plum jam and bread from the fire; everything they had.

Warm smiles for lost words, *lijepo* said it all as we gazed up to the August-benign mountain. 'Crna Gora!', exclaimed the senior, raising her fist triumphantly skyward in the manner of a Montenegrin who has just scored the winning goal. The spirit is indomitable.

BEYOND GUSINJE Drive on through the hamlet of **Vusanje** to where the road peters out at a small Montenegrin checkpoint (a local companion could be useful). From here a long valley (Ropojana) stretches apparently to oblivion, but actually to the neighbouring country. As you pause here you will become aware of an unceasing sloosh, for only a short distance beyond the post a magnificent waterfall hides itself, diving in several stages to an unseen canyon floor far below. **Skakavica** is its name and the rocks surrounding it make an ideal picnic spot – caution advised when trying to get the best photograph. At a diminutive dry-stone village, perched on the mountainside opposite, the donkey is still the everyday means of transport.

Retracing the way to Gusinje and turning west takes you past a modern whitewashed Catholic church on the right. Within 500m there is a Catholic church, an Orthodox church and, between them, a mosque. And all are friends. (The name of the street is Grbajska.) At the end of this road is an ancient water mill, in spring prettily framed by plum blossom (*sljiva*). The mill at **Dolja** has a tradition that every 5 May the little girls from the village come to its stream to celebrate the end of winter. They collect water and gather the white flowers that grow there: a type of hellebore. These they soak overnight in the water and the following morning their mothers must bathe the children with this water to ensure good health for the year ahead. This is an area not unexpectedly infused with superstition and ritual.

BORDER CROSSING WITH ALBANIA Travelling from Plav, turn west at the intersection just before the bridge at Gusinje. Beyond Grnčar, 8km from here, the road is asphalt only for a very short distance (see page 305).

PLAV TO KOLAŠIN

Unless you are ascending to the Čakor Pass for Peć and Kosovo (which is technically closed, and very tricky; see box, pages 286–7), it is now necessary to return from Plav with the Lim to Andrijevica. If the weather is favourable, consider the 50km route from Andrijevica to Kolašin through the Komovi Mountains (the final part of the route is along a newer highway section between Mateševo and Kolašin).

Though it's accessible in summer only, it considerably shortens the journey back to Kolašin and the Belgrade–Podgorica–Bar highway or the corresponding railway link. It also makes an excellent bike ride for the energetic.

> It is not, as the school books have it, that Montenegro is barren: that is the delusion of those who only see it from the sea. Its inland half, if it has little for the plough, has many woods and pastures. But they are held in a cup of rock.

This was Rebecca West's impression after taking this road in 1939.

At the top of the **Trešnjevik Pass** there are views to Kom Vasojevički (2,461m), Kom Kučki (2,487m) and Kom Ljevoriječki (2,483m), and a small restaurant.

Kom Vasojevički is the easiest of the three peaks to climb, a fairly tough, and very steep, hike. Kom Kučki is considerably more difficult and exposed, and should not be attempted without climbing gear. **Komovi** could be described as the Switzerland of Crna Gora; while its peaks are as lofty as the others, they share neither the admonition of Lovćen, the abruptness of Durmitor nor the hauteur of Prokletije. Like Durmitor their green uplands shelter *katuni*, the shepherds' summer retreat. Through the beechwoods, repeating corkscrew glimpses reveal far-off snowcaps as the totally beautiful road climbs ever higher before finally roller-coasting down to Kolašin and a jolting reminder of violence sustained.

⌂ Where to stay and eat *Map, page 266.*

Over the last few years more small places offering food and accommodation have sprung up along the latter section of what was once little more than a lane. If you wish to stay overnight in this lovely wild place, try the contact details below, or book through one of the agencies in Kolašin (page 294).

⌂ **Eko Katun Štavna** (10 huts, camping) 6km from Trešnjevik Pass; m 067 380532; e ekostavna@ gmail.com; www.ekokatunstavna.com. From the pass, a rough gravel track leads in the direction of the *katuni* village of Štavna. Designed for hikers, especially those tempted to climb the neighbouring Mt Komovi, & blessed with an eco-spartan streak. Each hut has 5 beds, kitchen & bathroom with warm

---

THE CROSS-BORDER BALKANS PEACE PARK PROJECT: B3P

One of the most beautiful and untouched areas of mountain wilderness in Europe is the Prokletije range, which straddles the borders of Kosovo, Albania and Montenegro. Here are unique rocky passes, meadows, pinewoods, distinct wildlife such as birds of prey and increasingly threatened brown bears.

This area has suffered from recent war as well as centuries of feuding, so it is an appropriate site for a trans-boundary protected area. Since 1999 various international and local organisations and individuals have been working to establish the Balkans Peace Park Project, following guidelines outlined by the World Conservation Union. The aims are to protect nature, promote peace and stability and provide employment for local communities. Since borders are a frequent cause of conflict and war, transcending them is a way to bring peace.

Since 2003, international treks have been sponsored by the Balkans Peace Park Project committee and its NGO partners. The Montenegrin zone of the Peace Park, Prokletije, was granted national park status in 2009.

Roads linking Prokletije to the Kosovar section of the proposed Peace Park run either over the Čakor Pass, extremely difficult on foot or bike and impossible in anything larger, or through the Rožaje Pass. Albania can be reached via the new border crossing at Grnčar and on to Vermosh and Lëpushë. All these roads are good on the Montenegrin side of the border, but only that leading from Rožaje to Peć has a surface fit for motor vehicles once you have crossed over.

In **Grnčar** there is a mountain hut available free of charge for the use of climbers and walkers. Sometimes it is full; if it is empty you will have to go to Gusinje for the key. A new hiking route, the epic Peaks of the Balkans trail, winds its way some 192km through the borderlands of these three countries (see page 326).

The Balkans Peace Park Project is a registered charity (No 1105447) and has been endorsed by the International Union for Conservation of Nature (IUCN) and the UN Environmental Programme (UNEP) as well as by the Research Unit in South-East European Studies, Peace Studies Dept, University of Bradford. Further details: e info@balkanspeacepark.org; www.balkanspeacepark.org.

water. Some meal facilities & camping also available. They can arrange mountain-bike rental, climbing & snowshoe hiking. €

🏠 **Trešnjevik** (1 hut) On Trešnjevik Pass, on road towards Kolašin; e pego@t-com.me. This 6-bed hut also caters for those of an ecologically athletic bent & a love of the open air. Owner runs a small eatery/café. €

✳ ✕ **Kafe Komovi** Kraljske Bare, approx 16km from Kolašin & 30km from Andrijevica. A welcoming refreshment spot on this beautiful route. No-one stops here very often & Mr & Mrs Djinović will be very happy if you do. The menu is short – in fact, there isn't one. It will be a case of what is on the hob. No English spoken. €€

KOLAŠIN

Positioned 960m above sea level, Kolašin has an excellent climate of long, mild, sunny summers and three to four months' winter snow coverage. After World War II the resort potential of the town was recognised in the construction below the memorial park of a sizeable alpine-style hotel called Bjelasica. It was an imposing building, though not especially aesthetically pleasing, and it became something of an icon. Gradually it fell into a state of disrepair and in 2006 it was privately purchased and completely renovated, leaving the exterior design, most likely with a degree of respect for local nostalgia, in the style of the original. Today it is one of Montenegro's smarter hotels.

But the town is tiny and compact, commanding on every side a wonderful outlook towards mountains over orchards, forests and rivers. There are no suburbs and much of the vicinity can be explored without recourse to any sort of transport. Within a few kilometres springs can be found bubbling out of the karst, and unexplored caves (though view these latter with caution).

During the last few years there has been considerable improvement to the infrastructure of what remains essentially a little market town, and work continues. Kolašin can now offer its visitors a wide variety of accommodation options.

Most urban activity takes place between two short streets running parallel east and upwards from the park square, where there are numerous small café-bars among the scattering of shops. Facing the square, a plaque marks the building that once held the Partisan headquarters and is now the town museum. At the end of Proletersk is a fine sturdy statue of Veljko Vlahović, Partisan comrade and friend of Tito.

HISTORY Over the course of its troubled history, the town of Kolašin has endured much brutality and changed hands repeatedly.

The Illyrian Autariata tribe were early inhabitants of this area; hence the **River Tara**. The Slavs first arrived in the 7th century. Between the 15th and 19th centuries the town was occupied and fortified by the Ottomans. All that remains from those four centuries are traces of the Turkish arsenal some 500m south of the centre. After 1878 and the Congress of Berlin, Kolašin became Montenegrin.

Most recently, heavy bombardment during World War II left the town smashed. In honour of its heroic role at the centre of Partisan resistance, a large **memorial hall** and **park** were created in the middle of the town. The gardens are fine and the many brave busts they hold are poignant reminders of the monstrous price they paid for freedom, but until recently the central building had become poignantly dilapidated and lost its message. It has, however, undergone a touch of sprucing up and now provides offices for the municipality. However you view the architecture, the fact remains that it is a monument and as such it should remain. Among the many men represented is a woman, **Jelica Mašković**. From a nearby village, she was 18 when she was killed 'fighting with a heavy man's gun' at Kupress, Bosnia, in 1942.

GETTING THERE AND AROUND The station for the Bar–Podgorica–Belgrade **railway** [off map 295 D4] (✆ *020 441492*) is 2km east of the centre, but incoming **trains** are met by taxis. The timetable (*www.zcg-prevoz.me*) may give some clues on arrivals and departures, but these trains are notoriously late. There are only two through trains a day. A taxi fare into town should not be more than €5.

The **bus station** [295 B1] (✆ *020 864033*) at Junaca Mojkovacke Bitke is close to the centre, shortly after the turn-off from the Podgorica–Belgrade highway. There are several buses a day from Podgorica (€6), starting at 08.30 and finishing at 19.50. Travel by independent shared kombi-bus can sometimes be locally arranged. Enquire at the tourist office or at one of the hotels.

Taxis are available from Lux Taxi (✆ *19501*), which can also provide 4x4s, and Taxi '081' (m *068 004400*).

TOURIST INFORMATION AND TOUR OPERATORS
Tourist information
⊠ Biogradska Gora National Park Office [295 B3] Buda Tomovića 7; ✆ 020 865625; e npbiogradskagora@t-com.me; www.nparkovi. me

⊠ Kolašin Tourist Organisation [295 B2] Mirka Vešovića bb; ✆ 020 864254; e tokolasin@ t-com.me; www.tokolasin.me; ⊕ 08.00–20.00. Quite a new office, a few doors west of Planinar café, headed by Markić Rakočević. Besides advice on local activities, they have details of a wide range of private accommodation, all described in a glossy illustrated catalogue subsidised by USAID.

⊠ Regional Tourism Organisation for Bjelasica and Komovi [295 B2] trg Boraca 2; ✆ 020 860670; e office@bjelasica-komovi.co.me; www.bjelasica-komovi.me; ⊕ 08.00–15.00. Just around the corner from the tourist office is this excellent office, founded in 2004 & supported by the Austrian Development Cooperation. Staff speak good English, as well as being extremely helpful & well informed. They have loads of leaflets & can give advice on accommodation, in particular small hotels & *sobe*. They can arrange snowshoe or traditional hikes; rock climbing; kayaking on the Lim, Tara & Morača rivers; visits to cheese or honey farms; jeep safaris, etc. Snowshoe hikes take place every Wed & Sat in winter; adult/student €15/10 inc guide & equipment. Book in the office. There is also internet access for the use of tourists.

Agencies specialising in responsible tourism
✳ Eco-Tours Kolašin [295 D2] ul Donje Đokić br 5; ✆ 020 860700; e eco-tours@t-com.me; www.eco-tours.co.me. Camping & canyoning

tours in the surrounding Morača Mountains, Sinjajevina & Bjelasica. Organises rafting – 1-, 2- & 3-day trips on either big rubber or traditional wooden rafts, with all equipment, food & transport provided. Pick-ups can be arranged in Kolašin, Mojkovac or Žabljak. Also mountain jeep tours, horseriding & fly-fishing packages, on the Tara & Morača rivers or in Kapetanovo Lake (the so-called 'bottomless lake'), high in the mountains above the Morača Canyon. This latter fishing package inc transport, fishing licence, food & a night by the lake. In addition there is a choice of 4 different climbs that can be made from the lake, inc an ascent to the summit of Kapa Morača (2,226m). Experienced & reliable, what they promise is what you'll get.

Explorer Mojkovačka bb; ✆ 020 864200; e explorer@t-com.me; www.montenegroexplorer. co.me. Also specialise in hiking & biking activities.

Jelka Tours (Vila Jelka) [295 D3] Corner of ul Braće Milošević & Palih Partizanski bb; ✆ 020 860150; e vilajelka@t-com.me; www.vilajelka. co.me. Organised camping in designated 2-person mountain huts (*katuni*) in the summer pastures of Bjelasica, close to the border of Biogradska Gora National Park (see Eco Summer Pasture Vranjak, page 296). All-organic meals are cooked on site with produce from their own land & there are opportunities to participate in all sorts of outdoor activities: riding (lessons can be arranged for beginners); mountain biking; hiking; photo safaris; rafting; controlled hunting; even soccer matches against shepherd families. Best of all is the clean healthy air & the easy silence, although during the night if you listen hard you might catch the evocative howling of a pack of wolves out there in the wilderness far beyond camp.

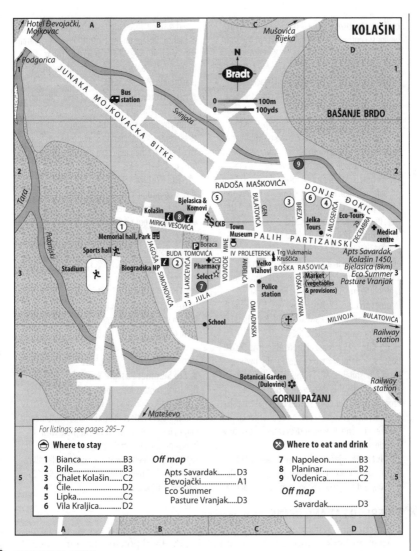

For listings, see pages 295–7

Where to stay

1	Bianca	B3
2	Brile	B3
3	Chalet Kolašin	C2
4	Čile	D2
5	Lipka	C2
6	Vila Kraljica	D2

Off map

Apts Savardak	D3
Đevojački	A1
Eco Summer	
Pasture Vranjak	D3

Where to eat and drink

7	Napoleon	B3
8	Planinar	B2
9	Vodenica	C2

Off map

Savardak	D3

WHERE TO STAY *Maps, above and page 273.*

In addition to the options given below, there's a useful list of private rooms and apartments on the tourist office website (*www.tokolasin.me/smjestaj/privatni-smjestaj/?lang=en*).

Hotels

Bianca (102 rooms, 15 suites) Mirka Vešovića just west of main sq; ☎ 020 863000; e reservations@biancaresort.com; www.biancaresort.com; www.kolasin1450.com. Surrounded by 10ha of pine forest, with mountain views, this is one of the very few hotels outside Podgorica & the coast that has serious pretensions.

This & the Lipka on the edge of town (as well as the ski centre) have been bought by the same group as the Grand Avala in Budva. Facilities are excellent, rooms comfortable & well appointed with cable TV, internet access, room safe & minibar (but in the absence of AC they really do need windows that open properly). 24hr room service; 2 restaurants (€€€€), coffee shop, shops, conference centre. Indoor & outdoor pools, gym, wellness centre all free to guests, except the spa. Gets full during the skiing season & at w/ends; booking in advance is wise. CCs accepted. €€€€€

🏠 **Hotel Lipka** (72 rooms) Mojkovačka 20; 📞020 863200; e sales@hotellipka.com. Opened 2008, slightly cheaper but comparable version of the Bianca under the same ownership, as is the new ski facility (to which there is a complimentary shuttle bus). Useful for those who may seek a degree of privacy; an excellent addition to the town's hotels. 5th-floor restaurant & bar, spa, gym, AC, safe, minibar, internet, plasma TV, supervised kindergarten. CCs accepted. Children under 2 stay free; up to 12, half price. €€€€

✳ 🏠 **Brile** (8 rooms) Buda Tomovića 2; 📞020 865021; www.brile.co. Clean & comfortable accommodation in a pretty building with nice views over central square. Friendly Italian wife & Montenegrin husband; good English. AC, internet access & TV. Restaurant (€€€). Sauna & jacuzzi. Visa & MasterCard accepted. Both hotel & restaurant recommended. €€€

✳ 🏠 **Čile** (15 rooms) ul Brace Miloševic; 📞020 865039; e zlatnido@t-com.me. Family-owned, clean & hospitable. AC, TV, free Wi-Fi, laundry service. Good-value restaurant & bar. Parking. Proprietor Čile Bulatović speaks minimal English but aims always to have his son or another English speaker on hand. In winter they cater particularly for skiers. €€€

🏠 **Hotel Đevojački** (10 rooms) Bakovići bb, 2km north of Kolašin on road to Mojkovac; 📞020 867100; e djevojackimost@t.com.me. Attractive

wood & stone décor; alpine architecture, after style of Bianca. Terrace on the Plašnica River. Restaurant, bar. TV, no AC, free Wi-Fi. Conference room. Nightclub (karaoke evenings); small children's playground. Parking. €€€

🏠 **Apartments Savardak** (2 apts) Biocinovici, na putu za skijalište; 📞020 865956. Lovely rural setting by small stream called Svinjača, on road to ski centre. Connected to & alongside restaurant (see below). Small log cabin units on 2 floors: €50 for 3 or 4 sharing. Visa & MasterCard. €€

🏠 **Vila Kraljica** (11 rooms) 📞020 860360; e vila-kraljica@t-com.me. Just behind Čile & owned by another member of the family. Basically a guesthouse but providing reasonable lodging with AC & cable TV. Shared kitchen facilities (or private if you take the large unit). Little English but reasonable French. No CCs. €€ (€ for 5 nights or more)

🏠 **Chalet Kolašin** (2 apts) ul Breza 10; m 069 015617; e chaletkolasin@gmail.com; www.chalet-kolasin.me. 150m from the main square; apts sleep up to 6. €€

Eco cottages

🏠 **Eco Summer Pasture Vranjak** (22 cabins) Bjelasica; contact Jelka Tours, page 294; 🕐 May–Oct. Set at 1,800m on the slopes of Bjelasica, this is designed to reflect the traditional Montenegrin way of life in the mountains, complete with horseriding, cheesemaking & other activities. Up to 80 people sleep in wooden chalet-style cabins, each with 2–7 beds & solar electricity. B&B €15 pp. €€ (HB & FB €€€)

✕ WHERE TO EAT AND DRINK   Map, page 295.

For picnic and self-catering needs there are three supermarkets as well as a farmers' market on Boška Rašovića. Bear in mind that the local potatoes are renowned. As well as the establishments below, there are a number of cafés and restaurants in and around Palih Partizanski.

Restaurants

✳ ✕ **Vodenica** ul Breza bb; m 069 241507. A sensitively restored, wooden-tiled watermill attractively set beside a small waterfall & run by a most affable host. Pretty good food at pretty modest prices in an atmospheric dining room. Specialities inc *cicvara* (a sort of cheese porridge) & river fish. The best non-hotel restaurant in town. €€€

✕ **Savardak** Biocinovici, na putu za skijalište; 📞020 865956; e savardak@t-com.me. On the road

to the ski centre, good, basic, national food in a traditional circular shepherd's hut beside a brook (Svinjača – Pig River) & an orchard. Tables set by the soothing stream in summer; log fire most of the year. Try the Montenegrin fondue – *kačamak* (mashed potato, cheese & cream). No English. No CCs. €€

✕ **Napoleon** ul 13 July; opposite the school; 🕐 07.00–01.00. Small, simple & affable. Opened 2010. Basically pizza, pasta & chicken. No CCs. €

✗ **Planinar** trg Boraca, on main sq; ⟍020 864454; ⌚ 07.00–22.00. Cheap & cheerful local food & largely local clientele. Wine at €7 a litre is about the most expensive thing on the menu. There is an English translation but take your phrasebook. €

Entertainment and nightlife

☆ **Select Nite Club** [295 C3] Corner of trg Palih Partizanski (main sq); ⌚ 01.00–03.00 Fri–Sat. No admission charge & no live music, but recommended by the locals as the best place to go for late-night action. No CCs.

OTHER PRACTICALITIES
Banks
$ **ATM** trg Boraca, beside the museum. Not Amex.
$ **CKB** [295 C3] trg Boraca bb; ⌚ 08.00–16.00
$ **Podgorička Banka** [295 C2] trg Boraca br 4; ⌚ 08.00–20.00

Medical facilities
✚ **Medical centre** [off map 295 D3] 29 Decembra bb; ⟍020 865140

✚ **Pharmacy** [295 C3] Montefarm; trg Boraca br 5; ⟍020 860480

Other
Automobile Association Mojkovačka bb; ⟍020 867060
✉ **Post office** [295 C3] trg Boraca br 4; ⌚ 07.00–20.00 Mon–Sat

WHAT TO SEE AND DO
Town Museum [295 C3] (*trg Boraca;* ⟍ *020 864344;* ⌚ *theoretically 08.00–12.00 & 17.00–21.00 Mon–Sat*) Who knows what's inside the pink building at the top of the square? The director and sole employee, who has run it for more than 20 years, invariably seems to be somewhere else and it's always locked. The collection is rumoured to cover World War II and the Tito days, but you can't see anything through the window.

Botanical Garden, Dulovine [295 C4] (⟍ *020 865477; tickets & further information from tourist office:* ⟍*020 864254;* e *tokolasin@t-com.me; www.tokolasin. me;* ⌚ *May–Aug with reservation only*) At Dulovine on the southeastern edge of the town, a little beyond the church (walk up the wooded hill leaving some tall painted railings on the left), there is a **botanical garden**, founded in the 1980s, with 300–400 species of mountain plants. Not much room for bushes or trees, but a 5ha arboretum is planned.

The garden is the property of Daniel Vincek. Croatian by birth, mountaineer, writer and botanist, he is charming and hospitable and speaks good English. He is one of the authors of the excellent *The Mountains of Montenegro* (see page 326). Flowers are at their best between mid-May and the end of June, but at other times the garden (and Mr Vincek) is well worth a visit.

Mr Vincek's knowledge is as great as his hospitality and I was delighted to deduce from him a link to a curious tradition. In the course of touring the garden he explained the medicinal qualities and folk uses of the herbs and plants. In mountain lore fresh cheese is wrapped in a leaf of hellebore to arrest the fermentation process. I remembered the children of Dolja (see page 291) and their ritual bathing in hellebore-infused water in the belief of its prophylactic properties.

For an overview of Montenegro's medicinal plants, see box, pages 8–9.

Winter sports Cross-country skiing could be initiated from town, but for downhill you must travel 9km to **Kolašin 1450** (*formerly the Jezerine Ski Centar: the number relates to the height of the start of the ski trails;* ⟍ *020 717845;* e *office@kolasin1450.com; www.kolasin1450.com – Montenegrin only*). There is a complimentary shuttle bus from the Hotel Lipka, which – like the Bianca Hotel – is under the same ownership. They expect snow between November and May but the road is kept open virtually whatever the conditions.

This small area has been comprehensively updated and now has a range of new equipment, including a snow canon, as well as the advantage of mainly north-facing slopes. There are five lifts (rising to 1,900m) and seven pistes (ranging from black to blue and green), including one not-unexciting 4.5km run. There's also a ski school.

Ski passes cost €20 per day for adults, €13 for children aged between five and 12, and €14 for those aged 65 or over. Five-day ski school passes (20 hours) are adult/child €145/72. Skis and snow mobiles are available to rent and there are facilities for snowboarding, floodlights for night skiing and a very respectable restaurant and café (€€€).

SOUTH FROM KOLAŠIN

Note: The highway between Morača Monastery and Podgorica (70km from Kolašin) has from time to time suffered landslides. During or after heavy rains, therefore, this route may be unsuitable.

The road passes first along the wooded **Pcinja Valley**, through the district of **Crkvine**, where there are several log cabins set beside a fast-flowing brook.

MORAČA MONASTERY After 17km the whitewashed walls of the pristine **Morača Monastery** come into view, and its little orchard where the long **Svetigora** ('Holy Mountain') waterfall plunges into the ravine below. The complex presents such an unspoilt appearance, with its rose-draped cloister, its beehives and its tidy lawn, that one might hesitate to enter, but that would be to miss some interesting 16th- and 17th-century frescoes, an icon (the work of Jovan Kir Kozama) and some exceptional 14th-century original depictions from the life of Sv Ilija (Prophet Elijah) and of the birth of St John the Baptist. The latter in the side chapel are all that has survived the Ottoman ravages of the first half of the 16th century. They are thought to be the handiwork of Father Jevstatije.

The monastery was founded in 1252 by Stefan, grandson of Serbian ruler Stefan Nemanja, and was dedicated to the Dormition of the Virgin. It used to be possible to stay overnight at this monastery and needless to say it is a very peaceful resting place, but at the time of writing accommodation has been suspended.

There's a **post office** (⏲ 08.00–14.30 Mon–Fri) beside Morača Monastery.

From here you will be following the emerald **Morača** downriver to the village of **Meduriječje**, about a third of the distance from Kolašin to Podgorica.

✕ Where to eat and drink

✕ **Restoran Počinak** Just north of monastery, on rd to Podgorica; ⏲ 12.00–24.00. A useful refreshment break. Hard-boiled eggs at the bar – like in Paris. €€

✕ **Konoba Meduriječje** Meduriječje. On the uphill side of the road, an attractive stone restaurant. Also a good place for a break from negotiating tricky bends, potentially hazardous tunnels, & long-haul trucks. €€

MRTVICA CANYON HIKE At 35km from Kolašin the **Mrtvica Canyon** runs west for 9km: a great hike. It takes in the bubbling springs of **Nerini** and the old stone bridge built in memory of Queen Milena by her son Danilo. Continuing a few kilometres would bring you at a height of 1,600m to the **Lake of Kapetanov**; some 480m long

Note: *For important practical hints on tackling Montenegro's back roads and byways, see box, page 50.*

The following expedition is not possible by public transport; you will need either a 4x4 or a mountain bike. (Jelka Tours in Kolašin – page 294 – can arrange a guided day excursion to the two lakes described at a cost of about €25 per head for a group of three or more.)

Leave **Kolašin** by the relatively new highway that swoops south to **Mateševo**, and at the cluster of buildings where the tributary Drcka joins the Tara, take the road south (signed Podgorica). At first it rigidly clings to the thickly wooded west bank of the sparkling Tara, which claims to be the cleanest river in Montenegro and potable too (caution advised, the latter assertion may at the very least have been overtaken by the passage of time). It is shallow here, with midstream strands of polished pebbles just inviting a cool summer picnic and a dip.

As the road climbs out of the valley, after about 15km turn left at Veruša and follow an obvious but very rough track through pastoral countryside and above the little Veruša River in the direction of a settlement called Mokro. After some 10km this route will bring you into the very heart of the lovely Komovi Mountains and to Bukumirsko, one of the smallest lakes in Montenegro. It is an enchanting setting, the surrounding peaks appearing deceptively benign, though in fact they present a number of challenging climbs for skilled mountaineers: Surdup and distinctive egg-shaped Pasjak to the south and Maglić to the north. Six kilometres or so further southeast along the track above Bukumirsko will take you to Širokar **katuni** where, it is usually suggested, one leaves the vehicle (mountain bikes can continue) and descends a very steep track (3km) to a second lake, Rikavačko, with behind it the soaring peak of Mt Vila and the Albanian border. It will be a stiff climb to rejoin your vehicle, even tougher by bike.

From Širokar it is possible to travel south by a continuing track (4x4 or mountain bike essential) through Orahovo, Ubli and Medun (see page 112), ultimately to Podgorica; or to retrace one's steps to Bukumirsko Lake and follow a different track leading southwest through the village of Brskut, then south through Donja Stravče and Kržanja to Medun. But without a guide, unless you're feeling very adventurous, it is probably wiser to retrace your steps to Veruša.

and 200m wide, and dropping to an astonishing depth of 37m, it is the deepest lake in Montenegro. It is possible to obtain provisions from the *katuni*. Remember the welcoming lady in Šavnik; her like is not so far from here.

If you have a tent, you may venture on in search of Utopia; it is waiting just over the rise. Otherwise, travel on down the road ahead.

ALONG THE MORAČA RIVER You and the Morača will now enter the Stygian Platije Canyon: in and out of tunnels, some lighted, some not. The river, where the sun never reaches, lies several hundred metres below, while across the gorge and high above, the railway races between Bar and Belgrade; first you see it, now you don't. Why the rush? We know *that* journey is going to take all day.

Eastern Highlands SOUTH FROM KOLAŠIN

8

RAFTING ON THE MORAČA Rafting on the Morača is in its infancy and extremely dangerous; just for starters, access to the river is infrequent and difficult. Smokovac is one such point. Go to www.raft.cz for more information.

✗ **WHERE TO EAT AND DRINK** As you draw closer to the capital, pit stops become more numerous. **Restoran Potaci** (*on the river side of the road at Milinovici, 18km short of Podgorica*) has a row of decent loos in the car park. Staff speak some English and they have a rotisserie, fruit and supply shop, as well as a useful café for snacks.

And so on to Podgorica … Such a country. But I am afraid the secret is out.

SEND US YOUR SNAPS!

We'd love to follow your adventures using our *Montenegro* guide – why not send us your photos and stories via Twitter (@BradtGuides) and Instagram (@bradtguides) using the hashtag #montenegro. Alternatively, you can upload your photos directly to the gallery on the Montenegro destination page via our website (*www.bradtguides.com*).

9

Borders and Beyond

I have always loved the moments of travel when, brought to a halt by a striped barrier, approached by unfamiliar uniforms, you feel yourself on the brink of somewhere unknown and possibly perilous.

Trieste and the Meaning of Nowhere, copyright Jan Morris, 2002
(quoted with kind permission from Faber and Faber Ltd)

Frontiers are enticing, intimating sights unseen, an altered perspective, the other side of the mountain. And now that Tito's old country has been all but fully dismantled these borders have a contemporary significance.

Interestingly, although opportunities derived from separate statehood are clear to see and quite possibly in even more abundance than anticipated by those who voted for it, there lingers a whiff of nostalgia for those united years when the greater Yugoslavia confidently maintained her balancing act, straddling the boundary of East and West, and when most of her people had little – but little seemed enough.

In this chapter I have endeavoured to demonstrate that it is not too difficult for travellers in Montenegro who may, like me, be curious to view the country not only inside out – but from the outside in.

Group cross-border excursions by coach to such destinations as Dubrovnik and Škodra are on offer from most of the main tourist towns along the coast, as well as from Kolašin, Cetinje and of course Podgorica, but this chapter is intended for individuals or small parties who would choose to take a more active role in the design of their adventures.

WARNING

While there is no evidence of unexploded ordnance within the boundaries of Montenegro, there are nevertheless rumours of possible uncleared landmines remaining from previous trans-border conflict. Therefore you are strongly advised to exercise due caution in travelling over border areas on foot or by bicycle and to stick to identifiable, if not waymarked trails. Pit stops and any ventures off the clear path should be made with particular attention to your surroundings.

A local guide who is thoroughly familiar with the terrain is essential and will in any case be able to assist with red tape in facilitating such expeditions.

Neither the author nor Bradt Travel Guides can accept any responsibility whatsoever for any mishap, accident or loss of life incurred in following the routes described herein.

On the borders of Montenegro today there are some 16 permanently controlled frontier posts, with an additional small number where passage is subject to a permit issued by the local authorities. In this chapter, unless otherwise stated, the crossing points described will be of the former variety and operational 24 hours a day.

Note that while most of the following trips could be achieved at least in one direction by an international bus journey, for neat round trips such as these described, a car – or in some cases a bicycle – is really the only realistic option.

TO ALBANIA (ON FOOT) AND BACK TO ULCINJ (WHEELS)

The small control post at **Vusanje** (page 291) is one of the frontier post exceptions, where passage is subject to a permit issued by the local authorities; application forms can be downloaded from www.montenegro.travel/en/border-crossings-and-visas. Beyond lies the beginning of a once-established mule trail leading over the **Qafa e Pejës** pass to remote **Okol** and ultimately to **Theth**, a village misplaced by time, deep within the Albanian highlands.

The route (*see map opposite; approx 20km; 8hrs min*), was vividly described a century ago by Edith Durham in *High Albania*, first published in 1909. To follow in her footsteps you will need the services of a **local guide**, not least to help with red tape at the police station in **Gusinje**. However the process has recently been made considerably more streamlined with the development of the Peaks of the Balkans trail (*www.peaksofthebalkans.com*), which includes this crossing. Ms Durham writes with humour of her struggles through deep snow on the col but the Theth Valley is essentially isolated winter through, with the handful of families who remain to tough it out supported only by their own stores.

It would be highly inadvisable to attempt this trek other than between the months of June and September, even then exercising caution with respect to predicted weather conditions.

Accommodation for your party, including the guide, and onward transport will both need to be negotiated. (The former military barracks at Zastan Koliba near the start of the trail in Montenegro, while at this time available for overnight camping, are run-down, frequently overcrowded and not recommended.) At the Albanian end of the trek, beyond Okol and in the village of Theth, an alternative to the 'boarding house', **Ćarqu** – a simple family-run outfit with hens scrabbling around the yard and located towards the edge of the village in the direction of **Bogë** – would be rooms in a private home. A few years ago a group who did this trek stayed overnight in the house in Okol where the intrepid writer Rose Wilder Lane is said to have been put up some 90 years earlier. See www.albanian-mountains.com for a good list of private accommodation available in this area. In a private home expect to pay between €10–20 full board per person.

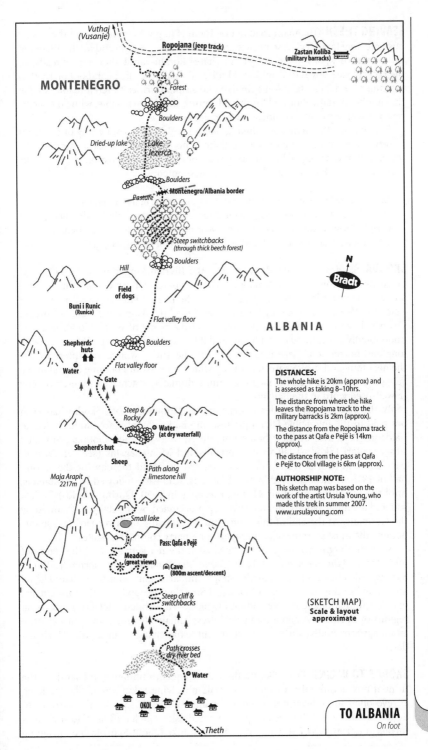

Vuthaj
(Vusanje)

Ropojana (jeep track)

Zastan Koliba
(military barracks)

MONTENEGRO

Forest

Boulders

Dried-up lake

Lake
Jezercä

Boulders

Pasture ✕✕✕ Montenegro/Albania border

Steep switchbacks
(through thick beech forest)

Boulders

Hill

**Field
of dogs**

**Buni i Runic
(Runica)**

Flat valley floor

ALBANIA

N

Bradt

**Shepherds'
huts**

Boulders

Water

Flat valley floor

Gate

Steep &
Rocky

Water
(at dry waterfall)

Shepherd's hut

Sheep

Path along
limestone hill

Maja Arapit
2217m

Small lake

DISTANCES:
The whole hike is 20km (approx) and
is assessed as taking 8–10hrs.

The distance from where the hike
leaves the Ropojama track to the
military barracks is 2km (approx).

The distance from the Ropojama track
to the pass at Qafa e Pejë is 14km
(approx).

The distance from the pass at Qafa
e Pejë to Okol village is 6km (approx).

AUTHORSHIP NOTE:
This sketch map was based on the
work of the artist Ursula Young, who
made this trek in summer 2007.
www.ursulayoung.com

Pass: Qafa e Pejë

Meadow
(great views)

Cave
(800m ascent/descent)

Steep cliff &
switchbacks

(SKETCH MAP)
**Scale & layout
approximate**

Path crosses
dry river bed

Water

OKOL

Theth

TO ALBANIA
On foot

9

LEAVING THETH The main road out of Theth is in poor condition and there is no bus or formal taxi service, so be prepared to do as the locals do and hitch a lift either in or on a truck, or look for a seat in a shared kombi-van. Either way be ready for the rackety ride down to **Koplik** or **Škodra**. Vehicular traffic in and out of Theth is infrequent and it can take some time to find a suitable ride; it therefore follows that the number of days allocated for this adventure should be flexible, while the scenic rewards will more than compensate for delays.

Koplik is on the main road linking Škodra and Podgorica, by way of the **Hani i Hotit** (note: at the time of writing there is no bus service back to Montenegro through that crossing) where overnight accommodation is possible at the quirky and pretty basic **Hotel Mirsadi**. A recent guest noted:

> there appeared to be only two showers in the whole of the building and these were situated back down the (exterior, winding) metal staircase out of the building and in a neighbouring entrance and into one of two bedrooms which fortunately for us were not occupied that evening … But what do you expect for €5 or €6 a night?

ŠKODRA Škodra was once the capital of the Illyrian kingdom. In 168BC it was taken by the Romans and developed as an important position on north–south and east–west trade routes. Captured by the Serbs in 1040 it became a centre of Zeta. The Venetians took it in 1396 and refortified the daunting citadel of Rozafat. Overshadowing the city from the south and the scene of much bloodshed, it is undoubtedly a feature to be explored (and it has a useful gift shop). After a notably long and horrendous siege it fell in 1479 to the Turks, who were a presence for the next four-and-a-bit centuries, during which time Škodra became central in the Sanjak, gradually increasing its powers until ultimately it achieved semi-autonomy (a well-used word in the Balkans).

By the 18th century, under Pasha Kara Mahmoud Bushati, Škodra had even put paid to the invincible Ulcinj pirates, who had suffered ignominious defeat at Valdanos Bay, west of their home port. In April 1913, after another protracted siege, Scutari (Škodra) fell to the Serbians and Montenegrins (see *Mt Taraboš*, page 222). In World War I, after Montenegro had held the city for the second half of 1915, it was occupied by the Austrians, who were followed by the Italians, until the establishment of an Albanian regency in 1920. During World War II it suffered a similar fate to Montenegro, being occupied by the Italians, followed by the Germans. At the end of this, under the dictatorship of Enver Hoxha, Albania became the most extreme of all European one-party communist states.

After thorough investigation of the citadel, the marketplace and the centre of town (*some 3km northeast via Vasil Shanto Street; market days normally Wed & Sat*), will also be of interest. Smaller shops, similar in character to those of Ulcinj, are located in the area around 13 Dhjetori Street, well supplied with fabrics, items of colourful national costume and locally produced wooden artefacts. In the rural regions of northern Albania traditional dress remains for some the normal attire and it appears, on the surface at least, that little has changed since Edith Durham's day.

ŠKODRA TO ULCINJ From Škodra there are frequent minibuses to **Ulcinj** via the frontier post at **Sukobin**, an attractive small town lying 14km west of Škodra. Keep an eye open for a beautiful green-and-white village mosque by the turn-off to **Selita**. Should you still have energy you could ask to be let off at **Vladimir**, 4km further on, from where it would be feasible to hike (about 5km) to the intriguing archaeological site at **Šas/Svač**. Much of the surrounding countryside consists of wetland and is a great area for bird activity, both endemic and migratory species.

Pick up the Ulcinj minibus in front of the **Rozafa Hotel** in Škodra; the journey should cost around €6. (For a full description of this lesser-known but spellbinding corner, see Gillian Gloyer's *Albania: The Bradt Travel Guide*.)

VIA GRNČAR TO ALBANIA AND BACK TO HANI I HOTIT

Back in the pocket of the **Prokletije**, there is an official border crossing into Albania at **Grnčar** (see page 292). But do not be misled by the uniformly perfect condition of the asphalt road leading from Gusinje, for after the briefest of stretches beyond the control post that same road is no longer surfaced and it deteriorates rapidly from there on into the **Vrmoša**.

The vast valley is a wild sequestered place, with those who live there and toil the land doing so in the same manner they have over the past hundred years. That said, a native speaker, travelling recently through the wilder reaches, recalls when hesitantly greeting a lone goatherd in his mountain fastness, his response in Albanian: 'Do you know what is the number I must call to top up my Vodafone?'

OTHER PRACTICALITIES Either a heavy-duty mountain bike along with a decent repair kit or a really sturdy 4x4 is essential if you are planning to travel for any appreciable distance into the gorge. It will probably be necessary to arrange car hire, with or without an attendant driver, either in Kolašin (you could try Vila Jelka, page 294) or even Podgorica. The per diem price is likely to be €25 per person minimum, plus food and any accommodation for the driver. But – and it's a big but – it is *vaut le détour*.

THE ROUTE To travel the full distance, through one civilisation and out into another, will be a journey approaching 60km. A tricky section comes early on the route, approaching the scattered settlement of **Vermoš**, where it is possible to find overnight accommodation, but where first the Vermoši torrent must be crossed. East of the village, and from tyre tracks in the pebbles, there appears to be a ford, but it is at a minimum 1m deep and would be more than that after heavy rain. Several

---

THUNDERSTORMS

Weather conditions in the mountains can change dramatically in a matter of minutes and the Balkans are no exception. Heeding regional forecasts and seeking local advice are both part of wise planning. You will find that people who live in the Balkan highlands are able to read the clouds, that they take the threat of extreme weather very seriously and will modify their intentions accordingly, even if it means losing a valuable day's guiding payment and despite your pleading that this is the final day of your stay and you might never have another opportunity to see this or that lake.

Lightning can be deadly and if you are unlucky and find yourself unable to reach safe shelter before a storm is overhead, do your best to move away from tall trees and on no account take refuge in the entrance of a cave or beneath overhanging rock. Rather sit tight on sloping, not soggy ground, head down and keeping yourself as small as you can until the worst of the storm has passed. Better soaked than dead.

years ago the timber bridge a little further on lay askew and semi-submerged and was judged too hazardous for a heavy vehicle. In 2011, a traveller who took this route reported the bridge to have been stabilised. But a bout of bad weather could easily tip it once again.

Once this obstacle has been overcome, one way or another, a short distance ahead an option presents itself: either continue straight ahead or make a hard left and turn uphill to see another self-contained village, **Lëpushë**. Here too there is hospitality on offer. The little pub/restaurant at the top of the village is a meeting place. It is where the men gather to philosophise while their women take care of the fields and the livestock. If you stay overnight in someone's home, your dinner will be a feast but he and his wife and their children will not eat with you; rather each will take a place in front of the table and watch intently to be sure you are happy with the food. Only after you are full to bursting may you be invited to join the family to drink their homemade *raki* and *kafe turke* in a small exterior room, midway between the house and its hyperactive kennel. This is the kitchen and the most meaningful room of the establishment. Even in summer it gets cold at night in the mountains but here in the lantern light it will be cosy, father stretched out in pole position by the fire, the children respectful in the background and mother breaking off from her quiet tatting only to fetch another log.

All around is wonderful countryside, black pine-wooded hills climbing to summer pastures and superlative views in every direction. Small wonder a local shepherd-cum-mountain guide has taught himself to paint these landscapes. He proudly displays the little gallery he has created within his house. All he lacks is a customer.

There is only one way back to rejoin the route through the gorge and that is the way you came. Many other diverting side turnings will present themselves and there are other hidden villages to be explored but, if you are making your way along the ups and downs of the stony and often downright difficult road to the border at Hani i Hotit, best to push ahead until you reach the community of **Tamarë**, where the road passes at some height above the translucent river **Cemit** and in the heat of the day you may be tempted to scramble down for a swim in the icy water.

Approximately 25km from the border the road becomes especially hazardous, rising up and up through a succession of almost vertical hairpins, a route it cannot be stressed too strongly requires total concentration and maximum caution. The reward is fresh breath in the lungs, a stupendous view to take it away again and an asphalt road for the last few kilometres to the border.

FROM ROŽAJE TO PEĆ IN KOSOVO

A trip to Peć in Kosovo from Rožaje, in the east of Montenegro, can be extended to make an interesting round trip, achievable by car in a day by returning to Montenegro over the border at **Dračenovac**.

In February 2008, as widely predicted, Kosovo's parliament unilaterally endorsed a declaration of independence from Serbia. The transition, which has been relatively peaceful, continues to be supervised by an international presence. In October 2008 Montenegro officially recognised the independent state of Kosovo. Serbia has yet to follow suit.

OTHER PRACTICALITIES At present there are no visa or entry fee requirements but passports will need to be produced at the borders. The currency is the euro.

There is now a regular bus service between Rožaje and Peć (see page 282) but none back over the border west of **Mitrovica**, so to make this a circular adventure a car will be necessary. If you are taking a hire car into Kosovo it is advisable to inform your rental company of your plans. It should be noted that this route will take you through parts of Kosovo where there continue to be isolated incidents of unrest, but as a foreign visitor you are unlikely to encounter any problems. In addition, since the dissolution of the Federation of Serbia and Montenegro, technically there is ambiguity. Leaving Kosovo by this route it is necessary to travel for a few kilometres through Serbia and in the past exit to Serbia was only permitted for those who had also entered from Serbia. Belgrade does not officially recognise a border between the two states, therefore those wishing to make this circular trip are strongly advised to consult the appropriate authorities in advance of travel.

THE ROUTE Take the main road leading east out of Rožaje (the bus station is on the left side of this road) and bear right to climb steadily through rocky, inhospitable moorland interspersed with darkest pine forest to reach the Montenegrin frontier, just before the pass. This is a busy crossing and passports and car papers of those travelling in both directions are routinely checked, which can result in delays, but it should still be possible to cover the distance between Rožaje and the outskirts of Peć (approximately 50km) within an hour. On a clear day the outlook on the descent is very fine and it is possible to see most of the country, but in bad weather you must watch out for cattle and their minders on the road. Cowherds carry umbrellas in these parts. Peć is a bustling town – the kind where, to the visitor, every day feels like market day and it can take rather a long time to traverse. If your intention is to visit the **Serbian Patriarchate** (something akin to the Vatican) on the western outskirts or to venture further in that direction and view the dramatic **Rugova Gorge**, it may take you a little time to navigate the crowded streets. Consider also a detour 15km south to the **Dečani** (Dečane) Orthodox Monastery with its lovely frescoes that somehow survived the Ottoman occupation.

In spite of today's frowsy appearance **Peć** is a town with an engrossing history and well worth exploring. Walls can still be seen bearing the unequivocal graffiti: *Jo negociata – Vetevendosje* ('No negotiations – Self-determination'). The population is almost entirely ethnic Albanian. Don't miss the bazaar section, a good place to find an unusual piece in silver or gold. (See a full description of the town in *Kosovo: The Bradt Travel Guide*, by Verena Knaus and Gail Warrander.) If you decide to stay here overnight, try the renovated **Hotel Royal Arda (€€€€)**; formerly the Hotel Metohija, it was at one time requisitioned by KFOR (the NATO Kosovo peacekeeping force).

The road that follows the bubbling **Bistrica River** on through the deep ravine of Rugova and ultimately leads to the **Čakor Pass** back into Montenegro (the pass is currently closed to vehicular traffic) gives access by way of mainly unsurfaced byroads to the **Bogë Mountain** area, virtually undiscovered by those who do not live in Kosovo but a wonderful alpine region with potential for hiking, climbing and winter sports. There are already a few small private hotels, charging around €20 a night, while along the course of the gorge itself one or two small restaurants and a campsite make convenient stopping places.

In the surrounding wilderness there are wolves and the farmers employ a large St Bernard-like dog to guard their animals. The Šarplaninac/Illyrian sheepdog breed originates from Šar Planina on the Macedonia–Kosovo border and is reputed to be the only dog capable of out-manoeuvring a wolf, itself a highly sophisticated animal with a complex pack hierarchy. In these parts you might encounter an older Šar mentoring a (not so) cuddly puppy.

The great **Hajla Mountain** (2,400m) rises to the north, a long but not too arduous trek for the fit. Ask locally for directions to the best access point for the summit and its stunning views down to Rožaje, Berane and beyond. It could then be possible, theoretically at least, to descend back into the Montenegrin valley connecting those two towns. That would make another, more ambitious, border story. And require a permit from both sets of authorities. The best place to start planning these things is at one of the police stations.

RETURNING TO ROŽAJE VIA MITROVICA Returning to the original plan for a day trip: you may choose to bypass the centre of Peć and continue on a circular tour by taking, as you first enter town, a left fork signed to Mitrovica. In contrast to the past 50km the road ahead is flat and the surroundings repetitive, hectare after hectare of smallholdings, and were it not for the poignant recognition that just about every structure is newly built, it would offer little of interest. One cannot forget that only a decade past this was the scene of violent conflict.

Several kilometres short of the mining town of Mitrovica, which remains both ethnically and physically divided – the Serbians to the north of the Ibar River and the Albanians to the south – the left turn back towards Montenegro is unsigned. If you reach the Mitrovica sign on the main road you will have just overshot the turn and will need to go back.

Once on the correct road the river will be on your right and soon you will pass a KFOR control post, indicating that you are entering the Serbian section of Kosovo. You may be asked to show your papers or simply be waved through. Soon you cross one long bridge followed by a second and the river, now on your left, becomes a sizeable lake, **Gazivodsko jezero**, with a large dam visible also on the left. The banks of the lake are thickly wooded and the views become increasingly attractive as you re-enter the mountainous region, passing through a series of short unlighted tunnels. The way is good and clear (though the maps are not). You will need to show your passport at the frontier control just beyond **Banje**, before entering Serbia itself. Some 8km further, in **Ribariće**, a newly restored mosque is noticeable beside a right fork to **Novi Pazar**, with a further mosque visible on the facing hillside, while the route you are following continues to wind down through pretty wooded countryside until a control post indicates you are leaving Serbia; another one at which you will most likely simply be waved on.

The official Montenegrin **Dračenovac** crossing follows shortly after **Špiljani** and here you will almost certainly be required to show your papers. Rožaje lies 30km away in the valley below, its approach tracing the edge of the precipitous Ibar Canyon (300m in depth) through which the river twists and tumbles from its source on Hajla Mountain. A large 'M' petrol station complex on the left side of a wide bend, shortly before entering town, makes an excellent pit stop with a welcoming and cosy restaurant (€€) offering, along with the usual soups and salads, more sustaining fare such as veal (€5). There is a small children's playground, the loos are decent and there is plenty of space to stretch the legs.

FROM BIJELO POLJE VIA SERBIA TO PLJEVLJA

From Bijelo Polje into Serbia and back to Pljevlja: another tour for which a car is really essential.

The road leaves Bijelo Polje in tandem with the railway line, passing the station and running northward through the wide fields of chamomile that give the town its name. The surrounding hills look as if they should be alive with the sound of music but alas, all you will be able to discern is the occasional tinkle of a cowbell, mostly drowned out by the thunder of Belgrade-bound juggernauts. Soon a very large church, its copper dome glittering in the sunlight, can be picked out in the far distance to the right. By crossing the **River Lim** and with a bit of fumbling it can be reached, but locked; standing alone and apparently recently built, it is not giving away any secrets. Even in late autumn the fields are dappled with yellow chamomile and by weaving through them, following small roads in the direction of **Bistrica**, village and river with the same name, you will be able to find both the old Ottoman bridge and the cottage-style church of **Sv Nikola** at **Podvrh** (page 277).

Continuing on the main road, there is a brown sign indicating 11km right to **Đalovića klisura** (Devil's Gorge). It is a frustrating feature of these newish signs to locations of special interest that although they set you in the right direction, there are frequently no follow-up markings at further intersections to keep you on the right track. This only partially explored cave system, thought to be one of the largest in Europe, is not easy to find. (Similar difficulties are encountered locating the **Crvena Stijena**, Red Rock Cave, on the other side of the country.)

Approaching the frontier, with the river and railway now on the right, two theatrically massive rocks dominate the view ahead. The border procedure is straightforward and amicable and feels very much a formality, but it should be borne in mind that this is a very major road linking many other parts of eastern Europe with the Adriatic coast, and there will inevitably be times when delays can arise, around public holidays being just one. At the Montenegrin exit area there is a cluster of kiosks for currency exchange, car hire, accessing taxis, etc, and from here until well beyond the Serbian crossing the road follows the course of the River Lim below, forcing its passage through a series of dramatic rocky outcrops, a stretch marked on some maps as *kumanička klisura*. The turbulence of the Lim is magnified as it is joined by its tributaries, **Vrbničkar** and **Dubočica**.

It should be noted that the dinar is the official monetary unit in Serbia. At the time of writing, euros may be exchanged for dinars at any petrol station near the Montenegrin border, and in practice euros will probably be accepted in most shops and restaurants near the frontier, but expect to receive any change in dinars, not necessarily at a favourable rate. There are no visa requirements for foreign visitors' short term visits to Serbia.

Over the border the road runs on in a somewhat alarming manner. A sign advises driving with care for 10km; *extreme care* would be a better way of putting it. Road markings suggesting suitable passing places allow far too short a margin for safety; traffic is heavy and in a hurry. Needless to add, cyclists should exercise great caution through all this section.

After a nice little town called **Brodarevo**, where you may find homemade apple juice and other local produce for sale beside the road, now gentler, greener slopes suggest good hiking. Gradually the valley widens and you must start to watch for a sign to the left indicating **Jabuka** and **Pljevlja**. It appears just after the one informing you that you are entering the city limits of **Prijepolje** and it directs you beneath a bridge and then hard right at a second sign to Pljevlja – and **Titograd** (Podgorica). From here begins the long westerly ascent to the border 38km ahead. Late in the year there will still be flowers by the roadside and the foliage – silver birch, oak and beech – is especially attractive in spring or autumn. As the height increases, pause and look back; the views over vast tracts of Serbia are great: to the north the **Zlatibor**, east to **Zlatar Mountain** and behind it the distinctive peaks of the **Kopaonik**, with **Pančićev vrb** at over 2,000m the highest in the country. (For more information, see *Serbia: The Bradt Travel Guide*, by Laurence Mitchell.)

The border process on re-entering Montenegro at **Ranče** again ought to be straightforward, but be warned, there are frequently quite long delays here, perhaps because non-commercial and local traffic favour this less hectic route. Whatever the reason, be prepared to sit it out if necessary. At least the setting is beautiful. On the high plateau, wide grassy swathes separate clusters of tall fir, swirled in gauzy mist; it has the appearance of parkland, dreamy parkland.

Once the bureaucratic hurdle is overcome, a lovely panorama unfolds as you cruise onward over open moorland, wild cornflower sheltering beneath craggy outcrop and strange arrangements of stone that an archaeologist might find significant, all of it framed by the distant jagged mountain crests: to the west **Prijevor** and **Maglić**, the latter at 2,386m the highest in Bosnia–Herzegovina; southwest to **Bobotov kuk**, 2,523m and the highest in the Durmitor; and directly south, **Sinjajevina**. Time out for refreshment at the only restaurant, **Nezaborav** (€), tiny and fuggy but hugely welcoming, its terrace commanding a gorgeous 270° view. The menu is in Cyrillic, the proprietor speaks only Serbian but roast of the day, salads, ham and cheese will all be there. And Vranac of course, a little jug of it not much more than €1.

> A jug of wine, a loaf of bread – and thou
> Beside me singing in the wilderness –
> Oh, wilderness were paradise enow
>
> Omar Khayyám

This is one you will remember, even if *thou* is not with thee.

Some 12km from the border, take a small turning to the left on a newish asphalt road to visit the **Dubočica Monastery**, sheltered in a hollow above a narrow lake formed at the confluence of three rivers: suma Dubočica, Čeotina and Maočnica. It is an idyllic setting, a meadow of gentian, velvet grass and then the whitewashed monastery, its *konak* framed with roses. Like Sv Nikola at Podvrh it was constructed to resemble a farm building, a strategem to dupe the Turks which in this case failed: in the 15th century it was destroyed. But a few decades later it was built again in a new and perceived safer position 2km from the original. Father Ciprian, the incumbent, relates how it is believed that somehow the frescoes were salvaged and replaced as before. Whatever the case, the present wall paintings are noteworthy and the artist unrecorded. It is interesting to learn that Sv Vasilije of Ostrog passed eight years in this monastery. During the harshest winter months Father Ciprian, who is in his 60s, and one other, a septuagenarian novice who 'doesn't yet feel *quite* ready to take his vows', retreat to Serbia, but at other times the monastery welcomes visitors – 'nobody ever comes here' – and you may well be offered tea and honey in the garden. The honey is dark and deep-flavoured and the father is uncertain which wildflowers the bees have been favouring, but if you would like a pot he will be only too happy to fetch it from the neighbouring farm. At €6 you may consider it more of a donation than a purchase. (No English spoken.)

Leaving the monastery, turn left to retrace your steps and rejoin the road into Pljevlja.

FROM PLUŽINE TO BOSNIA VIA ŠĆEPAN POLJE

*Over the border to Bosnia at **Šćepan Polje**, by bicycle or car; a 4x4 would allow more versatility.*

Approaching **Plužine** from the Nikšić–Plužine road, continue past a turning left, leading down to Plužine town, and an Eko petrol station also on the left. Brown signs indicate historic sites (still frequently hard to pinpoint) and there is one here indicating 'church under Soko' 22km ahead. The road runs along the shore of the sapphire **Piva Lake** (Pivsko jezero) and before long plunges into the nether regions of the Piva Canyon. If the Prokletije range in the east is the amphitheatre of the gods, in stormy weather this gorge could surely be described as Dante's Inferno. What a fabulous country this is! The sepulchral peak of Bosnian Maglić looming up from the west and the beetling canyon face riddled with caves only serve to intensify the sensation. But you must keep alert, for the road is narrow and there are large freight vehicles sharing it. First one bridge, then another (the dam itself) swings you from one side of the abyss to the other and then back again. (Take a sharp turn left after the first one if you wish to visit the village of **Mratinje**, a good starting place for wilderness hikes along the Bosnian borders; see below. But note well, the trails are unmarked and you will need your compass, better still a guide.)

As you draw near to Šćepan Polje and the **Hum** border controls, there is a sign right to **Crvka pod Sokolom** (Church Beneath the Falcon) and to **Tara Canyon**, and up a rough and narrow gravel road you will discover the ruins of the 15th-century fortress that gave its name to this place, its church and some scattered tombstones. Here was the residence of *herceg* (duke) **Stjepan Vukšić Kosača,** once ruler of all Bosnia and Hum (Herzegovina).

The border marks the confluence of the **Piva** and **Tara rivers**, now to flow on for 345km as the **Drina** and ultimately to join the **Sava River**. No visa is required for EU, American or Canadian citizens to enter Bosnia–Herzegovina. Other nationalities should consult a Bosnia–Herzegovina diplomatic mission before travel. The Podgorica Embassy is at Atinska 35 (✆ *020 618105*). Everyone intending to enter the country should carry a valid passport; Bosnia–Herzegovina border authorities do not accept any other type of personal ID. (Note: some maps still refer to this section of Bosnia as 'Republika Srpska'.)

On both sides of the border there are facilities for rafting expeditions but it is a good idea to make prior arrangements for such trips through an agency in Žabljak or Podgorica. On the Montenegro side there is **Café Budva**, and some simple accommodation is available. Once in Bosnia an asphalt road, overdue for resurfacing, follows the winding course of the Drina through dense scrub towards **Foca** (Srbinje). This is a popular hunting area and you may well pass pedestrians with guns and dogs. To the southwest is the **Sutjeska National Park**, a rugged paradise for hikers; it too can boast a primeval forest, **Perućica**. Compare it to Biogradska (pages 271–4). It also holds the highest mountains in the country, **Maglić** (2,386m) and close on its heels **Volujak** (2,336m), both of them slap bang on the Montenegrin border. (For a complete description of the park, see *Bosnia and Herzegovina: The Bradt Travel Guide,* by Tim Clancy.) To reach the park, turn sharp left on to the road for **Gacko** and **Trebinje**, 20km after Šćepan Polje and 4km short of Foca.

To return to Montenegro and avoid retracing your journey, an option would be to continue south through the Sutjeska Canyon and on in the Trebinje–Dubrovnik direction to re-enter Montenegro by either of the crossings suggested in the following round trip. It will be a decent road all the way. Alternatively – and it should be stressed, this is one to consider only if you have with you a guide who is familiar with the area, are in a 4x4 and there is enough light left in the day – you *could* turn east just short of Gacko, on a minor road leading to the border at **Krstac**, after which a byroad will eventually take you back to join the main Plužine–Nikšić road at **Vir**. But the section after the border zigzags through the mountains, over the Prenka Pass (1,065m), and it is all too easy to take a wrong turn and be seriously lost. It is also a long, slow, lonely way. Beautiful, of course …

THE SUTJESKA RIVER BATTLE

The battle on the Sutjeska River in early June 1943 was a massive and decisive confrontation between the main Partisan operational army and the encircling German and Italian divisions, supported by Ustaše and some Chetnik troops and with overwhelming numerical superiority in arms and men and total control of the air. Bill Deakin, in *The Embattled Mountain* (page 324), has written an enthralling account of this battle in the mountains of Durmitor and the surrounding valleys and of Tito's success, comparable to Dunkirk, in evacuating the main body of his National Liberation Army before the Axis ring closed.

Deakin's tiny British liaison party attached to Tito's headquarters had only sporadic radio contact with the Commander British Forces in Cairo but on 8 June they passed on to Tito a message from Cairo saying:

Hold on ... the Second Front is not a dream ... Your struggle will be of even greater importance in the coming months.

By 16 June, Tito and over 10,000 surviving Partisans had broken out (though Deakin's deputy, Captain Bill Stuart, had been killed in the air attack that also wounded Deakin and Tito himself) and the main battle was over. The Axis troops concentrated on mopping up the wounded and their nurses, executing them and the villagers suspected of being Partisan sympathisers. With fine precision, they counted 5,697 Partisan dead and 50 villages destroyed.

FROM NIKŠIĆ TO HERZEGOVINA VIA VILUSI

A round trip from Nikšić to Herzegovina and back, by car or bike. A relatively flat run, with the exception of a long climb from Trebinje back to the border.

It is 40km from the centre of **Nikšić** to the settlement of **Vilusi**, the route traversing a scarcely populated scrubby landscape. In the 19th century when eastern Herzegovina was still under Ottoman rule, the whole region was subject to repeated episodes of strife and somehow even today it is as if this plateau has taken enough hammering; why should it produce more flowers and fruit to be trampled upon?

At Vilusi there is an intersection, where it is straight ahead on a widened road to the new border post at **Ilijino brdo**. This is the way you will return. For now, take the signed road to the right to **Bileća** (27km). There is also a brown sign for **Crvena Stijena** (Red Rock Cave; see below) but then no follow-on directions. Continue in the direction of **Broćanac Grahovski** and, 13km after Vilusi, take a left fork signed to **Petrovići**. Passing through the village, soon you will arrive at a rectangle of grass not unlike a village green and behind it the **Kosijerevo Monastery** and a small chapel. You can try asking for a key at the house next door.

The **Red Rock Cave** is not easy to find, it does not appear on many maps and when it does it is placed incorrectly. Here is how you find it:

With the monastery on your left go straight in an easterly direction for 1.5km, ignoring any other turnings, until the end of the asphalt and bearing right on a small road that runs in front of an imposing modern house. Ahead and slightly to the left you will see a steep cliff of red-hued rock rising high above a lake, Bilećko jezero, that marks the border with Herzegovina. From here you will need to walk

400–500m across a steep slope with a fair amount of scree (appropriate footwear essential) to take a proper look at the yawning cave entrance. At the time of the author's visit, the padlock to the gate in the fence enclosing the excavation hole was hanging open and no palaeopathologists were at work, so a close-up view of the long flight of metal steps leading down through the black mouth was easy. But one false step and you could join the bats.

Return by the way you came, through Petrovići, and turn left to follow the road on to Bileća, the official border. There are many other pot-holes and caves in the rock-strewn hillsides around here but you would need a guide to know where to find them.

Make a right at **Vraćenovići**, approximately 3km before the control post, and follow that road for a further 10km or so if you are curious to pass through the battlefield of **Vučji Do**, scene of the 1876 turning-point in centuries of warfare with the Turks. A tattered Montenegrin banner and a painting of the scene can be viewed at the State Museum at Cetinje (page 87). The battlefield is set against a backdrop of crests, **Vardar** (1,130m), **Čućurača** (1,220m) and **Jelovica** (1,284m). There is little to see today but, as at Agincourt, somehow you can still smell the action.

Back to the Bileća road and cross into Herzegovina (procedure and requirements as at Šćepan Polje; see above). In the town turn left beside a field (on the right) containing a defunct aeroplane, and now with the lake you will have seen below Crvena Stijena, on the left. The road leading down to **Trebinje** (about 40km), and soon passing through a forest of pylons, is a good one though not notably scenic. When you reach the outskirts of the city you will be less than 30km from the Croatian border and Dubrovnik. (For a description of historic Trebinje, see Tim Clancy's *Bosnia and Herzegovina: The Bradt Travel Guide*.)

Leaving the town on your right, turn hard left back in the direction of Montenegro. The route follows the **Trebišnjica River** and then begins a long spiral ascent through a handful of villages and increasingly alpine woodland to the border. Look over your shoulder for fine views over southeast Herzegovina. Re-entering Montenegro at the **Ilijino brdo** crossing, the buffer zone between the two control points is mountainous and wild. And you are back in Vilusi, with Nikšić straight ahead.

FROM HERCEG NOVI TO THE PREVLAKA PENINSULA IN CROATIA

A round trip from Herceg Novi to Croatia, by car or bike (bearing in mind the Adriatic Highway linking Montenegro with Dubrovnik is a busy interstate road), reveals a secret.

From Herceg Novi bus station follow the main road (Adriatic Highway) west in the direction of **Debeli Brjeg**, the principal border crossing into Croatia, leading to Dubrovnik and Čilipi Airport – *but*, as you are leaving town, just before a petrol station take a fork to the left signed to **Njivice** and **Prevlaka**. This second road follows the curve of the bay, running above it through the flowery suburb of Njivice and passing a slip road down to the seafront Riviera Hotel (page 124). Pause when you can, to take in the view of Herceg Novi descending from the folds of mighty **Orjen** to the sparkling sea. A short distance further and the road makes a wide right curve to reveal below a dark green finger reaching out as if to close the entrance to the Boka Kotorska, once and for all. This is the long-contested Prevlaka Peninsula, still a bit of a sore point and best not raised by visitors. Oddly *prevlaka* translates as 'isthmus' …

The secret is the tiny border control post, here at the top of the hill, open 24 hours a day (at the time of writing) but not marked on most maps, and where there is usually – though not always – no queue. (The main border crossing on the Adriatic Highway at Debeli Brjeg can at busy times be subject to substantial delays.)

Visas are not required for citizens of the EU, the USA, Canada, Australia or New Zealand to enter Croatia. A list of countries whose citizens will need a visa is available from the Consular Department of the Croatian Foreign Ministry (*www. mvp.hr*). Every foreign national entering Croatia must carry a valid passport.

You are now roughly 6km south of Herceg Novi and 40km southeast of Dubrovnik and at the foot of a short hill you can turn left if you wish to visit **Prevlaka Park**. The entire peninsula, its vegetation chiefly *garrigue*, has been developed as a recreational facility, an adventure park, with rock climbing, organised paint-ball games, kayaking, swimming spots, picnic areas and at the headland an old fort (*oštri*) to explore. The entrance fee is 15 kuna (€2.20); you may rent a bike (*15 kuna for two hours*), or there is a little train that runs hourly from 10.00 to 18.00 and travels around the park, making five stops. Parking costs 15 kuna. **Konoba Gusari** (*beside the entrance;* ⊕ *summer only 10.00–22.00*) has snacks and drinks. There is also a currency exchange.

But to push on in the direction of Dubrovnik, leave Prevlaka on your left and follow the road in a westerly direction uphill. It is a pretty route, not many houses but rich in meadows and orchards, trees heavy with apples and figs, little groves of olive trees and cypresses. This southernmost corner of Croatia is the region of **Konavle** and the setting is typical. Pass through the village of **Vitaljina** and close by **Višnjići** and **Đurinići**. Off to the left, **Molunat** is a small seaside resort with good snorkelling. Continue on through **Pločice** before once more (15km from Prevlaka Park) rejoining the main Adriatic Highway at a T-junction, with Dubrovnik and the airport (from here 19km) to the left and the principal crossing at Debeli Brjeg, back to Montenegro and Herceg Novi, to the right.

There is plenty to explore in this rather less frequented region, with its long-maintained tradition for embroidery. Meticulous and precise, the style is called *poprsnica*. Originally it featured just in the decoration of national costume but nowadays its applications have been extended to household items, napkins, mats and tablecloths, which could make useful last-minute gifts if you are killing time before the plane. There is **Konavoski Dvori,** a nice old watermill restaurant at **Ljuta**, if you are feeling hungry, and an attractive 15th-century monastery at **Pridvorje**, should you prefer spiritual sustenance. More time in hand and you could explore the port of **Cavtat**, a Roman settlement south of **Zupa Bay** and also a short distance from Čilipi Airport.

And of course, had you a day or three, the lovely walled city of Ragusa – **Dubrovnik**. (For a full description, see Piers Letcher's *Croatia: The Bradt Travel Guide.*)

Appendix 1

LANGUAGE

PRONUNCIATION AND TRANSLITERATION In Montenegrin, which is identical to Serbian, almost every word is pronounced exactly as it is written. There are 30 letters in the alphabet, which is written in both Roman and Cyrillic forms.

Roman		Serbian Cyrillic		Pronunciation
Capital	*Lower case*	*Capital*	*Lower case*	
A	a	А	а	'a' as in ask
B	b	Б	б	'b' as in boy
C	c	Ц	ц	'c' as 'ts' in flotsam
Č	č	Ч	ч	'ch' as in church
Ć	ć	̈	̈	'tch' like 't' in future
D	d	Д	д	'd' as in dog
Dž	dž	Џ	џ	'j' as in just
Đ	đ	Ђ	ђ	'dj' as in endure
E	e	Е	е	'e' as in egg
F	f	Ф	ф	'f' as in father
G	g	Г	г	'g' as in girl
H	h	Х	х	'h' as in hot; as 'ch' in loch before another consonant
I	i	И	и	'i' as in machine
J	j	Ј	ј	'y' as in young
K	k	К	к	'k' as in king
L	l	Л	л	'l' as in like
Lj	lj	Љ	љ	'ly' like the 'lli' in million
M	m	М	м	'm' as in man
N	n	Н	н	'n' as in nest
Nj	nj	Њ	њ	'nj' like 'ny' in canyon
O	o	О	о	'o' between 'o' in bone and 'aw' in shawl
P	p	П	п	'p' as in perfect
R	r	Р	р	'r' as in rough
S	s	С	с	's' as in Serbia
Š	š	Ш	ш	'sh' as in lush
T	t	Т	т	't' as in test
U	u	У	у	'oo' as in boot
V	v	В	в	'v' as in victory
Z	z	З	з	'z' as in zebra
Ž	ž	Ж	ж	'zh' like 's' in pleasure

GRAMMAR Nouns may be masculine, feminine or neuter, as in German. Masculine nouns end in a consonant in the singular and generally end in '-i' in the plural. A few feminine nouns end in a consonant but most end in '-a' in the singular and '-e' in the plural. Neuter nouns end in '-e' or '-o' in the singular and generally in '-a' in the plural. There is no definite or indefinite article ('the' or 'a'). Adjectives agree with nouns.

WORDS AND PHRASES
Basics
The two most important Montenegrin adjectives to remember are *katastrofalan* (catastrophic) and *lijepo* (beautiful). On a more serious note:

Yes	*da*	bathroom	*kupatilom*
No	*ne*	Here you are/	*izvolite*
Maybe	*možda*	it's for you	
OK	*važi/može*	Do you speak	*govorite li engleski?*
Hello	*zdravo or cao*	English?	
Goodbye	*do videnja*	I am English/	*ja sam Englez*
Good morning	*dobro jutro*	American	*(… leskinja)/*
(until 10.00)			*Amerikanac (… anka)*
Good afternoon	*dobar dan*	You are	*vi ste*
(until 17.00)		How are you?	*kako ste?*
Good evening	*dobar večer*	good (I'm)	*dobro (sam)*
Good night	*laku noć*	bad	*loš*
Excuse me	*oprostite or izvinite*	not much	*slabo or malo*
Sorry	*pardon*	Mr	*gospodin (g.)*
You're welcome	*u redu je*	Mrs	*gospoda (gđa.)*
Please	*molim*	Miss	*gospođice (gdica.)*
(also answering the telephone)		married	*oženjen (man)*
Thank you	*hvala*		*udata (woman)*
How much is it?	*koliko košta?*	airmail	*avionski*
I do not understand	*ja ne razume*	not potable	*ne pijaci*
It happens/It's just		cold	*hladna*
one of those things	*dogadati se*	hot	*topla*

When sending an email or letter to a Montenegrin, you could conclude: *srdačan pozdrav* ('sincere greetings').

The body

ache	*bol*	head	*glava*
arm or hand	*ruka*	leg	*noga*
blood	*krv*	pain	*muka*
chest	*grudi*	shoulder	*rame*
foot	*stopalo*	stomach	*trbuh or stomak*

Directions

Where is …?	*gde je …?*	near/far	*blizu/daleko*
avenue	*bulevar*	petrol	*benzin*
street	*ulica*	puncture	*ubod*
bridge	*most*	go straight ahead	*idite pravo napred*
turn left/right	*skrenite lijevo/desno*	map	*mapa or karta*
north/south	*sever*/jug*	traffic	*saobracaj*
east/west	*istok/zapad*	traffic light	*semafor*

(*Note that *sever* – 'north' – confusingly abbreviates to 'S')

Signs

safe journey	*srećan put*	prohibited	*zabranjeno*
arrivals	*dolazak*	(no) rooms available	*(nema) slobodne sobe*
departures	*polasci*	(but 'room/s to let' is often abbreviated to
entrance/exit	*ulaz/izlaz*	'soba/e' on signs)
information	*informacije*	toilets	*toaleti* or *wc*
open/closed	*otvoreno/zatvoreno*	men/women	*muški/ženski*

Places

airport	*aerodrom*	lower	*donji*
bank	*banka*	market	*pijaca*
bay, gulf	*boka/zaliv*	mountain/hill/	*gora*
beach	*plaža*	forest	
beer hall	*pivnica*	mountain, peak	*vrh*
black	*crno*	museum	*muzej*
boats/cruises	*kristarenje*	new town	*novi grad*
bus station	*autobus stanica*	open 24 hours	*nonstop*
castle	*dvorac/zamak*	(shop)	
centre	*centar*	police	*milicija*
chapel	*gospe/kapela*	post office	*posta*
chemist	*apoteka*	railway station	*zdjeznička stanica*
church	*crkva*	restaurant	*restoran*
city	*varoš*	river	*rijka*
dentist	*zubar*	rooms	*sobe*
doctor	*ljekar*	sea	*more*
field	*polje*	square	*trg*
garage	*garaža*	tavern	*konoba*
gate	*porta/kapija*	tower	*kula*
inn	*hanovi*	(old) town	*(stari) grad*
island	*ada*	town hall	*opstina*
kiosk	*trafika*	train	*voz*
lake	*jezero*	undergrowth	*šiblje*
laundry	*perionica*	upper	*gornji*

Food and drink
In a restaurant

bill	*račun*	glass	*casa*
boil	*vrenje*	grill	*roštilj*
bottle	*flaše*	ice	*led*
breakfast	*doručak*	knife	*nož*
cup	*šolja*	lunch	*ručak*
dinner	*večera*	menu	*jelovnik*
fork	*viljuš*	plate	*tanjir*
fry/roast	*pečenje*	spoon	*kašika*

Basics

bread	*hleb*	pancakes	*palačinke*
butter	*maslac*	pepper/salt	*biber/sol*
cheese	*sir*	sour cream	*kajmak*
doughballs	*priganice*	sugar	*šecer*
egg	*jaje*	(veal) soup	*(teleca) čorba*

honey	med	vinegar	sirce
mustard	senf	yoghurt	jogurt
olive oil	maslinovo ulje		

Fish (riba) It is impossible to come up with a definitive list of English/Serbian fish, especially with regard to the bass/bream families. As Alan Davidson explained in his authoritative *Oxford Companion to Food* (1999), 'confusion [is] caused by the fact that even within one language, indeed sometimes within one dialect, the fish will have a range of different names'. So restaurants may speak with conviction, but not with one voice. Their labelled pictures differ. What follows is an attempted guide, but don't worry: most of them are good, and you may discover a new taste.

angler fish	grdoba	lobster	jastog/rarog
carp	krap	octopus	hobotnica
cod	bakalar	pike	štuka
cuttlefish	sipa	salmon	šaran
dentex*	dentex	scampi	gambori
eel	jegulja	sea bass	brancin
fish soup	riblja corba	sea bream	orata
gilt-head bream	podlanica	shrimp	morski račić
grey mullet	cipal	sole	losos
herring	haringa	squid	lignja
john dory	sanpjero	trout	pastrmka

*large Mediterranean fish resembling a large bream; features on most menus; well regarded

Meat (meso)

beef	govedina	lamb	jagnje
chicken	piletina	pork	svinjetina
duck	patka	sausage	kobasica
goose	guska	veal	teletina
ham	šunku/pršuta	hamburger	hamburger
homemade	domaca goveda supa		
('domestic') beef soup			

Vegetables (povrće)

artichoke	artišoka	green salad	zelena salate
asparagus	špargla	lettuce	zelena/salata
cabbage	kupus	mushroom	pečurka
capsicum	paprika	olives	masline
carrot	šargarepa	onion	crni luk
chips	pomfrit	potato	krompir
cucumber	krastavac	spinach	spanać
green beans	boranija	tomato	paradajz

There are two salads that you'll find on almost any Montenegrin menu which are very refreshing and composed of chopped cucumber and tomato. Mixed with grated cheese it is called *Šopska salata*; without cheese it is *Šrpska salata*.

Fruit (voće)

| apple | jabuka | lemon | limun |
| banana | banana | orange | pomorandža |

cherry	višnja	peach	breskva
fig	smokva	plum	šljiva
grapes	grožde	strawberry	jagoda

Drinks (piće)

beer	pivo	mineral water	mineralna voda
coffee	kafa	tap water	pijaća voda
fizzy water	kisela voda	tea	čaj
juice	sok	whisky	viski
milk	mlijeko	(red/white) wine	(crno/belo) vino

Countries

Australia	Australija	Netherlands	Holandija
Canada	Kanada	New Zealand	Novi Zelanda
England	Engleska	Russia	Rusija
France	Francuska	Scotland	Škotska
Germany	Nemačka	Spain	Spanija
Great Britain	Velika Brtanija	UK	Ujedinjeno Kraljevstvo
Ireland	Irrska	USA	Amerika
Italy	Italija	Wales	Vels

Numbers

0	nula	16	šesnaest
1	jedan	17	sedamnaest
2	dva	18	osamnaest
3	tri	19	devatnaest
4	četiri	20	dvadeset
5	pet	21	dvadeset jedan
6	šest	100	sto
7	sedam	200	dvesto
8	osam	300	tri stotine
9	devet	400	četiri stotine
10	deset	one thousand	hiljadu
11	jedanaest	one million	milion
12	dvanaest	a quarter	jedna četvrtina
13	trinaest	a half	pola
14	četnaest	three-quarters	tri četvrtina
15	petnaest		

The calendar Alongside the standard Serbian calendar, the central coastal region has its own idiosyncratic and poetic list of months, which are also used in Croatian – and which are too pretty to be omitted.

Months

January	januar	sječani ('cutting wood')
February	februar	veljača ('big winter')
March	mart	ožujak ('wind blows')
April	april	travanj ('mowing')
May	maj	svibanj ('dawning')
June	juni	lipanj ('flowers')
July	juli	srpanj ('harvest')

August	*avgust*	*kolovoz* ('back from holiday')	
September	*septembar*	*rujan* ('everything is red like wine')	
October	*oktobar*	*listopad* ('leaves fall')	
November	*novembar*	*studeni* ('cold')	
December	*decembar*	*prosinac* ('gathering')	

Weekdays

Monday	*ponedeljak*	Friday	*petak*
Tuesday	*utorak*	Saturday	*subota*
Wednesday	*srijeda*	Sunday	*nedjelja*
Thursday	*četvrtak*		

Appendix 2

GLOSSARY

apse	vaulted semicircle at east end of a church
Austro-Hungary	the dual state established in 1867 by Emperor Franz-Josef
Balkans	from Turkish word for 'mountains'; area of land in southeast Europe, south of the Danube and stretching to the Adriatic in the west, the Aegean in the east and the Mediterranean in the south
Balkanise	to divide a territory into small autonomous states; fragment
Bankada	Paštrovići Court
basilica	early Christian church, originally a colonnaded Roman variant of a Greek temple, subsequently adopted for Christian use
benzin	petrol
Beograd	Belgrade
Bogomil	member of a heretical Balkan sect, a variant of Manichaeism
bura	fierce northeasterly gale
Byzantine Empire	southeast European part of the Roman Empire after its division in AD395 following the death of Emperor Theodosius
Cattaro	Kotor (Italian)
centar	centre
Chetniks	Royalist resistance
Crna Gora	Montenegro
Crnagorski	Montenegrins
čun	flat-bottomed boat
Cyclopean masonry	ancient walls built of huge, rough-edged blocks of stone
Cyrillic	Script devised by disciples of St Cyril and St Methodius in the 9th century
diacritic marks	accents
Diatreton cup	Roman glass cup
Dormition	Orthodox term for the Assumption of the Virgin Mary
donja	lower
dubrava	grove
duga	rainbow
ex-voto	tablet or small painting expressing gratitude to a saint
fresco	a wall or ceiling painting created on 'fresh' wet plaster to achieve a deep-set result
frula dvojica	double flute (used by mountain shepherds)
garrigue	stunted, dense scrub
gljiva	mushroom
gluvi ples	deaf (= silent) dance

gorje	upper
Gornje Polimje	historically disputed territory along the banks of the Lim River
gospodar	prince
grad	town
gradina	massive stone employed in early fortifications
Grmožur	Montenegro's 'Alcatraz' prison on Skadar Lake
gusle	single-stringed violin
heldja	buckwheat pancakes
herceg	duke
hram	Orthodox basilica-like church, temple
hrast	oak
iconostasis	screen bearing icons
Illyrians	pre-Roman inhabitants of the Adriatic littoral
ispod	cooking method where coals are placed on the lid of the pot
izmirenje	reconciliation
izvor	spring (of water)
jadnik	poor thing
Jadran	Adriatic
jaz	inlet
Jekavian	Montenegrin dialect of Serbian
jezero	lake
junaštvo	courage
kajmak	sour cream
kalamera	willow rods used for supporting fishnets near Ulcinj (from the Albanian 'to take as it passes')
karst	porous limestone
kaštel	castle
katun	shepherd's tall wooden upland hut
Kolo-oro	traditional circular dance
konak	monks' sleeping quarters
konoba	tavern
kopriva	nettles
koziji sur	goat's cheese
Krstač	white wine
kufin	historic borderline between Montenegrin and Turkish territory
kuk	mountain, peak
kula	tower
lovor	laurel, bay
maestral	cooling west wind
mali	small
Manichaeism	dualistic religious system based on the primeval conflict between Light and Darkness
maquis	high, dense scrub
med	honey
Metropolitan	senior Orthodox bishop between archbishop and patriarch
more	sea
murva	mulberry (sometimes flavouring for *rakija*)
muzej	museum
narthex	church antechamber
namet	eternal snow
Orlov Krs	Eagle's Crag

Ottoman Empire	Turkish Islamic empire established in late 13th century; collapsed after World War I
Partisans	communist resistance led by Tito
paštrovici	territory, formerly semi-autonomous, based around Sveti Stefan
patriarch	head of an autocephalous or independent Orthodox Church
pelen	wormwood
pećina	cave
plaža	beach
plot	woven wicker support fencing of *vrba* (willow)
polje	field
porta	gate
Porte	also the Sublime or Turkish Porte; the Ottoman Court (from the French La Sublime Porte)
poskok	type of viper
priganice	fried doughballs
rakija	white grape brandy
rat	war
rijeka	river
rt	cape, headland
sač	special pot for *ispod*
Sanjak	an administrative district in the Ottoman Empire
šarka	type of viper
satkula	clocktower
Savarelji	Balkan/African dance
Sclavorum Regi	King of the Slavs; Pope Gregory VII's name for King Mihailo
šiblja	brushwood/*maquis*
Slavic	Indo-European language family comprising Russian and Ukrainian (Eastern Slavic); Polish, Czech and Slovak (Western Slavic); Serbo-Croat, Bulgarian, Macedonian and Slovene (Southern Slavic)
sljiva	plum blossom
slobode	freedom
sobe	rooms
Srpski	Serbian
stećci	Manichean gravestones
stari/stara	old
sveći	saints' days – days when you do not labour in the fields
sveti	saint
threshing floor	the cultural and agricultural centre of village life
tramontana	a north/northwesterly wind, strong and cold, bringing freshness from the mountains
trg	square
trikonhos	triangular church
ulica	street
Ustaše	Croatian Nazi movement formed in 1942
velik	big
vladika	prince-bishop
Vranac	red wine
yugo	warm, southerly wind (also known as sirocco)
zadruge	extended family group
župan	patriarch, circa 7th century

Appendix 3

FURTHER INFORMATION
HISTORY AND BIOGRAPHY

Adžić, Novak *Foreign Missions in Montenegro, 1878-1921* Cetinje, 2002

Allcock, John B and Young, Antonia (editors) *Black Lambs & Grey Falcons: Women Travellers in the Balkans* Bradford University Press, 1991

Angell, Henrik *The Sons of the Black Mountains* (translated from Norwegian 1896 original text) Montenegrin International Press, Nikšić, 2010

Azemović, Zaim *Pamet Je U Narodu* Podgorica, 2000

Butler, Hubert *The Sub-Prefect Should Have Held His Tongue, and Other Essays* (see in particular 'The Last Izmerenje') Penguin Press, London, 1990

Deakin, F W D *The Embattled Mountain* Oxford University Press, London, 1971

Destani, B (editor) *Montenegro: Political and Ethnic Boundaries 1840-1920* Archive Editions, Slough, 2001

Djilas, Milovan *Land Without Justice* Harcourt Brace Jovanovich, New York, 1958; *Montenegro* Methuen, London, 1964

Dukagjini, Leke, Gjecov, Shtjefen and Fox, Leonard *The Code of Leke* Bronx, NY, 1989

Glenny, Misha *The Balkans 1804-1999, Nationalism, War and the Great Powers* Granta, London, 2000; *The Fall of Yugoslavia: The Third Balkan War* Penguin Press, London, 1992

Hodgkinson, Harry *The Adriatic Sea* Jonathan Cape, London, 1955

Houston, Marco *Nikola and Milena: King and Queen of the Black Mountains* Leppi Publications, London, 2003

Ignatieff, Michael *The Warrior's Honour: Ethnic War and the modern conscience* Vintage, London, 1999

Jelavich, Barbara *History of the Balkans, Twentieth Century* Cambridge University Press, 1999

Jelušić, Božena and Mato *Dreaming about the Mediterranean* Argonaut, Budva, 1996

Jezernik, Božidar *Wild Europe: The Balkans in the Gaze of Western Travellers* Saqi Books, London, 2004

Judah, Tim *The Serbs, History Myth and the Destruction of Yugoslavia* Yale University Press, 1997

Kaplan, Robert D *Balkan Ghosts, A Journey Through History* St Martin's Press, New York, 1993

Laffan, R G D *The Serbs: The Guardians of the Gate* Dorset Press, New York, 1989

Le Bor, Adam *Milošević, A Biography* Bloomsbury, London, 2002

Mazower, Mark *The Balkans from the End of Byzantium to the Present Day* Weidenfeld and Nicolson, London, 2000

McConville, Michael *A Small War in the Balkans, British Military Involvement in Wartime Yugoslavia 1941-1945* Macmillan, London, 1986

Milich, Zorka *A Stranger's Supper: An Oral History of Centenarian Women in Montenegro* Simon and Schuster Macmillan, New York, 1995

Montefiore, Simon Sebag *The Life of Potemkin, Prince of Princes* Weidenfeld and Nicolson, London, 2000

Ogata, Sadako *The Turbulent Decade: Confronting the Refugee Crisis of the 1990s* W W Norton, New York, 2005

Owen, David *Balkan Odyssey* Victor Gollancz, London, 1995

Pettifer, James and Cameron, Averil *The Enigma of Montenegrin History: The Example of Svać* Bota Shqiptare, Tirana, 2008; *The South Slav Journal* Vol 28, London, 2008

Pillement, Georges *Unknown Yugoslavia* Johnson, London, 1969

Radović, Miljan and Cerović, Gavro *Durmitor, The Land and the People* Žabljak, 1996

Ramsbotham, Oliver and Woodhouse, Tom *Humanitarian Intervention in Contemporary Conflict* Polity Press, Cambridge, 1996

Roberts, Elizabeth *Realm of the Black Mountain* Hurst, London, 2006

Šćekić, Draško *Travelling through Montenegro* Podgorica, 1996

Silber, Laura and Little, Alan *Death of Yugoslavia* Penguin Press, London, 1995 (revised 1996)

Sugar, Peter *Southeastern Europe under Ottoman Rule, 1354–1804* University of Washington Press, 2000

Thompson, Milena Petrović Njegoš *My Father, the Prince* Xlibris Corp, USA, 2000

Tomašević, Ratko *Life and Death in the Balkans* Hurst, London, 2008

Vugdelić, Dragan M *Nyegosh's Last Hour* Podgorica, 1999

Vukanović, Dr Jovan *Paštrovici: Antropogeografska Studija* Cetinje, 1960

Warren, Whitney *Montenegro: The Crime of the Peace Conference* Brentano's, New York, 1922

Winchester, Simon *The Fracture Zone, A Return to the Balkans* Viking, London, 1999

Woodhouse, Tom and Ramsbotham, Oliver *Peacekeeping and Conflict Resolution* Frank Cass, Ilford, 2000

Woodward, Susan *Balkan Tragedy: Chaos and Dissolution after the Cold War* Brookings Institution, Washington DC, 1995

TRAVEL LITERATURE

Carnimeo, Nicolò *Montenegro, A Timeless Voyage* Mondadori, Rome, 1999

Carver, Robert *The Accursed Mountains: Journeys in Albania* John Murray, London, 1998

Durham, M Edith *High Albania* Phoenix Press, London, 2000; *Through the Lands of the Serb* Edward Arnold, London, 1904

Gordon, Mrs Will *A Woman in the Balkans* Hutchinson, London, 1916

Mackenzie, Muir G and Irby, A P *Travels in the Slavinic Provinces of Turkey-in-Europe* Dalby, Isbister, London, 1877

Maclean, Fitzroy *Eastern Approaches* Penguin Press, London, 1991

Miller, William *The Balkans, Roumania, Bulgaria, Serbia and Montenegro* T Fisher Unwin, London, 1896

Neale, Rev J M *Notes, Ecclesiological and Picturesque, on Dalmatia, Croatia, Istria, Styria, with a Visit to Montenegro* J T Hayes, Lyall Place, Eaton Square, London, 1861

West, Rebecca *Black Lamb and Grey Falcon, a Journey through Yugoslavia* Canongate, Edinburgh, 1993

White, Tony *Another Fool in the Balkans: In the Footsteps of Rebecca West* Cadogan, London, 2006

Wyon, Reginald, and Prance, Gerald *Land of Black Mountain: Adventures of Two Englishmen in Montenegro* Methuen, London, 1903

ART

Lucie-Smith, Edward *Dictionary of Art Terms* Thames and Hudson, London, 1984

Manojlović, Radoman-Risto (editor) *Review of the Pljevlja Regional Museum* Pljevlja, 2001

Seferović, Lazar *The Art Treasure of Herceg Novi* Herceg Novi, 1987

NATURAL HISTORY

Gorman, Gerard *Central and Eastern European Wildlife* Bradt Travel Guides, 2008

Polunin, Oleg *Flowers of Greece and the Balkans, a Field Guide* Oxford University Press, Oxford, 1980

HIKING, CLIMBING AND BIKING

Abraham, Rudolf *The Mountains of Montenegro* Cicerone, Milnthorpe, first published 2007; revised edn due 2015; *Peaks of the Balkans Trail* Cicerone, due out 2015

Cerović, Branislav *Durmitor and the Tara Canyon* Durmitor National Park, Žabljak, 1986

Montenegro Mountaineering Association *Coastal Mountaineering Transversal Route: Orjen–Lovćen–Rumija* Podgorica, 2006

Starčević, Željko and Komar, Dr Goran *Guide to the Orjen Massif: Backpacking & Mountain Hiking & Biking Guide* Herceg Novi, 2006

Vincek, Daniel, Popović, Ratko and Kovačević, Mijo *The Mountains of Montenegro, A Mountaineering Guide* Podgorica, 2004

Zindel, Christian and Hausammann, Barbara *Hiking Guide Northern Albania – Thethi and Kelmendi* Huber, 2009

TRAVEL GUIDES TO NEIGHBOURING COUNTRIES

Abraham, Rudolf *The Islands of Croatia* Cicerone, 2014; *Walking in Croatia* (2nd edition) Cicerone, 2010

Abraham, Rudolf and Evans, Thammy *Istria* Bradt Travel Guides, 2013

Clancy, Tim *Bosnia and Herzegovina* Bradt Travel Guides, 2013

Cuddon, J A *The Companion Guide to Jugoslavia* Collins, London, 1968. Out of date but still worth having.

Evans, Thammy *Macedonia* Bradt Travel Guides, 2015

Gloyer, Gillian *Albania* Bradt Travel Guides, 2015

Knaus, Verena and Warrander, Gail *Kosovo* Bradt Travel Guides, 2010

Letcher, Piers *Croatia* Bradt Travel Guides, 2013

Mitchell, Laurence *Serbia* Bradt Travel Guides, 2013

And for a little light relief:

Cilauro, Santo, Gleisner, Tom and Sitch, Rob *The Jetlag Travel Guide to Molvania* Hardie Grant Books, South Yarra, 2003

MAPS

Green Path Trekking Map: Bjelasica, Komovi and Biogradska National Park OSCE in conjunction with Siemens, Naturefriends International and the Norwegian government, 2002. Available from Montenegrin tourist offices, price €2.

Nautical and Touristic Catalogue of the Montenegro Coast South Adriatic Izdavac, Belgrade, 1998

Peaks of the Balkans: cross border hiking Albania – Kosovo – Montenegro Huber, 2012

PHRASEBOOKS

Eastern European Phrasebook Lonely Planet, Victoria, Australia, 2001, includes a 50-page Serbian section along with ten other languages and is about the cheapest Serbian pocket phrasebook.

Awde, Nicholas and Radosavljević, Duška *Serbian Dictionary & Phrasebook* Hippocrene Books Inc, New York, 2004, costs £11.99 in the UK or US$13.95 in the US, is excellent and a more manageable size if you can find it.

Norris, David A *Teach Yourself Serbian, A Complete Course for Beginners* Hodder Headline, London, 2003

FICTION

Kiš, Danilo *A Tomb for Boris Davidovich* Faber, London, 1985; *The Encyclopedia of the Dead* Faber, London, 1989; *Hourglass* Faber, London, 1990
Lawrence, Starling *Montenegro, a Novel* Transworld, London, 1998

WEBSITES Here is a selection of some of the more interesting and relevant websites:

Balkans Peace Park Project www.balkanspeacepark.org
Birdwatching www.birdwatchingmn.org
Black Mountain Adventure Travel (Herceg Novi) www.montenegroholiday.com
CIA World Factbook www.cia.gov/library/publications/the-world-factbook
CTU – Tourism Association of Montenegro www.ctu-montenegro.org
Diving Association of Montenegro www.mdiving.org.me
Ecological Tours in Montenegro www.eco-tours.co.me
Ferries www.viamare.com
Foreign and Commonwealth Office Travel Advice www.fco.gov.uk
GIZ (cross-border development of mountain tourism in the border triangle of Albania, Kosovo and Montenegro) www.giz.de
Gorbis Travel www.gorbis.com
International Union for Conservation of Nature www.iucn.org
Montenegro Adventures www.montenegro-adventures.com
Montenegro Culture www.montenet.org/culture
Montenegro History www.montenegro.org/history.html
Montenegro Tourism www.visit-montenegro.com
Montenegro Travel www.montenet.org
Montenegro Yellow Pages www.cgyellow.com
Mountaineering Association of Montenegro www.pscg.me
Mountains of Bjelasica and Komovi www.bjelasica-komovi.co.me
National Parks of Montenegro www.nparkovi.me
National Tourism Organisation of Montenegro www.montenegro.travel
Ornithology www.fatbirder.com/links_geo/europe/montenegro.html
Peaks of the Balkans www.peaksofthebalkans.com
Sailing Association of Montenegro www.sailmontenegro.com
Skiing Associations in Montenegro www.tourism-montenegro.com/directory/active/skiing
SOS www.sospecies.org (global initiative to support threatened species and their habitats; founded 2010 by IUCN, GEF and the World Bank)
Undiscovered Montenegro (Virpazar) www.undiscoveredmontenegro.com
US Travel Warnings http://travel.state.gov/travel/cis_pa_tw/tw/tw_1764.html

FOLLOW BRADT

For the latest news, special offers and competitions, subscribe to the Bradt newsletter via the website www.bradtguides.com and follow Bradt on:

 www.facebook.com/BradtTravelGuides
 @BradtGuides
 @bradtguides
 pinterest.com/bradtguides

Index

Page numbers in **bold** indicate major entries; those in *italics* indicate maps

INDEX OF ADVERTISERS